ISBN 978-0-266-03326-4
PIBN 11031663

This book is a reproduction of an important historical work. Forgotten Books uses
state-of-the-art technology to digitally reconstruct the work, preserving the original format
whilst repairing imperfections present in the aged copy. In rare cases, an imperfection in
the original, such as a blemish or missing page, may be replicated in our edition. We do,
however, repair the vast majority of imperfections successfully; any imperfections that
remain are intentionally left to preserve the state of such historical works.

1 MONTH OF
FREE
READING

at
www.ForgottenBooks.com

By purchasing this book you are eligible for one month membership to ForgottenBooks.com, giving you unlimited access to our entire collection of over 1,000,000 titles via our web site and mobile apps.

To claim your free month visit:

www.forgottenbooks.com/free1031663

English
Français
Deutsche
Italiano
Español
Português

www.forgottenbooks.com

Mythology Photography **Fiction**
Fishing Christianity **Art** Cooking
Essays Buddhism Freemasonry
Medicine **Biology** Music **Ancient**
Egypt Evolution Carpentry Physics
Dance Geology **Mathematics** Fitness
Shakespeare **Folklore** Yoga Marketing
Confidence Immortality Biographies
Poetry **Psychology** Witchcraft
Electronics Chemistry History **Law**
Accounting **Philosophy** Anthropology
Alchemy Drama Quantum Mechanics
Atheism Sexual Health **Ancient History**
Entrepreneurship Languages Sport
Paleontology Needlework Islam
Metaphysics Investment Archaeology
Parenting Statistics Criminology
Motivational

JOURNAL

OF THE

SENATE OF THE UNITED STATES OF AMERICA,

BEING THE

SECOND SESSION OF THE FIFTY-SECOND CONGRESS,

BEGUN AND HELD

AT THE CITY OF WASHINGTON

DECEMBER 5, 1892,

IN THE ONE HUNDRED AND SEVENTEENTH YEAR OF THE INDEPENDENCE OF THE UNITED STATES.

WASHINGTON:
GOVERNMENT PRINTING OFFICE.
1893.

CONGRESS OF THE UNITED STATES.

The SECOND SESSION OF THE FIFTY-SECOND CONGRESS commenced this day, conformably to the Constitution of the United States, and the Senate assembled in its Chamber at the City of Washington.

MONDAY, DECEMBER 5, 1892.

PRESENT.

From the State of Alabama:
Messrs. John T. Morgan and James L. Pugh.

From the State of Arkansas:
Messrs. James H. Berry and James K. Jones.

From the State of California:
Mr. Charles N. Felton.

From the State of Colorado:
Messrs. Henry M. Teller and Edward O. Wolcott.

From the State of Connecticut:
Mr. Orville H. Platt.

From the State of Delaware:
Mr. Anthony Higgins.

From the State of Florida:
Messrs. Wilkinson Call and Samuel Pasco.

From the State of Georgia:
Mr. John B. Gordon.

From the State of Idaho:
Messrs. Fred. T. Dubois and George L. Shoup.

From the State of Illinois:
Messrs. Shelby M. Cullom and John M. Palmer.

From the State of Indiana:
Mr. Daniel W. Voorhees.

From the State of Iowa:
Mr. James F. Wilson.

From the State of Kansas:
Mr. William A. Peffer.

From the State of Kentucky:
Messrs. Joseph C. S. Blackburn and John G. Carlisle.

From the State of Louisiana:
Mr. Edward D. White.

From the State of Maine:
Messrs. William P. Fry and Eugene Hale.

From the State of Maryland:
Mr. Arthur P. Gorman.

From the State of Massachusetts:
Messrs. Henry L. Dawes and George F. Hoar.

From the State of Michigan:
Messrs. James McMillan and Francis B. Stockbridge.

From the State of Minnesota:
Messrs. Cushman K. Davis and William D. Washburn.

From the State of Mississippi:
Messrs. James Z. George and Edward C. Walthall.

From the State of Missouri:
Messrs. Francis M. Cockrell and George G. Vest.

From the State of Montana:
Mr. Thomas C. Power.

From the State of Nebraska:
Messrs. Charles F. Manderson and Algernon S. Paddock.

From the State of Nevada:
Mr. William M. Stewart.

From the State of New Hampshire:
Messrs. William E. Chandler and Jacob H. Gallinger.

From the State of New Jersey:
Messrs. Rufus Blodgett and John R. McPherson.

From the State of North Carolina:
Mr. Zebulon B. Vance.

From the State of North Dakota:
Messrs. Lyman R. Casey and Henry C. Hansbrough.

From the State of Ohio:
Messrs. Calvin S. Brice and John Sherman.

From the State of Oregon:
Messrs. Joseph N. Dolph and John H. Mitchell.

From the State of Pennsylvania:
Messrs. James Donald Cameron and Matthew S. Quay.

From the State of Rhode Island and Providence Plantations:
Messrs. Nelson W. Aldrich and Nathan F. Dixon.

From the State of South Carolina:
Mr. Matthew C. Butler.

From the State of South Dakota:
Messrs. James H. Kyle and Richard F. Pettigrew.

From the State of Tennessee:
Messrs. William B. Bate and Isham G. Harris.

From the State of Texas:
Messrs. Richard Coke and Roger Q. Mills.

From the State of Vermont:
Messrs. Justin S. Morrill and Redfield Proctor.

From the State of Virginia:
Messrs. John W. Daniel and Eppa Hunton.

From the State of Washington:
Mr. John B. Allen.

From the State of West Virginia:
Mr. Charles J. Faulkner.

From the State of Wisconsin:
Messrs. Philetus Sawyer and William F. Vilas.

From the State of Wyoming:
Mr. Joseph M. Carey.

The honorable Levi P. Morton, Vice-President of the United States and President of the Senate, resumed the chair.

CREDENTIALS OF A SENATOR.

Mr. Morrill presented the credentials of Redfield Proctor, elected a Senator by the legislature of Vermont to fill the vacancy occasioned by the resignation of George F. Edmunds, in the term expiring March 4, 1893; which were read.

Mr. Proctor appeared, and the oath prescribed by law having been administered to him by the Vice-President, he took his seat in the Senate.

Mr. Morrill presented the credentials of Redfield Proctor, elected a Senator by the legislature of the State of Vermont for the term of six years commencing March 4, 1893; which were read and placed on file.

NOTIFICATION TO THE HOUSE.

Mr. Sherman submitted the following resolution; which was considered by unanimous consent and agreed to:

Resolved, That the Secretary inform the House of Representatives that a quorum of the Senate is assembled, and that the Senate is ready to proceed to business.

NOTIFICATION TO THE PRESIDENT.

Mr. Hale submitted the following resolution; which was considered by unanimous consent and agreed to:

Resolved, That a committee consisting of two members be appointed, to join such committee as may be appointed by the House

foreign trade of London during 1890 amounted to 13,480,767 tons, and of Liverpool 10,941,800 tons, a total for these two great shipping ports of 24,422,568 tons, only slightly in excess of the vessel tonnage passing through the Detroit River. And it should be said that the season for the Detroit River was but 228 days, while, of course, in London and Liverpool the season was for the entire year. The vessel tonnage passing through the St. Marys Canal for the fiscal year 1892 amounted to 9,828,874 tons, and the freight tonnage of the Detroit River is estimated for that year at 25,000,000 tons, against 23,209,619 tons in 1891. The aggregate traffic on our railroads for the year 1891 amounted to 704,398,609 tons of freight, compared with 691,344,437 tons in 1890, an increase of 13,054,172 tons.

Another indication of the general prosperity of the country is found in the fact that the number of depositors in savings banks increased from 693,870 in 1860 to 4,258,893 in 1890, an increase of 513 per cent, and the amount of deposits from $149,277,504 in 1860 to $1,524,844,506 in 1890, an increase of 921 per cent. In 1891 the amount of deposits in savings banks was $1,623,079,749. It is estimated that 90 per cent of these deposits represent the savings of wage-earners. The bank clearances for nine months ending September 30, 1891, amounted to $41,049,390,808. For the same months in 1892 they amounted to $45,189,601,947, an excess for the nine months of $4,140,211,139.

There never has been a time in our history when work was so abundant or when wages were as high, whether measured by the currency in which they are paid or by their power to supply the necessaries and comforts of life. It is one of the unfavorable incidents of agriculture that the farmer can not produce upon orders. He must sow and reap in ignorance of the aggregate production of the year, and is peculiarly subject to the depreciation which follows overproduction. But, while the fact I have stated is true as to the crops mentioned, the general average of prices has been such as to give to agriculture a fair participation in the general prosperity. The value of our total farm products has increased from $1,363,646,866 in 1860 to $4,500,000,000 in 1891, as estimated by statisticians, an increase of 230 per cent. The number of hogs January 1, 1891, was 50,625,106 and their value $210,193,925; on January 1, 1892, the number was 52,398,019 and the value $241,031,415. On January 1, 1891, the number of cattle was 36,875,648 and the value $544,127,908; on January 1, 1892, the number was 37,651,239 and the value $570,749,155.

If any are discontented with their state here; if any believe that wages or prices, the returns for honest toil, are inadequate, they should not fail to remember that there is no other country in the world where the conditions that seem to them hard would not be accepted as highly prosperous. The English agriculturist would be glad to exchange the returns of his labor for those of the American farmer, and the Manchester workmen their wages for those of their fellows at Fall River.

I believe that the protective system, which has now for something more than thirty years continuously prevailed in our legislation, has been a mighty instrument for the development of our national wealth and a most powerful agency in protecting the homes of our workingmen from the invasion of want. I have felt a most solicitous interest to preserve to our working people rates of wages that would not only give daily bread but supply a comfortable margin for those home attractions and family comforts and enjoyments without which life is neither hopeful nor sweet. They are American citizens—a part of the great people for whom our Constitution and Government were framed and instituted—and it can not be a perversion of that Constitution to so legislate as to preserve in their homes the comfort, independence, loyalty, and sense of interest in the Government which are essential to good citizenship in peace, and which will bring this stalwart throng, as in 1861, to the defense of the flag when it is assailed.

It is not my purpose to renew here the argument in favor of a protective tariff. The result of the recent election must be accepted as having introduced a new policy. We must assume that the present tariff, constructed upon the lines of protection, is to be repealed, and that there is to be substituted for it a tariff law constructed solely with reference to revenue; that no duty is to be higher because the increase will keep open an American mill or keep up the wages of an American workman, but that in every case such a rate of duty is to be imposed as will bring to the Treasury of the United States the largest returns of revenue. The contention has not been between schedules, but between principles, and it would be offensive to suggest that the prevailing party will not carry into legislation the principles advocated by it and the pledges given to the people. The tariff bills passed by the House of Representatives at the last session were, as I suppose—even in the opinion of their promoters—inadequate, and justified only by the fact that the Senate and House of Representatives were not in accord and that a general revision could not, therefore, be undertaken.

I recommend that the whole subject of tariff revision be left to the incoming Congress. It is matter of regret that this work must be delayed for at least three months; for the threat of great tariff changes introduces so much uncertainty that an amount, not easily estimated, of business inaction and of diminished production will

necessarily result. It is possible, also, that this uncertainty may result in decreased revenues from customs duties, for our merchants will make cautious orders for foreign goods in view of the prospect of tariff reductions and the uncertainty as to when they will take effect. Those who have advocated a protective tariff can well afford to have their disastrous forecasts of a change of policy disappointed. If a system of customs duties can be framed that will set the idle wheels and looms of Europe in motion and crowd our warehouses with foreign-made goods, and at the same time keep our own mills busy; that will give us an increased participation in the "markets of the world" of greater value than the home market we surrender; that will give increased work to foreign workmen upon products to be consumed by our people without diminishing the amount of work to be done here; that will enable the American manufacturer to pay to his workmen from 50 to 100 per cent more in wages than is paid in the foreign mill and yet to compete in our market and in foreign markets with the foreign producer; that will further reduce the cost of articles of wear and food without reducing the wages of those who produce them; that can be celebrated, after its effects have been realized, as its expectation has been, in European as well as in American cities, the authors and promoters of it will be entitled to the highest praise. We have had in our history several experiences of the contrasted effects of a revenue and of a protective tariff; but this generation has not felt them, and the experience of one generation is not highly instructive to the next. The friends of the protective system, with undiminished confidence in the principles they have advocated, will await the results of the new experiment.

The strained and too often disturbed relations existing between the employés and the employers in our great manufacturing establishments have not been favorable to a calm consideration by the wage-earner of the effect upon wages of the protective system. The facts that his wages were the highest paid in like callings in the world and that a maintenance of this rate of wages, in the absence of protective duties upon the product of his labor, was impossible, were obscured by the passion evoked by these contests. He may now be able to review the question in the light of his personal experience under the operation of a tariff for revenue only. If that experience shall demonstrate that present rates of wages are thereby maintained or increased either absolutely or in their purchasing power, and that the aggregate volume of work to be done in this country is increased, or even maintained, so that there are more or as many days' work in a year at as good or better wages for the American workman as has been the case under the protective system, everyone will rejoice. A general process of wage reduction can not be contemplated by any patriotic citizen without the gravest apprehension. It may be, indeed I believe it is, possible for the American manufacturer to compete successfully with his foreign rival in many branches of production without the defense of protective duties, if the pay rolls are equalized; but the conflict that stands between the producer and that result and the distress of our working people when it is attained are not pleasant to contemplate. The Society of the Unemployed, now holding its frequent and threatening parades in the streets of foreign cities, should not be allowed to acquire an American domicile.

The reports of the heads of the several Executive Departments, which are herewith submitted, have very naturally included a résumé of the whole work of the administration with the transactions of the last fiscal year. The attention not only of Congress but of the country is again invited to the methods of administration which have been pursued and to the results which have been attained. Public revenues amounting to $1,414,079,292.28 have been collected and disbursed without loss from misappropriation, without a single defalcation of such importance as to attract the public attention, and at a diminished per cent of cost for collection. The public business has been transacted not only with fidelity, but progressively, and with a view to giving to the people in the fullest possible degree the benefits of a service established and maintained for their protection and comfort.

Our relations with other nations are now undisturbed by any serious controversy. The complicated and threatening differences with Germany and England relating to Samoan affairs, with England in relation to the seal fisheries in the Bering Sea, and with Chile growing out of the Baltimore affair have been adjusted.

There have been negotiated and concluded, under section 3 of the tariff law, commercial agreements relating to reciprocal trade with the following countries: Brazil, Dominican Republic, Spain for Cuba and Puerto Rico, Guatemala, Salvador, the German Empire, Great Britain for certain West Indian Colonies and British Guiana, Nicaragua, Honduras, and Austria-Hungary.

Of these, those with Guatemala, Salvador, the German Empire, Great Britain, Nicaragua, Honduras, and Austria-Hungary have been concluded since my last annual message. Under these trade arrangements a free or favored admission has been secured in every case for an important list of American products. Especial care has been taken to secure markets for farm products in order to relieve that great underlying industry of the depression which the lack of an adequate foreign market for our surplus often brings. An opening has also been made for manufactured products that will undoubtedly, if this policy is maintained, greatly augment our export trade. The full benefits of these arrangements can not be realized instantly. New lines of trade are to be opened. The commercial traveler must survey the field. The manufacturer must adapt his goods to the new markets and facilities for exchange must be established. This work has been well begun, our merchants and manufacturers having entered the new fields with courage and enterprise. In the case of food products, and especially with Cuba, the trade did not need to wait, and the immediate results have been most gratifying. If this policy and these trade arrangements can be continued in force and aided by the establishment of American steamship lines, I do not doubt that we shall within a short period secure fully one-third of the total trade of the countries of Central and South America, which now amounts to about $600,000,000 annually. In 1885 we had only 8 per cent of this trade.

The following statistics show the increase in our trade with the countries with which we have reciprocal trade agreements from the date when such agreements went into effect up to September 30, 1892, the increase being in some almost wholly and in others in an important degree the result of these agreements.

The domestic exports to Germany and Austria-Hungary have increased in value from $47,673,756 to $57,993,064, an increase of $10,319,308, or 21.63 per cent. With American countries the value of our exports has increased from $44,160,285 to $54,613,598, an increase of $10,453,313, or 23.67 per cent. The total increase in the value of exports to all the countries with which we have reciprocity agreements has been $20,772,621. This increase is chiefly in wheat, flour, meat, and dairy products, and in manufactures of iron and steel and lumber. There has been a large increase in the value of imports from all these countries since the commercial agreements went into effect, amounting to $74,294,525, but it has been entirely in imports from the American countries, consisting mostly of sugar, coffee, india rubber, and crude drugs. The alarmed attention of our European competitors for the South American market has been attracted to this new American policy and to our acquisition and their loss of South American trade.

A treaty providing for the arbitration of the dispute between Great Britain and the United States as to the killing of seals in the Bering Sea was concluded on the 29th of February last. This treaty was accompanied by an agreement prohibiting pelagic sealing pending the arbitration, and a vigorous effort was made during this season to drive out all poaching sealers from the Bering Sea. Six naval vessels, three revenue cutters, and one vessel from the Fish Commission, all under the command of Commander Evans, of the Navy, were sent into the sea, which was systematically patrolled. Some seizures were made, and it is believed that the catch in the Bering Sea by poachers amounted to less than 500 seals. It is true, however, that in the North Pacific, while the seal herds were on their way to the passes between the Aleutian Islands, a very large number, probably 35,000, were taken. The existing statutes of the United States do not restrain our citizens from taking seals in the Pacific Ocean, and perhaps should not, unless the prohibition can be extended to the citizens of other nations. I recommend that power be given to the President, by proclamation, to prohibit the taking of seals in the North Pacific by American vessels, in case either as the result of the findings of the tribunal of arbitration, or otherwise, the restraints can be applied to the vessels of all countries. The case of the United States for the tribunal of arbitration has been prepared with great care and industry by the Hon. John W. Foster, and the counsel who represent this Government express confidence that a result substantially establishing our claims and preserving this great industry for the benefit of all nations will be attained.

During the past year a suggestion was received through the British minister that the Canadian Government would like to confer as to the possibility of enlarging, upon terms of mutual advantage, the commercial exchanges of Canada and of the United States, and a conference was held at Washington, with Mr. Blaine acting for this Government, and the British minister at this capital and three members of the Dominion cabinet acting as commissioners on the part of Great Britain. The conference developed the fact that the Canadian Government was only prepared to offer to the United States, in exchange for the concessions asked, the admission of natural products. The statement was frankly made that favored rates could not be given to the United States as against the mother country. This admission, which was foreseen, necessarily terminated the conference upon this question. The benefits of an exchange of natural products would be almost wholly with the people of Canada. Some other topics of interest were considered in the conference, and have resulted in the making of a convention for examining the Alaskan boundary and the waters of Passamaquoddy Bay adjacent to Eastport, Me., and in the initiation of an arrangement for the protection of fish life in the coterminous and neighboring waters of our northern border.

The controversy as to tolls upon the Welland Canal, which was presented to Congress at the last session by special message, having failed of adjustment, I felt constrained to exercise the authority conferred by the act of July 26, 1892, and to proclaim a suspension of the free use of St. Marys Falls Canal to cargoes in transit to ports in Canada. The Secretary of the Treasury established such tolls as were thought to be equivalent to the exactions unjustly levied upon our commerce in the Canadian canals.

If, as we must suppose, the political relations of Canada and the disposition of the Canadian Government are to remain unchanged, a somewhat radical revision of our trade relations should, I think, be made. Our relations must continue to be intimate, and they should be friendly. I regret to say, however, that in many of the controversies, notably those as to the fisheries on the Atlantic, the sealing interests on the Pacific, and the canal tolls, our negotiations with Great Britain have continuously been thwarted or retarded by unreasonable and unfriendly objections and protests from Canada. In the matter of the canal tolls, our treaty rights were flagrantly disregarded. It is hardly too much to say that the Canadian Pacific and other railway lines which parallel our northern boundary are sustained by commerce having either its origin or terminus, or both, in the United States. Canadian railroads compete with those of the United States for our traffic, and without the restraints of our interstate-commerce act. Their cars pass almost without detention into and out of our territory.

The Canadian Pacific Railway brought into the United States from China and Japan, via British Columbia, during the year ended June 30, 1892, 23,239,689 pounds of freight, and it carried from the United States to be shipped to China and Japan, via British Columbia, 24,068,346 pounds of freight. There were also shipped from the United States over this road from eastern ports of the United States to our Pacific ports, during the same year, 13,912,073 pounds of freight, and there were received over this road at the United States eastern ports from ports on the Pacific coast 13,293,315 pounds of freight. Mr. Joseph Nimmo, jr., former Chief of the Bureau of Statistics, when before the Senate Select Committee on Relations with Canada, April 26, 1890, said that "the value of goods thus transported between different points in the United States across Canadian territory probably amounts to $100,000,000 a year."

There is no disposition on the part of the people or Government of the United States to interfere in the smallest degree with the political relations of Canada. That question is wholly with her own people. It is time for us, however, to consider whether, if the present state of things and trend of things is to continue, our interchanges upon lines of land transportation should not be put upon a different basis, and our entire independence of Canadian canals and of the St. Lawrence as an outlet to the sea secured by the construction of an American canal around the Falls of Niagara and the opening of ship communication between the Great Lakes and one of our own seaports. We should not hesitate to avail ourselves of our great natural trade advantages. We should withdraw the support which is given to the railroads and steamship lines of Canada by a traffic that properly belongs to us, and no longer furnish the earnings which lighten the otherwise crushing weight of the enormous public subsidies that have been given to them. The subject of the power of the Treasury to deal with this matter without further legislation has been under consideration, but circumstances have postponed a conclusion. It is probable that a consideration of the propriety of a modification or abrogation of the article of the Treaty of Washington relating to the transit of goods in bond is involved in any complete solution of the question.

Congress at the last session was kept advised of the progress of the serious and for a time threatening difference between the United States and Chile. It gives me now great gratification to report that the Chilean Government, in a most friendly and honorable spirit, has tendered and paid as an indemnity to the families of the sailors of the Baltimore who were killed and to those who were injured in the outbreak in the city of Valparaiso the sum of $75,000. This has been accepted, not only as an indemnity for a wrong done, but as a most gratifying evidence that the Government of Chile rightly appreciates the disposition of this Government to act in a spirit of the most absolute fairness and friendliness in our intercourse with that brave people. A further and conclusive evidence of the mutual respect and confidence now existing is furnished by the fact that a convention submitting to arbitration the mutual claims of the citizens of the respective Governments has been agreed upon. Some of these claims have been pending for many years and have been the occasion of much unsatisfactory diplomatic correspondence.

I have endeavored in every way to assure our sister republics of Central and South America that the United States Government and its people have only the most friendly disposition toward them all. We do not covet their territory. We have no disposition to be oppressive or exacting in our dealings with any of them, even the weakest. Our interests and our hopes for them all lie in the direction of stable governments by their people and of the largest development of their great commercial resources. The mutual benefits of enlarged commercial exchanges and of a more familiar and friendly intercourse between our peoples we do desire, and in this have sought their friendly coöperation.

I have believed, however, while holding these sentiments in the greatest sincerity, that we must insist upon a just responsibility for any injuries inflicted upon our official representatives or upon our citizens. This insistence, kindly and justly, but firmly made, will, I believe, promote peace and mutual respect.

Our relations with Hawaii have been such as to attract an increased interest, and must continue to do so. I deem it of great importance that the projected submarine cable, a survey for which has been made, should be promoted. Both for naval and commercial uses we should have quick communication with Honolulu. We should before this have availed ourselves of the concession, made many years ago to this Government, for a harbor and naval station at Pearl River. Many evidences of the friendliness of the Hawaiian Government have been given in the past, and it is gratifying to believe that the advantage and necessity of a continuance of very close relations is appreciated.

The friendly act of this Government in expressing to the Government of Italy its reprobation and abhorrence of the lynching of Italian subjects in New Orleans, by the payment of 125,000 francs, or $24,330.90, was accepted by the King of Italy with every manifestation of gracious appreciation, and the incident has been highly promotive of mutual respect and good will.

In consequence of the action of the French Government in proclaiming a protectorate over certain tribal districts of the west coast of Africa, eastward of the San Pedro River, which has long been regarded as the southeastern boundary of Liberia, I felt constrained to make protest against this encroachment upon the territory of a Republic which was founded by citizens of the United States and toward which this country has for many years held the intimate relation of a friendly counselor.

The recent disturbances of the public peace by lawless foreign marauders on the Mexican frontier have afforded this Government an opportunity to testify its good will for Mexico and its earnest purpose to fulfill the obligations of international friendship by pursuing and dispersing the evil-doers. The work of relocating the boundary of the treaty of Gaudalupe Hidalgo, westward from El Paso, is progressing favorably.

Our intercourse with Spain continues on a friendly footing. I regret, however, not to be able to report as yet the adjustment of the claims of the American missionaries arising from the disorders at Ponape, in the Caroline Islands, but I anticipate a satisfactory adjustment in view of renewed and urgent representations to the Government at Madrid.

The treatment of the religious and educational establishments of American citizens in Turkey has of late called for a more than usual share of attention. A tendency to curtail the toleration which has so beneficially prevailed is discernible and has called forth the earnest remonstrance of this Government. Harassing regulations in regard to schools and churches have been attempted in certain localities, but not without due protest and the assertion of the inherent and conventional rights of our countrymen. Violations of domicile and search of the persons and effects of citizens of the United States by apparently irresponsible officials in the Asiatic vilayets have from time to time been reported. An aggravated instance of injury to the property of an American missionary at Bourdour, in the province of Konia, called forth an urgent claim for reparation, which I am pleased to say was promptly heeded by the government of the Porte. Interference with the trading ventures of our citizens in Asia Minor is also reported, and the lack of consular representation in that region is a serious drawback to instant and effective protection. I can not believe that these incidents represent a settled policy, and shall not cease to urge the adoption of proper remedies.

International copyright has been extended to Italy by proclamation in conformity with the act of March 3, 1891, upon assurance being given that Italian law permits to citizens of the United States the benefit of copyright on substantially the same basis as to subjects of Italy. By a special convention, proclaimed January 15, 1892, reciprocal provisions of copyright have been applied between the United States and Germany. Negotiations are in progress with other countries to the same end.

I repeat with great earnestness the recommendation which I have made in several previous messages that prompt and adequate support be given to the American company engaged in the construction of the Nicaragua Ship Canal. It is impossible to overstate the value from every standpoint of this great enterprise, and I hope that there may be time, even in this Congress, to give to it an impetus that will insure the early completion of the canal and secure to the United States its proper relation to it when completed.

The Congress has been already advised that the invitations of this Government for the assembling of an International Monetary Conference to consider the question of an enlarged use of silver were accepted by the nations to which they were addressed. The conference assembled at Brussels on the 22d of November and has entered upon the consideration of this great question. I have not doubted, and have taken occasion to express that belief, as well in the invitations issued for this conference as in my public messages, that the free coinage of silver upon an agreed international ratio would greatly promote the interests of our people and equally those of other nations. It is too early to predict what results may be accomplished by the conference. If any temporary check or delay intervenes, I believe that very soon commercial conditions will compel the now reluctant Governments to unite with us in this movement

to secure the enlargement of the volume of coined money needed for the transaction of the business of the world.

The report of the Secretary of the Treasury will attract especial interest in view of the many misleading statements that have been made as to the state of the public revenues. Three preliminary facts should not only be stated, but emphasized, before looking into details: First, that the public debt has been reduced since March 4, 1889, $259,074,200, and the annual interest charge $11,684,469; second, that there have been paid out for pensions during this administration up to November 1, 1892, $432,564,178.70, an excess of $114,466,386.09 over the sum expended during the period from March 1, 1885, to March 1, 1889; and third, that under the existing tariff up to December 1 about $93,000,000 of revenue, which would have been collected upon imported sugars if the duty had been maintained, has gone into the pockets of the people and not into the public treasury, as before. If there are any who still think that the surplus should have been kept out of circulation by hoarding it in the Treasury, or deposited in favored banks without interest while the Government continued to pay to these very banks interest upon the bonds deposited as security for the deposits, or who think that the extended pension legislation was a public robbery, or that the duties upon sugar should have been maintained, I am content to leave the argument where it now rests, while we wait to see whether these criticisms will take the form of legislation.

The revenues for the fiscal year ending June 30, 1892, from all sources were $425,868,260.22, and the expenditures for all purposes were $415,953,806.56, leaving a balance of $9,914,453.66. There were paid during the year upon the public debt $40,570,467.98. The surplus in the Treasury and the bank redemption fund, passed by the act of July 14, 1890, to the general fund, furnished in large part the cash available and used for the payments made upon the public debt. Compared with the year 1891, our receipts from customs duties fell off $42,069,241.08, While our receipts from internal revenue increased $8,284,823.13, leaving the net loss of revenue from these principal sources $33,784,417.95. The net loss of revenue from all sources was $32,675,972.81.

The revenues, estimated and actual, for the fiscal year ending June 30 1893, were placed by the Secretary at $463,336,350.44 and the expenditures at $461,336,350.44, showing a surplus of receipts over expenditure of $2,000,000. The cash balance in the Treasury at the end of the fiscal year, it is estimated, will be $20,992,377.03.

So far as these figures are based upon estimates of receipts and expenditures for the remaining months of the current fiscal year, there are not only the usual elements of uncertainty, but some added elements. New revenue legislation, or even the expectation of it, may seriously reduce the public revenues during the period of uncertainty and during the process of business adjustment to the new conditions when they become known. But the Secretary has very wisely refrained from guessing as to the effect of possible changes in our revenue laws, since the scope of those changes and the time of their taking effect can not in any degree be forecast or foretold by him. His estimates must be based upon existing laws and upon a continuance of existing business conditions, except so far as these conditions may be affected by causes other than new legislation.

The estimated receipts for the fiscal year ending June 30, 1894, are $490,121,365.38, and the estimated appropriations $457,261,335.33, leaving an estimated surplus of receipts over expenditures of $32,860,030.05. This does not include any payment to the sinking fund. In the recommendation of the Secretary that the sinking-fund law be repealed I concur. The redemption of bonds since the passage of the law to June 30, 1892, has already exceeded the requirements by the sum of $990.510,681.49. The retirement of bonds in the future before maturity should be a matter of convenience, not of compulsion. We should not collect revenue for that purpose, but only use any casual surplus. To the balance of $32,-860,030.05 of receipts over expenditures for the year 1894 should be added the estimated surplus at the beginning of the year, $20,192,-377.03; and from this aggregate there must be deducted, as stated by the Secretary, about $44,000,000 of estimated unexpended appropriations.

The public confidence in the purpose and ability of the Government to maintain the parity of all of our money issues, whether coin or paper, must remain unshaken. The demand for gold in Europe and the consequent calls upon us are in a considerable degree the result of the efforts of some of the European governments to increase their gold reserves, and these efforts should be met by appropriate legislation on our part. The conditions that have created this drain of the Treasury gold are in an important degree political and not commercial. In view of the fact that a general revision of our revenue laws in the near future seems to be probable, it would be better that any changes should be a part of that revision rather than of a temporary nature.

During the last fiscal year the Secretary purchased under the act of July 14, 1890, 54,355,748 ounces of silver, and issued in payment therefor $51,106,608 in notes. The total purchases since the passage of the act have been 120,479,981 ounces, and the aggregate of notes issued $116,783,590. The average price paid for silver during the year was 94 cents per ounce, the highest price being $1.02¼ July

1, 1891, and the lowest $0.83 March 21, 1892. In view of the fact that the monetary conference is now sitting and that no conclusion has yet been reached, I withhold any recommendation as to legislation upon this subject.

The report of the Secretary of War brings again to the attention of Congress some important suggestions as to the reorganization of the infantry and artillery arms of the service, which his predecessors have before urgently presented. Our Army is small, but its organization should all the more be put upon the most approved modern basis. The conditions upon what we have called the "frontier" have heretofore required the maintenance of may small posts, but now the policy of concentration is obviously the right one. The new posts should have the proper strategic relations to the only "frontiers" we now have, those of the seacoast and of our northern and part of our southern boundary. I do not think that any question of advantage to localities or to States should determine the location of the new posts. The reorganization and enlargement of the bureau of military information which the Secretary has effected is a work the usefulness of which will become every year more apparent. The work of building heavy guns and the construction of coast defenses has been well begun and should be carried on without check.

The report of the Attorney-General is by law submitted directly to Congress, but I can not refrain from saying that he has conducted the increasing work of the Department of Justice with great professional skill. He has in several directions secured from the courts decisions giving increased protection to the officers of the United States and bringing some classes of crime that escaped local cognizance and punishment into the tribunals of the United States, where they could be tried with impatiality.

The numerous applications for Executive clemency presented in behalf of persons convicted in United States courts and given penitentiary sentences have called my attention to a fact referred to by the Attorney-General in his report, namely, that a time allowance for good behavior for such prisoners is prescribed by the Federal statutes only where the State in which the penitentiary is located has made no such provision. Prisoners are given the benefit of the provisions of the State law regulating the penitentiary to which they may be sent. These are various, some perhaps too liberal and some perhaps too illiberal. The result is that a sentence for five years means one thing if the prisoner is sent to one State for confinement and quite a different thing if he is sent to another. I recommend that a uniform credit for good behavior be prescribed by Congress.

I have before expressed my concurrence in the recommendation of the Attorney-General that degrees of murder should be recognized in the Federal statutes as they are, I believe, in all the States. These grades are founded on correct distinctions in crime. The recognition of them would enable the courts to exercise some discretion in apportioning punishment, and would greatly relieve the Executive of what is coming to be a very heavy burden—the examination of these cases on application for commutation.

The aggregate of claims pending against the Government in the Court of Claims is enormous. Claims to the amount of nearly $400,000,000 for the taking of or injury to the property of persons claiming to be loyal during the war are now before that court for examination. When to these are added the Indian depredation claims and the French spoliation claims an aggregate is reached that is indeed startling. In the defense of all these cases the Government is at great disadvantage. The claimants have preserved their evidence, whereas the agents of the Government are sent into the field to rummage for what they can find. This difficulty is peculiarly great where the fact to be established is the disloyalty of the claimant during the war. If this great threat against our revenues is to have no other check, certainly Congress should supply the Department of Justice with appropriations sufficiently liberal to secure the best legal talent in the defense of these claims and to pursue its vague search for evidence effectively.

The report of the Postmaster-General shows a most gratifying increase and a most efficient and progressive management of the great business of that Department. The remarkable increase in revenues, in the number of post-offices, and in the miles of mail carriage furnishes further evidence of the high state of prosperity which our people are enjoying. New offices mean new hamlets and towns, new routes mean the extension of our border settlements, and increased revenues mean an active commerce. The Postmaster-General reviews the whole period of his administration of the office and brings some of his statistics down to the mouth of November last. The postal revenues have increased during the last year nearly $5,000,000. The deficit for the year ending June 30, 1892, is $848,341 less than the deficiency of the preceding year. The deficiency of the present fiscal year it is estimated will be reduced to $1,552,423, which will not only be extinguished during the next fiscal year, but a surplus of nearly $1,000,000 should then be shown. In these calculations the payments to be made under the contracts for ocean mail service have not been included. There have been added 1,590 new mail routes during the year, with a mileage of 8,563 miles; and the total number of new miles of mail trips added during the year is nearly 17,000,000. The number of miles of mail journeys added

during the last four years is about 76,000,000, this addition being 21,000,000 of miles more than were in operation in the whole country in 1861.

The number of post-offices has been increased by 2,790 during the year; and during the past four years and up to October 29 last the total increase in the number of offices has been nearly 9,000. The number of free-delivery offices has been nearly doubled in the last four years, and the number of money-order offices more than doubled within that time.

For the three years ending June 30, 1892, the postal revenue amounted to $197,744,359, which was an increase of $52,263,150 over the revenue for the three years ending June 30, 1888, the increase during the last three years being more than three and a half times as great as the increase during the three years ending June 30, 1888. No such increase as that shown for these three years has ever previously appeared in the revenues of the Department. The Postmaster-General has extended to the post-offices in the larger cities the merit system of promotion, introduced by my direction into the Departments here, and it has resulted there, as in the Departments, in a larger volume of work and that better done.

Ever since our merchant marine was driven from the sea by the rebel cruisers during the war of the rebellion the United States has been paying an enormous annual tribute to foreign countries in the shape of freight and passage moneys. Our grain and meats have been taken at our own docks and our large imports there laid down by foreign ship masters. An increasing torrent of American travel to Europe has contributed a vast sum annually to the dividends of foreign shipowners. The balance of trade shown by the books of our custom-houses has been very largely reduced and in many years altogether extinguished by this constant drain. In the year 1892 only 12.3 per cent of our imports were brought in American vessels. These great foreign steamships maintained by our traffic are many of them under contracts with their respective Governments by which in time of war they will become a part of their armed naval establishments. Profiting by our commerce in peace, they will become the most formidable destroyers of our commerce in time of war. I have felt and have before expressed the feeling that this condition of things was both intolerable and disgraceful. A wholesome change of policy, and one having in it much promise, as it seems to me, was begun by the law of March 3, 1891. Under this law contracts have been made by the Postmaster-General for eleven mail routes. The expenditure involved by these contracts for the next fiscal year approximates $954,123.33. As one of the results already reached sixteen American steamships, of an aggregate tonnage of 57,400 tons, costing $7,400,000, have been built or contracted to be built in American shipyards.

The estimated tonnage of all steamships required under existing contracts is 165,802, and when the full service required by these contracts is established there will be 41 mail steamers under the American flag, with the probability of further necessary additions in the Brazilian and Argentine service. The contracts recently let for transatlantic service will result in the construction of five ships of 10,000 tons each, costing $9,000,000 to $10,000,000, and will add, with the City of New York and City of Paris, to which the Treasury Department was authorized by legislation at the last session to give American registry, seven of the swiftest vessels upon the sea to our naval reserve. The contracts made with the lines sailing to Central and South American ports have increased the frequency and shortened the time of the trips, added new ports of call, and sustained some lines that otherwise would almost certainly have been withdrawn. The service to Buenos Ayres is the first to the Argentine Republic under the American flag. The service to Southhampton, Boulogne, and Antwerp is also new, and is to be begun with the steamships City of New York and City of Paris in February next.

I earnestly urge a continuance of the policy inaugurated by this legislation, and that the appropriations required to meet the obligations of the Government under the contracts may be made promptly, so that the lines that have entered into these engagements may not be embarrassed. We have had, by reason of connections with the transcontinental railway lines constructed through our own territory, some advantages in the ocean trade of the Pacific that we did not possess on the Atlantic. The construction of the Canadian Pacific Railway and the establishment under large subventions from Canada and England of fast steamship service from Vancouver with Japan and China seriously threaten our shipping interests in the Pacific. This line of English steamers receives, as is stated by the Commissioner of Navigation, a direct subsidy of $400,000 annually or $30,767 per trip for thirteen voyages, in addition to some further aid from the Admiralty in connection with contracts under which the vessels may be used for naval purposes. The competing American Pacific mail line, under the act of March 3, 1891, receives only $6,389 per roun trip.

Efforts have been made within the last year, as I am informed, to establish under similar conditions a line between Vancouver and some Australian port, with a view of seizing there a trade in which we have had a large interest. The Commissioner of Navigation states that a very large per cent of our imports from Asia are now brought to us by English steamships and their connecting railways in Canada. With a view of promoting this trade, especially in tea,

Canada has imposed a discriminating duty of 10 per cent upon tea and coffee brought into the Dominion from the United States. If this unequal contest between American lines without subsidy, or with diminished subsidies, and the English Canadian line to which I have referred is to continue, I think we should at least see that the facilities for customs entry and transportation across our territory are not such as to make the Canadian route a favored one, and that the discrimination as to duties, to which I have referred, is met by a like discrimination as to the importation of these articles from Canada.

No subject, I think, more nearly touches the pride, the power, and the prosperity of our country than this of the development of our merchant marine upon the sea. If we could enter into conference with other competitors and all would agree to withhold Government aid, we could perhaps take our chances with the rest, but our great competitors have established and maintained their lines by government subsidies until they now have practically excluded us from participation. In my opinion no choice is left to us but to pursue, moderately at least, the same lines.

The report of the Secretary of the Navy exhibits great progress in the construction of our new Navy. When the present Secretary entered upon his duties only three modern steel vessels were in commission. The vessels since put in commission and to be put in commission during the winter will make a total of 19 during his administration of the Department. During the current year 10 war vessels and 3 navy tugs have been launched, and during the four years 25 vessels will have been launched. Two other large ships and a torpedo boat are under contract and the work upon them well advanced, and the 4 monitors are awaiting only the arrival of their armor, which has been unexpectedly delayed, or they would have been before this in commission.

Contracts have been let during this administration, under the appropriations for the increase of the Navy, including new vessels and their appurtenances, to the amount of $35,000,000, and there has been expended during the same period for labor at navy-yards upon similar work $8,000,000 without the smallest scandal or charge of fraud or partiality. The enthusiasm and interest of our naval officers, both of the staff and line, have been greatly kindled. They have responded magnificently to the confidence of Congress and have demonstrated to the world an unexcelled capacity in construction, in ordnance, and in everything involved in the building, equipping, and sailing of great war ships.

At the beginning of Secretary Tracy's administration several difficult problems remained to be grappled with and solved before the efficiency in action of our ships could be secured. It is believed that as the result of new processes in the construction of armor plate our later ships will be clothed with defensive plates of higher resisting power than are found on any war vessels afloat. We were without torpedoes. Tests have been made to ascertain the relative efficiency of different constructions, a torpedo has been adopted, and the work of construction is now being carried on successfully. We were without armor-piercing shells, and without a shop instructed and equipped for the construction of them. We are now making what is believed to be a projectile superior to any before in use. A smokeless powder has been developed, and a slow-burning powder for guns of large caliber. A high explosive, capable of use in shells fired from service guns, has been found, and the manufacture of gun cotton has been developed so that the question of supply is no longer in doubt.

The development of a naval militia, which has been organized in eight States and brought into cordial and coöperative relations with the Navy, is another important achievement. There are now enlisted in these organizations 1,800 men, and they are likely to be greatly extended. I recommend such legislation and appropriations as will encourage and develop this movement. The recommendations of the Secretary will, I do not doubt, receive the friendly consideration of Congress, for he has enjoyed, as he has deserved, the confidence of all those interested in the development of our Navy, without any division upon partisan lines. I earnestly express the hope that a work which has made such noble progress may not now be stayed. The wholesome influence for peace and the increased sense of security which our citizens domiciled in other lands feel when these magnificent ships appear under the American flag appear is already most gratefully apparent. The ships from our Navy which will appear in the great naval parade next April in the harbor of New York will be a convincing demonstration to the world that the United States is again a naval power.

The work of the Interior Department, always very burdensome, has been larger than ever before during the administration of Secretary Noble. The disability pension law, the taking of the Eleventh Census, the opening of vast areas of Indian lands to settlement, the organization of Oklahoma, and the negotiations for the cession of Indian lands, furnish some of the particulars of the increased work; and the results achieved testify to the ability, fidelity, and industry of the head of the Department and his efficient assistants.

Several important agreements for the cession of Indian lands negotiated by the commission appointed under the act of March 2, 1889, are awaiting the action of Congress. Perhaps the most important of these is that for the cession of the Cherokee strip. This region has been the source of great vexation to the Executive Department and of great friction and unrest between the settlers who desire to occupy it and the Indians who assert title. The agreement which has been made by the commission is perhaps the most satisfactory that could have been reached. It will be noticed that it is conditioned upon its ratification by Congress before March 4, 1893. The Secretary of the Interior, who has given the subject very careful thought, recommends the ratification of the agreement, and I am inclined to follow his recommendation. Certain it is that some action by which this controversy shall be brought to an end and these lands opened to settlement is urgent.

The form of government provided by Congress on May 17, 1884, for Alaska was, in its frame and purpose, temporary. The increase of population and the development of some important mining and commercial interests make it imperative that the law should be revised and better provision made for the arrest and punishment of criminals.

The report of the Secretary shows a very gratifying state of facts as to the condition of the General Land Office. The work of issuing agricultural patents, which seemed to be hopelessly in arrear when the present Secretary undertook the duties of his office, has been so expedited that the Bureau is now upon current business. The relief thus afforded to honest and worthy settlers upon the public lands, by giving to them an assured titled to their entries, has been of incalculable benefit in developing the new States and the Territories.

The court of private land claims, established by Congress for the promotion of this policy of speedily settling contested land titles, is making satisfactory progress in its work, and when the work is completed a great impetus will be given to the development of those regions where unsettled claims under Mexican grants have so long exercised their repressive influence. When to these results are added the enormous cessions of Indian lands which have been opened to settlement, aggregating during this administration nearly 26,000,000 acres, and the agreements negotiated and now pending in Congress for ratification by which about 10,000,000 additional acres will be opened to settlement, it will be seen how much has been accomplished.

The work in the Indian Bureau, in the execution of the policy of recent legislation, has been largely directed to two chief purposes: First, the allotment of lands in severalty to the Indians and the cession to the United States of the surplus lands; and, secondly, to the work of educating the Indian for his own protection in his closer contact with the white man and for the intelligent exercise of his new citizenship. Allotments have been made and patents issued to 5,900 Indians under the present Secretary and Commissioner, and 7,600 additional allotments have been made for which patents are now in process of preparation. The school attendance of Indian children has been increased during that time over 13 per cent, the enrollment for 1892 being nearly 20,000. A uniform system of school text-books and of study has been adopted and the work in these national schools brought as near as may be to the basis of the free common schools of the States. These schools can be transferred and merged into the common-school systems of the States when the Indian has fully assumed his new relation to the organized civil community in which he resides and the new States are able to assume the burden.

I have several times been called upon to remove Indian agents appointed by me, and have done so promptly upon every sustained complaint of unfitness or misconduct. I believe, however, that the Indian service at the agencies has been improved and is now administered on the whole with a good degree of efficiency. If any legislation is possible by which the selection of Indian agents can be wholly removed from all partisan suggestions or considerations, I am sure it would be a great relief to the Executive and a great benefit to the service. The appropriation for the subsistence of the Cheyenne and Arapaho Indians made at the last session of Congress was inadequate. This smaller appropriation was estimated for by the Commissioner upon the theory that the large fund belonging to the tribe in the public Treasury could be and ought to be used for their support. In view, however, of the pending depredation claims against this fund and other considerations, the Secretary of the Interior on the 12th of April last submitted a supplemental estimate for $50,000. This appropriation was not made, as it should have been, and the oversight ought to be remedied at the earliest possible date.

In a special message to this Congress at the last session I stated the reasons why I had not approved the deed for the release to the United States by the Choctaws and Chickasaws of the lands formerly embraced in the Cheyenne and Arapaho Reservation and remaining after allotments to that tribe. A resolution of the Senate expressing the opinion of that body that, notwithstanding the facts stated in my special message, the deed should be approved and the money, $2,991,450, paid over, was presented to me May 10, 1892. My special message was intended to call the attention of Congress to the subject, and in view of the fact that it is conceded that the appropriation proceeded upon a false basis as to the amount of lands to be paid for, and is by $50,000 in excess of the amount they are entitled to (even if their claim to the land is given full recognition at the rate agreed upon), I have not felt willing to approve the deed, and shall not do so, at least until both Houses of Congress have acted upon the subject. It has been informally proposed by the claimants to release this sum of $50,000, but I have no power to demand or accept such a release, and such an agreement would be without consideration and void.

I desire further to call the attention of Congress to the fact that the recent agreement concluded with the Kiowas and Comanches relates to lands which were a part of the "leased district," and to which the claim of the Choctaws and Chickasaws is precisely that recognized by Congress in the legislation I have referred to. The surplus lands to which this claim would attach in the Kiowa and Comanche Reservation is 2,500,000 acres, and at the same rate the Government will be called upon to pay to the Choctaws and Chickasaws for these lands $3,125,000. This sum will be further augmented, especially if the title of the Indians to the tract now Grier County, Texas, is established. The duty devolved upon me in this connection was simply to pass upon the form of the deed; but as in my opinion the facts mentioned in my special message were not adequately brought to the attention of Congress in connection with the legislation, I have felt that I would not be justified in acting without some new expression of the legislative will.

The report of the Commissioner of Pensions, to which extended notice is given by the Secretary of the Interior in his report, will attract great attention. Judged by the aggregate amount of work done the last year has been the greatest in the history of the office. I believe that the organization of the office is efficient, and that the work has been done with fidelity. The passage of what is known as the disability bill has, as was foreseen, very largely increased the annual disbursements of the disabled veterans of the civil war. The estimate for this fiscal year was $144,956,000, and that amount was appropriated. A deficiency amounting to $10,508,621 must be provided for at this session. The estimate for pensions for the fiscal year ending June 30, 1894, is $165,000,000. The Commissioner of Pensions believes that, if the present legislation and methods are maintained and further additions to the pensions laws are not made, the maximum expenditure for pensions will be reached June 30, 1894, and will be at the highest point $188,000,000 per annum.

I adhere to the views expressed in previous messages that the care of the disabled soldiers of the war of the rebellion is a matter of national concern and duty. Perhaps no emotion cools sooner than that of gratitude, but I can not believe that this process has yet reached a point with our people that would sustain the policy of remitting the care of these disabled veterans to the inadequate agencies provided by local laws. The parade on the 20th of September last upon the streets of this capital of 60,000 of the surviving Union veterans of the war of the rebellion was a most touching and thrilling episode, and the rich and gracious welcome extended to them by the District of Columbia and the applause that greeted their progress from tens of thousands of people from all the States did much to revive the glorious recollections of the grand review, when these men and many thousand others now in their graves were welcomed with grateful joy as victors in a struggle in which the national unity, honor, and wealth were all at issue.

In my last annual message I called attention to the fact that some legislative action was necessary in order to protect the interests of the Government in its relations with the Union Pacific Railway. The Commissioner of Railroads has submitted a very full report, giving exact, information as to the debt, the liens upon the company's property and its resources. We must deal with the question as we find it, and take that course which will, under existing conditions, best secure the interests of the United States. I recommended in my last annual message that a commission be appointed to deal with this question, and I renew that recommendation, and suggest that the commission be given full power.

The report of the Secretary of Agriculture contains not only a most interesting statement of the progressive and valuable work done under the administration of Secretary Rusk, but many suggestions for the enlarged usefulness of this important Department. In the successful effort to break down the restrictions to the free introduction of our meat products in the countries of Europe, the Secretary has been untiring from the first, stimulating and aiding all other Government officers, at home and abroad, whose official duties enable them to participate in the work. The total trade in hog products with Europe in May, 1892, amounted to 82,000,000 pounds, against 46,900,000 in the same month of 1891; in June, 1892, the export aggregated 85,700,000 pounds, against 46,500,000 pounds in the same month of the previous year; in July there was an increase of 41 per cent and in August of 55 per cent over the corresponding months of 1891. Over 40,000,000 pounds of inspected pork have been exported since the law was put into operation, and a comparison of the four months of May, June, July, and August, 1892, with the same months of 1891 shows an increase in the number of pounds of our export of pork products of 62 per cent, and an increase in value of 66½ per cent. The exports of dressed beef increased from 137,900,000 pounds in 1889 to 220,500,000 pounds in 1892, or about 60 per cent. During the past year there have been exported 394,607 head of live cattle as against 205,786 exported in 1889. This

increased exportation has been largely promoted by the inspection authorized by law and the faithful efforts of the Secretary and his efficient subordinates to make that inspection thorough and to carefully exclude from all cargoes diseased or suspected cattle. The requirement of the English regulations that live cattle arriving from the United States must be slaughtered at the docks had its origin in the claim that pleuro-pneumonia existed among American cattle and that the existence of the disease could only certainly be determined by a post-mortem inspection.

The Department of Agriculture has labored with great energy and faithfulness to extirpate this disease; and on the 26th day of September last a public announcement was made by the Secretary that the disease no longer existed anywhere within the United States. He is entirely satisfied, after the most searching inquiry, that this statement was justified, and that by a continuance of the inspection and quarantine now required of cattle brought into this country the disease can be prevented from again getting any foothold. The value to the cattle industry of the United States of this achievement can hardly be estimated. We can not, perhaps, at once insist that this evidence shall be accepted as satisfactory by other countries; but if the present exemption from the disease is maintained and the inspection of our cattle arriving at foreign ports, in which our own veterinarians participate, confirms it, we may justly expect that the requirement that our cattle shall be slaughtered at the docks will be revoked, as the sanitary restrictions upon our pork products have been. If our cattle can be taken alive to the interior the trade will be enormously increased.

Agricultural products constituted 78.1 per cent of our unprecedented exports for the fiscal year which closed June 30, 1892, the total exports being $1,030,278,030 and the value of the agricultural products $793,717,676, which exceeds by more than $150,000,000 the shipment of agricultural products in any previous year.

An interesting and a promising work for the benefit of the American farmer has been begun through agents of the Agricultural Department in Europe, and consists in efforts to introduce the various products of Indian corn as articles of human food. The high price of rye offered a favorable opportunity for the experiment in Germany of combining corn meal with rye to produce a cheaper bread. A fair degree of success has been attained, and some mills for grinding corn for food have been introduced. The Secretary is of the opinion that this new use of the products of corn has already stimulated exportations, and that if diligently prosecuted large and important markets can presently be opened for this great American product.

The suggestions of the Secretary for an enlargement of the work of the Department are commended to your favorable consideration. It may, I think, be said without challenge that in no corresponding period has so much been done as during the last four years for the benefit of American agriculture.

The subject of quarantine regulations, inspection, and control was brought suddenly to my attention by the arrival at our ports in August last of vessels infected with cholera. Quarantine regulations should be uniform at all our ports. Under the Constitution they are plainly within the exclusive federal jurisdiction when and so far as Congress shall legislate. In my opinion the whole subject should be taken into national control, and adequate power given to the Executive to protect our people against plague invasions. On the 1st of September last I approved regulations establishing a twenty-day quarantine for all vessels bringing immigrants from foreign ports. This order will be continued in force. Some loss and suffering have resulted to passengers, but a due care for the homes of our people justifies in such cases the utmost precaution. There is danger that with the coming of spring cholera will again appear, and a liberal appropriation should be made at this session to enable our quarantine and port officers to exclude the deadly plague.

But the most careful and stringent quarantine regulations may not be sufficient absolutely to exclude the disease. The progress of medical and sanitary science has been such, however, that, if approved precautions are taken at once to put all of our cities and towns in the best sanitary condition, and provision is made for isolating any sporadic cases and for a thorough disinfection, an epidemic can, I am sure, be avoided. This work appertains to the local authorities, and the responsibility and the penalty will be appalling if it is neglected or unduly delayed.

We are peculiarly subject in our great ports to the spread of infectious diseases by reason of the fact that unrestricted immigration brings to us out of European cities, in the overcrowded steerages of great steamships, a large number of persons whose surroundings make them the easy victims of the plague. This consideration, as well as those affecting the political, moral, and industrial interests of our country, lead me to renew the suggestion that admission to our country and to the high privileges of its citizenship should be more restricted and more careful. We have, I think, a right and owe a duty to our own people, and especially to our working people, not only to keep out the vicious, the ignorant, the civil disturber, the pauper, and the contract laborer, but to check the too great flow of immigration now coming by further limitations.

The report of the World's Columbian Exposition has not yet been submitted. That of the board of management of the Government exhibit has been received and is herewith transmitted. The work of construction and of preparation for the opening of the Exposition in May next has progressed most satisfactorily and upon a scale of liberality and magnificence that will worthily sustain the honor of the United States.

The District of Columbia is left, by a decision of the supreme court of the District, without any law regulating the liquor traffic. An old statute of the legislature of the District, relating to the licensing of various vocations, has hitherto been treated by the Commissioners as giving them power to grant or refuse licenses to sell intoxicating liquors, and as subjecting those who sold without licenses to penalties; but in May last the supreme court of the District held aga nst this view of the powers of the Commissioners. It is of urgent importance, therefore, that Congress should supply, either by direct enactment or by conferring discretionary powers upon the Commissioners, proper limitations and restraints upon the liquor traffic in the District. The District has suffered in its reputation by many crimes of violence, a large per cent of them resulting from drunkenness and the liquor traffic. The capital of the nation should be freed from this reproach by the enactment of stringent restrictions and limitations upon the traffic.

In renewing the recommendation which I have made in three preceding annual messages that Congress should legislate for the protection of railroad employés against the dangers incident to the old and inadequate methods of braking and coupling which are still in use upon freight trains, I do so with the hope that this Congress may take action upon the subject. Statistics furnished by the Interstate Commerce Commission show that during the year ending June 30, 1891, there were forty-seven different styles of car-couplers reported to be in use, and that during the same period there were 2,060 employés killed and 26,140 injured. Nearly 16 per cent of the deaths occurred in the coupling and uncoupling of cars, and over 36 per cent of the injuries had the same origin.

The Civil Service Commission ask for an increased appropriation for needed clerical assistance, which I think should be given. I extended the classified service March 1, 1892, to include physicians, superintendents, assistant superintendents, school teachers, and matrons in the Indian service, and have had under consideration the subject of some further extensions, but have not as yet fully determined the lines upon which extensions can most properly and usefully be made.

I have in each of the three annual messages which it has been my duty to submit to Congress called attention to the evils and dangers connected with our election methods and practices as they are related to the choice of officers of the National Government. In my last annual message I endeavored to invoke serious attention to the evils of unfair apportionments for Congress. I can not close this message without again calling attention to these grave and threatening evils. I had hoped that it was possible to secure a non-partisan inquiry, by means of a commission, into evils the existence of which is known to all, and that out of this might grow legislation from which all thought of partisan advantage should be eliminated and only the higher thought appear of maintaining the freedom and purity of the ballot and the equality of the elector, without the guaranty of which the Government could never have been formed and without the continuance of which it can not continue to exist in peace and prosperity.

It is time that mutual charges of unfairness and fraud between the great parties should cease, and that the sincerity of those who profess a desire for pure and honest elections should be brought to the test of their willingness to free our legislation and our election methods from everything that tends to impair the public confidence in the announced result. The necessity for an inquiry, and for legislation by Congress, upon this subject is emphasized by the fact that the tendency of the legislation in some States in recent years has in some important particulars been away from and not toward free and fair elections and equal apportionment. Is it not time that we should come together upon the high plane of patriotism while we devise methods that shall secure the right of every man qualified by law to cast a free ballot and give to every such ballot an equal value in choosing our public officers and in directing the policy of the Government?

Lawlessness is not less such, but more, where it usurps the functions of the peace officer and of the courts. The frequent lynching of colored people accused of crime is without the excuse which has sometimes been urged by mobs for a failure to pursue the appointed methods for the punishment of crime, that the accused have an undue influence over courts and juries. Such acts are a reproach to the community where they occur, and so far as they can be made the subject of federal jurisdiction the strongest repressive legislation is demanded. A public sentiment that will sustain the officers of the law in resisting mobs and in protecting accused persons in their custody should be promoted by every possible means. The officer who gives his life in the brave discharge of this duty is worthy of special honor. No lesson needs to be so urgently impressed upon our people as this, that no worthy end or cause can be promoted by lawlessness.

This exhibit of the work of the Executive Departments is submitted to Congress and to the public in the hope that there will be

found in it a due sense of responsibility and an earnest purpose to maintain the national honor and to promote the happiness and prosperity of all our people. And this brief exhibit of the growth and prosperity of the country will give us a level from which to note the increase or decadence that new legislative policies may bring to us. There is no reason why the national influence, power, and prosperity should not observe the same rates of increase that have characterized the past thirty years. We carry the great impulse and increase of these years into the future. There is no reason why in many lines of production we should not surpass all other nations as we have already done in some. There are no near frontiers to our possible development. Retrogression would be a crime.

BENJ. HARRISON.

EXECUTIVE MANSION, *December 6, 1892.*

The message was read.

Ordered, That it lie on the table and be printed.

Mr. Manderson, from the Committee on Printing, reported the following resolution; which was considered by unanimous consent and agreed to:

Resolved, That 10,000 copies of the President's message be printed in pamphlet form for the use of the Senate.

EXECUTIVE COMMUNICATIONS.

The Vice-President laid before the Senate four communications from the Secretary of State, transmitting, in pursuance of the provisions of the act of February 3, 1887, certified copies of the final ascertainment of electors for President and Vice-President of the States of Georgia, New Hampshire, Arkansas, and Maryland.

Ordered, That they be printed and, with the accompanying papers, lie on the table.

The Vice-President laid before the Senate a letter of the Secretary of the Interior, transmitting the original report of the Maritime Canal Company of Nicaragua; which was referred to the Committee on Foreign Relations and ordered to be printed.

The Vice-President laid before the Senate a letter of the Secretary of the Treasury, communicating, in answer to a resolution of the Senate of July 30, 1892, certain information relative to the payment of customs duties and the currency system of the United States; which was referred to the Committee on Finance and ordered to be printed.

The Vice-President laid before the Senate a letter of the Secretary of the Interior, transmitting a copy of the report of the Government directors of the Union Pacific Railway Company for the year 1892; which was referred to the Select Committee on Pacific Railways and ordered to be printed.

The Vice-President laid before the Senate the annual report of the board of management and control of the Industrial Christian Home Association of the Territory of Utah; which was referred to the Committee on Territories and ordered to be printed.

The Vice-President laid before the Senate a letter of the Commissioner of Fish and Fisheries, transmitting, in obedience to law, a statement showing expenditures under all appropriations for propagation of food fishes during the fiscal year ending June 30, 1892; which was referred to the Committee on Appropriations and ordered to be printed.

The Vice-President laid before the Senate a letter of the Secretary of the Senate, submitting a full and complete account of all property belonging to the United States in his possession December 5, 1892.

Ordered, That it lie on the table and be printed.

The Vice-President laid before the Senate a letter of the Secretary of the Senate, submitting a statement of receipts and expenditures of the Senate from July 1, 1891, to June 30, 1892.

Ordered, That it lie on the table and be printed.

The Vice-President laid before the Senate a letter of the Chief of Engineers, transmitting a report upon the construction of the building for the Library of Congress during the year ending December 1, 1892; which was referred to the Select Committee on Additional Accommodations for the Library of Congress and ordered to be printed.

The Vice-President laid before the Senate a letter of the Sergeant-at-Arms of the Senate, submitting a full and complete account of all property of the United States in his possession December 5, 1892.

Ordered, That it lie on the table and be printed.

The Vice-President laid before the Senate a letter of the clerk of the Court of Claims, transmitting a statement showing judgments rendered by said court during the year ended December 3, 1892, amounts thereof, parties in whose favor, etc.

Ordered, That it lie on the table and be printed.

The Vice-President laid before the Senate the following communications from the clerk of the Court of Claims, transmitting the conclusions of fact and of law filed by said court in the following French spoliation claims:

In the matter of the brig *Endeavor;*

In the matter of the sloop *New York;* and

In the matter of the ship *Suffolk.*

Ordered, That they be referred to the Committee on Claims and printed.

The Vice-President laid before the Senate a letter of the Acting Secretary of War, transmitting a statement of the expenditures at the Springfield armory, Springfield, Mass., for the fiscal year ending June 30, 1892, which was referred to the Committee on Military Affairs and ordered to be printed.

The Vice-President laid before the Senate a letter of the Sergeant-at-Arms, submitting a full and complete account of all condemned property sold by him, and showing the disposition of the money received therefrom.

Ordered, That it lie on the table and be printed.

PETITIONS AND MEMORIALS.

Petitions, memorials, etc., were presented and referred as follows:

By Mr. Mitchell: A memorial of Jason Wheeler, of Albany, Oregon, late United States Indian agent at Warm Springs Agency, Oregon, praying relief on account of property lost and stolen during his administration of such office; to the Committee on Claims.

A petition of citizens of Umatilla County, Oregon, praying that the unsold portion of the agricultural lands of the Umatilla Indian Reservation be sold to actual settlers thereon in tracts not to exceed 160 acres, and that those lands unfit for cultivation be sold in tracts to suit settlers, not to exceed 640 acres, at the appraised value thereof; to the Committee on Indian Affairs.

By Mr. Sherman: A petition of Aden Benedict, praying to be reimbursed for commutation money paid by him in 1864 for exemption from service in the Army, he having subsequently enlisted; to the Committee on Military Affairs.

A petition of Philip Hawk, of Ohio, praying the passage of a law granting him a pension of $125 per month; to the Committee on Pensions.

Three petitions of citizens of Ohio, praying the passage of the bill to limit the free entry of wearing apparel to $100 in value; to the Committee on Finance.

A resolution of the Board of Trade of Zanesville, Ohio, praying an amendment of the immigration laws so as to give the President power to suspend all traffic between this country and countries where contagious diseases are epidemic; to the Committee on Immigration.

By Mr. Peffer: A petition of citizens of Kansas, praying the passage of a law to prevent the sale of intoxicating liquors at the National Soldiers' Home in Leavenworth, Kans.; to the Committee on Military Affairs.

A memorial of citizens of Kansas remonstrating against the closing of the World's Fair on the Sabbath day; and

Three petitions of citizens of Kansas praying for the closing of the World's Fair or the Sabbath day, and to prevent the sale of intoxicating liquors on the Fair grounds; to the Select Committee on the Quadro-Centennial.

By Mr. Paddock: A petition of citizens of Nebraska praying the passage of the bill requiring all railroad companies to equip their cars with automatic couplers and continuous brakes; to the Committee on Interstate Commerce.

By Mr. Call: A petition of citizens of Florida praying for the construction of a harbor of refuge at Cape Canaveral, Florida; to the Committee on Commerce.

By Mr. Sherman: Papers relating to the application of Mary A. L. Eastman to be allowed an increase of pension; to the Committee on Pensions to accompany the bill S. 3501.

Papers relating to the application of Frank Rabiska to be allowed a pension; to the Committee on Pensions, to accompany the bill S. 3502.

A petition of citizens of Ohio in behalf of Christian Vogt praying that he be allowed a pension; to the Committee on Pensions, to accompany the bill S. 3503.

By Mr. Paddock: Papers relating to the application of George Miller for the removal of the charge of desertion from his military record; to the Committee on Military Affairs, to accompany the bill S. 3505.

By Mr. Frye: An argument in relation to the establishment of communication from light-ships and outlying light-houses to the shore; to the Committee on Commerce, to accompany the bill S. 3512.

By Mr. Cullom: A petition of Ira Bacon praying the passage of a law granting him an additional bounty; to the Committee on Military Affairs, to accompany the bill S. 3618.

By the Vice-President: A petition of citizens of the United States praying the repeal of the provision providing for the closing of the World's Fair on the Sabbath day; to the Select Committee on the Quadro-Centennial.

Memorials remonstrating against the passage of the "antioption bill" were presented as follows:

By the Vice-President: Several memorials of citizens of the United States.

By Mr. George: Four memorials of citizens of Mississippi.

By Mr. Paddock: A memorial of the Memphis Cotton Exchange.

Ordered, That they lie on the table.

Mr. Mitchell presented a resolution of the legislature of the State of Iowa in favor of the passage of the "antioption bill."

Ordered, That it lie on the table.

Mr. Paddock presented a resolution of the legislature of Iowa in favor of the passage of the "antioption bill."

Ordered, That it lie on the table.

Petitions praying the appointment of a committee to investigate an alleged combine formed to depreciate the price of grain and now existing between the elevators, millers, and railroads at Minneapolis and St. Louis, and asking the postponement of the antioption bill until said committee reports, were presented as follows:

By Mr. Peffer: A petition of citizens of Kansas.

By Mr. Kyle: Three petitions of citizens of South Dakota.

By Mr. Paddock: Several petitions of citizens of Nebraska.

Ordered, That they be referred to the Committee on Agriculture and Forestry.

Memorials remonstrating against the repeal of the law providing for the closing of the World's Fair on the Sabbath were presented as follows:

By Mr. Cullom: A memorial of citizens of Illinois.

By Mr. Sherman: Several memorials of citizens of Ohio.

Ordered, That they be referred to the Select Committee on the Quadro-Centennial.

Petitions praying the passage of the bill to limit the amount of wearing apparel to be admitted free of duty were presented as follows:

By Mr. McMillan: A petition of citizens of Minnesota.

By Mr. Paddock: Two petitions of citizens of Nebraska.

By Mr. Cullom: A petition of citizens of Illinois.

Ordered, That they be referred to the Committee on Finance.

INTRODUCTION OF BILLS AND JOINT RESOLUTIONS.

Bills and joint resolutions were introduced, read the first and second times by unanimous consent, and referred as follows:

By Mr. Butler: A bill (S. 3500) to amend an act entitled "An act to credit and pay to the several States and Territories, and the District of Columbia, all moneys collected under the direct tax levied by the act of Congress approved August 5, 1861," approved March 2, 1891; to the Committee on Finance.

By Mr. Sherman: A bill (S. 3501) granting an increase of pension to Mary A. L. Eastman;

A bill (S. 3502) granting a pension to Frank Rabiska; and

A bill (S. 3503) granting a pension to Christian Vogt; to the Committee on Pensions.

By Mr. Paddock: A bill (S. 3505) to remove the charge of desertion from the military record of George Miller;

A bill (S. 3506) for the relief of John Palmier, Pine Ridge, Shannon County, South Dakota; and

A bill (S. 3507) for the relief of George H. Jewett of Arlington, Washington County, Nebraska; to the Committee on Military Affairs.

By Mr. Hunton: A bill (S. 3508) to incorporate the Washington and Marlboro Electric Railway Company of the District of Columbia; to the Committee on the District of Columbia.

A bill (S. 3509) for the relief of the heirs of the late Mrs. Mary Ann Randolph Custis Lee, of Fairfax County, Virginia; to the Committee on Claims.

By Mr. Frye: A bill (S. 3510) to amend section 4347 of the Revised Statutes of the United States; to the Committee on Commerce.

A bill (S. 3511) granting a pension to Mrs. Annie A. Townsend; to the Committee on Pensions.

A bill (S. 3512) to provide communication from light-ships and outlying light-houses to the shore; to the Committee on Commerce.

By Mr. Chandler: A bill (S. 3513) for the suspension of immigration for one year; to the Committee on Immigration.

By Mr. Peffer: A bill (S. 3514) to prohibit the collection of special liquor taxes from persons other than those who are duly authorized by State laws to traffic in intoxicating liquors; to the Committee on Finance.

A bill (S. 3515) for the relief of Charles Williamson, late assistant surgeon Twelfth Kansas State Militia; to the Committee on Pensions.

A bill (S. 3516) to fix the rank of officers and enlisted men of the Army of the United States retiring after long and faithful service; to the Committee on Military Affairs.

By Mr. Cullom: A bill (S. 3517) for the relief of Augustus G. Kellogg; to the Committee on Naval Affairs.

A bill (S. 3518) granting to Ira Bacon, of Company A, Fifty-second Regiment Indiana Volunteers, an additional bounty of $100; to the Committee on Military Affairs.

By Mr. Call: A bill (S. 3519) for the construction of a breakwater and harbor of refuge at or near Cape Canaveral, State of Florida; to the Committee on Commerce.

By Mr. Mitchell: A bill (S. 3520) for the relief of Jason Wheeler, late United States Indian agent at Warm Springs Agency, Oregon; to the Committee on Claims.

By Mr. Sherman: A bill (S. 3521) to amend the charter of the Eckington and Soldiers' Home Railway Company of the District of Columbia; to the Committee on the District of Columbia.

By Mr. Vest: A bill (S. 3522) to create a bureau in the Department of Agriculture for the giving public information of the production and shipping of live stock; to the Select Committee on the Transportation and Sale of Meat Products.

By Mr. Hale: A bill (S. 3523) to further increase the naval establishment; to the Committee on Naval Affairs.

By Mr. Kyle: A joint resolution (S. R. 116) extending the powers of the United States Government Exhibit Board; to the Committee on Education and Labor.

By Mr. Cockrell: A joint resolution (S. R. 118) to print the fifteenth number of the Statistical Abstract of the United States for the year 1892; to the Committee on Printing.

Mr. Bate introduced a bill (S. 3504) to repeal all statutes relating to supervisors of elections and special deputies; which was read the first and second times by unanimous consent and ordered to lie on the table.

Mr. Vest introduced a joint resolution (S. R. 117) authorizing the appointment of a Commission to treat with the five civilized tribes of the Indian Territory with a view of making agreements to induce them to take homesteads in severalty; which was read the first and second times by unanimous consent and ordered to lie on the table.

EXTRA COPIES OF BILL.

On motion by Mr. Chandler and by unanimous consent,

Ordered, That 2,000 extra copies of the bill (S. 3513) for the suspension of immigration for one year be printed for the use of the Senate.

WITHDRAWAL OF PAPERS.

On motion by Mr. Sherman,

Ordered, That James Petty have leave to withdraw his papers from the files of the Senate.

COMMITTEE SERVICE.

Mr. Vance having resumed his place upon the Committee to Audit and Control the Contingent Expenses of the Senate.

Mr. Gorman was excused from further service on the said committee.

CIVIL SERVICE COMMISSION REPORT.

Mr. Cockrell submitted the following concurrent resolution; which was referred to the Committee on Printing:

Resolved by the Senate (the House of Representatives concurring), That 23,000 copies of the ninth annual report of the United States Civil Service Commission, with appendices, be printed, of which 1,000 copies shall be for the use of the Senate, 2,000 copies for the use of the House of Representatives, and 20,000 copies for the use of the United States Civil Service Commission.

COMPENSATION OF LETTER-CARRIERS.

Mr. Hoar submitted the following resolution; which was considered by unanimous consent and agreed to:

Resolved, That the Postmaster-General be directed to inform the Senate of the facts, so far as known to his Department, affecting the claim of letter-carriers in cities which contain a population of 75,000 inhabitants to a larger compensation than they have received under the act of January 3, 1887, section 2; and, if in his opinion such letter-carriers are legally or in justice entitled to a compensation larger than they have received, to communicate to the Senate an estimate of the amount which will be necessary for the purpose.

KILLING OF FRANK RILEY.

Mr. Mitchell submitted the following resolution; which was referred to the Committee on Foreign Relations and ordered to be printed:

Resolved, That the President be, and he hereby is, requested, if not incompatible with the public interests, to transmit to the Senate, at his earliest convenience, copies of all correspondence on file in the Department of State, if any, relating to the alleged killing of Frank Riley, an American sailor of the United States steamship *Newark,* in Genoa, Italy, in August or September last.

RAILROAD INTERESTS.

Mr. Peffer submitted the following resolution; which was ordered to lie on the table and be printed:

Resolved by the Senate, That the Committee on Interstate Commerce be, and it is hereby, instructed to inquire and report as follows:

First. What is the separate and what the aggregate capitalization of the railroad corporations of the United States which are engaged in interstate commerce?

Second. What was the actual original cost of constructing and equipping said roads?

Third. What is the present value of the roads; that is, what would be the cost of building and stocking roads as good as they and on the same lines at the present value of materials and labor?

Fourth. What is the average number of salaried officers employed and paid by the several railroad companies; what is the total amount of money paid such officers annually as salaries; what is the average yearly wages paid locomotive engineers, firemen, and passenger conductors, and what is the average daily or monthly wages paid all other employés?

Fifth. What has been the general effect of the operation of the interstate-commerce law on the business and the net earnings of roads; has the cost of transportation been reduced; has the reduc-

tion, if any, been on through traffic or on local traffic; has the effect been uniform throughout the country?

Sixth. What has been the aggregate annual gross earnings and the aggregate net earnings of the roads during the last five years, and freight on said roads during the last five years, computing by distance and weight?

Seventh. What has been the average cost of moving passengers and freight on said roads during the last five years, computing by distance and weight?

Eighth. What is the actual and the relative cost of moving passengers and freight in different parts of the country, indicating the sections where such differences exist?

Ninth. Basing the estimate on the traffic of the last five years, and allowing an annual interest rate of 5 per cent on the actual present value of the roads, what would be equitable charges for carrying passengers and freight in the United States, said charges to be the same on all the roads?

Tenth. Would it be practicable to consolidate the interstate railroad business so as to establish and maintain uniform charges for carriage in all parts of the country and to fairly settle at one place all just differentials?

The committee will report as early as practicable. It may act by subcommittee of two or more of its members, may sit during sessions of the Senate, and if it be found that any part of the information asked for by this resolution can not be procured without the use of money specially appropriated, the committee will report that fact to the Senate, setting out what can not be so procured.

ADDITIONAL SENATE EMPLOYÉ.

Mr. McMillan submitted the following resolution; which was referred to the Committee to Audit and Control the Contingent Expenses of the Senate:

Resolved, That, until further ordered, the Sergeant-at-Arms is directed to employ one attendant in ladies' retiring room, Senate wing of the Capitol, at the rate of $720 per annum, said employé to be paid from the miscellaneous items of the contingent fund of the Senate.

CENSUS ENUMERATORS.

Mr. Vest submitted the following resolution for consideration; which was ordered to be printed:—

Whereas it has been charged by the public press that officials of the Government employed in the Census Bureau of the Interior Department have been guilty of gross misconduct for partisan purposes, and especially that the enumerators appointed to make the enrollment of population for the census of 1890 in the State of Missouri and elsewhere, did, under instructions from certain officers of the Bureau, make at the same time lists of voters for partisan use;

And also, that certain clerks and accountants employed in said Bureau were sent to the State of New York during the recent canvass to perform partisan service while drawing pay from the Government: Therefore,

Resolved, That the Committee on the Census is directed to investigate said charges, and to report by bill or otherwise; that said committee have power to send for persons and papers, and to employ a stenographer, the expenses to be paid out of the contingent fund of the Senate.

EXECUTIVE SESSION.

On motion by Mr. Sherman,

The Senate proceeded to the consideration of executive business; and

After the consideration of executive business the doors were reopened, and

On motion by Mr. Sherman, at 2 o'clock and 45 minutes p. m.,

The Senate adjourned.

WEDNESDAY, DECEMBER 7, 1892.

Mr. Frank Hiscock, from the State of New York, attended.

MESSAGE FROM THE PRESIDENT.

The following message was received from the President of the United States, by Mr. Pruden, his secretary:

To the Senate:

In response to the resolution of the Senate of April 11, 1892, requesting information in regard to the agreement between the United States and Great Britain of 1817, concerning the naval forces to be maintained by the two Governments on the Great Lakes, I transmit herewith a report of the Secretary of State and accompanying papers, giving all the information existing in that Department in regard to the agreement in question.

BENJ. HARRISON.

EXECUTIVE MANSION, *December 7, 1892.*

The message was read.

Ordered, That it be referred to the Committee on Foreign Relations and printed.

EXECUTIVE COMMUNICATIONS.

The Vice-President laid before the Senate the annual report of the Attorney-General for the year ending December 1, 1892.

Ordered, That it lie on the table and be printed.

The Vice-President laid before the Senate the annual report of the Secretary of the Treasury on the state of the finances for the year 1892; which was referred to the Committee on Finance and ordered to be printed.

The Vice-President laid before the Senate a letter of the Treasurer of the United States transmitting copies of accounts rendered to and settled with the First Comptroller of the Treasury, for the fiscal year ended June 30, 1892; which was ordered to be printed, and, with the accompanying documents, referred to the Committee on Printing.

PETITIONS AND MEMORIALS.

Petitions, memorials, etc., were presented and referred as follows:

By Mr. Dawes: A petition of citizens of Massachusetts, praying that the moral, intellectual, and industrial progress and development of the colored people during the first quarter century of their freedom be made part of the Government exhibit at the World's Columbian Exposition; which was referred to the Select Committee on the Quadro-Centennial.

By Mr. Dolph: A petition of citizens of Oregon, praying the passage of a law extending the time of payment by settlers for lands within the limits of the forfeited Northern Pacific land grant; to the Committee on Public Lands.

A petition of citizens of Oregon, praying the repeal of the provision for the closing of the World's Columbian Exposition on the Sabbath day; to the Select Committee on the Quadro-Centennial.

A petition of Cynthia J. Bloomfield, praying to be allowed a pension; and

A petition of Lorenzo Wyett Mulvany, praying to be allowed a pension; to the Committee on Pensions.

By Mr. Perkins: A petition of W. Spratt Scott, praying the protection of the rights of citizenship in the Cherokee Nation to his wife, Sarah Oregonia Bell; to the Committee on Indian Affairs.

Two petitions of citizens of Kansas, praying for the restriction of immigration by consular examination; to the Committee on Immigration.

A petition of citizens of Kansas, praying that the moral, intellectual and industrial progress and development of the colored people during the first quarter century of their freedom be made part of the Government exhibit at the World's Columbian Exposition; to the Select Committee on the Quadro-Centennial.

By Mr. Brice: Two petitions from citizens of Ohio, praying an amendment to the immigration laws, so as to authorize the President of the United States to suspend all traffic between this country and countries where contagious diseases are epidemic; to the Committee on Immigration.

A memorial of citizens of Ohio, remonstrating against the closing of the World's Columbian Exposition on the Sabbath day; to the Select Committee on the Quadro-Centennial.

By Mr. Wilson: A petition of citizens of Iowa, praying the passage of a law for the closing of the World's Columbian Exposition on the Sabbath Day; to the Select Committee on the Quadro-Centennial.

By Mr. Quay: A petition of Julius Bates, praying to be allowed a pension; to the Committee on Pensions.

By Mr. Manderson: Papers relating to the application of Eliza Ferguson to be restored to the pension rolls; to the Committee on Pensions, to accompany the bill S. 3532.

By Mr. Vilas: A petition of Caroline Borchers, praying to be allowed a pension; to the Committee on Pensions, to accompany the bill S. 3535.

Petitions praying the appointment of a committee to investigate an alleged combine formed to depreciate the price of grain and now existing between the elevators, millers, and railroads at Minneapolis and St. Louis, and praying for the postponement of the "antioption bill" until said committee can report, were presented as follows:

By Mr. Hansbrough: Four petitions of citizens of North Dakota.
By Mr. Manderson: Several petitions of citizens of Nebraska.
By Mr. Wilson: Several petitions of citizens of Iowa.
By Mr. Perkins: Four petitions of citizens of Kansas.

Ordered, That they be referred to the Committee on Agriculture and Forestry.

Petitions praying the passage of the bill to limit the free entry of wearing apparel of foreign manufacture were presented as follows:

By Mr. Wilson: Three petitions of citizens of Iowa.
By Mr. Faulkner: Two petitions of citizens of West Virginia.
By Mr. Cameron: Several petitions of citizens of Pennsylvania.
By Mr. Perkins: Two petitions of citizens of Kansas.
By Mr. Cullom: A petition of citizens of Illinois.
By Mr. Brice: Four petitions of citizens of Ohio.
By Mr. Teller: Two petitions of citizens of Colorado.

Ordered, That they be referred to the Committee on Finance.

Petitions praying the passage of the "antioption bill" were presented as follows:

By Mr. Harris: Three petitions of citizens of Tennessee.
By Mr. Washburn: A petition of citizens of Ohio.
By Mr. Perkins: A petition of citizens of Kansas.

By Mr. Allen: A petition of citizens of Washington.
By Mr. Washburn: Resolution of the Board of Trade of Minneapolis, Minn.

Ordered, That they lie on the table.

Memorials remonstrating against the passage of the "antioption bill" were presented as follows:

By the Vice-President: Several memorials of citizens of the United States.
By Mr. Mills: A memorial of citizens of Texas.
By Mr. Vance: Two memorials of citizens of North Carolina.
By Mr. Harris: A memorial of the Cotton Exchange of Memphis, Tenn., and a memorial of citizens of Tennessee.
By Mr. Gordon: A memorial of the Cotton Exchange of Savannah, Ga.
By Mr. Daniel: A memorial of citizens of Virginia.
By Mr. Brice: A memorial of the Toledo Produce Exchange.

Ordered, That they lie on the table.

Memorials remonstrating against the repeal of the provision for the closing of the World's Columbian Exposition on the Sabbath day were presented as follows:

By Mr. Cameron: A memorial of citizens of Pennsylvania.
By Mr. Brice: Several memorials of citizens of Ohio.

Ordered, That they be referred to the Select Committee on the Quadro-Centennial.

By Mr. Cameron: Papers relating to the application of L. H. Frink to be allowed a pension; to the Committee on Pensions, to accompany the bill S. 3551.

REPORTS OF COMMITTEES.

Mr. Paddock, from the Committee to Audit and Control the Contingent Expenses of the Senate, to whom was referred the resolution yesterday submitted by Mr. McMillan, providing for the employment of one attendant in the ladies' retiring room, Senate wing of the Capitol, reported it without amendment.

The Senate, proceeded by unanimous consent, to consider the said resolution; and

Resolved, That the Senate agree thereto.

Mr. Cameron, from the Committee on Military Affairs, to whom was referred the bill (S. 2739) for the relief of James Petty, submitted a report (No. 1117) thereon, with the recommendation that the committee be discharged from the further consideration thereof and that the said bill be referred to the Committee on Pensions; which was agreed to.

Mr. Peffer, from the Committee on Claims, to whom was referred the bill (S. 1447) for the relief of Secor & Co., Perine, Secor & Co., and the executors of Zeno Secor, submitted an adverse report (No. 1118) thereon.

Mr. Mitchell, from the Committee on Claims, to whom was referred the bill (S. 1421) for the relief of Lewis D. Allen, submitted an adverse report (No. 1119) thereon.

INTRODUCTION OF BILLS.

Bills were introduced, read the first and second times by unanimous consent, and referred as follows:

By Mr. Blackburn: A bill (S. 3524) to incorporate the East End Electric Railway Company of the District of Columbia; to the Committee on the District of Columbia.

By Mr. Harris: A bill (S. 3525) to authorize the construction of bridges across the Hiawassee, the Tennessee, and the Clinch rivers in the State of Tennessee; to the Committee on Commerce.

By Mr. Paddock: A bill (S. 3526) granting an increase of pension to Benjamin F. Chambers;

A bill (S. 3527) granting an increase of pension to Winfield S. Smith; and

A bill (S. 3528) granting a pension to John D. Keller; to the Committee on Pensions.

By Mr. Stockbridge: A bill (S. 3529) for the relief of William H. Hugo; to the Committee on Military Affairs.

By Mr. McMillan: A bill (S. 3530) to create a board of charities for the District of Columbia; and

A bill (S. 3531) to amend the charter of the Brightwood Railway Company; to the Committee on the District of Columbia.

By Mr. Manderson: A bill (S. 3532) to restore to the pension roll the name of Eliza Ferguson, widow of Hans Ferguson, Company I, Thirty-third Iowa Infantry Volunteers; to the Committee on Pensions.

A bill (S. 3533) to amend sections 4488 and 4489, Revised Statutes, for the greater safety to navigation; to the Committee on Commerce.

By Mr. Hill: A bill (S. 3534) to repeal the act of July 14, 1890, entitled "An act directing the purchase of silver bullion and the issue of Treasury notes thereon, and for other purposes;" to the Committee on Finance.

By Mr. Vilas: A bill (S. 3535) for the relief of Caroline Borchers, widow of John Frederick Borchers; to the Committee on Pensions.

A bill (S. 3536) for the relief of Lorenzo Wyett Mulvany; to the Committee on Pensions.

A bill (S. 3537) for the relief of M. P. Deady; to the Committee on the Judiciary.

By Mr. Perkins: A bill (S. 3538) granting a pension to Mrs. Hannah Kessenger;

A bill (S. 3539) granting a pension to Nancy C. Taylor;
A bill (S. 3540) granting a pension to Mattie M. Kersey;
A bill (S. 3541) granting a pension to Henry Synnamon;
A bill (S. 3542) granting a pension to Charlotte Ross;
A bill (S. 3543) granting a pension to James Bemis;
A bill (S. 3544) granting a pension to Jesse L. Knight;
A bill (S. 3545) granting an increase of pension to John Maloney;
A bill (S. 3546) granting an increase of pension to Levi W. Dikeman; and
A bill (S. 3547) granting an increase of pension to James Gauly; to the Committee on Pensions.
A bill (S. 3548) granting an honorable discharge to C. Frederickson;
A bill (S. 3549) granting an honorable discharge to Henry B. Rizzer; and
A bill (S. 3550) granting an honorable discharge to St. Clair Watts; to the Committee on Military Affairs.
By Mr. Cameron: A bill (S. 3551) granting a pension to L. H. Frink; to the Committee on Pensions.
By Mr. Gallinger: A bill (S. 3552) to remove the charge of desertion from the military record of George J. Barnes; to the Committee on Military Affairs.

JAMES F. SIMMONS.

Mr. Call submitted the following resolution; which was referred to the Committee on the Judiciary:

Resolved, That the Committee on the Judiciary be, and they are hereby, instructed to inquire and report to the Senate the facts in relation to the trial, conviction, and sentence of James F. Simmons in the circuit court of the southern district of New York, under an indictment for a conspiracy to wreck the Sixth National Bank of New York City, and further to report by bill or otherwise whether any legislation, and if so, what, is necessary to prevent the punishment of innocent persons wrongfully accused of crime in the courts of the United States, and that the committee have the authority to send for persons and papers and to have the record of the case printed for the use of the committee and the Senate.

MESSAGE FROM THE HOUSE.

A message from the House of Representatives, by Mr. Towles, its chief clerk:

Mr. President: The House of Representatives has passed the following bills and joint resolutions, in which it requests the concurrence of the Senate:

H. R. 1096. An act granting a pension to Julia Hood;
H. R. 1283. An act to pension Harriet Woodbury, Windsor, Vt.;
H. R. 1422. An act for the relief of George M. Henry;
H. R. 2128. An act granting a pension to John Fields;
H. R. 2407. An act granting a pension to Samuel Luttrell;
H. R. 2493. An act granting a pension to Jesse Cleaveland;
H. R. 3118. An act to pension John S. Dunham;
H. R. 3676. An act for the relief of R. L. Jennings, late postmaster at Marshall, Tex.;
H. R. 3845. An act to increase the pension of Edward R. Chapman;
H. R. 4366. An act granting a pension to Jacob Hall;
H. R. 4804. An act to place the name of Sarah L. Van Nest on the pension list;
H. R. 4955. An act granting a pension to Susannah Chadwick;
H. R. 5022. An act for the relief of Lucy Sprotberry;
H. R. 5509. An act to place the name of Mrs. E. M. Banister, an army nurse, on the pension rolls;
H. R. 5705. An act to increase the pension of Amelia Graham;
H. R. 6030. An act granting a pension to French W. Thornhill;
H. R. 6345. An act granting an honorable discharge to Frederick E. Kolter;
H. R. 6508. An act granting a pension to Joseph Fortier;
H. R. 6511. An act to pension Rebecca M. Youngblood;
H. R. 6914. An act granting a pension to Druke Nettie Barnett;
H. R. 6969. An act for the relief of Elisha Brown;
H. R. 6970. An act to remove the charge of desertion from the record of Montgomery M. Tuttle;
H. R. 7226. An act granting a pension to Julia P. Wright;
H. R. 7257. An act granting a pension to Alonzo D. Barber;
H. R. 7510. An act for the relief of Mrs. Mary A. Moorhead;
H. R. 7662. An act granting a pension to Marion Kern Sharman;
H. R. 8017. An act granting a pension to Elizabeth Voss;
H. R. 8106. An act for the correction of the army record of David R. Wallace, deceased;
H. R. 8221. An act granting a pension to Geo. W. Boyd;
H. R. 8275. An act granting a pension to Abraham B. Simmons, of Capt. Thomas Tripp's company, in Col. Brisbane's regiment South Carolina Volunteers, in the Florida Indian war;
H. R. 8409. An act granting a pension to Mary Danahay, mother of Daniel Danahay, late a private, Company H, Eighteenth New York Cavalry;
H. R. 9011. An act to grant a pension to Ida A. Taylor;

H. R. 9139. An act to pension Mrs. Eliza T. Palmatier;
H. R. 9585. An act for the relief of Harriett E. Niles; and
H. R. 157. A joint resolution providing for the calling of an international arbitration congress.

The House of Representatives has passed the following resolutions, which I am directed to communicate to the Senate:

Resolved, That this House has heard with deep sorrow of the death of the honorable Edward F. McDonald, late a Representative from the State of New Jersey.

Resolved, That a copy of the foregoing resolution be transmitted to the family of the dead member.

Resolved, That the Clerk be directed to communicate a copy of these resolutions to the Senate.

Resolved, That as a further mark of respect for the dead, this House do now adjourn.

It has also passed the following resolutions, which I am directed to communicate to the Senate:

Resolved, That the House has heard with profound sorrow of the death of honorable John G. Warwick, late a Representative from the State of Ohio.

Resolved, That the Clerk be directed to communicate a copy of these resolutions to the Senate.

Resolved, That as a mark of respect to his memory the House do now adjourn.

CENSUS BUREAU OFFICIALS.

The Vice-President laid before the Senate the resolution yesterday submitted by Mr. Vest, directing an investigation of certain charges by the public press against officials of the Census Bureau; and

Ordered, That it be referred to the Committee to Audit and Control the Contingent Expenses of the Senate.

RAILROAD INTERESTS.

The Vice-President laid before the Senate the resolution yesterday submitted by Mr. Peffer, providing for an inquiry into certain matters connected with railroad corporations engaged in interstate commerce; and

Ordered, That it be referred to the Committee on Interstate Commerce.

THE FIVE CIVILIZED TRIBES.

On motion by Mr. Vest,

The Senate proceeded to consider, as in Committee of the Whole, the joint resolution (S. R. 117) authorizing the appointment of a commission to treat with the five civilized tribes of the Indian Territory with a view of making agreements to induce them to take homesteads in severalty; and

After debate,

Ordered, That the further consideration thereof be postponed to to-morrow.

DEATH OF EDWARD F. M'DONALD.

The Vice-President laid before the Senate the resolutions of the House of Representatives announcing the death of the honorable Edward F. McDonald; which were read;

When

Mr. McPherson submitted the following resolutions:

Resolved, That the Senate has heard with deep sensibility the announcement of the death of Hon. Edward F. McDonald, late a Representative from the State of New Jersey.

Resolved, That the Secretary communicate this resolution to the House of Representatives.

Resolved, That as a mark of respect to the memory of the deceased the Senate do now adjourn.

The resolutions were considered by unanimous consent and unanimously agreed to;

Whereupon

The Senate adjourned.

THURSDAY, DECEMBER 8, 1892.

Mr. Charles H. Gibson, from the State of Maryland, and Mr. David Turpie, from the State of Indiana, attended.

HOUSE BILLS AND JOINT RESOLUTION REFERRED.

The bills and joint resolution yesterday received from the House of Representatives for concurrence were severally read the first and second times by unanimous consent.

Ordered, That the bills H. R. 1096, H. R. 1283, H. R. 2128, H. R. 2407, H. R. 2493, H. R. 3118, H. R. 3845, H. R. 4366, H. R. 4804, H. R. 4955, H. R. 5022, H. R. 5509, H. R. 5705, H. R. 6030, H. R. 6508, H. R. 6511, H. R. 6914, H. R. 6969, H. R. 7226, H. R. 7257, H. R. 7510, H. R. 7662, H. R. 8017, H. R. 8221, H. R. 8275, H. R. 8409, H. R. 9011, H. R. 9139, and H. R. 9585, be referred to the Committee on Pensions; that the bills H. R. 1422, H. R. 6345, H. R. 6970 and H. R. 8106 be referred to the Committee on Military Affairs; that the bill H. R. 3676 be referred to the Committee on Post-Offices and Post-Roads, and that the joint resolution H. R. 157 be referred to the Committee on Foreign Relations.

in 1890, and suspended in 1891, to provide accommodation for the Government Printing Office; which was read the first and second times by unanimous consent.

Mr. Dolph, from the Committee on Public Lands, to whom was referred the bill (S. 3382) to authorize a corrected patent to be issued for the donation land claim of Wheelock Simmonds and wife, reported it with amendments and submitted a report (No. 1121) thereon.

On motion by Mr. Hale,
Ordered, That the Committee on the Census be discharged from the further consideration of the bill (H. R. 8582) to provide for the publication of the Eleventh Census, and that it be referred to the Committee on Printing.

Mr. Hoar, from the Committee on the Judiciary, to whom was referred the bill (S. 2625) to provide for the punishment of offenses upon the high seas, reported it with amendments.

The Senate proceeded, by unanimous consent, to consider the said bill as in Committee of the Whole; and the reported amendments having been agreed to, the bill was reported to the Senate and the amendments were concurred in.

Ordered, That the bill be engrossed and read a third time.
The said bill was read the third time.
Resolved, That it pass, and that the title thereof be as aforesaid.
Ordered, That the Secretary request the concurrence of the House of Representatives therein.

INTRODUCTION OF BILLS.

Bills were introduced, read the first and second times by unanimous consent, and referred as follows:

By Mr. Vest: A bill (S. 3561) to encourage the construction of electric railroads, to facilitate the rapid transportation of the mails, to promote the interests of commerce and travel, and to aid in demonstrating the feasibility of the distribution of electrical power for agricultural and other purposes along the line of electric roads, and especially to aid in the construction of a pioneer electric railroad between the cities of Chicago and St. Louis by the Chicago and St. Louis Electric Railroad Company, and to secure to the Government the use of the same for postal, military, and other purposes at existing rates; to the Committee on Commerce.

By Mr. Cameron: A bill (S. 3562) for the relief of Nicholas Marshall; to the Committee on Claims.

A bill (S. 3563) to authorize the sale to the Schuylkill River East Side Railroad Company of a lot of ground belonging to the United States Naval Asylum in the city of Philadelphia, Pa.; to the Committee on Naval Affairs.

By Mr. Hoar: A bill (S. 3564) for the relief of Josiah Pickett; to the Committee on Post-Offices and Post-Roads.

By Mr. Proctor: A bill (S. 3565) to pension Mary Brown, of Berlin, Vt.; to the Committee on Pensions.

By Mr. Hale: A bill (S. 3566) for the relief of Almon Springsteen, of Binghamton, N. Y.; to the Committee on Pensions.

By Mr. Callom: A bill (S. 3567), for the relief of Rev. Moses M. Longley; to the Committee on Military Affairs.

By Mr. Frye: A bill (S. 3568), providing for the establishment and enforcement of rules and regulations for the use and navigation of United States canals and similar works of navigation, and for other purposes; to the Committee on Commerce.

REPORT ON IMMIGRATION.

Mr. Chandler submitted the following resolution; which was referred to the Committee on Printing:

Resolved by the Senate (*the House of Representatives concurring*), That the Public Printer be, and he is hereby, directed to print, with a title page, 13,000 additional copies of the report of Immigrant Commissioner H. J. Schultels, contained in Part I, House Executive Document No. 235, first session, Fifty-first Congress, pages 263 to 323, inclusive, 2,000 to be for the use of the Treasury Department, 2,000 for the use of the House Committee on Immigration, 2,000 for the use of the Senate Committee on Immigration, 2,000 for the use of the Senate, and 4,000 for the use of the House.

INTRODUCTION OF CHOLERA.

Mr. Chandler submitted the following resolution; which was considered by unanimous consent and agreed to:

Resolved, That the Secretary of the Treasury be directed to transmit to the Senate any communications recently received from the port physician of the city of Philadelphia concerning the danger of the introduction of cholera into this country during the coming season, and also to inform the Senate whether during the past summer any immigrants shipped back to Europe by the United States immigration officers were retaken from the vessels by their owners, contrary to law; and, if so, to state the circumstances of such reception, and whether or not prosecutions were instituted to punish the violators of law.

ENTRANCE TO FERNANDINA HARBOR.

Mr. Call submitted the following resolution; which was considered by unanimous consent and agreed to:

Resolved, That the Secretary of War be, and is hereby, directed to furnish to the Senate any information in possession of the Chief of Engineers as to the condition of the present ship channel between Cumberland Island, Georgia, and Fernandina, Fla., and the injury to it from the construction of the north jetty, and its present unfinished condition, and as to the danger of the closing of the channel on account of the obstruction created by this work, and the necessity for an immediate appropriation to prevent the closing of the channel.

COMMITTEE SERVICE.

Mr. Cullom submitted the following resolution; which was considered by unanimous consent and agreed to:

Resolved, That Senators Peffer and Call be appointed as additional members of the Committee on Immigration during the present session of Congress.

MESSAGE FROM THE HOUSE.

A message from the House of Representatives, by Mr. Towles, its chief clerk:

Mr. President: The House of Representatives has passed the following bills, in which it requests the concurrence of the Senate:
H. R. 2034. An act for the relief of Susan T. Salisbury;
H. R. 2478. An act for the relief of David Sarsfield;
H. R. 2901. An act to pension Ida Cassell;
H. R. 6564. An act to remove the charge of desertion against Charles H. Behle;
H. R. 7036. An act granting a pension to Lillie Rice, late a nurse at Jefferson Barracks;
H. R. 7099. An act granting an increase of pension to Samuel S. Anderson;
H. R. 7375. An act granting a pension to Mary Hollis;
H. R. 8054. An act to increase the pension of Mary L. Bacon, widow of the late George B. Bacon, late lieutenant-commander of the United States Navy;
H. R. 8780. An act to restore to the pension roll Mary Eleanor White, as former widow of Capt. George W. Hazzard; and
H. R. 8925. An act to increase the pension of Harvey Lyon.

The Speaker of the House of Representatives having signed an enrolled joint resolution (H. R. 167), I am directed to bring it to the Senate for the signature of its President.

ENROLLED JOINT RESOLUTION SIGNED.

Mr. Sanders reported from the committee that they had examined and found duly enrolled the joint resolution (H. R. 167) relating to the discharge of certain official duties in the office of the Register of the Treasury;

Whereupon
The Vice-President signed the same, and it was delivered to the committee to be presented to the President of the United States.

HOUSE BILLS REFERRED.

The bills last received from the House of Representatives for concurrence were severally read the first and second times by unanimous consent.

Ordered, That the bills H. R. 2478 and H. R. 6564 be referred to the Committee on Military Affairs; and that the residue of the said bills be referred to the Committee on Pensions.

HOUSE AMENDMENT TO SENATE BILL.

The Presiding Officer (Mr. Gallinger in the chair) laid before the Senate the amendment of the House of Representatives to the bill (S. 2612) granting a pension to Tendoy, chief of the Bannocks, Shoshones, and Sheepeaters tribe of Indians; and

On motion by Mr. Shoup,
Resolved, That the Senate agree thereto.
Ordered, That the Secretary notify the House of Representatives thereof.

INDIANS ON WHITE EARTH RESERVATION.

The Senate proceeded to consider, as in Committee of the Whole, the bill (S. 3184) to provide for allotments to Indians on White Earth Reservation in Minnesota; and, having been amended on the motion of Mr. Dawes, the bill was reported to the Senate and the amendments were concurred in.

Ordered, That it be engrossed and read a third time.
The said bill was read the third time.
Resolved, That it pass, and that the title thereof be as aforesaid.
Ordered, That the Secretary request the concurrence of the House of Representatives therein.

FIVE CIVILIZED TRIBES OF INDIANS.

On motion by Mr. Berry,
The Senate resumed, as in Committee of the Whole, the consideration of a commission to treat with the five civilized tribes of the Indian Territory, with a view of making agreements to induce them to take homesteads in severalty; and,

Pending debate,

"OPTIONS" AND "FUTURES."

The Presiding Officer announced that the hour of 2 o'clock had arrived, and laid before the Senate the bill (H. R. 7845) defining "options" and "futures," imposing special taxes on dealers therein, and requiring such persons engaged in selling certain products to obtain license, and for other purposes, made the unfinished business of the Senate by its order of the 30th of July last; and

The Senate resumed, as in Committee of the Whole, the consideration of the bill; and

After debate,

On motion by Mr. Harris,

Ordered, That the bill be reprinted, showing the amendments agreed to in Committee of the Whole and the amendment proposed.

EXECUTIVE SESSION.

On motion by Mr. Cullom,

The Senate proceeded to the consideration of executive business; and

After the consideration of executive business the doors were reopened, and

On motion by Mr. Cullom, at 3 o'clock and 5 minutes p. m.,

The Senate adjourned.

TUESDAY, DECEMBER 13, 1892.

PUBLIC PRINTING AND BINDING.

The Vice-President laid before the Senate the amendments of the House of Representatives to the bill (S. 1549) providing for the public printing and binding and distribution of public documents.

On motion by Mr. Manderson,

Resolved, That the Senate disagree to the amendments of the House of Representatives to the said bill, and ask a conference with the House on the disagreeing votes of the two Houses thereon.

Ordered, That the conferees on the part of the Senate be appointed by the Vice-President; and

The Vice-President appointed Mr. Manderson, Mr. Hawley, and Mr. Gorman.

Ordered, That the Secretary notify the House of Representatives thereof.

EXECUTIVE COMMUNICATION.

The Vice-President laid before the Senate five communications from the Secretary of State, transmitting, in pursuance of the provisions of the act of February 3, 1887, certified copies of the final ascertainment of the electors for President and Vice-President in the States of Texas, North Carolina, Alabama, Illinois, and Maine.

Ordered, That they lie on the table.

PETITIONS AND MEMORIALS.

Petitions, memorials, etc., were presented and referred as follows:

By Mr. Daniel: Several petitions of citizens of Virginia, praying the repeal of the provision in the revenue law of 1890 providing for the sale of leaf tobacco free of tax; to the Committee on Finance.

By Mr. Mitchell: A petition of William E. Stevenson, praying to be allowed a pension; to the Committee on Pensions.

By Mr. Wilson: A petition of citizens of Iowa praying for the closing of the Columbian Exposition on the Sabbath day; for the passage of the "antioption bill;" to prohibit the sale of intoxicating liquors on the grounds of the Columbian Exposition; for the restriction of immigration, etc.; to the Select Committee on the Quadro-Centennial.

By Mr. Paddock: A memorial of the Chamber of Commerce of Duluth, Minn., praying the construction by the United States of a canal from the Great Lakes to the Hudson River; to the Committee on Commerce.

By Mr. Felton: A petition of Dr. Edmund P. Tierney, praying to be allowed a pension; to the Committee on Pensions.

By Mr. Hill: A petition of citizens of New York, praying the passage of the bill authorizing the New York and New Jersey Bridge Companies to construct and maintain a bridge across the Hudson River between New York City and the State of New Jersey.

Ordered, That it lie on the table and be printed.

By Mr. Felton: A petition of James Joyes, praying the passage of a law authorizing his appointment to the Army of the United States as a first lieutenant, and to be placed on the retired list: to the Committee on Military Affairs, to accompany the bill S. 3573.

Petitions praying for the appointment of a committee to investigate an alleged combine formed to depreciate the price of grain, and now existing between the elevators, millers, and railroads at Minneapolis and St. Louis, and asking for the postponement of the antioption bill until said committee can report, were presented as follows:

By Mr. Perkins: Several petitions of citizens of Kansas.

By Mr. Paddock: Several petitions of citizens of Nebraska.

Mr. Peffer: Several petitions of citizens of Kansas.

Ordered, That they be referred to the Committee on Agriculture and Forestry.

Memorials remonstrating against the passage of any law for closing of the Columbian Exposition on the Sabbath day were presented as follows:

By Mr. Daniel: A memorial of citizens of Virginia.

By Mr. Mitchell: A memorial of citizens of Oregon.

Ordered, That they be referred to the Select Committee on the Quadro-Centennial.

Petitions praying the closing of the Columbian Exposition on the Sabbath day were presented as follows:

By Mr. Cullom: A petition of citizens of Illinois.

By Mr. Wilson: A petition of citizens of Iowa.

Ordered, That they be referred to the Select Committee on the Quadro-Centennial.

Petitions praying the passage of the bill limiting the amount of wearing apparel that may be admitted free of duty were presented as follows:

By Mr. Allen: A petition of citizens of Washington.

By Mr. Wilson: A petition of citizens of Iowa.

By Mr. Perkins: A petition of citizens of Kansas.

Ordered, That they be referred to the Committee on Finance.

Memorials remonstrating against the passage of the "antioption bill" were presented as follows:

By Mr. Daniel: A memorial of the Chamber of Commerce of Richmond, Va., and a memorial of citizens of Virginia.

By Mr. Irby: Two memorials of citizens of South Carolina.

Ordered, That they lie on the table.

Mr. Kyle presented a petition of citizens of South Dakota, praying the passage of the "antioption bill."

Ordered, That it lie on the table.

REPORTS OF COMMITTEES.

Mr. Sanders reported from the committee that on the 12th instant they presented to the President of the United States an enrolled bill (S. 1661) granting an increase of pension to John Hallam.

Mr. Manderson, from the Committee on Printing, to whom was referred the letter of the Treasurer of the United States transmitting copies of accounts rendered to and settled with the First Comptroller, reported the same back with the recommendation that they be not printed; which was agreed to.

Mr. Manderson, from the Committee on Printing, to whom was referred the joint resolution (S. R. 118) to print the fifteenth number of the Statistical Abstract of the United States for the year 1892, reported in lieu thereof the following resolution; which was considered by unanimous consent and agreed to:

Resolved by the Senate (the House of Representatives concurring), That there be printed 20,000 copies of the Statistical Abstract of the United States for the year 1892, prepared by the Bureau of Statistics, Treasury Department—6,000 copies for the use of the members of the Senate, 12,000 copies for the use of the members of the House of Representatives, and 2,000 copies for the use of the Bureau of Statistics, Treasury Department.

Ordered, That the Secretary request the concurrence of the House of Representatives therein.

INTRODUCTION OF BILLS.

Bills were introduced, read the first and second times by unanimous consent, and referred as follows:

By Mr. Bate: A bill (S. 3569) for the relief of D. W. and Minna H. Glassie and Joseph C. Nash; to the Committee on Claims.

By Mr. Gallinger: A bill (S. 3570) for the suspension of immigration under certain circumstances; to the Committee on Immigration.

By Mr. Peffer: A bill (S. 3571) to facilitate promotion in the Navy; to the Committee on Naval Affairs.

By Mr. Perkins: A bill (S. 3572) providing for the purchase of certain property therein named; to the Committee on Appropriations.

By Mr. Felton: A bill (S. 3573) for the relief of James Joyes, late lieutenant, United States Army; to the Committee on Military Affairs.

By Mr. Mitchell: A bill (S. 3574) to provide for a national encampment of the Army and militia at the World's Columbian Exposition; to the Select Committee on the Quadro-Centennial.

A bill (S. 3575) granting a pension to William E. Stevenson; to the Committee on Pensions.

A bill (S. 3576) to remove the charge of desertion from the military record of Henry Von Hess, of Portland, Oregon; to the Committee on Military Affairs.

By Mr. Cullom: A bill (S. 3577) to amend an act entitled "An act to regulate commerce," approved February 4, 1887; to the Committee on Interstate Commerce.

By Mr. Platt: A bill (S. 3578) granting a pension to Susan E. Cunningham; to the Committee on Pensions.

By Mr. Vest: A bill (S. 3579) to extend the jurisdiction of courts in Oklahoma Territory, and of the United States court in the Indian Territory; to the Committee on the Judiciary.

By Mr. Sawyer: A bill (S. 3580) to amend the proviso to be found in connection with the free-delivery service, page 569, 24th volume, Statutes at Large; to the Committee on Post-Offices and Post Roads.

By Mr. Dolph: A bill (S. 3581) to amend an act entitled "An act to forfeit certain lands heretofore granted for the purpose of aiding in the construction of railroads, and for other purposes;" to the Committee on Public Lands.

REPORT OF COMMISSIONER OF FISH AND FISHERIES.

Mr. Manderson submitted the following resolution; which was referred to the Committee on Printing:

Resolved by the Senate (the House of Representatives concurring therein), That the report of the Commissioner of Fish and Fisheries, covering the operations of the Commission for the fiscal year ending June 30, 1892, be printed; and that there be printed 8,000 extra copies, of which 2,000 shall be for the use of the Senate, 4,000 for the use of the House of Representatives, and 2,000 for the use of the Commissioner of Fish and Fisheries; the illustrations to be obtained by the Public Printer under the direction of the Joint Committee on Printing.

POSITIONS IN THE CIVIL SERVICE.

Mr. Daniel submitted the following resolution; which was ordered to lie on the table:

Resolved, That the Civil Service Commission be, and it is hereby, requested to furnish the Senate with a succinct statement of the positions in the Government service now embraced under civil service regulations, including their number and kind, and of the methods of application and examination; the said statement also to specify the quota of each State, whether filled or vacant, and what positions in number and kind are open to appointment outside of civil service regulations, with their number and kind, the design of this resolution being to procure in a compact form information for the use of those desiring to enter the service of the Government.

MESSAGE FROM THE HOUSE.

A message from the House of Representatives by Mr. Towles, its chief clerk.

Mr. President: The House of Representatives has passed without amendment the following bills of the Senate:

S. 2275. An act for the relief of purchasers of timber and stone lands under the act of June 3, 1878; and

S. 3418. An act making Saturday a half-holiday for banking and trust-company purposes in the District of Columbia.

The House of Representatives has passed the bill (S. 2093) to provide for the disposal of certain abandoned military reservations in the State of Wyoming with amendments, in which it requests the concurrence of the Senate; and

It has passed the following bills, in which it requests the concurrence of the Senate:

H. R. 6180. An act to establish an additional land office in the Territory of New Mexico;

H. R. 6644. An act to amend an act entitled "An act authorizing the sale of title of the United States in lot 3 in square south of square 990, approved, March 3, 1891;"

H. R. 6922. An act to amend section 452 of the Revised Statutes relating to the District of Columbia concerning conveyance of real estate;

H. R. 7625. An act for relief of certain settlers on public land in the Tucson land district in Arizona;

H. R. 8268. An act to amend chapter 559, page 1095, volume 26, United States Statutes at Large.

H. R. 8815. An act to extend North Capitol street to the Soldiers' Home;

H. R. 8956. An act establishing a fog signal at Tibbets Point, Lake Ontario, New York, and

H. R. 9758. An act to amend the charter of the Eckington and Soldiers' Home Railway Company of the District of Columbia.

HOUSE BILLS REFERRED.

The bills last received from the House of Representatives for concurrence were severally read the first and second times by unanimous consent.

Ordered, That the bills H. R. 6180, H. R. 7625, and H. R. 8268 be referred to the Committee on Public Lands; that the bills H. R. 6644, H. R. 6922, H. R. 8815, and H. R. 9758 be referred to the Committee on the District of Columbia; and that the bill H. R. 8956 be referred to the Committee on Commerce.

FIVE CIVILIZED TRIBES OF INDIANS.

On motion by Mr. Jones, of Arkansas,

The Senate resumed, as in Committee of the Whole, the consideration of the joint resolution (S. R. 117) authorizing the appointment of a commission to treat with the five civilized tribes of the Indian Territory, with a view of making agreements to induce them to take homesteads in severalty; and

After debate,

Ordered, That the further consideration thereof be postponed until to-morrow.

DEALINGS IN OPTIONS AND FUTURES.

On motion by Mr. Washburn,

The Senate resumed, as in Committee of the Whole, the consideration of the bill (H. R. 7845) defining "options" and "futures," imposing special taxes on dealers therein, and requiring such persons engaged in selling certain products to obtain license, and for other purposes; and

The question being on the amendment proposed by Mr. Daniel to strike out section 10,

Pending debate,

EXECUTIVE SESSION.

On motion by Mr. Platt,

The Senate proceeded to the consideration of executive business; and

After the consideration of executive business the doors were reopened, and

On motion by Mr. Manderson, at 3 o'clock and 30 minutes p. m., The Senate adjourned.

WEDNESDAY, DECEMBER 14, 1892.

EXECUTIVE COMMUNICATIONS.

The Vice-President laid before the Senate a letter of the Secretary of State, transmitting, in pursuance of the provisions of the act of February 3, 1887, a certified copy of the final ascertainment of the electors for President and Vice-President in the State of Florida.

Ordered, That it lie on the table.

The Vice-President laid before the Senate a letter of the Secretary of the Interior, transmitting, in obedience to law, a report of the Commissioner of Education on the schools in the District of Columbia; which was referred to the Committee on Appropriations and ordered to be printed.

The Vice-President laid before the Senate a letter of the Secretary of the Treasury, transmitting, in answer to a resolution of the 12th instant, a communication from the Philadelphia Board of Health concerning the suspension of immigration during the existence of cholera in Europe, prepared by the port physician at Philadelphia, Pa., on December 5, 1892; which was referred to the Committee on Immigration and ordered to be printed.

PETITIONS AND MEMORIALS.

Petitions, memorials, etc., were presented and referred as follows:

By Mr. Paddock: A petition of William O. McDowell, praying an amendment to the election laws changing the age of the right to vote from 21 to 18 years; to the Committee on Privileges and Elections.

A petition of citizens of New York, praying the passage of the bill limiting the amount of wearing apparel that may be admitted free of duty; to the Committee on Finance.

By Mr. Wilson: A memorial of the board of managers of the National Temperance Association, praying that the sale of intoxicating liquors be prohibited on the grounds of the Columbian Exposition; to the Select Committee on the Quadro-Centennial.

By Mr. Vest: Papers relating to the application of Robert McGee for compensation out of any moneys due the Sioux Indians on account of damages sustained by him by having been scalped and otherwise injured by the Brule-Sioux Indians; to the Select Committee on Indian Depredation, to accompany the bill S. 3582.

By Mr. Hawley: Three petitions of citizens of Connecticut, praying the passage of the bill to limit the amount of wearing apparel that may be admitted free of duty; to the Committee on Finance.

Petitions praying the passage of the "antioption bill" were presented as follows:

By Mr. Paddock: A petition of citizens of Nebraska.

By Mr. Harris: A petition of citizens of Tennessee.

Ordered, That they lie on the table.

Memorials remonstrating against the passage of the "antioption bill" were presented as follows:

By the Vice-President: A memorial of the New York Mercantile Exchange, and a memorial of citizens of South Carolina.

By Mr. Jones, of Arkansas: A memorial of citizens of Arkansas.

Ordered, That they lie on the table.

Papers in the case of Susan E. Cunningham, to accompany the bill S. 3578, were taken from the files and referred under the rule to the Committee on Pensions.

REPORTS OF COMMITTEES.

Mr. Vilas, from the Committee on Claims, to whom was referred the bill (H. R. 3804) to confer jurisdiction upon the Court of Claims to hear and determine the claim of David Ryan against the United States, submitted an adverse report (No. 1124) thereon.

Ordered, That it be placed on the Calendar.

Mr. Dawes, from the Committee on Indian Affairs, to whom was referred the bill (S. 3146) authorizing the removal of the Indians of the Papago or Gila Bend Reservation in Maricopa County, Arizona, to the Papago Reservation in Pima County, or to one of the Pima and Maricopa reservations, known as the Gila River and Salt River Indian reservations, reported it with amendments.

Mr. McPherson, from the Committee on Naval Affairs, to whom was referred the bill (H. R. 8760) to provide for the sale of navy-yard lands in the city of Brooklyn, reported it without amendment.

INTRODUCTION OF BILLS.

Bills were introduced, read the first and second times by unanimous consent, and referred as follows:

By Mr. Vest: A bill (S. 3582) for the relief of Robert McGee; to the Select Committee on Indian Depredations.

By Mr. Paddock: A bill S. 3583) to place John F. Adams on the pension roll; to the Committee on Pensions.

By Mr. Gallinger: A bill (S. 3584) to prohibit the interment of bodies in Graceland Cemetery, in the District of Columbia; to the Committee on the District of Columbia.

By Mr. Perkins: A bill (S. 3585) to amend and modify section 3480 of the Revised Statutes of the United States; to the Committee on the Judiciary.

By Mr. Hansbrough: A bill (S. 3586) to establish a military post at or near the city of Grand Forks, in Grand Forks County, in the State of North Dakota; to the Committee on Military Affairs.

By Mr. Paddock: A bill (S. 3587) to amend section 1514 of the Revised Statutes of the United States, in relation to the appointment of cadets at the Naval Academy at Annapolis, in the State of Maryland; to the Committee on Naval Affairs.

By Mr. Chandler: A bill (S. 3588) to amend an act entitled "An act to perfect the quarantine service of the United States;" to the Committee on Epidemic Diseases.

By Mr. McMillan: A bill (S. 3589) to amend an act entitled "An act to regulate commerce," approved February 4, 1887; to the Committee on Interstate Commerce.

METZEROTT HALL.

Mr. Hawley submitted the following resolution; which was considered by unanimous consent and agreed to:

Whereas many complaints have been publicly made concerning the safety of Metzerott Hall;

Resolved, That the Committee on the District of Columbia be, and it hereby is, instructed to report to the Senate whatever information it may have received relating to that subject.

MRS. DORA MARSHALL.

Mr. Dawes submitted the following resolution; which was referred to the Committee to Audit and Control the Contingent Expenses of the Senate:

Resolved, That the Secretary of the Senate be, and he is hereby, authorized and directed to pay, out of the miscellaneous items of the contingent fund of the Senate, to Mrs. Dora Marshall, widow of James H. Marshall, deceased, late a messenger of the United States Senate, the sum of $720, being an amount equal to six months' salary at the rate per annum allowed by law to the messenger aforesaid, said sum to be considered as including the funeral expenses and all allowances.

COMMITTEE ON IMMIGRATION.

Mr. Chandler submitted the following resolution; which was considered by unanimous consent and agreed to:

Resolved, That the Committee on Immigration be authorized to continue during the present session the inquiries directed by resolution of the Senate of July 16, 1892, with all the powers conferred by said resolution.

COMMITTEE ON FAILED NATIONAL BANKS.

Mr. Chandler submitted the following resolution; which was considered by unanimous consent and agreed to:

Resolved, That the Committee on Failed National Banks be authorized to continue during the present session the inquiries directed by resolutions of the Senate of June 2, 1892, and July 19, 1892, with all the powers conferred by said resolutions.

POSITIONS IN THE CIVIL SERVICE.

On motion by Mr. Daniel,

The Senate proceeded to consider the resolution yesterday submitted by him calling upon the Civil Service Commission for certain information relative to positions in the Government service; and The resolution was agreed to.

MESSAGE FROM THE HOUSE.

A message from the House of Representatives, by Mr. Towles, its chief clerk:

Mr. President: The House of Representatives has passed without amendment the following bills of the Senate:

S. 539. An act to amend and enlarge the act approved June 18, 1878, entitled "An act to provide for the distribution of the awards made under the convention between the United States of America and the Republic of Mexico, concluded on the 4th day of July, 1868."

S. 606. An act to amend and enlarge the act approved June 18, 1878, entitled "An act to provide for the distribution of the awards made under the convention between the United States of America and the Republic of Mexico, concluded on the 4th day of July, 1878."

The Speaker of the House of Representatives having signed three enrolled bills, S. 139, S. 1940, and S. 2612, I am directed to bring them to the Senate for the signature of its President.

ENROLLED BILLS SIGNED.

Mr. Sanders reported from the committee that they had examined and found duly enrolled the following bills:

S. 139. An act terminating the reduction in the numbers of the Engineer Corps of the Navy;

S. 1940. An act for the relief of R. B. Woodson; and

S. 2612. An act granting a pension to Tendoy, chief of the Bannocks, Shoshones, and Sheepeaters tribe of Indians;

The Vice-President signed the same, and they were delivered to the committee to be presented to the President of the United States.

PUBLIC PRINTING AND BINDING.

On motion by Mr. Cockrell,

Ordered, That the bill (S. 1549) providing for the public printing and binding and distribution of public documents be printed as passed by the House of Representatives.

BILL RECOMMITTED.

On motion by Mr. Peffer,

Ordered, That the bill (S. 1447) for the relief of Secor & Co., Perine, Secor & Co., and the executors of Zeno Secor, be recommitted to the Committee on Claims.

COMMITTEE SERVICE.

Mr. Morgan, at his own request, was excused from further service as a member of the Committee on Public Lands.

Ordered, That the vacancy be filled by the Presiding Officer; and The Presiding Officer (Mr. Harris in the chair) appointed Mr. Vilas.

MILITARY RESERVATIONS IN WYOMING.

The Presiding Officer laid before the Senate the amendments of the House of Representatives to the bill (S. 2093) to provide for the disposal of certain abandoned military reservations in the State of Wyoming; and

On motion by Mr. Carey,

Resolved, That the Senate agree thereto.

Ordered, That the Secretary notify the House of Representatives thereof.

CLAIM OF WILLIAM M'GARRAHAN.

On motion by Mr. Teller,

The Senate resumed the reconsideration of the bill (S. 1958) to submit to the Court of Private Land Claims, established by an act of Congress approved March 3, 1891, the title of William McGarrahan to the Rancho Panoche Grande, in the State of California, and for other purposes, returned by the President of the United States to the Senate with his objections thereto; and Pending debate,

DEALINGS IN OPTIONS AND FUTURES.

The Presiding Officer announced that the hour of 2 o'clock had arrived, and laid before the Senate the unfinished business at its adjournment yesterday, viz, the bill (H. R. 7845) defining "options" and "futures," imposing special taxes on dealers therein, and requiring such persons engaged in selling certain products to obtain license, and for other purposes; and

The Senate resumed, as in Committee of the Whole, the consideration of the bill; and

The question being on the amendment proposed by Mr. Daniel, Pending debate,

EXECUTIVE SESSION.

On motion by Mr Sawyer,

The Senate proceeded to the consideration of executive business; and

After the consideration of executive business the doors were reopened, and

On motion by Mr. Sawyer, at 4 o'clock and 20 minutes p. m., The Senate adjourned.

THURSDAY, DECEMBER 15, 1892.

EXECUTIVE COMMUNICATIONS.

The Vice-President laid before the Senate a letter of the Secretary of State, transmitting, in pursuance of the provisions of the act of February 3, 1887, a certified copy of the final ascertainment of the electors for President and Vice-President in the State of Delaware.

Ordered, That it lie on the table.

The Vice-President laid before the Senate a letter of the Secretary of the Treasury, transmitting, in compliance with a resolution of the Senate of the 8th instant, copies of all correspondence between the Third Auditor of the Treasury and the mayor of Baltimore, relating to the claim of the city of Baltimore for advances in the war of 1812, between the United States and Great Britain; which was referred to the Committee on Claims and ordered to be printed.

Petitions, memorials, etc., were presented and referred as follows:

By Mr. Morrill: A petition of Willis L. Roberts, praying to be allowed a pension; to the Committee on Pensions.

By Mr. Perkins: A petition of the heirs of Miguel Salinas, praying compensation for the use and occupancy of their property by the United States Army; to the Committee on Claims.

By Mr. Cockrell: A memorial of the Interstate Convention of Cattlemen, praying for the establishment of a bureau of information and statistics in live stock; to the Select Committee on the Transportation and Sale of Meat Products.

By Mr. Paddock: A petition of working men of the District of Columbia, praying the passage of a law for an effective eight-hour law for workingmen; to the Committee on Education and Labor.

By Mr. Hiscock: A petition of colored citizens of New York, praying that the moral, intellectual, and industrial progress and development of the colored people during the first quarter of a century of their freedom should be made a part of the Government exhibit at the Columbian Exposition; to the Select Committee on the Quadro-Centennial.

By Mr. Pugh: A memorial of John A. Rollings and James Gilfillan, praying payment of their claim against the Choctaw Nation out of the so-called "net proceeds" claim; to the Committee on Indian Affairs, to accompany the bill S. 3599.

By Mr. Teller: Papers relating to the application of Cyrus Payne for the passage of a law granting him an honorable discharge; to the Committee on Military Affairs, to accompany the bill S. 3600.

By Mr. Hiscock: Papers relating to the application of Ira Doane to be allowed a pension; to the Committee on Pensions to accompany the bill S. 3606.

By Mr. Cullom: A petition of citizens of Illinois in behalf of Johanna Cashman, praying that she be allowed a pension; to the Committee on Pensions, to accompany the bill S. 3607.

By Mr. Quay: A paper relating to the application of Veronica McGuire to be allowed a pension; to the Committee on Pensions, to accompany the bill S. 3593.

By Mr. Cockrell: Two petitions of citizens of Missouri, praying the appointment of a committee to investigate an alleged combine formed to depreciate the price of grain, and now existing between the elevators, millers, and railroads at Minneapolis and St. Louis, and asking for the postponement of the antioption bill until said committee can make report; to the Committee on Agriculture and Forestry.

By Mr. White: A memorial of the several commercial bodies of New Orleans, La., praying the completion of the Nicaragua Canal under the direction of the United States Government; to the Committee on Foreign Relations.

By Mr. Cockrell: A memorial of citizens of Missouri, remonstrating against the closing of the Columbian Exposition on the Sabbath day; to the Select Committee on the Quadro-Centennial.

Mr. Hiscock presented a petition of business men of the city of New York supplemental to the petition heretofore presented, praying the passage of the bill authorizing the New York and New Jersey Bridge Company to construct a bridge across the Hudson River; praying further that the location of the said bridge shall not be fixed by said bill, but be left to the free determination of the Secretary of War.

Ordered, That it lie on the table and be printed.

Mr. Bate presented a memorial of certain members of the Memphis Cotton Exchange, remonstrating against the action taken by said exchange in opposition to the "antioption bill."

Ordered, That it lie on the table.

Petitions praying the closing of the Columbian Exposition on the Sabbath day, for the prevention of the sale of liquors on the Fair grounds, for the passage of the "antioption bill," to prohibit State legislatures from passing any law respecting religion, etc., were presented as follows:

By Mr. Quay: A petition of citizens of Pennsylvania.
By Mr. Brice: A petition of citizens of Ohio.
By Mr. Paddock: A petition of citizens of Nebraska.

Ordered, That they be referred to the Select Committee on the Quadro-Centennial.

Memorials remonstrating against the repeal of the provision for the closing of the Columbian Exposition on the Sabbath day were presented as follows:

By Mr. Sherman: Two memorials of citizens of Ohio.
By Mr. Cockrell: A memorial of citizens of Missouri.
By Mr. Vest: A memorial of citizens of Missouri.
By Mr. Brice: Three petitions of citizens of Ohio.
By Mr. Cullom: A memorial of citizens of Illinois.

Ordered, That they be referred to the Select Committee on the Quadro-Centennial.

Petitions praying the passage of the "antioption bill" were presented as follows:

By Mr. Frye: A petition of citizens of Maine.
By Mr. Allen: A petition of citizens of Washington.
By Mr. Brice: Two petitions of citizens of Ohio.
By Mr. Harris: A petition of citizens of Tennessee.

Ordered, That they lie on the table.

Memorials remonstrating against the passage of the "antioption bill" were presented as follows:

By Mr. Hiscock: A memorial of the New York Mercantile Exchange.

By Mr. Jones, of Arkansas: A memorial of citizens of Arkansas.

Ordered, That they lie on the table.

Petitions praying the passage of the bill to limit the amount of wearing apparel that may be admitted free of duty were presented as follows:

By Mr. Sanders: A petition of citizens of Montana.
By Mr. Teller: A petition of citizens of Colorado.
By Mr. Brice: A petition of citizens of Ohio.

Ordered, That they be referred to the Committee on Finance.

Mr. McPherson, from the Committee on Naval Affairs, submitted a report (No. 1131) to accompany the bill (H. R. 8760) providing for the sale of navy-yard lands in the city of Brooklyn, heretofore reported.

Mr. Sanders reported from the committee that they this day presented to the President of the United States the following enrolled bills:

S. 139. An act terminating the reduction in the numbers of the Engineer Corps of the Navy;

S. 1940. An act for the relief of R. B. Woodson; and

S. 2612. An act granting a pension to Tendoy, chief of the Bannocks, Shoshones, and Sheepeaters tribe of Indians.

Mr. Manderson, from the Committee on Printing, to whom was referred the following resolution, received from the House of Representatives for concurrence July 30, 1892, reported it without amendment and submitted a report (No. 1128) thereon:

Resolved by the House of Representatives (the Senate concurring), That there be printed of the eulogies delivered upon the Hon. Francis B. Spinola, late a Representative from the State of New York, 8,000 copies, which shall include 50 copies to be bound in full morocco, to be delivered to the family of the deceased; and of these remaining, 2,600 copies shall be for the use of the Senate and 5,350 copies for the use of the House of Representatives; and the Secretary of the Treasury is directed to have engraved and printed a portrait of the said Francis B. Spinola to accompany said eulogies.

The Senate proceeded, by unanimous consent, to consider the said resolution; and

Resolved, That the Senate agree thereto.

Ordered, That the Secretary notify the House of Representatives thereof.

Mr. Manderson, from the Committee on Printing, to whom was referred the resolution submitted by Mr. Cockrell on the 6th instant, to print 23,000 copies of the Ninth Annual Report of the United States Civil Service Commission, reported it without amendment and submitted a report (No. 1129) thereon.

The Senate proceeded, by unanimous consent, to consider the said resolution; and

Resolved, That the Senate agree thereto.

Ordered, That the Secretary request the concurrence of the House of Representatives therein.

Mr. Manderson, from the Committee on Printing, to whom was referred the resolution submitted by Mr. Chandler on the 12th instant, to print 12,000 additional copies of the report of Immigrant Commissioner H. J. Schulties, contained in Part 1, House Ex. Doc. No. 235, 52d Congress, 1st session, pages 263 to 325, inclusive, reported it without amendment and submitted a report (No. 1130) thereon.

The Senate proceeded, by unanimous consent, to consider the said resolution; and

Resolved, That the Senate agree thereto.

Ordered, That the Secretary request the concurrence of the House of Representatives therein.

Mr. Turpie, from the Committee on Pensions, to whom was referred the bill (H. R. 6024) for the relief of William H. Taylor, reported it without amendment and submitted a report (No. 1125) thereon.

The Senate proceeded, by unanimous consent, to consider the said bill as in Committee of the Whole; and no amendment being made it was reported to the Senate.

Ordered, That it pass to a third reading.

The said bill was read the third time.

Resolved, That it pass.

Ordered, That the Secretary notify the House of Representatives thereof.

Mr. Turpie, from the Committee on Pensions, to whom was referred the bill (H. R. 6737) granting a pension to Delzell R. Bradford, Twenty-fourth Michigan Volunteers, reported it without amendment and submitted a report (No. 1126) thereon.

Mr. Frye, from the Committee on Commerce, to whom was referred the bill (S. 3583) to amend sections 4488 and 4489, Revised Statutes, for the greater safety to navigation, reported adversely thereon.

Ordered, That it be postponed indefinitely.

Mr. Frye, from the Committee on Commerce, to whom was referred the following bills, reported them without amendment:

H. R. 8956. An act establishing a fog signal at Tibbets Point, Lake Ontario, New York; and

S. 3510. A bill to amend section 4347 of the Revised Statutes of the United States.

Mr. Voorhees, from the Committee on the Library, to whom was referred the bill (S. 2089) to purchase the portrait of Daniel D. Tompkins, late Vice-President of the United States, painted by Jarvis in 1812, reported it without amendment and submitted a report (No. 1127) thereon.

Mr. Paddock, from the Committee to Audit and Control the Contingent Expenses of the Senate, to whom was referred the resolution submitted by Mr. Dawes on the 14th instant, to pay Mrs. Dora Marshall, widow of James H. Marshall, deceased, an amount equal to six months of his pay as messenger of the Senate, reported it without amendment.

The Senate proceeded, by unanimous consent, to consider the said resolution; and

Resolved, That the Senate agree thereto.

INTRODUCTION OF BILLS AND JOINT RESOLUTIONS.

Bills and joint resolutions were introduced, read the first and second times by unanimous consent, and referred as follows:

By Mr. Carlisle: A bill (S. 3590) for the benefit of Mrs. Anna C. Supplee, of Harrison, Ohio; to the Committee on Patents.

By Mr. Cameron: A bill (S. 3591) to authorize the allowance of commutation for quarters to officers of the Navy on shore duty; to the Committee on Naval Affairs.

By Mr. Quay: A bill (S. 3592) to provide an American register for the steamer *Oceano,* of Philadelphia; to the Committee on Commerce.

A bill (S. 3593) granting a pension to Veronica McGuire; to the Committee on Pensions.

By Mr. McMillan: A bill (S. 3594) to confirm title to lots 13 and 14 in square 959, in Washington, D. C.; to the Committee on the District of Columbia.

By Mr. Casey: A bill (S. 3595) to amend an act entitled "An act for the relief of settlers upon certain lands in the States of North Dakota and South Dakota," approved August 5, 1892; to the Committee on Public Lands.

By Mr. Power: A bill (S. 3596) to provide for the examination and classification of certain mineral lands in the States of Montana and Idaho; to the Committee on Public Lands.

By Mr. Proctor: A bill (S. 3597) to establish companies of the Hospital Corps, United States Army, and for other purposes; and

A bill (S. 3598) to discontinue the Signal Corps and devolve the duties thereof upon other branches of the Army; to the Committee on Military Affairs.

By Mr. Pugh: A bill (S. 3599) for the relief of John A. Rollings and James Gilfillan; to the Committee on Indian Affairs.

By Mr. Teller: A bill (S. 3600) granting an honorable discharge to Cyrus Payne; to the Committee on Military Affairs.

By Mr. Perkins: A bill (S. 3601) granting to the Chicago, Rock Island and Pacific Railway Company the use of certain lands at Chichasha Station, in the Indian Territory; and

A bill (S. 3602) to grant to the Chicago, Rock Island and Pacific Railway Company a right of way through the Indian Territory, and for other purposes; to the Committee on Indian Affairs.

By Mr. Hiscock: A bill (S. 3603) for the relief of B. J. Van Vleck, administrator of Henry Van Vleck, deceased;

A bill (S. 3604) authorizing the Secretary of the Treasury to adjust and settle the account of the heirs of Alfred G. Benson with the United States and pay said heirs such sum of money as they may be justly and equitably entitled to; and

A bill (S. 3605) in relation to refunding certain sums to port wardens; to the Committee on Claims.

A bill (S. 3606) for the relief of Ira Doane; to the Committee on Pensions.

By Mr. Cullom: A bill (S. 3607) granting a pension to Mrs. Johanna Cashman; to the Committee on Pensions.

By Mr. Cockrell: A bill (S. 3608) granting a pension to Herbert Vanderberg; to the Committee on Pensions.

By Mr. Sawyer: A bill (S. 3609) to punish robbery upon or wrecking trains engaged in interstate commerce; to the Committee on Interstate Commerce.

By Mr. Pugh: A bill (S. 3610) regulating the sale of paints, white lead, colors, and linseed oil; to the Committee on Manufactures.

By Mr. Hunton: A joint resolution (S.R.121) authorizing payment, under act of August 30, 1890, to the State of Virginia, upon the assent of the governor heretofore given until adjournment of next session of the legislature thereof; to the Committee on Education and Labor.

A joint resolution (S.R.122) to receive drawback certificates in payment of arrears of general taxes under act of June 2, 1890; to the Committee on the District of Columbia.

INDIAN DEPREDATION CLAIMS.

Mr. Platt submitted the following resolution for consideration; which was ordered to be printed:

Resolved, That the Secretary of the Interior be, and he is hereby, directed to inform the Senate—

First. Of the amounts of the different funds held in trust by the United States for the benefit of the Indian tribes.

Second. Of the amount of Indian depredation claims which has hitherto received the approval of the Department of the Interior.

Third. If within his knowledge, the whole amount of Indian depredation claims have been presented to the Court of Claims.

Fourth. Whether any judgments rendered by the Court of Claims against Indian tribes for depredations have yet been paid out of funds held in trust by the United States for the benefit of Indian tribes.

Fifth. To what extent the funds held in trust for Indian tribes by the United States are likely to be depleted by the payment of judgments rendered or to be rendered by the Court of Claims for Indian depredations.

REPORT ON FOREIGN STREETS AND HIGHWAYS.

Mr. Manderson submitted the following concurrent resolution; which was referred to the Committee on Printing:

Resolved by the Senate (the House of Representatives concurring), That there be printed —— thousand copies of the special consular report relating to streets and highways in foreign countries, heretofore published by the Department of State, of which —— thousand copies shall be for the use of the Senate and —— thousand copies for the use of the House of Representatives.

MESSAGE FROM THE HOUSE.

A message from the House of Representatives, by Mr. Towles, its chief clerk:

Mr. President: The House of Representatives insists upon its amendments to the bill (S. 1549) providing for the public printing and binding and the distribution of public documents disagreed to by the Senate. It agrees to the conference asked by the Senate on the disagreeing votes of the two Houses thereon, and has appointed Mr. Richardson, Mr. McKaig, and Mr. Broderick, managers at the same on its part.

The House of Representatives has passed without amendment the following bills and joint resolution of the Senate:

S. 869. An act to provide an American register for the barge *Sea Bird,* of Perth Amboy, N. J.;

S. 1647. An act to authorize the Alabama Grand Trunk Railroad Company to bridge across the Tallapoosa and Coosa rivers;

S. 1956. An act to make Punta Gorda a subport of entry;

S. 2451. An act authorizing the Secretary of the Treasury to reconvey to Lucius U. Maltby and Louise W. Maltby, his wife, Margaret Elizabeth Lucas, and the Sea Girt Land Improvement Company a piece of land selected as a site for the Squan Inlet light-station, New Jersey, but found to be unsuitable for the purpose of said station; and

S. R. 73. Joint resolution authorizing the Secretary of War to receive for instruction at the Military Academy at West Point Francisco Alcantara, of Venezuela.

The House of Representatives has passed the bill (S. 3188) to extend to Duluth, Minn., the privileges of the first section of an act entitled "An act to amend the statutes in relation to immediate transportation of dutiable goods, and for other purposes," approved June 10, 1888, with an amendment to the title in which it requests the concurrence of the Senate; and

It has passed the following bills and joint resolution, in which it requests the concurrence of the Senate:

H. R. 3184. An act correcting the muster of Lieut. Gilman L. Johnston;

H. R. 5752. An act to amend an act approved August 6, 1888, entitled "An act to authorize the construction of a bridge across the Alabama River;"

H. R. 8602. An act to authorize the construction of a bridge across the Mobile River by the Chicago, Mobile and Gulf Ports Railroad Company;

H. R. 9487. An act to amend an act approved April 22, 1890, authorizing the Natchitoches Cane River Bridge Company to construct and maintain a bridge across Cane River in Louisiana;

H. R. 9488. An act to amend an act approved March 2, 1891, authorizing the construction of a bridge across the Red River, Louisiana, by the Rapides Bridge Company limited; and

H. R. 170. Joint resolution to pay the officers and employés of the Senate and House of Representatives their respective salaries for the month of December, 1892, on the 21st day of said month.

The House of Representatives has passed the following resolution, in which it requests the concurrence of the Senate:

Resolved by the House of Representatives (the Senate concurring), That when the two Houses adjourn on Thursday, December 22, they will stand adjourned until Wednesday, January 4, 1893.

The Speaker of the House of Representatives having signed two enrolled bills, S. 2275 and S. 3418, I am directed to bring them to the Senate for the signature of its President.

ENROLLED BILLS SIGNED.

Mr. Sanders reported from the committee that they had examined and found duly enrolled the following bills:

S. 2275. An act for the relief of purchasers of timber and stone land under the act of June 3, 1878; and

S. 3418. An act making Saturday a half holiday for banking and trust company purposes in the District of Columbia;

Whereupon

The Vice-President signed the same, and they were delivered to the committee to be presented to the President of the United States.

HOLIDAY RECESS.

The resolution of the House of Representatives providing for the adjournment of the two Houses from the 22d instant to January 4, 1893, was read and referred to the Committee on Appropriations.

HOUSE BILLS AND JOINT RESOLUTION REFERRED.

The bills and joint resolution last received from the House of Representatives for concurrence were severally read the first and second times by unanimous consent.

Ordered, That the bill H. R. 3184 be referred to the Committee on Military Affairs; that the bills H. R. 5752, H. R. 8602, H. R. 9487, and H. R. 9488 be referred to the Committee on Commerce; and that the joint resolution H. R. 170 be referred to the Committee on Appropriations.

DUTIABLE GOODS IN BOND.

The Vice-President laid before the Senate the amendment of the House of Representatives to the title of the bill (H. R. 3188) to extend to Duluth, Minn., the privileges of the first section of an act entitled "An act to amend the statutes in relation to the immediate transportation of dutiable goods, and for other purposes," approved June 10, 1888; and

Resolved, That the Senate agree thereto.

Ordered, That the Secretary notify the House of Representatives thereof.

ADJOURNMENT TO MONDAY.

On motion by Mr. Cameron that when the Senate adjourn it be to Monday next,

The yeas were 27 and the nays were 27.

On motion by Mr. Washburn,

The yeas and nays being desired by one-fifth of the Senators present, Those who voted in the affirmative are,

Messrs. Blackburn, Blodgett, Cameron, Carlisle, Dixon, Dolph, Faulkner, Gordon, Gorman, Harris, Hawley, Hiscock, Hoar, Jones of Arkansas, McMillan, Manderson, Mills, Morrill, Pasco, Platt, Quay, Vance, Vest, Vilas, Voorhees, White, Wolcott.

Those who voted in the negative are,

Messrs. Allen, Bate, Berry, Butler, Call, Carey, Casey, Coke, Dawes, Gallinger, George, Hunton, Kyle, Paddock, Peffer, Perkins, Pettigrew, Power, Proctor, Pugh, Sanders, Sawyer, Sherman, Teller, Walthall, Warren, Washburn.

The Senate being equally divided,

The Vice-President voted in the affirmative.

So the motion was agreed to.

MESSAGE FROM THE HOUSE.

A message from the House of Representatives, by Mr. Towles, its chief clerk:

Mr. President: The House of Representatives has passed the following bill and joint resolution, in which it requests the concurrence of the Senate:

H. R. 9825. An act making appropriations for the support of the Army for the fiscal year ending June 30, 1894, and for other purposes; and

H. R. 166. Joint resolution to authorize the Secretary of the Treasury to cover back into the Treasury $48,800 of the appropriation to Choctaw and Chickasaw Indians.

The Speaker of the House of Representatives having signed three enrolled bills, S. 539, S. 606, and S. 2093, I am directed to bring them to the Senate for the signature of its President.

PRESENTATION OF BILLS.

Mr. Sanders reported from the committee that they this day presented to the President of the United States the following enrolled bills:

S. 2275. An act for the relief of purchasers of timber and stone lands under the act of June 3, 1878; and

S. 3418. An act making Saturday a half holiday for banking and trust-company purposes in the District of Columbia.

CLAIM OF WILLIAM M'GARRAHAN.

On motion by Mr. Teller,

The Senate resumed the reconsideration of the bill (S. 1958) to submit to the Court of Private Land Claims, established by an act of Congress approved March 3, 1891, the title of William McGarrahan to the Rancho Panoche Grande, in the State of California, and for other purposes, returned by the President of the United States to the Senate, with his objections thereto; and,

Pending debate,

DEALINGS IN OPTIONS AND FUTURES.

The Presiding Officer (Mr. Harris in the chair) announced that the hour of 2 o'clock had arrived, and laid before the Senate the unfinished business at its adjournment yesterday, viz, the bill (H. R. 7845) defining "options" and "futures," imposing special taxes on dealers therein, and requiring such persons engaged in selling certain products to obtain license, and for other purposes; and

The Senate resumed, as in Committee of the Whole, the consideration of the bill; and

The question being on the amendment proposed by Mr. Daniel,

Pending debate,

EXECUTIVE SESSION.

On motion by Mr. Wolcott,

The Senate proceeded to the consideration of executive business; and

After the consideration of executive business the doors were reopened, and

On motion by Mr. Butler, at 3 o'clock and 40 minutes p. m.,

The Senate adjourned.

MONDAY, DECEMBER 19, 1892.

Mr. Gorman announced the death of the Hon. Randall Lee Gibson, late a Senator from the State of Louisiana, which occurred Thursday, the 15th instant, at Hot Springs, Ark., and submitted the following resolutions:

Resolved, That the Senate has heard with profound sorrow the announcement of the death of the Hon. Randall Lee Gibson, late a Senator from the State of Louisiana.

Resolved, That a committee of five Senators be appointed by the Presiding Officer to join such committee as may be appointed by the House of Representatives, to attend the funeral at Lexington, Ky., and that the necessary expenses attending the execution of this order be paid out of the contingent fund of the Senate.

Resolved, That the Secretary communicate these resolutions to the House of Representatives.

Resolved, That, as a further mark of respect to the memory of the deceased, the Senate do now adjourn.

The resolutions were considered by unanimous consent and unanimously agreed to;

Whereupon

The Vice-President announced the appointment of Mr. White, Mr. Butler, Mr. Gordon, Mr. Pettigrew; and Mr. Shoup as members of the committee; and

The Senate adjourned.

TUESDAY, DECEMBER 20, 1892.

Mr. Watson C. Squire, from the State of Washington, attended.

The bill H. R. 8925 and the joint resolution H. R. 166, received from the House of Representatives for concurrence on Thursday last, were read the first and second times by unanimous consent.

Ordered, That the bill H. R. 8925 be referred to the Committee on Appropriations, and that the joint resolution H. R. 166 lie on the table.

EXECUTIVE COMMUNICATIONS.

The Vice-President laid before the Senate a letter of the Secretary of War, recommending the appointment of an associate professor of mathematics at the Military Academy at West Point, N. Y.; which was referred to the Committee on Military Affairs and ordered to be printed.

The Vice-President laid before the Senate a letter of the Secretary of the Treasury, transmitting the annual report of the superintendent of the Coast and Geodetic Survey for the fiscal year ended June 30, 1892; which was ordered to be printed and, with the accompanying papers, referred to the Committee on Printing.

The Vice-President laid before the Senate a letter of the clerk of the Court of Claims, transmitting the conclusions of fact and law in the French spoliation claim for the loss of the brig *Horatio*; which was referred to the Committee on Claims and ordered to be printed.

PETITIONS AND MEMORIALS.

Petitions, memorials, etc., were presented and referred as follows:

By Mr. Wilson: Resolutions of the National Farmers' Congress, praying for the removal of all obstructions to the full administration of the interstate commerce law; for the establishment of experimental stations for the maintenance of scientific work by the Agricultural Department; for the establishment of reservoirs for the purposes of irrigation; for the establishment of waterways and the improvement of navigable rivers; and for the closing of the Columbian Exposition on the Sabbath day; to the Committee on Agriculture and Forestry and ordered to be printed.

By the Vice-President: Resolutions adopted at the Southwest Silver Convention, held at El Paso, Tex., remonstrating against the demonetization of silver, and praying for the restoration of the double standard by the immediate passage of the free coinage act; to the Committee on Finance.

By Mr. Sherman: A petition of Irvin B. Wright, praying to be allowed a pension of $25 per month; to the Committee on Pensions.

A petition of the Rank and File Garrison, of Cleveland, Ohio, praying the passage of the several measures now pending in the interest of the enlisted men of the United States Army; to the Committee on Military Affairs.

A petition of citizens of Ohio, praying the enactment of more stringent laws for the restriction of immigration; to the Committee on Immigration.

A petition of the N. P. and Memphis Packet Company, praying that the steamboat inspection service below the grade of supervising inspector be wholly nonpartisan; to the Committee on Commerce.

By Mr. Mitchell: A petition of Robert Williams, sergeant of ordnance, United States Army, praying the passage of a law authorizing his appointment as a second lieutenant of infantry in the Army and for his retirement as of that grade; to the Committee on Military Affairs.

A petition of citizens of Oregon, praying for an extension of the time for the payment of lands embraced within the limits of the lands forfeited by the act of September 29, 1890; to the Committee on Public Lands.

A memorial of citizens of Oregon, remonstrating against the closing of the Columbian Exposition on the Sabbath day; to the Select Committee on the Quadro-Centennial.

By Mr. Davis: A memorial of the Minnesota Editors and Publishers' Association, remonstrating against the passage of any law providing for the furnishing of stamped envelopes at the cost of the stamps; to the Committee on Post-Offices and Post-Roads.

By Mr. Perkins: A petition of Andrew J. Arnlett, praying to be allowed an increase of pension; to the Committee on Pensions.

By Mr. Cullom: A memorial of the National Transportation Association praying certain amendments to the interstate commerce law; to the Committee on Interstate Commerce.

By Mr. Pasco: A petition of citizens of Florida, praying an appropriation to continue the improvement of Cumberland Sound and to protect the entrance to the port of Fernandina; to the Committee on Commerce.

A resolution of the Board of Trade of Jacksonville, Fla., praying the passage of the Torrey bankruptcy bill; to the Committee on the Judiciary.

By Mr. Dawes: A petition of citizens of Massachusetts, praying the passage of the bill providing for the retirement of privates in the Army after a continuous service of twenty-five years; to the Committee on Military Affairs.

By Mr. Vest: A memorial of citizens of South McAlester, Ind. T., praying certain legislation for the relief of citizens residing in said Territory; to the Committee on the Judiciary.

By Mr. Cameron: Resolutions of the Trades League of Philadelphia, praying the enactment of laws encouraging reciprocity among nations; to the Committee on Finance.

By Mr. Turpie: Two petitions of citizens of South Bend, Ind., praying the correction of certain evils complained of at the Government works at the arsenal at West Troy, N. Y.; to the Committee on Appropriations.

By Mr. Aldrich: A memorial of colored citizens of Rhode Island, praying that the moral, intellectual, and industrial progress and development of the colored people during the first quarter of a century of their freedom should be made part of the Government exhibit at the World's Columbian Exposition; to the Select Committee on the Quadro-Centennial.

By Mr. Allen: A petition of citizens of Washington, praying the passage of the bill providing for the retirement of enlisted men of the Army after a continuous service of twenty-five years; to the Committee on Military Affairs.

By Mr. Hale: A memorial of the Maine State Board of Trade, praying the passage of a law providing for the consolidation of the second, third, and fourth class mail matter under the second-class rating; to the Committee on Post-Offices and Post-Roads.

By Mr. Jones, of Arkansas: A petition of Amanda Ellington, praying to be allowed a pension; to the Committee on Pensions.

By Mr. Hoar: A petition of citizens of Massachusetts, praying an amendment to the Constitution of the United States providing for the right of suffrage to women; to the Select Committee on Woman Suffrage.

By Mr. Manderson: A petition of citizens of Nebraska, praying the passage of a law for the retirement of enlisted men of the Army after a continuous service of twenty-five years; to the Committee on Military Affairs.

By Mr. Bate: Papers relating to the application of Capt. Thomas H. Reeves for the correction of his military record; to the Committee on Military Affairs, to accompany the bill S. 3611.

By Mr. Dawes: A petition of Henry M. Everest, praying for the removal of the charge of desertion from his military record; to the Committee on Military Affairs, to accompany the bill S. 3612.

By Mr. Sherman: A petition of Nicholas Krier and others, praying to have refunded them an amount required of them to become exempt

from a draft held May 16, 1864, and alleged to have been illegal; to the Committee on Military Affairs, to accompany the bill S. 3630.

By Mr. Manderson: A paper relating to the equalization of the pay of officers of the Navy; to the Committee on Naval Affairs, to accompany the bill S. 3632.

Papers relating to the application of George W. McCloughan for the removal of the charge of desertion from his military record; to the Committee on Military Affairs, to accompany the bill S. 3633.

By Mr. Stockbridge: A paper relating to the application of Mrs. John G. Mallery to be allowed a pension; to the Committee on Pensions, to accompany the bill S. 3635.

By Mr. Hale: A paper relating to the application of N. J. Coffin for the payment of certain moneys claimed to be due him under suspended law; to the Committee on Military Affairs, to accompany the bill S. 3638.

By Mr. Aldrich: Papers relating to the application of Alice Warren to be allowed a pension; to the Committee on Pensions, to accompany the bill S. 3639.

Papers relating to the application of Eliza A. Fiske to be allowed a pension; to the Committee on Pensions, to accompany the bill S. 3640.

Papers relating to the application of Sarah M. Phillips to be allowed a pension; to the Committee on Pensions, to accompany the bill S. 3641.

Papers relating to the application of Honora Breslin to be allowed a pension; to the Committee on Pensions, to accompany the bill S. 3642.

Petitions praying the passage of the bill limiting the amount of clothing that may be admitted free of duty were presented as follows:

By Mr. Palmer: Several petitions of citizens of Illinois.

By Mr. Allen: Two petitions of citizens of Washington.

Ordered, That they be referred to the Committee on Finance.

Memorials praying for the completion of the Nicaragua Canal under the direction of the Government of the United States were presented as follows:

By Mr. Allen: A memorial of the Chamber of Commerce of Seattle, Wash.

By Mr. Pasco: A memorial of the Board of Trade of Jacksonville, Fla.

By Mr. Cullom: A memorial of the Board of Trade of Chicago, Ill.

Ordered, That they be referred to the Committee on Foreign Relations.

Mr. Palmer presented a petition of J. George Seltzer, praying the passage of the bill requiring railroads to use an universal system of automatic brakes and couplers.

Ordered, That it lie on the table.

Mr. Walthall presented several petitions of citizens of Mississippi, praying the postponement of the "antioption bill" until after the present cotton crop is marketed.

Ordered, That they lie on the table.

Petitions praying for the closing of the World's Fair on the Sabbath day were presented as follows:

By Mr. Palmer: A petition of citizens of Illinois.

By Mr. Cullom: Two petitions of citizens of Illinois.

By Mr. Sherman: Three petitions of citizens of Ohio.

By Mr. Proctor: A petition of citizens of Vermont.

By Mr. Peffer: A petition of citizens of Kansas.

By Mr. Cameron: A petition of citizens of Pennsylvania.

By Mr. Aldrich: A petition of citizens of Rhode Island.

By Mr. Sanders: A petition of citizens of Montana.

By Mr. Turpie: Two petitions of citizens of Indiana.

By Mr. Quay: A petition of citizens of Pennsylvania.

Ordered, That they be referred to the Select Committee on the Quadro-Centennial.

Petitions praying the passage of the "antioption bill" were presented as follows:

By the Vice-President: A petition of citizens of Arkansas.

By Mr. Palmer: Two petitions of citizens of Illinois.

By Mr. Dubois: A petition of citizens of Idaho.

By Mr. Casey: A petition of citizens of North Dakota.

By Mr. Vest: A petition of citizens of Missouri.

By Mr. Sherman: A petition of citizens of Ohio.

By Mr. Mills: A petition of citizens of Texas.

By Mr. Allen: Three petitions of citizens of Washington.

By Mr. Hale: A petition of citizens of Maine.

By Mr. Walthall: Two petitions of citizens of Mississippi.

By Mr. Coke: Four petitions of citizens of Texas.

By Mr. Harris: Three petitions of citizens of Tennessee.

By Mr. Bate: A petition of citizens of Tennessee.

Ordered, That they lie on the table.

Memorials remonstrating against the passage of the "antioption bill" were presented as follows:

By the Vice-President: A memorial of citizens of Mississippi.

By Mr. Pasco: A memorial of the Board of Trade of Jacksonville, Fla.

By Mr. Walthall: Three memorials of citizens of Mississippi.

Ordered, That they lie on the table.

Petitions praying for the appointment of a committee to investigate an alleged combine formed to depreciate the price of grain, and now existing between the millers, elevators, and railroads at Minneapolis and St. Louis, and asking for a postponement of the anti-option bill till said committee can make report, were presented as follows:

By Mr. Bate: A petition of citizens of Tennessee.
By Mr. Palmer: Five petitions of citizens of Illinois.
By Mr. Wilson: Seven petitions of citizens of Iowa.
By Mr. Casey: Several petitions of citizens of North Dakota.
By Mr. Manderson: Several petitions of citizens of Nebraska.
By Mr. Cullom: Five petitions of citizens of Illinois.
By Mr. Jones, of Arkansas: Three petitions of citizens of Arkansas.

By Mr. Mills: Three petitions of citizens of Texas.
By Mr. Vest: Several petitions of citizens of Missouri.
By Mr. Sherman: Two petitions of citizens of Ohio.
By Mr. Dawes: A petition of citizens of Massachusetts.
By Mr. Davis: A petition of citizens of Minnesota.
By Mr. Hoar: A petition of citizens of Massachusetts.
By Mr. Turpie: Seven petitions of citizens of Indiana.
By Mr. Peffer: Several petitions of citizens of Kansas.
By Mr. Paddock: Several petitions of citizens of Nebraska.
By Mr. Coke: Four petitions of citizens of Texas.
By Mr. Hansbrough: Three petitions of citizens of North Dakota.
By Mr. Sanders: A petition of citizens of Moutana.
By Mr. Harris: Three petitions of citizens of Tennessee.
Ordered, That they be referred to the Committee on Agriculture and Forestry.

MESSAGE FROM THE HOUSE.

A message from the House of Representatives, by Mr. Towles, its chief clerk:

Mr. President: The House of Representatives has passed, without amendment, the following bills of the Senate:

S. 570. An act to provide for the removal of the remains of the late Ensign D. F. Terrell, United States Navy, from Sitka, Alaska, to his home in the State of Mississippi;

S. 1675. An act granting increase of pension to soldiers of the Mexican war in certain cases;

S. 2981. An act for the relief the Citadel Academy of Charleston, S. C.; and

S. 3059. An act for the relief of the Old Dominion Steamship Company.

The House of Representatives has passed without amendment the resolution of the Senate to print 20,000 copies of the Statistical Abstract of the United States for the year 1892; and

It has passed the following bill and joint resolution of the Senate, with amendments, in which it requests the concurrence of the Senate:

S. 985. An act to provide for the enlargement of the military post at Fort Wayne, Mich; and

S. R. 112. Joint resolution to print and bind 1,000 extra copies each of the drill regulations for infantry, cavalry, and artillery.

The House of Representatives has passed the following bills, in which it requests the concurrence of the Senate:

H. R. 456. An act to limit the jurisdiction of the district and circuit courts of the United States;

H. R. 5697. An act for the relief of William Smith and others;

H. R. 6753. An act for the relief of Nimrod J. Smith, ex-chief of the Eastern Band of Cherokee Indians;

H. R. 6796. An act to authorize the construction of a bridge across the Warrior River by the Montgomery, Tuscaloosa and Memphis Railway Company;

H. R. 7633. An act to ratify and confirm an agreement with the Kickapoo Indians in Oklahoma Territory, and to make appropriations for carrying the same into effect;

H. R. 9176. An act relating to contracts of common carriers and to certain obligations, duties, and rights in connection with the carriage of property;

H. R. 9417. An act to incorporate the Protestant Episcopal Cathedral Foundation of the District of Columbia; and

H. R. 9030. An act for the construction and maintenance of a bridge across the St. Lawrence River.

The Speaker of the House of Representatives having signed six enrolled bills, S. 869, S. 1647, S. 1956, S. 2451, S. 3188, and H. R. 6024, and an enrolled joint resolution, S. R. 73, I am directed to bring them to the Senate for the signature of its President.

PRESIDENTIAL APPROVALS.

A message from the President of the United States, by Mr. Pruden, his secretary:

Mr. President: The President of the United States approved and signed on the 16th instant the following acts:

S. 139. An act terminating the reduction of the numbers of the Engineer Corps of the Navy;

S. 1661. An act granting an increase of pension to John Hallam;

S. 1940. An act for the relief ot R. B. Woodson; and

He yesterday approved and signed an act (S. 3612) granting a pension to Tendoy, chief of the Bannocks, Shoshones, and Sheepeaters tribe of Indians.

Ordered, That the Secretary notify the House of Representatives thereof.

HOUSE BILLS REFERRED.

The bills last received from the House of Representatives for concurrence were severally read the first and second times by unanimous consent.

Ordered, That the bill H. R. 456 be referred to the Committee on the Judiciary; that the bill H. R. 5597 be referred to the Committee on Military Affairs; that the bills H. R. 6796, H. R. 9176, and H. R. 9630 be referred to the Committee on Commerce; that the bills H. R. 6753 and H. R. 7633 be referred to the Committee on Indian Affairs, and that the bill H. R. 9417 be referred to the Committee on the District of Columbia.

ENROLLED BILLS SIGNED.

Mr. Sanders reported from the committee that they had examined and found duly enrolled the following bills and joint resolution:

S. 539. An act to amend and enlarge the act approved June 18, 1878, entitled "An act to provide for the distribution of the awards made under the convention between the United States of America and the Republic of Mexico, concluded on the 4th day of July, 1868;"

S. 606. An act to amend and enlarge the act approved June 18, 1878, entitled "An act to provide for the distribution of the awards made under the convention between the United States of America and the Republic of Mexico, concluded on the 4th day of July, 1868;"

S. 2093. An act to provide for the disposal of certain abandoned military reservations in the State of Wyoming;

S. 869. An act to provide an American register for the barge Sea Bird, of Perth Amboy, N. J.;

S. 1647. An act to authorize the Alabama Grand Trunk Railroad Company to bridge across the Tallapoosa and Coosa rivers;

S. 1956. An act to make Punta Gorda a subport of entry;

S. 2451. An act authorizing the Secretary of the Treasury to reconvey to Lucius U. Maltby and Louise W. Maltby, his wife, Margaret Elizabeth Lucas, and the Sea Girt Land Improvement Company a piece of land selected as a site for the Squan Inlet light-station, New Jersey, but found to be unsuitable for the purpose of said station;

S. 3188. An act to extend to Duluth, Minn., the privileges of the first section of an act entitled "An act to amend the statutes in relation to immediate transportation of dutiable goods, and for other purposes," approved June 10, 1880;

S. 6024. An act for the relief of William H. Taylor; and

S. R. 73. Joint resolution authorizing the Secretary of War to receive for instruction at the Military Academy at West Point, Francisco Alcantara, of Venezuela;

Whereupon

The Vice President signed the same, and they were delivered to the committee to be presented to the President of the United States.

REPORTS OF COMMITTEES.

Mr. Chandler, from the Committee on Immigration, reported the following reslution; which was considered by unanimous consent and agreed to:

Resolved, That the Secretary of State be directed to transmit to the Senate the report on the condition of labor in Europe recently made by Mr. Walter T. Griffin, United States commercial agent at Limoges, France.

Mr. McMillan, from the Committee on the District of Columbia, who were instructed by the resolution of the Senate of the 14th instant to report upon the complaints made concerning the safety of Metzerott Hall, submitted a report (No. 1137) thereon.

Mr. Gallinger, from the Committee on the District of Columbia, to whom was referred the bill (H. R. 6644) to amend an act entitled "An act authorizing the sale of title of the United States in lot 3, in square south of square 990," approved March 3, 1891, reported it without amendment.

The Senate proceeded, by unanimous consent, to consider the said bill as in Committee of the Whole, and no amendment being made, it was reported to the Senate.

Ordered, That it pass to a third reading.

The said bill was read the third time.

Resolved, That it pass.

Ordered, That the Secretary notify the House of Representatives thereof.

On motion by Mr. Gallinger,

The Senate proceeded to consider, as in Committee of the Whole, the bill (S. 3453) to amend an act entitled "An act authorizing the sale of title of the United States in lot 3, in square south of square 990," approved March 3, 1891;

Ordered, That it be postponed indefinitely.

Mr. McMillan, from the Committee on the District of Columbia, to whom was referred the joint resolution (S. 110) conferring the control of the bridges in the District of Columbia on the Commissioners of the District of Columbia, reported it with au amendment and submitted a report (No. 1132) thereon.

Mr. Pasco, from the Committee on Public Lands, to whom was

referred the bill (S. 3316) to restore the Fort Jupiter military reservation, in the State of Florida, to entry, reported it with amendments and submitted a report (No. 1133) thereon.

Mr. Dawes, from the Committee on Appropriations, to whom was referred the joint resolution (H. R. 170) to pay the officers and employés of the Senate and the House of Representatives their respective salaries for the month of December, 1892, on the 21st day of said month, reported it without amendment.

The Senate proceeded, by unanimous consent, to consider the said resolution as in Committee of the Whole; and no amendment being made, it was reported to the Senate.

Ordered, That it pass to a third reading.

The said resolution was read the third time.

Resolved, That it pass.

Ordered, That the Secretary notify the House of Representatives thereof.

Mr. Dawes, from the Committee on Appropriations, to whom was referred the resolution received from the House of Representatives for concurrence, on the 15th instant, providing for the adjournment of the two Houses of Congress during the Christmas holidays, reported it without amendment.

Mr. Harris, from the Committee on the District of Columbia, to whom was referred the bill (H. R. 9758) to amend the charter of the Eckington and Soldiers' Home Railroad Company of the District of Columbia, reported it with an amendment and submitted a report (No. 1134) thereon.

Mr. Jones, of Arkansas, from the Committee on Indian Affairs, to whom was referred the joint resolution (S. 119) authorizing the Secretary of the Treasury to retain and cover into the Treasury certain moneys, etc., reported it without amendment.

Mr. Mitchell, from the Committee on the Judiciary, to whom was referred the bill (S. 3537) for the relief of M. P. Deady, reported it with amendments and submitted a report (No. 1135) thereon.

Mr. Sawyer, from the Committee on Pensions to whom was referred the bill (H. R. 8907) to increase the pension of John Malloy, reported it without amendment and submitted a report (No. 1136) thereon.

The Senate proceeded, by unanimous consent, to consider the said bill as in Committee of the Whole; and no amendment being made, it was reported to the Senate.

Ordered, That it pass to a third reading.

The said bill was read the third time.

Resolved, That it pass.

Ordered, That the Secretary notify the House of Representatives thereof.

Mr. Vest, from the Committee on Commerce, to whom were referred the following bills, reported them severally without amendment:

H. R. 9487. An act to amend an act approved April 22, 1890, authorizing the Natchitoches Cane River Bridge Company to construct and maintain a bridge across Cane River, in Louisiana;

H. R. 8602. An act to authorize the construction of a bridge across the Mobile River by the Chicago, Mobile and Gulf Ports Railroad Company;

H. R. 9488. An act to amend an act approved March 2, 1891, authorizing the construction of a bridge across the Red River, Louisiana, by the Rapides Bridge Company, limited; and

H. R. 5752. An act to amend an act approved August 6, 1888, entitled "An act to authorize the construction of a bridge across the Alabama River."

Mr. Manderson, from the Committee on Printing, to whom was referred the resolution submitted by him on the 13th instant to print the report of the Commissioner of Fish and Fisheries covering the operations of the Commission for the fiscal year ending June 30, 1892, and extra copies thereof, reported it without amendment and submitted a report (No. 1138) thereon.

The Senate proceeded, by unanimous consent, to consider the resolution; and

Resolved, That the Senate agree thereto.

Ordered, That the Secretary request the concurrence of the House of Representatives therein.

Mr. Hoar, from the Committee on Privileges and Elections, who were instructed by the resolution of the Senate of February 28, 1891, to cause to be prepared a new edition of the book entitled "Senate Election Cases," reported that they had complied with the order and submitted the work to the Senate for its acceptance.

Ordered, That it be printed.

He also submitted the following resolution, which was referred to the Committee on Printing:

Resolved by the Senate (the House of Representatives concurring), That there be printed and bound, in addition to the usual number, 3,100 copies of the compilation entitled "Senate Privileges and Elections" prepared by the Committee on Privileges and Elections under resolution of the Senate passed February 28, 1891, of which 1,500 copies shall be for the use of the Senate and 1,500 copies for the use of the House of Representatives and 100 for the compiler.

INTRODUCTION OF BILLS AND JOINT RESOLUTION.

Bills and a joint resolution were introduced, read the first and second times by unanimous consent, and referred as follows:

By Mr. Bate: A bill (S. 3611) to amend the record of Capt. Thomas H. Reeves, United States Army, retired; to the Committee on Military Affairs.

By Mr. Dawes: A bill (S. 3612) for the relief of Henry M. Everest, late a private of the Fifteenth Battery, Massachusetts Artillery Volunteers; to the Committee on Military Affairs.

By Mr. Cameron: A bill (S. 3613) amending section 1443 of the Revised Statutes of the United States.

A bill (S. 3614) authorizing the Secretary of the Navy to make certain rules and regulations in relation to the naval rendezvous in April next, and for other purposes; and

A bill (S. 3615) amendatory of an act making appropriations for the naval service for the fiscal year ending June 30, 1893, and for other purposes, approved July 19, 1892; to the Committee on Naval Affairs.

A bill (S. 3616) for the relief of Lieut. T. R. Kennedy, Company F, Ninth Pennsylvania Reserves; to the Committee on Military Affairs.

By Mr. Cullom: A bill (S. 3617) concerning the testimony of witnesses before the Interstate Commerce Commission; and,

A bill (S. 3618) to amend an act entitled "An act to regulate commerce," approved February 4, 1887; to the Committee on Interstate Commerce.

Br. Mr. Dawes; A bill (S. 3619) for the relief of Nathaniel McKay; to the Committee on Claims.

By Mr. Proctor: A bill (S. 3620) to amend the act of Congress of February 12, 1887, entitled, "An act to amend section 1661 of the Revised Statutes, making an annual appropriation to provide arms and equipments for the militia;" and

A bill (S. 3621) to reduce the number of officers in, and the expenses of the Signal Corps of the Army; to the Committee on Military Affairs.

By Mr. Davis: A bill (S. 3622) for the relief of Anna W. Osborne; to the Committee on Claims.

By Mr. McMillan: A bill (S. 3623) to amend the act of March 3, 1873, for the relief of the Columbian University, in the District of Columbia; to the Committee on the District of Columbia.

By Mr. Perkins: A bill (S. 3624) to pay Thompson McKinley $375 for service voucher issued to him during the late war by Capt. George W. Harrison, assistant quartermaster, United States Army; and

A bill (S. 3625) granting an honorable discharge to Walter Mitchell; to the Committee on Military Affairs.

By Mr. Platt: A bill (S. 3626) granting a pension to Mrs. Honora Hennessey; and

A bill (S. 3627) granting a pension to Britton Brant; to the Committee on Pensions.

By Mr. Warren: A bill (S. 3628) donating to the county of Laramie, Wyoming, certain bridges on the abandoned Fort Laramie military reservation, and for other purposes; to the Committee on Public Lands.

By Mr. Sherman: A bill (S. 3629) to extend to the North Pacific Ocean the provisions of the statutes for the protection of fur seals and other fur-bearing animals; to the Committee on Foreign Relations.

A bill (S. 3630) for the relief of Nicholas Krier, and others; to the Committee on Military Affairs.

A bill (S. 3631) granting a pension to Irvin B. Wright; to the Committee on Pensions.

By Mr. Manderson: A bill (S. 3632) to equalize the pay of officers of the Navy; to the Committee on Naval Affairs.

A bill (S. 3633) to remove the charge of desertion from the military record of George W. McCloughan, late of Company B, Second United States Cavalry; to the Committee on Military Affairs.

By Mr. Teller: A bill (S. 3634) to provide for building and maintaining an Indian industrial school at Unalaska, Alaska; to the Committee on Military Affairs.

By Mr. Stockbridge: A bill (S. 3635) granting a pension to Mrs. John G. Mallery; to the Committee on Pensions.

By Mr. Paddock: A bill (S. 3636) granting a pension to Mrs. Attie Grubb; and

A bill (S. 3637) granting an increase of pension to John Grady; to the Committee on Pensions.

By Mr. Hale: A bill (S. 3638) for the relief of N. J. Coffin; to the Committee on Military Affairs.

By Mr. Aldrich: A bill (S. 3639) granting a pension to Alice Warren;

A bill (S. 3640) granting a pension to Eliza A. Fiske;

A bill (S. 3641) granting a pension to Sarah M. Phillips; and

A bill (S. 3642) granting a pension to Honora Breslin; to the Committee on Pensions.

By Mr. Carey: A bill (S. 3643) to provide for the disposal of the Fort Bridger abandoned military reservation, in the State of Wyoming; to the Committee on Public Lands.

By Mr. Hansbrough: A bill (S. 3644) for the relief of the families of certain Indian policemen, who were killed during the engagement at Sitting Bull's camp on Grand River, December 15, 1890, and for the relief of Alexander Middle, who was wounded in said engagement; and

A bill (S. 3645) granting medals to certain Indian policemen of the Standing Rock Agency, N. Dak.; to the Committee on Indian Affairs.

By Mr. McMillan: A joint resolution (S. R. 124) directing the Secretary of War to investigate the subject of raft-towing on the Great Lakes and their connecting waters; to the Committee on Commerce.

REGENTS OF THE SMITHSONIAN INSTITUTION.

Mr. Morrill introduced a joint resolution (S. R. 123) to fill vacancies in the board of regents of the Smithsonian Institution; which was read the first and second times by unanimous consent and considered as in Committe of the Whole; and no amendment being made, it was reported to the Senate.

Ordered, That it be engrossed and read a third time.

The said resolution was read the third time by unanimous consent.

Resolved, That it pass, and that the title thereof be as aforesaid.

Ordered, That the Secretary request the concurrence of the House of Representatives therein.

The Vice-President appointed Mr. Gray a member of the board of regents of the Smithsonian Institution to fill the vacancy occasioned by the death of Mr. Gibson.

COUNT OF THE ELECTORAL VOTE.

Mr. Teller submitted the following resolution; which was referred to the Committee on Privileges and Elections:

Resolved by the Senate (the House of Representatives concurring), That the two Houses of Congress shall assemble in the Hall of the House of Representatives on Wednesday, the 8th day of February, 1893, at 1 o'clock in the afternoon, pursuant to the requirement of the Constitution and laws relating to the election of President and Vice-President of the United States, and the President of the Senate shall be the presiding officer; that two persons be appointed tellers on the part of the Senate, and two on the part of the House of Representatives, to make a list of the votes as they shall be declared; that the result shall be delivered to the President of the Senate, who shall announce the state of the vote and the persons elected, to the two Houses assembled as aforesaid, which shall be deemed a declaration of the persons elected President and Vice-President of the United States; and, together with a list of the votes, be entered on the Journals of the two Houses.

MRS. MARY A. MERRITT.

Mr. Davis submitted the following resolution; which was referred to the Committee to Audit and Control the Contingent Expenses of the Senate:

Resolved, That the Secretary of the Senate be, and he is hereby, authorized and directed to pay, out of the miscellaneous items of the contingent fund of the Senate, to Mrs. Mary A. Merritt, widow of John G. Merritt, deceased, late a messenger acting as assistant doorkeeper of the United States Senate, the sum of $900, being an amount equal to six months' salary at the rate per annum allowed by law to the aforesaid messenger acting as assistant doorkeeper. Said sum to be considered as including the funeral expenses and all allowances.

HEARINGS ON INDIAN DEPREDATION CLAIMS.

Mr. Dawes submitted the following resolution; which was referred to the Committee to Audit and Control the Contingent Expenses of the Senate:

Resolved, That the Committee on Indian Affairs have authority for the employment of a stenographer to report the hearing before said committee on the 16th instant relative to payment of Indian depredation claims; also that said committee be authorized to employ a stenographer to report hearings before said committee whenever the committee shall so order; the expense of such employment to be paid out of the contingent fund of the Senate.

INDIAN DEPREDATION CLAIMS.

Mr. Faulkner submitted the following resolution; which was considered by unanimous consent and agreed to:

Resolved, That the Attorney-General be, and he is hereby, directed to report to the Senate the total number of Indian depredation claims already filed in the Court of Claims, with the total amount claimed therein; the number of cases claimed as entitled to priority of consideration and the amount claimed therein; the number to which such consideration has been given and the amount claimed therein; and the number and amount of judgments rendered in such cases; with a list of the cases in which the Department of Justice has made a defense, and the reason and result thereof; a list of all cases in which there has been allowed by the Secretary of the Interior or the Court of Claims or by either, or has been conceded by the Department of Justice an amount greater than the amount recommended by the Commissioner of Indian Affairs, with a statement of the differences between such allowances and recommendations; and a statement of the judgments, if any, which, after they were paid, were found to be unjust; and, in addition, to inform the Senate whether any attorneys for claimants have also been employed as agents or counsel for the Government in other cases; and whether any claims have been at any time allowed by the court or their priority of consideration conceded by the Department which were not covered by the clause in the act of March 3, 1891, providing that only such cases shall have priority as were allowed by the Secretary of the Interior under the act of March 3, 1885, and the subsequent Indian appropriation acts.

The Vice-President laid before the Senate the resolution submitted by Mr. Platt on the 15th instant, calling for information in relation to Indian trust funds and Indian depredation claims; and having been modified by Mr. Platt by inserting at the end of the first clause the following words: *and the approximate amount which will be added to such trust funds under agreement recently made with Indian tribes,*

The resolution as modified was agreed to.

RECOMMITTAL OF BILL.

On motion by Mr. Palmer, and by unanimous consent,

Ordered, That the vote of the Senate whereby the bill (S. 1754) for the relief of Herbert Cushman was postponed indefinitely, be reconsidered, and the bill recommitted to the Committee on Military Affairs.

MESSAGE FROM THE HOUSE.

A message from the House of Representatives, by Mr. Towles, its chief clerk:

Mr. President: The House of Representatives has passed, without amendment, the resolution of the Senate to print 23,000 copies of the ninth annual report of the United States Civil Service Commission; and

It has passed the bill of the Senate (S. 3298) authorizing the sale of land in the vicinity of Fort Mifflin, on the river Delaware, with amendments, in which it requests the concurrence of the Senate.

The Speaker of the House of Representatives having signed an enrolled joint resolution, (H. R. 170,) I am directed to bring it to the Senate for the signature of its president.

ENROLLED JOINT RESOLUTION SIGNED.

Mr. Sanders reported from the Committee that they had examined and found duly enrolled the joint resolution (H. R. 170) to pay the officers and employés of the Senate and House of Representatives their respective salaries for the month of December, 1892, on the 21st day of said month;

Whereupon

The Vice-President signed the same, and it was delivered to the committee to be presented to the President of the United States.

HOUSE AMENDMENTS TO SENATE BILL.

The Senate proceeded to consider the amendments of the House of Representatives to the bill (S. 3298) authorizing the sale of land in the vicinity of Fort Mifflin on the river Delaware; and

On motion by Mr. Cameron,

Resolved, That the Senate agree thereto.

Ordered, That the Secretary notify the House of Representatives thereof.

CALENDAR BILLS CONSIDERED.

On motion by Mr. McPherson,

The Senate proceeded to consider, as in Committee of the Whole, the bill (H. R. 8760) to provide for the sale of navy-yard lands in the city of Brooklyn; and no amendment being made, it was reported to the Senate.

Ordered, That it pass to a third reading.

The said bill was read the third time.

Resolved, That it pass.

Ordered, That the Secretary notify the House of Representatives thereof.

On motion by Mr. Bate,

The Senate proceeded to consider as, in Committee of the Whole, the bill (S. 3504) to repeal all statutes relating to supervisors of elections and special deputies; and

After debate,

Ordered, That it lie on the table.

EXECUTIVE SESSION.

On motion by Mr. Hoar,

The Senate proceeded to the consideration of executive business; and

After the consideration of executive business the doors were reopened.

DEALINGS IN OPTIONS AND FUTURES.

The Presiding Officer (Mr. Harris in the chair) announced that the hour of 2 o'clock had arrived and laid before the Senate the unfinished business at its last adjournment, viz, the bill (H. R. 7845) defining "options" and "futures," imposing taxes on dealers therein, and requiring such persons engaged in selling certain products to obtain license, and for other purposes; when,

On motion by Mr. Blackburn that the Senate proceed to the consideration of the bill (S. 2626) to authorize the New York and New Jersey Bridge companies to construct and maintain a bridge across the Hudson River between New York City and the State of New Jersey,

It was determined in the negative, { Yeas 13
{ Nays 41

On motion by Mr. Washburn, ·
The yeas and nays being desired by one-fifth of the Senators present,
Those who voted in the affirmative are,
Messrs. Aldrich, Blackburn, Blodgett, Brice, Gibson, Gray, Harris, Hunton, Mills, Sanders, Stewart, Vest, Vilas.
Those who voted in the negative are,
Messrs. Allen, Bate, Berry, Call, Casey, Chandler, Coke, Cullom, Davis, Dawes, Dolph, Dubois, Frye, Gallinger, George, Hale, Hansbrough, Hiscock, Hoar, Jones of Arkansas, McMillan, Manderson, Mitchell, Morgan, Morrill, Pasco, Peffer, Perkins, Platt, Proctor, Pugh, Ransom, Sawyer, Sherman, Stockbridge, Teller, Turpie, Vance, Washburn, Wilson, Wolcott.
So the motion was not agreed to.
The Senate resumed, as in Committee of the Whole, the consideration of the bill H. R. 7845; and
The question being on the amendment proposed by Mr. Daniel,
Pending debate,
On motion by Mr. Quay, at 3 o'clock and 57 minutes p. m.,
The Senate adjourned.

WEDNESDAY, DECEMBER 21, 1892.

The Vice-President laid before the Senate the sixth annual report of the Interstate Commerce Commission.
Ordered, That it lie on the table and be printed.

PETITIONS AND MEMORIALS.

Mr. Morgan presented a memorial of the legislature of Alabama, and a memorial of the National Nicaragua Canal Convention in favor of the speedy completion of the Nicaragua Canal under the direction and control of the United States.
Ordered, That they lie on the table and be printed.
Mr. Hiscock presented a petition of citizens of New York, praying the appointment of a committee to investigate an alleged combine formed to depreciate the price of grain, and now existing between the millers, elevators and railroads at Minneapolis and St. Louis, and asking for a postponement of the passage of the antioption bill until said committee can make report; which was referred to the Committee on Agriculture and Forestry.
Mr. Hiscock presented resolutions adopted by the Board of Aldermen of Buffalo, N. Y., praying an extension of the breakwater at that place to Stony Point, N. Y.; which were referred to the Committee on Commerce.
Mr. Sherman presented a petition of citizens of Ohio, praying for the appointment of a committee to investigate an alleged combine, formed to depreciate the price of grain, now existing between the millers, elevators, and railroads at Minneapolis and St. Louis, and asking for a postponement of the antioption bill until after said committee can make report; which was referred to the Committee on Agriculture and Forestry.
Petitions praying the passage of the "antioption bill" were presented as follows:
By Mr. Sherman: Three petitions of citizens of Ohio.
By Mr. Harris: A petition of citizens of Tennessee.
By Mr. McPherson: A petition of the New Jersey State Horticultural Society.
By Mr. Bate: Two petitions of citizens of Tennessee.
Ordered, That they lie on the table.
Memorials remonstrating against the repeal of the provision providing for the closing of the Columbian Exposition on the Sabbath day were presented as follows:
By Mr. Proctor: A memorial of citizens of Vermont.
By Mr. Hiscock: A memorial of citizens of New York.
By Mr. Quay: A memorial of citizens of Pennsylvania.
Ordered, That they be referred to the Select Committee on the Quadro-Centennial.
Mr. Cullom presented a petition of William Martin, praying for the removal of the charge of desertion from his military record; which was referred to the Committee on Military Affairs, to accompany the bill S. 3647.
Mr. Felton presented a petition of colored citizens of California, praying that the moral, intellectual, and industrial progress and development of the colored people during the first quarter century of their freedom should be made part of the Government exhibit at the Columbian Exposition; which was referred to the Select Committee on the Quadro-Centennial.

MESSAGE FROM THE HOUSE.

A message from the House of Representatives, by Mr. Towles, its chief clerk:
Mr. President: The House of Representatives has passed, without amendment, the resolution of the Senate to print the report of the Commissioner of Fish and Fisheries for the fiscal year ending June 30, 1892, and extra copies of the same.
The House of Representatives has passed the following bills, in which it requests the concurrence of Senate:
H. R. 1484. An act for the relief of Mary A. Lewis;
H. R. 8915. An act granting an increase of pension to Joseph Coffman; and

H. R. 9649. An act to provide for the purchase of Fort Brown, Tex.
The Speaker of the House of Representatives having signed three enrolled bills, H. R. 6644, H. R. 8760, and H. R. 8907, I am directed to bring them to the Senate for the signature of its President.

ENROLLED BILL SIGNED.

Mr. Sanders reported from the committee that they had examined and found duly enrolled the bill (H. R. 8760) to provide for the sale of navy-yard lands in the city of Brooklyn;
Whereupon
The Vice-President signed the same, and it was delivered to the committee to be presented to the President of the United States.

BILLS PRESENTED.

Mr. Sanders reported from the committee that they yesterday presented to the President of the United States the following enrolled bills and joint resolution:
S. 539. An act to amend and enlarge the act approved June 18, 1878, entitled "An act to provide for the distribution of the awards made under the convention between the United States of America and the Republic of Mexico, concluded on the 4th of July, 1868;"
S. 606. An act to amend and enlarge the act approved June 18, 1878, entitled "An act to provide for the distribution of the awards made under the convention between the United States of America and the Republic of Mexico, concluded on the 4th day of July, 1868;"
S. 2093. An act to provide for the disposal of certain abandoned military reservations in the State of Wyoming;
S. 869. An act to provide an American register for the barge *Sea Bird*, of Perth Amboy, N. J.;
S. 1647. An act to authorize the Alabama Grand Trunk Railroad Company to bridge across the Tallapoosa and Coosa rivers;
S. 1936. An act to make Punta Gorda a subport of entry;
S. 2451. An act authorizing the Secretary of the Treasury to reconvey to Lucius U. Maltby and Louise W. Maltby, his wife, Margaret Elizabeth Lucas, and the Sea Girt Land Improvement Company, a piece of land selected as a site for the Squan Inlet light-station, New Jersey, but found to be unsuitable for the purpose of said station;
S. 3188. An act to extend to Duluth, Minn., the privileges of the first section of an act entitled "An act to amend the statutes in relation to immediate transportation of dutiable goods, and for other purposes," approved June 10, 1880; and
S. R. 73. A joint resolution authorizing the Secretary of War to receive for instruction at the Military Academy at West Point Francisco Alcantara, of Venezuela,

REPORTS OF COMMITTEES.

Mr. Turpie, from the Committee on Pensions, to whom was referred the bill (H. R. 5012) to increase the pension of Thomas Enlow, reported it without amendment and submitted a report (No. 1139) thereon.
Mr. Vilas, from the Committee on Claims, to whom was referred the bill (S. 3028) for the relief of William P. Dunwoody, submitted an adverse report (No. 1140) thereon.
Ordered, That it be postponed indefinitely.
Mr. Dawes, from the Committee on Indian Affairs, to whom was referred the bill (S. 2594) for the adjustment of the rights of the Indians and the Indian tribes to lands owned or occupied by them in the Indian Territory, and for other arrangements with a view to the creation of a State embracing such territory, reported it with amendments.
Mr. Sherman, from the Committee on Foreign Relations, to whom was referred the bill (S. 1218) to amend the act entitled "An act to incorporate the Maritime Canal Company of Nicaragua," approved February 20, 1889, reported it with amendments.
On motion by Mr. Stewart,
Ordered, That the Committee on Claims be discharged from the further consideration of the bill (S. 1353) for the relief of Morgan Everts, and that it be referred to the Committee on Military Affairs.
Mr. McMillan, from the Committee on the District of Columbia, to whom was referred the bill (H. R. 9417) to incorporate the Protestant Episcopal Cathedral Foundation of the District of Columbia, reported it without amendment.
The Senate, proceeded, by unanimous consent, to consider the said bill as in Committee on the Whole; and no amendment being made, it was reported to the Senate.
Ordered, That it pass to a third reading.
The said bill was read the third time.
Resolved, That it pass.
Ordered, That the Secretary notify the House of Representatives thereof.
On motion by Mr. McMillan,
The Senate proceeded to consider, as in Committee of the Whole, the bill (S. 3391) to incorporate the Protestant Episcopal Cathedral Foundation of the District of Columbia; and
Ordered, That it be postponed indefinitely.
Mr. Manderson, from the Committee on Printing, to whom was re-

ferred the resolution submitted by him on the 15th instant to print —— copies of the consular report relating to streets and highways in foreign countries, reported it without amendment and submitted a report (No. 1141) thereon.

The Senate proceeded, by unanimous consent, to consider the said resolution; and having been amended, on the motion of Mr. Manderson, the resolution as amended was agreed to as follows:

Resolved by the Senate (the House of Representatives concurring), That there be printed 30,000 copies of the special consular report relating to streets and highways in foreign countries, heretofore published by the Department of State, of which 10,000 copies shall be for the use of the Senate and 20,000 copies for the use of the House of Representatives.

Ordered, That the Secretary request the concurrence of the House of Representatives therein.

Mr. Vance, from the Committee to Audit and Control the Contingent Expenses of the Senate, to whom was referred the resolution submitted by Mr. Vest on the 6th instant, directing the Committee on the Census to investigate certain charges made against the employés of the Census Bureau, reported it without amendment.

The Senate proceeded, by unanimous consent, to consider the said resolution; and

Resolved, That the Senate agree thereto.

Mr. Paddock, from the Committee to Audit and Control the Contingent Expenses of the Senate, to whom was referred the resolution yesterday submitted by Mr. Davis, to pay to Mrs. Mary A. Merritt, widow of John G. Merritt, deceased, an amount equal to six months of his salary as messenger of the Senate, reported it without amendment.

The Senate proceeded, by unanimous consent, to consider the said resolution; and

Resolved, That the Senate agree thereto.

INTRODUCTION OF BILLS AND JOINT RESOLUTIONS.

Bills were introduced, read the first and second times by unanimous consent, and referred as follows:

By Mr. Perkins: A bill (S. 3646) to remove the charge of desertion against Alfred Rebsamen; to the Committee on Military Affairs.

By Mr. Callom: A bill (S. 3647) for the relief of William Martin; to the Committee on Military Affairs.

By Mr. Felton: A bill (S. 3648) for the improvement of San Pedro Bay; to the Committee on Commerce.

Mr. Call introduced a joint resolution (S. R. 125) to suspend approval of lists of public lands to States or corporations until the further action of Congress; which was read the first and second times by unanimous consent.

Ordered, That it lie on the table.

Mr. McPherson introduced a joint resolution (S. R. 126) authorizing and directing the Secretary of the Treasury to suspend all purchases of silver bullion as provided in the act of July 14, 1890; which was read the first and second times by unanimous consent.

Ordered, That it lie on the table.

UNLAWFUL DISPOSAL OF PUBLIC LANDS.

Mr. Call submitted the following resolution; which was ordered to lie on the table and be printed.

Resolved, That it be, and is hereby, referred to a special committee of five Senators, to be appointed by the President of the Senate, to inquire and report to the Senate whether there have been approvals of land by the Secretary of the Interior to States or railroad corporations in violation of the acts of Congress, and to report by bill or otherwise the measures necessary for the opening of such land to the use and occupation of citizens of the United States under the homestead laws and for the protection of actual settlers on said land.

MESSAGE FROM THE HOUSE.

A message from the House of Representatives, by Mr. Towles, its chief clerk:

Mr. President: The House of Representatives has passed a bill (H. R. 9826) granting certain rights and privileges to the commissioners of water works in the city of Erie, Pa., in which it requests the concurrence of the Senate.

The Speaker of the House of Representatives having signed five enrolled bills, S. 570, S. 1675, S. 2981, S. 3059, and S. 3278, I am directed to bring them to the Senate for the signature of its president.

ADJOURNMENT FOR THE HOLIDAYS.

The Vice-President laid before the Senate the resolution of the House of Representatives providing for the adjournment of the two Houses from the 22d instant to January 4, 1893; and

On motion by Mr. Dawes,

Resolved, That the Senate agree thereto.

Ordered, That the Secretary notify the House of Representatives thereof.

CONSIDERATION OF BILLS ON THE CALENDAR.

On motion by Mr. Stockbridge,

The Senate proceeded to consider, as in Committee of the Whole, the bill (H. R. 6737) granting a pension to Delzell R. Bradford,

Twenty-fourth Michigan Volunteers; and no amendment being made, it was reported to the Senate.

Ordered, That it pass to a third reading.

The said bill was read the third time.

Resolved, That it pass.

Ordered, That the Secretary notify the House of Representatives thereof.

On motion by Mr. Paddock,

The Senate proceeded to consider, as in Committee of the Whole, the bill (S. 1674) incorporating the Society of American Florists; and the reported amendments having been agreed to, and the bill further amended on the motion of Mr. Mills, it was reported to the Senate and the amendments were concurred in.

Ordered, That it be engrossed and read a third time.

The said bill was read the third time.

Resolved, That it pass, and that the title thereof be as aforesaid.

Ordered, That the Secretary request the concurrence of the House of Representatives therein.

On motion by Mr. Sanders,

The Senate proceeded to consider, as in Committee of the Whole, the bill (S. 2576) for the relief of C. L. Coder; and having been amended on the motion of Mr. Sanders, the bill was reported to the Senate and the amendment was concurred in.

Ordered, That it be engrossed and read a third time.

The said bill was read the third time.

Resolved, That it pass, and that the title thereof be as aforesaid.

Ordered, That the Secretary request the concurrence of the House of Representatives therein.

On motion by Mr. Hale,

The Senate proceeded to consider, as in Committee of the Whole, the bill (S. 3221) to provide for the adjustment and payment of the claim of Thomas Rhys Smith for work done and materials furnished for the breakwater at Bar Harbor, Me.; and the reported amendment having been agreed to, the bill was reported to the Senate and the amendment was concurred in.

Ordered, That it be engrossed and read the third time.

The said bill was read the third time.

Resolved, That it pass, and that the title thereof be as aforesaid.

Ordered, That the Secretary request the concurrence of the House of Representatives therein.

On motion by Mr. White,

The Senate proceeded to consider, as in Committee of the Whole, the following bills; and no amendment being made, they were reported to the Senate:

H. R. 9487. An act to amend an act approved April 22, 1890, authorizing the Natchitoches Cane River Bridge Company to construct and maintain a bridge across Cane River, in Louisiana; and

H. R. 9488. An act to amend an act approved March 2, 1891, authorizing the construction of a bridge across the Red River, Louisiana, by the Rapides Bridge Company, limited.

Ordered, That they pass to a third reading.

The said bills were read the third time.

Resolved, That they pass.

Ordered, That the Secretary request the concurrence of the House of Representatives therein.

CHANGE OF REFERENCE OF BILL.

On motion by Mr. Teller.

Ordered, That the Committee on Military Affairs be discharged from the further consideration of the bill (S. 3634) to provide for building and maintaining an Indian industrial school at Unalaska, and that it be referred to the Committee on Indian Affairs.

CLAIM OF WILLIAM M'GARRAHAN.

The Senate resumed the reconsideration of the bill (S. 1958) to submit to the Court of Private Land Claims, established by an act of Congress approved March 3, 1891, the title of William McGarrahan to the Rancho Panoche Grande, in the State of California, and for other purposes, returned by the President of the United States to the Senate with his objections thereto; and

Pending debate,

DEALINGS IN OPTIONS AND FUTURES.

The Presiding Officer (Mr. Platt in the chair) announced that the hour of 2 o'clock had arrived, and laid before the Senate the unfinished business at its adjournment yesterday, viz, the bill (H. R. 7815) defining "options" and "futures," imposing special taxes on dealers therein, and requiring such persons engaged in selling certain products to obtain license, and for other purposes; and

The Senate resumed, as in Committee of the Whole, the consideration of the bill; and

The question being on the amendment proposed by Mr. Daniel; and

Pending debate,

EXECUTIVE SESSION.

On motion by Mr. Manderson,

The Senate proceeded to the consideration of executive business; and

After the consideration of executive business the doors were reopened, and

On motion by Mr. Manderson, at 4 o'clock and 22 minutes p. m., The Senate adjourned.

THURSDAY, DECEMBER 22, 1892.

The Vice-President being absent, the President pro tempore, Mr. Charles F. Manderson, from the State of Nebraska, assumed the chair.

ENROLLED BILLS SIGNED.

Mr. Sanders reported from the committee that they had examined and found duly enrolled the following bills:

S. 570. An act to provide for the removal of the remains of the late Ensign D. F. Terrell, United States Navy, from Sitka, Alaska, to his home in the State of Mississippi;

S. 1675. An act granting increase of pension to soldiers of the Mexican war in certain cases;

S. 2981. An act for the relief of the Citadel Academy of Charleston, S. C.;

S. 3059. An act for the relief of the Old Dominion Steamship Company;

S. 3298. An act authorizing the sale of land in the vicinity of Fort Mifflin, on the river Delaware;

H. R. 6644. An act to amend an act entitled "An act authorizing the sale of title of the United States in lot 3 in square south of square 990," approved March 3, 1891; and

H. R. 8907. An act to increase the pension of John Malloy.

Whereupon,

The President pro tempore signed the same, and they were delivered to the committee to be presented to the President of the United States.

HOUSE BILLS REFERRED.

The bills yesterday received from the House of Representatives for concurrence were severally read the first and second times by unanimous consent.

Ordered, That the bill H. R. 1484 be referred to the Committee on Claims; that the bill H. R. 8915 be referred to the Committee on Pensions; that the bill H. R. 9649 be referred to the Committee on Military Affairs, and that the bill H. R. 9826 be referred to the Committee on Public Buildings and Grounds.

DRILL REGULATIONS FOR THE ARMY.

The President pro tempore laid before the Senate the amendments of the House of Representatives to the joint resolution (S. R. 112) to print and bind 1,000 copies each of the drill regulations for infantry, cavalry, and artillery; and

On motion by Mr. Cockrell,

Resolved, That the Senate agree thereto.

Ordered, That the Secretary notify the House of Representatives thereof.

MESSAGE FROM THE HOUSE.

A message from the House of Representatives, by Mr. Towles, its chief clerk:

Mr. President: The House of Representatives has passed a bill (H. R. 9527) to restore to the public domain a portion of the White Mountain Apache Indian Reservation, in the Territory of Arizona, and for other purposes, in which it requests the concurrence of the Senate.

The Speaker of the House of Representatives having signed two enrolled bills, H. R. 6737 and H. R. 9417, I am directed to bring the same to the Senate for the signature of its President.

The bill H. R. 9527, last received from the House of Representatives for concurrence, was read the first and second time by unanimous consent and referred to the Committee on Indian Affairs.

PETITIONS AND MEMORIALS.

Petitions, memorials, etc., were presented and referred as follows:

By the President pro tempore: A resolution of the legislature of Vermont in favor of the passage of a law establishing a uniform policy of immigration from foreign nations and of migration from State to State; to the Committee on Immigration.

By Mr. Blackburn: A resolution of the legislature of Kentucky in favor of legislation to increase the efficiency of the Weather Bureau; to the Committee on Agriculture and Forestry.

By Mr. Proctor: A resolution of the legislature of Vermont in favor of the passage of a law establishing a uniform policy of immigration from foreign nations and of migration from State to State; to the Committee on Immigration.

A resolution of the legislature of Vermont in favor of the passage of a law for the free delivery of the mails in all the towns of the United States; to the Committee on Post-Offices and Post Roads.

A resolution of the legislature of Vermont in favor of an amendment to the Constitution of the United States prohibiting any State

from passing any law respecting religion or the free exercise thereof; to the Committee on the Judiciary.

By Mr. Pasco: A memorial of the Board of Trade of Jacksonville, Fla., praying the passage of a law to restrict immigration into this country for one year; to the Committee on Immigration.

Two memorials of citizens of Florida, praying an immediate appropriation for continuing the work of improvement of Cumberland Sound and to protect the entrance to the port of Fernandina; to the Committee on Commerce.

By Mr. Carlisle: A memorial of the Chamber of Commerce of Phœnix, Ariz., praying the passage of a law for the admission of the Territory of Arizona into the Union as a State; to the Committee on Territories.

By Mr. Casey: A petition of citizens of North Dakota, praying the passage of the bill providing for the retirement of enlisted men of the Army after a continuous service of twenty-five years; to the Committee on Military Affairs.

By Mr. Washburn: A petition of citizens of Minnesota, praying the passage of the bill limiting the amount of wearing apparel that may be admitted free of duty; to the Committee on Finance.

By Mr. Dawes: A memorial of the National League for the Protection of American Industries, praying that no further appropriation be made for the support of sectarian schools among the Indians; to the Committee on Appropriations.

By Mr. Cullom: A memorial of the Kilo, Club, of Chicago, Ill., remonstrating against the closing of the Columbian Exposition on the Sabbath day; to the Select Committee on the Quadro-Centennial.

By Mr. Wilson: A petition of citizen of citizens of Iowa in behalf of George Wallace Jones, praying the passage of a law for his relief; to the Committee on Foreign Relations.

By Mr. Cameron: Two petitions of citizens of Pennsylvania, praying the passage of a law for the closing of the Columbian Exposition on the Sabbath day; to the Select Committee on the Quadro-Centennial.

By Mr. Dolph: Papers relating to the application of William J. Carnell and Joseph M. Carnell to have refunded them the amount of an overpayment on a certain land entry in the State of Oregon; to the Committee on Public Lands, to accompany the bill S. 3649.

By Mr. Cullom: Papers relating to the application of Frederick Dise for the removal of the charge of desertion from his military record; to the Committee on Military Affairs, to accompany the bill S. 3652.

By Mr. Cockrell: A petition of citizens of the District of Columbia, owners of lands in the Petworth Addition to the city of Washington, praying an appropriation for the completion of the sewerage in said tract of land; to the Committee on Appropriations.

By Mr. Mitchell: A petition of S. Heydenfeldt, jr., praying the passage of a law to prohibit the use of electricity on human beings where it affects others; to the Committee on the Judiciary, to accompany the bill S. 3658.

Petitions praying for the appointment of a committee to investigate an alleged combine formed to depreciate the price of grain, and now existing between the millers, elevators, and railroads at Minneapolis and St. Louis, and asking for the postponement of the antioption bill until said committee can make report, were presented as follows:

By Mr. Bate: A petition of citizens of Tennessee.

By Mr. Cameron: A petition of citizens of Pennsylvania.

By Mr. Cockrell: Several petitions of citizens of Missouri.

By Mr. Cullom: Several petitions of citizens of Illinois.

Ordered, That they be referred to the Committee on Agriculture and Forestry.

Memorials remonstrating against the repeal of the provision providing for the closing of the Columbian Exposition on the Sabbath day were presented as follows:

By Mr. Casey: A memorial of citizens of North Dakota.

By Mr. Cullom: A memorial of citizens of Illinois.

Ordered, That they be referred to the Select Committee on the Quadro-Centennial.

Petitions praying the passage of the "antioption bill," were presented as follows:

By Mr. Cullom: A petition of citizens of Illinois.

By Mr. Morgan: Two petitions of citizens of Alabama.

Ordered, That they lie on the table.

Mr. Squire presented a memorial of the Chamber of Commerce of Seattle, Washington, praying for the speedy completion of the Nicaragua Canal under the direction and control of the United States Government.

Ordered, That it lie on the table.

COMMITTEE SERVICE.

Mr. White, at his own request, was excused from further service as a member of the Committee on Epidemic Diseases.

Ordered, That the vacancy in the said committee be filled by the President pro tempore; and

The President pro tempore appointed Mr. Gibson.

PAPERS REFERRED FROM FILES.

Papers in the following named cases, to accompany bills introduced, were taken from the files and referred, under the Rule, as follows:

Miguel Salinas; to the Committee on Claims.

N. J. Coffin, Wm. Martin; to the Committee on Naval Affairs.

REPORTS OF COMMITTEES.

Mr. Chandler, from the Committee on Immigration, to whom was referred the bill (S. 3513) for the suspension of immigration for one year, reported it with amendments.

Mr. Harris, from the Committee on Epidemic Diseases, to whom was referred the bill (S. 2707) granting additional quarantine powers and imposing additional duties upon the Marine-Hospital Service, reported it with amendments.

Mr. Sherman, from the Committee on Foreign Relations, submitted a report (No. 1142) to accompany the bill (S. 1218) to amend the act entitled "An act to incorporate the Maritime Canal Company of Nicaragua," approved February 20, 1889, heretofore reported.

ENROLLED BILLS SIGNED.

Mr. Sanders reported from the committee that they had examined and found duly enrolled the following bills:

H. R. 6737. An act granting a pension to Delzell R. Bradford, Twenty-fourth Michigan Volunteers; and

H. R. 9417. An act to incorporate the Protestant Episcopal Cathedral Foundation of the District of Columbia;

Whereupon,

The President pro tempore signed the same, and they were delivered to the committee to be presented to the President of the United States.

INTRODUCTION OF BILLS AND JOINT RESOLUTION.

Bills and a joint resolution were introduced, read the first and second times by unanimous consent, and referred as follows:

By Mr. Dolph: A bill (S. 3649) for the relief of William J. Cornell and Joseph M. Cornell; to the Committee on Public Lands.

By Mr. Casey: A bill (S. 3650) to reduce the fees on domestic money orders, and for other purposes; to the Committee on Post Offices and Post-Roads.

By Mr. Cameron: A bill (S. 3651) to amend the articles for the government of the Navy; to the Committee on Naval Affairs.

By Mr. Cullom: A bill (S. 3652) to remove the charge of desertion from the military record of Frederick Diss; to the Committee on Military Affairs.

A bill (S. 3653) for the relief of Joseph W. Parish; and

A bill (S. 3654) for the relief of Elias E. Barnes; to the Committee on Claims.

By Mr. Gorman: A bill (S. 3655) to incorporate the Washington, Burnt Mills and Sandy Springs Railway Company; to the Committee on the District of Columbia.

By Mr. Perkins: A bill (S. 3656) to enable the people of the Territory of Oklahoma and the Indian Territory to form a constitution and State government and to be admitted into the Union on an equal footing with the original States, and for other purposes; to the Committee on Territories.

By Mr. Allen: A bill (S. 3657) to provide for the survey of public lands in the State of Washington; to the Committee on Public Lands.

By Mr. Mitchell: A bill (S. 3658) to prohibit electromagnetizing, mesmerizing, or hypnotizing human beings, or affecting one person through another by electricity, and to declare the same to be a crime against the law of nations, and to define its punishment; to the Committee on the Judiciary.

Mr. Casey introduced a joint resolution (S. R. 127) authorizing the Smithsonian Institution to lend to the North Dakota World's Fair Commission the Red River cart, now in the National Museum; which was read the first and second times by unanimous consent and considered as in Committee of the Whole; and no amendment being made, it was reported to the Senate.

Ordered, That it be engrossed and read a third time.

The said resolution was read the third time by unanimous consent.

Resolved, That it pass, and that the title thereof be as aforesaid.

Ordered, That the Secretary request the concurrence of the House of Representatives therein.

NICARAGUA CANAL.

Mr. Sherman submitted the following resolution; which was referred to the Committee on Printing:

Resolved, That 5,000 extra copies of the report of the Committee on Foreign Relations on Senate bill No. 1218, relating to the Nicaragua Canal, and the accompanying documents, be printed for the use of the Senate.

REGULATION OF IMMIGRATION.

Mr. Chandler submitted the following resolution; which was considered by unanimous consent and agreed to:

Resolved, That 1,000 copies be printed for the use of the Senate of the immigration act, Public No. 152, of March 3, 1891.

PRESIDENTIAL APPROVALS.

A message from the President of the United States, by Mr. Pruden, his secretary:

Mr. President: The President of the United States this day approved and signed the following acts and joint resolution:

S. 869. An act to provide an American register for the barge Sea Bird, of Perth Amboy, N. J.;

S. 1956. An act to make Punta Gorda a subport of entry;

S. 2451. An act authorizing the Secretary of the Treasury to reconvey to Lucius U. Maltby and Louise W. Maltby, his wife, Margaret Elizabeth Lucas, and the Sea Girt Land Improvement Company, a piece of land selected as a site for the Squan Inlet light-station, New Jersey, but found to be unsuitable for the purpose of said station;

S. 3188. An act to extend to Duluth, Minn., the privileges of the first section of an act entitled "An act to amend the statutes in relation to immediate transportation of dutiable goods and for other purposes," approved June 10, 1888;

S. 3418. An act making Saturday a half holiday for banking and trust company purposes in the District of Columbia; and

S. R. 73. Joint resolution authorizing the Secretary of War to receive for instruction at the military academy at West Point, Francisco Alcantara, of Venezuela.

Ordered, That the Secretary notify the House of Representatives thereof.

CONSIDERATION OF CALENDAR BILLS.

On motion by Mr. Stewart,

The Senate resumed, as in Committee of the Whole, the consideration of the bill (S. 54) to amend chapter 6 of title 32 of the Revised Statutes relating to mineral lands and mining resources; and having been further amended on the motion of Mr. Stewart, the bill was reported to the Senate and the amendments were concurred in.

Ordered, That it be engrossed and read a third time.

The said bill was read the third time.

Resolved, That it pass, and that the title thereof be as aforesaid.

Ordered, That the Secretary request the concurrence of the House of Representatives therein.

On motion by Mr. Wilson,

The Senate proceeded to consider, as in Committee of the Whole, the bill (S. 2730) granting an honorable discharge to William Barnes; and no amendment being made, it was reported to the Senate.

Ordered, That it be engrossed and read a third time.

The said bill was read the third time.

Resolved, That it pass, and that the title thereof be as aforesaid.

Ordered, That the Secretary request the concurrence of the House of Representatives therein.

CLAIM OF WILLIAM M'GARRAHAN.

The Senate resumed the reconsideration of the bill (S. 1938) to submit to the Court of Private Land Claims, established by an act of Congress approved March 3, 1891, the title of William McGarrahan to the Rancho Panoche Grande in the State of California, and for other purposes, returned by the President of the United States to the Senate with his objections thereto; and

Pending debate,

DEALINGS IN "OPTIONS" AND "FUTURES."

The President pro tempore announced that the hour of 2 o'clock had arrived, and laid before the Senate the unfinished business at its adjournment yesterday, viz, the bill (H. R. 7745) defining "options" and "futures," imposing special taxes on dealers therein, and requiring such persons engaged in selling certain products to obtain license, and for other purposes; and

The Senate resumed, as in Committee of the Whole, the consideration of the bill; and

The question being on the amendment proposed by Mr. Daniel,

Pending debate,

EXECUTIVE SESSION.

On motion by Mr. Washburn,

The Senate proceeded to the consideration of executive business; and

After the consideration of executive business the doors were reopened, and

On motion by Mr. Quay, at 2 o'clock and 45 minutes p. m.,

The Senate adjourned.

WEDNESDAY, JANUARY 4, 1893.

The Vice-President resumed the chair.

Mr. William B. Allison, from the State of Iowa, attended.

MESSAGES FROM THE PRESIDENT.

The following messages were received from the President of the United States, by Mr. Pruden, his secretary:

To the Senate and House of Representatives:

I transmit herewith, for the consideration of Congress, a communication of the 23d of December, 1892, from the Secretary of the

Interior, accompanied by an agreement concluded by and between the Cherokee Commission and the Comanche, Kiowa, and Apache tribes of Indians in the Territory of Oklahoma, for the cession of certain lands, and for other purposes.

BENJ. HARRISON.

EXECUTIVE MANSION, *January 4, 1893.*

To the Senate and House of Representatives:

I transmit herewith for the consideration of Congress a communication of the 23d of December, 1892, from the Secretary of the Interior, accompanied by an agreement concluded by and between the Cherokee Commission and the Pawnee tribe of Indians, in the Territory of Oklahoma, for the cession of certain lands, and for other purposes.

BENJ. HARRISON.

EXECUTIVE MANSION, *January 4, 1893.*

The messages were read.

Ordered, That they be referred to the Committee on Indian Affairs and printed.

EXECUTIVE COMMUNICATIONS.

The Vice-President laid before the Senate a letter of the Secretary of the Interior, transmitting, in answer to a resolution of the Senate of December 20, 1892, a report of the Commissioner of Indian Affairs relative to the amount of Indian depredation claims paid from Indian trust funds; which was referred to the Committee on Indian Affairs and ordered to be printed.

The Vice-President laid before the Senate ten communications from the Secretary of State, transmitting, in pursuance of the provisions of the act of February 3, 1887, certified copies of the final ascertainment of the electors for President and Vice-President in the States of Mississippi, Iowa, Vermont, Rhode Island, Massachusetts, Nevada, West Virginia, Idaho, Virginia, and Pennsylvania.

Ordered, That they lie on the table.

REPORT OF PUBLIC PRINTER.

The Vice-President laid before the Senate the annual report of the Public Printer for the fiscal year ended June 30, 1892; which was referred to the Committee on Printing and ordered to be printed.

PETITIONS AND MEMORIALS.

Petitions, memorials, etc., were presented and referred as follows:

By the Vice-President: A memorial of the New York Board of Trade and Transportation, praying the passage of a law to prevent the importation of undesirable immigrants; to the Committee on Immigration.

By Mr. Cullom: A resolution of the State Grange of Illinois, praying the passage of a law placing the control of all railroads under the Government of the United States, and providing for the election of all officers of control by the people; to the Committee on Interstate Commerce.

Resolutions of the State Grange of Illinois praying the passage of a law for the establishment of United States postal savings banks; and

Resolutions of the State Grange of Illinois, praying the passage of a law extending the free delivery of the mails to the rural districts; to the Committee on Post-Offices and Post-Roads.

Resolutions of the State Grange of Illinois, praying the passage of a law providing for the lending of money by the Government to the people at the rate of 2 per cent per annum;

Resolutions of the State Grange of Illinois, praying for the free coinage of silver;

Resolutions of the State Grange of Illinois, praying the passage of a law for the issuance of paper money limited in amount to the needs of the people; and

Resolutions of the State Grange of Illinois, praying for the revival of the income-tax law; to the Committee on Finance.

By Mr. Vest: Resolutions of the Bar Association of the First Judicial Division of the Indian Territory in regard to the jurisdiction and work of the United States courts in the Indian Territory; to the Committee on the Judiciary.

Two petitions of citizens of Missouri, praying the passage of the Conger lard bill; to the Committee on Agriculture and Forestry.

A petition of citizens of Missouri, praying an amendment to the Constitution of the United States limiting the term of President of the United States to one term of six years; to the Committee on Privileges and Elections.

By Mr. Mitchell: A petition of Marshall R. Hathaway, praying to be allowed a pension; to the Committee on Pensions.

A memorial of citizens of Oregon, remonstrating against the passage of the bill providing for the admission of foreign vessels to American registry; to the Committee on Commerce.

By Mr. Dolph: A petition of citizens of Oregon, praying for an extension of the time to settlers in which to make payment for lands within the limits of the forfeited land grant to the Northern Pacific Railroad Company; to the Committee on Public Lands.

By Mr. Teller: A memorial of citizens of Colorado, remonstrating against the removal of the Southern Ute Indians from their present reservation; to the Committee on Indian Affairs.

By Mr. Warren: Resolutions adopted by the Irrigation Convention, held at Las Vegas, N. Mex., praying certain legislation for the development of the arid region by irrigation; to the Committee on Irrigation and Reclamation of Arid Lands.

By Mr. Peffer: A resolution of the International Association of Machinists, remonstrating against any reduction of the rate of duty on machinery used in the manufacture of sugar; to the Committee on Finance.

By Mr. Cockrell: A memorial of Caroline F. Corbin, remonstrating against the passage of the proposed amendment to the Constitution of the United States extending the right of suffrage to women; to the Select Committee on Woman Suffrage.

By Mr. McMillan: A memorial of citizens of Michigan, remonstrating against the closing of the Columbian Exposition on the Sabbath day; to the Select Committee on the Quadro-Centennial.

Petitions praying the passage of the bill limiting the amount of clothing that may be admitted free of duty were presented as follows:

By Mr Quay: A petition of citizens of Pennsylvania.
By Mr. Perkins: A petition of citizens of Kansas.
By Mr. McMillan: A petition of citizens of Michigan.
By Mr. Teller: A petition of citizens of Colorado.

Ordered, That they be referred to the Committee on Finance.

Resolutions praying the speedy completion of the Nicaragua Canal under the direction and control of the United States were presented as follows:

By the Vice-President: A resolution of the Chamber of Commerce of San Diego, Cal.
By Mr. Sherman: A resolution of the Chamber of Commerce of Cincinnati, Ohio.
By Mr. Mitchell: A resolution of the Chamber of Commerce of Portland, Oregon.

Ordered, That they lie on the table.

Mr. Perkins presented a petition of citizens of Kansas praying the passage of the antilottery bill; the antioption bill; for the exclusion of liquor selling on the grounds of the Columbian Exposition; for the restriction of immigration, etc.

Ordered, That it lie on the table.

Petitions praying the passage of the Paddock pure food bill were presented as follows.

By Mr. Cullom: A petition of citizens of Illinois.
By Mr. Vest: A petition of citizens of Missouri.
By Mr. Sherman: A petition of citizens of Ohio.

Ordered, That they be referred to the Committee on Agriculture and Forestry.

Petitions praying the passage of the antioption bill were presented as follows:

By Mr. Cullom: Two petitions of citizens of Illinois.
By Mr. Cockrell: Two petitions of citizens of Missouri.
By Mr. Coke: Six petitions of citizens of Texas.
By Mr. Vest: Four petitions of citizens of Missouri.
By Mr. McMillan: A petition of citizens of Michigan.
By Mr. Sherman: Seven petitions of citizens of Ohio.
By Mr. Harris: A petition of citizens of Tennessee.

Ordered, That they lie on the table.

Memorials remonstrating against the repeal of the provision providing for the closing of the Columbian Exposition on the Sabbath day were presented as follows:

By the Vice-President: A memorial of citizens of Illinois.
By Mr. Quay: Several memorials of citizens of Pennsylvania.
By Mr. Cockrell: Five memorials of citizens of Missouri.
By Mr. McMillan: Five memorials of citizens of Michigan.
By Mr. Harris: A memorial of citizens of Tennessee.
By Mr. Peffer: A memorial of citizens of Kansas.
By Mr. Sherman: A memorial of citizens of Ohio.

Ordered, That they be referred to the Select Committee on the Quadro-Centennial.

Petitions praying for the appointment of a committee to investigate an alleged combine formed for the depreciation of the price of grain by the millers, elevators, and railroads at St. Louis and Minneapolis, were presented as follows:

By Mr. Cullom: Several petitions of citizens of Illinois.
By Mr. Teller: A petition of citizens of Colorado.
By Mr. McMillan: A petition of citizens of Michigan.
By Mr. Peffer: Several petitions of citizens of Kansas.

Ordered, That they be referred to the Committee on Agriculture and Forestry.

PRESENTATION OF BILLS.

Mr. Sanders reported from the committee that they yesterday presented to the President of the United States the following enrolled bills:

S. 570. An act to provide for the removal of the remains of the late Ensign D. F. Terrell, United States Navy, from Sitka, Alaska, to his home in the State of Mississippi;

S. 1675. An act granting increase of pension to soldiers of the Mexican war in certain cases;

S. 2981. An act for the relief of the Citadel Academy of Charleston, S. C.;

5 s

S. 3059. An act for the relief of the Old Dominion Steamship Company; and

S. 3298. An act authorizing the sale of land in the vicinity of Fort Mifflin, on the river Delaware.

REPORTS OF COMMITTEES.

Mr. Quay, from the Committee on Public Buildings and Grounds, to whom was referred the bill (H. R. 9826) granting certain rights and privileges to the commissioners of waterworks in the city of Erie, Pa., reported it with amendments.

The Senate proceeded, by unanimous consent, to consider the said bill as in Committee of the Whole, and the reported amendments having been agreed to, the bill was reported to the Senate and the amendments were concurred in.

Ordered, That the amendments be engrossed and the bill read a third time.

The said bill as amended was read the third time.

Resolved, That it pass, and that the Senate request a conference with the House of Representatives on the said bill and amendments.

Ordered, That the conferees on the part of the Senate be appointed by the Vice-President; and

The Vice-President appointed Mr. Quay, Mr. Morrill, and Mr. Vest.

Ordered, That the Secretary notify the House of Representatives thereof.

Mr. Vest, from the Committee on Commerce, to whom was referred the bill (S. 3525) to authorize the construction of bridges across the Hiawassee, the Tennessee, and the Clinch rivers, in the State of Tennessee, reported it with amendments.

Mr. Warren, from the Select Committee on Woman Suffrage, submitted a report (No. 1143) accompanied by a joint resolution (S. R.129) proposing an amendment to the Constitution of the United States extending the right of suffrage to women; which was read the first and second times by unanimous consent.

Mr. Vance asked and obtained leave to submit the views of a minority of the Select Committee on Woman Suffrage on the foregoing joint resolution; which were ordered to be printed, to accompany the report No. 1143.

Mr. Harris, from the Committee on Epidemic Diseases, submitted a report (No. 1144) to accompany the bill (S. 2707) granting additional quarantine powers and imposing additional duties upon the Marine-Hospital Service, heretofore reported.

Mr. Vest, from the Committee on Commerce, to whom was referred the bill (H. R. 6798) to authorize the construction of a bridge across the Warrior River by the Montgomery, Tuscaloosa and Memphis Railway Company, reported it with amendments.

PRESIDENTIAL APPROVALS.

A message from the President of the United States, by Mr. Pruden, his secretary:

Mr. President: The President of the United States approved and signed, December 22, 1892, an act (S. 2093) to provide for the disposal of certain abandoned military reservations in the State of Wyoming; and

He approved and signed, December 28, 1892, the following acts:

S. 599. An act to amend and enlarge the act approved June 18, 1878, entitled "An act to provide for the distribution of the awards made under the convention between the United States of America and the Republic of Mexico, concluded on the 4th day of July, 1868;"

S. 606. An act to amend and enlarge the act approved June 18, 1878, entitled "An act to provide for the distribution of the awards made under the convention between the United States of America and the Republic of Mexico, concluded on the 4th day of July, 1868;" and

S. 1647. An act to authorize the Alabama Grand Trunk Railroad Company to bridge across the Tallapoosa and Coosa rivers.

Ordered, That the Secretary notify the House of Representatives thereof.

MESSAGE FROM THE HOUSE.

A message from the House of Representatives, by Mr. Towles, its chief clerk:

Mr. President: The House of Representatives has passed, without amendment, the following bills of the Senate:

S. 1786. An act granting a pension to Mrs. Jennie Gray;

S. 1831. An act to admit free of duty the wreckage of the ships Trenton and Vandalia presented by the United States to the King of Samoa;

S. 3029. An act authorizing the construction of a bridge across the Columbia River in the State of Washington; and

S. 3048. An act granting to the Blue Mountain Irrigation and Improvement Company a right of way for reservoir and canals through the Umatilla Indian Reservation in the State of Oregon.

The House of Representatives has passed the following bills, in which it requests the concurrence of the Senate:

H. R. 2395. An act granting a pension to D. M. Lang; and

H. R. 9824. An act to amend "An act to promote the construction of a safe deep-water harbor on the coast of Texas," approved February 9, 1891.

INTRODUCTION OF BILLS AND JOINT RESOLUTIONS.

Bills and joint resolutions were introduced, read the first and second times by unanimous consent, and referred as follows:

By Mr. Frye: A bill (S. 3659) authorizing the appointment of a commission to make a settlement of the claims growing out of the issue of bonds by the United States to aid in the construction of certain railroads, and to secure to the United States payment of all indebtedness of certain railroad companies therein mentioned; to the Select Committee on Pacific Railroads.

By Mr. Coke: A bill (S. 3660) for the establishment of a lighthouse, fog signal, and line lights at or near the mouth of the Brazos River, Texas; to the Committee on Commerce.

By Mr. Dawes: A bill (S. 3661) for the relief of the estate of John R. Bigelow; to the Committee on Claims.

By Mr. Chandler: A bill (S. 3662) to prohibit unlawful military organizations; to the Select Committee on the Employment of Armed Bodies of Men for Private Purposes.

A bill (S. 3663) establishing additional regulations concerning immigration to the United States; to the Committee on Immigration.

By Mr. McMillan: A bill (S. 3664) creating form of real estate deed for the District of Columbia; to the Committee on the District of Columbia.

By Mr. Quay: A bill (S. 3665) for the relief of George R. Burnett; to the Committee on Military Affairs.

A bill (S. 3666) enlarging the limit for the construction of a post-office building at Allegheny, Pa.; to the Committee on Public Buildings and Grounds.

By Mr. Perkins: A bill (S. 3667) granting a pension to Willis Clayton;

A bill (S. 3668) granting a pension to Mrs. Sarah Beardsley; and A bill (S. 3669) granting a pension to Isaac Newman; to the Committee on Pensions.

By Mr. Sawyer: A bill (S. 3670) granting an increase of pension to Charles A. Lang; to the Committee on Pensions.

By Mr. McMillan: A joint resolution (S. R. 130) to amend an act entitled "An act making Saturday a half holiday for banks and trust companies in the District of Columbia," approved December 22, 1892; to the Committee on the District of Columbia.

By Mr. Cullom: A joint resolution (S. R. 131) giving the views of Congress on the swamp-land grant approved September 28, 1850; to the Committee on Public Lands.

Mr. Gorman introduced a joint resolution (S. R. 128) to authorize the Secretary of War to grant permits for the use of reservations and public spaces in the city of Washington, and for other purposes; which was read the first and second times by unanimous consent, and considered as in Committee of the Whole; and no amendment being made, it was reported to the Senate.

Ordered, That it be engrossed and read a third time.

The said resolution was read the third time by unanimous consent.

Resolved, That it pass, and that the title thereof be as aforesaid.

Ordered, That the Secretary request the concurrence of the House of Representatives therein.

WITHDRAWAL OF PAPERS.

On motion by Mr. Perkins,

Ordered, That Louis Volkhausen have leave to withdraw his petition and papers from the files of the Senate.

INTRODUCTION OF CHOLERA.

On motion by Mr. Chandler, and by unanimous consent,

Ordered, That on Friday next, after the routine business of the morning hour is transacted, and on Saturday if necessary, bills on the Calendar reported by the Committees on Epidemic Diseases and Immigration, having relation to the danger of the introduction of cholera into this country during the present year, shall be the special orders and have exclusive consideration on those days without displacing the present unfinished business.

HOUSE BILLS REFERRED.

The bills this day received from the House of Representatives for concurrence were read the first and second times by unanimous consent.

Ordered, That the bill H. R. 2395 be referred to the Committee on Pensions; and that the bill H. R. 9824 be referred to the Committee on Commerce.

CONSIDERATION OF BILLS ON CALENDAR.

On motion by Mr. Stewart,

The Senate proceeded to consider, as in Committee of the Whole, the joint resolution (S. R. 126) authorizing and directing the Secretary of the Treasury to suspend all purchases of silver bullion, as provided in the act of July 14, 1890; and an amendment having been proposed by Mr. Stewart,

After debate,

Ordered, That the further consideration thereof be postponed to to-morrow.

The Senate proceeded to consider, as in Committee of the Whole, the bill (S. 1664) for the relief of Lester Noble; and the reported amendments having been agreed to, the bill was reported to the Senate and the amendments were concurred in.

Ordered, That it be engrossed and read a third time.

The said bill was read the third time.

Resolved, That it pass, and that the title thereof be as aforesaid.

Ordered, That the Secretary request the concurrence of the House of Representatives therein.

The Senate proceeded to consider, as in Committee of the Whole, the bill (S. 29) for the relief of Wetmore & Brother, of St. Louis, Mo.; and no amendment being made, it was reported to the Senate.

Ordered, That it be engrossed and read a third time.

The said bill was read the third time.

Resolved, That it pass, and that the title thereof be as aforesaid.

Ordered, That the Secretary request the concurrence of the House of Representatives therein.

DEALINGS IN "OPTIONS" AND "FUTURES."

The Presiding Officer (Mr. Platt in the Chair) announced that the hour of 2 o'clock had arrived, and laid before the Senate the unfinished business at its last adjournment, viz, the bill (H. R. 7845) defining "options" and "futures," imposing special taxes on dealers therein, and requiring such persons engaged in selling certain products to obtain license, and for other purposes; and

The Senate resumed, as in Committee of the Whole, the consideration of the bill; and

The question being on the amendment proposed by Mr. Daniel, to strike out section 10,

The amendment was, by unanimous consent, temporarily laid aside.

The bill having been further amended on the motion of Mr. Washburn and the motion of Mr. White,

On motion by Mr. White to further amend the bill by striking out on page 3 the following proviso:

"*Provided, however,* That such contract or agreement shall not be made, settled for by delivery, or by settlement of differences, or by any other mode of performance or settlement, in or upon any board of trade, produce, cotton, merchants', or other exchange, or other commercial association, or in any place or upon any premises where price quotations of said articles are announced, bulletined, or published, nor be subject to the rules or regulations of any such board, exchange, or other commercial association,"

The yeas were 12 and the nays were 20.

On motion by Mr. Washburn,

, The yeas and nays being desired by one-fifth of the Senators present,

Those who voted in the affirmative are,

Messrs. Call, Carlisle, Daniel, Gorman, Hoar, Hunton, Mitchell, Platt, Stewart, Vilas, White, Wolcott.

Those who voted in the negative are,

Messrs. Berry, Blodgett, Cockrell, Coke, Dawes, Dubois, Frye, George, Morgan, Pasco, Peffer, Proctor, Pugh, Quay, Sherman, Teller, Vance, Warren, Washburn, Wilson.

The number of Senators voting not constituting a quorum,

The Presiding Officer directed the roll to be called; When

Forty-four Senators answered to their names.

A quorum being present,

EXECUTIVE SESSION.

On motion by Mr. Sherman,

The Senate proceeded to the consideration of executive business; and

After the consideration of executive business the doors were reopened, and

On motion by Mr. Sherman, at 3 o'clock and 15 minutes p. m., The Senate adjourned.

THURSDAY, JANUARY, 5, 1893.

The Vice-President laid before the Senate a letter of the Secretary of War, transmitting, in answer to a resolution of the Senate of December 12, 1892, a copy of a report of the Chief of Engineers as to the condition of the present ship channel between Cumberland Island, Georgia, and Fernandina, Fla.; which, with the accompanying documents, excepting the maps, was ordered to be printed and referred to the Committee on Commerce.

The Vice-President laid before the Senate a letter of the Secretary of Agriculture, transmitting the annual report of the operations of the Bureau of Animal Industry for the year 1892.

Ordered, That it lie on the table and be printed.

The Vice-President laid before the Senate a letter of the Secretary of the Interior, transmitting, in answer to a resolution of the Senate of June 1, 1892, a copy of a communication from the Commissioner of Indian Affairs relative to the employment of attorneys or agents by Indians for obtaining recognition of claims against the United States; which was ordered to be printed and, together with the accompanying documents, referred to the Committee on Indian Affairs.

The Vice-President laid before the Senate a letter of the Secretary of the Interior, communicating, in answer to a resolution of

the Senate of September 22, 1890, information as to whether lands granted to the State of California under the act of June 30, 1864, have been apoliated or otherwise diverted from the public use contemplated by said grant; which was referred to the Committee on Public Lands and ordered to be printed.

The Vice-President laid before the Senate a letter of the Attorney-General, transmitting, in answer to a resolution of the Senate of December 20, 1892, a list of Indian depredation claims already filed in the Court of Claims, the number of cases entitled to priority of consideration, and the amounts of judgments rendered, etc.; which was referred to the Select Committee on Indian Depredation Claims and ordered to be printed.

PETITIONS AND MEMORIALS.

Petitions, memorials, etc., were presented and referred as follows:

By Mr. George: A memorial of Warren T. Holland, William L. Hardy, and John L. Carter, of Jackson, Miss., praying the intervention of the United States to secure them indemnity from the Government of Spain occasioned by their illegal arrest on board the brig *Georgiana,* off the coast of Yucatan, by a Spanish man-of-war in May, 1850; to the Committee on Foreign Relations.

By Mr. Perkins: A petition of citizens of Kansas, praying an amendment to the Constitution of the United States prohibiting any State from passing any law respecting religion or the free exercise thereof; to the Committee on the Judiciary.

By Mr. Sherman: Resolutions of the Board of Trade of Cleveland, Ohio, praying such legislation as will protect the United States from the introduction of cholera; to the Committee on Epidemic Diseases.

By Mr. Berry: A memorial of citizens of the Cherokee Nation residing upon the Cherokee Outlet, praying the passage of a law protecting them in their rights to their lands; to the Committee on Indian Affairs.

By Mr. Hoar: A memorial of merchants and business men of Boston, Mass., praying for the repeal of the law providing for the purchase of silver bullion, etc.; to the Committee on Finance.

By Mr. Cockrell: A petition of Mrs. Effie G. Snow, of Schell City, Mo., praying an investigation into the circumstances of the death of her daughter Lora Snow, at Richfield, Utah, October 4, 1889; to the Committee on Education and Labor.

By Mr. Cameron: A memorial of the Select and Common Councils of Philadelphia, Pa., praying an appropriation for an examination, survey, and report for a channel between the Delaware River and Raritan Bay; to the Committee on Commerce.

A memorial of the Maritime Exchange of Philadelphia, Pa., praying the passage of a national quarantine law; to the Committee on Epidemic Diseases.

By Mr. Quay: A petition of Bernard Brennan, praying the removal of the charge of desertion from his military record; to the Committee on Military Affairs.

A memorial of the Select and Common Councils of Philadelphia, Pa., praying an appropriation for an examination, survey, and report for a channel between the Delaware River and Raritan Bay; to the Committee on Commerce.

By Mr. Felton: A memorial of survivors of the crew of the late United States steamer *Rodgers,* of the *Jeannette* search expedition, praying extra compensation for services and sufferings while on said search; to the Committee on Naval Affairs.

By Mr. Allison: A memorial of J. Wesley Brown, of Emery, S. Dak., remonstrating against the importation of tea and coffee free of duty; to the Committee on Finance.

A memorial of J. Wesley Brown, of South Dakota, praying the passage of a law making persons committing perjury in Federal courts and before registers and receivers of United States land officers responsible in damages to the party injured by the same; to the Committee on the Judiciary.

By Mr. Voorhees: A petition of citizens of South Bend, Ind., praying the correction of certain evils complained of at the Government works at the arsenal at West Troy, N. Y.; to the Committee on Appropriations.

Resolutions of the International Association of Machinists, remonstrating against the admission, free of duty, of machinery used in the manufacture of sugar; to the Committee on Finance.

By Mr. Irby: A petition of Louisa G. Heyward and others, praying compensation for property taken and used by the United States military authorities during the late war; to the Committee on Claims, to accompany the bill S. 3671.

By Mr. Cockrell: A petition of citizens of Missouri, in behalf of Eli Browning, praying that he be allowed a pension; to the Committee on Pensions, to accompany the bill S. 3673.

Papers relating to the application of Lucy F. Watson to be allowed a pension; to the Committee on Pensions, to accompany the bill S. 3674.

A petition of Maria Hall, praying to be allowed a pension; to the Committee on Pensions, to accompany the bill S. 3675.

A petition of James G. Crump, praying to be allowed a pension; to the Committee on Pensions, to accompany the bill S. 3676.

A petition of John G. Hanna, praying to be allowed a pension; to the Committee on Pensions, to accompany the bill S. 3677.

A petition of Eliza Dickerhoff, praying to be allowed a pension; to the Committee on Pensions, to accompany the bill S. 3679.

By Mr. Quay: A petition of Lieut. Col. James Cooper McKee, surgeon United States Army, retired, praying the passage of a law placing him on the retired list with the full rank of colonel; to the Committee on Military Affairs, to accompany the bill S. 3681.

By Mr. Allison: A petition of citizens of Iowa, praying the passage of a law to correct the military record of Bernt G. Anderson; to the Committee on Military Affairs, to accompany the bill S. 3684.

Five petitions of citizens of Iowa, praying the passage of the bill limiting the amount of clothing that may be admitted free of duty; to the Committee on Finance.

By Mr. Brice: A petition of citizens of Ohio, praying the passage of the bill providing for the retirement of enlisted men of the Army after a continuous service of twenty-five years; to the Committee on Military Affairs.

Resolutions of the Board of Trade of Cleveland, Ohio, praying the passage of a national quarantine law; to the Committee on Epidemic Diseases.

A memorial of the Builders' Exchange of Cincinnati, Ohio, praying the passage of the Torrey bankruptcy bill; to the Committee on the Judiciary.

A memorial of A. Hurd, of Findlay, Ohio, praying certain reforms in the pension system; to the Committee on Pensions.

Mr. Allison presented a resolution of the legislature of Iowa, in favor of the passage of the antioption bill.

Ordered, That it lie on the table.

Resolutions praying the passage of the bill for the speedy construction of the Nicaragua Canal under the direction and control of the Government were presented as follows:

By Mr. Brice: Resolutions of the Chamber of Commerce of Cincinnati, Ohio.

By Mr. Voorhees: Resolutions adopted at a meeting of business men of Evansville, Ind.

Ordered, That they lie on the table.

Petitions praying the appointment of a committee to investigate an alleged combine formed to depreciate the price of grain by the millers, elevators, and railroads at St. Louis and Minneapolis, were presented as follows:

By Mr. Cullom: Five petitions of citizens of Illinois.

By Mr. Voorhees: Several petitions of citizens of Indiana.

By Mr. Brice: Several petitions of citizens of Ohio.

Ordered, That they be referred to the Committee on Agriculture and Forestry.

Petitions praying the passage of the antioption bill were presented as follows:

By Mr. George: A petition of citizens of Mississippi.

By Mr. Allison: Three petitions of citizens of Iowa.

By Mr. Sherman: Six petitions of citizens of Ohio.

By Mr. Brice: Several petitions of citizens of Ohio.

Ordered, That they lie on the table.

Memorials remonstrating against the repeal of the provision providing for the closing of the Columbian Exposition on the Sabbath day, were presented as follows:

By Mr. Cameron: Two memorials of citizens of Pennsylvania.

By Mr. Proctor: A memorial of citizens of Vermont.

By Mr. Voorhees: Several memorials of citizens of Indiana.

By Mr. Sherman: Five memorials of citizens of Ohio.

By Mr. Allison: Four memorials of citizens of Iowa.

By Mr. Quay: Several memorials of citizens of Pennsylvania.

By Mr. Brice: Several memorials of citizens of Ohio.

Ordered, That they be referred to the Select Committee on the Quadro-Centennial.

REPORTS OF COMMITTEES.

Mr. Frye, from the Committee on Commerce, to whom was referred the joint resolution (S. R. 124) directing the Secretary of War to investigate the subject of raft-towing on the Great Lakes and their connecting waters, reported it without amendment.

The Senate proceeded, by unanimous consent, to consider the said resolution as in Committee of the Whole; and no amendment being made, it was reported to the Senate.

Ordered, That it be engrossed and read a third time.

The said resolution was read the third time.

Resolved, That it pass, and that the title thereof be as aforesaid.

Ordered, That the Secretary request the concurrence of the House of Representatives therein.

Mr. Dolph, from the Committee on Commerce, to whom was referred the bill (S. 3568) providing for the establishment and enforcement of rules and regulations for the use and navigation of United States canals and similar works of navigation, and for other purposes, reported it with amendments.

Mr. Coke, from the Committee on Commerce, to whom was referred the bill (H. R. 9824) to amend "An act to promote the construction of a safe deep-water harbor on the coast of Texas," approved February 9, 1891, reported it with amendments.

Mr. Vest, from the Committee on Commerce, to whom was referred the bill (H. R. 9930) for the construction and maintenance of a bridge across the St. Lawrence River, reported it with an amendment.

INTRODUCTION OF BILLS.

Bills were introduced, read the first and second time by unanimous consent, and referred as follows:

By Mr. Irby: A bill (S. 3671) for the relief of Louisa G. Heyward and others; to the Committee on Claims.

By Mr. Cameron: A bill (S. 3672) to amend the act approved June 8, 1880, relating to the pay of the Judge-Advocate-General of the Navy; to the Committee on Naval Affairs.

By Mr. Cockrell: A bill (S. 3673) granting a pension to Eli Browning;

A bill (S. 3674) granting a pension to Lucy F. Watson, widow of Joseph W. Melton, deceased;

A bill (S. 3675) granting a pension to Maria Hall, widow of Joseph E. Doak, deceased;

A bill (S. 3676) granting a pension to James F. Crump;

A bill (S. 3677) granting a pension to John G. Hanna;

A bill (S. 3678) granting a pension to Margaret Garrison, widow of James Garrison; and

A bill (S. 3679) for the relief of Eliza Dickerhoff, widow of Louis Dickerhoff, deceased, of Company A, Cape Girardeau Missouri Home Guards; to the Committee on Pensions.

A bill (S. 3680) for the relief of Bernard J. D. Irwin; to the Committee on Claims.

By Mr. Quay: A bill (S. 3681) to provide for the retirement of Lieut. Col. James Cooper McKee, surgeon, United States Army, retired, as full colonel; to the Committee on Military Affairs.

By Mr. Teller: A bill (S. 3682) to narrow California avenue within Belair Heights, District of Columbia; to the Committee on the District of Columbia; and

A bill (S. 3683) to prevent the abatement of action against officers of the United States; to the Committee on the Judiciary.

By Mr. Allison: A bill (S. 3684) authorizing the Secretary of War to correct the military record of Bernt G. Anderson; to the Committee on Military Affairs.

By Mr. Cockrell: A bill (S. 3685) to permit Anna M. Colman; widow, to prosecute a claim; to the Committee on Claims.

PROPOSED SUSPENSION OF IMMIGRATION.

Mr. Hill submitted the following resolution for consideration; which was ordered to be printed:

Resolved, That the Clerk of the Senate be directed to transmit to the honorable the Secretary of State a copy of Senate bill No. 3513, now pending in this body, entitled "A bill for the suspension of immigration for one year," and that the Secretary of State be, and is hereby, respectfully requested to inform the Senate at his earliest convenience whether the provisions of the said bill absolutely suspending immigration for the period of one year are in conflict with any treaties now existing between the United States and any foreign countries, and, if so, with what countries; and any further information which he may deem necessary for the information of the Senate in relation to the propriety of the enactment of the said bill in its present form.

CLAIM OF W. L. HARDY AND OTHERS.

Mr. George submitted the following resolution; which was referred to the Committee on Foreign Relations:

Resolved, That the Secretary of State be, and he is hereby, directed to communicate to the Senate the present status of the claim of W. L. Hardy, John L. Carter, and William T. Holland against the Government of Spain for damages occasioned by their illegal arrest on board the brig *Georgiana* off the coast of Yucatan by a Spanish war ship in May, 1850, and their subsequent imprisonment; what obstacles exist to the enforcement of said claim, and what action, if any, is needed to be taken by Congress in reference to the settlement of the same.

GERMAN LABOR STATISTICS.

Mr. Chandler submitted the following resolution; which was considered by unanimous consent and agreed to:

Resolved, That the Secretary of State be directed to transmit to the Senate the report of Mr. W. H. Edwards, consul-general at Berlin, on the labor statistics of the German trades unions for the year 1891.

MESSAGE FROM THE HOUSE.

A message from the House of Representatives, by Mr. Towles, its chief clerk:

Mr. President: The House of Representatives has passed, without amendment, the following bills of the Senate:

S. 2187. An act granting a pension to Margaret M. Rice; and

S. 2593. An act granting an increase of pension to Samuel M. Campbell.

The Speaker of the House of Representatives having signed two enrolled bills, H. R. 9487 and H. R. 9488, and an enrolled joint resolution, S. R. 112, I am directed to bring them to the Senate for the signature of its President.

ENROLLED BILLS SIGNED.

Mr. Sanders reported from the committee that they had examined and found duly enrolled the following bills and joint resolution:

H. R. 9487. An act to amend an act approved April 22, 1890, authorizing the Natchitoches Cane River Bridge Company to construct and maintain a bridge across Cane River, in Louisiana;

H. R. 9488. An act to amend an act approved March 2, 1891, authorizing the construction of a bridge across the Red River, Louisiana, by the Rapides Bridge Company, limited; and

S. R. 112. Joint resolution to print and bind 2,000 extra copies each of the drill regulations for infantry, cavalry, and artillery;

Whereupon,

The Vice-President signed the same, and they were delivered to the committee to be presented to the President of the United States.

PRESIDENTIAL APPROVAL.

A message from the President of the United States, by Mr. Pruden, his secretary:

Mr. President: The President of the United States this day approved and signed the following acts:

S. 570. An act to provide for the removal of the remains of the late Ensign D. F. Terrill, United States Navy, from Sitka, Alaska, to his home in the State of Mississippi; and

S. 3059. An act for the relief of the Old Dominion Steamship Company.

Ordered, That the Secretary notify the House of Representatives thereof.

CONSIDERATION OF BILLS ON CALENDAR.

On motion by Mr. Mitchell,

The Senate proceeded to consider, as in Committee of the Whole, the bill (S. 3537) for the relief of M. P. Deady; and the reported amendment having been agreed to, the bill was reported to the Senate and the amendment was concurred in.

Ordered, That it be engrossed and read a third time.

The said bill was read the third time.

Resolved, That it pass, that the preamble be stricken out, and that the title thereof be as aforesaid.

Ordered, That the Secretary request the concurrence of the House of Representatives therein.

On motion by Mr. Jones, of Arkansas,

The Senate proceeded to consider, as in Committee of the Whole, the joint resolution (H. Res. 166) to authorize the Secretary of the Treasury to cover back into the Treasury $48,000 of the appropriation to Choctaw and Chickasaw Indians; and having been amended on the motion of Mr. Platt, the resolution was reported to the Senate and the amendment was concurred in.

Ordered, That the amendment be engrossed and the resolution read a third time.

The said resolution as amended was read the third time.

Resolved, That it pass, and that the Senate request a conference with the House of Representatives on the said resolution and the amendment.

Ordered, That the conferees on the part of the Senate be appointed by the Vice-President; and

The Vice-President appointed Mr. Jones of Arkansas, Mr. Dawes, and Mr. Platt.

Ordered, That the Secretary notify the House of Representatives thereof.

On motion by Mr. Jones, of Arkansas,

The Senate proceeded to consider, as in Committee of the Whole, the joint resolution (S. R. 119) authorizing the Secretary of the Treasury to retain and cover into the Treasury certain moneys, etc.; and

Ordered, That it be postponed indefinitely.

On motion by Mr. Dolph,

The Senate proceeded to consider, as in Committee of the Whole, the bill (S. 3382) to authorize a corrected patent to be issued for the donation land claim of Wheelock Simmons and wife; and the reported amendments having been agreed to, the bill was reported to the Senate and the amendments were concurred in.

Ordered, That it be engrossed and read a third time.

The said bill was read the third time.

Resolved, That it pass, and that the title thereof be as aforesaid.

Ordered, That the Secretary request the concurrence of the House of Representatives therein.

On motion by Mr. Wilson,

The Senate proceeded to consider, as in Committee of the Whole, the bill (S. 1933) to amend section 860 of the Revised Statutes of the United States; and the reported amendment having been agreed to, the bill was reported to the Senate and the amendment was concurred in.

Ordered, That it be engrossed and read a third time.

The said bill was read the third time.

Resolved, That it pass, and that the title be amended so as to read: "A bill concerning testimony in criminal cases or proceedings based upon or growing out of alleged violations of an act entitled 'An act to regulate commerce,' approved February 4, 1887, as amended March 2, 1889, and February 10, 1891."

Ordered, That the Secretary request the concurrence of the House of Representatives therein.

The Senate proceeded to consider, as in Committee of the Whole, the bill (S. 457) for the relief of the assignees or legal representatives of John Roach, deceased, to pay balance due on the United States steamer Dolphin; and the reported amendment having been agreed to,

Pending debate,

DEALINGS IN OPTIONS AND FUTURES.

The Presiding Officer (Mr. Pasco in the chair) announced that the hour of 2 o'clock had arrived, and laid before the Senate the unfinished business at its adjournment yesterday, viz, the bill (H. R. 7845) defining "options" and "futures," imposing special taxes on dealers therein, and requiring such persons engaged in selling certain products to obtain license, and for other purposes; and

The Senate resumed, as in Committee of the Whole, the consideration of the bill, and

The question being on the amendment yesterday proposed by Mr. White,

Pending debate,

EXECUTIVE SESSION.

On motion by Mr. Washburn,

The Senate proceeded to the consideration of executive business, and

After the consideration of executive business the doors were reopened, and

On motion by Mr. Sawyer, at 4 o'clock and 30 minutes p. m.,

The Senate adjourned.

FRIDAY, JANUARY 6, 1893.

EXECUTIVE COMMUNICATIONS.

The Vice-President laid before the Senate a letter of the Secretary of State, transmitting, in pursuance of the provisions of the act of Congress approved February 3, 1887, a certified copy of the final ascertainment of the electors for President and Vice-President appointed in the State of Washington.

Ordered, That it lie on the table.

The Vice-President laid before the Senate a letter of the Secretary of the Interior, transmitting, in answer to a resolution of the Senate of July 12, 1892, a detailed statement showing amounts paid to attorneys out of appropriations made for Indians by the Fifty-first Congress, and also the contracts made between Indian tribes and attorneys for recovery of moneys, etc.; which was referred to the Committee on Indian Affairs and ordered to be printed.

PETITIONS AND MEMORIALS.

Petitions, memorials, etc., were presented and referred as follows:

By Mr. Pasco: Six petitions of citizens of Florida, praying an appropriation for the completion of the work for the protection of the entrance to Cumberland Sound and the improvement of the harbor of Fernandina; to the Committee on Commerce.

By Mr. Hansbrough: A petition of citizens of North Dakota, praying the passage of the bill for the retirement of enlisted men of the Army after a continuous service of twenty-five years; to the Committee on Military Affairs.

By Mr. Hoar: A petition of business men of Boston, Mass., praying the repeal of the law providing for the purchase of silver bullion; to the Committee on Finance.

By Mr. Cullom: Two petitions of citizens of Illinois, praying for the appointment of a committee to investigate an alleged combine formed to depreciate the price of grain by millers, elevators, and railroads at St. Louis and Minneapolis; to the Committee on Agriculture and Forestry.

By Mr. Hunton: A petition of Thomas H. G. Todd, praying the passage of a law to correct and confirm his title to certain property in the city of Washington, D. C.; to the Committee on the Judiciary.

Memorials remonstrating against the repeal of the provision providing for the closing of the Columbian Exposition on the Sabbath day were presented as follows:

By Mr. Sherman: Two memorials of citizens of Ohio.

By Mr. Quay: A memorial of citizens of Pennsylvania.

By Mr. Perkins: A memorial of citizens of Kansas.

Ordered, That they be referred to the Select Committee on the Quadro-Centennial.

Mr. Wilson presented a petition of citizens of Iowa praying the passage of the antioption bill.

Ordered, That it lie on the table.

Petitions praying the passage of a law to prevent the sale of intoxicating liquors on the grounds of the Columbian Exposition were presented as follows:

By Mr. Sherman: A petition of citizens of Ohio;

By Mr. Quay: A petition of citizens of Pennsylvania.

Ordered, That they be referred to the Select Committee on the Quadro-Centennial.

REPORTS OF COMMITTEES.

Mr. McMillan, from the Committee on the District of Columbia, to whom was referred the joint resolution (S. R. 130) to amend an act entitled "An act making Saturday a half holiday for banking and trust companies in the District of Columbia," approved December 22, 1892, reported it with an amendment.

Mr. Hansbrough, from the Committee on the District of Columbia, to whom was referred the bill (S. 2265) for the removal of snow and ice from the side walks, cross walks, and gutters in the cities of Washington and Georgetown. and for other purposes, reported it with amendments and submitted a report (No. 1145) thereon.

INTRODUCTION OF BILLS AND JOINT RESOLUTION.

Bills and a joint resolution were introduced, read the first and second times by unanimous consent, and referred as follows:

By Mr. Butler: A bill (S. 3686) for the relief of John B. McElhose; to the Committee on Claims.

By Mr. Hunton: A bill (S. 3687) for the relief of Thomas H. G. Todd; to the Committee on the Judiciary.

By Mr. McMillan: A bill (S. 3688) to authorize the Washington and Marlboro Electric Railway Company to extend its line within the District of Columbia; to the Committee on the District of Columbia.

By Mr. Higgins: A bill (S. 3689) for the relief of the owners of the schooner *Henry R. Tilton*, and of personal effects thereon; to the Committee on Claims.

By Mr. Cockrell: A joint resolution (S. R. 132) to print 100,000 copies of the special report of the Bureau of Animal Industry on Diseases of Cattle and on Cattle Feeding; to the Committee on Printing.

INTRODUCTION OF REINDEER IN ALASKA.

Mr. Teller submitted the following resolution; which was considered by unanimous consent and agreed to:

Resolved, That the Commissioner of Education be directed to transmit a copy of the latest report of Dr. Sheldon Jackson on the introduction of domesticated reindeer into Alaska.

PROPOSED SUSPENSION OF IMMIGRATION.

The Vice-President laid before the Senate the resolution yesterday submitted by Mr. Hill calling upon the Secretary of State for certain information respecting the pending bill providing for the suspension of immigration for one year; and having been amended on the motion of Mr. Chandler,

The resolution, as amended, was agreed to as follows:

Resolved, That the Secretary of the Senate be directed to transmit to the Secretary of State a copy of Senate bill numbered 3513, now pending in this body, entitled "A bill for the suspension of immigration for one year," and that the Secretary of State be, and is hereby, directed to inform the Senate whether the provisions of the said bill absolutely suspending immigration for the period of one year are in conflict with any treaties now existing between the United States and any foreign countries; and, if so, with what countries, and any further information which he may deem necessary for the information of the Senate during the consideration of said bill.

COMMITTEE SERVICE.

Mr. Gibson, at his own request, was excused from further service as a member of the Committee on Epidemic Diseases,

Ordered, That the vacancy be filled by the Vice-President; and The Vice-President appointed Mr. White.

REPRINT OF BILL.

On motion by Mr. Morgan, and by unanimous consent,

Ordered, That 3,000 copies of the bill (S. 1218) to amend the act entitled "An act to incorporate the Maritime Canal Company of Nicaragua," approved February 20, 1889, be printed for the use of the Senate.

MESSAGE FROM THE HOUSE.

A message from the House of Representatives, by Mr. Towles, its chief clerk:

Mr. President: The House of Representatives has passed, without amendment, the joint resolution (S. R. 123) to fill vacancies in the Board of Regents of the Smithsonian Institution.

The House of Representatives has agreed to the amendment of the Senate to the joint resolution (H. R. 166) to authorize the Secretary of Treasury to cover back into the Treasury $18,800 of the appropriation to Choctaw and Chickasaw Indians.

The House of Representatives has passed a bill (H. R. 9923) making appropriations for fortifications and other works of defense, for the armament thereof, for the procurement of heavy ordnance for trial and service, and for other purposes, in which it requests the concurrence of the Senate.

HOUSE BILL REFERRED.

The bill H. R. 9923, last received from the House of Representatives for concurrence, was read the first and second times by unanimous consent, and referred to the Committee on Appropriations.

EXECUTIVE SESSION.

On motion by Mr. Sherman,

The Senate proceeded to the consideration of executive business; and

After the consideration of executive business the doors were reopened.

ADDITIONAL QUARANTINE POWERS.

Pursuant to the order of the 4th instant

The Senate proceeded to consider, as in Committee of the Whole, the bill (S. 2707) granting additional quarantine powers and imposing additional duties upon the Marine-Hospital Service; and the reported amendments having been agreed to in part, and the bill further amended on the motion of Mr. Harris, the motion of Mr. Dolph, the motion of Mr. Vest, the motion of Mr. McPherson, and the motion of Mr. Teller; and

A further amendment having been proposed by Mr. Vest,

On motion by Mr. Allison,

Ordered, That the bill as amended be reprinted.

On motion by Mr. Allison, at 5 o'clock and 20 minutes p. m., The Senate adjourned.

SATURDAY, JANUARY 7, 1893.

EXECUTIVE COMMUNICATIONS.

The Vice-President laid before the Senate four communications from the Secretary of State, transmitting, in pursuance of the provisions of the act of February 3, 1887, certified copies of the final ascertainment of electors for President and Vice-President of the United States in the States of Kansas, Missouri, Nebraska, and Minnesota.

Ordered, That they lie on the table.

The Vice-President laid before the Senate a letter of the Secretary of War, recommending the passage of a law providing for the encampment of 100,000 United States and State troops, to be held at Chicago on the occasion of the World's Columbian Exposition; which was referred to the Select Committee on the Quadro-Centennial and ordered to be printed.

PETITIONS AND MEMORIALS.

Petitions, memorials, etc., were presented and referred as follows:

By Mr. Cameron: A petition of William Ledyard Ellsworth, praying for an extension of his patent for improvement in fire-extinguishers; to the Committee on Patents.

A memorial of the Board of Trade of Philadelphia, Pa., praying an amendment to the interstate-commerce law so as to allow pool agreements between railways, subject to the approval of the Interstate Commerce Commissioners; to the Committee on Interstate Commerce.

By Mr. McMillan: A petition of citizens of the District of Columbia, praying the passage of a law granting the use of the Aqueduct Bridge for street-car purposes; to the Committee on the District of Columbia.

By Mr. Kyle: Four petitions of citizens of the District of Columbia praying the passage of the bill authorizing the board of management and control of the United States Government exhibit to collect and publish certain facts pertaining to the moral, educational, and industrial development of the American negro for the past thirty years; to the Committee on Education and Labor.

By Mr. Sherman: A petition of citizens of Ohio, praying the repeal of the act of July 14, 1890, directing the purchase of silver bullion, and the issue of Treasury notes thereon, and for other purposes; to the Committee on Finance.

By Mr. Hoar: A resolution of the Chamber of Commerce of Boston, Mass., praying that no obstructions be permitted to be placed upon the advantages now enjoyed by the Canadian railways in their operations between Canadian points and New England; to the Committee on Interstate Commerce.

Resolutions of the Chamber of Commerce of Boston, Mass., praying the immediate repeal of the silver-purchase act of 1890; to the Committee on Finance.

By Mr. Sherman: Four memorials of the citizens of Ohio, remonstrating against the repeal of the provision providing for the closing of the Columbian Exposition on the Sabbath day; to the Select Committee on the Quadro-Centennial.

Mr. Cameron presented a memorial of the Maritime Exchange of Philadelphia, Pa., praying the passage of a federal quarantine law.

Ordered, That it lie on the table.

Mr. Cameron presented a memorial of the Board of Trade of Philadelphia, Pa., praying for the speedy completion of the Nicaragua Canal under the direction and control of the United States Government.

Ordered, That it lie on the table.

Mr. Cameron presented resolutions of the Chinese Equal Rights League, of Philadelphia, Pa., praying the repeal of the act for the restriction of the coming of Chinese into the United States; which were referred to the Committee on Foreign Relations.

Mr. Quay also submitted similar resolutions for a like purpose; which were similarly referred.

Petitions praying the passage of the antioption bill were presented as follows:

By Mr. Sherman: A petition of citizens of Ohio.

By Mr. Harris: A petition of citizens of Tennessee.

Ordered, That they lie on the table.

Petitions praying the appointment of a committee to investigate an alleged combine formed to depreciate the price of grain by the millers, elevators, and railroads at St. Louis and Minneapolis, were presented as follows:

By Mr. Cullom: Three petitions of citizens of Illinois.

By Mr. Kyle: Several petitions of citizens of South Dakota.

Ordered, That they be referred to the Committee on Agriculture an l Forestry.

Mr. Kyle presented a petition of citizens of South Dakota, praying the passage of the antioption bill

Ordered, That it lie on the table.

Mr. Cockrell presented a memorial of the Merchants' Exchange of St. Louis, Mo., remonstrating against the passage of the anti-option bill.

Ordered, That it lie on the table.

Mr. Cockrell presented a memorial of members of the Confederated Kaskaskia, Peoria, Wea, and Piankeshaw Indians, and a memorial of members of the Peoria and Miami Indians, all of the Quapaw Agency, in the Indian Territory, remonstrating against the passage of the bill (S. 3030) to provide for the allotment of lands among the several Indian tribes in the Quapaw Agency, in the Indian Territory, and for the sale of surplus lands of such tribes; and for the creation of the county of Cayuga, in the Territory of Oklahoma, and for other purposes.

Ordered, That it lie on the table.

Mr. Cockrell presented a petition of citizens of Missouri, praying for the closing of the Columbian Exposition on the Sabbath day; which was referred to the Select Committee on the Quadro-Centennial.

REPORTS OF COMMITTEES.

Mr. Quay, from the Committee on the Library, to whom was referred the bill (S. 1425) to provide for the erection of a monument to Maj. Gen. Nathanael Greene on the battlefield of the battle of Guilford Court-House, North Carolina, fought March 15, 1781, and for other purposes, reported it with amendments and submitted a report (No. 1147) thereon.

Mr. Higgins, from the Committee on the District of Columbia, to whom was referred the bill (S. 3623) to amend the act of March 3, 1873, for the relief of the Columbian University, in the District of Columbia, reported it without amendment and submitted a report (No. 1146) thereon.

The Senate proceeded, by unanimous consent, to consider the said bill as in Committee of the Whole; and no amendment being made, it was reported to the Senate.

Ordered, That it be engrossed and read a third time.

The said bill was read the third time.

Resolved, That it pass, and that the title thereof be as aforesaid.

Ordered, That the Secretary request the concurrence of the House of Representatives therein.

INTRODUCTION OF BILLS.

Bills were introduced, read the first and second times by unanimous consent, and referred as follows:

By Mr. Vance: A bill (S. 3690) to incorporate the Tabernacle Society of the District of Columbia; to the Committee on the District of Columbia.

By Mr. McMillan: A bill (S. 3691) regulating the employment of certain persons in manufactories, workshops, and stores in the District of Columbia; to the Committee on the District of Columbia.

By Mr. Platt: A bill (S. 3692) to provide a temporary government for Alaska, and for other purposes; to the Committee on Territories.

By Mr. Sawyer: A bill (S. 3693) granting a pension to Fred. S. Chamberlain; to the Committee on Pensions.

By Mr. Mitchell: A bill (S. 3694) for the relief of certain purchasers of public lands within the limits of Congressional land grants; to the Committee on Public Lands.

TREATY WITH INDIANS OF OREGON.

Mr. Mitchell submitted the following resolution for consideration; which was ordered to be printed:

Resolved, That the Secretary of the Interior be, and he is hereby, directed to transmit to the Senate a copy of a treaty negotiated by Joel Palmer, then superintendent of Indian affairs for the Territory of Oregon, on or about the 11th day of August, 1855, with the various tribes inhabiting the coast of Oregon from the Columbia River to the California line, consisting of Tillamook, Coos Bay, Coquille, Too-too-to-ney, Chetco, Siuslaw, Clatsop, and Lower Umpqua Indians, and whereby they, it is alleged, ceded all the country claimed by them between the country theretofore ceded by various other treaties and the Pacific Ocean, estimated to contain 5,000,000 acres of land, and by the terms of which it is alleged there was a reservation of a tract of country on the coast within the limits of the coast reservation established by the President, estimated to contain 750,000 acres; and that the Secretary of the Interior be further directed to advise the Senate whether such treaty was ever transmitted to the Senate for ratification; also whether the United States, if said treaty was not ratified, has acted upon the terms stipulated therein and received the benefits of the ces-

sion therein provided; and if so, whether said Indians were ever paid the amounts stipulated in such treaty to be paid to them for and on account of the lands so ceded, and if so, when were such payments made; and further, that he advise the Senate fully whether such treaty became operative and whether the terms thereof or any of them have been enforced against the Indians, or the stipulations therein complied with by the United States.

MESSAGE FROM THE PRESIDENT.

The following message was received from the President of the United States, by Mr. Pruden, his Secretary:

To the Senate:

In response to the resolution of the Senate of January 6, 1893, calling on the Secretary of State for information whether the provisions of Senate bill No. 3513, absolutely suspending immigration for the period of one year, are in conflict with any treaties now existing between the United States and any foreign countries, I transmit herewith a report from the Secretary of State giving the information called for.

BENJ. HARRISON.

EXECUTIVE MANSION, *Washington, January 7, 1893.*

The message was read.

Ordered, That it lie on the table and be printed.

DEEP-WATER HARBOR ON TEXAS COAST.

On motion by Mr. Coke,

The Senate proceeded to consider, as in Committee of the Whole, the bill (H. R. 9824) to amend "An act to promote the construction of a deep-water harbor on the coast of Texas," approved February 9, 1891; and the reported amendment having been agreed to, the bill was reported to the Senate and the amendment was concurred in.

Ordered, That the amendment be engrossed and the bill read a third time.

The said bill as amended was read the third time.

Resolved, That it pass.

Ordered, That the Secretary request the concurrence of the House of Representatives in the amendment.

SATURDAY HALF HOLIDAY.

The Senate proceeded to consider, as in Committee of the Whole, the joint resolution (S. R. 130) to amend an act entitled "An act making Saturday a half holiday for banking and trust companies in the District of Columbia," approved December 22, 1892; and the reported amendment having been agreed to, the resolution was reported to the Senate and the amendment was concurred in.

Ordered, That it be engrossed and read a third time.

The said resolution was read the third time.

Resolved, That it pass, and that the title thereof be as aforesaid.

Ordered, That the Secretary request the concurrence of the House of Representatives therein.

PRESIDENTIAL APPROVALS.

A message from the President of the United States, by Mr. Pruden, his secretary:

Mr. President: The President of the United States approved and signed, on the 5th instant, an act (S. 1675) granting an increase of pension to soldiers of the Mexican war in certain cases; and

He approved and signed on the 6th instant the following acts:

S. 2981. An act for the relief of the Citadel Academy of Charleston, S. C.; and

S. 3298. An act authorizing the sale of land in the vicinity of Fort Mifflin on the river Delaware.

Ordered, That the Secretary notify the House of Representatives thereof.

MESSAGE FROM THE HOUSE.

A message from the House of Representatives, by Mr. Towles, its chief clerk:

Mr. President: The House of Representatives has passed, without amendment, the following bills of the Senate:

S. 317. An act granting an increase of pension to John M. Roberts;

S. 2592. An act granting an increase of pension to William C. Tarkington; and

S. 2890. An act for the relief of George W. McKinney.

S. 3314. An act for the relief of E. Darwin Gage, late lieutenant-colonel of the One Hundred and Forty-eighth New York Infantry.

The House of Representatives has passed the bill (S. 1303) to increase the pension of Mrs. S. A. Farquharson, with an amendment, in which it requests the concurrence of the Senate; and

It has passed the following bills, in which it requests the concurrence of the Senate:

H. R. 1318. An act granting a pension to Martha A Harris;

H. R. 2077. An act for the relief of William B. Price;

H. R. 2592. An act for the relief of Andrew B. Knapp;

H. R. 2912. An act to pension John T. Fleenor;

H. R. 3713. An act for increase of pension of Francis P. Gardener;

H. R. 4047. An act granting a pension to Ellen Hewett;

H. R. 4320. An act granting a pension to Thomas S. Kennedy;

H. R. 4916. An act granting a pension to Thomas Tucker, of Battery A, Fourth United States Artillery;

H. R. 6272. An act to pension Susan S. Murphy;

H. R. 6649. An act to extend the provisions of an act to provide for the muster and pay of certain officers and enlisted men of the volunteer forces;

H. R. 7234. An act granting a pension to Mary Millard;

H. R. 7238. An act granting a pension to Amanda Atherton;

H. R. 7713. An act granting a pension to Benajah Morgan, late private in Capt. Burn's company, Third Regiment, Third Brigade of Mounted Volunteers in the Black Hawk war;

H. R. 8498. An act to pension Sophia Kagwatch;

H. R. 8574. An act granting an honorable discharge to James C. Jennings;

H. R. 8924. An act granting a pension to the widow of James A. Kelly;

H. R. 8069. An act to grant a pension to Lydia Bollman, a dependent sister;

H. R. 9215. An act granting a pension to Eliza Holmes;

H. R. 9220. An act granting a pension to Mrs. Caroline Hardee Dyall, widow of James R. Dyall, veteran of the Florida war, 1836;

H. R. 9233. An act to grant a pension to Harriet Cota; and

H. R. 9590. An act granting a pension to Cornelius Day.

The Speaker of the House of Representatives having signed six enrolled bills, S. 1786, S. 1831, S. 2187, S. 2593, S. 3029, and S. 3048, and two enrolled joint resolutions, S. R. 123 and H. R. 166, I am directed to bring them to the Senate for the signature of its President.

HOUSE BILLS REFERRED.

The bills last received from the House of Representatives for concurrence were severally read the first and second times by unanimous consent.

Ordered, That the bills H. R. 2077, H. R. 2592, H. R. 6649, and H. R. 8574 be referred to the Committee on Military Affairs; and that the residue of the said bills be referred to the Committee on Pensions.

ENROLLED BILLS SIGNED.

Mr. Dubois reported from the committee that they had examined and found duly enrolled the following bills and joint resolutions:

S. 2187. An act granting a pension to Margaret M. Rice;

S. 2593. An act granting an increase of pension to Samuel M. Campbell;

S. 1786. An act granting a pension to Mrs. Jennie Gray;

S. 1831. An act to admit free of duty the wreckage of the ships Trenton and Vandalia, presented by the United States to the King of Samoa;

S. 3029. An act authorizing the construction of a bridge across the Columbia River in the State of Washington;

S. 3048. An act granting to the Blue Mountain Irrigation and Improvement Company a right of way for reservoir and canals through the Umatilla Indian Reservation in the State of Oregon;

S. R. 123. A joint resolution to fill vacancies in the Board of Regents of the Smithsonian Institution; and

H. R. 166. A joint resolution to authorize the Secretary of the Treasury to cover back into the Treasury $48,800 of the appropriation to Choctaw and Chickasaw Indians;

Whereupon,

The Vice-President signed the same, and they were delivered to the committee to be presented to the President of the United States.

ADDITIONAL QUARANTINE POWERS.

The Senate resumed, as in Committee of the Whole, the consideration of the bill (S. 2707) granting additional quarantine powers and imposing additional duties upon the Marine-Hospital Service; and

The question being on the amendment yesterday proposed by Mr. Vest,

It was determined in the affirmative.

The bill having been further amended on the motion of Mr. Harris; and

The question recurring on agreeing to the last amendment reported by the Committee on Epidemic Diseases, viz: Insert an additional section, numbered 7,

On motion by Mr. Kyle to amend the amendment,

It was determined in the affirmative; when

The amendment as amended was agreed to.

The bill having been further amended, on the motion of Mr. Harris, the motion of Mr. Chandler, the motion of Mr. Platt, and the motion of Mr. Call, and a further amendment having been proposed by Mr. Harris,

By unanimous consent, it was agreed that the order of the 4th instant, providing for the consideration of the bill, be extended to and include Monday next.

EXECUTIVE SESSION.

On motion by Mr. Allison,

The Senate proceeded to the consideration of executive business; and

After the consideration of executive business the doors were reopened, and

On motion by Mr. Sawyer, at 3 o'clock and 25 minutes p. m.,

The Senate adjourned.

MONDAY, JANUARY 9, 1893.

PETITIONS AND MEMORIALS.

Petitions, memorials, etc., were presented and referred as follows:

By Mr. Manderson: Papers relating to the application of Brig. Gen. John R. Brooke, United States Army, to be relieved from the payment of a judgment rendered in favor of Andrew Cameron and John Smith against him for alleged trespass and false imprisonment; to the Committee on Military Affairs, to accompany the bill S. 3696.

By Mr. Cullom: A petition of citizens of Illinois in behalf of Wade H. Newman, praying the passage of a law for the removal of the charge of desertion from his military record; to the Committee on Military Affairs, to accompany the bill S. 3697.

Mr. McMillan presented a memorial of the Board of Trade of Detroit, Mich., praying the passage of the bill for the completion of the Nicaragua Canal under the direction and control of the United States.

Ordered, That it lie on the table.

Memorials praying the passage of a national quarantine law, and for the restriction of immigration, were presented as follows:

By Mr. Pasco: A memorial of the Board of Trade of Jacksonville, Fla.

By Mr. Teller: A memorial of the Chamber of Commerce of Denver, Colo.

Ordered, That they lie on the table.

Petitions, etc., praying the immediate repeal of the law providing for the purchase of silver bullion, were presented as follows:

By Mr. McPherson: A petition of citizens of New Jersey.

By Mr. Hoar: A petition of citizens of Massachusetts.

By Mr. Cullom: A petition of citizens of Illinois.

By Mr. Sherman: A petition of citizens of Ohio, and a resolution of the Chamber of Commerce of Cincinnati, Ohio.

Ordered, That they be referred to the Committee on Finance.

Petitions praying the passage of the antioption bill were presented as follows:

By Mr. Sherman: A petition of citizens of Ohio.

By Mr. Hansbrough: A petition of citizens of North Dakota.

By Mr. Gallinger: Two petitions of citizens of New Hampshire.

By Mr. Frye: A petition of citizens of Maine.

Ordered, That they lie on the table.

Petitions praying the appointment of a committee to investigate an alleged combine formed to depreciate the price of grain by the millers, elevators, and railroads at St. Louis and Minneapolis, were presented as follows:

By Mr. Butler: A petition of citizens of South Carolina.

By Mr. Cullom: Six petitions of citizens of Illinois.

Ordered, That they be referred to the Committee on Agriculture and Forestry.

Memorials remonstrating against the repeal of the provision providing for the closing of the Columbian Exposition were presented as follows:

By Mr. Hansbrough: A memorial of citizens of North Dakota.

By Mr. Hoar: A memorial of citizens of Massachusetts.

By Mr. Sherman: Six memorials of citizens of Ohio.

By Mr. Quay: Four memorials of citizens of Pennsylvania.

By Mr. Gallinger: A memorial of citizens of New Hampshire.

By Mr. Berry: A memorial of citizens of Arkansas.

Ordered, That they be referred to the Select Committee on the Quadro-Centennial.

Petitions praying the passage of the bill to limit the amount of wearing apparel that may be admitted free of duty were presented as follows:

By the Vice President: A petition of citizens of New York.

By Mr. Hoar: A petition of citizens of Massachusetts.

By Mr. Gallinger: A petition of citizens of New Hampshire.

Ordered, That they be referred to the Committee on Finance.

PRESENTATION OF BILLS.

Mr. Dubois reported from the committee that on the 7th instant they presented to the President of the United States the following enrolled bills and joint resolutions:

S. 1786. An act granting a pension to Mrs. Jennie Gray;

S. 1831. An act to admit free of duty the wreckage of the ships Trenton and Vandalia, presented to the United States by the King of Samoa;

S. 2593. An act granting an increase of pension to Samuel M. Campbell;

S. 2187. An act granting a pension to Margaret M. Rice;

S. 3029. An act authorizing the construction of a bridge across the Columbia River, in the State of Washington;

S. 3048. An act granting to the Blue Mountain Irrigation and Improvement Company a right of way for reservoir and canals through the Umatilla Indian Reservation in the State of Oregon;

S. R. 112. A joint resolution to print and bind 2,000 extra copies each of the drill regulations for infantry, cavalry, and artillery; and

S. R. 123. A joint resolution to fill vacancies in the Board of Regents of the Smithsonian Institution.

REPORTS OF COMMITTEES.

Mr. Manderson, from the Committee on Printing, to whom was referred the resolution submitted by Mr. Sherman December 22,

1892, to print 5,000 extra copies of the report of the Committee on Foreign Relations on the bill S. 1218, relating to the Nicaragua Canal, reported it without amendment and submitted a report (No. 1148) thereon.

The Senate proceeded, by unanimous consent, to consider the said resolution; and

Resolved, That the Senate agree thereto.

INTRODUCTION OF BILLS AND JOINT RESOLUTION.

Bills and a joint resolution were introduced, read the first and second times by unanimous consent, and referred as follows:

By Mr. Dawes: A bill (S. 3695) to ratify and confirm an agreement with the Pawnee tribe of Indians in Oklahoma Territory, and to make appropriations for carrying the same into effect; to the Committee on Indian Affairs.

By Mr. Manderson: A bill (S. 3696) for the relief of Brig. Gen. John R. Brooke, United States Army; to the Committee on Military Affairs.

By Mr. Cullom: A bill (S. 3697) to remove the charge of desertion from the record of Wade H. Newman; to the Committee on Military Affairs.

By Mr. Quay: A bill (S. 3698) granting an increase of pension to Mrs. Olivia Betton; to the Committee on Pensions.

By Mr. Gallinger: A joint resolution (S. R. 133) instructing the Secretary of War to cause an examination to be made of the piers of the Aqueduct Bridge, and the District Commissioners to furnish a statement of expenditures on account of said bridge since it became the joint property of the United States and the District of Columbia; to the Committee on the District of Columbia.

REPORT ON CATTLE DISEASES.

Mr. McMillan submitted the following concurrent resolution; which was referred to the Committee on Printing:

Resolved by the Senate (the House of Representatives concurring therein), That there be printed of the special report on the diseases of cattle, and cattle feeding, prepared by the Bureau of Animal Industry of the Department of Agriculture, 100,000 copies, of which number 30,000 shall be for the use of the Senate, 60,000 for the use of the House of Representatives, and 10,000 to be distributed by the Secretary of Agriculture.

REPORT ON SHEEP INDUSTRY.

Mr. McMillan submitted the following concurrent resolution; which was referred to the Committee on Printing:

Resolved by the Senate (the House of Representatives concurring therein), That there be printed of the special report on the sheep industry of the United States, prepared by the Bureau of Animal Industry of the Department of Agriculture, 35,000 copies, of which number 10,000 shall be for the use of the Senate, 20,000 for the use of the House of Representatives, and 5,000 for distribution by the Secretary of Agriculture.

OBSERVATIONS OF NAVAL OBSERVATORY.

Mr. Manderson submitted the following concurrent resolution; which was referred to the Committee on Printing:

Resolved by the Senate of the United States (the House of Representatives concurring), That the annual volumes of the observations of the Naval Observatory, commonly known as the "Washington Observations," for the years 1889, 1890, 1891, and 1892, be printed, and that 1,800 additional copies of each volume be printed, of which 300 shall be for the use of the Senate, 700 for the use of the House, and 800 for the use of the Naval Observatory; and, furthermore, that 1,200 separate copies of each of the astronomical appendices, and 1,000 separate copies of the meteorological and magnetic observations, extracted from each of the above volumes, be printed for the use of the Naval Observatory.

TREATY WITH INDIANS OF OREGON.

The Vice-President laid before the Senate the resolution submitted by Mr. Mitchell on the 7th instant, calling for information relative to a treaty negotiated by Joel Palmer with various Indian tribes in Oregon in 1855; and,

The resolution was considered and agreed to.

PRESIDENTIAL APPROVALS.

A message from the President of the United States, by Mr. Pruden, his secretary:

Mr. President: The President of the United States approved and signed on the 7th inst. the joint resolution (S. R. 112) to print and bind 2,000 extra copies each of the drill regulations for infantry, cavalry, and artillery; and

He this day approved and signed the joint resolution (S. R. 123) to fill vacancies in the Board of Regents of the Smithsonian Institution.

Ordered, That the Secretary notify the House of Representatives thereof.

MESSAGE FROM THE HOUSE.

A message from the House of Representatives, by Mr. Towles, its chief clerk:

6 S

Mr. President: The House of Representatives has passed, without amendment, the following bills:

S. 118. An act for the relief of the estate of Isaac W. Talkington, deceased; and

S. 3623. An act to amend the act of March 3, 1873, for the relief of the Columbian University in the District of Columbia.

The House of Representatives has passed a bill (H. R. 10038) making appropriations for the expenses of the government of the District of Columbia for the fiscal year ending June 30, 1894, and for other purposes, in which it requests the concurrence of the Senate.

The Speaker of the House of Representatives having signed four enrolled bills, S. 317, S. 2592, S. 2990, and S. 3314, I am directed to bring them to the Senate for the signature of its President.

SUSPENSION OF PURCHASE OF SILVER BULLION.

On motion by Mr. McPherson,

The Senate resumed, as in Committee of the Whole, the consideration of the joint resolution (S. R. 126) authorizing and directing the Secretary of the Treasury to suspend all purchases of silver bullion as provided in the act of July 14, 1890; and

The question being on the amendment proposed by Mr. Stewart, After debate,

Ordered, That it lie on the table.

ADDITIONAL QUARANTINE POWERS.

The Senate resumed, as in Committee of the Whole, the consideration of the bill (S. 2707) granting additional quarantine powers and imposing additional duties upon the Marine-Hospital Service; and

The question being on the amendment proposed by Mr. Harris, It was determined in the affirmative.

The bill having been further amended on the motion of Mr. Harris and the motion of Mr. White, and

A further amendment having been proposed by Mr. White, Pending debate,

EXECUTIVE SESSION.

On motion by Mr. Sawyer,

The Senate proceeded to the consideration of executive business; and

After the consideration of executive business the doors were reopened, and

On motion by Mr. Sawyer, at 5 o'clock and 10 minutes p. m., The Senate adjourned.

TUESDAY, JANUARY 10, 1893.

HOUSE BILL REFERRED.

The bill H. R. 10038, yesterday received from the House of Representatives for concurrence, was read the first and second times by unanimous consent, and referred to the Committee on Appropriations.

EXECUTIVE COMMUNICATIONS.

The Vice-President laid before the Senate three communications from the Secretary of State, transmitting, in pursuance of the provisions of the act of February 3, 1887, certified copies of the final ascertainment of the electors for President and Vice-President appointed in the States of Kentucky, California, and Indiana.

Ordered, That they lie on the table.

The Vice-President laid before the Senate a letter of the Secretary of the Interior, transmitting, in compliance with a resolution of the Senate of the 6th instant, a copy of the latest report of Dr. Sheldon Jackson on the introduction of domesticated reindeer into Alaska; which was referred to the Committee on Appropriations and ordered to be printed.

The Vice-President laid before the Senate a letter of the Chief of Engineers, transmitting, in answer to a resolution of the Senate of July 22, 1892, estimates of the cost of converting Rock Creek into a closed sewer; which was referred to the Committee on the District of Columbia and ordered to be printed.

PETITIONS AND MEMORIALS.

Petitions, memorials, etc., were presented and referred as follows:

Resolutions of the Republican Territorial Central Committee of Arizona, praying the admission of that Territory into the Union; to the Committee on Territories;

A memorial of the Business Men's Association of Davenport, Iowa, praying the reduction of the rate of letter postage to one cent per ounce; to the Committee on Post-Offices and Post-Roads.

A resolution of the Iowa State Grange, praying that manufacturers of oleomargarine, butterine, and like compounds be compelled to color their manufactures pink; to the Committee on Agriculture and Forestry.

By Mr. Washburn: A memorial of the Commissioners of the Sinking Fund of the city of New York, remonstrating against the passage of a law authorizing the construction of a bridge over the Hudson River with approaches at or above Seventieth street in said city; to the Committee on Commerce.

By Mr. Felton: A memorial of the American Brotherhood of Steamboat Pilots, of San Francisco, Cal., remonstrating against the admission of alien officers to American registry; to the Committee on Commerce.

By Mr. Wilson: Papers relating to the claim of John Bryson for compensation for the use of his property at Red Oak, Iowa, by the Post-Office Department; to the Committee on Post-Offices and Post Roads, to accompany the bill S. 3699.

By Mr. Chandler: A petition of Arthur C. Heffenger, a passed assistant surgeon on the retired list of the Navy, praying to be promoted to the grade of surgeon on the retired list with the rank and pay of such grade; to the Committee on Naval Affairs, to accompany the bill S. 3700.

By Mr. Butler: Papers relating to the application of Franklin A. Stoddard to be allowed a pension; to the Committee on Pensions, to accompany the bill S. 3701.

By Mr. Chandler: A memorial of the United Brotherhood of Carpenters and Joiners of America, praying the passage of a law to suspend immigration into the United States indefinitely; to the Committee on Immigration, and ordered to be printed.

Mr. Felton presented a memorial of the Chamber of Commerce of San Francisco, Cal., and a memorial of the Geographical Society of the Pacific, praying the speedy passage of the bill for the completion of the Nicaragua Canal under the direction and control of the United States.

Ordered, That they lie on the table.

Mr. Morgan presented a memorial of citizens of Alabama, remonstrating against the passage of the antioption bill.

Ordered, That it lie on the table.

Petitions praying the passage of the antioption bill were presented as follows:

By Mr. Washburn: Three petitions of citizens of Minnesota.

By Mr. Stockbridge: A petition of citizens of Michigan.

By Mr. Wilson: Three petitions of citizens of Iowa.

Ordered, That they lie on the table.

Memorials remonstrating against the repeal of the provision providing for the closing of the Columbian Exposition on the Sabbath day were presented as follows:

By Mr. Quay: Four memorials of citizens of Pennsylvania.

By Mr. Washburn: A memorial of citizens of Minnesota.

By Mr. Sawyer: Two memorials of citizens of Wisconsin.

By Mr. Wilson: Two memorials of citizens of Iowa.

By Mr. Teller: A memorial of citizens of Colorado.

Ordered, That they be referred to the Select Committee on the Quadro-Centennial.

ENROLLED BILLS SIGNED.

Mr. Dubois reported from the committee that they had examined and found duly enrolled the following bills:

S. 317. An act granting an increase of pension to John M. Roberts;

S. 2592. An act granting an increase of pension to William C. Tarkington;

S. 2990. An act for the relief of George W. McKinney; and

S. 3314. An act for the relief of E. Darwin Gage, late lieutenant-colonel of the One hundred and forty-eighth New York Infantry.

Whereupon,

The Vice-President signed the same, and they were delivered to the committee to be presented to the President of the United States.

REPORTS OF COMMITTEES.

Mr. Blodgett, from the Committee on Pensions, to whom was referred the bill (H. R. 9433) granting a pension to Mrs. Ann Mercer Slaughter, reported it without amendment and submitted a report (No. 1150) thereon.

Mr. Vilas, from the Committee on Pensions, to whom was referred the bill (H. R. 1795) to increase the pension of A. J. Copenhaver, late a soldier in the Mexican war, reported it with an amendment and submitted a report (No. 1151) thereon.

Mr. Vilas, from the Committee on Pensions, to whom was referred the bill (H. R. 8038) granting a pension to William M. Watson, of Walker County, Georgia, reported it without amendment and submitted a report (No. 1152) thereon.

Mr. Stewart, from the Committee on Mines and Mining, to whom was referred the bill (H. R. 9286) to create the California Débris Commission and regulate hydraulic mining in the State of California, reported it with amendments.

Mr. Mills, from the Committee on Post-Offices and Post-Roads, to whom was referred the bill (H. R. 3676) for the relief of R. L. Jennings, late postmaster at Marshall, Tex., reported it with an amendment and submitted a report (No. 1153) thereon.

Mr. Dawes, from the Committee on Indian Affairs, to whom was referred the bill (H. R. 7633) to ratify and confirm an agreement with the Kickapoo Indians in Oklahoma Territory, and to make appropriations for carrying the same into effect, reported it with an amendment.

Mr. Dawes, from the Committee on Indian Affairs, to whom was referred the bill (S. 3329) to increase the area of the Northern Cheyenne or Tongue River Indian Reservation, Mont., and to authorize the Secretary of the Interior to settle the claims of bona fide settlers within the present reservation and the addition thereto, and

to make appropriation for that purpose, reported it without amendment.

Mr. Sawyer, from the Committee on Pensions, to whom was referred the bill (S. 2243) for the relief of W. G. Piper, of Moscow, Idaho, submitted an adverse report (No. 1154) thereon.

Ordered, That it be postponed indefinitely.

Mr. Sawyer, from the Committee on Pensions, to whom was referred the bill (S. 3670) granting an increase of pension to Charles A. Lang, reported it without amendment and submitted a report (No. 1155) thereon.

Mr. Sawyer, from the Committee on Post-Offices and Post-Roads, to whom was referred the bill (S. 3564) for the relief of Josiah Pickett, reported it with an amendment and submitted a report (No. 1156) thereon.

The Senate proceeded, by unanimous consent, to consider the said bill as in Committee of the Whole; and the reported amendment having been agreed to, the bill was reported to the Senate and the amendment was concurred in.

Ordered, That the bill be engrossed and read a third time.

The said bill was read the third time.

Resolved, That it pass, and that the title thereof be as aforesaid.

Ordered, That the Secretary request the concurrence of the House of Representatives therein.

Mr. Daniel, from the Committee on Claims, to whom was referred the bill (S. 651) for the relief of Aaron Van Camp and V. P. Chapin & Co., submitted an adverse report (No. 1157) thereon.

Ordered, That it be postponed indefinitely

Mr. Dolph, from the Committee on Public Lands, to whom was referred the bill (S. 3649) for the relief of William J. Cornell and Joseph M. Cornell, reported it with amendments and submitted a report (No. 1149) thereon.

The Senate proceeded, by unanimous consent, to consider the said bill as in Committee of the Whole; and the reported amendments having been agreed to, the bill was reported to the Senate and the amendments were concurred in.

Ordered, That the bill be engrossed and read a third time.

The said bill was read the third time.

Resolved, That it pass, and that the title thereof be amended so as to read, "A bill for the relief of William J. Carnell and Joseph M. Carnell."

Ordered, That the Secretary request the concurrence of the House of Representatives therein.

Mr. Manderson, from the Committee on Printing, reported the following resolution; which was considered by unanimous consent and agreed to:

Resolved, That 500 copies of the bill S. 1 be printed, as reported by the Committee on Agriculture of the House, for the use of the Committee on Agriculture and Forestry.

INTRODUCTION OF BILLS.

Bills were introduced, read the first and second times by unanimous consent, and referred as follows:

By Mr. Wilson: A bill (S. 3699) for the relief of John Bryson; to the Committee on Post-offices and Post-Roads.

By Mr. Chandler: A bill (S. 3700) for the relief of Arthur C. Heffenger; to the Committee on Naval Affairs.

By Mr. Butler: A bill (S. 3701) granting a pension to Franklin A. Stoddard; to the Committee on Pensions.

By Mr. Dawes: A bill (S. 3702) granting to the Chicago, Rock Island and Pacific Railway Company the use of certain lands at Chickasha Station, and for a "Y" in the Chickasaw Nation, Indian Territory; to the Committee on Indian Affairs.

By Mr. Voorhees: A bill (S. 3703) for the relief of John Spicer; to the Committee on Claims.

By Mr. Peffer: A bill (S. 3704) to amend "An act to provide a temporary government for the Territory of Oklahoma, to enlarge the jurisdiction of the United States court in the Indian Territory, and for other purposes," approved May 2, 1890; to the Committee on the Judiciary.

By Mr. Morgan: A bill (S. 3705) to ratify and confirm an agreement with the Wichita and affiliated bands of Indians in Oklahoma Territory, and to make appropriations for carrying the same into effect; to the Committee on Indian Affairs.

CALENDAR BILLS CONSIDERED.

On motion by Mr. Cockrell,

The Senate proceeded to consider, as in Committee of the Whole, the bill (S. 21) for the relief of J. C. Irwin & Co. and C. A. Perry & Co.; and

Ordered, That it be recommitted to the Committee on Claims.

On motion by Mr. Cockrell,

The Senate proceeded to consider, as in Committee of the Whole, the bill (S. 1421) for the relief of Lewis D. Allen; and

Ordered, That it be postponed indefinitely.

PRESENTATION OF BILLS.

Mr. Dubois reported from the committee that they this day presented to the President of the United States the following enrolled bills:

S. 317. An act granting an increase of pension to John M. Roberts;

S. 2592. An act granting an increase of pension to William C. Tarkington;

S. 2990. An act for the relief of George W. McKinney; and

S. 3314. An act for the relief of E. Darwin Gage, late lieutenant-colonel of the One hundred and forty-eighth New York Infantry.

ADDITIONAL COPIES OF BILL.

On motion by Mr. Washburn,

Ordered, That 2,000 copies of the bill (H. R. 7845) defining "options" and "futures," imposing special taxes on dealers therein, and requiring such persons engaged in selling certain products to obtain license, and for other purposes, be printed for the use of the Senate.

ADDITIONAL QUARANTINE POWERS.

The Senate resumed, as in Committee of the Whole, the consideration of the bill (S. 2707) granting additional quarantine powers and imposing additional duties upon the Marine-Hospital Service; and

The question being on the amendment yesterday proposed by Mr. White, viz: *All the provisions of this act shall expire on the first day of January, eighteen hundred and ninety-five.*

It was determined in the negative, { Yeas .... 13 { Nays 33

On motion by Mr. White,

The yeas and nays being desired by one-fifth of the Senators present,

Those who voted in the affirmative are,

Messrs. Blodgett, Butler, Gallinger, George, Gibson, Gorman, Gray, Mills, Palmer, Platt, Vance, Vilas, White.

Those who voted in the negative are,

Messrs. Aldrich, Allison, Berry, Cameron, Chandler, Cockrell, Coke, Dixon, Dolph, Dubois, Felton, Frye, Hansbrough, Harris, Higgins, Hoar, Hunton, Irby, McMillan, McPherson, Mitchell, Peffer, Pettigrew, Proctor, Sawyer, Sherman, Shoup, Stewart, Stockbridge, Teller, Walthall, Washburn, Wolcott.

So the amendment was not agreed to.

The bill having been further amended on the motion of Mr. Vilas and the motion of Mr. Gallinger, it was reported to the Senate and the amendments were, in part, concurred in.

On the question to concur in the following amendment made in Committee of the Whole, viz: Insert as an additional section the following words:

SEC. 7. *That whenever it shall be shown to the satisfaction of the President that, by reason of the existence of cholera or other infectious or contagious diseases in a foreign country, there is serious danger of the introduction of the same into the United States, and that, notwithstanding the quarantine defense, this danger is so increased by immigration that a suspension of the same is demanded in the interest of the public health, the President shall have power to suspend immigration from such countries or places as he shall designate and for such period of time as he may deem necessary,*

On motion by Mr. Vilas to amend the amendment by striking out the word "immigration" where it first occurs, and in lieu thereof inserting the words *passenger travel,* and by striking out the word "immigration" where it occurs the second t.me, and in lieu thereof inserting the words *all passenger travel, but not immigration alone,*

It was determined in the negative, { Yeas .... 17 { Nays 27

On motion by Mr. Vilas,

The yeas and nays being desired by one-fifth of the Senators present,

Those who voted in the affirmative are,

Messrs. Berry, Blodgett, Butler, Cockrell, George, Gibson, Harris, Jones of Arkansas, Kyle, Mills, Morgan, Palmer, Vance, Vilas, Voorhees, Walthall, White.

Those who voted in the negative are,

Messrs. Call, Cameron, Chandler, Dawes, Dixon, Dolph, Dubois, Frye, Gallinger, Gray, Hansbrough, Higgins, Hunton, McMillan, McPherson, Mitchell, Morrill, Platt, Proctor, Sawyer, Sherman, Shoup, Stockbridge, Teller, Washburn, Wolcott.

So the amendment to the amendment was not agreed to.

The amendment having been amended on the motion of Mr. Palmer,

On the question to concur in the amendment as amended, as follows: Insert as an additional section the following words:

SEC. 7. *That whenever it shall be shown to the satisfaction of the President that, by reason of the existence of cholera or other infectious or contagious diseases in a foreign country, there is serious danger of the introduction of the same into the United States, and that, notwithstanding the quarantine defense, this danger is so increased by the introduction of persons or property from such country that a suspension of the right to introduce the same is demanded in the interest of the public health, the President shall have power to prohibit, in whole or in part, the introduction of persons and property from such countries or places as he shall designate and for such period of time as he may deem necessary,*

It was determined in the affirmative, { Yeas .... 37 { Nays 10

On motion by Mr. Vilas,

The yeas and nays being desired by one-fifth of the Senators present,

Those who voted in the affirmative are,

Messrs. Call, Cameron, Chandler, Cockrell, Dawes, Dixon. Dolph, Dubois, Frye, Gallinger, George, Hansbrough, Harris, Higgins, Hoar, Irby, Kyle, McMillan, McPherson, Mitchell, Morrill, Palmer, Peffer, Pettigrew, Platt, Proctor, Pugh, Sawyer, Sherman, Shoup, Stockbridge, Teller, Vance, Voorhees, Walthall, Washburn, Wolcott.

Those who voted in the negative are,

Messrs. Berry, Blodgett, Butler, Coke, Gray, Hunton, Mills, Morgan, Vilas, White.

So the amendment was concurred in.

On motion by Mr. Morgan, to amend the bill by inserting an additional section, as follows:

SEC. —. *Nothing in this act contained shall be so construed as to authorize the United States, or any officer thereof in its behalf, to take into its ownership or control for quarantine purposes any place in any State and to exercise therein exclusive jurisdiction, without the consent of such State,*

It was determined in the negative, { Yeas .... 19 { Nays 28

On motion by Mr. Morgan,

The yeas and nays being desired by one-fifth of the Senators present,

Those who voted in the affirmative are,

Messrs. Berry, Blodgett, Butler, Coke, Daniel, Gorman, Gray, Hunton, Kyle, McPherson, Mills, Morgan, Palmer, Pugh, Vance, Vilas, Voorhees, Walthall, White.

Those who voted in the negative are,

Messrs. Call, Cameron, Chandler, Cockrell, Dawes, Dolph, Dubois, Frye, Gallinger, George, Hansbrough, Harris, Higgins, Hoar, Irby, McMillan, Mitchell, Morrill, Peffer, Pettigrew, Platt, Proctor, Sawyer, Sherman, Shoup, Stockbridge, Teller, Washburn.

So the amendment was not agreed to.

No further amendment being proposed,

Ordered, That the bill be engrossed and read a third time.

The said bill was read the third time.

Resolved, That it pass, and that the title be amended so as to read, "A bill granting additional quarantine powers and imposing additional duties upon the Secretary of the Treasury and the Marine-Hospital Service, and for other purposes."

Ordered, That the Secretary request the concurrence of the House of Representatives therein.

DEALINGS IN "OPTIONS" AND "FUTURES."

The Senate resumed, as in Committee of the Whole, the consideration of the bill (H. R. 7845), defining "options" and "futures," imposing special taxes on dealers therein, and requiring such persons engaged in selling certain products to obtain license, and for other purposes; and

The question being on the amendment proposed by Mr. White, viz: Strike out the proviso at the end of section 2, as follows:

"*Provided, however,* That such contract or agreement shall not be made, settled for by delivery or settlement of differences, or by any other mode of performance or settlement in or upon any board of trade, produce, cotton, merchants', or other exchange, or other commercial association, or in any place or upon any premises where price quotations of said articles are announced, bulletined, or published, nor be subject to the rules or regulations of any such board, exchange, or other commercial association,"

After debate,

On the question to agree to the amendment,

The yeas were 10 and the nays were 21.

The yeas and nays having been heretofore ordered,

Those who voted in the affirmative are,

Messrs. Blodgett, Dixon, Gorman, Hunton, McPherson, Mills, Mitchell, Palmer, Vilas, White.

Those who voted in the negative are,

Messrs. Allison, Call, Cockrell, Coke, Dubois, Frye, Gallinger, George, Hansbrough, Higgins, Kyle, McMillan, Manderson, Pasco, Peffer, Pettigrew, Pugh, Teller, Walthall, Washburn, Wilson.

The number of Senators voting not constituting a quorum,

On motion by Mr. Butler, at 4 o'clock and 37 minutes p. m.,

The Senate adjourned.

WEDNESDAY, JANUARY 11, 1893.

DEATH OF THE HON. JOHN E. KENNA.

Mr. Blackburn announced the death of the honorable John E. Kenna, late a Senator from the State of West Virginia, which occurred at his residence in this city at 3 o'clock this morning; and

He submitted the following resolutions; which were considered by unanimous consent and unanimously agreed to:

Resolved, That the Senate has heard with great sorrow of the death of the Hon. John E. Kenna, late a Senator from the State of West Virginia.

Resolved, That a committee of seven Senators be appointed by the Vice-President to take order for superintending the funeral of Mr. Kenna, which will take place to-morrow, Thursday, in the Senate Chamber, at 1 o'clock p. m., and that the Senate will attend the same.

Resolved, That as a further mark of respect entertained by the Senate for his memory, his remains be removed from Washington to West Virginia in charge of the Sergeant-at-Arms, and attended by the committee, who shall have full power to carry this resolution into effect.

Resolved, That the Secretary communicate these proceedings to the House of Representatives, and invite the House of Representatives to attend the funeral to-morrow, Thursday, at 1 o'clock p. m., and to appoint a committee to act with the committee of the Senate.

The Vice-President appointed as members of the committee Mr. Faulkner, Mr. Blackburn, Mr. Ransom, Mr. Daniel, Mr. Walthall, Mr. Manderson, and Mr. Squire.

Mr. Blackburn submitted the following resolutions:

Resolved, That invitations be extended to the President of the United States and the members of his Cabinet, the Chief Justice and the Associate Justices of the Supreme Court of the United States, the Diplomatic Corps, the Major-General commanding the Army, and the Senior Admiral of the Navy, to attend the funeral of the Hon. John E. Kenna, late a Senator from the State of West Virginia, in the Senate Chamber, to-morrow, Thursday, at 1 o'clock p. m.

Resolved, That as a further mark of respect, the Senate do now adjourn.

The resolutions were considered by unanimous consent and unanimously agreed to.

Whereupon,

The Senate adjourned.

THURSDAY, JANUARY 12, 1893.

FUNERAL OF THE LATE SENATOR KENNA.

On motion by Mr. Faulkner, and by unanimous consent,

Ordered, That the privileges of the floor for to-day be granted to the committee appointed by the legislature of West Virginia to attend the funeral of the late Senator Kenna and escort his remains to the place of burial.

On motion by Mr. Manderson,

The Senate took a recess until 12 o'clock and 45 minutes p. m.

AT TWELVE O'CLOCK AND FORTY-FIVE MINUTES P. M.

A message from the House of Representatives, by Mr. Towles, its chief clerk:

The House of Representatives has passed the following resolutions, which I am directed to communicate to the Senate:

Resolved, That the House has learned with profound sorrow of the death of Hon. John E. Kenna, a Senator of the United States from the State of West Virginia.

Resolved, That the Speaker of the House appoint a committee of ten members, to act in conjunction with the committee appointed by the Senate to take order for superintending the funeral, and to accompany the remains to their last resting place.

Resolved, That the House accept the invitation of the Senate to attend the funeral to-morrow, Thursday, at 1 o'clock p. m., and that the Clerk of the House communicate these proceedings to the Senate.

Resolved, That as a further tribute and mark of respect to the memory of the deceased this House do now adjourn.

The Speaker appointed as the committee under the second resolution Mr. Alderson, Mr. Pendleton, Mr. Wilson of West Virginia, Mr. Capehart, Mr. Outhwaite, Mr. Tucker, Mr. Dungan, Mr. Mansur, Mr. Henderson of Illinois, and Mr. Bingham.

The Speaker and the House of Representatives, the General Commanding the Army, the Diplomatic Corps, the Chief Justice and the Associate Justices of the Supreme Court of the United States, the President and members of his Cabinet, entered the Senate Chamber and were escorted to the seats assigned them.

After appropriate funeral ceremonies, the remains were intrusted to the custody of the committee appointed by the two Houses for superintending the funeral, to be attended by them to the Pennsylvania Railroad station, and from thence to the place of interment in the State of West Virginia.

When,

The persons invited to be present having retired,

On motion by Mr. Allison, at 1 o'clock and 47 minutes p. m.,

The Senate adjourned.

FRIDAY, JANUARY 13, 1893.

MESSAGE FROM THE PRESIDENT.

The following message was received from the President of the United States, by Mr. Pruden, his secretary:

To the Senate:

In response to the resolutions of the Senate, dated December 20, 1892, and January 5, 1893, respectively, I transmit herewith a report from the Secretary of State of the 10th instant, accompanying the reports of Mr. Walter T. Griffin, United States commercial agent at Limoges, France, and Mr. W. H. Edwards, United States consul-general at Berlin, Germany, which were called for by the aforesaid resolutions.

BENJ. HARRISON.

EXECUTIVE MANSION, *Washington, January 11, 1893.*

The message was read.

Ordered, That it be referred to the Committee on Immigration.

EXECUTIVE COMMUNICATIONS.

The Vice-President laid before the Senate two communications from the Secretary of State, transmitting, under the provisions of the act of February 3, 1887, certified copies of the final ascertainment of electors for President and Vice-President in the States of New York and South Carolina.

Ordered, That they lie on the table.

The Vice-President laid before the Senate a letter of the Secretary of the Treasury relative to the purchase of a site for an appraiser's warehouse and custom-house in the city of New York, under the act of September 14, 1888, and the acts amendatory thereof; which was referred to the Committee on Public Buildings and Grounds and ordered to be printed.

CREDENTIALS OF A SENATOR.

Mr. White presented the credentials of Donelson Caffery, appointed a Senator by the governor of the State of Louisiana to fill the vacancy occasioned by the death of the honorable Randall Lee Gibson; which were read.

PETITIONS AND MEMORIALS.

Petitions, memorials, etc., were presented and referred as follows:

By the Vice-President: A memorial of the Federation of Labor of Washington, D. C., praying the passage of a law prohibiting foreign immigration for the next five years; to the Committee on Immigration.

By Mr. Quay: Resolutions of the city council of Oklahoma City, Okla., praying the passage of a law donating to that city the Oklahoma military reservation for school purposes; to the Committee on Territories.

By Mr. Peffer: A memorial of licensed officers of the American merchant marine, remonstrating against the passage of the bill granting American registry and license to the alien officers heretofore employed on the steamships *City of New York* and *City of Paris*; to the Committee on Naval Affairs.

By Mr. Proctor: A resolution of the Board of Trade of Rutland, Vt., praying the establishment of a road department, or such other legislation as will promote the building and maintaining of improved highways in the United States; to the Committee on Interstate Commerce.

By Mr. Wolcott: A resolution of the Chamber of Commerce and Board of Trade of Denver, Colo., praying that that place be selected for the headquarters for the Department of the West, United States Army; to the Committee on Military Affairs.

By Mr. Washburn: A resolution of the Board of Trade of Minneapolis, Minn., remonstrating against any restrictions being placed upon the traffic of the Northwest to the seaboard by way of Canada; to the Committee on Commerce.

By Mr. Stockbridge: A memorial of the Engineers, Beneficial Association, of San Francisco, Cal., remonstrating against the passage of the bill granting American registry and license to the alien officers heretofore employed on the steamships *City of New York* and *City of Paris*; to the Committee on Commerce.

By Mr. Hiscock: A petition of citizens of New York, praying the passage of the bill limiting the amount of clothing that may be admitted free of duty; to the Committee on Finance.

Resolutions of the Chamber of Commerce of New York, praying the passage of a law placing the quarantine at New York under national control; to the Committee on Immigration.

By Mr. Jones, of Arkansas: A petition of Mrs. E. L. Eblen, of Tahlequah, Ind. T., praying compensation for the use and occupancy of certain property belonging to her by the United States military forces during the late war; and

A petition of the legal representatives of Capt. Charles Willey, deceased, praying compensation for the use of certain steamboats belonging to said Willey by the United States authorities during the late war; to the Committee on Claims.

By Mr. Wolcott: Resolutions of the Trades League of Philadelphia, Pa., praying the passage of a law to promote reciprocity with foreign nations; to the Committee on Finance.

By Mr. Morrill: The twenty-ninth annual report of the National Association for the Relief of Destitute Colored Women and Children, for the year ending January 1, 1892, and urging an appropriation for additional accommodations for school purposes; to the Committee on Appropriations, to accompany an amendment intended to be proposed to the bill H. R. 10038.

Mr. Vest presented a memorial of the Merchants' Exchange of St. Louis, Mo., remonstrating against the passage of the antioption bill.

Ordered, That it lie on the table.

Mr. Stockbridge presented a memorial of the Board of Trade of Detroit, Mich., praying the passage of a law for the completion of the Nicaragua Canal under the direction and control of the United States.

Ordered, That it lie on the table.

Mr. Vest presented resolutions of the Merchants' Exchange of St. Louis, Mo., praying the passage of the bill providing for the purchase of the Cherokee Strip and opening the same up to settlement.

Ordered, That they lie on the table.

Mr. Cockrell also presented similar resolutions for the same purpose; which were also ordered to lie on the table.

The Vice-President laid before the Senate a resolution of the Democratic and Republican Territorial Central Committees, praying the passage of a law for the admission of the Territory of Arizona into the Union as a State; which was referred to the Committee on Territories.

Mr. Sherman presented a similar resolution for the same purpose; which was similarly referred.

Memorials, etc., praying the passage of the bill to restrict immigration into the United States, were presented as follows:

By Mr. Sherman: A memorial of citizens of Ohio.

By Mr. Quay: Resolutions of the Chamber of Commerce of Pittsburg, Pa.

By Mr. Wolcott: Resolutions of the Chamber of Commerce and Board of Trade of Denver, Colo.

Ordered, That they lie on the table.

Memorials, etc., praying the repeal of the law providing for the purchase of silver bullion, were presented as follows:

By Mr. Hill: A memorial of citizens of New York.

By Mr. Hiscock: A memorial of members of the New York Cotton Exchange.

By Mr. Gallinger: Resolutions of the Board of Trade of Manchester, N. H.

By Mr. Quay: A resolution of the Chamber of Commerce of Pittsburg, Pa.

By Mr. Hoar: Two petitions of citizens of Massachusetts.

By the Vice-President: A resolution of the Board of Trade of Minneapolis, Minn.

Ordered, That they be referred to the Committee on Finance.

Petitions praying the passage of the antioption bill were presented as follows:

By the Vice-President: A petition of citizens of Washington.

By Mr. Hale: A petition of citizens of Maine.

By Mr. Sherman: A petition of citizens of Ohio.

By Mr. Frye: A petition of citizens of Maine.

By Mr. Vest: A petition of citizens of Missouri.

By Mr. Peffer: A petition of citizens of Kansas.

Ordered, That they lie on the table.

Memorials remonstrating against the repeal of the provision providing for the closing of the Columbian Exposition on the Sabbath day were presented as follows:

By the Vice-President: A memorial of citizens of Georgia.

By Mr. Hoar: Eight memorials of citizens of Massachusetts.

By Mr. Vilas: A memorial of citizens of Wisconsin.

By Mr. Kyle: A memorial of citizens of South Dakota.

By Mr. Sherman: Several memorials of citizens of Ohio.

By Mr. Washburn: A memorial of citizens of Minnesota.

By Mr. Dawes: Three memorials of citizens of Massachusetts.

By Mr. Wilson: Six memorials of citizens of Iowa.

By Mr. Stockbridge: Five memorials of citizens of Michigan.

By Mr. Cockrell: Several memorials of citizens of Missouri.

By Mr. Quay: Seven memorials of citizens of Pennsylvania.

By Mr. Hiscock: A memorial of citizens of New York.

Ordered, That they be referred to the Select Committee on the Quadro-Centennial.

Petitions praying for the appointment of a committee to investigate an alleged combine formed to depreciate the price of grain, by the millers and others of St. Louis and Minneapolis, were presented as follows:

By Mr. Wolcott: A petition of citizens of Colorado.

By Mr. Pettigrew: Several petitions of citizens of South Dakota.

Ordered, That they be referred to the Committee on Agriculture and Forestry.

REPORTS OF COMMITTEES.

Mr. Sherman, from the Committee on Foreign Relations, to whom was referred the bill (S. 3629) to extend to the North Pacific Ocean the provisions of the statutes for the protection of fur seals and other fur-bearing animals, reported it without amendment and submitted a report (No. 1158) thereon.

The Senate proceeded, by unanimous consent, to consider the said bill as in Committee of the Whole; and no amendment being made, it was reported to the Senate.

Ordered, That it be engrossed and read a third time.

The said bill was read the third time.

Resolved, That it pass, and that the title thereof be as aforesaid.

Ordered, That the Secretary request the concurrence of the House of Representatives therein.

Mr. Sawyer, from the Committee on Pensions, to whom was referred the bill (H. R. 6069) for the relief of Elisha Brown, reported it without amendment and submitted a report (No. 1159) thereon.

Mr. Pasco, from the Committee on Claims, to whom was referred the following bills, submitted written adverse reports thereon as follows:

H. R. 915. An act for the relief of the heirs of Noah Noble, deceased; Report No. 1160.

H. R. 2281. An act for the relief of Miss Jane Linn; Report No. 1161.

Ordered, That they be postponed indefinitely.

Mr. McMillan, from the Committee on the District of Columbia, to whom was referred the following bills, reported them each with an amendment, and submitted written reports thereon as follows:

S. 3691. A bill regulating the employment of certain persons in manufactories, workshops, and stores in the District of Columbia; Report No. 1162.

S. 3682. A bill to narrow California avenue within Bel Air Heights, District of Columbia; Report No. 1163.

Mr. Mitchell, on behalf of Mr. Daniel, from the Committee on Claims, to whom was referred the bill (H. R. 1036) for the benefit of Logan, Simpson, Hardin, and Hart counties, and of the city of Louisville, Ky., and of Sumner and Davidson counties, Tennessee, reported it with amendments and submitted a report (No. 1164) thereon.

Mr. Sawyer, from the Committee on Pensions, to whom were referred the following bills, reported them without amendment and submitted written reports thereon, as follows:

H. R. 5705. An act to increase the pension of Amelia Graham; Report No. 1165.

H. R. 8925. An act to increase the pension of Harvey Lyon; Report No. 1167.

Mr. Sawyer, from the Committee on Pensions, to whom was referred the bill (H. R. 7099) granting an increase of pension to Samuel S. Anderson, reported it with an amendment and submitted a report (No. 1166) thereon.

Mr. Hansbrough, from the Committee on the District of Columbia, who were instructed by a resolution of April 19, 1892, to investigate the manner and methods by which the appropriation for the removal of garbage in the District of Columbia has been expended, submitted a report (No. 1167).

INTRODUCTION OF BILLS.

Bills were introduced, read the first and second times by unanimous consent, and referred as follows:

By Mr. Frye: A bill (S. 3706) providing for a commission on the subject of the social vice; to the Committee on Education and Labor.

A bill (S. 3707) making an appropriation for the establishing of buoyage on the water front of Chicago, Lake Michigan, Illinois; to the Committee on Commerce.

By Mr. Wolcott: A bill (S. 3708) granting a pension to Helen L. Dent; to the Committee on Pensions.

By Mr. McMillan: A bill (S. 3709) granting a pension to John E. Burnes; to the Committee on Pensions.

By Mr. Wilson: A bill (S. 3710) to incorporate the Chesapeake and Washington Underground Electric Railway Company; to the Committee on the District of Columbia.

By Mr. Berry, on behalf of Mr. Blodgett: A bill (S. 3711) granting the right of way through the Arlington reservation for railroad purposes; to the Committee on Military Affairs.

By Mr. Hill: A bill (S. 3712) to grant the right of way for electric-railroad purposes through certain lands of the United States in Richmond County, New York; and

A bill (S. 3713) to provide an American register for the steam yacht *Golden Fleece*; to the Committee on Commerce.

By Mr. Dawes: A bill (S. 3714) to ratify and confirm an agreement with the Comanche, Kiowa, and Apache tribes of Indians in Oklahoma Territory, and to make appropriations for carrying the same into effect; to the Committee on Indian Affairs.

By Mr. Proctor: A bill (S. 3715) to authorize the appointment of an associate professor of mathematics at the Military Academy; to the Committee on Military Affairs.

NICARAGUA CANAL.

Mr. Morgan submitted the following resolution for consideration; which was ordered to be printed:

Resolved, That the Committee on Commerce is instructed to inquire and report to the Senate the advantages, if any, that will accrue to the productions, industries, coastwise and foreign commerce, immigration, and other interests of the United States, by means of the additional facilities of transportation, and the reduction of the cost thereof, that would be afforded by the building of a ship canal to connect the waters of the Atlantic and Pacific oceans through Lake Nicaragua.

DISTRIBUTION OF SOUVENIR COINS.

Mr. Wilson submitted the following resolution; which was considered by unanimous consent and agreed to:

Resolved, That the Secretary of the Treasury be directed to transmit to the Senate a copy of the opinion of the law officer of the Government for his Department under which he is disbursing the $2,500,000 in souvenir coins in aid of the World's Columbian Exposition, appropriated by the act of Congress approved August 5, 1892, and conditioned upon Sunday closing; and also to transmit a copy of such regulations relative to the issuance and delivery of said coins as he may have established in pursuance of said opinion.

REPRINT OF BILL.

On motion by Mr. Harris,

Ordered, That the bill (S. 2707) granting additional quarantine powers and imposing additional duties upon the Secretary of the Treasury and the Marine-Hospital Service, and for other purposes, be printed as passed by the Senate.

PRESIDENTIAL APPROVALS.

A message from the President of the United States, by Mr. Pruden, his secretary:

Mr. President: The President of the United States approved and signed on the 10th instant the following acts:

S. 1831. An act to admit free of duty the wreckage of the ships *Trenton* and *Vandalia*, presented by the United States to the King of Samoa; and

S. 3029. An act authorizing the construction of a bridge across the Columbia River in the State of Washington.

He approved and signed on the 11th instant the following acts:

S. 1786. An act granting a pension to Mrs. Jennie Gray;

S. 2187. An act granting a pension to Margaret M. Rice; and

S. 2593. An act granting an increase of pension to Samuel M. Campbell.

He approved and signed on the 12th instant the following acts:

S. 3048. An act granting to the Blue Mountain Irrigation and Improvement Company a right of way for reservoirs and canals through the Umatilla Indian Reservation in the State of Oregon;

S. 317. An act granting an increase of pension to John M. Roberts;

S. 2592. An act granting an increase of pension to William C. Tarkington.

S. 2990. An act for the relief of George W. McKinney; and

S. 3314. An act for the relief of E. Darwin Gage, late lieutenant-colonel of the One hundred and forty-eighth New York Infantry.

Ordered, That the Secretary notify the House of Representatives thereof.

MESSAGE FROM THE HOUSE.

A message from the House of Representatives, by Mr. Towles, its chief clerk:

Mr. President: The House of Representatives has passed, without amendment, the following bill and joint resolution of the Senate:

S. 3195. An act granting to the Yuma Pumping Irrigation Company the right of way for two ditches across that part of the Yuma Indian Reservation lying in Arizona; and

S. R. 113. Joint resolution for the printing of the Agricultural Report for 1892.

The House of Representatives has agreed to the amendment of the Senate to the bill (H. R. 9824) to amend "An act to promote the construction of a safe deep-water harbor on the coast of Texas," approved February 9, 1891.

The House of Representatives has passed the following bills, in which it requests the concurrence of the Senate:

H. R. 3591. An act to authorize the Norfolk and Western Railroad Company, of Virginia, to extend its line of road into and within the District of Columbia, and for other purposes; and

H. R. 10015. An act to authorize the construction of bridges across the Hiawassee, the Tennessee and the Clinch rivers in the State of Tennessee.

The Speaker of the House of Representatives having signed two enrolled bills, S. 118 and S. 3623, I am directed to bring them to the Senate for the signature of its President.

ENROLLED BILLS SIGNED.

Mr. Dubois reported from the committee, that they had examined and found duly enrolled the following bills:

S. 118. An act for the relief of the estate of Isaac W. Talkington, deceased; and

S. 3623. An act to amend the act of March 3, 1873, for the relief of the Columbian University in the District of Columbia;

Whereupon,

The Vice-President signed the same, and they were delivered to the committee to be presented to the President of the United States.

HOUSE BILLS REFERRED.

The bills last received from the House of Representatives for concurrence were read the first and second times by unanimous consent.

Ordered, That the bill H. R. 3591 be referred to the Committee on the District of Columbia, and that the bill H. R. 10015 be referred to the Committee on Commerce.

MESSAGE FROM THE PRESIDENT.

The following message was received from the President of the United States, by Mr. Pruden, his secretary:

To the Senate and House of Representatives:

I transmit herewith, for your information, a letter from the Secretary of State, inclosing the annual report of the Bureau of American Republics for the year ending June 30, 1892.

BENJ. HARRISON.

EXECUTIVE MANSION, *January 13, 1893.*

The message was read.

Ordered, That it be referred to the Committee on Appropriations and be printed.

CONSIDERATION OF BILLS ON THE CALENDAR.

On motion by Mr. Wolcott,

The Senate proceeded to consider, as in Committee of the Whole, the bill (S. 1491) to establish a free public and departmental library and reading room; and

After debate,

On motion by Mr. Morgan,

Ordered, That it be referred to the Committee on the Library.

On motion by Mr. Teller,

The Senate resumed the reconsideration of the bill (S. 1958) to submit to the Court of Private Land Claims, established by an act of Congress approved March 3, 1891, the title of William McGarrahan to the Rancho Panoche Grande, in the State of California, and for other purposes, returned by the President of the United States to the Senate with his objections; and

After debate,

Ordered, That the further consideration thereof be postponed to Monday next.

On motion by Mr. Gordon,

The Senate proceeded to consider, as in Committee of the Whole, the bill (H. R. 8038) granting a pension to William M. Watson, of Walker County, Georgia; and no amendment being made, it was reported to the Senate.

Ordered, That it pass to a third reading.

The said bill was read the third time.

Resolved, That it pass.

Ordered, That the Secretary notify the House of Representatives thereof.

On motion by Mr. Sawyer,

The Senate proceeded to consider, as in Committee of the Whole, the bill (S. 3670) granting an increase of pension to Charles A. Lang; and no amendment being made, it was reported to the Senate.

Ordered, That it be engrossed and read a third time.

The said bill was read the third time.

Resolved, That it pass, and that the title thereof be as aforesaid.

Ordered, That the Secretary request the concurrence of the House of Representatives therein.

On motion by Mr. Hansbrough,

The Senate proceeded to consider, as in Committee of the Whole, the bill (S. 2265) for the removal of snow and ice from the sidewalks, cross walks, and gutters in the cities of Washington and Georgetown, and for other purposes; and the reported amendments having been agreed to, the bill was reported to the Senate and the amendments were concurred in.

Ordered, That it be engrossed and read a third time.

The said bill was read the third time.

Resolved, That it pass, and that the title thereof be as aforesaid.

Ordered, That the Secretary request the concurrence of the House of Representatives therein.

DEALINGS IN "OPTIONS" AND "FUTURES."

The Presiding Officer (Mr. Pasco in the chair) announced that the hour of 2 o'clock had arrived, and laid before the Senate its unfinished business, viz, the bill (H. R. 7845) defining "options" and "futures," imposing special taxes on dealers therein, and requiring such persons engaged in selling certain products to obtain license, and for other purposes; and

The Senate resumed, as in Committee of the Whole, the consideration of the bill; and

The question being on the amendment proposed by Mr. White, viz: At the end of section 2 strike out the following proviso:

"*Provided, however,* That such contract or agreement shall not be made, settled for by delivery or settlement of differences, or by any other mode of performance or settlement in or upon any board of trade, produce, cotton, merchants' or other exchange, or other commercial association, or in any place or upon any premises where price quotations of said articles are announced, bulletined, or published, nor be subjected to the rules or regulations of any such board, exchange, or other commercial association,"

The yeas were 10 and the nays were 31.

The yeas and nays having been heretofore ordered,

Those who voted in the affirmative are,

Messrs. Brice, Cameron, Dixon, Gorman, Hunton, Palmer, Quay, Vilas, White, Wolcott.

Those who voted in the negative are,

Messrs. Berry, Butler, Call, Carey, Chandler, Cockrell, Coke, Dawes, Dubois, Frye, Gallinger, George, Hale, Hansbrough, Harris, Kyle, McMillan, Morrill, Pasco, Peffer, Pettigrew, Pugh, Ransom,

Sherman, Shoup, Stewart, Teller, Vance, Voorhees, Washburn, Wilson.

The number of Senators voting not constituting a quorum,
The Presiding Officer directed the roll to be called;
When,
Forty-five Senators answered to their names.
A quorum being present, and
The question being again taken on the amendment,

It was determined in the negative, { Yeas 15
{ Nays 32

Those who voted in the affirmative are,
Messrs. Brice, Cameron, Dixon, Felton, Gibson, Gorman, Hiscock, Hunton, Mills, Mitchell, Palmer, Quay, Vilas, White, Wolcott.

Those who voted in the negative are,
Messrs. Allison, Berry, Butler, Call, Carey, Chandler, Cockrell, Coke, Dawes, Dubois, Frye, Gallinger, George, Hale, Hansbrough, Harris, Irby, Kyle, McMillan, Pasco, Peffer, Proctor, Pugh, Ransom, Sherman, Shoup, Stockbridge, Teller, Vance, Voorhees, Washburn, Wilson.

So the amendment was not agreed to.
A further amendment having been proposed by Mr. Vilas,
After debate,
On motion by Mr. Wolcott that the Senate proceed to the consideration of the first bill on the calendar under Rule 8, viz, the bill (S. 88) for the relief of Hiram Somerville,

It was determined in the negative, { Yeas 9
{ Nays 36

On motion by Mr. Washburn,
The yeas and nays being desired by one-fifth of the Senators present,
Those who voted in the affirmative are,
Messrs. Dixon, Hill, Hiscock, Hoar, McMillan, Mills, Palmer, Vilas, White.

Those who voted in the negative are,
Messrs. Allison, Berry, Butler, Call, Carey, Chandler, Cockrell, Coke, Dawes, Dubois, Frye, Gallinger, George, Gordon, Hale, Hansbrough, Hunton, Irby, Jones of Arkansas, Kyle, Mitchell, Morgan, Pasco, Pettigrew, Proctor, Pugh, Quay, Ransom, Sawyer, Sherman, Shoup, Teller, Vance, Voorhees, Washburn, Wilson.

So the motion was not agreed to.
The question recurring on the amendment proposed by Mr. Vilas, viz: After the words "owner thereof" in line 15, section 2, insert the following words: *And does not in good faith intend to purchase and deliver the articles contracted to be sold and delivered according to the terms and requirements of such contract,*
On motion by Mr. White,
The yeas and nays were ordered; and
Pending debate on the amendment,

EXECUTIVE SESSION.

On motion by Mr. Washburn,
The Senate proceeded to the consideration of executive business; and
After the consideration of executive business the doors were reopened, and
On motion by Mr. Sawyer, at 5 o'clock and 16 minutes p. m.,
The Senate adjourned.

SATURDAY, JANUARY 14, 1893.

MESSAGE FROM THE HOUSE.

A message from the House of Representatives, by Mr. Towles, its chief clerk:

Mr. President: The House of Representatives has passed a bill (H. R. 10007) to provide for lowering the height of a bridge proposed to be constructed across the Ohio River between Cincinnati, Ohio, and Covington, Ky., by the Cincinnati and Covington Rapid Transit Bridge Company, in which it requests the concurrence of the Senate.

The House of Representatives has passed the following resolutions, in which it requests the concurrence of the Senate:

Resolved by the House of Representatives (the Senate concurring), That there be printed and bound of the special report of the Bureau of Animal Industry on Diseases of Cattle and Cattle Feeding 60,000 copies, of which 20,000 shall be for the use of the Senate and 40,000 for the use of the House.

Resolved by the House of Representatives (the Senate concurring), That there be printed and bound of the special report of the Sheep Industry of the United States 60,000 copies, of which 20,000 copies shall be for the use of the Senate and 40,000 for the use of the House.

The Speaker of the House of Representatives having signed two enrolled bills, H. R. 9824 and S. 3195, and an enrolled joint resolution, S. R. 113, I am directed to bring the same to the Senate for the signature of its President.

ENROLLED BILLS EXAMINED AND SIGNED.

Mr. Dubois reported from the committee that they had examined and found duly enrolled the following bills and joint resolution:

S. 3195. An act granting to the Yuma Pumping Irrigation Company the right of way for two ditches across that part of the Yuma Indian Reservation lying in Arizona;

H. R. 9824. An act to amend "An act to promote the construction of a safe deep-water harbor on the coast of Texas," approved February 9, 1891; and

S. R. 113. A joint resolution providing for the printing of the Agricultural Report for 1892;

Whereupon,
The Vice-President signed the same, and they were delivered to the committee to be presented to the President of the United States.

SENATOR SWORN.

Mr. Caffery, whose credentials were heretofore presented, appeared, and the oath prescribed by law having been administered to him by the Vice-President, he took his seat in the Senate.

EXECUTIVE COMMUNICATONS.

The Vice-President laid before the Senate two communications from the Secretary of State, transmitting, in pursuance of the provisions of the act of February 3, 1887, certified copies of the final ascertainment of electors for President and Vice-President in the States of South Dakota and Oregon.

Ordered, That they lie on the table.

The Vice-President laid before the Senate a letter of the Secretary of the Treasury, recommending the passage of a resolution conferring exclusive control upon the Secretary of the Treasury in all matters pertaining to the custody, care, etc., the assignment of rooms, etc., of public buildings erected under his direction; which was referred to the Committee on Public Buildings and Grounds and ordered to be printed.

The Vice-President laid before the Senate the report of the Anacostia and Potomac River Railroad Company for the year ending December 31, 1892; which was referred to the Committee on the District of Columbia and ordered to be printed.

PETITIONS AND MEMORIALS.

Petitions, memorials, etc., were presented and referred as follows:

By Mr. Cameron: A memorial of the Chamber of Commerce of Pittsburg, Pa., praying the passage of the bill creating an Ohio River commission; to the Committee on Commerce.

A memorial of the Board of Trade of Philadelphia, Pa., praying the passage of a law for the creation of a Bureau to be known as the Department of Roads; to the Committee on Interstate Commerce.

By Mr. Brice: Three petitions of citizens of Ohio, praying the passage of a bill relating to contracts of common carriers, and to certain obligations, duties, and rights in connection with the carriage of property; to the Committee on Interstate Commerce.

By Mr. Peffer: Papers relating to the application of James Richardson for the removal of the charge of desertion from his military record; to the Committee on Military Affairs, to accompany the bill S. 3716.

By Mr. Gallinger: Papers relating to the application of George J. Barnes for the correction of his military record; to the Committee on Military Affairs, to accompany the bill S. 3720.

By Mr. Cameron: A petition of George Rushburger, praying compensation for the discovery and capture of Santa Anna's money at Cerro Gordo, Mexico, in April, 1847; to the Committee on Claims, to accompany the bill S. 3721.

By Mr. Sherman: A memorial of the American Cotton Oil Company, of Cincinnati, Ohio, praying the establishment of a department of roads, and for a road exhibit at the Columbian Exposition at the expense of the Government; to the Select Committee on the Quadro-Centennial.

Memorials, etc., praying the repeal of the law providing for the purchase of silver bullion, were presented as follows:

By Mr. Sherman: A memorial of the Trust National Bank, of Hamilton, Ohio.

By Mr. Hoar: A memorial of the Cold Cut Club, Waltham, Mass.

By Mr. Brice: Resolutions of the Chamber of Commerce of Cincinnati, Ohio.

Ordered, That they lie on the table.

Petitions praying the passage of the bill providing for the opening up of the Cherokee Strip to settlement were presented as follows:

By Mr. Coke: A petition of citizens of Texas.

By Mr. Mills: A petition of citizens of Texas.

By Mr. Vest: A petition of the Commercial Club of Kansas City, Mo.

By Mr. Cockrell: A petition of the Commercial Club of Kansas City, Mo.

Ordered, That they lie on the table.

Memorials, etc., praying the passage of the bill to restrict immigration into the United States, were presented as follows:

By Mr. Teller: A memorial of the Board of Trade of Denver, Colo.

By Mr. Sherman: A resolution of the State Board of Health of Ohio.

By Mr. Cameron: A petition of citizens of Pennsylvania.

By Mr. Brice: A resolution of the Ohio State Board of Health.

Ordered, That they lie on the table.

Mr. Sherman presented resolutions of the boards of health of certain cities of Ohio, praying the passage of a law conferring the control of the quarantine service to the United States, and for ample appropriations to prevent the introduction of cholera into the United States;

Ordered, That it lie on the table.

Mr. Cockrell presented a petition of Henry Hahman, praying to be allowed a pension; which was referred to the Committee on Pensions, to accompany the bill S. 3724.

Mr. Cockrell presented papers relating to the application of Mrs. Gabrilla P. Moody to be allowed a pension; which was referred to the Committee on Pensions.

Petitions praying the passage of the antioption bill were presented as follows:

By Mr. Brice: Several petitions of citizens of Ohio.

By Mr. Coke: A petition of citizens of Texas.

By Mr. Cockrell: A petition of citizens of Missouri.

Ordered, That they lie on the table.

Memorials remonstrating against the repeal of the provision providing for the closing of the Columbian Exposition on the Sabbath day were presented as follows:

By Mr. Stockbridge: Several memorials of citizens of Michigan.

By Mr. Frye: A memorial of citizens of Maine.

By Mr. Quay: Two memorials of citizens of Pennsylvania.

By Mr. Sherman: Four memorials of citizens of Ohio.

By Mr. Vest: A memorial of citizens of Missouri.

By Mr. Brice: Several memorials of citizens of Ohio.

By Mr. Cameron: Five memorials of citizens of Pennsylvania.

By Mr. Butler: A memorial of citizens of South Carolina.

By Mr. George: Two memorials of citizens of Mississippi.

Ordered, That they be referred to the Select Committee on the Quadro-Centennial.

REPORTS OF COMMITTEES.

Mr. Vest, from the Committee on Commerce, to whom was referred the bill (H. R. 10015) to authorize the construction of bridges across the Hiawassee, the Tennessee, and Clinch rivers, in the State of Tennessee, reported it without amendment.

On motion by Mr. Vest,

The Senate proceeded to consider, as in Committee of the Whole, the bill (S. 3525) to authorize the construction of bridges across the Hiawassee, the Tennessee, and Clinch rivers, in the State of Tennessee; and

Ordered, That it be postponed indefinitely.

Mr. Sawyer, from the Committee on Pensions, to whom was referred the bill (H. R. 8162) to pension Mary E. Trimble, widow of Montague N. Trimble, of Mexican war, submitted an adverse report (No. 1169) thereon.

Ordered, That it be placed on the Calendar.

INTRODUCTION OF BILLS AND JOINT RESOLUTION.

Bills and a joint resolution were introduced, read the first and second times by unanimous consent, and referred as follows:

By Mr. Peffer: A bill (S. 3716) for the relief of James Richardson; and

A bill (S. 3717) for the relief of John Kircher; to the Committee on Military Affairs.

By Mr. Berry: A bill (S. 3718) to authorize the Oklahoma Midland Railway Company to construct and operate a railway, telegraph, and telephone lines through the Indian and Oklahoma Territories, and for other purposes; to the Committee on Indian Affairs.

By Mr. Higgins: A bill (S. 3719) for the relief of Jasper Hanson; to the Committee on Claims.

By Mr. Gallinger: A bill (S. 3720) to set aside the verdict of a court-martial in the case of George J Barnes, late private in Company F, Second Regiment United States Sharpshooters, and Company H, Fifth New Hampshire Volunteer Infantry; to the Committee on Military Affairs.

By Mr. Cameron: A bill (S. 3721) for the relief of George Rushburger; to the Committee on Claims.

By Mr. Voorhees: A bill (S. 3722) to increase the pension of William G. Smith; to the Committee on Pensions.

A bill (S. 3723) to reimburse the Miami Indians of Indiana for money improperly withheld from them; to the Committee on Indian Affairs.

By Mr. Cockrell: A bill (S. 3724) granting a pension to Henry Hahman; to the Committee on Pensions.

By Mr. Quay: A joint resolution (S. R. 134) authorizing the exhibition at the World's Columbian Exposition of the picture entitled "The Recall of Columbus," by Angustus G. Heaton; to the Committee on the Library.

NICARAGUA CANAL.

Mr. Wolcott submitted the following resolution for consideration; which was ordered to be printed:

Be it resolved, That the Committee on Foreign Relations be directed to inquire what sums, if any, have been expended by the Maritime Canal Company, the Nicaragua Canal Construction Company, or any company allied to either of said companies, in and about the construction of said canal or otherwise, with the items of said expenditure, since the accounts of expenditure heretofore rendered to said committee.

The Vice-President laid before the Senate the resolution yesterday submitted by Mr. Morgan, instructing the Committee on Commerce to inquire and report what advantages, if any, will accrue to the interests of the United States by the building of a ship canal to connect the waters of the Atlantic and Pacific oceans through Lake Nicaragua; and

After debate,

Ordered, That it lie on the table.

HOUSE BILL AND RESOLUTIONS REFERRED.

The bill H. R. 10007, this day received from the House of Representatives for concurrence, was read the first and second times by unanimous consent, and referred to the Committee on Commerce.

The resolution to print 60,000 copies of the special report of the Bureau of Animal Industry on Diseases of Cattle and Cattle Feeding, and the resolution to print 60,000 copies of the special report on the Sheep Industry of the United States, this day received from the House of Representatives for concurrence, were read and referred to the Committee on Printing.

ELISHA BROWN.

On motion by Mr. Sawyer,

The Senate proceeded to consider, as in Committee of the Whole, the bill (H. R. 6969) for the relief of Elisha Brown; and no amendment being made, it was reported to the Senate.

Ordered, That it pass to a third reading.

The said bill was read the third time.

Resolved, That it pass.

Ordered, That the Secretary notify the House of Representatives thereof.

PRESENTATION OF BILLS.

Mr. Dubois reported from the committee that they this day presented to the President of the United States the following bills:

S. 3623. An act to amend the act of March 3, 1873, for the relief of the Columbian University in the District of Columbia; and

S. 118 An act for the relief of the estate of Isaac W. Talkington, deceased.

DEALINGS IN "OPTIONS" AND "FUTURES."

The Vice-President laid before the Senate the unfinished business at its adjournment yesterday. viz, the bill (H. R. 7845) defining "options" and "futures," imposing special taxes on dealers therein, and requiring such persons engaged in selling certain products to obtain license, and for other purposes;

When,

On motion by Mr. Wolcott, that the Senate proceed to the consideration of the first bill on the Calendar under Rule 8, viz, the bill (S. 88) for the relief of Hiram Somerville,

The yeas were 9 and the nays were 31.

On motion by Mr. Washburn,

The yeas and nays being desired by one-fifth of the Senators present,

Those who voted in the affirmative are,

Messrs. Brice, Caffery, Dixon, Palmer, Stewart, Vest, Vilas, White, Wolcott.

Those who voted in the negative are,

Messrs. Allison, Berry, Call, Carey, Chandler, Cockrell. Coke, Dawes, Dubois, Felton, Frye, Gallinger, George, Hansbrough, Higgins, Irby, Kyle, McMillan, Morgan, Peffer, Pettigrew, Pugh, Quay, Sawyer, Sherman, Shoup, Stockbridge, Teller, Vance, Washburn, Wilson.

The number of Senators voting not constituting a quorum,

On motion by Mr. Wolcott that the Senate adjourn,

It was determined in the negative, { Yeas .... 11 / Nays .... 31 }

On motion by Mr. Washburn,

The yeas and nays being desired by one-fifth of the Senators present,

Those who voted in the affirmative are,

Messrs. Brice, Caffery, Dixon, Hiscock, Hoar, Palmer, Quay, Vest, Vilas, White, Wolcott.

Those who voted in the negative are,

Messrs. Allison, Berry, Call, Carey, Chandler, Coke, Dawes, Dubois, Frye, Gallinger, George, Hale, Hansbrough, Higgins, Irby, Kyle, McMillan, Morgan, Peffer, Pettigrew. Proctor, Pugh, Sawyer, Sherman, Shoup, Stockbridge, Teller, Vance, Washburn, Wilson.

So the motion was not agreed to.

No quorum having voted,

The Vice-President directed the roll to be called;

When,
Forty-six Senators answered to their names.
A quorum being present,

EXECUTIVE SESSION.

On motion by Mr. Quay,
The Senate proceeded to the consideration of executive business; and
After the consideration of executive business the doors were re-opened, and
On motion by Mr. Quay, at 3 o'clock p. m.,
The Senate adjourned.

MONDAY, JANUARY 16, 1893.

EXECUTIVE COMMUNICATIONS.

The Vice-President laid before the Senate a letter of the Secretary of the Treasury, communicating further information relative to the purchase of a site for an appraisers' warehouse and custom-house in the city of New York, under the act of September 14, 1888; which was referred to the Committee on Public Buildings and Grounds and ordered to be printed.

The Vice-President laid before the Senate a letter of the Secretary of War, transmitting a report on the condition of the Mackinac National Park for the year ending December 31, 1893; which was referred to the Committee on Public Lands and ordered to be printed.

The Vice-President laid before the Senate a report of the Eckington and Soldiers' Home Railway Company of the District of Columbia for the year ending December 31, 1892; which was referred to the Committee on the District of Columbia and ordered to be printed.

PETITIONS AND MEMORIALS.

Petitions, memorials, etc., were presented and referred as follows:

By Mr. Peffer: Two petitions of citizens of Kansas, praying the passage of a law to prevent the sale of intoxicating liquors at the Soldiers' Home at Leavenworth; to the Committee on Military Affairs.

By Mr. Wilson: A resolution of the Republican and Democratic Territorial Central Committees, praying the passage of a law for the admission of the Territory of Arizona into the Union as a State; to the Committee on Territories.

By Mr. Manderson: A petition of citizens of Nebraska, praying the passage of a law so as to include within the boundaries of that State certain lands lying in the Missouri River; to the Committee on the Judiciary.

By Mr. Sawyer: A resolution of the Boston Associated Board of Trade, praying the passage of a law adding the telephone and telegraph to the postal system of the United States; to the Committee on Post-Offices and Post-Roads.

A resolution of the Association for the Advancement of Milwaukee, Wis., praying the repeal of the provision of law providing for the purchase of silver bullion; to the Committee on Finance.

By Mr. Washburn: A resolution of the Board of Trade of Minneapolis, Minn., praying the passage of a law for the encouragement of reciprocity with foreign nations; and

A petition of citizens of Minnesota, praying the passage of the bill limiting the amount of clothing that may be admitted free of duty; to the Committee on Finance.

A petition of citizens of Minnesota, praying the passage of a law creating a retired list for enlisted men after a continuous service of twenty-five years; to the Committee on Military Affairs.

By Mr. Manderson: Papers relating to the application of the Omaha Bridge and Terminal Railway Company for an extension of time for the completion of the bridge across the Missouri River near Council Bluffs, Iowa, and Omaha, Nebr.; to the Committee on Commerce, to accompany the bill S. 3727.

The Vice-President laid before the Senate a petition of citizens of the United States, praying the passage of the bill granting to women the right of suffrage.

Ordered, That it lie on the table.

Mr. Blackburn presented a resolution of the Kentucky State Nicaragua Canal Convention, praying the passage of the bill for the completion of the Nicaragua Canal under the direction and control of the Government.

Ordered, That it lie on the table.

Mr. Dolph presented a resolution of the legislature of Oregon, in favor of an extension of time to settlers upon lands within the limits of the forfeited land grant to the Northern Pacific Railroad Company in which to make final proof in all cases, to January 1, 1894; which was referred to the Committee on Public Lands.

Mr. Teller presented papers relating to the application of the citizens of Ouray, Colo., for the passage of a law authorizing the mayor of Ouray to enter in trust certain lands for township purposes; which were referred to the Committee on Public Lands, to accompany the bill S. 3729.

Mr. Washburn presented a petition of citizens of Minnesota, praying the passage of the antioption bill.

7 s

Ordered, That it lie on the table.

Memorials remonstrating against the repeal of the provision providing for the closing of the Columbian Exposition on the Sabbath day were presented as follows:

By Mr. Quay: Five memorials of citizens of Pennsylvania.

By Mr. Platt: A memorial of the Woman's Christian Temperance Union of the District of Columbia.

By Mr. Harris: Two memorials of citizens of Tennessee.

By Mr. Berry: Two memorials of citizens of Arkansas.

By Mr. Pettigrew: A memorial of citizens of South Dakota.

By Mr. Wilson: Several memorials of citizens of Iowa.

By Mr. Hoar: A memorial of citizens of Massachusetts.

By Mr. Peffer: Two memorials of citizens of Kansas.

By Mr. Kyle: Two memorials of citizens of South Dakota.

Ordered, That they be referred to the Select Committee on the Quadro-Centennial.

PRESENTATION OF BILLS.

Mr. Dubois reported from the committee that they this day presented to the President of the United States the following enrolled bill and resolution:

S. 3195. An act granting to the Yuma Pumping and Irrigation Company the right of way for two ditches across that part of the Yuma Indian Reservation lying in Arizona; and

S. R. 113. A joint resolution for the printing of the Agricultural Report for 1891.

REPORTS OF COMMITTEES.

Mr. Gallinger, from the Committee on Pensions, to whom was referred the bill (S. 3340) granting a pension to Elizabeth Ellery, reported it with amendments and submitted a report (No. 1170) thereon.

Mr. Proctor, from the Committee on Military Affairs, to whom was referred the bill (H. R. 4844) to authorize the Secretary of War to convey to school district No. 12, of Kittery, Me., a portion of Fort McClary military reservation, in exchange for other land, reported it without amendment.

The Senate proceeded, by unanimous consent, to consider the said bill as in Committee of the Whole; and no amendment being made, it was reported to the Senate.

Ordered, That it pass to a third reading.

The said bill was read the third time.

Resolved, That it pass.

Ordered, That the Secretary notify the House of Representatives thereof.

Mr. Proctor, from the Committee on Military Affairs, to whom was referred the bill (S. 3244) to authorize the Secretary of War to convey to school district No. 12, of Kittery, Me., a portion of Fort McClary military reservation, in exchange for other land, reported adversely thereon.

Ordered, That it be postponed indefinitely.

Mr. Manderson from the Committee on Printing, to whom was referred the resolution submitted by Mr. Hoar December 21, 1892, to print and bind 3,100 extra copies of the compilation entitled "Senate Privileges and Elections," prepared by the Committee on Privileges and Elections, reported it with amendments and submitted a report (No. 1171) thereon.

The Senate proceeded, by unanimous consent, to consider the said resolution; and the reported amendments having been agreed to, the resolution as amended was agreed to, as follows:

Resolved by the Senate (the House of Representatives concurring), That there be printed and bound, in addition to the usual number, 4,600 copies of the compilation entitled "Senate Privileges and Elections," prepared by the Committee on Privileges and Elections under a resolution of the Senate passed February 28, 1891, said work to be bound in two volumes, the first to contain all Senate election cases to date and the second to contain all matter pertaining to Senate privileges, of which 1,500 copies shall be for the use of the Senate, 3,000 copies for the use of the House of Representatives, and 100 for the compiler.

Ordered, That the Secretary request the concurrence of the House of Representatives therein.

Mr. Manderson, from the Committee on Printing, to whom was referred the report of the Superintendent of the Coast and Geodetic Survey for the fiscal year ending June 30, 1892, reported in favor of printing the same, and submitted a report (No. 1172); which was agreed to.

Mr. Vest, from the Committee on Commerce, to whom was referred the bill (H. R. 10097) to provide for lowering the height of a bridge proposed to be constructed across the Ohio River between Cincinnati, Ohio, and Covington, Ky., by the Cincinnati and Covington Rapid Transit Bridge Company, reported it without amendment.

INTRODUCTION OF BILLS.

Bills were introduced, read the first and second times by unanimous consent, and referred as follows:

By Mr. Jones, of Arkansas: A bill (S. 3725) authorizing the construction of a free bridge across the Arkansas River, connecting Little Rock and Argenta; to the Committee on Commerce.

By Mr. Manderson: A bill (S. 3726) for the relief of Harrison Wagner; to the Committee on Pensions.

A bill (S. 3727) to amend "An act authorizing the construction of a railway, street-railway, motor, wagon, and pedestrian bridge over the Missouri River near Council Bluffs, Iowa, and from Omaha, Nebr., and to extend the time for the completion of the bridge therein provided for; to the Committee on Commerce.

By Mr. Dolph: A bill (S. 3728) for the relief of the Blalock Wheat Growing Company; to the Committee on Public Lands.

By Mr. Teller: A bill (S. 3729) for the relief of the citizens of Ouray, in the State of Colorado; to the Committee on Public Lands.

By Mr. Chandler: A bill (S. 3730) in amendment of the provisions of the Revised Statutes relative to national banks; to the Select Committee on Failed National Banks.

By Mr. Squire: A bill (S. 3731) for the purpose of increasing the efficiency of the coast defenses; to the Committee on Naval Affairs.

MESSAGE FROM THE HOUSE.

A message from the House of Representatives, by Mr. Towles, its chief clerk:

Mr. President: The House of Representatives has passed the following bills, in which it requests the concurrence of the Senate:

H. R. 9190. An act to ratify and confirm an agreement with the Cherokee Nation of Indians of the Indian Territory, to make appropriation for carrying out the same, and for other purposes; and

H. R. 10189. An act relating to proof of citizenship of applicants for Indian war pensions under the act of Congress approved July 27, 1892.

HOUSE BILLS REFERRED.

The bills last received from the House of Representatives for concurrence were read the first and second times by unanimous consent.

Ordered, That the bill H. R. 10189 be referred to the Committee on Pensions, and that the bill H. R. 9190 lie on the table.

FUNERAL OF SENATOR KENNA.

Mr. Blackburn submitted the following resolution; which was referred to the Committee to Audit and Control the Contingent Expenses of the Senate:

Resolved, That the expenses incurred by the select committee appointed to take order for the funeral of the late Senator Kenna be paid from the contingent fund of the Senate.

PARIS EXPOSITION REPORTS.

Mr. Manderson submitted the following concurrent resolution; which was referred to the Committee on Printing:

Resolved by the Senate (the House of Representatives concurring), That in addition to the usual number, there shall be printed 5,000 extra copies of the reports of the Commissioners of the United States to the Paris Exposition of 1889, 1,000 copies for the use of the Senate, 2,000 copies for the use of the House, and 2,000 copies for the use of the Department of State.

EMPLOYMENT OF ARMED MEN FOR PRIVATE PURPOSES.

Mr. Gallinger submitted the following resolution; which was considered by unanimous consent and agreed to:

Resolved, That the select committee to investigate the facts in relation to the employment of armed bodies of men for private purposes be authorized to continue during the present session the inquiries directed by resolution of the Senate of August 2, 1892, with all the powers conferred by said resolution.

NICARAGUA CANAL.

The Vice-President laid before the Senate the resolution submitted by Mr. Wolcott on the 14th instant, directing the Committee on Foreign Relations to inquire what sums have been expended by the Maritime Canal Company of Nicaragua; and

The resolution was considered and agreed to.

CLAIMS OF NEW YORK INDIANS.

On motion by Mr. Hiscock,

The Senate, proceeded to consider, as in Committee of the Whole the bill (S. 3407) to authorize the Court of Claims to hear and determine the claims of certain New York Indians against the United States; and no amendment being made, it was reported to the Senate.

Ordered, That it be engrossed and read a third time.

The said bill was read the third time.

Resolved, That it pass, and that the title thereof be as aforesaid.

Ordered, That the Secretary request the concurrence of the House of Representatives therein.

FUNERAL OF SENATOR KENNA.

Mr. Vance, from the Committee to Audit and Control the Contingent Expenses of the Senate, to whom was referred the resolution submitted by Mr. Blackburn to pay the expenses of the committee appointed to take order for the funeral of the late Senator Kenna, reported it without amendment; and

The resolution was considered by unanimous consent and agreed to.

CLAIM OF WILLIAM M'GARRAHAN.

The Senate resumed the reconsideration of the bill (S. 1958) to submit to the Court of Private Lands Claims, established by an act of Congress approved March 3, 1891, the title of William McGarrahan to the Rancho Panoche Grande, in the State of California, and for other purposes, returned by the President of the United States to the Senate with his objections thereto; and

After debate,

Ordered, That the further consideration thereof be postponed to to-morrow.

R. L. JENNINGS.

On motion by Mr. Mills,

The Senate proceeded to consider, as in Committee of the Whole, the bill (H. R. 3676) for the relief of R. L. Jennings, late postmaster at Marshall, Tex.; and the reported amendment having been agreed to, the bill was reported to the Senate and the amendment was concurred in.

Ordered, That the amendment be engrossed and the bill read a third time.

The said bill as amended was read the third time.

Resolved, That it pass, and that the Senate request a conference with the House of Representatives on the bill and amendment.

Ordered, That the conferees on the part of the Senate be appointed by the Vice-President; and

The Vice-President appointed Mr. Sawyer, Mr. Mills, and Mr. Irby.

Ordered, That the Secretary notify the House of Representatives thereof.

THE PRESIDENTAL TERM.

On motion by Mr. Peffer,

The Senate proceeded to consider, as in Committee of the Whole, the joint resolution (S. R. 96) to limit the office of President to one term for each incumbent; and

Pending debate,

DEALINGS IN "OPTIONS" AND "FUTURES."

The Presiding Officer (Mr. Platt in the chair) announced that the hour of 2 o'clock had arrived, and laid before the Senate the unfinished business at its last adjournment, viz, the bill (H. R. 7845) defining "options" and "futures," imposing special taxes on dealers therein, and requiring such persons engaged in selling certain products to obtain license, and for other purposes; and

The Senate resumed, as in Committee of the Whole, the consideration of the bill; and

The question being on the amendment proposed by Mr. Vilas,

After debate,

Mr. Platt raised a question as to the presence of a quorum;

Whereupon,

The Vice-President directed the roll to be called;

When,

Forty-six Senators answered to their names,

A quorum being present,

On the question to agree to the amendment proposed by Mr. Vilas, viz: In line 15, section 2, after the words "owner thereof" insert *and does not in good faith intend to purchase and deliver the articles contracted to be sold and delivered according to the terms and requirements of such contract,*

It was determined in the negative, { Yeas .... 12 | Nays 33

The yeas and nays having been heretofore ordered.

Those who voted in the affirmative are,

Messrs. Caffery, Dixon, Gibson, Jones of Arkansas, McPherson, Mills, Palmer, Power, Stewart, Vest, Vilas, White.

Those who voted in the negative are,

Messrs. Allison, Berry, Blackburn, Call, Carey, Chandler, Cockrell, Coke, Dawes, Dolph, Dubois, Gallinger, George, Gordon, Hale, Hansbrough, Higgins, Hunton, Kyle, McMillan, Manderson, Morgan, Peffer, Pugh, Quay, Ransom, Sherman, Stockbridge, Vance, Voorhees, Walthall, Washburn, Wilson.

So the amendment was not agreed to.

The bill having been further amended on the motion of Mr. Washburn, and

The question recurring on the amendment proposed by Mr. Daniel, viz: Strike out the tenth section of the bill in the following words:

"SEC. 10. Whenever any contract or agreement for the sale and future delivery of any of the articles mentioned in section 3 of this act shall be made, and the making thereof shall not be reported by the collector of internal revenue, as required by section 9, and it shall come to the knowledge of such collector, or he shall have reasonable cause to believe that the party by whom such contract or agreement was made as vendor was not, at the time of the making thereof, the owner of the article or articles which were the subject of, embraced in, or covered by such contract or agreement, and had not then acquired, and was not then entitled to the right to the future possession of such article or articles under and by virtue of a contract or agreement for the sale and future delivery thereof previously made by the owner of such article or articles, it shall be the duty of such collector to require the party who shall have made such contract or agreement as vendor to forthwith furnish to such collector proof of such vendor's ownership, or right or title to the future possession of the article or articles so embraced in or covered by such contract or agreement, and said party shall thereupon make, and file with such collector, an affidavit stating by whom the said article or articles were owned at the time said contract or agreement was made, and, if affiant was not at that time such owner, whether at the time of making such contract or agreement affiant was entitled to the right to the future possession of said article or articles, and how such right was acquired. Such affidavit shall also state the warehouse, elevator, or other place where said article or articles are stored, or, if the same be then in the possession of a vessel, railroad, or other carrier for transportation, the name of such vessel, railroad, or carrier, and the number and date of each separate bill of lading or receipt issued by such vessel, railroad, or carrier thereof, and the amount or quantity of such article or articles called for by such bill of lading or receipt; and such affidavit shall further state the amount or quantity of other articles of the kind embraced in and covered by such contract or agreement which said affiant is then the owner of, or entitled to the possession of, and any and all contracts or agreements which affiant may have made, and which are then outstanding and remaining uncanceled, for the sale and future delivery of any such article or articles of such kind. And said party is further required, if demanded by such collector, to exhibit to the collector the original receipt of the warehouse or elevator where the aforesaid article or articles are then stored, or the bill of lading or receipt of the vessel, railroad, or other carrier having possession of said article or articles for transportation. And in case said party shall fail or refuse to make and file with the collector the said affidavit when so required, or shall fail or refuse to exhibit the said warehouse or elevator receipt or said bill of lading, when so demanded, such failure or refusal shall constitute and be deemed and held to be prima facie evidence that the contract or agreement so made by said party was a 'futures' contract or agreement as described and defined in section 2 of this act, and said party shall thereupon become liable and be required to pay to said collector upon the article or articles which are the subject of, embraced in, or covered by such contract or agreement, the amount or amounts of special taxes imposed and required by section 4 of this act to be paid for and upon an article or articles of the same kind when sold under any 'futures' contract or agreement; and if when such contract was made the party making the same was not authorized, by a certificate issued to him under the provisions of section 5 of this act, to make 'futures' contracts or agreements, then said party shall also become liable and be required to pay the further sum of $1,000 prescribed by said section 5 of this act as a license fee for conducting the business of dealer in 'futures,'"

It was determined in the negative, { Yeas .... 13 / Nays 32

On motion by Mr. Palmer,
The yeas and nays being desired by one-fifth of the Senators present, Those who voted in the affirmative are,
Messrs. Brice, Caffery, Dixon, Gibson, Hill, Jones of Arkansas, Mills, Palmer, Pugh, Sawyer, Stewart, Vest, White.
Those who voted in the negative are,
Messrs. Allison, Berry, Blackburn, Call, Carey, Chandler, Cockrell, Coke, Dawes, Dubois, Felton, Frye, Gallinger, George, Gordon, Hansbrongh, Hunton, Kyle, McMillan, Manderson, Peffer, Power, Quay, Sherman, Squire, Stockbridge, Teller, Vance, Voorhees, Walthall, Washburn, Wilson.
So the amendment was not agreed to.
A further amendment having been proposed by Mr. George,
Pending debate,
On motion by Mr. Stewart, at 5 o'clock and 27 minutes p. m.,
The Senate adjourned.

TUESDAY, JANUARY 17, 1893.

EXECUTIVE COMMUNICATIONS.

The Vice-President laid before the Senate two communications from the Secretary of State, transmitting, in pursuance of the provisions of the act of February 3, 1887, certified copies of the final ascertainment of the electors for President and Vice-President in the States of Wisconsin and Wyoming.
Ordered, That they lie on the table.
The Vice-President laid before the Senate a letter of the Secretary of the Treasury, transmitting, in compliance with a resolution of the Senate of the 13th instant, a copy of the opinion of the law officer of the Treasury Department relative to the issuance and de-

livery of the souvenir coins in aid of the World's Columbian Exposition; which was referred to the Committee on the Quadro-Centennial and ordered to be printed.

PETITIONS AND MEMORIALS.

Petitions, memorials, etc., were presented and referred as follows:
By the Vice-President: Resolutions of the California Board of Lady Managers of the World's Fair Commission, praying the passage of a law to permit the opening of the Exposition of Sundays; to the Select Committee on the Quadro-Centennial.
By Mr. Quay: A petition of citizens of Pennsylvania, praying the passage of the bill to limit the amount of clothing that may be admitted free of duty; to the Committee on Finance.
By Mr. Felton: Resolutions of the legislature of California in favor of the passage of the bill to create the California Mining Débris Commission, and to regulate hydraulic mining in said State; to the Committee on Mines and Mining.
Mr. Sherman presented a petition of citizens of Ohio, praying the passage of the antioption bill
Ordered, That it lie on the table.
Mr. Sherman presented resolutions of the boards of health of certain towns in Ohio, praying the passage of a law for the establishment of a national quarantine and for the suspension of immigration until the quarantine defenses of the country shall have been placed in a condition for protection against contagious diseases.
Ordered, That they lie on the table.
Mr. Sherman presented a petition of citizens of Ohio, praying the passage of a law for the restriction of immigration into the United States.
Ordered, That it lie on the table.
Mr. Dolph presented a petition of citizens of Oregon, praying the passage of the bill extending the time for settlers to make final proof and payment for lands within the limits of the forfeited land grant to the Northern Pacific Railroad Company.
Ordered, That it lie on the table.
Mr. Mills presented a petition of citizens of Texas, praying the passage of a law for the opening up of the Cherokee Outlet to settlement.
Ordered, That it lie on the table.
Petitions, etc., praying the repeal of the provision of law providing for the purchase of silver bullion, were presented as follows:
By Mr. Aldrich: A petition of citizens of Rhode Island.
By Mr. Sawyer: Resolutions of the Merchants' Association of Milwaukee, and resolutions of the Bankers' Association of Superior, Wis.
By Mr. Sherman: A memorial of the Board of Trade of Dayton, Ohio.
Ordered, That they be referred to the Committee on Finance.
Petitions praying the repeal of the provision providing for the opening of the Columbian Exposition on the Sabbath day were presented as follows:
By Mr. Pettigrew: Three petitions of citizens of South Dakota.
By Mr. McMillan: A petition of citizens of Michigan.
By Mr. Kyle: A petition of citizens of South Dakota.
By Mr. Dubois: A petition of citizens of Idaho.
By Mr. Dolph: A petition of citizens of Oregon.
By Mr. Hiscock: A petition of citizens of New York.
By Mr. Mitchell: Two petitions of citizens of Oregon.
By Mr. Mills: Two petitions of citizens of Texas.
By Mr. Vest: A petition of citizens of Missouri.
By Mr. Cockrell: A petition of citizens of Missouri.
Ordered, That they be referred to the Select Committee on the Quadro-Centennial.
Memorials remonstrating against the repeal of the provision providing for the closing of the Columbian Exposition on the Sabbath day were presented as follows:
By the Vice-President: Several memorials of citizens of the United States.
By Mr. Quay: Several memorials of citizens of Pennsylvania.
By Mr. Stockbridge: Four memorials of citizens of Michigan.
By Mr. Cockrell: A memorial of citizens of Missouri.
By Mr. Vest: A memorial of citizens of Missouri.
By Mr. Pettigrew: Several memorials of citizens of South Dakota.
Ordered, That they be referred to the Select Committee on the Quadro-Centennial.

MESSAGE FROM THE HOUSE.

A message from the House of Representatives, by Mr. Towles, its chief clerk:
Mr. President: The House of Representatives has passed, without amendments, the bill (S. 1292) to remit the penalties on the light-house steamer Pansy.
The House of Representatives has passed the following joint resolutions, in which it requests the concurrence of the Senate.
H. R. 71. Joint resolution to authorize the Secretary of the Interior to continue the report on wages by Joseph D. Weeks; and
H. R. 90. Joint resolution proposing an amendment to the Constitution providing that Senators shall be elected by the people of the several States.

The Speaker of the House of Representatives having signed an enrolled bill, H. R. 8038, I am directed to bring it to the Senate for the signature of its President.

The President of the United States has informed the House of Representatives that he has approved and signed acts and joint resolutions as follows:

On December 13, 1892:

H. R. 167. Joint resolution relating to the discharge of certain official duties in the office of Register of the Treasury.

On December 16:

H. R. 8868. An act granting increase of pension to Mary North, a widow of a soldier of the war of 1812, and who is 100 years old.

On December 20:

H. R. 170. Joint resolution to pay the officers and employés of the Senate and House of Representatives their respective salaries for the month of December, 1892, on the 21st day of said month.

On December 22:

H. R. 8760. An act to provide for the sale of navy-yard lands in the city of Brooklyn; and

H. R. 6024. An act for the relief of William H. Taylor.

On January 5, 1893:

H. R. 9417. An act to incorporate the Protestant Episcopal Cathedral Foundation of the District of Columbia.

On January 7:

H. R. 6644. An act to amend an act entitled "An act authorizing the sale of title of the United States in lot 3 in square south of square 990," approved March 3, 1891.

On January 9:

H. R. 6737. An act granting a pension to Delzell R. Bradford, Twenty-fourth Michigan Volunteers;

H. R. 8907. An act to increase the pension of John Malloy;

H. R. 9487. An act to amend an act approved April 22, authorizing the Natchitoches Cane River Bridge Company to construct and maintain a bridge across Cane River in Louisiana; and

H. R. 9488. An act to amend an act approved March 2, 1891, authorizing the construction of a bridge across the Red River, Louisiana, by the Rapides Bridge Company, limited.

HOUSE JOINT RESOLUTIONS REFERRED.

The joint resolutions last received from the House of Representatives for concurrence were read the first and second times by unanimous consent.

Ordered, That the joint resolution H. R. 71 be referred to the Committee on Education and Labor, and that the joint resolution H. R. 90 be referred to the Committee on Privileges and Elections.

ENROLLED BILL SIGNED.

Mr. Dubois reported from the committee that they had examined and found duly enrolled the bill (H. R. 8038) granting a pension to William M. Watson, of Walker County, Georgia.

Whereupon,

The Vice-President signed the same, and it was delivered to the committee to be presented to the President of the United States.

REPORTS OF COMMITTEES.

Mr. Dolph, from the Committee on Public Lands, to whom was referred the bill (S. 3581) to amend an act entitled "An act to forfeit certain lands heretofore granted for the purpose of aiding in the construction of railroads, and for other purposes," reported it with amendments and submitted a report (No. 1173) thereon.

The Senate proceeded, by unanimous consent, to consider the said bill as in Committee of the Whole; and the reported amendments having been agreed to, and the bill further amended on the motion of Mr. Dolph, it was reported to the Senate and the amendments were concurred in.

Ordered, That the bill be engrossed and read a third time.

The said bill was read the third time.

Resolved, That it pass, and that the title thereof be as aforesaid.

Ordered, That the Secretary request the concurrence of the House of Representatives therein.

Mr. Sherman, from the Committee on Finance, to whom was referred the bill (S. 3423) for the repeal of certain parts of the act directing the purchase of silver bullion and the issue of Treasury notes thereon, and for other purposes, approved July 14, 1890, reported it with amendments.

Mr. Hunton, from the Committee on Education and Labor, to whom was referred the joint resolution (S. R. 121) authorizing payment, under act of August 30, 1890, to the State of Virginia, upon the assent of the governor, heretofore given, until adjournment of next session of legislature thereof, reported it without amendment.

The Senate proceeded, by unanimous consent, to consider the said resolution as in Committee of the Whole; and no amendment being made, it was reported to the Senate.

Ordered, That it be engrossed and read a third time.

The said resolution was read the third time.

Resolved, That it pass, and that the title thereof be as aforesaid.

Ordered, That the Secretary request the concurrence of the House of Representatives therein.

Mr. Kyle, from the Committee on Education and Labor, to whom was referred the joint resolution (S. R. 116) extending the powers of the United States Government Exhibit Board, reported it without amendment.

Mr. Pettigrew, from the Committee on Indian Affairs, to whom was referred the bill (S. 3459) to secure the relinquishment of the Indian title to a portion of the Pyramid Lake Reservation, in Nevada, and to the entire Walker River Reservation, in said State, and for other purposes, reported it without amendment.

Mr. McMillan, from the Committee on the District of Columbia, reported a joint resolution (S. R. 135) making an appropriation of $5,000 for clearing the Potomac River of ice; which was read the first and second times by unanimous consent and considered as in Committee of the Whole; and no amendment being made, it was reported to the Senate.

Ordered, That it be engrossed and read a third time.

The said resolution was read the third time by unanimous consent.

Resolved, That it pass, and that the title thereof be as aforesaid.

Ordered, That the Secretary request the concurrence of the House of Representatives therein.

Mr. Carey, from the Committee on Public Lands, to whom was referred the bill (S. 3643) to provide for the disposal of the Fort Bridger abandoned military reservation, in the State of Wyoming, reported it without amendment.

The Senate proceeded, by unanimous consent, to consider the said bill as in Committee of the Whole; and no amendment being made, it was reported to the Senate.

Ordered, That it be engrossed and read a third time.

The said bill was read the third time.

Resolved, That it pass, and that the title thereof be as aforesaid.

Ordered, That the Secretary request the concurrence of the House of Representatives therein.

Mr. Sawyer, from the Committee on Post-Offices and Post-Roads, to whom was referred the bill (S. 3580) to amend the proviso to be found in connection with the free-delivery service, page 569, twenty-fourth volume, Statutes at Large, reported it without amendment and submitted a report (No. 1175) thereon.

The Senate proceeded, by unanimous consent, to consider the said bill as in Committee of the Whole; and no amendment being made, it was reported to the Senate.

Ordered, That it be engrossed and read a third time.

The said bill was read the third time.

Resolved, That it pass, and that the title thereof be as aforesaid.

Ordered, That the Secretary request the concurrence of the House of Representatives therein.

INTRODUCTION OF BILLS AND JOINT RESOLUTION.

Bills and a joint resolution were introduced, read the first and second times by unanimous consent, and referred as follows:

By Mr. Hale: A bill (S. 3732) to amend the act approved June 8, 1880, relating to the pay of the Judge-Advocate-General of the Navy; to the Committee on Naval Affairs.

By Mr. Butler: A bill (S. 3733) to empower Robert Adger and others to bring suit in the Court of Claims for rent alleged to be due them; to the Committee on Claims.

A joint resolution (S. R. 136) providing for the disposition of arrears of pay and bounty due the estates of deceased colored soldiers; to the Committee on Military Affairs.

ARTESIAN-WELL AND IRRIGATION MACHINERY.

Mr. Cockrell submitted the following resolution; which was referred to the Committee on Irrigation and Reclamation of Arid Lands:

Resolved, That the Secretary of Agriculture be directed to submit to the Senate as early as practicable the report on artesian well and irrigation machinery now in course of preparation under his direction, the expense of completing said report to be paid out of the money appropriated in the act of July 5, 1892: "To enable the Secretary of Agriculture to collect information as to the best modes of agriculture by irrigation, $6,000."

PAPERS WITHDRAWN AND REFERRED.

On motion by Mr. Dolph,

Ordered, That the petition and papers of Mrs. Susan A. Shelby be withdrawn from the files of the Senate and referred to the Committee on Claims.

PRESIDENTIAL TERM.

On motion by Mr. Peffer,

The Senate resumed, as in Committee of the Whole, the consideration of the joint resolution (S. R. 96) to limit the office of President to one term for each incumbent; and

After debate,

Ordered, That the further consideration thereof be postponed to to-morrow.

CLAIM OF WILLIAM M'GARRAHAN.

The Senate resumed the reconsideration of the bill (S. 1958) to submit to the Court of Private Land Claims, established by an act of Congress approved March 3, 1891, the title of William McGarrabau to the Rancho Panoche Grande, in the State of California, and for other purposes, returned by the President of the United States to the Senate with his objections thereto, and,

After debate,

On the question, Shall the bill pass, the objections of the President notwithstanding?

It was determined in the negative, { Yeas .... 29 / Nays 18

Those who voted in the affirmative are,

Messrs. Blodgett, Brice, Butler, Call, Carey, Chandler, Coke, Dawes, Dubois, Gallinger, George, Gibson, Gordon, Gorman, Hansbrough, Hunton, Jones of Arkansas, Kyle, Mitchell, Morgan, Peffer, Pettigrew, Power, Pugh, Teller, Vance, Voorhees, Washburn, Wilson.

Those who voted in the negative are,

Messrs. Allison, Caffery, Dixon, Dolph, Frye, Higgins, Hoar, McMillan, Mills, Morrill, Palmer, Platt, Sawyer, Sherman, Stewart, Stockbridge, Walthall, White.

So it was

Resolved, That the bill do not pass, two-thirds of the Senators present not having voted in the affirmative.

MESSAGE FROM THE HOUSE.

A message from the House of Representatives, by Mr. Towles, its chief clerk:

Mr. President: The House of Representatives has passed, without amendment, the following bills of the Senate:

S. 2625. An act to provide for the punishment of offenses on the high seas; and

S. 3537. An act for the relief of M. P. Deady.

The House of Representatives has passed the joint resolution (S. R. 128) to authorize the Secretary of War to grant permits for the use of reservations and public spaces in the city of Washington, and for other purposes, with amendments, in which it requests the concurrence of the Senate.

The House of Representatives has agreed to the amendment of the Senate to the bill (H. R. 3676) for the relief of R. L. Jennings, late postmaster at Marshall, Tex.

The House of Representatives has passed the following resolution, in which it requests the concurrence of the Senate:

Resolved by the House of Representatives (the Senate concurring), That the two Houses of Congress shall assemble in the Hall of the House of Representatives on Wednesday, the 8th day of February, 1893, at 1 o'clock in the afternoon, pursuant to the requirement of the Constitution and laws relating to the election of President and Vice-President of the United States, and the President of the Senate shall be the presiding officer; that two persons be appointed tellers on the part of the Senate, and two on the part of the House of Representatives, to make a list of the votes as they shall be declared; that the result shall be delivered to the President of the Senate, who shall announce the state of the vote and the persons elected to the two Houses assembled as aforesaid, which shall be deemed a declaration of the persons elected President and Vice-President of the United States, and, together with a list of the votes, be entered on the journals of the two Houses.

BRIDGES IN TENNESSEE.

On motion by Mr. Gordon,

The Senate proceeded to consider, as in Committee of the Whole, the bill (H. R. 10015) to authorize the construction of bridges across the Hiawassee, the Tennessee, and Clinch rivers, in the State of Tennessee; and no amendment being made, it was reported to the Senate.

Ordered, That it pass to a third reading.

The said bill was read the third time.

Resolved, That it pass.

Ordered, That the Secretary notify the House of Representatives thereof.

HOUSE AMENDMENTS AGREED TO.

The Senate proceeded to consider the amendments of the House of Representatives to the joint resolution (S. R. 128) to authorize the Secretary of War to grant permits for the use of reservations and public spaces in the city of Washington, and for other purposes; and

On motion by Mr. Gorman,

Resolved, That the Senate agree thereto.

Ordered, That the Secretary notify the House of Representatives thereof.

HOUSE RESOLUTION REFERRED.

The resolution providing for counting the votes for President and Vice-President, last received from the House of Representatives for concurrence, was read and referred to the Committee on Privileges and Elections.

DEALINGS IN OPTIONS AND FUTURES.

The Senate resumed, as in Committee of the Whole, the consideration of the bill (H. R. 7845) defining "options" and "futures," imposing special taxes on dealers therein, and requiring such persons engaged in selling certain products to obtain license, and for other purposes; and

The question being on the amendment proposed by Mr. George, Pending debate,

EXECUTIVE SESSION.

On motion by Mr. Sawyer,

The Senate proceeded to the consideration of executive business; and

After the consideration of executive business the doors were reopened, and

On motion by Mr. Sawyer, at 5 o'clock and 10 minutes p. m., The Senate adjourned.

WEDNESDAY, JANUARY 18, 1893.

The Vice-President being absent, the President *pro tempore* assumed the chair.

DEATH OF EX-PRESIDENT HAYES.

Mr. Sherman announced the death of the honorable Rutherford Birchard Hayes, ex-President of the United States, which occurred last evening at his residence at Fremont, Ohio; and he moved that out of respect to his memory the Senate do now adjourn.

The motion was unanimously agreed to; and

The Senate adjourned.

THURSDAY, JANUARY 19, 1893.

EXECUTIVE COMMUNICATIONS.

The President *pro tempore* laid before the Senate a letter of the Secretary of the Interior, transmitting the fifth annual report of the commissioner of schools of Utah Territory; which was referred to the Committee on Territories and ordered to be printed.

The President *pro tempore* laid before the Senate a communication of the Secretary of State, transmitting, in pursuance of the provisions of the act of February 3, 1887, certified copies of the final ascertainment of electors in the State of Tennessee.

Ordered, That it lie on the table.

The President *pro tempore* laid before the Senate the report of the Washington and Arlington Railway Company of the District of Columbia and the report of the District of Columbia Suburban Railway Company of the District of Columbia; which were referred to the Committee on the District of Columbia and ordered to be printed.

PETITIONS AND MEMORIALS.

Petitions, memorials, etc., were presented and referred as follows:

By Mr. Blackburn: A resolution of the legislature of Kentucky in favor of the repeal of the Federal election law; to the Committee on Privileges and Elections and ordered to be printed.

By Mr. Cameron: A memorial of the Board of Trade of Philadelphia, Pa., praying the passage of the Torrey bankruptcy bill; to the Committee on the Judiciary.

By Mr. McMillan: Ten petitions of citizens of the District of Columbia, praying the passage of the bill to incorporate the Washington, Fairfax and Alexandria Railway Company; to the Committee on the District of Columbia.

By Mr. Frye: Several memorials of citizens of the United States, praying an amendment to the Constitution prohibiting the manufacture, importation, and sale of intoxicating liquors throughout the United States; to the Committee on Education and Labor.

By Mr. Cullom: Several petitions of citizens of Illinois, praying for the appointment of a committee to investigate an alleged combine, formed to depreciate the price of grain by the millers, elevators, and railways at St. Louis and Minneapolis; to the Committee on Agriculture and Forestry.

Papers relating to the application of Sarah B. Stebbins to be allowed a pension; to the Committee on Pensions, to accompany the bill S. 3739.

Mr. White presented a resolution of the National Board of Trade, remonstrating against the passage of the antioption bill.

Ordered, That it lie on the table.

Mr. Cockrell presented a memorial of Caroline F. Corbin in behalf of herself and other remonstrants, remonstrating against the passage of the amendment to the Constitution proposing to give to women the right of suffrage.

Ordered, That it lie on the table and be printed.

Mr. Peffer presented a petition of settlers of lands ceded to the United States by the Pottawatomie, the Shawnee, and Cheyenne and Arapaho Indians of Oklahoma Territory, praying for an extension of time in which to make payment for their lands.

Ordered, That it lie on the table.

Mr. Felton presented a memorial of fruit-growers of California, praying the passage of the bill for the completion of the Nicaragua Canal under the direction and control of the United States.

Ordered, That it lie on the table.

Petitions praying the passage of a law for the creation of a bureau to be known as the Department of Roads were presented as follows:

By Mr. Felton: A petition of citizens of California.

By Mr. Brice: Two petitions of citizens of Ohio.

Ordered, That they be referred to the Committee on Agriculture and Forestry.

Memorials, etc., praying the repeal of the provision of law providing for the purchase of silver bullion, were presented as follows:

By Mr. Dawes: A resolution of the Boston Stock Exchange, and two memorials of citizens of Massachusetts.

By Mr. Hoar: A memorial of the Westminster National Bank.

By Mr. Cameron: A memorial of the Chamber of Commerce of Pittsburg, Pa.; a memorial of the Commercial Exchange of Philadelphia, Pa.

By Mr. Brice: A memorial of the Board of Trade of Dayton, Ohio.

Ordered, That they lie on the table.

Memorials, etc., praying the passage of a national quarantine law and for the restriction of immigration into the United States, were presented as follows:

By Mr. Cameron: A memorial of the Chamber of Commerce of Pittsburg, Pa.

By Mr. Sherman: Resolutions of boards of health of certain towns in Ohio.

By Mr. Brice: Resolutions of boards of health of certain towns in Ohio.

Ordered, That they lie on the table.

Petitions praying the passage of the antioption bill were presented as follows:

By Mr. Sherman: A petition of citizens of Ohio.

By Mr. Cameron: A petition of citizens of Pennsylvania.

By Mr. Brice: A petition of citizens of Ohio.

Ordered, That they lie on the table.

Petitions praying the passage of a law for the suspension of immigration into the United States for one year, and for the appointment of a commission to investigate the subject of immigration, were presented as follows:

By Mr. Quay: Several petitions of citizens of Pennsylvania.

By Mr. Dawes: A petition of citizens of Massachusetts.

By Mr. Sawyer: Several petitions of citizens of Wisconsin.

By Mr. Cameron: Four petitions of citizens of Pennsylvania.

By Mr. Hawley: A petition of citizens of Connecticut.

By Mr. McPherson: Several petitions of citizens of New Jersey.

By Mr. Sherman: A petition of citizens of Ohio.

Ordered, That they be referred to the Committee on Immigration.

Petitions praying the repeal of the provision providing for the closing of the Columbian Exposition on the Sabbath day were presented as follows:

By Mr. Wilson: A petition of citizens of Iowa.

By Mr. Cullom: Two petitions of citizens of Illinois.

By Mr. Harris: Two petitions of citizens of Tennessee.

By Mr. Shoup: Two petitions of citizens of Idaho.

By Mr. Cameron: Several petitions of citizens of Pennsylvania.

By Mr. Dolph: Two petitions of citizens of Oregon.

By Mr. Dawes: Four petitions of citizens of Massachusetts.

By Mr. Sawyer: Several petitions of citizens of Wisconsin.

By Mr. Brice: A petition of citizens of Ohio.

Ordered, That they be referred to the Select Committee on the Quadro-Centennial.

Memorials remonstrating against the repeal of the provision providing for the closing of the Columbian Exposition were presented as follows:

By Mr. Quay: A memorial of citizens of Pennsylvania.

By Mr. Cullom: Several memorials of citizens of Illinois.

By Mr. Stockbridge: A memorial of citizens of Michigan.

By Mr. Proctor: A memorial of citizens of Vermont.

By Mr. Wilson: A memorial of citizens of Iowa.

By Mr. Sherman: A memorial of citizens of Ohio.

By Mr. Dubois: A memorial of citizens of Idaho.

By Mr. Shoup: A memorial of citizens of Idaho.

By Mr. Hoar: A memorial of citizens of Massachusetts.

By Mr. Cameron: Two memorials of citizens of Pennsylvania.

By Mr. Peffer: A memorial of citizens of Kansas.

By Mr. Brice: Two memorials of citizens of Ohio.

Ordered, That they be referred to the Select Committee on the Quadro-Centennial.

REPORTS OF COMMITTEES.

Mr. Cockrell, from the Committee on Military Affairs, to whom were referred the following bills, submitted written adverse reports thereon, as follows:

S. 3350. A bill donating a Napoleon gun to the Society of the Sons of the Revolution of Pennsylvania; Report No. 1176.

S. 2687. A bill authorizing the Secretary of War to issue to the governor of Colorado four 3-inch Rodman guns in exchange for two brass Napoleon guns; Report No. 1177.

S. 2767. A bill to deliver to the State of Colorado certain guns; Report No. 1177.

Ordered, That they be postponed indefinitely.

Mr. Cockrell, from the Committee on Military Affairs, to whom was referred the bill (H. R. 5049) to remove the charge of desertion against Lucius L. Dyer, reported it with amendments and submitted a report (No. 1178) thereon.

Mr. Vilas, from the Committee on Claims, to whom was referred the bill (S. 3181) for the relief of Luster P. Chester and Freeland Chester, and Luster P. Chester and Freeland Chester, executors of Thomas R. Chester, submitted an adverse report (No. 1179) thereon.

Ordered, That it be postponed indefinitely.

Mr. Dolph, from the Committee on Foreign Relations, to whom was referred the bill (S. 3555) for the relief of George W. Jones, reported it with amendments.

Mr. Cullom, from the Committee on Interstate Commerce, reported a bill (S. 3734) to amend an act entitled "An act to regulate commerce," approved February 4, 1887; which was read the first and second times by unanimous consent.

Mr. Cameron, from the Committee on Military Affairs, to whom was referred the bill (H. R. 5649) for the relief of Lieut. F. W. Davis, and granting him an honorable discharge, reported it with amendments and submitted a report (No. 1181) thereon.

Mr. Cameron, from the Committee on Military Affairs, to whom were referred the following bills, reported them each with an amendment and submitted written reports thereon as follows:

H. R. 730. An act for the relief of James A. Finley; Report No. 1180.

H. R. 4758. An act for the relief of Charles E. Heuston; Report No. 1182.

Mr. Cullom, from the Committee on Commerce, to whom was referred the bill (S. 3707) making an appropriation for establishing buoyage on the water front of Chicago, Lake Michigan, Illinois, reported it without amendment.

The Senate proceeded, by unanimous consent, to consider the said bill as in Committee of the Whole; and no amendment being made, it was reported to the Senate.

Ordered, That it be engrossed and read a third time.

The said bill was read the third time.

Resolved, That it pass and that the title thereof be as aforesaid.

Ordered, That the Secretary request the concurrence of the House of Representatives therein.

INTRODUCTION OF BILLS AND JOINT RESOLUTION.

Bills were introduced, read the first and second times by unanimous consent, and referred as follows:

By Mr. McMillan: A bill (S. 3735) to amend an act entitled "An act to provide for semiannual statements by foreign corporations doing business in the District of Columbia;" to the Committee on the District of Columbia.

By Mr. Pettigrew: A bill (S. 3736) requiring the Secretary of the Treasury to secure a bond from the corporation known as the World's Columbian Exposition before the coins provided for by chapter 381, statutes of the United States, first session, Fifty-first Congress, are delivered to said corporation; to the Select Committee on the Quadro-Centennial.

By Mr. Cameron: A bill (S. 3737) to prevent desertions from the Navy, and for other purposes; to the Committee on Naval Affairs.

By Mr. Sawyer: A bill (S. 3738) granting a pension to Fred. S. Chamberlain; to the Committee on Pensions.

By Mr. Cullom: A bill (S. 3739) granting a pension to Miss Sarah B. Stebbins; to the Committee on Pensions.

By Mr. McMillan: A bill (S. 3740) for the relief of S. J. Block and A. P. Baurman, of the District of Columbia; to the Committee on the District of Columbia.

By Mr. Teller: A bill (S. 3741) to submit to the Court of Private Land Claims, established by an act of Congress approved March 3, 1891, the title of William McGarrahan to the Rancho Panoche Grande, in the State of California, and for other purposes; to the Committee on the Judiciary.

By Mr. Cockrell: A bill (S. 3742) granting a pension to Evarts Ewing; to the Committee on Pensions.

Mr. Wolcott introduced a joint resolution (S. R. 137) instructing the Postmaster-General to discontinue the sale of the so-called Columbian stamps; which was read the first and second times by unanimous consent.

Ordered, That it lie on the table.

SALMON FISHERIES OF ALASKA.

Mr. Dolph submitted the following resolution; which was considered by unanimous consent and agreed to:

Resolved, That the Secretary of the Treasury be, and he is hereby, directed to transmit to the Senate a copy of the report of the special agent having in charge the protection of the salmon fisheries of Alaska.

MESSAGE FROM THE HOUSE.

A message from the House of Representatives, by Mr. Towles, its chief clerk:

Mr. President: The House of Representatives has disagreed to the report of the committee of conference on the disagreeing votes of the two Houses on the amendments of the House of Representatives to the bill (S. 1307) to provide a permanent system of highways in that part of the District of Columbia lying outside of cities. It further insists upon its amendments to the said bill, asks a further conference with the Senate on the disagreeing votes of the two Houses thereon, and has appointed Mr. Hemphill, Mr. Heard, and Mr. Post managers at the same on its part.

The House of Representatives has passed, without amendment, the bill (S. 3580) to amend the proviso to be found in connection with the free delivery, page 569, twenty-fourth volume, Statutes at Large.

The House of Representatives has passed the following bills, in which it requests the concurrence of the Senate:

H. R. 6797. An act to authorize the construction of a bridge across the Cahawba River, in Bibb County, Alabama, by the Montgomery, Tuscaloosa and Memphis Railway;

H. R. 9053. An act to punish trespassers on the lands of either of the five civilized tribes;

H. R. 9069. An act for the further continuance of the publication of the Supplement to the Revised Statutes of the United States;

H. R. 9610. An act to amend section 1014 of the Revised Statutes of the United States, relating to offenses against the United States;

H. R. 9611. An act to amend section 847 of the Revised Statutes of the United States, relating to commissioners' fees;

H. R. 9612. An act to amend section 833 of the Revised Statutes of the United States, relating to semiannual returns of fees by district attorneys, marshals, and clerks;

H. R. 9613. An act to amend section 828 of the Revised Statutes of the United States, relating to clerks' fees.

H. R. 9979. An act to regulate the right of appeal in certain cases; and

H. R. 10062. An act to authorize the construction of a bridge across the Osage River, between the mouths of the Pomme de Terre River and Buffalo Creek, in Benton County, Missouri.

The Speaker of the House of Representatives having signed four enrolled bills, S. 1292, H. R. 3676, H. R. 4844, and H. R. 6969, I am directed to bring them to the Senate for the signature of its President.

ENROLLED BILLS SIGNED.

Mr. Dubois reported from the committee that they had examined and found duly enrolled the following bills:

S. 1292. An act to remit the penalties on the light-house steamer Pansy;

H. R. 3676. An act for the relief of R. L. Jennings, late postmaster at Marshall, Tex.;

H. R. 4844. An act to authorize the Secretary of War to convey to school district numbered 12, of Kittery, Me., a portion of Fort Mc-Cleary military reservation in exchange for other land; and

H. R. 6969. An act for the relief of Elisha Brown;

Whereupon,

The President pro tempore signed the same, and they were delivered to the committee to be presented to the President of the United States.

HOUSE BILLS REFERRED.

The bills last received from the House of Representatives for concurrence were severally read the first and second times by unanimous consent.

Ordered, That the bill H. R. 9053 be referred to the Committee on Indian Affairs; that the bill H. R. 9069 be referred to the Committee on the Revision of the Laws of the United States; that the bills H. R. 6797 and H. R. 10062 be referred to the Committee on Commerce; and that the bills H. R. 9610, H. R. 9611, H. R. 9612, H. R. 9613, and H. R. 9979 be referred to the Committee on the Judiciary.

PRESIDENTIAL APPROVALS.

A message from the President of the United States, by Mr. Pruden, his secretary:

Mr. President: The President of the United States approved and signed on the 14th instant the act (S. 3623) to amend the act of March 3, 1873, for the relief of the Columbian University of the District of Columbia; and

He approved and signed on the 16th instant the joint resolution (S. R. 113) providing for the printing of the Agricultural Report for 1892.

Ordered, That the Secretary notify the House of Representatives thereof.

HIGHWAYS IN THE DISTRICT.

The Presiding Officer (Mr. Hale in the chair) laid before the Senate the amendments of the House of Representatives to the bill (S. 1307) to provide a permanent system of highways in that part of the District of Columbia lying outside of cities, insisted upon by the House; and

On motion by Mr. Harris,

Resolved, That the Senate further insist upon its disagreement to the amendments of the House of Representatives to the said bill, and agree to the further conference asked by the House on the disagreeing votes of the two Houses thereon.

Ordered, That the conferees on the part of the Senate be appointed by the Presiding Officer; and

The Presiding Officer appointed Mr. Harris, Mr. McMillan, and Mr. Perkins.

Ordered, That the Secretary notify the House of Representatives thereof.

On motion by Mr. Peffer,

The Senate resumed, as in Committee of the Whole, the consideration of the joint resolution (S. R. 96) to limit the office of President to one term for each incumbent; and,

After debate,

Ordered, That it lie on the table.

DEALINGS IN "OPTIONS" AND "FUTURES."

The Presiding Officer announced that the hour of 2 o'clock had arrived, and laid before the Senate its unfinished business, viz, the bill (H. R. 7845) defining "options" and "futures," imposing special taxes on dealers therein, and requiring such persons engaged in selling certain products to obtain license, and for other purposes; and

The Senate resumed, as in Committee of the Whole, the consideration of the bill; and,

The question being on the amendment proposed by Mr. George,

After debate,

Mr. Wolcott raised a question as to the presence of a quorum;

Whereupon,

The President pro tempore directed the roll to be called;

When,

Fifty-five senators answered to their names.

A quorum being present,

After further debate,

An amendment to the amendment having been proposed by Mr. Vilas,

Pending debate,

On motion by Mr. Washburn, at 5 o'clock and 57 minutes p. m.,

The Senate adjourned.

FRIDAY, JANUARY 20, 1893.

EXECUTIVE AND OTHER COMMUNICATIONS.

The President pro tempore laid before the Senate a certificate signed by the presiding officers of the two branches of the legislature of the State of Delaware, certifying to the election of George Gray as Senator from said State for the term of six years commencing March 4, 1893; which was read.

The President pro tempore laid before the Senate the annual report of the Capitol, North O Street and South Washington Railway Company, and the annual report of the Rock Creek Railway Company of the District of Columbia; which were referred to the Committee on the District of Columbia and ordered to be printed.

The President pro tempore laid before the Senate a resolution of the National League for Good Roads, praying for the printing and distribution of certain consular reports on roads in foreign countries; which was referred to the Committee on Agriculture and Forestry and ordered to be printed.

PETITIONS AND MEMORIALS.

Petitions, memorials, etc., were presented and referred as follows:

By the President pro tempore: A memorial of the Presbyterian Ministers' Association of Baltimore, Md., remonstrating against the use of intoxicating liquors, opium, and firearms as articles of trade by American traders on the islands of the western Pacific; to the Committee on Foreign Relations.

By Mr. Vest: Resolutions of a convention of delegates from certain States and Territories, praying for the opening of the Cherokee Strip to settlement, and the formation of a State from the Indian and Oklahoma Territories, for the giving of full jurisdiction to the United States courts in the Indian Territory over all litigation, civil and criminal, in said Territory; to the Committee on Indian Affairs.

Resolutions of District Assembly No. 4, Knights of Labor, of Missouri, praying for the establishment of a permanent census bureau, and for the collection and distribution of statistics in regard to mortgages and so forth on farm property; to the Committee on the Census.

By Mr. Proctor: A petition of citizens of Vermont, praying the passage of a law for the creation of a bureau to be known as the Road Department; to the Committee on Agriculture and Forestry.

By Mr. Hale: A memorial of the Board of Trade of Bangor, Me., praying the passage of the Torrey bankruptcy bill; to the Committee on the Judiciary.

Mr. Washburn presented resolutions of the Board of Trade of Winona, Minn., praying the establishment of a national quarantine.

Ordered, That they lie on the table.

Mr. Sherman presented resolution of boards of health of certain towns in Ohio, praying for a national quarantine and for the restriction of immigration into the United States.

Ordered, That they lie on the table.

Memorials, etc., praying the repeal of the provision of the act of 1890 providing for the purchase of silver bullion, were presented as follows:

By Mr. Hale: A memorial of the First National Bank of Augusta, Me.

By Mr. Dixon: Resolutions of the Board of Trade of Providence, R. I.

By Mr. Washburn: Resolutions of the Board of Trade of Winona, Min.; resolutions of the Chamber of Commerce of Minneapolis, Min., and a memorial of business men of Minneapolis, Minn.

Ordered, That they lie on the table.

Mr. Washburn presented a petition of citizens of Minnesota, praying the passage of the antioption bill.

Ordered, That it lie on the table.

Petitions praying the repeal of the provision providing for the closing of the Columbian Exposition on the Sabbath day were presented as follows:

By Mr. Washburn: Several petitions of citizens of Minnesota.

By Mr. Stockbridge: Five petitions of citizens of Michigan.

By Mr. Wilson: Several petitions of citizens of Iowa.

By Mr. Harris: A petition of citizens of Tennessee.

By Mr. George: A petition of citizens of Mississippi.

By Mr. Cullom: Several petitions of citizens of Illinois.

By Mr. Sherman: Several petitions of citizens of Ohio.

By Mr. Peffer: Several petitions of citizens of Kansas.

Ordered, That they be referred to the Select Committee on the Quadro-Centennial.

Memorials remonstrating against the repeal of the provision of the law providing for the closing of the Columbian Exposition on the Sabbath day were presented as follows:

By the President *pro tempore:* Three memorials of citizens of the United States.

By Mr. Stockbridge: A memorial of citizens of Michigan.

By Mr. Sherman: A memorial of citizens of Ohio.

Ordered, That they be referred to the Select Committee on the Quadro-Centennial.

Mr. Cullom presented three petitions of citizens of Illinois, praying the appointment of a committee to investigate an alleged combine to depreciate the price of grain by the millers, elevators, and railroads at St. Louis and Minneapolis; which were referred to the Committee on Agriculture and Forestry.

PETITION REFERRED.

On motion by Mr. Peffer,

Ordered, That the petition of certain settlers on lands in Oklahoma, praying an extension of time in which to make payment for their lands, be referred to the Committee on Public Lands.

REPORTS OF COMMITTEES.

Mr. Vest, from the Committee on Commerce, to whom was referred the bill (S. 3561) to encourage the construction of electric railroads, to facilitate the rapid transportation of the mails, to promote the interests of commerce and travel, and to aid in demonstrating the feasibility of the distribution of electrical power for agricultural and other purposes along the line of electric roads, and especially to aid in the construction of a pioneer electric railroad between the cities of Chicago and St. Louis, by the Chicago and St. Louis Electric Railroad Company, and to secure to the Government the use of the same for postal, military, and other purposes, at existing rates, reported it with amendments.

Mr. Vest, from the Committee on Commerce, to whom was referred the bill (H. R. 10062) to authorize the construction of a bridge across the Osage River between the mouths of the Pomme de Terre River and Buffalo Creek, in Benton County, Missouri, reported it without amendment.

MESSAGE FROM THE HOUSE.

A message from the House of Representatives, by Mr. Towles, its chief clerk:

Mr. President: The House of Representatives has passed, without amendment, the bill (S. 3407) to authorize the Court of Claims to hear and determine the claims of certain New York Indians against the United States; and

It has passed the following bills, with amendments, in which it requests the concurrence of the Senate:

S. 1933. An act concerning testimony in criminal cases or proceedings based upon or growing out of alleged violations of an act entitled "An act to regulate commerce," approved February 4, 1887, as amended March 2, 1889, and February 10, 1891; and

S. 2345. An act to authorize the construction of a bridge across the Mississippi River above New Orleans.

The House of Representatives has passed the following bills, in which it requests the concurrence of the Senate:

H. R. 9531. An act to make Rockport, Tex., a subport of entry;

H. R. 9955. An act providing for sundry light-houses and other aids to navigation;

H. R. 10010. An act to establish a court of appeals for the District of Columbia, and for other purposes; and

H. R. 10063. An act to amend "An act authorizing the construction of a high wagon bridge across the Missouri River at or near Sioux City, Iowa," etc.

The Speaker of the House of Representatives having signed an enrolled bill, H. R. 10015, I am directed to bring it to the Senate for the signature of its President.

ENROLLED BILL EXAMINED.

Mr. Dubois reported from the committee that they had examined and found duly enrolled the bill (H. R. 10015) to authorize the construction of bridges across the Hiawassee, the Tennessee, and the Clinch rivers, in the State of Tennessee.

DEATH OF EX-PRESIDENT HAYES.

Mr. Brice submitted the following resolution:

Resolved, That the Senate has heard with deep regret of the death of Rutherford Birchard Hayes, formerly Chief Magistrate of the United States, and as a further mark of respect to his memory on this the day of his funeral, the Senate do now adjourn.

The resolution was considered by unanimous consent and unanimously agreed to.

Whereupon,

The Senate adjourned.

SATURDAY, JANUARY 21, 1893.

ENROLLED BILL SIGNED.

The President *pro tempore* signed the enrolled bill, H. R. 10015, yesterday reported to have been examined, and it was delivered to the committee to be presented to the President of the United States.

HOUSE BILLS REFERRED.

The bills yesterday received from the House of Representatives for concurrence were severally read the first and second times by unanimous consent.

Ordered, That the bill H. R. 10010 be referred to the Committee on the Judiciary; that the bills H. R. 9531, H. R. 9955, and H. R. 10063 be referred to the Committee on Commerce.

HOUSE AMENDMENTS TO SENATE BILL.

The President *pro tempore* laid before the Senate the amendments of the House of Representatives to the bill (S. 2345) to authorize the construction of a bridge across the Mississippi River above New Orleans; and

On motion by Mr. Frye,

Resolved, That the Senate agree thereto.

Ordered, That the Secretary notify the House of Representatives thereof.

The President *pro tempore* laid before the Senate the amendment of the House of Representatives to the bill (S. 1933) concerning testimony in criminal cases or proceedings based upon or growing out of alleged violations of an act entitled "An act to regulate commerce," approved February 4, 1887, as amended March 2, 1889, and February 10, 1891.

On motion, by Mr. Wilson,

Resolved, That the Senate disagree to the amendment of the House of Representatives to the said bill, and ask a conference with the House on the disagreeing votes of the two Houses thereon.

Ordered, That the conferees on the part of the Senate be appointed by the President *pro tempore;* and

The President *pro tempore* appointed Mr. Wilson, Mr. Teller, and Mr. Pugh.

Ordered, That the Secretary notify the House of Representatives thereof.

CREDENTIALS OF SENATORS.

The President *pro tempore* laid before the Senate the credentials of Matthew S. Quay, elected a Senator by the legislature of Pennsylvania for the term of six years commencing March 4, 1893; which were read and placed on file.

Mr. Frye presented the credentials of Eugene Hale, elected a Senator by the legislature of Maine for the term of six years commencing March 4, 1893; which were read and placed on file.

Mr. Voorhees presented the credentials of David Turpie, elected a Senator by the legislature of Indiana for the term of six years commencing March 4, 1893; which were read and placed on file.

PETITIONS AND MEMORIALS.

Petitions, memorials, etc., were presented and referred as follows;

By Mr. Vest: Resolutions of the Merchants Exchange of St. Louis, Mo., and resolutions of the Trades and Labor Union of St. Louis, Mo., praying the establishment of a permanent Census Bureau, and for the collection and publication of statistics relating to mortgages on farm property; to the Committee on the Census.

A petition of Archbishop Kenrick, of St. Louis, Mo., praying for the opening of the Columbian Exposition after 12 o'clock m. on Sunday; to the Select Committee on the Quadro Centennial.

A petition of citizens of Wichita Falls, Tex., praying the passage of a law for the opening up to settlement lands in the Indian Territory; to the Committee on Indian Affairs.

By Mr. McMillan: A petition of citizens of Florence, Ariz., praying for the admission of that Territory into the Union upon an equal footing with the original States; to the Committee on Territories.

By Mr. Washburn: A resolution of the Commercial Club of St. Paul, Minn., praying the passage of a law regulating the classification of immigrants; to the Committee on Immigration.

By Mr. Sherman: A petition of citizens of Ohio, praying the passage of a law for the suspension of immigration for one year and for the appointment of a commission to thoroughly investigate the subject of immigration; to the Committee on Immigration.

By Mr. Quay: Resolutions of the Chamber of Commerce of Pittsburg, Pa., praying for the appointment of a commission to be known as the Ohio River Commission, to have general supervision of the improvement of the river from Pittsburg, Pa, to Cairo, Ill.; to the Committee on Commerce.

By Mr. Cockrell: A resolution of the Merchants' Exchange of St. Louis, Mo., praying for the establishment of a permanent census bureau, and for the collection and publication of statistics concerning mortgages on farm property; to the Committee on the Census

By Mr. Cullom: Three petitions of citizens of Illinois, praying the appointment of a committee to investigate an alleged combine formed to depreciate grain by the millers, elevators, and railroads at St. Louis and Minneapolis; to the Committee on Agriculture and Forestry.

A petition of citizens of Illinois, praying for passage of the antioption bill; the Paddock pure-food bill; for Government postal savings banks; the free delivery of mail matter in the rural districts, etc.; to the Committee on Post-Offices and Post-Roads.

By Mr. Hansbrough: A resolution of the Chamber of Commerce of Grand Forks, N. Dak., praying the establishment of a national timber reservation to include the Turtle Mountain region in that State; to the Committee on Public Lands.

By Mr. Quay: A paper relating to the application of Julia E. Lock to be allowed a pension; to the Committee on Pensions, to accompany the bill S. 3743.

By Mr. Brice: Papers relating to the application of Thomas M. Elliott for the correction of his military record; to the Committee on Military Affairs, to accompany the bill S. 3745.

By Mr. Stockbridge: A petition of B. C. Goodhue, praying to be allowed a pension; to the Committee on Pensions, to accompany the bill S. 3748.

By Mr. Quay: Several petitions of citizens of Pennsylvania, praying the passage of a law to suspend immigration for one year, and for the appointment of a commission to investigate the subject of immigration; to the Committee on Immigration.

Mr. Hunton presented a memorial of the Cotton Exchange of Norfolk and Portsmouth, Va., remonstrating against the passage of the antioption bill.

Ordered, That it lie on the table.

Mr. Teller presented a memorial of the German-American Central Verein of Arapahoe County, Colorado, remonstrating against the passage of the bill for the restriction of immigration into the United States.

Ordered, That it lie on the table.

Mr. Teller presented a memorial of citizens of Colorado, remonstrating against the repeal of the provision providing for the purchase of silver bullion.

Ordered, That it lie on the table.

Mr. Sherman presented resolutions of the boards of health of certain towns in Ohio, praying the passage of a law to suspend immigration for one year.

Ordered, That they lie on the table.

Mr. Wolcott presented a memorial of the German-American Central Verein of Arapahoe County, Colo., remonstrating against the suspension of immigration into the United States.

Ordered, That it lie on the table.

Memorials, etc., praying for the repeal of the law providing for the purchase of silver bullion, were presented, as follows:

By Mr. Cullom: A petition of citizens of Illinois.

By Mr. Sawyer: A petition of citizens of Wisconsin.

By Mr. Hunton: A resolution of the Chamber of Commerce of Norfolk, Va., and a petition of citizens of Norfolk, Va.

By Mr. Frye: A memorial of citizens of Portland, Me.

Ordered, That they lie on the table.

Petitions praying the passage of the antioption bill were presented as follows:

By Mr. Washburn: Two petitions of citizens of Minnesota.

By Mr. Palmer: A petition of citizens of Illinois.

By Mr. Stockbridge: A petition of citizens of Michigan.

Ordered, That they lie on the table.

Mr. Quay presented a resolution of the National Board of Trade, praying for the early completion of the Nicaragua Canal under the direction and control of the United States.

Ordered, That it lie on the table and be printed.

Petitions praying the repeal of the provision providing for the

8 s

closing of the Columbian Exposition on the Sabbath day were presented as follows:

By Mr. Mills: Two petitions of citizens of Texas.

By Mr. Vest: Several petitions of citizens of Missouri.

By Mr. Stockbridge: Four petitions of citizens of Michigan.

By Mr. Power: Several petitions of citizens of Montana.

By Mr. Cockrell: Several petitions of citizens of Missouri.

By Mr. Harris: A petition of citizens of Tennessee.

By Mr. Platt: A petition of citizens of Connecticut.

By Mr. Sherman: A petition of citizens of Ohio.

By Mr. Hansbrough: A petition of citizens of North Dakota.

Ordered, That they be referred to the Select Committee on the Quadro-Centennial.

Memorials remonstrating against the repeal of the provision providing for the closing of the Columbian Exposition on the Sabbath day were presented as follows:

By the President *pro tempore*: Four memorials of citizens of the United States.

By Mr. Quay: Several memorials of citizens of Pennsylvania.

By Mr. Stockbridge: A memorial of citizens of Michigan.

By Mr. Vest: A memorial of citizens of Missouri.

By Mr. Hansbrough: A memorial of citizens of North Dakota.

Ordered, That they be referred to the Select Committee on the Quadro-Centennial.

PAPERS REFERRED FROM FILES.

Papers in the cases hereinafter mentioned, to accompany bills introduced, were taken from the files and referred under the rule as follows:

Robert Adger *et al.* and Joseph Hanson; to the Committee on Claims.

REPORTS OF COMMITTEES.

Mr. Sherman, from the Committee on Foreign Relations, to whom was referred the resolution submitted by Mr. Mitchell December 6, 1892, calling for copies of all correspondence on file in the Department of State relating to the killing of Frank Riley, an American sailor, in Genoa, Italy, in August or September, 1892, reported it without amendment.

The Senate proceeded, by unanimous consent, to consider the said resolution; and

Resolved, That the Senate agree thereto.

Mr. Frye, from the Committee on Commerce, to whom was referred the bill (S. 3727) to amend "An act authorizing the construction of a railway, street-railway, motor, wagon, and pedestrian bridge over the Missouri River, near Council Bluffs, Iowa, and Omaha, Nebr., and to extend the time for completion of the bridge therein provided for," reported it with an amendment.

The Senate proceeded, by unanimous consent, to consider the said bill as in Committee of the Whole; and the reported amendment having been agreed to, the bill was reported to the Senate and the amendment was concurred in.

Ordered, That the bill be engrossed and read a third time.

The said bill was read a third time.

Resolved, That it pass, and that the title thereof be as aforesaid.

Ordered, That the Secretary request the concurrence of the House of Representatives therein.

Mr. Hunton, from the Committee on the District of Columbia, to whom was referred the bill (S. 3383) to amend the act of May 6, 1890, fixing the rate of interest to be charged on arrearages of general and special taxes now due the District of Columbia, reported it without amendment and submitted a report (No. 1183) thereon.

The Senate proceeded, by unanimous consent, to consider the said bill as in Committee of the Whole; and no amendment being made, it was reported to the Senate.

Ordered, That it be engrossed and read a third time.

The said bill was read the third time.

Resolved, That it pass, and that the title thereof be as aforesaid.

Ordered, That the Secretary request the concurrence of the House of Representatives therein.

Mr. Morrill, from the Committee on Public Buildings and Grounds, to whom was referred the bill (S. 535) to provide for the construction of a public building at Baker City, Oregon, reported it with an amendment.

Mr. Harris, from the Committee on the District of Columbia, to whom was referred the bill (S. 3521) to amend the charter of the Eckington and Soldiers' Home Railway Company of the District of Columbia, reported adversely thereon.

Ordered, That it be postponed indefinitely.

Mr. Vance, from the Committee on the District of Columbia, to whom was referred the bill (S. 3690) to incorporate the Tabernacle Society of the District of Columbia, reported it with an amendment.

The Senate proceeded, by unanimous consent, to consider the said bill as in Committee of the Whole; and the reported amendment having been agreed to, the bill was reported to the Senate and the amendment was concurred in.

Ordered, That the bill be engrossed and read a third time.

The said bill was read the third time.

Resolved, That it pass and that the title thereof be as aforesaid.

Ordered, That the Secretary request the concurrence of the House of Representatives therein.

Mr. Quay, from the Committee on the Library, to whom was referred the joint resolution (S. R. 134) authorizing the exhibition at the World's Columbian Exposition of the picture entitled "The Recall of Columbus," by Augustus G. Heaton, reported it with an amendment.

The Senate proceeded, by unanimous consent, to consider the said resolution as in Committee of the Whole; and the reported amendment having been agreed to, the resolution was reported to the Senate and the amendment was concurred in.

Ordered, That the resolution be engrossed and read a third time. The said resolution was read the third time.

Resolved, That it pass, and that the little thereof, as reported by the Committee on the Library, be amended so as to read: "A joint resolution authorizing the loan for exhibition at the World's Columbian Exposition, of the picture entitled 'The Recall of Columbus,' by Augustus C. Heaton.'"

Ordered, That the Secretary request the concurrence of the House of Representatives therein.

Mr. Gallinger, from the Committee on the District of Columbia, to whom was referred the joint resolution (S. R. 133) instructing the Secretary of War to cause an examination to be made of the piers of the Aqueduct Bridge, and the District Commissioners to furnish a statement of expenditures on account of said bridge since it became the property of the United States and the District of Columbia, reported in lieu thereof the following resolution; which was considered by unanimous consent and agreed to:

Whereas by the annual report of the Commissioners of the District of Columbia for the year ending June 30, 1889, it is made to appear that the masonry composing the piers of the Aqueduct Bridge was largely in need of repair and at least one of the piers thereof had settled 4 inches to the north, and large cavities caused by erosion existed in more than one of said piers, and that a large sum of money was expended in the repair of the same: Therefore,

Resolved, That the Secretary of War is hereby authorized and directed to cause to be made a thorough examination of the piers of said bridge by some competent officer of the Engineer Corps of the United States Army, and report to Congress at an early day—

First. If any one of said piers of said bridge has so settled as to be out of plumb; and, if so, which way it leans.

Second. What cavities, if any, exist in any of the piers of said bridge requiring repairs or in any way impairing the supporting capacity of said piers, or either of them, making specific report of defects, if any, in each pier.

Third. That he transmit a copy of the report of the officer of the Engineer Corps charged with the duty of constructing the piers of the said bridge, showing as minutely as may be the plans and processes used in the construction thereof.

And be it further resolved, That the Commissioners of the District of Columbia be required to transmit to Congress a detailed report of any and all expenses incurred in the repair of the piers of said bridge since the same became the joint property of the United States and the District of Columbia, and by whom said repairs, if any, were made, and under whose direction or supervision the same were made, and, as fully as may be practicable, a detailed account of the work of making the same, and a copy of the report of any officer of the District or employé thereof, engaged in the said work, or upon any part thereof, including a statement as to whether the said Commissioners have ever caused either or all of the piers of said bridge to be tested with plumb and level, or any other suitable instrument, to see if either or all of them, are out of plumb, and, if so, the result of such examination.

Ordered, That the joint resolution S. R. 133 be postponed indefinitely.

Mr. Peffer, from the Committee on Claims, to whom was referred the bill (S. 988) for the relief of Mrs. Emilie M. Ferriere, widow and representative of Louis L. Ferriere, deceased, submitted an adverse report (No. 1184) thereon.

Ordered, That it be postponed indefinitely.

Mr. Vest, from the Select Committee on the Transportation and Sale of Meat Products, to whom was referred the bill (S. 3522) to create a bureau in the Department of Agriculture for the giving public information of the production and shipping of live stock, reported it without amendment.

Mr. Vest, from the Committee on Commerce, to whom was referred the bill (H. R. 6797) to authorize the construction of a bridge across the Cahaba River, in Bibb County, Alabama, by the Montgomery, Tuscaloosa and Memphis Railway, reported it without amendment.

Mr. Mitchell, from the Committee on Claims, to whom was referred the bill (S. 1954) for the relief of Lewis D. Allen, submitted an adverse report (S. 1185) thereon.

Ordered, That it be postponed indefinitely.

Mr. Mitchell, from the Committee on Claims, to whom was referred the bill (S. 3520) for the relief of Jason Wheeler, late United States Indian agent at Warm Springs Agency, Oregon, reported it without amendment and submitted a report (No. 1186) thereon.

MESSAGE FROM THE HOUSE.

A message from the House of Representatives, by Mr. Towles, its chief clerk:

Mr. President: The House of Representatives has passed, without amendment, the following bills and joint resolution of the Senate:

S. 3117. An act relating to post traderships;

S. 3581. An act to amend an act entitled "An act to forfeit certain lands heretofore granted for the purpose of aiding in the construction of railroads, and for other purposes;" and

S. R. 135. Joint resolution making appropriation of $5,000 for clearing the Potomac River of ice.

The House of Representatives has passed the following bills, in which it requests the concurrence of the Senate:

H. R. 1419. An act for the relief of Catharine Caine;

H. R. 5504. An act to permit the withdrawal of certain papers and the signing of certain receipts by John Finn or his attorney;

H. R. 9925. An act to establish companies of the Hospital Corps, United States Army, and for other purposes;

H. R. 10206. An act to ratify and confirm an agreement made between the Seneca Nation of Indians and William B. Barker;

H. R. 10042. An act to amend an act entitled "An act to regulate commerce," approved February 4, 1887, as amended March 2, 1889; and

H. R. 10163. An act to amend an act entitled "An act to regulate commerce," approved February 4, 1887.

The Speaker of the House of Representatives having signed three enrolled bills, S. 2625, S. 3537, and S. 3580, and an enrolled joint resolution, S. R. 128, I am directed to bring them to the Senate for the signature of its president.

HOUSE BILLS REFERRED.

The bills last received from the House of Representatives for concurrence were severally read the first and second times by unanimous consent.

Ordered, That the bills H. R. 1419 and H. R. 9925 be referred to the Committee on Military Affairs; that the bill H. R. 5504 be referred to the Committee on Finance; that the bill H. R. 10206 be referred to the Committee on Indian Affairs, and that the bills H. R. 10042 and H. R. 10163 be referred to the Committee on Inter-state Commerce.

ENROLLED BILLS AND JOINT RESOLUTION SIGNED.

Mr. Dubois reported from the committee that they had examined and found duly enrolled the following bills and joint resolution:

S. 2625. An act to provide for the punishment of offenses on the high seas;

S. 3537. An act for the relief of M. P. Deady;

S. 3580. An act to amend the proviso to be found in connection with the free-delivery service, page 569, twenty-fourth volume, Statutes at Large; and

S. R. 128. Joint resolution to authorize the Secretary of War to grant permits for the use of reservations and public spaces in the city of Washington, and for other purposes;

Whereupon,

The President *pro tempore* signed the same, and they were delivered to the committee to be presented to the President of the United States.

INTRODUCTION OF BILLS AND JOINT RESOLUTION.

Bills and a joint resolution were introduced, read the first and second times by unanimous consent, and referred as follows:

By Mr. Teller: A bill (S. 3743) granting a pension to Julia E. Lock, formerly widow of the late Gen. Daniel McCook; to the Committee on Pensions.

By Mr. Chandler: A bill (S. 3744) granting a pension to Alice K. Potter, widow of Gen. Joseph H. Potter, deceased; to the Committee on Pensions.

By Mr. Brice: A bill (S. 3745) to amend the military record of Thomas M. Elliott; to the Committee on Military Affairs.

By Mr. Wolcott: A bill (S. 3746) granting a pension to William J. Eaton; to the Committee on Pensions.

By Mr. Peffer: A bill (S. 3747) for the relief of William K. Copeland; to the Committee on Pensions.

By Mr. Stockbridge: A bill (S. 3748) granting a pension to B. C. Goodhue; to the Committee on Pensions.

By Mr. Cullom: A bill (S. 3749) to place William H. Bailhache on the retired list of the Army; to the Committee on Military Affairs.

By Mr. Call: A bill (S. 3750) granting an increase of pension to Benjamin F. Perry; and

A bill (S. 3751) granting a pension to John Hatcher; to the Committee on Pensions.

By Mr. White: A bill (S. 3752) for the relief of Mrs. Mattie S. Holland; to the Committee on Claims.

By Mr. Wilson: A joint resolution (S. R. 138) to recover the value of the Columbian souvenir coins in certain contingencies; to the Select Committee on the Quadro-Centennial.

SALMON FISHERIES OF ALASKA.

Mr. Platt submitted the following resolution; which was considered by unanimous consent and agreed to:

Resolved, That the Secretary of the Treasury be, and he is hereby, directed to transmit to the Senate a copy of the report of date January 19, 1893, of the special agent of the Treasury Department, detailed under the act of March 2, 1889, to carry into effect the provisions of the laws pertaining to the protection of the salmon fisheries of Alaska.

INDIAN DEPREDATION CLAIMS.

Mr. Chandler submitted the following resolution; which was considered by unanimous consent and agreed to:

Resolved, That the Attorney-General be directed to transmit to the Senate a copy of the decision mentioned in his communication to the Senate of the 3d instant, announced by the Court of Claims, that two specified classes of Indian depredation claims are entitled to priority of consideration under section 4 of the act of March 3, 1891.

COLUMBIAN STAMPS.

On motion by Mr. Wolcott,

The Senate proceeded to consider, as in Committee of the Whole, the joint resolution (S. R. 137) instructing the Postmaster-General to discontinue the sale of the so-called Columbian stamps; and

Ordered, That it be referred to the Committee on Post-Offices and Post-Roads.

PRESENTATION OF BILLS AND JOINT RESOLUTION.

Mr. Dubois reported from the committee that they this day presented to the President of the United States the following enrolled bills and joint resolution: .

S. 2625. An act to provide for the punishment of offenses on the high seas;

S. 3637. An act for the relief of M. P. Deady;

S. 3580. An act to amend the proviso to be found in connection with the free-delivery service, page 569, twenty-fourth volume, Statutes at Large; and

S. R. 128. Joint resolution to authorize the Secretary of War to grant permits for the use of reservations and public spaces in the city of Washington, and for other purposes.

PRESIDENTIAL APPROVALS.

A message from the President of the United States, by Mr. Pruden, his secretary:

Mr. President: The President of the United States approved and signed on the 20th instant the following acts:

S. 118. An act for the relief of the estate of Isaac W. Talkington, deceased; and

S. 3195. An act granting to the Yuma Pumping Irrigation Company the right of way for two ditches across that part of the Yuma Indian Reservation lying in Arizona.

Ordered, That the Secretary notify the House of Representatives thereof.

PRESENTATION OF BILL.

Mr. Dubois reported from the committee that they yesterday presented to the President of the United States the bill (S. 1292) to remit the penalties on the light-house steamer *Pansy.*

SOUTHERN KANSAS RAILWAY.

On motion by Mr. Jones, of Arkansas,

The Senate proceeded to consider, as in Committee of the Whole, the bill (S. 1948) to authorize the Southern Kansas Railway Company to construct and maintain a pipe line from the North Fork of the Canadian River, Indian Territory, to said railroad; and no amendment being made, it was reported to the Senate.

Ordered, That it be engrossed and read a third time.

The said bill was read the third time.

Resolved, That it pass, and that the title thereof be as aforesaid.

Ordered, That the Secretary request the concurrence of the House of Representatives therein.

EXECUTIVE SESSION.

On motion by Mr. Sherman,

The Senate proceeded to the consideration of executive business; and

After the consideration of executive business the doors were reopened.

DEALINGS IN OPTIONS AND FUTURES.

The President *pro tempore* laid before the Senate the unfinished business, viz, the bill (H. R. 7845) defining "options" and "futures," imposing special taxes on dealers therein, and requiring such persons engaged in selling certain products to obtain license, and for other purposes; and

The Senate resumed, as in Committee of the Whole, the consideration of the bill; and

The question being on the amendment proposed by Mr. Vilas to the amendment of Mr. George,   •

Pending debate,

Mr. Pugh raised a question as to the presence of a quorum;

Whereupon,

The Presiding Officer (Mr. Jones, of Arkansas, in the chair) directed the roll to be called;

When,

Forty-seven Senators answered to their names.

A quorum being present,

After further debate,

On motion by Mr. George, at 3 o'clock and 37 minutes p. m., The Senate adjourned.

MONDAY, JANUARY 23, 1893.

The Vice-President resumed the chair.

MESSAGE FROM THE HOUSE.

A message from the House of Representatives, by Mr. Towles, its chief clerk:

Mr. President: The House of Representatives has passed, without amendment, the bill (S. 1631) to establish a life-saving station at Gay Head, on the coast of Massachusetts.

The Speaker of the House of Representatives having signed two enrolled bills, S. 2345 and S. 3407, I am directed to bring the same to the Senate for the signature of its President.

ENROLLED BILLS SIGNED.

Mr. Dubois reported from the committee that they had examined and found duly enrolled the following bills:

S. 2345. An act to authorize the construction of a bridge across the Mississippi River above New Orleans; and

S. 3407. An act to authorize the Court of Claims to hear and determine the claims of certain New York Indians against the United States;

Whereupon,

The Vice-President signed the same, and they were delivered to the committee to be presented to the President of the United States.

EXECUTIVE COMMUNICATIONS.

The Vice-President laid before the Senate a communication from the Secretary of State, transmitting, in pursuance to the provisions of the act of February 3, 1887, certified copies of the final ascertainment of electors for President and Vice-President in the State of Louisiana.

Ordered, That it lie on the table.

The Vice-President laid before the Senate a letter of the Acting Secretary of the Interior, transmitting a statement of the Commissioner of Indian Affairs, showing open-market purchases of goods and supplies for the Indian service for the fiscal year 1892 in excess of $500; which was referred to the Committee on Indian Affairs and ordered to be printed.

CREDENTIALS OF SENATORS.

The Vice-President laid before the Senate the credentials of Francis Marion Cockrell, elected a Senator by the legislature of the State of Missouri for the term of six years commencing March 4, 1893; which were read and placed on file.

Mr. Washburn presented the credentials of Cushman K. Davis, elected a Senator by the legislature of the State of Minnesota for the term of six years commencing March 4, 1893; which were read and placed on file.

PETITIONS AND MEMORIALS.

Petitions, memorials, etc., were presented and referred as follows:

By Mr. Turpie: A resolution of the legislature of California, in favor of the election of United States Senators by a direct vote of the people; to the Committee on Privileges and Elections.

By Mr. Perkins: A petition of citizens of Kansas, in behalf of Henry Carter, praying that he be allowed a pension; to the Committee on Pensions.

By Mr. Gallinger: Additional papers relating to the application of George J. Barnes for the removal of the charge of desertion from his military record; to the Committee on Military Affairs, to accompany the bill S. 3720.

By Mr. Cullom: Three petitions of citizens of Illinois, praying the appointment of a committee to investigate an alleged combine formed to depreciate the price of grain by millers, elevators, and railroads at St. Louis and Minneapolis; to the Committee on Agriculture and Forestry.

By Mr. Davis: A petition of the village council of La Prairie, Minn., praying that said village be made one of the objective points for a preliminary survey for a canal connecting the waters of Lake Superior with those of the Mississippi River; to the Committee on Commerce.

By Mr. Squire: A memorial of A. H. Nickerson, praying to be restored to the retired list of the Army with the rank of major; and
A petition of citizens of Washington, praying the passage of a law for the retirement of enlisted men after a continuous service of twenty-five years; to the Committee on Military Affairs.

By Mr. Voorhees: Papers relating to the proposed extension of California avenue, in the District of Columbia; to the Committee on the District of Columbia, to accompany the bill S. 3759.

Papers relating to the application of Samuel J. Rhoades to be allowed a pension; and
A paper relating to the application of John Helfrich to be allowed a pension; to the Committee on Pensions, to accompany the bills S. 3760 and S. 3761.

Mr. Brice presented resolutions of boards of health of certain towns in Ohio praying the passage of a law to suspend immigration into the United States.

Ordered, That they lie on the table.

Mr. Davis presented resolutions of the Board of Trade of Winona, Minn., praying the passage of a law for the establishment of a national quarantine.

Ordered, That they lie on the table.

Mr. Perkins presented a petition of citizens of Kansas, praying for the opening up to settlement of the Cherokee Outlet.

Ordered, That it lie on the table.

Petitions praying the passage of a law for the creation of a bureau to be known as the Department of Roads were presented as follows:

By Mr. Sherman: A petition of citizens of Ohio.
By Mr. Brice: A petition of citizens of Ohio.
Ordered, That they be referred to the Committee on Agriculture and Forestry.

Memorials, etc., praying for the repeal of the law providing for the purchase of silver bullion, were presented as follows:

By Mr. Sawyer: Two memorials of citizens of Wisconsin.
By Mr. Carlisle: A memorial of national banks and trust companies of Louisville, Ky.
By Mr. Stockbridge: A memorial of citizens of Michigan.
By Mr. Davis: A resolution of the Chamber of Commerce of Minneapolis, Minn., and a resolution of the Board of Trade of Winona, Minn.
By Mr. Turpie: A memorial of citizens of Indiana.
By Mr. Gallinger: A memorial of citizens of New Hampshire.
Ordered, That they lie on the table.

Petitions praying the passage of the antioption bill were presented as follows:

By Mr. Squire: Two petitions of citizens of Washington.
By Mr. Brice: Three petitions of citizens of Ohio.
By Mr. Coke: Three petitions of citizens of Texas.
By Mr. Sherman: A petition of citizens of Ohio.
Ordered, That they lie on the table.

Petitions praying the repeal of the provision providing for the closing of the Columbian Exposition on the Sabbath day were presented as follows:

By Mr. Manderson: Several petitions of citizens of Nebraska.
By Mr. Perkins: A petition of citizens of Kansas.
By Mr. Squire: Several petitions of citizens of Washington.
By Mr. Brice: Several petitions of citizens of Ohio.
By Mr. Sherman: A petition of citizens of Ohio.
By Mr. Peffer: A petition of citizens of Kansas.
By Mr. Davis: A petition of citizens of Minnesota.
By Mr. Turpie: Several petitions of citizens of Indiana.
By Mr. Washburn: Two petitions of citizens of Minnesota.
Ordered, That they be referred to the Select Committee on the Quadro-Centennial.

Memorials remonstrating against the repeal of the provision providing for the closing of the Columbian Exposition on the Sabbath day were presented as follows:

By the Vice-President: Three memorials of citizens of Pennsylvania.
By Mr. Manderson: Two memorials of citizens of Nebraska.
By Mr. Perkins: Three memorials of citizens of Kansas.
By Mr. Brice: Several memorials of citizens of Ohio.
By Mr. Blackburn: Several memorials of citizens of Kentucky.
By Mr. Sherman: A memorial of citizens of Ohio.
By Mr. Davis: Several memorials of citizens of Minnesota.
Ordered, That they be referred to the Select Committee on the Quadro-Centennial.

Mr. Sherman presented two petitions of citizens of Ohio, praying for the suspension of immigration for one year and for the appointment of a commission to investigate the subject of immigration; which were referred to the Committee on Immigration.

Mr. Jones, of Arkansas, presented a resolution of the legislative assembly of the Territory of New Mexico for the admission of that Territory into the Union upon an equal footing with the original States.

Ordered, That it lie on the table.

CHANGE OF REFERENCE OF BILL.

On motion by Mr. Peffer,
Ordered, That the Committee on Pensions be discharged from the further consideration of the bill (S. 3747) for the relief of William K. Copeland, and that it be referred to the Committee on Military Affairs.

REPRINT OF REPORT.

On motion by Mr. Platt,
Ordered, That the report No. 1079, accompanying Senate bill No. 2870, for the opening of the Cherokee Outlet to settlement, be reprinted.

REPORTS OF COMMITTEES.

Mr. Manderson, from the Committee on Military Affairs, to whom was referred the bill (S. 2110) for the relief of Henry Halteman, reported it without amendment and submitted a report (No. 1187) thereon.

On motion by Mr. Manderson,
Ordered, That the Committee on Military Affairs be discharged from the further consideration of the bill (S. 3506) for the relief of John Palmier, Pine Ridge, Shannon County, South Dakota, and that it be referred to the Committee on Indian Affairs.

Mr. Manderson, from the Committee on Printing, to whom was referred the resolution received from the House of Representatives for concurrence on the 14th instant, to print 60,000 copies of the special report on Sheep Industry in the United States, reported it without amendment and submitted a report (No. 1190) thereon.

The Senate proceeded, by unanimous consent, to consider the said resolution; and
Resolved, That the Senate agree thereto.
Ordered, That the Secretary notify the House of Representatives thereof.

Mr. Manderson, from the Committee on Printing, to whom was referred the joint resolution (S. R. 132) to print 100,000 copies of the special report of the Bureau of Animal Industry on diseases of cattle and on cattle feeding, submitted an adverse report (No. 1191) thereon.

Ordered, That it be postponed indefinitely.

Mr. Manderson, from the Committee on Printing, to whom were referred the resolutions submitted by Mr. McMillan on the 9th instant, to print 35,000 copies of the special report of the Sheep Industry of the United States, and 100,000 copies of the report on cattle diseases and cattle feeding, submitted an adverse report (No. 1191) thereon.

Ordered, That they be postponed indefinitely.

Mr. Manderson, from the Committee on Printing, to whom was referred the resolution received from the House of Representatives for concurrence on the 14th instant to print 60,000 copies of the special report on diseases of cattle and cattle feeding, reported it without amendment and submitted a report (No. 1192) thereon.

The Senate proceeded, by unanimous consent, to consider the said resolution; and
Resolved, That the Senate agree thereto.
Ordered, That the Secretary notify the House of Representatives thereof.

Mr. Butler, on behalf of Mr. Cameron, from the Committee on Naval Affairs, to whom was referred the bill (S. 3672) to amend the act approved June 18, 1880, relating to the pay of the Judge-Advocate-General of the Navy, reported it without amendment and submitted a report (No. 1188) thereon.

Mr. Wilson, from the Committee on the Revision of the Laws of the United States, to whom was referred the bill (H. R. 9069) for the further continuance of the publication of the supplement to the Revised Statutes of the United States, reported it without amendment and submitted a report (No. 1189) thereon.

Mr. Dolph, from the Committee on Public Lands, to whom was referred the bill (S. 3728) for the relief of the Blalock Wheat-Growing Company, reported it without amendment.

INTRODUCTION OF BILLS.

Bills were introduced, read the first and second times by unanimous consent, and referred as follows:

By Mr. Cullom: A bill (S. 3753) relating to the anchorage and movement of vessels in the port of Chicago; to the Committee on Commerce.

By Mr. Squire: A bill (S. 3754) to amend an act entitled "An act to provide for the times and places to hold terms of the United States courts in the State of Washington;" to the Committee on the Judiciary.

A bill (S. 3755) for the relief of Col. Azor H. Nickerson; to the Committee on Military Affairs.

A bill (S. 3756) providing for the manufacture of steel high-power rifled guns under the designs of R. J. Gatling for coast defenses; to the Committee on Coast Defenses.

By Mr. Perkins: A bill (S. 3757) granting a pension to Henry Curtis; and

A bill (S. 3758) granting a pension to Robert Parker; to the Committee on Pensions.

By Mr. Voorhees: A bill (S. 3759) to extend California avenue, in West Washington, D. C.; to the Committee on the District of Columbia.

A bill (S. 3760) granting a pension to Samuel J. Rhoads; and
A bill (S. 3761) granting a pension to John Helfrich; to the Committee on Pensions.

By Mr. Dolph: A bill (S. 3762) for the relief of Mrs. M. P. Sawtelle; to the Select Committee on Indian Depredations.

By Mr. Mitchell: A bill (S. 3763) for the relief of the Oregon Improvement Company; to the Committee on Appropriations.

COAST AND GEODETIC SURVEY REPORT.

Mr. Manderson submitted the following concurrent resolution; which was referred to the Committee on Printing:

Resolved by the Senate (the House of Representatives concurring), That there be printed and bound in cloth, of the report of the Superintendent of the United States Coast and Geodetic Survey for the fiscal year 1892, 1,500 extra copies of part 1, in quarto form, of which 200 copies shall be for the use of the Senate, 600 copies for the use of the House, and 700 copies for distribution by the Superintendent of the Coast and Geodetic Survey; and of part 2, in octavo form, 2,800 extra copies, of which 200 copies shall be for the use of the Senate, 600 for the use of the House, and 2,000 copies for distribution by said Superintendent.

PROHIBITION OF CHINESE IMMIGRATION.

Mr. Call submitted the following resolution; which was considered, by unanimous consent, and agreed to:

Resolved, That the Secretary of State be, and he is hereby, directed, if not incompatible with the public interest, to send to the Senate the official correspondence of the Government of China with the United States relating to the acts of Congress forbidding the emigration of Chinese and the treaty stipulations between the two countries, and that the same shall be printed for the use of the Senate.

BRIDGE ACROSS THE OHIO RIVER.

On motion by Mr. Blackburn,

The Senate proceeded to consider, as in Committee of the Whole, the bill (H. R. 10007) to provide for lowering the height of a bridge proposed to be constructed across the Ohio River between Cincinnati, Ohio, and Covington, Ky., by the Cincinnati and Covington Rapid Transit Bridge Company; and no amendment being made, it was reported to the Senate.

Ordered, That it pass to a third reading.

The said bill was read the third time.

Resolved, That it pass.

Ordered, That the Secretary notify the House of Representatives thereof.

PRESENTATION OF BILLS.

Mr. Dubois reported from the committee that they this day presented to the President of the United States the following enrolled bills:

S. 2345. An act to authorize the construction of a bridge across the Mississippi River above New Orleans; and

S. 3407. An act to authorize the Court of Claims to hear and determine the claims of certain New York Indians against the United States.

DEALINGS IN OPTIONS AND FUTURES.

On motion by Mr. Washburn,

The Senate resumed, as in Committee of the Whole, the consideration of the bill (H. R. 7845) defining "options" and "futures," imposing special taxes on dealers therein, and requiring such persons engaged in selling certain products to obtain license, and for other purposes; and

The question being on the amendment proposed by Mr. Vilas to the amendment of Mr. George,

Pending debate,

CHEROKEE OUTLET.

On motion by Mr. Platt, and by unanimous consent,

The Senate proceeded to consider, as in Committee of the Whole, the bill (H. R. 9190) to ratify and confirm an agreement with the Cherokee Nation of Indians of the Indian Territory, to make appropriation for carrying out the same, and for other purposes; and an amendment having been proposed by Mr. Platt, and the same having been amended on the motion of Mr. Berry,

EXECUTIVE SESSION.

On motion by Mr. Platt,

The Senate proceeded to the consideration of executive business; and

After the consideration of executive business the doors were reopened, and

On motion by Mr. Sawyer, at 5 o'clock and 20 minutes p. m., The Senate adjourned.

EXECUTIVE COMMUNICATIONS.

The Vice-President laid before the Senate a communication from the Secretary of State, transmitting, in pursuance of the provisions of the act of February 3, 1887, a certified copy of the final ascertainment of electors in the State of Michigan.

Ordered, That it lie on the table.

The Vice-President laid before the Senate a letter of the Secretary of the Treasury, transmitting, in answer to a resolution of the Senate of the 19th instant, a copy of the report of the special agent having in charge the protection of the salmon fisheries of Alaska; which was referred to the Committee on Appropriations and ordered to be printed.

The Vice-President laid before the Senate a letter of the Attorney-General, transmitting, in answer to a resolution of the Senate of the 21st instant, copies of the decisions of the Court of Claims in the Indian depredation claims of John T. Mitchell, administrator, and of James S. Valk, executor; which was referred to the Select Committee on Indian Depredation Claims and ordered to be printed.

The Vice-President laid before the Senate the report of the Brightwood Railroad Company of the District of Columbia; which was referred to the Committee on the District of Columbia and ordered to be printed.

CREDENTIALS OF SENATORS.

The Vice-President laid before the Senate the credentials of George Gray, elected a Senator by the legislature of the State of Delaware for the term of six years commencing March 4, 1893; which were read and placed on file.

Mr. Harris presented the credentials of William B. Bate, elected a Senator by the legislature of the State of Tennessee for the term of six years commencing March 4, 1893; which were read and placed on file.

PETITIONS AND MEMORIALS.

Petitions, memorials, etc., were presented and referred as follows:

By Mr. Quay: A petition of the Regular Army and Navy Union of the United States, praying an amendment to the act providing a retired list for enlisted men of the Army so as to include enlisted men of the Navy; to the Committee on Military Affairs.

Resolutions of the Trade League of Philadelphia, and resolution of the Paint and Drug Club of Pittsburg, Pa., praying the passage of the Torrey bankruptcy bill; to the Committee on the Judiciary.

By Mr. Cullom: Several petitions of citizens of Illinois, praying for the appointment of a committee to investigate an alleged combine formed to depreciate the price of grain by the millers, elevators, and railroads at St. Louis and Minneapolis; to the Committee on Agriculture and Forestry.

Mr. Sherman presented resolutions of boards of health of certain towns in Ohio, praying the passage of a law for the suspension of immigration into the United States.

Ordered, That they lie on the table.

Petitions, etc., praying the repeal of the provision of law providing for the purchase of silver bullion, were presented as follows:

By Mr. Quay: Resolutions of the Board of Trade of Philadelphia, Pa.

By Mr. Sawyer: A petition of citizens of Wisconsin.

By Mr. Vilas: Resolutions of the Manufacturers and Jobbers' Union of La Crosse, Wis.

By Mr. Daniel: A petition of business men of Norfolk, Va.

By Mr. Cullom: A petition of business men of Mendota, Ill.

Ordered, That they lie on the table.

Petitions praying the repeal of the provision providing for the closing of the Columbian Exposition on the Sabbath day were presented as follows:

By Mr. Wilson: Two petitions of citizens of Iowa.

By Mr. Cullom: Two petitions of citizens of Illinois.

Ordered, That they be referred to the Select Committee on the Quadro-Centennial.

Memorials remonstrating against the repeal of the provision providing for the closing of the Columbian Exposition on the Sabbath day were presented as follows:

By the Vice-President: Two memorials of citizens of the United States.

By Mr. Sherman: A memorial of citizens of Ohio.

Ordered, That they be referred to the Select Committee on the Quadro-Centennial.

Petitions praying the passage of the antioption bill were presented as follows:

By Mr. Cullom: Two petitions of citizens of Illinois.

By Mr. Wilson: A petition of citizens of Iowa.

By Mr. Sherman: A petition of citizens of Ohio.

Ordered, That they lie on the table.

REPORTS OF COMMITTEES.

Mr. Morrill, from the Committee on Finance, to whom was referred the bill (S. 3500) to amend an act entitled "An act to credit and to pay to the several States and Territories and the District of Columbia all moneys collected under the direct tax levied by the act of Congress approved August 5, 1861," approved March 2, 1891, reported adversely thereon.

Ordered, That it be placed on the Calendar.

On motion by Mr. Morrill,

Ordered, That the Committee on Finance be discharged from the further consideration of the bill (H. R. 5504) to permit the withdrawal of certain papers and the signing of certain receipts by John Finn or his attorney, and that it be referred to the Committee on Claims.

Mr. McMillan, from the Committee on the District of Columbia, submitted a report (No. 1193) accompanied by a bill (S. 3764) to authorize reassessments for local improvements in the District of Columbia, and for other purposes; which was read the first and second times by unanimous consent and referred to the Committee on Appropriations.

Mr. Sawyer, from the Committee on Pensions, to whom was referred the bill (H. R. 929) granting a pension to Mrs. Mary E. Donaldson, reported it with an amendment striking out the preamble and submitted a report (No. 1194) thereon.

Mr. Sawyer, from the Committee on Pensions, to whom were referred the following bills, reported them severally without amendment and submitted written reports thereon as follows:

H. R. 7036. An act granting a pension to Lillie Ries, late nurse at Jefferson Barracks; Report No. 1195.

H. R. 4047. An act granting a pension to Ellen Hewett; Report No. 1196.

H. R. 2407. An act granting a pension to Samuel Luttrell; Report No. 1197.

H. R. 2400. An act granting a pension to Willis Luttrell; Report No. 1198.

Mr. Sawyer, from the Committee on Pensions, to whom was referred the bill (H. R. 10189) relating to proof of citizenship of applicants for Indian war pensions under the act of Congress approved July 27, 1892, reported it without amendment.

The Senate proceeded, by unanimous consent, to consider the said bill as in Committee of the Whole; and no amendment being made, it was reported to the Senate.

Ordered, That it pass to a third reading.

The said bill was read the third time.

Resolved, That it pass.

Ordered, That the Secretary notify the House of Representatives thereof.

Mr. Davis, from the Committee on Pensions, to whom were referred the following bills, reported them without amendment and submitted written reports thereon as follows:

H. R. 8275. An act granting a pension to Abraham B. Simmons, of Capt. Thomas Tripp's Company, in Col. Brisbane's regiment, South Carolina Volunteers, in the Florida Indian war; Report No. 1199.

H. R. 6508. An act granting a pension to Joseph Fortier; Report No. 1200.

DEATH OF MR. JUSTICE LAMAR.

The Vice-President laid before the Senate the following letter from the Chief Justice of the United States:

SUPREME COURT OF THE UNITED STATES,
Washington, January 24, 1893.

The VICE-PRESIDENT:

It becomes my painful duty to inform the Vice-President and the Senate of the death of Mr. Justice Lamar, which occurred at 8:50 o'clock last night, at Macon, Ga.

I have the honor to be, your obedient servant,
MELVILLE W. FULLER,
Chief Justice of the United States.

The letter was read; and after remarks by Mr. Walthall and Mr. Gordon,

On motion by Mr. Wilson, as a mark of respect to the memory of the deceased,

The Senate adjourned.

WEDNESDAY, JANUARY 25, 1893.

CREDENTIALS OF A SENATOR.

Mr. Platt presented the credentials of Joseph R. Hawley, elected a Senator by the legislature of the State of Connecticut for the term of six years commencing March 4, 1893; which were read and placed on file.

MESSAGE FROM THE HOUSE.

A message from the House of Representatives, by Mr. Towles, its chief clerk:

Mr. President: The House of Representatives has passed, without amendment, the bill (S. 3727) to amend "An act authorizing the construction of a railway, street-railway, motor, wagon, and pedestrian bridge over the Missouri River, near Council Bluffs, Iowa, and

Omaha, Nebr., and to extend the time for the completion of the bridge therein provided for."

The House of Representatives insists upon its amendments to the bill (S. 1933) concerning testimony in criminal cases or proceedings based upon, or growing out of alleged violations of an act entitled "An act to regulate commerce," approved February 4, 1887, as amended March 2, 1889, and February 10, 1891, disagreed to by the Senate. It agrees to the conference asked by the Senate on the disagreeing votes of the two Houses thereon, and has appointed Mr. Wise, Mr. Patterson, and Mr. Storer, managers at the same on its part.

The House of Representatives has passed a bill (H. R. 9757) granting additional quarantine powers and imposing additional duties upon the Marine-Hospital Service, in which it requests the concurrence of the Senate.

The Speaker of the House of Representatives having signed four enrolled bills, S. 1631, S. 3117, S. 3581, and H. R. 10007, and an enrolled joint resolution, S. R. 135, I am directed to bring the same to the Senate for the signature of its President.

ENROLLED BILLS SIGNED.

Mr. Dubois reported from the committee that they had examined and found duly enrolled the following bills and joint resolution:

S. 1631. An act to establish a life-saving station at Gay Head, on the coast of Massachusetts;

S. 3117. An act relating to post traderships;

S. 3581. An act to amend an act entitled "An act to forfeit certain lands heretofore granted for the purpose of aiding in the construction of railroads, and for other purposes;"

H. R. 10007. An act to provide for lowering the height of a bridge proposed to be constructed across the Ohio River between Cincinnati, Ohio, and Covington, Ky., by the Cincinnati and Covington Rapid Transit Company; and

S. R. 135. A joint resolution making an appropriation of $5,000 to clear the Potomac River of ice;

Whereupon,

The Vice-President signed the same, and they were delivered to the committee to be presented to the President of the United States.

EXECUTIVE COMMUNICATIONS.

The Vice-President laid before the Senate a letter of the Secretary of the Interior, transmitting statements of the Commissioner of Indian Affairs, showing property transferred from one reservation to another, and also showing property sold at the various agencies and schools during the fiscal year ended June 30, 1892; which was referred to the Committee on Indian Affairs and ordered to be printed.

The Vice-President laid before the Senate a letter of the Secretary of the Interior, transmitting, in answer to a resolution of the Senate of the 9th instant, a copy of a treaty negotiated by Juel Palmer, for the Territory of Oregon, with the various Indian tribes inhabiting the coast of Oregon from the Columbia River to the California line; which was referred to the Committee on Indian Affairs and ordered to be printed.

PETITIONS AND MEMORIALS.

Petitions, memorials, etc., were presented and referred as follows:

By the Vice-President: A memorial of the Board of Trade of Santa Fe, N. Mex., and a memorial of the Bar Association of the Territory of New Mexico, praying the passage of a bill for the admission of that Territory and other Territories into the Union; to the Committee on Territories.

By Mr. Quay: Resolutions of the Board of Trade of Philadelphia, Pa., praying the passage of the bill allowing national banks to issue notes up to the full amount of the bonds deposited with the Secretary of the Treasury to secure said notes; to the Committee on Finance.

By Mr. Harris: A memorial of the Post-Office Clerks' Association of the first and second class post-offices of Tennessee, praying the passage of the bill providing for the classification of the clerks, fixing the salaries, etc., of certain post-office clerks; to the Committee on Post-Offices and Post-Roads.

By Mr. Turpie: A petition of citizens of Indiana, praying the passage of a law for the appointment of an Ohio River Commission; to the Committee on Commerce.

By Mr. Dolph: A resolution of the Ministerial Association of Portland, Oregon, praying the repeal of the law restricting the immigration; to the Committee on Foreign Relations.

By Mr. Peffer: A memorial of the Yearly Meeting of Friends of Iowa, praying an amendment to the internal-revenue laws prohibiting the issuance of a United States internal-revenue license to anyone until he has complied with the laws of the State in regard to the sale of intoxicating liquors; to the Committee on Finance.

By Mr. Frye: A memorial of citizens of Maine, demonstrating against the passage of the bill (H. R. 9176) relating to contracts of common carriers and to certain obligations, duties, and rights in connection with the carriage of property; to the Committee on Commerce.

By Mr. Hiscock: A memorial of the Scientific Publishing Company of New York, praying an appropriation for the publication of a report of the mineral industry of the United States; to the Committee on Printing.

By Mr. Wilson: A memorial of the Yearly Meeting of Friends of Iowa, praying an amendment to the internal-revenue laws prohibiting the issuance of a United States internal-revenue license to any one until he has complied with the laws of the State in regard to the sale of intoxicating liquors; to the Committee on Finance.

The Vice-President laid before the Senate a resolution of the legislative assembly of the Territory of New Mexico, praying the passage of the bill for the admission of that Territory into the Union upon an equal footing with the original States.

Ordered, That it lie on the table.

Mr. Felton presented a memorial of the Stockton Grange of California praying for the early completion of the Nicaragua Canal under the control and direction of the United States.

Ordered, That it lie on the table.

Mr. Perkins presented a resolution of the legislature of Kansas in favor of the passage of the antioption bill.

Ordered, That it lie on the table.

Mr. Perkins presented a resolution of the legislature of Kansas; a resolution of the Commercial Club of Kansas City, Kans.; and resolution adopted at a meeting of citizens of Kansas, in favor of the ratification of the Cherokee treaty providing for the opening up to settlement of the Cherokee Outlet.

Ordered, That they lie on the table.

Petitions praying the passage of the bill for the suspension of immigration into the United States for one year were presented as follows:

By Mr. Quay: A petition of citizens of Pennsylvania.

By Mr. Sherman: Two petitions of citizens of Ohio.

Ordered, That they lie on the table.

Petitions praying the repeal of the law providing for the purchase of silver bullion were presented as follows:

By Mr. Hiscock: A petition of business men of Buffalo, N. Y.

By Mr. Turpie: A petition of citizens of Indiana.

Ordered, That they lie on the table.

Mr. Sherman presented a petition of citizens of Ohio, praying the passage of the antioption bill.

Ordered, That it lie on the table.

Petitions praying the repeal of the provision providing for the closing of the Columbian Exposition on the Sabbath day were presented as follows:

By Mr. Frye: A petition of citizens of Maine.

By Mr. Quay: A petition of citizens of Pennsylvania.

By Mr. Vest: A petition of citizens of Missouri.

By Mr. Perkins: A petition of citizens of Kansas.

By Mr. Dubois: A petition of citizens of Idaho.

Ordered, That they be referred to the Select Committee on the Quadro-Centennial.

Memorials remonstrating against the repeal of the provision providing for the closing of the Columbian Exposition on the Sabbath day were presented as follows:

By Mr. Quay: Several memorials of citizens of Pennsylvania.

By Mr. Stockbridge: A memorial of citizens of Michigan.

By Mr. Hiscock: A memorial of citizens of New York.

By Mr. Perkins: A memorial of citizens of Kansas.

Ordered, That they be referred to the Select Committee on the Quadro-Centennial.

Mr. Manderson presented papers relating to the proposed settlement of the outstanding indebtedness of the Genoa Indian School for the year 1892; which were referred to the Committee on Appropriations, to accompany an amendment intended to be proposed to the Indian appropriation bill.

REPORTS OF COMMITTEES.

Mr. McMillan, from the Committee on the District of Columbia, to whom was referred the bill (S.3531) to amend the charter of the Brightwood Railway Company, reported it with amendments and submitted a report (No. 1201) thereon.

Mr. McMillan, from the Committee on the District of Columbia, submitted a report (No. 1202) accompanied by a bill (S. 3765) to provide for annual reports by certain corporations in the District of Columbia; which was read the first and second times by unanimous consent.

Mr. Manderson, from the Committee on Military Affairs, to whom was referred the bill (H. R. 6649) to extend the provisions of an act to provide for the muster and pay of certain officers and enlisted men of the volunteer forces, reported it without amendment and submitted a report (No. 1203) thereon.

Mr. Manderson, from the Committee on Indian Affairs, to whom was referred the bill (S. 3506) for the relief of John Palmier, Pine Ridge, Shannon County, South Dakota, reported it without amendment and submitted a report (No. 1204) thereon.

Mr. Butler, from the Committee on Naval Affairs, to whom was referred the bill (S. 66) for the relief of Commodore Oscar C. Badger, reported it without amendment and submitted a report (No. 1205) thereon.

Mr. Sawyer, from the Committee on Pensions, to whom were referred the following bills, reported them severally without amendment and submitted written reports thereon as follows:

H. R. 7234. An act granting a pension to Mary Millard; Report No. 1206.

H. R. 9220. An act granting a pension to Mrs. Caroline Hardee Dyall, widow of James R. Dyall, veteran of the Florida war, 1836; Report No. 1207.

H. R. 1318. An act granting a pension to Martha A. Harris; Report No. 1208.

H. R. 7257. An act granting a pension to Alonzo D. Barber; Report No. 1209.

Mr. Walthall, from the Committee on Public Lands, to whom was referred the bill (H. R. 7625) for the relief of certain settlers on public land in the Tucson land district in Arizona, reported it without amendment and submitted a report (No. 1210) thereon.

Mr. Walthall, from the Committee on Public Lands, to whom was referred the bill (H. R. 8268) to amend chapter 559, page 1095, volume 26, United States Statutes at Large, reported it with amendments and submitted.a report (No. 1211) thereon.

Mr. Turpie, from the Committee on Pensions, to whom was referred the bill (H. R. 6272) to pension Susan S. Murphy, reported it without amendment and submitted a report (No. 1212) thereon.

Mr. Gallinger, from the Committee on the District of Columbia, to whom was referred the bill (S. 3530) to create a board of charities for the District of Columbia, reported it without amendment and submitted a report (No. 1213) thereon.

Mr. Harris, on behalf of Mr. Hunton, from the Committee on the District of Columbia, to whom was referred an amendment intended to be proposed to the District of Columbia appropriation bill, to regulate the collection of garbage in the District of Columbia, submitted a report (No. 1214) thereon; which, together with the proposed amendment, was referred to the Committee on Appropriations.

Mr. Hoar, from the Committee on the Judiciary, to whom was referred the bill (H. R. 10010) to establish a court of appeals for the District of Columbia, and for other purposes, reported it with an amendment.

The Senate proceeded, by unanimous consent, to consider the said bill as in Committee of the Whole; and the reported amendment having been agreed to, the bill was reported to the Senate and the amendment was concurred in.

Ordered, That the amendment be engrossed and the bill read a third time.

The said bill as amended was read the third time.

Resolved, That it pass, and that the Senate request a conference with the House of Representatives on the said bill and the amendment.

Ordered, That the conferees on the part of the Senate be appointed by the Vice-President; and

The Vice-President appointed Mr. Hoar, Mr. Wilson, and Mr. Pugh.

Ordered, That the Secretary notify the House of Representatives thereof.

Mr. Manderson, from the Committee on Printing, to whom was referred the resolution submitted by him on the 15th instant, to print 5,000 extra copies of the Reports of the United States Commissioners to the Paris Exposition of 1889, reported it with amendments and submitted a report (No. 1215) thereon.

The Senate proceeded, by unanimous consent, to consider the said resolution; and the reported amendments having been agreed to, the resolution as amended was agreed to, as follows:

Resolved by the Senate (the House of Representatives concurring), That in addition to the usual number, there shall be printed 5,500 extra copies of the Reports of the Commissioners of the United States to the Paris Exposition of 1889—1,500 copies for the use of the Senate, 3,000 copies for the use of the House, and 1,000 copies for the use of the Department of State.

Ordered, That the Secretary request the concurrence of the House of Representatives therein.

INTRODUCTION OF BILLS AND JOINT RESOLUTION.

Bills and a joint resolution were introduced, read the first and second times by unanimous consent, and referred as follows:

By Mr. Faulkner: A bill (S. 3766) to enable the people of Utah to form a constitution and State government, and to be admitted into the Union on an equal footing with the original States; to the Committee on Territories.

A bill (S. 3767) to amend "An act to provide for the incorporation of trust, loan, mortgage, and certain other corporations within the District of Columbia;" to the Committee on the District of Columbia; and

A bill (S. 3768) relative to voluntary assignments by debtors for the benefit of creditors, in the District of Columbia, and to amend section 782 of the Revised Statutes of the United States, relating to the District of Columbia; to the Committee on the Judiciary.

By Mr. Davis: A bill (S. 3769) relative to voluntary assignments by debtors for the benefit of creditors, in the District of Columbia, and to amend section 782 of the Revised Statutes of the United

States, relating to the District of Columbia; to the Committee on the Judiciary.

By Mr. Manderson: A bill (S. 3770) for the appointment of officers of the United States Army on the retired list, as Indian agents; to the Committee on Indian Affairs.

A bill (S. 3771) to change the name of a portion of reservation No. 1 in the District of Columbia; to the Committee on the District of Columbia.

By Mr. Hiscock: A bill (S. 3772) for the relief of Maj. Gen. John C. Robinson, authorizing the Secretary of War to place him on the retired list of the Army with the full rank and pay of a major-general; to the Committee on Military Affairs.

A bill (S. 3773) to ratify and confirm an agreement made between the Seneca Nation of Indians and William B. Barker; to the Committee on Indian Affairs.

By Mr. Platt: A bill (S. 3774) authorizing the Secretary of the Navy to contract for the building of an Ericsson "destroyer"; to the Committee on Naval Affairs.

By Mr. Vest: A bill (S. 3775) to authorize the construction of a bridge across the St. Louis River between the States of Minnesota and Wisconsin, near the village of West Duluth; to the Committee on Commerce.

By Mr. Harris: A bill (S. 3776) to amend the charter of the District of Columbia Railway Company; to the Committee on the District of Columbia.

By Mr. Hiscock: A joint resolution (S. 139) authorizing the Secretary of War to make use of an unexpended balance in deepening the harbor at Oswego, New York; to the Committee on Commerce.

CONSULAR FEES.

Mr. Dolph submitted the following resolution; which was considered by unanimous consent and agreed to:

Resolved, That the Secretary of State be directed to inform the Senate what fees of officers in the consular service of the United States are regulated by law and the rules of the Department, the amount of fees allowed in such cases, and what rules have been made on that subject; what fees are required by law and regulations of the Department to be reported to the Department; what fees or charges, if any, are collected by such officers not required to be reported and not reported to the Department; the aggregate amount of fees reported by each of said officers for the last fiscal year; what fees, if any, were collected by such officers which are not fixed by law or the regulations of the Department; whether the fees should not be reduced at the principal consulates; and what further legislation is required to regulate the amount of fees and charges collected by such officers, and prevent unjust and unreasonable charges.

NORTHERN PACIFIC INDEMNITY LANDS, ETC.

Mr. Hansbrough submitted the following resolution; which was considered by unanimous consent and agreed to:

Resolved, by the Senate, That the Secretary of the Interior be, and he hereby is, directed to report to the Senate the area of lands excluded from the grant to the Northern Pacific Railroad Company in each State traversed by said railroad because reserved, granted, or otherwise appropriated, or to which claims or rights had attached prior to July 2, 1864; also the area of lands excluded from said grant by similar causes arising subsequent to July 2, 1864, the area of the different reservations and grants by reason of which lands are held excluded from such grant to be separately given; also the estimated area of lands excluded from said grant as mineral.

Also the area of surveyed lands within the first indemnity limits of said grant in each State selected by said railroad company; the area of such surveyed first indemnity lands in each State now remaining subject to its right of selection; and the estimated area of the unsurveyed first indemnity lands in each State which will probably become subject to said right of selection.

WITHDRAWAL OF PAPERS.

On motion by Mr. Sherman,

Ordered, That Philip Hawk be permitted to withdraw his papers from the files of the Senate.

ELECTRIC RAILROADS.

On motion by Mr. Morrill,

The Senate proceeded to consider, as in Committee of the Whole, the bill (S. 3561) to encourage the construction of electric railroads, to facilitate the rapid transportation of the mails, to promote the interests of commerce and travel, and to aid in demonstrating the feasibility of the distribution of electrical power for agricultural and other purposes along the line of electric roads, and especially to aid in the construction of a pioneer electric railroad between the cities of Chicago and St. Louis, by the Chicago and St. Louis Electric Railroad Company, and to secure to the Government the use of the same for postal, military, and other purposes at the existing rates; and

Ordered, That it be referred to the Committee on Finance.

PRESIDENTIAL APPROVALS.

A message from the President of the United States, by Mr. Pruden, his secretary,

Mr. President: The President of the United States approved and signed on the 23d instant the following acts:

S. 1292. An act to remit the penalties on the light-house steamer Pansy;

S. 3580. An act to amend the proviso to be found in connection with the free-delivery service, page 569, twenty-fourth volume, Statutes-at-Large; and

He this day approved and signed the act (S. 3537) for the relief of M. P. Deady.

Ordered, That the Secretary notify the House of Representatives thereof.

HOUSE BILL REFERRED.

The bill H. R. 9757, last received from the House of Representatives for concurrence, was read the first and second times by unanimous consent and referred to the Committee on Epidemic Diseases.

PRESENTATION OF BILLS AND JOINT RESOLUTION.

Mr. Dubois reported from the committee that they this day presented to the President of the United States the following enrolled bills and joint resolution:

S. 1631. An act to establish a life-saving station at Gay Head, on the coast of Massachusetts;

S. 3117. An act relating to post traderships;

S. 3581. An act to amend an act entitled "An act to forfeit certain lands heretofore granted for the purpose of aiding in the construction of railroads, and for other purposes;" and

S. R. 135. Joint resolution making an appropriation of $5,000 for clearing the Potomac River of ice.

EXECUTIVE SESSION.

On motion by Mr. Mitchell,

The Senate proceeded to the consideration of executive business; and

After the consideration of executive business the doors were reopened; and

On motion by Mr. Hale, at 5 o'clock and 5 minutes p. m.,

The Senate adjourned.

THURSDAY, JANUARY 26, 1893.

MESSAGE FROM THE PRESIDENT.

The following message was received from the President of the United States, by Mr. Pruden, his secretary:

To the Senate of the United States:

In response to the resolution of the Senate of the 21st instant, relating to the alleged killing of Frank B. Riley, a sailor of the United States steamship Newark, in Genoa, Italy, I transmit herewith a report on the subject from the Secretary of State.

BENJ. HARRISON.

EXECUTIVE MANSION,
Washington, January 25, 1893.

The message was read.

Ordered, That it be referred to the Committee on Foreign Relations and printed.

EXECUTIVE COMMUNICATION.

The Vice-President laid before the Senate a letter of the Secretary of the Treasury, recommending an increase of the appropriation for the erection of a custom-house and post-office building at St. Albans, Vt., which was referred to the Committee on Appropriations and ordered to be printed.

CREDENTIALS OF A SENATOR.

Mr. Hoar presented the credentials of Henry Cabot Lodge, elected a Senator by the legislature of the Commonwealth of Massachusetts for the term of six years commencing March 4, 1893; which were read and placed on file.

PETITIONS AND MEMORIALS.

Petitions, memorials, etc., were presented and referred as follows:

By the Vice-President: A petition of citizens of Indiana, praying the passage of the bill to limit the amount of wearing apparel that may be admitted free of duty; to the Committee on Finance.

By Mr. McMillan: A petition of citizens of Michigan, praying the passage of a law for the establishment of a retired list for enlisted men of the Army after a continuous service of twenty-five years; to the Committee on Military Affairs.

By Mr. Sherman: A petition of citizens of Ohio, praying the passage of a law for the establishment of a permanent census bureau, and for the collection and publication of statistics relating to farm mortgages, etc.; to the Committee on the Census.

By Mr. Dawes: A memorial of citizens of New Mexico in behalf of the Navajo Indians, praying an appropriation for the irrigation of the lands of the Navajo Indian Reservation in that Territory; to the Committee on Indian Affairs.

By Mr. Harris: Two memorials of the Post-office Clerks' Association of the first and second class post-offices of Tennessee, praying the passage of the bill providing for the classification of the clerks, fixing the salaries, etc., of certain post-office clerks; to the Committee on Post-Offices and Post-Roads.

By Mr. Hunton: A resolution of the Board of Trade of Roanoke, Va., praying the passage of the bill extending the line of the Norfolk and Western Railroad into the city of Washington, D. C.; to the Committee on the District of Columbia.

By Mr. McMillan: A petition of citizens of the District of Columbia, praying for the widening of G street, in the city of Washington, D. C.; to the Committee on Appropriations.

By Mr. Hawley: A petition of citizens of Connecticut, praying the passage of the bill to limit the amount of wearing apparel that may be admitted free of duty; to the Committee on Finance.

Resolutions of the Board of Trade of Hartford, Conn., praying the passage of the Torrey bankruptcy bill; to the Committee on the Judiciary.

By Mr. Hoar: A petition of Sarah Bennett, praying to be allowed a pension; to the Committee on Pensions.

By Mr. Cullom: Several petitions of citizens, of Illinois, praying for the appointment of a committee to investigate an alleged combine formed to depreciate the price of grain at St. Louis and Minneapolis; to the Committee on Agriculture and Forestry.

By Mr. Sherman: Several resolutions of boards of health of certain towns in Ohio, praying the passage of a law for the suspension of immigration; to the Committee on Immigration.

By Mr. Call: Papers relating to the construction of a harbor of refuge at Cape Canaveral; in the State of Florida; to the Committee on Naval Affairs, to accompany the bill S. 2777.

Mr. Washburn presented resolutions of the legislature of Minnesota in favor of the passage of the antioption bill.

Ordered, That they lie on the table.

Mr. Vest presented resolutions of the Commercial Exchange of Kansas City, Mo., praying the passage of the bill providing for the opening up to settlement of the Cherokee Outlet.

Ordered, That they lie on the table.

Petitions praying the passage of the antioption bill were presented as follows:

By Mr. Sherman: A petition of citizens of Ohio.

Ry Mr. Kyle: A petition of citizens of South Dakota.

Ordered, That they lie on the table.

Petitions praying the repeal of the provision providing for the closing of the Columbian Exposition on the Sabbath day were presented as follows:

. By Mr. Faulkner: A petition of citizens of West Virginia.

By Mr. Hawley: Two petitions of citizens of Connecticut.

By Mr. Perkins: A petition of citizens of Kansas.

By Mr. Hoar: Three petitions of citizens of Massachusetts.

By Mr. Quay: Two petitions of citizens of Pennsylvania.

Ordered, That they be referred to the Select Committee on the Quadro-Centennial.

Memorials remonstrating against the repeal of the provision providing for the closing of the Columbian Exposition on the Sabbath day were presented as follows:

By Mr. Dawes: A memorial of citizens of Massachusetts.

By Mr. Higgins: Two memorials of citizens of Delaware.

By Mr. Kyle: A memorial of citizens of South Dakota.

By Mr. Butler: A memorial of citizens of South Carolina.

By Mr. Hawley: A memorial of citizens of Connecticut.

By Mr. Perkins: A memorial of citizens of Kansas.

By Mr. Hoar: Three memorials of citizens of Massachusetts.

Ordered, That they be referred to the Select Committee on the Quadro-Centennial.

Petitions praying the passage of a law for the suspension of immigration, and for the appointment of a commission to investigate the subject of immigration, were presented as follows:

By Mr. Blodgett: Several petitions of citizens of New Jersey.

By Mr. Cockrell: A petition of citizens of Missouri.

By Mr. Faulkner: A petition of citizens of West Virginia.

By Mr. Sherman: A petition of citizens of Ohio.

· By Mr. Hiscock: Several petitions of citizens of New York.

· By Mr. Higgins: Several petitions of citizens of Delaware.

By Mr. Platt: Several petitions of citizens of Connecticut.

By Mr. Quay: Several petitions of citizens of Pennsylvania.

Ordered, That they be referred to the Committee on Immigration.

Petitious, etc., praying the repeal of the law providing for the purchase of silver bullion, were presented as follows:

By Mr. Davis: A resolution of the Board of Trade of Mankato, Minn.

By Mr. Sherman: A petition of citizens of Ohio.

By Mr. Hunton: A petition of citizens of Virginia.

By Mr. Washburn: A resolution of the Board of Trade of Mankato, Minn.

By Mr. Hoar: A petition of the Boston Savings Bank.

By Mr. Hawley: Two petitions of citizens of Connecticut.

By Mr. Quay: A petition of citizens of Pennsylvania.

Ordered, That they lie on the table.

Mr. Teller presented a memorial of citizens of Colorado, remonstrating against the passage of the bill to repeal the provision of law providing for the purchase of silver bullion.

Ordered, That it lie on the table.

9 s

On motion by Mr. Sherman,

Ordered, That Philip Hawk have leave to withdraw his petition and papers from the files of the Senate.

HOUSE AMENDMENTS TO SENATE BILLS.

The Vice-President laid before the Senate the amendment of the House of Representatives to the bill (S. 985) to provide for the enlargement of the military post at Fort Wayne, Mich.; and

On motion by Mr. Hawley,

Resolved, That the Senate agree thereto.

Ordered, That the Secretary notify the House of Representatives thereof.

The Vice-President laid before the Senate the amendment of the House of Representatives to the bill (S. 1303) to increase the pension of Mrs. S. A. Farquharson.

On motion by Mr. Turpie,

Resolved, That the Senate disagree to the amendment of the House of Representatives to the said bill and ask a conference with the House on the disagreeing votes of the two Houses thereon.'

Ordered, That the conferees on the part of the Senate be appointed by the Vice-President; and

The Vice-President appointed Mr. Davis, Mr. Turpie, and Mr. Palmer.

Ordered, That the Secretary notify the House of Representatives thereof.

REPORTS OF COMMITTEES.

Mr. Cullom, from the Committee on Interstate Commerce, to whom was referred the bill (H. R. 10163) to amend an act entitled "An act to regulate commerce," approved February 4, 1887, reported it with amendments.

Mr. Teller, from the Committee on Privileges and Elections, to whom was referred the resolution received from the House of Representatives for concurrence on the 17th instant, providing for the meeting of the two Houses of Congress on Wednesday, February 8, 1893, and for the order of counting the electoral votes for President and Vice-President of the United States, reported it without amendment.

The Senate proceeded, by unanimous consent, to consider the said resolution; and

Resolved, That the Senate agree thereto.

Ordered, That the Secretary notify the House of Representatives thereof.

Mr. Davis, from the Committee on Military Affairs, to whom was referred the bill (H. R. 5597) for the relief of William Smith and others, reported it without amendment.

The Senate proceeded, by unanimous consent, to consider the said bill as in Committee of the Whole; and no amendment being made, it was reported to the Senate.

Ordered, That it pass to a third reading.

The said bill was read the third time.

Resolved, That it pass.

Ordered, That the Secretary notify the House of Representatives thereof.

On motion by Mr. Davis,

Ordered, That the Secretary be directed to request the House of Representatives to return to the Senate the bill (S. 1678) for the relief of William Smith and others.

Mr. Cockrell, from the Committee on Military Affairs, to whom was referred the bill (H. R. 6345) granting an honorable discharge to Frederick E. Kolter, reported it without amendment and submitted a report (No. 1216) thereon.

Mr. Coke from the Committee on Commerce to whom was referred the bill (H. R. 9531) to make Rockport, Tex., a subport of entry, reported it without amendment.

Mr. Hawley, from the Committee on Military Affairs, to whom was referred the bill (H. R. 8106) for the correction of the army record of David R. Wallace, deceased, reported it without amendment and submitted a report (No. 1217) thereon. •

Mr. Sawyer, from the Committee on Pensions, to whom were referred the following bills, reported them severally without amendment and submitted written reports thereon as follows:

H. R. 7238. An act granting a pension to Amanda Atherton; Report No. 1218.

H. R. 7226. An act granting a pension to Julia P. Wright; Report No. 1219.

H. R. 7662. An act granting a pension to Marion Kern Sharman; Report No. 1220.

Mr. Frye, from the Committee on Commerce, to whom was referred the bill (S. 3512) to provide communication for light-ships and outlying light-houses to the shore, reported it without amendment.

Mr. Palmer, from the Committee on Military Affairs, to whom was referred the bill (S. 3573) for the relief of James Joyce, late lieutenant United States Army, reported adversely thereon.

Ordered, That it be postponed indefinitely.

Mr. Mitchell, from the Committee on Claims, to whom was referred the bill (S. 746) to settle and readjust the claims of any State for expenses incurred in its defense of the United States, reported it without amendment and submitted a report (No. 1221) thereon.

Mr. Sawyer, from the Committee on Pensions, to whom was referred the bill (H. R. 6507) granting a pension to Sarah A. Hagan, reported it without amendment and submitted a report (No. 1222) thereon.

Mr. Dolph, from the Committee on Commerce, to whom was referred the bill (H. R. 9935) providing for sundry light-houses and other aids to navigation, reported it with amendments.

Mr. Mitchell, from the Committee on Claims, to whom was referred the amendment intended to be proposed by Mr. Turpie to the bill (H. R. 10258) making appropriations to supply general deficiencies, etc., for the settlement of the claim of Silas Q. Howe, surviving partner of W. T. Pate & Co., submitted a report (No. 1223) thereon; which, together with the proposed amendment, was referred to the Committee on Appropriations.

MESSAGE FROM THE HOUSE.

A message from the House of Representatives, by Mr. Towles, its chief clerk:

Mr. President: The House of Representatives has passed, without amendment, the joint resolution (S. R. 124) directing the Secretary of War to investigate the subject of raft-towing on the Great Lakes and their connecting waters.

The House of Representatives has disagreed to the amendment of the Senate to the bill (H. R. 10010) to establish a court of appeals for the District of Columbia, and for other purposes. It agrees to the conference asked by the Senate on the disagreeing votes of the two Houses thereon, and has appointed Mr. Culberson, Mr. Oates, and Mr. E. B. Taylor managers at the same on its part.

The Speaker of the House of Representatives having signed two enrolled bills, S. 3727 and H. R. 10189, I am directed to bring them to the Senate for the signature of its President.

ENROLLED BILLS SIGNED.

Mr. Dubois reported to the committee that they had examined and found duly enrolled the following bills:

S. 3727. An act to amend "An act authorizing the construction of a railway, street-railway, motor, wagon, and pedestrian bridge over the Missouri River near Council Bluffs, Iowa, and Omaha, Nebr,, and to extend the time for the completion of the bridge therein provided for;" and

H. R. 10189. An act relating to proof of citizenship of applicants for Indian war pensions under the act of Congress approved July 27, 1892;

Whereupon,

The Vice-President signed the same, and they were delivered to the committee to be presented to the President of the United States.

INTRODUCTION OF BILLS AND JOINT RESOLUTIONS.

Bills and joint resolutions were introduced, read the first and second times by unanimous consent, and referred as follows:

By Mr. Call: A bill (S. 3777) for the construction of works to render the Bight of Canaveral, in the State of Florida, available for the use of the Navy; to the Committee on Naval Affairs.

By Mr. Cullom: A bill (S. 3778) granting a pension Mrs. Elisha Kent Kane, widow of Dr. Elisha Kent Kane, the Arctic explorer; to the Committee on Pensions.

By Mr. Sherman: A bill (S. 3779) authorizing the purchase of oil paintings for the Executive Mansion; to the Committee on the Library.

By Mr. Jones, of Arkansas: A bill (S. 3780) to authorize the loyal Creek Indians, Indian Territory, to bring suit in the Court of Claims for damages committed upon their property; to the Committee on Indian Affairs.

By Mr. Pettigrew: A bill (S. 3781) to establish a military post at or near the city of Pierre, Hughes County, in the State of South Dakota; to the Committee on Military Affairs.

A bill (S. 3782) to authorize the construction of a bridge across the St. Louis River between the States of Minnesota and Wisconsin, near the village of West Duluth; to the Committee on Commerce.

By Mr. Hiscock: A bill (S. 3783) to amend the several acts of Congress relating to the acquisition of property for a site and for the construction of a building for the custom-house in the city of New York; to the Committee on Public Buildings and Grounds.

By Mr. Washburn: A bill (S. 3784) to authorize the construction of a bridge across the St. Louis River between the States of Minnesota and Wisconsin, near the village of West Duluth; to the Committee on Commerce.

By Mr. Jones, of Arkansas: A bill (S. 3785) to provide for the condemnation of land for a military post near the city of Little Rock, Ark.; to the Committee on the Judiciary.

By Mr. Cullom: A joint resolution (S. R. 141) requesting the municipal authorities of Philadelphia to loan to the United States Government, the "liberty bell" for exhibition as therein stated; to the Committee on the Library.

By Mr. Hiscock: A joint resolution (S. R. 142) authorizing the control of matters pertaining to the assignment, occupation, etc., of

rooms occupied by officers and employés of the Government, to be vested in the Secretary of the Treasury; to the Committee on Public Buildings and Grounds.

Mr. Gorman introduced a joint resolution (S. R. 140) authorizing the Secretaries of War and of the Navy to loan to the committee on inaugural ceremonies flags, etc.; which was read the first and second times by unanimous consent and considered as in Committee of the Whole; and no amendment being made, it was reported to the Senate.

Ordered, That it be engrossed and read a third time.

The said resolution was read the third time by unanimous consent.

Resolved, That it pass, and that the title thereof be as aforesaid.

Ordered, That the Secretary request the concurrence of the House of Representatives therein.

INAUGURATION ARRANGEMENTS.

Mr. Gorman submitted the following resolution; which was considered by unanimous consent and agreed to:

Resolved, That a committee of three Senators be appointed by the Vice-President to make the necessary arrangements for the inauguration of the President-elect of the United States on the 4th day of March next.

LIQUOR TRUST.

Mr. Chandler submitted the following resolution; which was referred to the Committee on Finance:

Resolved, That the Committee on Finance is hereby directed to make inquiry whether or not a trust exists to control and monopolize the business of producing and selling high wines and alcohol or other distilled liquors, and to restrain the freedom of trade and commerce therein, which trust is maintained in violation of the laws of the United States; whether the purpose of said trust is accomplished in whole or in part by giving rebate certificates for the payment of 5 cents per gallon on all such liquors sold by the persons or company maintaining the trust, payable only on condition that the purchasers and their successors and assigns shall make all their future purchases solely from said persons or company, and if so, what amount of rebate certificates have been issued from time to time and how many are now outstanding unpaid;

Whether any portion of such liquors produced or handled by said trust has been at any time adulterated with any poisonous or deleterious drugs or other additions and thereafter sold or used as a beverage;

What portion of such liquors produced or handled by said trust is used as a beverage and what portion in the arts or for medicinal purposes;

Whether such adulteration is practiced under licenses issued to rectifiers under the internal-revenue laws or under the protection of special taxes imposed by said laws; and

Whether any legal proceedings have been commenced against the persons or company maintaining said trust, and to investigate any and all other facts connected with said trust which the committee may deem material, said committee to have power to send for persons and papers and examine witnesses, and to act as a full committee or by a subcommittee or subcommittees during the present session of Congress and after its expiration and until the next regular meeting of Congress on the first Monday in December next, the expenses of making said inquiry to be paid from the appropriation for the contingent expenses of the Senate.

ATTORNEYS' FEES IN INDIAN CLAIMS.

Mr. Dawes submitted the following resolution; which was referred to the Committee on Printing:

Resolved, That the copies of contracts made with Indian tribes or Indians since January 1, 1889, by which compensation was agreed to be paid to attorneys, agents, or other persons for obtaining the recognition, allowance, or payment of claims in favor of such tribes or Indians against the United States, and other papers furnished to the Senate by the Secretary of the Interior, January 5, 1893, in response to the Senate resolution of June 1, 1892, be printed.

MARITIME OFFENSES.

Mr. Hoar submitted the following concurrent resolution; which was considered by unanimous consent, and agreed to:

Resolved by the Senate (the House of Representatives concurring), That the President be requested to return to the Senate the bill (S. 2625) to provide for the punishment of offenses on the high seas.

Ordered, That the Secretary request the concurrence of the House of Representatives therein.

MESSAGE FROM THE PRESIDENT.

The following message was received from the President of the United States, by Mr. Pruden, his secretary:

To the Senate and House of Representatives:

I transmit herewith, for the information of Congress, the third regular report of the World's Columbian Commission and the report of the president of the Board of Lady Managers, with the accompanying papers.

                                        BENJ. HARRISON.

EXECUTIVE MANSION, *January 26, 1893.*

The message was read.

Ordered, That it be referred to the Select Committee on the Quadro-Centennial and be printed.

SUPERVISORS OF ELECTIONS.

On motion by Mr. Bate,

Ordered, That the bill (S. 3504) to repeal all statutes relating to supervisors of elections and special deputies be referred to the Committee on the Judiciary.

CONSIDERATION OF BILLS ON CALENDAR.

On motion by Mr. Platt,

The Senate proceeded to consider, as in Committee of the Whole, the bill (H. R. 5049) to remove the charge of desertion against Lucius L. Dyer; and the reported amendment having been agreed to, the bill was reported to the Senate and the amendment was concurred in.

Ordered, That the amendment be engrossed and the bill read a third time.

The said bill as amended was read the third time.

Resolved, That it pass, and that the title be amended to read, "An act to amend the military record of Lucius L. Dyer."

Ordered, That the Secretary request the concurrence of the House of Representatives in the amendments.

On motion by Mr. Vest,

The Senate proceeded to consider, as in Committee of the Whole, the bill (H. R. 10062) to authorize the construction of a bridge across the Osage River between the mouths of Pomme de Terre River and Buffalo Creek, in Benton County, Missouri; and no amendment being made, it was reported to the Senate.

Ordered, That it pass to a third reading.

The said bill was read the third time.

Resolved, That it pass.

Ordered, That the Secretary notify the House of Representatives thereof.

The Senate proceeded, to consider, as in Committee of the Whole, the following bills; and the reported amendments having been agreed to, the bills were severally reported to the Senate and the amendments were concurred in:

S. 88. A bill for the relief of Hiram Somerville;

S. 2173. A bill to authorize the Missouri River Power Company, of Montana, to construct a dam across the Missouri River;

S. 2869. A bill to provide for the reservation of certain timber lands upon the Siletz Indian Reservation for the benefit of the Indians; and

S. 3568. A bill providing for the establishment and enforcement of rules and regulations for the use and navigation of United States canals and similar works of navigation, and for other purposes.

Ordered, That they be engrossed and read a third time.

The said bills were severally read the third time.

Resolved, That they pass, and that the respective titles thereof be as aforesaid.

Ordered, That the Secretary request the concurrence of the House of Representatives therein.

The Senate proceeded to consider, as in Committee of the Whole, the bill (S. 1790) for the relief of Thomas Antisell; and the reported amendment having been agreed to, and the bill further amended on the motion of Mr. Mitchell, it was reported to the Senate and the amendments were concurred in.

On the question, Shall the bill be engrossed and read a third time?

Ordered, That the further consideration thereof be postponed to to-morrow.

The Senate proceeded to consider, as in Committee of the Whole, the bill (S. 2657) granting right of way to the Watertown, Sioux City and Duluth Railroad Company through the Sisseton and Wahpeton Indian Reservation; and the reported amendments having been agreed to, and the bill further amended on the motion of Mr. Cockrell, it was reported to the Senate and the amendments were concurred in.

Ordered, That it be engrossed and read a third time.

The said bill was read the third time.

Resolved, That it pass and that the title thereof be as aforesaid.

Ordered, That the Secretary request the concurrence of the House of Representatives therein.

PRESIDENTIAL APPROVALS.

A message from the President of the United States, by Mr. Pruden, his secretary:

Mr. President: The President of the United States approved and signed on the 25th instant the joint resolution (S. R. 135) making an appropriation of $5,000 for clearing the Potomac River of ice; and

He this day approved and signed the following act and joint resolution:

S. 2345. An act to authorize the construction of a bridge across the Mississippi River above New Orleans; and

S. R. 128. Joint resolution to authorize the Secretary of War to grant permits for the use of reservations and public spaces in the city of Washington, and for other purposes.

Ordered, That the Secretary notify the House of Representatives thereof.

ALCOHOLIC LIQUOR TRAFFIC.

The Senate resumed the consideration of the bill (S. 749) to provide for a commission on the subject of the alcoholic liquor traffic; and

The question being, Shall the bill pass?

On motion by Mr. Vest,

The yeas and nays were ordered.

Pending debate on the bill,

DEALINGS IN OPTIONS AND FUTURES.

The Presiding Officer (Mr. Harris in the chair) announced that the hour of 2 o'clock had arrived, and laid before the Senate its unfinished business, viz, the bill (H. R. 7845) defining "options" and "futures," imposing special taxes on dealers therein, and requiring such persons engaged in selling certain products to obtain license, and for other purposes; and

The Senate resumed, as in Committee of the Whole, the consideration of the bill; and

The question being on the amendment proposed by Mr. Vilas to the amendment of Mr. George,

Pending debate,

Mr. Blackburn raised a question as to the presence of a quorum;

Whereupon,

The Presiding Officer (Mr. Faulkner in the chair), directed the roll to be called;

When,

Thirty-seven Senators answered to their names.

No quorum being present,

On motion by Mr. Manderson, at 4 o'clock and 45 minutes p. m., The Senate adjourned.

FRIDAY, JANUARY 27, 1893.

Mr. Hale announced the death of the honorable James G. Blaine, which occurred at his residence in this city at 11 o'clock this morning.

On motion by Mr. Cockrell, as a mark of respect to the memory of the deceased,

The Senate adjourned.

SATURDAY, JANUARY 28, 1893.

CREDENTIALS OF SENATORS.

The Vice-President laid before the Senate the credentials of Charles J. Faulkner, elected a Senator by the legislature of the State of West Virginia for the term of six years commencing March 4, 1893; which were read and placed on file.

Mr. McMillan presented the credentials of Francis B. Stockbridge, elected a Senator by the legislature of the State of Michigan for the term of six years commencing March 4, 1893; which were read and placed on file.

Mr. Faulkner presented the credentials of Johnson N. Camden, elected a Senator by the legislature of the State of West Virginia, to fill the vacancy occasioned by the death of John E. Kenna, for the term expiring March 3, 1895; which were read and placed on file.

SENATOR SWORN.

Mr. Camden appeared, and the oath prescribed by law having been administered to him by the Vice-President, he took his seat in the Senate.

PETITIONS AND MEMORIALS.

Petitions, memorials, etc., were presented and referred as follows:

By the Vice-President: A memorial of the Commercial Club of Albuquerque, N. Mex., praying the passage of a law for the admission of the Territories of New Mexico, Arizona, Utah, and Oklahoma into the Union; to the Committee on Territories.

Resolutions of the New York Typothetæ praying the passage of a law to provide means for adequate postal facilities in the city of New York; to the Committee on Post-Offices and Post-Roads.

By Mr. Cullom: Two petitions, praying for the appointment of a committee to investigate an alleged combine formed to depreciate the price of grain in the cities of St. Louis and Minneapolis; to the Committee on Agriculture and Forestry.

By Mr. Stockbridge: A petition of citizens of Michigan, praying the passage of a law for the establishment of a retired list for enlisted men of the United States Army after a continuous service of twenty-five years; to the Committee on Military Affairs.

By Mr. Pasco: A memorial of citizens of Florida, remonstrating against the passage of the bill granting American registry to foreign-built vessels and granting license to alien officers; to the Committee on Commerce.

By Mr. Platt: A memorial of the State Board of Trade of Connecticut, praying the repeal of the Chinese exclusion act; to the Committee on Foreign Relations.

By Mr. Voorhees: A memorial of the board of managers of the Home for Incurables, praying for the opening of California avenue, in the District of Columbia; to the Committee on the District of Columbia.

A resolution of the legislature of the State of Indiana, in favor of the repeal of the provision providing for the closing of the Columbian Exposition on the Sabbath day; to the Select Committee on the Quadro-Centennial.

By Mr. Teller: A petition of members of Col. McLane's Erie Three Months' Regiment, of Pennsylvania, praying that said regiment be placed upon the same basis as other regiments that responded to the call of the President in 1861; to the Committee on Military Affairs.

By Mr. Dixon: A petition of Charles G. Gilliat, praying payment of an award of the Court of Claims of a certain French spoliation claim; to the Committee on Claims, to accompany the joint resolution S. R. 143.

By Mr. Dolph: A letter of the surveyor-general of Oregon, addressed to him, recommending an increase of the clerical force in his office; to the Committee on Appropriations, to accompany an amendment intended to be proposed to the legislative, executive, and judicial appropriation bill, No. 10331.

The Vice-President laid before the Senate a memorial of the Washington World's Fair Commission, praying such legislation as will prevent the introduction and spread of cholera into the United States; which was referred to the Committee on Immigration.

Resolutions praying the passage of the bill for the opening up to settlement of the Cherokee Outlet were presented as follows:

By Mr. Cockrell: Resolutions of the Kansas City Live Stock Exchange, of Kansas City, Mo., and resolutions of the Commercial Exchange, of Kansas City, Mo.

By Mr. Vest: Resolutions of the Kansas City Live Stock Exchange.

Ordered, That they lie on the table.

Mr. Coke presented a petition of citizens of Texas, praying the passage of the antioption bill.

Ordered, That it lie on the table.

Memorials remonstrating against the passage of the antioption bill were presented as follows:

By Mr. Cockrell: A memorial of the Commercial Club of Kansas City, Mo.

By Mr. Washburn: A memorial of the Chamber of Commerce of Minneapolis, Minn.

Ordered, That they lie on the table.

Petitions, etc., praying for the establishment of a national quarantine, and for the suspension of immigration into the United States, etc., were presented as follows:

By Mr. Sherman: Resolutions of boards of health of certain towns in Ohio.

By Mr. Palmer: A petition of citizens of Illinois.

By Mr. Chandler: Three petitions of citizens of the United States, and a resolution of the National Board of Trade.

By Mr. Cullom: A petition of citizens of Illinois.

Ordered, That they be referred to the Committee on Immigration.

Memorials, etc., praying for the repeal of the provision of law providing for the purchase of silver bullion, were presented as follows:

By Mr. Peffer: A petition of citizens of Kansas.

By Mr. Platt: Resolutions of the State Board of Trade of Connecticut.

By Mr. Washburn: A memorial of the Duluth Stock Exchange, and a petition of citizens of Minnesota.

By Mr. Dawes: A petition of citizens of Massachusetts.

Ordered, That they lie on table.

Petitions praying the repeal of the provision providing for the opening of the Columbian Exposition on the Sabbath day were presented as follows:

By Mr. Washburn: Several petitions of citizens of Minnesota.
By Mr. Cockrell: Three petitions of citizens of Missouri.
By Mr. Stockbridge: Several petitions of citizens of Michigan.
By Mr. Vest: Four petitions of citizens of Missouri.
By Mr. Higgins: Two petitions of citizens of Delaware.
By Mr. Sherman: Two petitions of citizens of Ohio.
By Mr. Hiscock: A petition of citizens of New York.
By Mr. Palmer: Several petitions of citizens of Illinois.
By Mr. Cullom: A petition of citizens of Illinois.

Ordered, That they be referred to the Select Committee on the Quadro-Centennial.

Memorials remonstrating against the repeal of the provision providing for the closing of the Columbian Exposition on the Sabbath day were presented as follows:

By the Vice-President: Four memorials of citizens of the United States.
By Mr. Irby: A memorial of citizens of South Carolina.
By Mr. Stockbridge: A memorial of citizens of Michigan.
By Mr. Higgins: A memorial of citizens of Delaware.
By Mr. Bate: A memorial of citizens of Tennessee.

By Mr. Pasco: A memorial of citizens of Florida.

Ordered, That they be referred to the Select Committee on the Quadro-Centennial.

On motion by Mr. Chandler,

Ordered, That all petitions and memorials relating to immigration be taken from the table and referred to the Committee on Immigration.

REPORTS OF COMMITTEES.

Mr. Faulkner, from the Committee on the District of Columbia, to whom was referred the bill (H. R. 6922) to amend section 452 of the Revised Statutes relating to the District of Columbia, concerning conveyance of real estate, reported it without amendment.

Mr. Faulkner, from the Committee on the District of Columbia, to whom was referred the bill (S. 3080) supplementary to an act entitled "An act to provide a government for the District of Columbia," approved February 21, 1871, and also an act entitled "An act for the government of the District of Columbia, and for other purposes," approved June 20, 1874, reported it with amendments.

Mr. Stewart, from the Committee on Appropriations, to whom was referred the bill (H. R. 9625) making appropriations for the support of the Army for the fiscal year ending June 30, 1894, and for other purposes, reported it with amendments and submitted a report (No. 1224) thereon.

Mr. Manderson, from the Committee on Military Affairs, to whom was referred the bill (S. 2782) to restore Eugene Wells to the Army, reported it without amendment and submitted a report (No. 1225) thereon.

Mr. Manderson, from the Committee on Military Affairs, to whom was referred the bill (S. 3696) for the relief of Brig. Gen. John R. Brooke, United States Army, reported it with amendments and submitted a report (No. 1226) thereon.

Mr. Chandler, from the Committee on Immigration, to whom the subject was referred, reported a bill (S. 3786) establishing additional regulations concerning immigration to the United States; which was read the first and second times by unanimous consent.

Mr. Frye, from the Committee on Commerce, to whom was referred the bill (H. R. 9176) relating to contracts of common carriers and to certain obligations, duties, and rights in connection with the carriage of property, reported it with amendments.

Mr. Dawes, from the Committee on Appropriations, to whom was referred the bill (H. R. 9923) making appropriations for fortifications and other works of defense, for the armament thereof, for the procurement of heavy ordnance for trial and service, and for other purposes, reported it with amendments and submitted a report (No. 1227) thereon.

Mr. Proctor, from the Committee on Military Affairs, to whom was referred the bill (H. R. 2582) for the relief of Andrew B. Knapp, reported it with an amendment and submitted a report (No. 1228) thereon.

Mr. Coke, from the Committee on Commerce, to whom was referred the bill (S. 3660) for the establishment of a light-house, fog signal, and line lights at or near the mouth of the Brazos River, Texas, reported it without amendment.

Mr. Cullom, from the Committee on Commerce, to whom was referred the bill (S. 3753) relating to the anchorage and movement of vessels in the port of Chicago, reported it with amendments.

The Senate proceeded, by unanimous consent, to consider the said bill as in Committee of the Whole; and the reported amendments having been agreed to, the bill was reported to the Senate and the amendments were concurred in.

Ordered, That the bill be engrossed and read a third time.

The said bill was read the third time.

Resolved, That it pass, and that the title thereof be as aforesaid.

Ordered, That the Secretary request the concurrence of the House of Representatives therein.

MESSAGE FROM THE HOUSE.

A message from the House of Representatives, by Mr. Towles, its chief clerk:

Mr President: I am directed to return to the Senate, in compliance with its request, the bill (S. 1678) for the relief of William Smith and others.

The House of Representatives has agreed to the resolution of the Senate requesting the President of the United States to return to the Senate the enrolled bill (S. 2625) to provide for the punishment of offenses on the high seas; and

It has agreed to the amendments of the Senate to the bill (H. R. 5049) to remove the charge of desertion against Lucius L. Dyer.

The House of Representatives has passed, without amendment, the bill (S. 3115) for the relief of Clement Reeves; and

It has passed the bill (S. 509) granting an increase of pension to Thomas J. Matlock, with an amendment in which it requests the concurrence of the Senate.

The House of Representatives has passed the following bills, in which it requests the concurrence of the Senate:

H. R. 2850. An act for the relief of F. Y. Ramsey, the heir at law and distributee of Joseph Ramsey; and

H. R. 10146. An act to authorize the Oklahoma Midland Railway Company to construct and operate a railway, telegraph, and telephone lines through the Indian and Oklahoma Territories, and for other purposes.

The Speaker of the House of Representatives, having signed an enrolled bill, H. R. 5597, I am directed to bring it to the Senate for the signature of its President.

INTRODUCTION OF BILLS AND JOINT RESOLUTION.

Bills and a joint resolution were introduced, read the first and second times by unanimous consent, and referred as follows:

By Mr. Pasco: A bill (S. 3787) to authorize the construction of a bridge across the St. Marys River between the States of Florida and Georgia; to the Committee on Commerce.

By Mr. Teller: A bill (S. 3788) granting right of way to the Colorado River Irrigation Company through the Yuma Indian Reservation, Cal. ; to the Committee on Indian Affairs.

By Mr. Harris: A bill (S. 3789) to authorize the investigation by the Attorney-General of certain claims alleged to be due the late proprietors of the Knoxville Whig for advertising, and authorizing the payment therefor by the Secretary of the Treasury of any amounts found by the Attorney-General to be legally or equitably due; to the Committee on Claims.

By Mr. Chandler: A bill (S. 3790) for the relief of William Dillon; to the Committee on Claims.

A bill (S. 3791) to define and to provide for the execution of the provisions of sections 1390, 1476, and 1480 of the Revised Statutes of the United States relative to the commissions of naval officers; to the Committee on Naval Affairs.

By Mr. Proctor: A bill (S. 3792) to incorporate the American University ; to the Committee on the District of Columbia.

By Mr. Dixon: A joint resolution (S. R. 143) for the more effectual carrying out of the provisions of the act approved March 3, 1891, entitled " An act making appropriations to supply deficiencies in the appropriations for the fiscal year ending June 30, 1891, and for prior years, and for other purposes;" to the Committee on Claims.

MEMORIAL OF C. C. MERRICK.

On motion by Mr. Cullom,

Ordered, That the Committee on the Judiciary be discharged from the further consideration of the memorial of C. C. Merrick, to inquire into the legality of the disposition of the 2 per cent fund by the legislature of the State of Alabama, and that he have leave to withdraw the same from the files of the Senate.

PREVENTION OF CONTAGIOUS OR INFECTIOUS DISEASES.

Mr. Chandler submitted the following resolution; which was considered by unanimous consent and agreed to:

Resolved, That the Secretary of the Treasury be directed to inform the Senate what rules and regulations, if any, are now in existence and in force at the port of New York for the prevention of the introduction into this country of contagious or infectious diseases; and to specifically state what precautions against such diseases are prescribed to be observed at the ports of departure, upon the vessels on their voyages, and in the harbor of arrival; and also to inform the Senate by what authority of law such rules and regulations have been established.

INVESTIGATION BY COMMITTEE ON COMMERCE.

Mr. Dolph submitted the following resolution; which was referred to the Committee on Commerce and ordered to be printed:

Resolved, That the Committee on Commerce be, and they are hereby, authorized to sit, by subcommittee or otherwise, during the recess of Congress, at such places in the United States as they may deem proper; and that they be, and they are hereby, authorized to inquire into the laws and regulations governing the expenditures of moneys appropriated for the improvement of rivers and harbors, and the supervision and auditing of the accounts for such expenditure, and the manner in which such expenditures are made and the accounts thereof audited, and the character, importance, and condition of the works in progress for the improvement of rivers and harbors, and all matters connected with the subject of the improvement of the water ways of the country, with power to administer oaths and take testimony, to employ a stenographer and a clerk, and to appoint a sergeant-at-arms from the messengers of the Senate; and that the actual necessary expenses of the said committee, properly incurred in the execution of this resolution, shall be paid out of the contingent fund of the Senate in the usual manner, upon the order of the chairman of the committee.

HOUSE BILLS REFERRED.

The bills last received from the House of Representatives for concurrence were read the first and second times by unanimous consent.

Ordered, That the bill H. R. 2850 be referred to the Committee on Claims, and that the bill H. R. 10146 be referred to the Committee on Indian Affairs.

ENROLLED BILL SIGNED.

Mr. Dubois reported from the committee that they had examined and found duly enrolled the bill (H. R. 5597) for the relief of William Smith and others;

Whereupon,

The Vice-President signed the same, and it was delivered to the committee to be presented to the President of the United States.

PRESENTATION OF BILL.

Mr. Dubois reported from the committee that on the 26th instant they presented to the President of the United States the enrolled bill (S. 3727) to amend " An act authorizing the construction of a railway, street-railway, motor, wagon, and pedestrian bridge over the Missouri River, near Council Bluffs, Iowa, and Omaha, Nebr., and to extend the time for the completion of the bridge therein provided for."

HOUR OF NEXT MEETING.

On motion by Mr. Hale,

Ordered, That when the Senate adjourn it be to 2 o'clock p. m. on Monday next.

PRESIDENTIAL APPROVALS.

A message from the President of the United States, by Mr. Pruden, his secretary:

Mr. President: The President of the United States approved and signed, on the 27th instant, an act (S. 1631) to establish a life-saving station at Gay Head, on the coast of Massachusetts; and

He this day approved and signed the following acts:

S. 3117. An act relating to post traderships; and

S. 3407. An act to authorize the Court of Claims to hear and determine the claims of certain New York Indians against the United States.

Ordered, That the Secretary notify the House of Representatives thereof.

ADDITIONAL COPIES OF BILL.

On motion by Mr. Chandler, and by unanimous consent,

Ordered, That 1,000 additional copies of the bill (S. 3786) establishing additional regulations concerning immigration to the United States be printed for the use of the Senate.

EXECUTIVE SESSION.

On motion by Mr. Sherman,

The Senate proceeded to the consideration of executive business; and

After the consideration of executive business the doors were reopened, and

On motion by Mr. Harris, at 4 o'clock and 25 minutes p. m.,

The Senate adjourned.

MONDAY, JANUARY 30, 1893.

The Vice-President being absent, the President *pro tempore* assumed the Chair.

MESSAGE FROM THE HOUSE.

A message from the House of Representatives, by Mr. Towles, its chief clerk :

Mr. President: The House of Representatives insists upon its amendment to the bill (S. 1303) to increase the pension of Mrs. S. A. Farquharson. It agrees to the conference asked by the Senate on the disagreeing votes of the two Houses thereon, and has appointed Mr. Wilson of Missouri Mr. Barwig, and Mr. Houk of Tennessee, managers at the same on its part.

The House of Representatives has passed the following resolutions, which I am directed to communicate to the Senate:

Resolved, That the business of the House be now suspended that opportunity may be given for tributes to the memory of the Hon. Eli T. Stackhouse, late a Representative from the State of South Carolina.

Resolved, That as a particular mark of respect to the memory of the deceased, and in recognition of his eminent abilities as a distinguished public servant, the House, at the conclusion of these memorial proceedings, shall stand adjourned.

Resolved, That the Clerk communicate these resolutions to the Senate.

Resolved, That the Clerk be instructed to send a copy of these resolutions to the family of the deceased.

The Speaker of the House of Representatives having signed three enrolled bills, S. 985, H. R. 5049, and H. R. 10062, and an enrolled joint resolution S. R. 124, I am directed to bring the same to the Senate for the signature of its President.

AQUEDUCT BRIDGE.

The President *pro tempore* laid before the Senate a letter of the Commissioners of the District of Columbia, transmitting, in answer to a resolution of the Senate of the 21st instant, a report relative to the condition of the piers of the Aqueduct Bridge; which was referred to the Committee on the District of Columbia and ordered to be printed.

PETITIONS AND MEMORIALS.

Petitions, memorials, etc., were presented and referred as follows:

By Mr. Cameron: A memorial of the Chinese Equal Rights League of Philadelphia, Pa., praying the repeal of the Chinese exclusion act; to the Committee on Foreign Relations.

A memorial of the Philadelphia Builders' Exchange, praying for the establishment of a permanent census bureau, and for the collection and publication of statistics relating to farm mortgages; to the Committee on the Census.

By Mr. Kyle: A memorial of the legislature of South Dakota in favor of the passage of a law giving preference to veterans of the late war in appointment to and retention in the civil service; to the Committee on Civil Service and Retrenchment.

By Mr. Vest: A resolution of the Commercial Club of Kansas City, Mo., praying the establishment of a road department; to the Committee on Agriculture and Forestry.

By Mr. Sherman: A petition of citizens of Ohio, praying for the free delivery of the mails in the rural districts; to the Committee on Post-Roads and Post-Roads.

A petition of citizens of Ohio, praying the passage of a law making certain issues of money a full legal tender in payment of all debts; to the Committee on Finance.

A petition of citizens of Ohio, praying the passage of a law for the encouragement of silk culture; and

A petition of citizens of Ohio, praying the passage of a law to prevent the manufacture of impure lard; to the Committee on Agriculture and Forestry.

By Mr. Cullom: A petition of citizens of Illinois, praying for the appointment of a committee to investigate an alleged combine formed to depreciate the price of grain at St. Louis and Minneapolis; to the Committee on Agriculture and Forestry.

By Mr. Perkins: A petition of citizens of Kansas, praying for a reduction of the appropriations in the river and harbor appropriation bill; to the Committee on Commerce.

A petition of citizens of Kansas, in behalf of William Lambert, praying that he be allowed a pension; to the Committee on Pensions.

By Mr. Harris: A petition of members of the legislature of Tennessee, praying the passage of the bill for the classification of post-office clerks; to the Committee on Post-Offices and Post-Roads.

A memorial of marble producers of Tennessee, remonstrating against unjust discrimination in favor of foreign marble used in the construction of public buildings; to the Select Committee on Additional Accommodations for the Library of Congress.

By Mr. Vilas: A resolution of the Lawrence University, of Appleton, Wis., praying for the establishment of a permanent census bureau and for the collection and publication of statistics relating to farm mortgages; to the Committee on the Census.

By Mr. Sawyer: A petition of citizens of Wisconsin, praying the passage of the bill to limit the amount of wearing apparel that may be admitted free of duty; to the Committee on Finance.

By Mr. Hawley: Resolutions of the Connecticut State Grange, praying the repeal of the so-called Chinese exclusion act; to the Committee on Foreign Relations.

By Mr. Cockrell: Resolutions of the Commercial Club of Kansas City, Mo., praying for the establishment of a road department; to the Committee on Agriculture and Forestry.

By Mr. Felton: A memorial of the Chamber of Commerce of San Francisco, Cal., praying the passage of a national quarantine law; to the Committee on Immigration.

A memorial of the Chamber of Commerce of San Francisco, Cal., praying that steps be taken looking to the laying of an ocean telegraph cable to Australia; to the Committee on Commerce.

Mr. Washburn presented resolutions of the House of Representative of the legislature of the State of Minnesota, praying the passage of the antioption bill.

Ordered, That they lie on the table.

Mr. Pettigrew presented a memorial of citizens of South Dakota, remonstrating against the repeal of the law providing for the purchase of silver bullion.

Ordered, That it lie on the table.

Petitions praying the repeal of the provision providing for the closing of the Columbian Exposition on the Sabbath day were presented as follows:

By Mr. Cameron: Several petitions of citizens of Pennsylvania.
By Mr. Cullom: A petition of citizens of Illinois.
By Mr. Pasco: A petition of citizens of Florida.
By Mr. Vilas: Several petitions of citizens of Wisconsin.

Ordered, That they be referred to the Select Committee on the Quadro Centennial.

Memorials remonstrating against the repeal of the provision providing for the closing of the Columbian Exposition on the Sabbath day were presented as follows:

By the President pro tempore: Two memorials of citizens of the United States.

By Mr. Cameron: Two memorials of citizens of Pennsylvania.
By Mr. Butler: A memorial of citizens of South Carolina.

Ordered, That they be referred to the Select Committee on the Quadro-Centennial.

Petitions praying the passage of the antioption bill were presented as follows:

By Mr. Sherman: A petition of citizens of Ohio.
By Mr. Cullom: A petition of citizens of Illinois.
By Mr. Sawyer: A petition of citizens of Wisconsin.
By Mr. Washburn: A petition of citizens of Minnesota.
By Mr. Hawley: A petition of citizens of Connecticut.

Ordered, That they lie on the table.

Memorials remonstrating against the passage of the antioption bill were presented as follows:

By Mr. Davis: A memorial of the Chamber of Commerce of Minneapolis, Minn.

By Mr. McMillan: A memorial of the Board of Trade of Detroit, Mich.

By Mr. Waltball: A memorial of citizens of Mississippi.

By Mr. Vest: A memorial of the Commercial Club of Kansas City, Mo.

Ordered, That they lie on the table.

Petitions praying the passage of a law to suspend immigration into the United States, for the appointment of a commission to investigate the subject of immigration, etc., were presented as follows:

By Mr. Cameron: Several petitions of citizens of Pennsylvania.
By Mr. Cullom: A petition of citizens of Illinois.
By Mr. Sherman: Resolutions of boards of health of certain towns in Ohio.

By Mr. Felton: A memorial of the Chamber of Commerce of San Francisco, Cal.

Ordered, That they be referred to the Committee on Immigration.

Memorials, etc., praying the repeal of the law providing for the purchase of silver bullion, were presented as follows:

By Mr. Dawes: A memorial of citizens of Massachusetts.
By Mr. Cameron: A memorial of citizens of Pennsylvania.
By Mr. Felton: A memorial of the Chamber of Commerce of San Francisco, Cal.

By Mr. Davis: Resolutions of the Duluth Stock Exchange, and a petition of citizens of Minnesota.

By Mr. Perkins: A memorial of citizens of Kansas.
By Mr. Washburn: A memorial of citizens of Minnesota.
By Mr. Hawley: A resolution of the Connecticut State Board of Trade.

Ordered, That they lie on the table.

Mr. Perkins presented a memorial of the Kansas City Live Stock Exchange, a memorial of the Kansas City Board of Trade, and a petition of citizens of Kansas, praying for the opening of the Cherokee Outlet to settlement.

Ordered, That they lie on the table.

ENROLLED BILLS EXAMINED.

Mr. Dubois reported from the committee that they had examined and found duly enrolled the following bills and joint resolution:

S. 985. An act to provide for the enlargement of the military post at Fort Wayne, Mich.;

H. R. 5049. An act to amend the military record of Lucius L. Dyer;

H. R. 10062. An act to authorize the construction of a bridge across the Osage River, between the mouths of the Pomme de Terre River and Buffalo Creek, in Benton County, Missouri; and

S. R. 124. A joint resolution directing the Secretary of War to investigate the subject of raft-towing on the Great Lakes and their connecting waters.

REPORTS OF COMMITTEES.

Mr. Allison, from the Committee on Appropriations, to whom was referred the bill (H. R. 10038) making appropriations for the government of the District of Columbia for the fiscal year ending June 30, 1894, and for other purposes, reported it with amendments and submitted a report (No. 1229) thereon.

Mr. Kyle, from the Select Committee on Indian Depredations, to whom was referred the bill (S. 3682) for the relief of Robert McGee, reported it with amendments and submitted a report (No. 1230) thereon.

Ordered, That it lie on the table.

Mr. Morrill, from the Committee on Public Buildings and Grounds, to whom was referred the bill (H. R. 9592) authorizing the Secretary of the Treasury to obtain plans and specifications for public buildings to be erected under the supervision of the Treasury Department, and providing for local supervision of the construction of the same, reported it with amendments.

Mr. McMillan, from the Committee on the District of Columbia, reported a joint resolution (S. R. 144) to provide for maintenance of order during inaugural ceremonies, March, 1893; which was read the first and second times by unanimous consent and considered as in Committee of the Whole; and no amendment being made, it was reported to the Senate.

Ordered, That it be engrossed and read a third time.

The said resolution was read the third time by unanimous consent.

Resolved, That it pass, and that the title thereof be as aforesaid.

Ordered, That the Secretary request the concurrence of the House of Representatives therein.

INTRODUCTION OF BILLS.

Bills were introduced, read the first and second times by unanimous consent, and referred as follows:

By Mr. Washburn: A bill (S. 3793) to authorize the construction of a bridge over the St. Louis River between the States of Wisconsin and Minnesota; to the Committee on Commerce.

By Mr. Wilson: A bill (S. 3794) for the relief of Enoch Davis; to the Committee on Military Affairs.

By Mr. Hunton: A bill (S. 3795) to authorize the Washington, Alexandria and Mount Vernon Electric Railway Company to construct a bridge across the Potomac River, and to construct a railroad over the same and through certain streets and reservations of Washington; to the Committee on the District of Columbia.

By Mr. Faulkner: A bill (S. 3796) to amend "An act to prevent the manufacture and sale of adulterated food or drugs in the District of Columbia," and transfer the execution thereof to the Department of Agriculture;" to the Committee on Agriculture and Forestry.

By Mr. Sawyer: A bill (S. 3797) establishing a fog signal at Kewaunee, Wis.; to the Committee on Commerce.

MATERIAL IN THE LIBRARY BUILDING.

Mr. Harris submitted the following resolution; which was considered, by unanimous consent and agreed to:

Resolved, That the Chief of Engineers of the Army be, and he is hereby, directed to inform the Senate whether or not he has used or is using, has contracted for or is contracting for or is proposing to contract for, any building material from foreign countries to be used in the construction of the Library building now in course of construction, and if such material is being used, or intended to be used, he will inform the Senate the character, quantity, and actual or probable cost of such imported material, and the reasons for such importation.

ANNEXATION OF THE HAWAIIAN ISLANDS.

Mr. Chandler submitted the following resolution for consideration:

Resolved by the Senate (the House of Representatives concurring), That the President be requested to enter into negotiations with the present provisional government of the late kingdom of Hawaii for the admission of the islands as a Territory into the United States, and to lay any convention which he may make before Congress for ratification by legislation.

MINING TROUBLES IN IDAHO.

Mr. Dubois submitted the following resolution; which was referred to the Committee on Education and Labor:

Be it resolved, That a select committee of seven Senators be appointed by the President of the Senate, whose duty it shall be to investigate and report to the Senate the facts in relation to the recent serious difficulties existing between the employing silver-mine owners and the working miners of Idaho, as to the employment, for private purposes, of armed bodies of men or detectives in connection with said difficulties.

The investigation shall extend to and embrace, in addition, an inquiry into the causes and necessity for the employment of United States soldiers, and the conduct of such soldiers.

The committee shall ascertain if present serious difficulties exist between employers and employés, or if justice has been or is being denied anyone through a suspension of the writ of habeas corpus, or through any dereliction of duty on the part of the United States courts.

The committee shall also inquire into the character, objects, and purposes of the Miners' Union, and whether the obligations required of its members conflict or conflicted with the obligations and duties these members owe to the State and Government as law-abiding citizens.

In addition to the testimony and conclusions of fact, the committee will consider and report, by bill or otherwise, what legislation, if any, will tend to prevent a recurrence of similar troubles.

Said committee, either as a full committee or through subcommittees thereof, shall have authority to send for persons and papers, administer oaths to witnesses, and take testimony in Washington or elsewhere, according to its discretion, during the present session or approaching recess of Congress, and to employ a clerk, messenger, and stenographer, the expenses of the investigation to be paid from the contingent fund of the Senate.

DEALINGS IN "OPTIONS" AND "FUTURES."

The Senate resumed, as in Committee of the Whole, the consideration of the bill (H. R. 7845) defining "options" and "futures," imposing special taxes on dealers therein, and requiring such persons engaged in selling certain products to obtain license, and for other purposes; and

The question being on the amendment proposed by Mr. Vilas to the amendment of Mr. George,

Pending debate,

On motion by Mr. Platt, at 5 o'clock and 45 minutes p. m.,

The Senate adjourned.

TUESDAY, JANUARY 31, 1893.

The Vice-President resumed the chair.

ENROLLED BILLS SIGNED.

The Vice-President signed the three enrolled bills, S. 985, H. R. 5049, and H. R. 10062, and the enrolled joint resolution, S. R. 124, yesterday reported to have been examined, and they were delivered to the committee to be presented to the President of the United States.

MESSAGE FROM THE HOUSE.

A message from the House of Representatives, by Mr. Towles, its chief clerk:

Mr. President: The House of Representatives has passed; without amendment, the following bills of the Senate:

S. 3311. An act to refer the claim of Jessie Benton Fremont to certain lands and the improvements thereon, in San Francisco, Cal., to the Court of Claims; and

S. 3753. An act relating to the anchorage and movement of vessels in the port of Chicago.

The House of Representatives has passed a bill (H. R. 8123) granting to the Santa Fe, Prescott and Phœnix Railway Company the right of way across the Whipple Barracks military reservation in Arizona, in which it requests the concurrence of the Senate.

The Speaker of the House of Representatives having signed an enrolled bill, S. 3115, I am directed to bring the same to the Senate for the signature of its President.

ENROLLED BILL SIGNED.

Mr. Dubois reported from the committee that they had examined and found duly enrolled the bill (S. 3115) for the relief of Clement Reeves;

Whereupon,

The Vice-President signed the same, and it was delivered to the committee to be presented to the President of the United States.

HOUSE BILL REFERRED.

The bill, H. R. 8123, last received from the House of Representatives for concurrence was read the first and second times by unanimous consent and referred to the Committee on Military Affairs.

THOMAS J. MATLOCK.

The Vice-President laid before the Senate the amendment of the House of Representatives to the bill (S. 509) granting an increase of pension to Thomas J. Matlock; and

On motion by Mr. Wilson,

Resolved, That the Senate agree thereto.

Ordered, That the Secretary notify the House of Representatives thereof.

EXECUTIVE COMMUNICATIONS.

The Vice-President laid before the Senate a letter of the Secretary of the Treasury, transmitting, in answer to the resolution of the Senate of July 26, 1892, a statement of the taxes collected on the outstanding circulation of national and State banks since 1863, the losses to stockholders, etc.; which was referred to the Committee on Finance and ordered to be printed.

The Vice-President laid before the Senate a report of the Commissioner of Patents for the year 1892, giving a detailed statement of all moneys received for patents and from other sources, and a detailed statement of all expenditures for contingent and miscellaneous expenses; which was referred to the Committee on Patents and ordered to be printed.

CREDENTIALS OF A SENATOR.

The Vice-President laid before the Senate the credentials of Roger Q. Mills, elected a Senator by the legislature of the State of Texas for the term of six years commencing March 4, 1893; which were read and placed on file.

PETITIONS AND MEMORIALS.

Petitions, memorials, etc., were presented and referred as follows:

By Mr. Teller: Resolutions of the State Beet Sugar Association, praying for the establishment of experimental stations in the State of Colorado for the purpose of encouraging the culture of sugar beets; to the Committee on Agriculture and Forestry.

By the Vice-President: A resolution of the legislature of South Dakota in favor of the passage of a law giving preference to veterans of the late war in appointment to and retention in the civil service; to the Committee on Civil Service and Retrenchment.

By Mr. Hale: A memorial of the Board of Trade of Portland, Me., praying for the establishment of a permanent census bureau and for the collection and publication of statistics relating to farm mortgages; to the Committee on the Census.

By Mr. Palmer: A memorial of the Pattern Makers' National League, remonstrating against the employment of unnaturalized citizens upon Government works; to the Committee on Education and Labor.

By Mr. Gorman: A petition of citizens of Maryland, praying the passage of a bill for the suspension of immigration into the United States; to the Committee on Immigration.

By Mr. Turpie: A memorial of the North American Turnerbund, remonstrating against the passage of the bill for the restriction of immigration into the United States; to the Committee on Immigration.

By Mr. Hill: A memorial on behalf of various religious bodies, praying for a refund on the duties paid on pictorial stained-glass windows for church edifices; to the Committee on Finance.

By Mr. Cullom: A petition of citizens of Illinois, praying for the appointment of a committee to investigate an alleged combine formed to depreciate the price of grain at St. Louis and Minneapolis; to the Committee on Agriculture and Forestry.

By Mr. Peffer: A petition of Eli Gilbert and others, members of the Kansas State militia, praying to be allowed pensions; to the Committee on Pensions.

A memorial of marble-producers of Tennessee, remonstrating against unjust discrimination in favor of foreign marble in the construction of the Congressional Library building; to the Select Committee on Additional Accommodations for the Library of Congress.

A resolution of District Assembly, No. 66, Washington, D. C., praying the passage of a bill for the demonetization of gold and for the issue of paper money sufficient to supply the demands of trade; to the Committee on Finance.

By Mr. Bate: A memorial of the Post-Office Clerks' Association of Tennessee, praying the passage of a bill for the classification of post-office clerks; to the Committee on Post-Offices and Post-Roads.

By Mr. Chandler: A memorial of citizens of the District of Columbia, remonstrating against authority being given to the Commissioners of the District of Columbia to reassess special assessments and taxes which have been or shall hereafter be declared void by the courts; to the Committee on the District of Columbia.

By Mr. Frye: A petition of citizens of the District of Columbia, praying the passage of a law for protection against mob violence; for an amendment of the law relating to the forfeiture of collateral before the police court of the District; and for the passage of the bill in relation to bond in real-estate cases appealed to the upper court; to the Committee on the Judiciary.

A memorial of the Lincoln Sailors' and Soldiers' National Monument Association of the District of Columbia, praying for authority to erect a monument in the park adjoining the Howard University to the memory of the colored soldiers and sailors of the late war; to the Committee on the District of Columbia.

A petition of citizens of Maine, praying an appropriation to aid in defraying the expenses of the Pan-American Medical Congress to be held in Washington in September, 1893; to the Committee on Foreign Relations.

A memorial of the Board of Trade of Portland, Me., praying for the establishment of a permanent census bureau and for the collection and publication of statistics relating to farm mortgages; to the Committee on the Census.

By Mr. Mitchell: A petition of Marshall R. Hathaway, praying to be allowed a pension; to the Committee on Pensions.

A resolution of the legislature of Oregon in favor of an increase of the appropriation for the improvement at the mouth of the Siuslaw River; to the Committee on Commerce.

By Mr. Pasco: Papers relating to the application of Aaron Daniel to be allowed a pension; to the Committee on Pensions, to accompany the bill S. 3801.

By Mr. Voorhees: A petition of Louis V. Schmidle, praying for the removal of the charge of desertion from his military record; to the Committee on Military Affairs, to accompany the bill S. 3802.

By Mr. Manderson: Papers relating to the application of veterinary Surgeon John Tempany, United States Army, to be placed on the retired list of the Army; to the Committee on Military Affairs, to accompany the bill S. 3803.

Mr. Stockbridge presented a resolution of the Lumber Trade Association of New York, praying the early completion of the Nicaragua Canal under the control and direction of the United States.

Ordered, That it lie on the table.

Mr. Butler presented a petition of citizens of South Carolina, praying the passage of the antioption bill.

Ordered, That it lie on the table.

Petitions praying the repeal of the provision providing for the closing of the Columbian Exposition on the Sabbath day were presented as follows:

By Mr. Palmer: A petition of citizens of Illinois.
By Mr. Peffer: A petition of citizens of Kansas.
By Mr. Stockbridge: A petition of citizens of Michigan.
By Mr. Hale: A petition of citizens of Maine.
By Mr. Butler: A petition of citizens of South Carolina.
By Mr. Voorhees: A petition of citizens of Indiana.

Ordered, That they may be referred to the Select Committee on the Quadro-Centennial.

Memorials remonstrating against the repeal of the provision providing for the closing of the Columbian Exposition on the Sabbath day, were presented as follows:

By Mr. Gorman: Six memorials of citizens of Maryland;
By Mr. George: A memorial of citizens of Mississippi;
By Mr. Cullom: A memorial of citizens of Illinois;
By Mr. Dawes: A memorial of citizens of Massachusetts.
By Mr. Voorhees: A memorial of citizens of Indiana;
By Mr. Turpie: A memorial of citizens of Indiana;

Ordered, That they be referred to the Select Committee on the Quadro Centennial.

Memorials, etc., praying for the repeal of the law providing for the purchase of silver bullion, were presented as follows:

By the Vice-President: A resolution of the republican club of Massachusetts.

By Mr. Hiscock: A petition of citizens of New York;
By Mr. Hill: Two petitions of citizens of New York;
By Mr. Washburn: A memorial of the Duluth Clearing-House Association;

By Mr. Blodgett: A petition of citizens of New Jersey.
By Mr. Butler: A memorial of the Chamber of Commerce of Charleston, S. C.
By Mr. Sawyer: A petition of citizens of Wisconsin.
Ordered, That they lie on the table.

REPORTS OF COMMITTEES.

Mr. Harris, from the Committee on Epidemic Diseases, to whom was referred the bill (H. R. 9757) granting additional quarantine powers and imposing additional duties upon the Marine-Hospital Service, reported it with an amendment.

Mr. Turpie, from the Committee on Pensions, to whom were referred the following bills, reported them severally without amendment and submitted written reports thereon as follows:

H. R. 8780. An act to restore to the pension roll Mary Eleanor White, as former widow of Capt. George W. Hazzard; Report No. 1231.

H. R. 8784. An act granting a pension to Edward Smitherman; Report No. 1232.

H. R. 8969. An act to grant a pension to Lydia Bollman, dependent sister; Report No. 1233, and

H. R. 8924. An act granting a pension to the widow of James A. Kelly; Report No. 1234.

Mr. Vilas, from the Committee on Pensions, to whom was referred the bill (H. R. 8054) to increase the pension of Mary L. Bacon, widow of the late George B. Bacon, late lieutenant-commander in the United States Navy, reported it without amendment and submitted a report (No. 1235) thereon.

Mr. Frye, from the Committee on Foreign Relations, to whom was referred the bill (S. 3429) for the relief of Charles T. Russell, reported it without amendment and submitted a report (No. 1236) thereon.

Mr. Jones, of Arkansas, from the Committee on Indian Affairs, to whom was referred the bill (H. R. 9527) to restore to the public domain a portion of the White Mountain Apache Indian Reservation in the Territory of Arizona, and for other purposes, reported it with amendments.

Mr. Manderson, from the Committee on Printing, to whom was referred the resolution submitted by him on the 23d instant, to print extra copies of Parts I and II of the Report of the Superintendent of the Coast and Geodetic Survey for the year 1892, reported it without amendment and submitted a report (No. 1237) thereon.

The Senate proceeded, by unanimous consent, to consider the said resolution; and

Resolved, That the Senate agree thereto.

Ordered, That the Secretary request the concurrence of the House of Representatives therein.

Mr. Vest, from the Committee on Commerce, to whom was referred the bill (H. R. 10063) to amend "An act authorizing the construction of a high wagon bridge across the Missouri River at or near Sioux City, Iowa, etc.," reported it without amendment.

The Senate proceeded, by unanimous consent, to consider the said bill as in Committee of the Whole; and no amendment being made, it was reported to the Senate.

Ordered, That it pass to a third reading.

The said bill was read the third time.

Resolved, That it pass.

Ordered, That the Secretary notify the House of Representatives thereof.

INTRODUCTION OF BILLS.

Bills were introduced, read the first and second times by unanimous consent, and referred as follows:

By Mr. Berry: A bill (S. 3798) to authorize the building of a railroad bridge at Little Rock, Ark.; to the Committee on Commerce.

By Mr. Faulkner: A bill (S. 3799) to amend an act to incorporate the Georgetown and Tennallytown Railway Company of the District of Columbia, which became a law August 10, A. D. 1888; to the Committee on the District of Columbia.

By Mr. Pugh: A bill (S. 3800) to authorize the construction of a bridge over the Tennessee River at or near Sheffield, Ala.,; to the Committee on Commerce.

By Mr. Pasco: A bill (S. 3801) granting a pension to Aaron Daniel, of Lafayette County, Florida; to the Committee on Pensions.

By Mr. Voorhees: A bill (S. 3802) to remove the charge of desertion from the military record of Lewis V. Schmidle; to the Committee on Military Affairs.

By Mr. Manderson: A bill (S. 3803) for the retirement of veterinary surgeon John Tempany, Ninth Cavalry, United States Army; to the Committee on Military Affairs.

By Mr. Mitchell: A bill (S. 3804) for the relief of Marshall R. Hathaway; to the Committee on Pensions.

By Mr. Sawyer: A bill (S. 3805) creating circuit courts of interstate commerce and for other purposes; to the Committee on Interstate Commerce.

INVESTIGATION BY THE COMMITTEE ON INDIAN AFFAIRS.

Mr. Dawes, from the Committee on Indian Affairs, reported the following resolution; which was referred to the Committee to Audit and Control the Contingent Expenses of the Senate:

Resolved, That the Committee on Indian Affairs be instructed, either by full committee or such subcommittee or committees as may be appointed by the chairman thereof, with the full power of such committee, to continue during the recess of Congress the investigations authorized by the resolutions of May 13, 1890, and February 27, 1891, with the authority and in the manner and to the extent provided in said resolutions, and in pursuance of such investigations to visit the several Indian reservations, Indian schools supported in whole or in part by the Government, and the five nations in the Indian Territory, or any reservation where, in the opinion of said committee, it may be necessary to extend their investigations.

2. That said committee or subcommittee shall have power to send for persons and papers, to administer oaths, and to examine witnesses under oath touching the matters whic . they are hereby empowered to investigate, and may hold their sessions during the recess of the Senate at such place or places as they may determine; and the necessary and proper expense incurred in the execution of this order shall be paid out of the contingent fund of the Senate upon vouchers approved by the chairman of said committee.

OZAMA RIVER BRIDGE.

Mr. Higgins submitted the following resolution; which was referred to the Committee on Foreign Relations:

Resolved, That the Secretary of State be directed to furnish the Senate with all the correspondence and other documents in connection with the building of the Ozama River bridge at Santo Domingo City by American citizens, and to inform the Senate of what steps have been taken by the State Department to protect the interests of said citizens, if it is not incompatible with the public service.

ANNEXATION OF THE HAWAIIAN ISLANDS.

The Vice President laid before the Senate the resolution yesterday submitted by Mr. Chandler relative to the admission of the Hawaiian Islands as a Territory into the United States; and

After debate,

Ordered, That the further consideration thereof be postponed to to-morrow.

THOMAS P. MORGAN, JR.

On motion by Mr. Gorman, and by unanimous consent,

The vote postponing indefinitely the bill (S. 1361) for the relief of Thomas P. Morgan, jr., was reconsidered, and the bill recommitted to the Committee on Claims.

PRESIDENTIAL APPROVALS.

A message from the President of the United States, by Mr. Pruden, his secretary:

Mr. President: The President of the United States approved and signed on the 28th instant an act (S. 3727) to amend "An act authorizing the construction of a railway, street-railway, motor, wagon, and pedestrian bridge over the Missouri River, near Council Bluffs, Iowa, and Omaha, Nebr., and to extend the time for the completion of the bridge therein provided for;" and

He this day approved and signed an act (S. 3581) to amend an act entitled "An act to forfeit certain lands heretofore granted for the purpose of aiding in the construction of railroads, and for other purposes."

Ordered, That the Secretary notify the House of Representatives thereof.

PRESENTATION OF BILLS.

Mr. Dubois reported from the committee that they this day presented to the President of the United States the following enrolled bills and joint resolution:

S. 3115. An act for the relief of Clement Reeves;

S. 985. An act to provide for the enlargement of the military post at Fort Wayne, Mich.; and

S. R. 124. Joint resolution directing the Secretary of War to investigate the subject of raft-towing on the Great Lakes and their connecting waters.

DEALINGS IN "OPTIONS" AND "FUTURES."

The Senate resumed, as in the Committee of the Whole, the consideration of the bill (H. R. 7845) defining "options" and "futures," imposing special taxes on dealers therein, and requiring such persons engaged in selling certain products to obtain license, and for other purposes; and

The question being on the amendment proposed by Mr. Vilas to the amendment of Mr. George, viz: Commencing in the first line of the part proposed to be inserted, strike out the following words: "'Options' and 'futures,' as hereinbefore defined, are hereby declared to be obstructions to and restraints upon commerce among the States and with foreign nations, and to be illegal and void; and"

It was determined in the negative, { Yeas 21
{ Nays 50

On motion by Mr. Mills,

The yeas and nays being desired by one-fifth of the Senators present,

Those who voted in the affirmative are

Messrs. Blodgett, Caffery, Cameron, Daniel, Dixon, Gibson, Gorman, Gray, Hill, Hiscock, Hoar, Jones of Arkansas, McPherson, Mills, Platt, Sawyer, Stewart, Vest, Vilas, White, Wolcott.

Those who voted in the negative are,

10 s

Messrs. Allison, Bate, Berry, Butler, Call, Carey, Chandler, Cockrell, Coke, Cullom, Davis, Dawes, Dolph, Dubois, Felton, Frye, Gallinger, George, Gordon, Hale, Hansbrough, Harris, Hawley, Higgins, Hunton, Irby, Kyle, McMillan, Manderson, Mitchell, Morgan, Morrill, Pasco, Peffer, Perkins, Power, Proctor, Pugh, Ransom, Sherman, Shoup, Squire, Stockbridge, Teller, Turpie, Vance, Voorhees, Walthall, Washburn, Wilson.

So the amendment to the amendment was not agreed to.

The question recurring on the amendment proposed by Mr. George, viz:

Strike out all after section 3 down to the last section of the bill, and in lieu thereof insert the following:

SEC. 4. *That "options" and "futures," as hereinbefore defined, are hereby declared to be obstructions to and restraints upon commerce among the States and with foreign nations, and to be illegal and void; and if any person shall be a party, either as buyer or seller, to any contract or agreement hereinbefore defined as "options" or "futures" he shall be deemed guilty of a misdemeanor, and on conviction therefor in either the proper district or circuit court of the United States shall be fined for every such offense in a sum not less than the whole sum paid or agreed to be paid or received, or agreed to be received on any such contract, if the sum shall amount to as much as one thousand dollars; but if the said sum shall not amount to one thousand dollars then he shall be fined one thousand dollars, and in addition thereto shall be imprisoned for a period not less than one year nor more than five years; and every distinct contract shall constitute a separate offense of the seller and also of the buyer.*

SEC. 5. *That any merchant or other exchange, board, or other association in or through which "options" or "futures," or both, shall be made, encouraged, settled, regulated, or adjusted, are hereby declared to be unlawful combinations to obstruct commerce among the States and with foreign nations. And if it shall appear that any such board, association, or exchange has encouraged, regulated, adjusted or promoted any such contract or settlement, the said board, association, or exchange shall be subject to proceedings to be instituted in the circuit court of the United States by bill in equity, by which such action of such association or exchange, or by any member thereof, shall be enjoined. Such proceedings shall be commenced by the proper district attorney of the United States or the Attorney-General, whenever there shall be reasonable ground to suspect that any such board, association, or exchange has violated this section. Such proceedings may also be instituted and maintained by any private person or persons, on leave of the court first had and obtained; and it shall be the duty of the court to grant such leave, upon proof made by affidavit that there is reasonable ground to believe that any such board, association, or exchange has violated this section. In cases of such suits by a private party or parties, the proceedings shall be in the name of the United States on the relation of such private party or parties. In case such proceedings are successful the court shall adjudge to the relator or relators full costs and also full attorney's fees for prosecuting such suit, together with reasonable compensation for his or their time spent, and expenses incurred in and about said suit. But such suit, at the relation of a private party, shall be subject to the control of the district attorney or Attorney-General.*

SEC. 6. *That any person who shall, in the United States, by letter or telegram or other communication sent from the United States to any foreign country, or by an agent, resident in a foreign country, enter into any contract hereinbefore described as "options" or "futures," or who shall do any other act aiding and encouraging the making of such contracts in any foreign country, or shall, in the United States, perform any such contract or pay any damages for nonperformance, or do any act in part performance of such contract or in part satisfaction of such damage, shall be deemed guilty of a misdemeanor, and be triable and punishable as provided for in section four of this act.*

SEC. 7. *That any contract herein defined as "options" or "futures," when made outside the jurisdiction of the United States, shall be held utterly null and void when attempted to be enforced in any court of the United States.*

SEC. 8. *That when any money or other valuable thing has been paid or delivered on any contract herein prohibited, or in satisfaction of any damages or any part of the damages claimed from a breach of any such contract, the title to such money or other valuable thing shall be held as not having been passed by such delivery or payment, and the same may be recovered back in the proper district or circuit court of the United States at the suit of the party making such delivery or payment, or by his legal representatives, if he be dead, and shall be subject to his creditors as their property; and there shall be no defense against any such proceeding by a creditor to subject said money or property to his debt arising out of any transaction between the parties to such payment or delivery, except the actual and bona fide return of the money paid or thing delivered before such proceeding had been commenced.*

It was determined in the negative, { Yeas 19
{ Nays 51

On motion by Mr. George,

The yeas and nays being desired by one-fifth of the Senators present,

Those who voted in the affirmative are,

Messrs. Berry, Blackburn, Butler, Call, Coke, Dolph, George, Gorman, Harris, Hunton, Jones of Arkansas, Morgan, Morrill, Pasco, Peffer, Pugh, Ransom, Vance, Walthall.

Those who voted in the negative are,

Messrs. Allison, Blodgett, Caffery, Cameron, Carey, Carlisle, Cockrell, Cullom, Daniel, Davis, Dawes, Dixon, Dubois, Felton, Gallinger,

Gibson, Gray, Hale, Hansbrough, Hawley, Higgins, Hill, Hiscock, Hoar, Irby, Kyle, McMillan, McPherson, Manderson, Mills, Mitchell, Palmer, Perkins, Platt, Power, Proctor, Sawyer, Sherman, Shoup, Squire, Stewart, Stockbridge, Teller, Turpie, Vest, Vilas, Voorhees, Washburn, White, Wilson, Wolcott.

So the amendment was not agreed to.

On motion by Mr. Mills to amend the bill by inserting as an additional section the following:

SEC.—. *That all railroad corporations, associations, or companies engaged in interstate commerce shall, within six months after the passage of this act, provide, at all stations established or that may be established on their roads, side-track facilities for all persons or parties to erect and maintain private elevators or warehouses, of a capacity of not less than five thousand bushels each, for the storage of grain while waiting shipment on such lines of railroad, and to permit such elevators and warehouses to be erected, maintained, controlled, and operated by any person or corporation desiring to erect, maintain, control, and operate the same for said persons. And it is hereby made the duty of said railroad companies to receive and carry over their lines all grain offered for shipment to and from such private elevators and warehouses, and they shall receive its their cars and carry over their lines of railroad all grain offered in carload lots at such stations without precious storage, and shall transport the same at the same rates charged for transporting grain for elevator and miller companies. And every railroad company that shall fail or refuse to comply with the provisions of this section shall be guilty of a misdemeanor, and on conviction shall be fined the sum of ten thousand dollars for each offense.*

It was determined in the negative, { Yeas .... 21 / Nays 46

On motion by Mr. Mills,

The yeas and nays being desired by one-fifth of the Senators present, Those who voted in the affirmative are,

Messrs. Berry, Butler, Call, Coke, Daniel, Gibson, Gordon, Gray, Harris, Hunton, Jones of Arkansas, Kyle, McPherson, Mills, Power, Pugh, Ransom, Vest, Vilas, Walthall, White.

Those who voted in the negative are,

Messrs. Allison, Blackburn, Blodgett, Caffery, Cameron, Carey, Chandler, Cockrell, Gullom, Davis, Dawes, Dixon, Dubois, Felton, Frye, Gallinger, Gorman, Hale, Hawley, Higgins, Hill, Hiscock, Irby, McMillan, Manderson, Mitchell, Morgan, Morrill, Palmer, Peffer, Perkins, Pettigrew, Platt, Proctor, Sawyer, Sherman, Shoup, Squire, Stewart, Stockbridge, Teller, Turpie, Voorhees, Washburn, Wilson, Wolcott.

So the amendment was not agreed to.

A further amendment having been proposed by Mr. Mills; and the same having been amended on the motion of Mr. Butler, the motion of Mr. Harris.

On the question to agree to the amendment as amended, viz: Insert as an additional section the following:

SEC. 15. *Any person, corporation, or company who shall enter into any combination or agreement to fix the price at which grain or cotton, or other agricultural product shall be bought or sold in any market in the United States, or to prevent competition in the sale and purchase of grain or cotton, or other agricultural product, in any market in the United States, shall be guilty of a misdemeanor, and on conviction shall be fined the sum of ten thousand dollars for each offense so committed,*

It was determined in the negative, { Yeas .... 26 / Nays 40

On motion by Mr. Butler,

The yeas and nays being desired by one-fifth of the Senators present, Those who voted in the affirmative are,

Messrs. Blackburn, Butler, Caffery, Call, Carey, Coke, Cullom, Daniel, Frye, Gallinger, Gibson, Gorman, Harris, Hiscock, Hunton, Jones of Arkansas, Kyle, Mills, Pugh, Ransom, Vest, Vilas, Walthall, White, Wolcott.

Those who voted in the negative are,

Messrs. Allison, Blodgett, Cameron, Chandler, Davis, Dixon, Dubois, Faulkner, Felton, Gordon, Gray, Hale, Hawley, Higgins, Hill, Irby, McMillan, McPherson, Manderson, Mitchell, Morgan, Morrill, Palmer, Peffer, Perkins, Pettigrew, Platt, Power, Proctor, Sawyer, Sherman, Shoup, Squire, Stewart, Stockbridge, Teller, Turpie, Voorhees, Washburn, Wilson.

So the amendment was not agreed to.

On motion by Mr. Power to amend the bill by inserting after the word "bacon," in line 4, section 3, the following words: *and silver bullion,*

It was determined in the negative, { Yeas .... 21 / Nays 44

On motion by Mr. Power,

The yeas and nays being desired by one-fifth of the Senators present, Those whose voted in the affirmative are,

Messrs. Carey, Chandler, Daniel, Dawes, Dolph, Dubois, Hansbrough, Jones of Arkansas, Mills, Mitchell, Palmer, Pettigrew, Power, Sawyer, Shoup, Squire, Stewart, Teller, Washburn, White, Wolcott.

Those who voted in the negative are,

Messrs. Allison, Berry, Blackburn, Blodgett, Butler, Caffery, Call, Cameron, Cockrell, Cullom, Davis, Dixon, Felton, Frye, Gallinger,

Gordon, Gray, Hale, Harris, Hawley, Higgins, Hill, Irby, Kyle, McMillan, McPherson, Manderson, Morgan, Morrill, Peffer, Perkins, Platt, Proctor, Pugh, Ransom, Sherman, Stockbridge, Turpie, Vest, Vilas, Voorhees, Walthall, Wilson.

So the amendment was not agreed to.

A further amendment having been proposed by Mr. Wolcott, On the question to agree thereto,

It was determined in the negative.

No further amendment being proposed to the bill, it was reported to the Senate and the amendments made in the Committee of the Whole were concurred in.

Ordered, That the amendments be engrossed and the bill be read a third time.

The said bill as amended was read the third time.

On the question, Shall the bill pass?

It was determined in the affirmative, { Yeas .... 40 / Nays 29

On motion by Mr. White,

The yeas and nays being desired by one-fifth of the Senators present, Those who voted in the affirmative are,

Messrs. Allison, Blackburn, Call, Carey, Chandler, Cockrell, Cullom, Davis, Dubois, Faulkner, Felton, Frye, Gallinger, Gordon, Hale, Hansbrough, Hawley, Higgins, Hunton, Irby, Kyle, McMillan, Manderson, Mitchell, Morgan, Morrill, Peffer, Perkins, Pettigrew, Proctor, Sherman, Shoup, Squire, Stockbridge, Teller, Turpie, Voorhees, Walthall, Washburn, Wilson.

Those who voted in the negative are,

Messrs. Berry, Blodgett, Butler, Caffery, Cameron, Coke, Daniel, Dawes, Dixon, Gibson, Gorman, Gray, Harris, Hill, Hiscock, Hoar, Jones of Arkansas, McPherson, Mills, Palmer, Platt, Pugh, Ransom, Sawyer, Stewart, Vest, Vilas, White, Wolcott.

So it was

Resolved, That the bill pass.

Whereupon,

Mr. Washburn submitted a motion that the Senate request a conference with the House of Representatives on the bill and amendments.

FORTIFICATION APPROPRIATION BILL.

On motion by Mr. Dawes,

The Senate proceeded to consider, as in Committee of the Whole, the bill (H. R. 9923) making appropriations for fortifications and other other works of defense, for the armament thereof, for the procurement of heavy ordnance for trial and service, and for other purposes; and

The reported amendments having been agreed to in part,

On motion by Mr. Dawes, at 5 o'clock and 50 minutes p. m.,

The Senate adjourned.

WEDNESDAY, FEBRUARY 1, 1893.

MESSAGE FROM THE HOUSE.

A message from the House of Representatives, by Mr. Towles, its chief clerk:

Mr. President: The House of Representatives has passed the following resolution, in which it requests the concurrence of the Senate:

Resolved by the House of Representatives (the Senate concurring), That there be printed 6,000 copies of House report No. 2309 on the sweating system, of which 2,000 copies shall be for the use of the Senate and 4,000 copies for the use of the House.

EXECUTIVE COMMUNICATION.

The Vice-President laid before the Senate a letter of the Secretary of the Interior, transmitting a copy of a communication from the Commissioner of Indian Affairs and accompanying agreement made by the commission appointed to treat with the Indians of the Siletz Reservation in Oregon for the cession of the surplus lands of the reservation upon which they reside; which was referred to the Committee on Indian Affairs and ordered to be printed.

COMMITTEE OF ARRANGEMENTS FOR THE INAUGURATION.

The Vice-President appointed Mr. Teller, Mr. Ransom, and Mr. McPherson members of the committee to make the necessary arrangements for the inauguration of the President-elect of the United States, on the 4th day of March next, under the resolution of the Senate of January 26.

MESSAGE FROM THE PRESIDENT.

The following message was received from the President of the United States, by Mr. Pruden, his secretary:

To the Senate of the United States:

In compliance with a resolution of the Senate (the House of Representatives concurring) I return herewith the bill (S. 3625) entitled "An act to provide for the punishment of offenses on the high seas."

BENJ. HARRISON.

EXECUTIVE MANSION, *January 31, 1893.*

The message was read.

Ordered, That it lie on the table.

PETITIONS AND MEMORIALS.

Petitions, memorials, etc., were presented and referred as follows:

By Mr. Vest: A petition of citizens of Missouri, praying the passage of an amendment to the Constitution providing for the election of Senators of the United States by a direct vote of the people; to the Committee on Privileges and Elections.

By Mr. Bate: A petition of members of the legislature of Tennessee, praying for the classification of post-office clerks; to the Committee on Post-Offices and Post-Roads.

By Mr. Felton: Resolutions of the Chamber of Commerce of San Francisco, Cal., praying for the establishment by the United States of a provisional government over the Hawaiian Islands; to the Committee on Foreign Relations and ordered to be printed.

Five petitions of citizens of Arizona, praying an appropriation for the construction of a deep-water harbor at San Pedro, Cal.; to the Committee on Commerce.

By Mr. Brice: A memorial of the Ohio Society of Engineers, praying an appropriation for the work of testing the strength of material of American woods; to the Committee on Appropriations.

A memorial of the Single Tax Club of Dayton, Ohio, praying for the establishment of a permanent census bureau, and for the collection and publication of statistics relating to farm mortgages; to the Committee on the Census.

A petition of Dr. James T. Whittaker, praying for the continuance of the publication of "The Index Medicus;" to the Committee on Appropriations.

A memorial of the Young Men's Christian Association of Toledo, Ohio, praying the passage of the bill (S. 2824) regulating rates of postage on second-class mail matter at letter-carrier offices; to the Committee on Post-Offices and Post-Roads.

A petition of citizens of Ohio, praying for the establishment of a bureau to be known as the Road Department; to the Committee on Agriculture and Forestry.

By Mr. Jones, of Arkansas: A paper relating to the application of Bertrand & Scull for compensation for certain property taken from them by the United States authorities during the late war; to the Committee on Claims, to accompany the bill S. 3810.

Mr. Sherman presented resolutions of the Chamber of Commerce of Cincinnati, Ohio, praying the passage of a law to enlarge the powers of the Interstate Commerce Commission.

Ordered, That they lie on the table.

Mr. Brice presented several petitions of citizens of Ohio, praying the passage of the antioption bill.

Ordered, That they lie on the table.

Mr. Brice presented a memorial of citizens of Ohio, remonstrating against the repeal of the provision providing for the closing of the Columbian Exposition on the Sabbath day; which was referred to the Select Committee on the Quadro-Centennial.

Petitions, etc., praying for the repeal of the law providing for the purchase of silver bullion, were presented as follows:

By Mr. Vilas: A petition of citizens of Wisconsin.

By Mr. Sherman: A petition of citizens of Ohio.

By Mr. Washburn: A memorial of the Chamber of Commerce of St. Paul, Minn.

By Mr. Brice: A petition of citizens of Ohio.

Ordered, That they lie on the table.

Petitions, etc., praying for the establishment of a national quarantine, for the suspension of immigration, etc., were presented as follows:

By Mr. Brice: Several petitions of citizens of Ohio.

By Mr. Sherman: Several petitions of citizens of Ohio.

By Mr. Bate: A memorial of the Merchants' Exchange of Memphis, Tenn.

Ordered, That they be referred to the Committee on Immigration.

Mr. Morgan presented papers relating to the application of the Mobile and Dauphin Island Railroad and Harbor Company for an extension of time for the construction of a trestle across the shoal water between Cedar Point and Dauphin Island; which were referred to the Committee on Commerce, to accompany the bill S. 3811.

REPORTS OF COMMITTEES.

Mr. Cullom, from the Committee on Interstate Commerce, to whom was referred the bill (H. R. 10042) to amend an act entitled "An act to regulate commerce," approved February 4, 1887, as amended March 2, 1889, reported it with amendments.

Mr. Hoar, from the Committee on the Judiciary, reported a bill (S. 3806) to provide for the punishment of offenses on the high seas; which was read the first and second times by unanimous consent, and considered as in Committee of the Whole; and no amendment being made, it was reported to the Senate.

Ordered, That it be engrossed and read a third time.

The said bill was read the third time by unanimous consent.

Resolved, That it pass, and that the title thereof be as aforesaid.

Ordered, That the Secretary request the concurrence of the House of Representatives therein.

Mr. Jones, from the Committee on Claims, to whom was referred the bill (S. 3363) for the relief of the heirs of Jacob R. Davis, submitted an adverse report (No. 1238) thereon.

Ordered, That it be postponed indefinitely.

Mr. Mitchell, from the Committee on Claims, to whom was referred the bill (S. 3789) to authorize the investigation by the Attorney-General of certain claims alleged to be due the late proprietors of the Knoxville Whig for advertising, and authorizing the payment therefor by the Secretary of the Treasury of any amounts found by the Attorney-General to be legally or equitably due, reported it without amendment and submitted a report (No. 1239) thereon.

Mr. Vest, from the Committee on Commerce, to whom was referred the bill (S. 3798) to authorize the building of a railroad bridge at Little Rock, Ark., reported it with an amendment.

The Senate proceeded, by unanimous consent, to consider the said bill as in Committee of the Whole; and the reported amendment having been agreed to, the bill was reported to the Senate and the amendment was concurred in.

Ordered, That the bill be engrossed and read a third time.

The said bill was read the third time.

Resolved, That it pass, and that the title be amended so as to read: "A bill to amend an act entitled 'An act to authorize the building of a railroad bridge at Little Rock, Ark.'"

Ordered, That the Secretary request the concurrence of the House of Representatives therein.

INTRODUCTION OF BILLS.

Bills were introduced, read the first and second times by unanimous consent, and referred as follows:

By Mr. Perkins: A bill (S. 3807) granting a pension to Margaret Brennan; to the Committee on Pensions.

By Mr. Gibson: A bill (S. 3808) amending the charter of the Maryland and Washington Railroad Company; to the Committee on the District of Columbia.

By Mr. Jones, of Arkansas: A bill (S. 3809) for the relief of the estate of James Scull, late of Arkansas; and

A bill (S. 3810) for the relief of the firm of Bertrand & Scull, late of Arkansas; to the Committee on Claims.

By Mr. Morgan: A bill (S. 3811) to amend an act entitled "An act to grant to the Mobile and Dauphin Island Railroad and Harbor Company the right to trestle across the shoal water between Cedar Point and Dauphin Island," approved September 26, 1890; to the Committee on Commerce.

HOUR OF MEETING.

On motion by Mr. Allison, and by unanimous consent,

Ordered, That on and after Friday next, until otherwise ordered, the hour of the daily meeting of the Senate be 11 o'clock a. m.

DEALINGS IN "OPTIONS" AND "FUTURES."

The Senate proceeded to consider the motion, yesterday submitted by Mr. Washburn, that the Senate ask a conference with the House of Representatives on the bill (H. R. 7845) defining "options" and "futures," imposing special taxes on dealers therein, and requiring such dealers and persons engaged in selling certain products to obtain license, and for other purposes, and the amendments of the Senate thereto; and

The motion was agreed to.

Ordered, That the conferees on the part of the Senate be appointed by the Vice-President; and

The Vice-President appointed Mr. Washburn, Mr. Mitchell, and Mr. George.

Ordered, That the Secretary notify the House of Representatives thereof.

CONSIDERATION OF APPROPRIATION BILLS.

On motion by Mr. Dawes,

The Senate resumed, as in Committee of the Whole, the consideration of the bill (H. R. 9923) making appropriations for fortifications and other works of defense, for the armament thereof, for the procurement of heavy ordnance for trial and service, and for other purposes; and the reported amendments having been further agreed to in part,

On the question to agree to the last reported amendment,

On motion by Mr. Cockrell to amend the same,

It was determined in the affirmative;

When,

The amendment as amended was agreed to.

The bill having been further amended on the motion of Mr. Teller, it was reported to the Senate and the amendments were concurred in.

Ordered, That the amendments be engrossed and the bill read a third time.

The said bill as amended was read the third time.

Resolved, That it pass.

Ordered, That the Secretary request the concurrence of the House of Representatives in the amendments.

On motion by Mr. Stewart,

The Senate proceeded to consider, as in Committee of the Whole, the bill (H. R. 9825) making appropriations for the support of the Army for the fiscal year ending June 30, 1894, and for other purposes; and the reported amendments having been agreed to, and the bill further amended, on the motion of Mr. Proctor, from the Committee on Military Affairs, it was reported to the Senate and the amendments were concurred in.

Ordered, That the amendments be engrossed and the bill read a third time.

The said bill as amended was read the third time.

Resolved, That it pass.

Ordered, That the Secretary request the concurrence of the House of Representatives in the amendments.

On motion by Mr. Allison.

The Senate proceeded to consider, as in Committee of the Whole, the bill (H. R. 10038) making appropriations for the expenses of the government of the District of Columbia for the fiscal year ending June 30, 1894, and for other purposes; and the reported amendments having been agreed to in part, and in part disagreed to, and the bill further amended on the motion of Mr. McMillan, and the motion of Mr. Allison, from the Committee on Appropriations,

Ordered, That the further consideration thereof be postponed to to-morrow.

CONSIDERATION OF HOUSE BILLS ON CALENDAR.

The Senate proceeded to consider, as in Committee of the Whole, the bill (H. R. 7028) to protect settlement rights when two or more persons settle upon the same subdivision of agricultural public lands before survey thereof; and an amendment having been proposed by Mr. Pettigrew, from the Committee on Public Lands,

Ordered, That the further consideration thereof be postponed to to-morrow.

The Senate proceeded to consider, as in Committee of the Whole, the following bills; and no amendment being made, they were severally reported to the Senate:

H. R. 8156. An act establishing a fog signal at Tibbets Point, Lake Ontario, New York;

H. R. 8602. An act to authorize the construction of a bridge across the Mobile River by the Chicago, Mobile and Gulf Ports Railroad Company;

H. R. 5752. An act to amend an act approved August 6, 1888, entitled "An act to authorize the construction of a bridge across the Alabama River;"

H. R. 5012. An act to increase the pension of Thomas Enlow; and

H. R. 9433. An act granting a pension to Mrs. Ann Mercer Slaughter.

Ordered, That they pass to a third reading.

The said bills were severally read the third time.

Resolved, That they pass.

Ordered, That the Secretary notify the House of Representatives thereof.

The Senate proceeded to consider, as in Committee of the Whole, the following bills; and the reported amendments having been agreed to, the bills were severally reported to the Senate and the amendments were concurred in:

H. R. 9758. An act to amend the charter of the Eckington and Soldiers' Home Railway Company of the District of Columbia;

H. R. 6798. An act to authorize the construction of a bridge across the Warrior River by the Montgomery, Tuscaloosa and Memphis Railway Company;

H. R. 9930. An act for the construction and maintenance of a bridge across the St. Lawrence River; and

H. R. 1795. An act to increase the pension of A. J. Copenhaver, late a soldier in the Mexican war.

Ordered, That the amendments be engrossed and the bills read a third time.

The said bills as amended were severally read the third time.

Resolved, That they pass.

Ordered, That the Secretary request the concurrence of the House of Representatives in the amendments.

CHEROKEE OUTLET.

On motion by Mr. Platt,

The Senate resumed, as in Committee of the Whole, the consideration of the bill (H. R. 9190) to ratify and confirm an agreement with the Cherokee Nation of Indians of the Indian Territory, to make appropriation for carrying out the same, and for other purposes.

When,

EXECUTIVE SESSION.

On motion by Mr. Sawyer,

The Senate proceeded to the consideration of executive business; and

After the consideration of executive business the doors were reopened, and

On motion by Mr. Cockrell, at 5 o'clock and 55 minutes, p. m.,

The Senate adjourned.

THURSDAY, FEBRUARY 2, 1893.

RESIGNATION OF HON. JOHN G. CARLISLE.

The Vice-President laid before the Senate a letter of Hon. John G. Carlisle, notifying the Senate that he had forwarded his resigna-

tion as a Senator of the United States from the State of Kentucky to the governor of that State, to take effect from the 4th day of February, 1893.

Ordered, That it lie on the table.

HOUSE RESOLUTION REFERRED.

The Vice-President laid before the Senate the resolution, yesterday received from the House of Representatives for concurrence, to print 6,000 copies of House Report No. 2309 on the "sweating system," which was read and referred to the Committee on Printing.

TELLERS FOR COUNTING THE ELECTORAL VOTE.

On motion by Mr. Teller,

Ordered, That the tellers on the part of the Senate, authorized by the concurrent resolution of the two Houses relating to the counting of the electoral votes for President and Vice-President of the United States, be appointed by the Vice-President; and

The Vice-President appointed Mr. Hale and Mr. Blackburn.

Ordered, That the Secretary notify the House of Representatives thereof.

PETITIONS AND MEMORIALS.

Petitions, memorials, etc., were presented and referred as follows:

By Mr. Dolph: A resolution of the legislature of Oregon in favor of legislation looking to the annexation of the Hawaiian Islands to the United States; to the Committee on Foreign Relations.

By Mr. Felton; A resolution of the Board of Trade of Pomona, Cal., and two petitions of citizens of New Mexico, praying an appropriation for the construction of a deep-water harbor at San Pedro, Cal.; to the Committee on Commerce.

By Mr. Quay: Resolution of the Master Builders' Exchange of Philadelphia, Pa., praying for the establishment of a permanent census bureau, and for the collection and publication of statistics relating to farm mortgages; to the Committee on the Census.

By Mr. Jones, of Arkansas: A petition of W. J. Murray, praying to be allowed a pension; to the Committee on Pensions.

By Mr. Washburn: Resolutions from the Brown County Agricultural Society of Minnesota, praying the passage of a law to place railroads and telegraph lines under the control of the Government; for a reduction of the tariff; for the encouragement of reciprocity with foreign nations; for the repeal of all internal-revenue taxes, and for a graduated income tax; to the Committee on Finance.

By Mr. McPherson: A petition of Mary E. Hutman in behalf of Ella Hatfield, praying that she be allowed a pension; to the Committee on Pensions.

By Mr. Sherman: Papers relating to the application of John Russell for the correction of his military record; to the Committee on Military Affairs, to accompany the bill S. 3813.

By Mr. McPherson: Papers relating to the application of Ella Hatfield to be allowed a pension; to the Committee on Pensions, to accompany the bill S. 3816.

By Mr. Quay: Several petitions of citizens of Pennsylvania, praying the passage of a law for the suspension of immigration into the United States; to the Committee on Immigration.

By Mr. Cullom: Six petitions of citizens of Illinois, praying for the appointment of a committee to investigate an alleged combine formed to depreciate the price of grain at St. Louis and Minnesota; to the Committee on Agriculture and Forestry.

Mr. Palmer presented a memorial of John Cowden relative to the improvement of the Mississippi River and its tributaries and the stopping of the overflow of their valley lands.

Ordered, That it lie on the table and be printed.

Mr. Sherman presented a memorial of the New York Lumber Trade Association, praying the completion of the Nicaragua Canal under the direction and control of the United States Government.

Ordered, That it lie on the table.

Mr. Peffer presented resolutions of the Board of Trade of Kansas City, Kans., praying the passage of the bill providing for the opening up to settlement of the Cherokee Outlet.

Ordered, That they lie on the table.

Memorials remonstrating against the repeal of the provision providing for the closing of the Columbian Exposition on the Sabbath day were presented as follows:

By Mr. Cockrell: A memorial of citizens of Missouri.

By Mr. Dawes: A memorial of citizens of Massachusetts.

By Mr. Quay: Several memorials of citizens of Pennsylvania.

By Mr. Sherman: Several memorials of citizens of Ohio.

Ordered, That they be referred to the Select Committee on the Quadro-Centennial.

REPORTS OF COMMITTEES.

Mr. Proctor, from the Committee on Military Affairs, to whom was referred the bill (H. R. 4375) for the relief of Charles S. Blood, reported it without amendment and submitted a report (No. 1240) thereon.

Mr. Davis, from the Committee on Military Affairs, to whom was referred the bill (H. R. 1162) for the relief of Harlow L. Street, reported it with an amendment and submitted a report (No. 1241) thereon.

Mr. Manderson, from the Committee on Military Affairs, to whom was referred the bill (S. 3711) granting the right of way through the Arlington reservation for railroad purposes, reported it with amendments and submitted a report (No. 1242) thereon.

Mr. Frye, from the Committee on Commerce, to whom was referred the joint resolution (S. R. 139) authorizing the Secretary of War to make use of an unexpended balance in deepening the harbor at Oswego, N. Y., reported it with an amendment.

Mr. Peffer, from the Committee on Claims, to whom was referred the bill (S. 376) for the relief of Thomas H. Russell, submitted an adverse report (No. 1243) thereon.

Ordered, That it be postponed indefinitely.

Mr. Palmer, from the Committee on Military Affairs, to whom was referred the bill (S. 1920) for the relief of the legal representatives of Orremus B. Boyd, reported it without amendment.

Mr. Bate, from the Committee on Military Affairs, to whom was referred the bill (H. R. 9437) for the removal of the charge of desertion against William H. Holloway, reported it without amendment and submitted a report (No. 1244) thereon.

Mr. Jones, of Arkansas, from the committee on Indian Affairs, to whom was referred the bill (H. R. 7762) to ratify and confirm agreement between the Puyallup Indians and the Northern Pacific Railroad Company for right of way through the Puyallup Indian Reservation, reported it with an amendment.

Mr. Proctor, from the Committee on Military Affairs, to whom was referred the bill (H. R. 4215; to correct the military record of Capt. William C. Knowlton, reported it without amendment and submitted a report (No. 1245) thereon.

Mr. Manderson, from the Committee on Military Affairs, to whom was referred the bill (H. R. 8727) for the relief of S. J. Brooks, reported it without amendment and submitted a report (No. 1246) thereon.

Mr. Manderson, from the Committee on Military Affairs, to whom was referred the bill (S. 3507) for the relief of George H. Jewett, of Arlington, Washington County, Nebraska, reported it without amendment and submitted a report (No. 1247) thereon.

Mr. Sherman, from the Committee on Foreign Relations, to whom was referred the resolution submitted by Mr. Higgins January 31, 1893, calling for the correspondence and information relating to the Osama River bridge at Santo Domingo city, reported it with amendments.

The Senate proceeded, by unanimous consent, to consider the said resolution; and the reported amendments having been agreed to, the resolution as amended was agreed to as follows:

Resolved, That the President, if not incompatible with the public service, be directed to furnish the Senate with all the correspondence and other documents in connection with the building of the Osama River bridge at Santo Domingo city by American citizens, and to inform the Senate what steps have been taken by the State Department to protect the interests of said citizens.

Mr. Felton, from the Select Committee on Forest Reservations in California, who were instructed by a resolution of the Senate of July 28, 1892, to inquire into the rights, and so forth, of settlers on lands within the limits of the Yosemite and Sequoia National Parks in California, submitted a report (No. 1248) thereon.

Mr. Manderson, from the Committee on Printing, to whom was referred the resolution submitted by him January 9, 1892, to print the annual volumes of the observations of the Naval Observatory for the years 1889, 1890, 1891, and 1892, reported it without amendment and submitted a report (No. 1249) thereon.

The Senate proceeded, by unanimous consent, to consider said resolution; and

Resolved, That the Senate agree thereto.

Ordered, That the Secretary request the concurrence of the House of Representatives therein.

INTRODUCTION OF BILLS.

Bills were introduced, read the first and second times by unanimous consent, and referred as follows:

By Mr. Dawes: A bill (S. 3812) to ratify and confirm an agreement with the Alsea and other bands of Indians located upon the Siletz Reservation, in the State of Oregon, and to make appropriations for carrying the same into effect; to the Committee on Indian Affairs.

By Mr. Sherman: A bill (S. 3813) granting an honorable discharge to John Russell; to the Committee on Military Affairs.

By Mr. Dubois: A bill (S. 3814) to establish a port of delivery at Bonners Ferry, Idaho; to the Committee on Commerce.

By Mr. Peffer: A bill (S. 3815) to readjust the salary and allowances of the postmasters at Guthrie, Oklahoma City, and Kingfisher, in Territory of Oklahoma; to the Committee on Post-Offices and Post-Roads.

By Mr. McPherson: A bill (S. 3816) granting a pension to Ella Hatfield, invalid daughter of Maj. David Hatfield, First Regiment New Jersey Infantry Volunteers; to the Committee on Pensions.

ADMISSION OF HAWAIIAN ISLANDS.

On motion by Mr. Chandler,

Ordered, That the resolution submitted by him January 30, relative to the admission of the Hawaiian Islands as a Territory into the United States, be referred to the Committee on Foreign Relations.

AIDS TO NAVIGATION.

On motion by Mr. Dolph,

The Senate proceeded to consider, as in Committee of the Whole, the bill (H. R. 9955) providing for sundry light-houses and other aids to navigation; and the reported amendments having been agreed to in part, and in part disagreed to, and the bill further amended on the motion of Mr. Coke, from the Committee on Commerce, and the motion of Mr. Sawyer, it was reported to the Senate and the amendments were concurred in.

When,

EXECUTIVE SESSION.

On motion by Mr. Sherman,

The Senate proceeded to the consideration of executive business; and

After the consideration of executive business the doors were reopened.

DISTRICT APPROPRIATION BILL.

On motion by Mr. Allison,

The Senate resumed, as in Committee of the Whole, the consideration of the bill (H. R. 10038) making appropriations for the expenses of the government of the District of Columbia for the fiscal year ending June 30, 1894, and for other purposes; and,

On the question to agree to the amendment reported from line 23, page 35, to line 10, page 36,

It was determined in the negative.

The bill having been further amended, on the motion of Mr. Allison, from the Committee on Appropriations; the motion of Mr. McMillan, from the Committee on the District of Columbia, and the motion of Mr. Gallinger, it was reported to the Senate and the amendments made in Committee of the Whole were concurred in.

Ordered, That the amendments be engrossed and the bill read a third time.

The said bill as amended was read the third time.

Resolved, That it pass.

Ordered, That the Secretary request the concurrence of the House of Representatives in the amendments.

CHEROKEE INDIAN LANDS.

The Senate resumed, as in Committee of the Whole, the consideration of the bill (H. R. 9190) to ratify and confirm an agreement with the Cherokee Nation of Indians of the Indian Territory, to make appropriation for carrying out the same, and for other purposes.

When,

On motion by Mr. Allison, at 6 o'clock and 10 minutes p. m.,

The Senate adjourned.

FRIDAY, FEBRUARY 3, 1893.

PETITIONS AND MEMORIALS.

Petitions, memorials, etc., were presented and referred as follows:

By the Vice-President: A memorial of the legislature of Minnesota in favor of the establishment of a national system of quarantine; to the Committee on Immigration; and

A petition of S. S. Daish & Son, of Washington, D. C., praying for the laying of an asphalt pavement from the Aqueduct Bridge to Arlington; to the Committee on the District of Columbia.

By Mr. Voorhees: A statement of J. M. Lee, captain Ninth United States Infantry, concerning alleged frauds upon the Cheyenne and Arapaho Indians of the Indian Territory; to the Committe on Indian Affairs.

By Mr. Hoar: A petition of Frederick Douglass and others, praying to be allowed a hearing before the Judiciary Committee of the Senate in respect to the lawless outrages committed in some of the Southern States upon persons accused of crime; to the Committee on the Judiciary.

By Mr. Gordon: A petition of citizens of Columbus, Ga., praying an additional appropriation for the completion of the public building at that place; to the Committee on Public Buildings and Grounds.

By Mr. Vance: A petition of W. W. Rollins, collector of internal revenue for the fifth district of North Carolina, praying to be relieved from liability for the loss of certain internal-revenue stamps destroyed by fire; to the Committee on Finance, to accompany the bill S. 3817.

By Mr. Gallinger: Papers relating to the application of George J. Barnes for the correction of his military record; to the Committee on Military Affairs, to accompany the bill S. 3720.

By Mr. Mitchell: A letter of the Secretary of the Interior, recommending an appropriation for the purchase of additional volumes of the Supreme Court reports to supply certain incomplete sets; to the Committee on Appropriations, to accompany an amendment intended to be proposed to the bill (H. R. 10238) making appropriations for sundry civil expenses, etc., and ordered to be printed.

By Mr. Cullom: A petition of citizens of Illinois, praying for the appointment of a committee to investigate an alleged combine formed to depreciate the price of grain by the millers and elevators at St. Louis and Minneapolis; to the Committee on Agriculture and Forestry.

By Mr. Mitchell: A petition of citizens of Oregon, praying the repeal of the provision providing for the closing of the Columbian Exposition on the Sabbath day; to the Select Committee on the Quadro-Centennial.

Memorials remonstrating against the repeal of the provision providing for the closing of the Columbian Exposition on the Sabbath day were presented as follows:

By the Vice-President: A memorial of citizens of the United States.

By Mr. Hiscock: A memorial of citizens of New York.

Ordered, That they be referred to the Select Committee on the Quadro-Centennial.

Petitions praying the passage of the bill for the restriction of immigration into the United States, and for the establishment of a national quarantine, were presented as follows:

By the Vice-President: A petition of citizens of the United States.

By Mr. Quay: A petition of citizens of Pennsylvania.

By Mr. Dixon: A petition of citizens of Rhode Island.

By Mr. Hoar: A petition of citizens of Massachusetts.

Ordered, That they be referred to the Committee on Immigration.

Mr. Gordon presented two petitions of citizens of Georgia, praying the repeal of the provision providing for the purchase of silver bullion.

Ordered, That they lie on the table.

Mr. Wolcott presented several petitions of citizens of Colorado, praying that the duty on lead bullion be allowed to stand, and also for the repeal of the duty on silver lead fluxing ores; which were referred to the Committee on Finance.

Mr. Teller presented three memorials of citizens of Colorado, remonstrating against the repeal of the provision of law providing for the purchase of silver bullion.

Ordered, That they lie on the table.

MESSAGE FROM THE PRESIDENT.

The following message was received from the President of the United States, by Mr. Pruden, his secretary:

To the Senate and House of Representatives:

On the 23d of July last, the following resolution of the House of Representatives was communicated to me:

Resolved, That the President be requested to inform the House, if not incompatible with the public interests, what regulations are now in force concerning the transportation of imported merchandise in bond or duty paid and products or manufactures of the United States from one port in the United States over Canadian territory to another port therein, under the provisions of section 3006 of the Revised Statutes, whether further legislation thereon is necessary or advisable, and especially whether a careful inspection of such merchandise should not be had at the frontiers of the United States upon the departure and arrival of such merchandise, and whether the interests of the United States do not require that each car containing such merchandise, while in Canadian territory, be in the custody and under the surveillance of an inspector of the Customs Department, the cost of such surveillance to be paid by the foreign carrier transporting such merchandise.

The resolution is limited in its scope to the subject of the transit of merchandise from one port in the United States, through Canadian territory, to another port in the United States, under the provision of section 3006 of the Revised Statutes; but I have concluded that a review of our treaty obligations, if any, and of our legislation upon the whole subject of the transit of goods from, to, or through Canada is desirable, and therefore address this message to the Congress.

It should be known, before new legislation is proposed, whether the United States is under any treaty obligations which affect this subject, growing out of the provisions of article 29 of the treaty of Washington. That article is as follows:

"It is agreed that, for the term of years mentioned in article 33 of this treaty, goods, wares, or merchandise arriving at the ports of New York, Boston, and Portland, and any other ports in the United States which have been or may, from time to time, be specially designated by the President of the United States, and destined for Her Britannic Majesty's possessions in North America, may be entered at the proper custom-house and conveyed in transit, without the payment of duties, through the territory of the United States, under such rules, regulations, and conditions for the protection of the revenue as the Government of the United States may from time to time prescribe; and under like rules, regulations, and conditions goods, wares, or merchandise may be conveyed in transit, without the payment of duties, from such possessions through the territory of the United States for export from the said ports of the United States.

"It is further agreed that, for the like period, goods, wares, or merchandise arriving at any of the ports of Her Britannic Majesty's possessions in North America and destined for the United States may be entered at the proper custom-house and conveyed in transit, without the payment of duties, through the said possessions, under such rules and regulations and conditions for the protection of the revenue as the government of the said possessions may from time to time prescribe; and under like rules, regulations, and conditions, goods, wares, or merchandise may be conveyed in transit, without payment of duties, from the United States through the said possessions to other places in the United States, or for export from ports in the said possessions."

It will be noticed that provision is here made—

First. For the transit in bond, without the payment of duties, of goods arriving at specified ports of the United States, and at others to be designated by the President, destined for Canada.

Second. For the transit from Canada to ports of the United States, without the payment of duties, of merchandise for export.

Third. For the transit of merchandise arriving at Canadian ports, destined for the United States, through Canada, to the United States, without the payment of duties to the Dominion government.

Fourth. For the transit of merchandise from the United States to Canadian ports for export, without the payment of duties.

And fifth. For the transit of merchandise, without the payment of duties, from the United States, through Canada, to other places in the United States.

The first and second of these provisions were concessions by the United States and were made subject to "such rules, regulations, and conditions for the protection of the revenue as the Government of the United States may from time to time prescribe." The third, fourth, and fifth provisions of the article are concessions on the part of the Dominion of Canada, and are made subject "to such rules, regulations, and conditions for the protection of the revenue as the governments of the said possessions may from time to time prescribe." The first and second and the third and fourth of these provisions are reciprocal in their nature. The fifth, which provides for the transit of merchandise from one point in the United States, through Canada, to another point in the United States, is not met by a reciprocal provision for the passage of Canadian goods from one point in Canada to another point in Canada through the United States. If this article of the treaty is in force the obligations assumed by the United States should be fully and honorably observed until such time as this Government shall free itself from them by methods provided in the treaty or recognized by international law.

It is, however, no part of the obligation resting upon the United States under the treaty that it will use the concessions made to it by Canada. This Government would undoubtedly meet its full duty by yielding, in an ample manner, the concessions made by it to Canada. There could be no just cause of complaint by Great Britain or Canada if the compensating concession to the United States should not be exercised. We have not stipulated in the treaty that we will permit merchandise to be moved through Canadian territory from one point of the United States to another at the will of the shipper; the stipulation is on the part of Canada that it will permit such merchandise to enter its territory from the United States, to pass through it and to return to the United States without the exaction of duties and without other burdens than such as may be necessary to protect its revenues.

The questions whether we shall continue to allow merchandise to pass from one point in the United States, through Canadian territory, to another point in the United States, and, if so, to what exactions and examinations it shall be subjected on reëntering our territory, are wholly within the power of Congress, without reference to the question whether article 29 is or is not in force.

The treaty of Washington embraced a number of absolutely independent subjects. Its purpose, as recited, was "to provide for an amicable settlement of all causes of difference between the two countries." It provided for four distinct arbitrations of unsettled questions, including the Alabama claims, for a temporary settlement of the questions growing out of the fisheries, and for various arrangements affecting commerce and intercourse between the United States and the British North American possessions. Some of its provisions were made terminable by methods pointed out in the treaty. Articles 1 to 17, inclusive, provide for the settlement of the Alabama claims and of the claims of British subjects against the United States, and have been fully executed. Articles 18 to 25, inclusive, relate to the subject of the fisheries and provide for a joint commission to determine what indemnity should be paid to Great Britain for the fishing privileges conceded. These articles have been terminated by the notice provided for in the treaty.

Article 26 provides for the free navigation of the St. Lawrence, Yukon, Porcupine, and Stickeen rivers. Article 27 provides for the equal use of certain frontier canals and waterways, and contains no provision for termination upon notice. Article 28 opens Lake Michigan to the commerce of British subjects, under proper regulations, and contains a provision for its abrogation, to which reference will presently be made. Article 30 provides for certain privileges of transshipment on the lakes and northern waterways, and contains the same provision as article 29 as to the method by which it may be terminated.

Article 31 provides for the nonimposition of a Canadian export

Canada. Neither government has placed itself under any restraint as to merchandise intended for the use of its own people when such merchandise comes within its own territory. The question, therefore, as to how we shall deal with merchandise imported by our own people through a Canadian port, and with merchandise passing from one place in the United States to another through Canadian territory, is wholly one of domestic policy and law.

I turn now to consider the legislation of Congress upon this subject, upon which, as it seems to me, the duties of the Treasury and the rights of our people as to those phases of the transportation question to which I have just alluded, wholly depend. Sections 3005 and 3006 of the Revised Statutes, which are taken from the act of July 28, 1866, entitled, "An act to protect the revenue, and for other purposes" (14 Stat. L., 328), are as follows:

SEC. 3005. All merchandise arriving at the ports of New York, Boston, Portland in Maine, or any other port specially designated by the Secretary of the Treasury, and destined for places in the adjacent British provinces or arriving at the port of (Point Isabel) (Brownsville), in Texas, or any other port specially designated by the Secretary of the Treasury, and destined for places in the Republic of Mexico, may be entered at the custom-house, and conveyed, in transit, through the territory of the United States, without the payment of duties, under such regulations as the Secretary of the Treasury may prescribe.

SEC. 3006. Imported merchandise in bond, or duty paid, and products or manufactures of the United States, may, with the consent of the proper authorities of the British provinces or Republic of Mexico, be transported from one port in the United States to another port therein, over the territory of such provinces or Republic, by such routes, and under such rules, regulations, and conditions as the Secretary of the Treasury may prescribe, and the merchandise so transported shall, upon arrival in the United States from such provinces or Republic, be treated in regard to the liability to or exemption from duty, or tax, as if the transportation had taken place entirely within the limits of the United States.

Section 3102 of the Revised Statutes is also related to this subject, and is as follows:

"To avoid the inspection at the first port of arrival, the owner, agent, master, or conductor of any such vessel, car, or other vehicle, or owner, agent, or other person having charge of any such merchandise, baggage, effects, or other articles, may apply to any officer of the United States duly authorized to act in the premises, to seal or close the same, under and according to the regulations hereinafter authorized, previous to their importation into the United States; which officer shall seal or close the same accordingly; and thereupon the same may proceed to their port of destination without further inspection. Every such vessel, car, or other vehicle shall proceed, without unnecessary delay, to the port of its destination, as named in the manifest of its cargo, freight, or contents, and be there inspected. Nothing contained in this section shall be construed to exempt such vessel, car, or vehicle, or its contents, from such examination as may be necessary and proper to prevent frauds upon the revenue and violations of this title."

It will be noticed that section 3005 does not provide for the transit of merchandise through our territory from Canada to ports of the United States for export, nor have I been able to find any other law now in force that does provide for such transit. It would seem, therefore, that as to this concession made by the United States in article 29 of the treaty, legislation to put it into force was necessary, and that there is no such legislation, unless section 3 of the act of 1873 was saved by the amendment to the joint resolution abrogating the fisheries articles and article 30, limiting the repeal to so much of said act as "relates to the articles of said treaty so to be terminated." The joint resolution certainly did not repeal section 3, and if that section has ceased to be operative it is by virtue of the limitation contained in the section itself. I think it did expire by its own express limitation.

The question has presented itself whether section 3 of the act of 1873 (R. S., 2866) repealed by implication that section of the act of July, 1866, which is now section 3005 of the Revised Statutes; but I am of the opinion that the last-named section was not repealed. Section 3 of the act of 1873 was expressly intended to carry into effect a treaty obligation and was limited as to time. It contained no express repeal of the act of 1866, and, while its provisions were broader than the last-named act, they were not inconsistent, save in the provision that while the act of 1873 was in force the additional ports in the United States at which Canadian goods might be received were to be designated by the President; whereas under the act of 1866 the designation was by the Secretary of the Treasury. This last-named act related also to intercourse with Mexico and, I think, was unaffected by the act of 1873.

It will be seen that the law permits merchandise arriving at the ports of New York, Boston, Portland in Maine, and at other ports specially designated by the Secretary of the Treasury, for places in the adjacent British provinces, to be entered at the custom-house and the port where it is landed and conveyed through the territory of the United States without the payment of duty, under regulations to be prescribed by the Secretary of the Treasury. As these goods come immediately and fully under the inspection of our customs officers at the principal ports, are entered there and remain until they cross our border into Canada fully under our supervision, there

is little or no danger involved to our revenue. The regulations prescribed by the Treasury for conducting this traffic seem to me to be adequate.

As to merchandise imported into the United States from a contiguous foreign country, it is provided by section 3104 that the inspection at the first port of arrival in the United States may be avoided if the vehicle in which the same arrives has been sealed or closed by some officer of the United States, duly authorized, at some point in the contiguous country. When the act of closing or sealing conformably to the regulations of the Treasury has been effected, the car or other vehicle may proceed without unnecessary delay to the port of its destination, as named in the manifest of its cargo, freight, or contents, and be there inspected. This privilege, however, is subject to such examination at the point of entry to the United States as may be necessary to prevent fraud. It is important to be noticed that the merchandise to which this section refers is described in section 3100 as merchandise, etc., "imported into the United States from any contiguous foreign country."

A practice has grown up, and a traffic of considerable dimensions under it, of allowing merchandise from China and Japan, purchased and imported from those countries by our own citizens, and landed at ports in the Dominion of Canada to be there loaded into cars which, being sealed by an officer of the United States, or some one supposed to represent him, are forwarded through the territory of Canada, across the entire continent, and allowed to cross our frontier without other inspection than an examination of the seals. The real fact is, that the American consul can not and does not either compare the manifest with the contents of the cars, or attach the seals. The agents of the transportation companies are furnished by the consul with the seals and place them upon the cars. The practice of sealing such merchandise, notwithstanding it has been allowed by the Treasury for some years, I think is unauthorized. Such merchandise is not imported from a "contiguous country," but from China and Japan.

It has never become subject to the Canadian revenue laws as an importation from Japan to Canada, but by force of the treaty or by the courtesy of that government has been treated as subject to the revenue laws of the United States from the time of landing at the Canadian port. Our Treasury seal has been placed upon it; Canada only gives it passage. It is no more an importation from Canada than is a train load of wheat that starts from Detroit and is transported through Canada to another port of the United States. Section 3102 was enacted in 1864, two years before sections 3005 and 3006, and could not have had reference to the later methods of importing merchandise through one country to the other.

The practice to which I have referred not only equalizes the advantages of Canadian seaports with our own in the importation of goods for our domestic consumption, but makes the Canadian ports favored ports of entry. The detentions under this system at the Canadian ports are less than when the merchandise is landed at a port of the United States to be forwarded in bond to another port therein. Full effect should be given to section 3102 as to merchandise imported into the United States from Canada, so far as the appropriations enable the Treasury to provide the officers to do the work of closing and sealing. It will, however, be required that all this kind of work be done, and carefully done, by an officer of the United States, and that the duty shall in no case be delegated to the employés of the transportation companies. The considerations that it is quite doubtful whether a fraud committed in Canada by one of our agents upon our revenue would be punishable in our courts, and that such a fraud committed by anyone else certainly would not be, and that even if such acts are made penal by our statutes the criminal would be secure against extradition, seem to me to be conclusive against the policy of attempting to maintain such revenue agents in Canadian territory.

I come now to discuss another element of this international traffic, namely, the transportation of merchandise from one "port" in the United States to another "port" therein, over the territory of Canada. This traffic is enormous in its dimensions, and very great interests have grown up in the United States in connection with it. Section 3006 authorizes this traffic, subject to "such rules, regulations, and conditions as the Secretary of the Treasury may prescribe." But the important limitation is from "port" to "port." Section 3007 of the Revised Statutes, which exempts sealed cars from certain fees, preserves the terms of the preceding section—from "port" to "port." It seems to me that sections 3006 and 3007 contemplate the delivery of the sealed cars at a "port" of the United States, there to be examined by a revenue officer and their contents verified. But in practice the car, if the seal is found at the border to be intact, is passed to places not "ports" and is opened and unloaded by the consignee, no officer being present. The bill or manifest accompanying the merchandise and the unbroken seal on the car may furnish prima facie evidence that the amount and kind of merchandise named in the manifest and said to be contained in the car came from a port in the United States, but certainly it was not intended that the merchandise should go to the owner without an official ascertainment of the correspondence between the bill and the actual contents of the car.

I pass at this point any discussion of the question whether, as a national policy, this traffic should be promoted. It is enough to say that as the law stands it is authorized between "ports" of the

By Mr. Mitchell: A joint resolution (S. R. 145) authorizing the issue of duplicate medals where the originals have been lost or destroyed; to the Committee on the Library.

COLONIAL CHARTERS AND STATE CONSTITUTIONS.

Mr. Quay submitted the following resolution; which was considered by unanimous consent and agreed to:

Resolved, That the Committee on the Library be, and it is hereby, authorized and instructed to inquire into and report to the Senate the advisability of preparing a new compilation of the various colonial charters and State constitutions of each State of the United States, together with all amendments thereto at any time in force.

TESTIMONY ON FAILED NATIONAL BANKS.

Mr. Chandler submitted the following resolution; which was referred to the Committee on Printing:

Resolved by the Senate (the House of Representatives concurring), That the Public Printer be, and he is hereby, directed to print and bind in muslin 7,000 copies of the testimony taken by the Senate Select Committee on Failed National Banks, together with the report of the committee, of which 2,000 copies shall be for the use of the House, 1,000 copies for the use of the Senate, and 4,000 copies to be distributed by the Comptroller of the Currency.

WITHDRAWAL OF PAPERS.

Mr. Cullom submitted the following order:

Ordered, That the rules be suspended, and that the Secretary of the Senate be directed to withdraw from the files of the Senate for exhibition at the World's Columbian Exposition, under the auspices of the Department of State, a memorial of Maria Helena America Vespucci, praying a donation of land, and that she be admitted to the rights of citizenship.

PRESIDENTIAL APPROVALS.

A message from the President of the United States, by Mr. Pruden, his secretary:

Mr. President: The President of the United States this day approved and signed the following act and joint resolution:

S. 3115. An act for the relief of Clement Reeves; and

S. R. 124. Joint resolution directing the Secretary of War to investigate the subject of raft-towing on the Great Lakes and their connecting waters.

Ordered, That the Secretary notify the House of Representatives thereof.

MESSAGE FROM THE HOUSE.

A message from the House of Representatives, by Mr. Towles, its chief clerk:

Mr. President: The House of Representatives has agreed to the report of the committee of conference on the amendment of the Senate to the bill (H. R. 10010) to establish a court of appeals for the District of Columbia, and for other purposes; and

It has agreed to the concurrent resolution of the Senate to print extra copies of Parts I and II of the Report of the Superintendent of the United States Coast and Geodetic Survey for the fiscal year ending June 30, 1892.

The House of Representatives has passed a bill (H. R. 10238) making appropriations for the sundry civil expenses of the Government for the fiscal year ending June 30, 1894, and for other purposes, in which it requests the concurrence of the Senate; and

It has passed the following resolution, in which it requests the concurrence of the Senate:

Resolved by the House of Representatives (the Senate concurring), That there be printed 4,500 copies of the report, which includes the testimony, of the Committee on Interstate and Foreign Commerce (Report No. 2278), relating to combinations between the Philadelphia and Reading Railroad Company, and other railroads—3,000 copies for the House, and 1,500 copies for the use of the Senate.

The House has announced the appointment of Mr. Chipman and Mr. Lodge as tellers on the part of the House to count the electoral vote at the joint session of the two Houses, February 8, 1893.

The House of Representatives has disagreed to the amendments of the Senate to the bill (H. R. 10038) making appropriations for the expenses of the government of the District of Columbia for the fiscal year ending June 30, 1894, and for other purposes. It asks a conference with the Senate on the disagreeing votes of the two Houses thereon, and has appointed Mr. Dockery, Mr. Compton, and Mr. Henderson, of Iowa, managers at the same on its part.

The Speaker of the House of Representatives having signed nine enrolled bills, S. 509, S. 3311, S. 3753, H. R. 5012, H. R. 5752, H. R. 8602, H. R. 8956, H. R. 9433, and H. R. 10063, I am directed to bring them to the Senate for the signature of its President.

The President of the United States has informed the House of Representatives that he has approved and signed acts and joint resolutions as follows:

On January 13, 1893:

H. R. 166. Joint resolution to authorize the Secretary of the Treasury to cover back into the Treasury $48,800 of the appropriation to Choctaw and Chickasaw Indians.

On January 23, 1893:

H. R. 9824. An act to amend "An act to promote the construction of a safe deep-water harbor on the coast of Texas," approved February 9, 1891;

H. R. 4844. An act to authorize the Secretary of War to convey to school district numbered 12, of Kittery, Me., a portion of Fort McClary military reservation, in exchange for other lands; and

H. R. 3676. An act for the relief of R. L. Jennings, late postmaster at Marshall, Tex.

On January 26, 1893:

H. R. 10015. An act to authorize the construction of bridges across the Hiawassee, the Tennessee, and the Clinch rivers, in the State of Tennessee; and

H. R. 6969. An act for the relief of Elisha Brown.

HOUSE BILL REFERRED.

The bill H. R. 10238, last received from the House of Representatives for concurrence, was read the first and second times by unanimous consent and referred to the Committee on Appropriations.

HOUSE RESOLUTION REFERRED.

The resolution to print 4,500 copies of the report and testimony relating to combinations between the Philadelphia and Reading Railroad Company and other railroads, this day received from the House of Representatives for concurrence, was read and referred to the Committee on Printing.

ENROLLED BILLS SIGNED.

Mr. Dubois reported from the committee that they had examined and found duly enrolled the following bills:

S. 509. An act granting an increase of pension to Thomas J. Matlock;

S. 3311. An act to refer claim of Jessie Benton Fremont to certain lands and the improvements thereon, in San Francisco, Cal., to the Court of Claims;

S. 3753. An act relating to the anchorage and movement of vessels in the port of Chicago;

H. R. 5012. An act to increase the pension of Thomas Enloe;

H. R. 5752. An act to amend the act approved August 6, 1888, entitled "An act to authorize the construction of a bridge across the Alabama River."

H. R. 8602. An act to authorize the construction of a bridge across the Mobile River by the Chicago, Mobile and Gulf Ports Railroad Company;

H. R. 8956. An act establishing a fog signal at Tibbets Point, Lake Ontario, New York;

H. R. 9433. An act granting a pension to Mrs. Ann Mercer Slaughter; and

H. R. 10063. An act to amend "An act authorizing the construction of a high wagon bridge across the Missouri River at or near Sioux City, Iowa," etc.;

Whereupon,

The Vice-President signed the same, and they were delivered to the committee to be presented to the President of the United States.

DISTRICT APPROPRIATION BILL.

The Presiding Officer (Mr. Gallinger in the chair) laid before the Senate the message from the House of Representatives announcing its disagreement to the amendments of the Senate to the bill (H. R. 10038) making appropriations for the expenses of the government of the District of Columbia for the fiscal year ending June 30, 1894, and for other purposes, and asking a conference with the Senate on the disagreeing votes of the two Houses thereon; and

On motion by Mr. Cockrell,

Resolved, That the Senate insist upon its amendments to the bill and agree to the conference asked by the House on the disagreeing votes of the two Houses thereon.

Ordered, That the conferees on the part of the Senate be appointed by the Presiding Officer; and

The Presiding Officer appointed Mr. Allison, Mr. Dawes, and Mr. Cockrell.

Ordered, That the Secretary notify the House of Representatives thereof.

DISTRICT COURT OF APPEALS.

Mr. Hoar, from the committee of conference on the disagreeing votes of the two Houses on the amendment of the Senate to the bill (H. R. 10010) to establish a court of appeals for the District of Columbia, and for other purposes, submitted the following report:

The committee of conference on the disagreeing votes of the two Houses on the amendments of the Senate to the bill (H. R. 10010) to establish a court of appeals for the District of Columbia, and for other purposes, having met, after full and free conference have agreed to recommend and do recommend to their respective Houses as follows:

That the Senate recede from its disagreement to the House bill and agree to the same with the following amendment: Strike out section 9 and in lieu thereof insert the following:

SEC. 9. *That the determination of appeals from the decision of the Commissioner of Patents, now vested in the general term of the su-*

preme court of the District of Columbia, in pursuance of the provisions of section seven hundred and eighty of the Revised Statutes of the United States relating to the District of Columbia, shall hereafter be, and the same is hereby, vested in the court of appeals created by this act; and, in addition, any party aggrieved by a decision of the Commissioner of Patents in any interference case may appeal therefrom to said court of appeals.

And the House agree to the same.

GEORGE F. HOAR,
JAMES F. WILSON,
JAMES L. PUGH,
Managers on the part of the Senate.

D. B. CULBERSON,
WILLIAM C. OATES,
Managers on the part of the House.

The Senate proceeded to consider the report; and
On motion by Mr. Hoar,
Resolved, That the Senate agree thereto.
Ordered, That the Secretary notify the House of Representatives thereof.

AGREEMENT WITH THE KICKAPOO INDIANS.

On motion by Mr. Dawes,
The Senate proceeded to consider, as in Committee of the Whole, the bill (H. R. 7633) to ratify and confirm an agreement with the Kickapoo Indians in Oklahoma Territory, and to make appropriations for carrying the same into effect; and the reported amendment having been amended on the motion of Mr. Dawes, was agreed to as amended, and the bill was reported to the Senate and the amendment concurred in.

Ordered, That the amendment be engrossed and the bill read a third time.
The said bill as amended was read the third time.
Resolved, That it pass, and that the Senate request a conference with the House of Representatives on the said bill and amendment.
Ordered, That the conferees on the part of the Senate be appointed by the Vice-President; and
The Vice-President appointed Mr. Dawes, Mr. Platt, and Mr. Jones, of Arkansas.
Ordered, That the Secretary notify the House of Representatives thereof.

SETTLEMENT RIGHTS ON PUBLIC LANDS.

On motion by Mr. Pettigrew,
The Senate resumed, as in Committee of the Whole, the consideration of the bill (H. R. 7028) to protect settlement rights when two or more persons settle upon the same subdivision of agricultural public lands before survey thereof; and
The question being on the amendment proposed by Mr. Pettigrew, from the Committee on Public Lands,
After debate,
The amendment was agreed to.
A further amendment having been proposed by Mr. Carey; and the same having been amended on the motion of Mr. Perkins, it was agreed to as amended;
When,
The bill was reported to the Senate and the amendments made in Committee of the Whole were concurred in.
Ordered, That the amendments be engrossed and the bill read a third time.
The said bill as amended was read the third time.
Resolved, That it pass, that the title be amended by adding thereto the words *and for other purposes,* and that the Senate request a conference with the House of Representatives on the bill and the amendments.
Ordered, That the conferees on the part of the Senate be appointed by the Vice-President; and
The Vice-President appointed Mr. Dolph, Mr. Pettigrew, and Mr. Berry.
Ordered, That the Secretary notify the House of Representatives thereof.

CHEROKEE INDIAN LANDS.

The Senate resumed, as in Committee of the Whole, the consideration of the bill (H. R. 9190) to ratify and confirm an agreement with the Cherokee Nation of the Indian Territory, to make appropriation for carrying out the same, and for other purposes; and
The question being on the amendment proposed by Mr. Platt as amended; and
The amendment having been further amended on the motion of Mr. Dawes, the motion of Mr. Vest, the motion of Mr. Perkins, and the motion of Mr. Butler,
Pending debate,

EULOGIES ON THE LATE SENATOR BARBOUR.

Pursuant to notice,
Mr. Daniel submitted the following resolutions; which were considered by unanimous consent and unanimously agreed to:
Resolved, That the Senate deplores the death of the Hon. John Strode Barbour, late a Senator from the State of Virginia.

Resolved, That as a mark of respect to the memory of the deceased, the business of the Senate be now suspended to enable his associates to pay proper tribute of regard to his high character and distinguished public service.
Resolved, That the Secretary of the Senate communicate these resolutions to the House of Representatives.
After addresses by Mr. Daniel, Mr. Manderson, Mr. Faulkner, Mr. Gallinger, Mr. Platt, Mr. Hill, Mr. Hiscock, and Mr. Hunton,
On motion by Mr. Hunton, as an additional mark of respect to the memory of the deceased,
The Senate adjourned.

SATURDAY, FEBRUARY 4, 1893.

EXECUTIVE COMMUNICATIONS.

The Vice-President laid before the Senate a letter of the Secretary of the Treasury, transmitting an estimate of appropriations for expenses of the Army incident to the International Naval Rendezvous and Review; which was referred to the Committee on Appropriations and ordered to be printed.
The Vice-President laid before the Senate a letter of the Secretary of the Treasury, transmitting the claim of George Q. Cannon, of Utah, to recover $25,000 covered in the Treasury of the United States on a forfeited bond; which was referred to the Committee on Claims and ordered to be printed.
The Vice-President laid before the Senate a letter of the Secretary of the Treasury, transmitting an estimate of the Secretary of War for the purchase of machine guns of small caliber for the fiscal year ending June 30, 1894; which was referred to the Committee on Appropriations and ordered to be printed.

PETITIONS AND MEMORIALS.

Petitions, memorials, etc., were presented and referred as follows:
By Mr. Davis: A memorial of the legislature of Minnesota in favor of the passage of a national quarantine law; to the Committee on Immigration.
Resolutions of the Brown County Agricultural Society of Minnesota, praying legislation for the assuming of Government control of all railroads, telegraph and telephone lines; for a reduction of the tariff; for the establishment of reciprocity with other nations; for the repeal of the internal-revenue laws, and for a graduated income tax, etc.; to the Committee on Finance.
By Mr. Sherman: A memorial of the Trades and Labor Assembly of Columbus, Ohio, praying for the establishment of permanent census bureau, and for the collection and publication of statistics relating to farm mortgages; to the Committee on the Census.
By Mr. Quay: A petition of citizens of Pennsylvania, praying for the repeal of the provision providing for the closing of the Columbian Exposition on the Sabbath day; to the Select Committee on the Quadro-Centennial.
By Mr. Cullom: A petition of citizens of Illinois, praying for the appointment of a committee to investigate an alleged combine formed to depreciate the prices of grain by millers and others at St. Louis and Minneapolis; to the Committee on Agriculture and Forestry.
Petitions praying the passage of a law for the restriction of immigration into the United States, and for the establishment of a national quarantine, were presented as follows:
By the Vice-President: A petition of citizens of the United States.
By Mr. Quay: Several petitions of citizens of Pennsylvania.
By Mr. Higgins: A petition of citizens of Delaware.
Ordered, That they be referred to the Committee on Immigration.
Memorials, etc., praying for the repeal of the provision of law providing for the purchase of silver bullion, were presented as follows:
By Mr. Sherman: A memorial of the Commercial Club of Cincinnati, Ohio.
By Mr. Platt: Resolutions of the Board of Trade of Birmingham, Conn.
By Mr. Davis: Resolutions of the Commercial Club of St. Paul, Minn.
By Mr. Hawley: Resolutions of the Board of Trade of Birmingham, Conn.
Ordered, That they lie on the table.
Memorials remonstrating against the repeal of the provision providing for the closing of the Columbian Exposition on the Sabbath day were presented as follows:
By Mr. Cullom: A memorial of citizens of Illinois.
By Mr. Quay: Several memorials of citizens of Pennsylvania.
By Mr. Higgins: Two memorials of citizens of Delaware.
Ordered, That they be referred to the Select Committee on the Quadro-Centennial.
Mr. Squire presented a letter of the Fourth Auditor of the Treasury relative to the claim of Capt. Norman H. Farquhar, United States Navy, for difference of pay while attached to the *Santee;* which was referred to the Committee on Naval Affairs, to accompany an amendment intended to be proposed to the general deficiency appropriation bill, and ordered to be printed.

REPORTS OF COMMITTEES.

Mr. Bate, from the Committee on Military Affairs, to whom was referred the bill (S. 1683) for the relief of Mrs. Fanny N. Belger, reported it without amendment and submitted a report (No. 1253) thereon.

Mr. Teller, from the Committee on the Judiciary, to whom was referred the bill (S. 3741) to submit to the Court of Private Land Claims, established by an act of Congress approved March 3, 1891, the title of William McGarrahan to the Rancho Panoche Grande, in the State of California, and for other purposes, reported it with amendments and submitted a report (No. 1254) thereon.

Mr. Vest, from the Committee on Commerce, to whom was referred the bill (S. 3787) to authorize the construction of a bridge across the St. Marys River, between the States of Florida and Georgia, reported it with amendments.

Mr. Peffer from the Committee on Claims, to whom was referred the bill (S. 3689) for the relief of the owners of the schooner Henry R. Tilton, and of personal effects thereon, reported it with an amendment and submitted a report (No. 1260) thereon.

Mr. Gallinger, from the Committee on Pensions, to whom were referred the following bills, reported them severally without amendment and submitted written reports thereon as follows:

H. R. 2427. An act granting a pension to Margaret Byron; Report No. 1257·

H. R. 9011. An act to grant a pension to Ida A. Taylor; Report No. 1258.

H. R. 8298. An act to pension Emma Johnson, blind and dependent daughter of Daniel D. Johnson, Company B, One hundred and forty-second New York Volunteers; Report No. 1259.

Mr. Hawley, from the Committee on Military Affairs, to whom was referred the bill (H. R. 6194) to commission David P. Cordray as second lieutenant, to date from June 12, 1892, reported it without amendment and submitted a report (No. 1255) thereon.

Mr. Turpie, from the Committee on Pensions, to whom was referred the bill (H. R. 8550) to increase the pension of W. H. Philpot, a pensioner of the Mexican war, reported it without amendment and submitted a report (No. 1256) thereon.

Mr. Hawley, from the Committee on Military Affairs, to whom was referred the bill (H. R. 8123) granting to the Santa Fe, Prescott and Phœnix Railway Company the right of way across the Whipple Barracks military reservation, in Arizona, reported it without amendment and submitted a report (No. 1261) thereon.

Mr. Sherman, from the Committee on Foreign Relations, who were instructed by a resolution of the Senate of January, 26, 1893, to inquire what sums, if any, have been expended in the construction of the Nicaragua Canal, submitted a report (No. 1262).

Mr. Call, from the Committee on Immigration, who were instructed by resolutions of the Senate of July 16 and December 14, 1892, to examine into the conditions of immigrants from Cuba and the West India Islands, and the danger of the importation of epidemic diseases into the United States from those islands, submitted a report (No. 1263).

MESSAGE FROM THE HOUSE.

A message from the House of Representatives, by Mr. Towles, its chief clerk:

Mr. President: The House of Representatives has passed, without amendment, the bill (S. 3798) to amend an act entitled "An act to authorize the building of a railroad bridge at Little Rock, Ark."

The House of Representatives has agreed to the amendment of the Senate to the bill (H. R. 9758) to amend the charter of the Eckington and Soldiers' Home Railway Company of the District of Columbia, with an amendment, in which it requests the concurrence of the Senate.

The House of Representatives has agreed to the amendments of the Senate to the following bills of the House:

H. R. 1795. An act to increase the pension of A. J. Copenhaver, late a soldier in the Mexican war;

H. R. 6798. An act to authorize the construction of a bridge across the Warrior River by the Montgomery, Tuscaloosa and Memphis Railroad Company; and

H. R. 9930. An act for the construction and maintenance of a bridge across the St. Lawrence River.

The House of Representatives has agreed to the report of the committee of conference on the disagreeing votes of the two Houses on the amendments of the House to the bill (S. 1933) concerning testimony in criminal cases or proceedings based upon or growing out of alleged violations of an act entitled "An act to regulate commerce," approved February 4, 1887, as amended March 2, 1889, and February 10, 1891.

The House of Representatives has disagreed to the amendments of the Senate to the bill (H. R. 9825) making appropriations for the support of the Army for the fiscal year ending June 30, 1894, and for other purposes. It requests a conference with the Senate on the disagreeing votes of the two Houses thereon, and has appointed Mr. Outhwaite, Mr. Newberry, and Mr. Bingham managers at the same on its part.

The Speaker of the House of Representatives having signed an enrolled bill, H. R. 1795, I am directed to bring the same to the Senate for the signature of its President.

ENROLLED BILL SIGNED.

Mr. Dubois reported from the committee that they had examined and found duly enrolled the bill (H. R. 1795) to increase the pension of A. J. Copenhaver, late a soldier in the Mexican war;

Whereupon,

The Vice-President signed the same, and it was delivered to the committee to be presented to the President of the United States.

ARMY APPROPRIATION BILL.

The Vice-President laid before the Senate the message of the House announcing its disagreement to the amendments of the Senate to the bill (H. R. 9825) making appropriations for the support of the Army for the fiscal year ending June 30, 1894, and for other purposes.

On motion by Mr. Allison,

Resolved, That the Senate insist upon its amendments to the said bill disagreed to by the House of Representatives and agree to the conference asked by the House on the disagreeing votes of the two Houses thereon.

Ordered, That the conferees on the part of the Senate be appointed by the Vice-President; and

The Vice-President appointed Mr. Stewart, Mr. Allison, and Mr. Gorman.

Ordered, That the Secretary notify the House of Representatives thereof.

INTRODUCTION OF BILLS AND JOINT RESOLUTION.

Bills and a joint resolution were introduced, read the first and second times by unanimous consent, and referred as follows:

By Mr. Stockbridge: A bill (S. 3823) to prevent fishing in the Mississippi River during the months of March, April, and May of each year; to the Committee on Fisheries.

By Mr. Proctor: A bill (S. 3824) to establish a national university; to the Select Committee to Establish the University of the United States.

By Mr. Quay: A bill (S. 3825) to authorize the Homestead and Pittsburg Bridge Company to construct a bridge over the Monongahela River from Pittsburg to Homestead; to the Committee on Commerce.

By Mr. Cullom: A bill (S. 3826) authorizing the Velasco and Surfside Terminal Railway Company to construct a bridge across the Galveston and Brazos Canal; to the Committee on Commerce.

By Mr. Hiscock: A bill (S. 3827) to ratify certain leases made with chartered companies existing under act of the Chickasaw legislature, approved September 27, 1893; to the Committee on Indian Affairs.

By Mr. Shoup: A bill (S. 3828) to correct the northern boundary line of the Cœur d'Alene Indian Reservation, in Kootenai County, Idaho; to the Committee on Indian Affairs.

By Mr. Call: A bill (S. 3829) to provide for light-houses and other aids to navigation; to the Committee on Commerce.

By Mr. Hawley: A bill (S. 3830) to provide for the detail of Army officers for the instruction of the militia of any State upon the application of the governor thereof; to the Committee on Military Affairs.

By Mr. Butler: A joint resolution (S. R. 146) for the restoration of the books of the Beaufort Library Society, of Beaufort, S. C; to the Committee on the Library.

INTEROCEANIC CANAL.

Mr. Higgins submitted the following resolution; which was considered by unanimous consent and agreed to:

Resolved, That the Secretary of War is hereby requested to transmit to the Senate a copy of the report upon the routes for a ship canal between the Atlantic and Pacific oceans known as the Nicaragua route and the Darien and Atrato route, made in March and April, 1874, by Maj. Walter McFarland, United States Engineers, under the direction of the United States Interoceanic Canal Company.

HAWAIIAN NEGOTIATIONS OF 1854.

Mr. Morgan submitted the following resolution; which was considered by unanimous consent and agreed to:

Resolved, That the President is requested, if in his opinion it is not inconsistent with the public interests, to send to the Senate the draft of a treaty, negotiated in 1854, but not completed, between the plenipotentiaries of the United States and the Kingdom of Hawaii, with the correspondence between the two Governments relating to said negotiation.

REFERENCE OF THE PRESIDENT'S MESSAGE RELATIVE TO CANADA.

On motion by Mr. Sherman,

Ordered, That so much of the message of the President in respect to the relations of the United States with Canada as refers to the treaty stipulations existing or alleged to exist between the United States and Great Britain be referred to the Committee on Foreign Relations, and so much as relates to the transportation of merchandise between the United States and the British Possessions, as affecting interstate commerce, be referred to the Committee on Commerce, and so much as relates to general relations with Canada be referred to the Select Committee on Relations with Canada.

CONSIDERATION OF CALENDAR BILLS.

The Senate proceeded to consider, as in Committee of the Whole, the following bills; and no amendments being made, they were severally reported to the Senate:

H. R. 5705. An act to increase the pension of Amelia Graham;

H. R. 8925. An act to increase the pension of Harvey Lyon;

H. R. 6797. An act to authorize the construction of a bridge across the Cahaba River, in Bibb County, Alabama, by the Montgomery, Tuscaloosa and Memphis Railway;

H. R. 7086. An act granting a pension to Lillie Rice, late a nurse at Jefferson Barracks;

H. R. 4047. An act granting a pension to Ellen Hewett;

H. R. 2407. An act granting a pension to Samuel Luttrell;

H. R. 2400. An act granting a pension to Willis Luttrell;

H. R. 8275. An act granting a pension to Abraham B. Simmons, of Capt. Thomas Tripp's company, in Col. Brisbane's regiment, South Carolina Volunteers, in the Florida Indian war;

H. R. 6508. An act granting a pension to Joseph Fortier;

H. R. 6649. An act to extend the provisions of "An act to provide for the muster and pay of certain officers and enlisted men of the volunteer forces;

H. R. 7234. An act granting a pension to Mary Millard;

H. R. 9220. An act granting a pension to Mrs. Caroline Hardee D. all, widow of James R. Dyall, veteran of the Florida war, 1836;

H. R. 1318. An act granting a pension to Martha A. Harris;

H. R. 7257. An act granting a pension to Alonzo D. Barber;

H. R. 6272. An act to pension Susan S. Murphy;

H. R. 6345. An act granting an honorable discharge to Frederick E. Kolter;

H. R. 9631. An act to make Rockport, Tex., a suport of entry;

H. R. 8106. An act for the correction of the army record of David R. Wallace, deceased;

H. R. 7238. An act granting a pension to Amanda Atherton;

H. R. 7226. An act granting a pension to Julia P. Wright;

H. R. 7662. An act granting a pension to Marion Kern Sharman; and

H. R. 6507. An act granting a pension to Sarah A. Hagan.

Ordered, That they pass to a third reading.

The said bills were severally read the third time.

Resolved, That they pass.

Ordered, That the Secretary notify the House of Representatives thereof.

MESSAGE FROM THE HOUSE.

A message from the House of Representatives, by Mr. Towles, its chief clerk:

Mr. President: The House of Representatives has agreed to the resolution of the Senate to print the annual volumes of the observations of the Naval Observatory, commonly known as the "Washington Observations," for the years 1889, 1890, 1891, and 1892.

The House of Representatives has passed a bill (H. R. 10258) making appropriations to supply deficiencies in the appropriations for the fiscal year ending June 30, 1893, and for prior years, and for other purposes, in which it requests the concurrence of the Senate.

HOUSE BILL REFERRED.

The bill H. R. 10258, last received from the House of Representatives for concurrence, was read the first and second times by unanimous consent and referred to the Committee on Appropriations.

PRESIDENTIAL APPROVAL.

A message from the President of the United States, by Mr. Pruden, his secretary:

Mr. President: The President of the United States this day approved and signed an act (S. 985) to provide for the enlargement of the military post at Fort Wayne, Mich.

Ordered, That the Secretary notify the House of Representatives thereof.

CONSIDERATION OF BILLS ON THE CALENDAR.

The Senate proceeded to consider, as in Committee of the Whole, the following bills; and the reported amendments having been agreed to, the bills were severally reported to the Senate and the amendments were concurred in:

H. R. 5649. An act for the relief of Lieut. F. W. Davis, and granting him an honorable discharge;

H. R. 730. An act for the relief of James A. Finley; and

H. R. 4758. An act for the relief of Charles E. Heuston.

Ordered, That the amendments be engrossed and the bills read a third time.

The said bills as amended were severally read the third time.

Resolved, That they pass, and that the Senate request conferences with the House of Representatives on the bills and amendments.

Ordered, That the conferees on the part of the Senate be appointed by the Vice-President; and

The Vice-President appointed Mr. Cameron, Mr. Manderson, and Mr. Cockrell.

Ordered, That the Secretary notify the House of Representatives thereof.

The Senate proceeded to consider, as in Committee of the Whole, the bill (H. R. 1036) for the benefit of Logan, Simpson, and Hardin counties, and of the city of Louisville, Ky., and of Sumner and Davidson counties, Tennessee; and the reported amendment having been disagreed to, and the bill amended on the motion of Mr. Mitchell, it was reported to the Senate and the amendment was concurred in.

Ordered, That the amendment be engrossed and the bill read a third time.

The said bill as amended was read the third time.

Resolved, That it pass, that the title thereof be amended so as to read, "An act for the benefit of the State of Kentucky, Logan and Simpson counties, and of Louisville, Ky., and of Sumner and Davidson counties, Tennessee," and that the Senate request a conference with the House of Representatives on the said bill and amendments.

Ordered, That the conferees on the part of the Senate be appointed by the Vice-President; and

The Vice-President appointed Mr. Mitchell, Mr. Peffer, and Mr. Vilas.

Ordered, That the Secretary notify the House of Representatives thereof.

The Senate proceeded to consider, as in Committee of the Whole, the bill (H. R. 8268) to amend chapter 559, page 195, volume 26, United States Statutes at Large; and the reported amendments having been agreed to, the bill was reported to the Senate and the amendments were concurred in.

Ordered, That the amendments be engrossed and the bill read a third time.

The said bill as amended was read the third time.

Resolved, That it pass, and that the title thereof be amended to read, "An act to extend the provisions of section 8 of the act entitled 'An act to repeal timber-culture laws, and for other purposes,' approved March 3, 1891, concerning prosecutions for cutting timber on public lands, to Wyoming, New Mexico, and Arizona."

On motion by Mr. Dolph,

Resolved, That the Senate request a conference with the House of Representatives on the said bill and amendments.

Ordered, That the conferees on the part of the Senate be appointed by the Vice-President; and

The Vice-President appointed Mr. Dolph, Mr. Carey, and Mr. Walthall.

Ordered, That the Secretary notify the House of Representatives thereof.

The Senate proceeded to consider, as in Committee of the Whole, the bill (H. R. 9176) relating to contracts of common carriers and to certain obligations, duties, and rights in connection with the carriage of property; and the reported amendments having been agreed to, the bill was reported to the Senate and the amendments were concurred in.

Ordered, That the amendments be engrossed and the bill read a third time.

The said bill as amended was read the third time.

Resolved, That it pass, and that the title thereof be amended to read, "An act relating to navigation of vessels, bills of lading, and to certain obligations, duties, and rights in connection with the carriage of property."

On motion by Mr. Frye,

Resolved, That the Senate request a conference with the House of Representatives on the said bill and amendments.

Ordered, That the conferees on the part of the Senate be appointed by the Vice-President; and

The Vice-President appointed Mr. Frye, Mr. Washburn, and Mr. Gorman.

Ordered, That the Secretary notify the House of Representatives thereof.

ECKINGTON AND SOLDIERS' HOME RAILWAY COMPANY.

The Senate proceeded to consider the amendment of the House of Representatives to the amendment of the Senate to the bill (H. R. 9758) to amend the charter of the Eckington and Soldiers' Home Railway Company of the District of Columbia; and

On motion by Mr. Harris,

Resolved, That the Senate agree thereto,

Ordered, That the Secretary notify the House of Representatives thereof.

REPORT OF COMMITTEE.

Mr. Vest, from the Committee on Commerce, to whom was referred the bill (S. 3825) to authorize the Homestead and Pittsburg Bridge Company to construct a bridge across the Monongahela River from Pittsburg to Homestead, reported it without amendment.

RECOMMITTAL OF BILL.

On motion by Mr. Mitchell,

The Senate proceeded to consider, as in Committee of the Whole, the bill (S. 1358) for the relief of Clara A. Graves, Lewis Smith Lee, Florence P. Lee, Mary S. Sheldon, and Elizabeth Smith, heirs of Lewis Smith deceased; and

Ordered, That it be recommitted to the Committee on Claims.

CONSIDERATION OF BILLS ON THE CALENDAR.

The Senate resumed the consideration of the bill (H. R. 9955) providing for sundry light-houses and other aids to navigation; and having been further amended on the motion of Mr. Gorman,

Ordered, That the amendments be engrossed and the bill read a third time.

The said bill as amended was read the third time.

Resolved, That it pass, and that the Senate request a conference with the House of Representatives on the said bill and amendments.

Ordered, That the conferees on the part of the Senate be appointed by the Vice-President; and

The Vice-President appointed Mr. Dolph, Mr. Sawyer, and Mr. Coke.

Ordered, That the Secretary notify the House of Representatives thereof.

The Senate proceeded to consider, as in Committee of the Whole, the bill (H. R. 9592) authorizing the Secretary of the Treasury to obtain plans and specifications for public buildings to be erected under the supervision of the Treasury Department, and providing for local supervision of the construction of the same; and the reported amendments having been agreed to, the bill was reported to the Senate and the amendments were concurred in.

Ordered, That the amendments be engrossed and the bill read a third time.

The said bill as amended was read the third time.

Resolved, That it pass, and that the Senate request a conference with the House of Representatives on the said bill and amendments.

Ordered, That the conferees on the part of the Senate be appointed by the Vice-President; and

The Vice-President appointed Mr. Morrill, Mr. Pasco, and Mr. Vest.

Ordered, That the Secretary notify the House of Representatives thereof.

The Senate proceeded to consider, as in Committee of the Whole, the bill (H. R. 9286) to create the California Débris Commission and regulate hydraulic mining in the State of California; and the reported amendments having been agreed to, the bill was reported to the Senate and the amendments were concurred in.

Ordered, That the amendments be engrossed and the bill read a third time.

The said bill as amended was read the third time.

Resolved, That it pass, and that the Senate request a conference with the House of Representatives on the said bill and amendments.

Ordered, That the conferees on the part of the Senate be appointed by the Vice-President; and

The Vice-President appointed Mr. Stewart, Mr. Felton, and Mr. Mills.

Ordered, That the Secretary notify the House of Representatives thereof.

The Senate proceeded to consider, as in Committee of the Whole, the bill (H. R. 929) granting a pension to Mrs. Mary E. Donaldson; and no amendment being made, it was reported to the Senate.

Ordered, That it pass to a third reading.

The said bill was read the third time.

Resolved, That it pass, and that the preamble be stricken out.

Ordered, That the Secretary request the concurrence of the House of Representatives in striking out the preamble.

The Senate resumed, as in Committee of the Whole, the consideration of the bill (H. R. 9190) to ratify and confirm an agreement with the Cherokee Nation of Indians, of the Indian Territory, to make appropriation for carrying out the same, and for other purposes; and

The question being on the amendment proposed by Mr. Platt, from the Committee on Indian Affairs, as amended; and the same having been further amended on the motion of Mr. Perkins, it was agreed to as amended; and

The bill was reported to the Senate and the amendment was concurred in.

Ordered, That the amendment be engrossed and the bill read a third time.

The said bill as amended was read the third time.

Resolved, That it pass, and that the Senate request a conference with the House of Representatives on the said bill and amendment.

Ordered, That the conferees on the part of the Senate be appointed by the Presiding Officer; and

The Presiding Officer (Mr. Berry in the chair) appointed Mr. Platt, Mr. Pettigrew, and Mr. Jones, of Arkansas.

Ordered, That the Secretary notify the House of Representatives thereof.

The Senate proceeded to consider, as in Committee of the Whole, the bill (H. R. 9592) for the relief of Andrew B. Knapp; and the reported amendment having been agreed to, the bill was reported to the Senate and the amendment was concurred in.

Ordered, That the amendment be engrossed and the bill read a third time.

The said bill as amended was read the third time.

Resolved, That it pass.

Ordered, That the Secretary request the concurrence of the House of Representatives in the amendment.

The Senate proceeded to consider, as in Committee of the Whole the following bills; and the reported amendments having been agreed to, the bills were severally reported to the Senate and the amendments were concurred in:

S. 1578. A bill for the relief of the First National Bank of Newton, Mass.;

S. 3787. A bill to authorize the construction of a bridge across the St. Marys River between the States of Florida and Georgia; and

S. 3812. A bill to ratify and confirm an agreement with the Alsea and other bands of Indians located upon the Siletz Reservation in the State of Oregon, and to make appropriation for carrying the same into effect.

Ordered, That they be engrossed and read a third time.

The said bills were severally read the third time.

Resolved, That they pass, and that the respective titles thereof be as aforesaid.

Ordered, That the Secretary request the concurrence of the House of Representatives therein.

MESSAGE FROM THE HOUSE.

A message from the House of Representatives, by Mr. Towles, its chief clerk:

Mr. President: The House of Representatives has passed a bill (H. R. 10267) making appropriations for the diplomatic and consular service of the United States for the fiscal year ending June 30, 1894, in which it requests the concurrence of the Senate.

HOUSE BILL REFERRED.

The bill H. R. 10267, last received from the House of Representatives for concurrence, was read the first and second times by unanimous consent and referred to the Committee on Appropriations.

CONFERENCE REPORT.

Mr. Teller, from the committee of conference on the disagreeing votes of the two Houses on the amendments of the House of Representatives to the bill S. 1933, submitted the following report:

The committee of conference on the disagreeing votes of the two Houses on the amendments of the House to the bill (S. 1933) concerning testimony in criminal cases or proceedings based upon or growing out of alleged violations of an act entitled "An act to regulate commerce," approved February 4, 1887, as amended March 2, 1889, and February 10, 1891, after full and free conference, have agreed to recommend and do recommend to their respective Houses:

That the Senate recede from its disagreement to the amendments of the House, and agree to the same with amendments as follows:

In line 5, after the words "subpœna of the Commission, whether" insert the words such subpœna be.

In line 8, after the words "violation of," strike out the word "said" and insert in lieu thereof the word the.

In line 16, add to the word "subject" the letters ed; and in the same line, after the word "penalty," insert the words or forfeiture.

In line 20, after the words "to its subpœna," insert the words or the subpœna of either of them.

And that the House do agree to the same.

> JAMES F. WILSON,
> H. M. TELLER,
> JAMES L. PUGH,
> *Conferees on the part of the Senate.*
> GEO. D. WISE,
> JOSIAH PATTERSON,
> BELLAMY STORER,
> *Conferees on the part of the House.*

The Senate proceeded to consider the said report; and

On motion by Mr. Teller,

Resolved, That the Senate agree thereto.

Ordered, That the Secretary notify the House of Representatives thereof.

RELIEF TO INDIAN CITIZENS.

The Senate proceeded to consider, as in Committee of the Whole, the bill (S. 2068) extending relief to Indian citizens, and for other purposes; and the reported amendment having been amended on the motion of Mr. Cockrell; and

A further amendment to the amendment having been proposed by Mr. Manderson,

Pending debate,

MEMORIAL ADDRESSES.

JOHN R. GAMBLE.

The Presiding Officer laid before the Senate the resolutions of the House of Representatives on the announcement of the death of the honorable John R. Gamble, as follows:

IN THE HOUSE OF REPRESENTATIVES,

March 12, 1892.

Resolved, That the business of the House be now suspended that an opportunity be given for tributes to the memory of Hon. John R. Gamble, late a Representative at Large from the State of South Dakota.

Resolved, That the Clerk be directed to communicate a copy of these resolutions to the Senate.

Resolved, That, as a further mark of respect to the memory of the deceased and his public services, the House, at the conclusion of these memorial proceedings, shall stand adjourned.

The resolutions were read;

When,

Mr. Pettigrew submitted the following resolutions:

Resolved, That the Senate has heard with profound sorrow the announcement of the death of the Hon. John R. Gamble, late a Representative from the State of South Dakota.

Resolved, That the business of the Senate be now suspended in order that fitting tribute may be paid to his memory.

Resolved, That a copy of these resolutions be transmitted by the Secretary of the Senate to the family of the deceased.

The Senate proceeded, by unanimous consent, to consider the resolutions; and

After addresses by Mr. Pettigrew, Mr. Hansbrough, Mr. Davis, and Mr. Kyle,

The resolutions were unanimously agreed to.

MELBOURNE H. FORD.

The Presiding Officer laid before the Senate the resolutions of the House of Representatives on the announcement of the death of the Hon. Melbourne H. Ford, as follows:

IN THE HOUSE OF REPRESENTATIVES, *April 9, 1892.*

Resolved, That the business of the House be now suspended, that opportunity may be given for tributes to the memory of the Hon. Melbourne H. Ford, late a Representative from the State of Michigan.

Resolved, That as a particular mark of respect to the memory of the deceased, and in recognition of his eminent abilities as a public servant, the House, at the conclusion of these memorial proceedings, shall stand adjourned.

Resolved, That the Clerk communicate these resolutions to the Senate.

Resolved, That the Clerk be instructed to send a copy of these resolutions to the family of the deceased.

The resolutions were read;

When,

Mr. Stockbridge submitted the following resolutions:

Resolved, That the Senate receives with sincere regret the announcement of the death of the Hon. Melbourne H. Ford, late a member of the House of Representatives from the State of Michigan, and tenders to the family of the deceased the assurance of its sympathy with them under the bereavement they have been called upon to sustain.

Resolved, That the Secretary of the Senate be directed to transmit to the family of Mr. Ford a certified copy of the foregoing resolution.

The Senate proceeded, by unanimous consent, to consider the resolutions; and

After addresses by Mr. Stockbridge, Mr. Daniel, and Mr. McMillan,

The resolutions were unanimously agreed to.

ELI T. STACKHOUSE.

The Presiding Officer laid before the Senate the resolutions of the House of Representatives on the announcement of the death of the Hon. Eli T. Stackhouse, as follows:

IN THE HOUSE OF REPRESENTATIVES, *January 28, 1893.*

Resolved, That the business of the House be now suspended that opportunity may be given for tributes to the memory of the Hon. Eli T. Stackhouse, late a Representative from the State of South Carolina.

Resolved, That as a particular mark of respect to the memory of the deceased, and in recognition of his eminent abilities as a distinguished public servant, the House, at the conclusion of these memorial proceedings, shall stand adjourned.

Resolved, That the Clerk communicate these resolutions to the Senate.

Resolved, That the Clerk be instructed to send a copy of these resolutions to the family of the deceased;

The resolutions were read,

When,

Mr. Butler submitted the following resolutions:

Resolved, That the Senate has received with deep regret the announcement of the death of the Hon. Eli T. Stackhouse, late a Representative from the State of South Carolina, and tenders to its family of the deceased the assurance of its sympathy in their bereavement.

Resolved, That the Secretary be directed to transmit to the family of Mr. Stackhouse a copy of the foregoing resolution.

The Senate proceeded, by unanimous consent, to consider the resolutions; and

After addresses by Mr. Butler, Mr. Gallinger, Mr. Kyle, and Mr. Irby,

The resolutions were unanimously agreed to.

When,

On motion by Mr. Irby, as an additional mark of respect to the memory of the deceased Representatives,

The Senate adjourned.

Mr. John P. Jones, from the State of Nevada, attended.

EXECUTIVE COMMUNICATION.

The Vice-President laid before the Senate a letter of the Secretary of State, transmitting, in answer to a resolution of the Senate of January 25, 1893, a report relative to the fees paid to consular officers of the United States; which was referred to the Committee on Commerce and ordered to be printed.

RESOLUTION OF LEGISLATURE.

The Vice-President laid before the Senate a resolution of the legislature of Colorado, remonstrating against the repeal of the law providing for the purchase of silver bullion.

Ordered, That it lie on the table.

PETITIONS AND MEMORIALS.

Petitions, memorials, etc., were presented and referred as follows:

By the Vice-President: A memorial of the New York Academy of Medicine, praying the passage of a law for the establishment of a national quarantine; to the Committee on Immigration.

By Mr. Allison: A petition of the Iowa State Grange, praying the passage of a law compelling the manufacturers of oleomargarine and like compounds to color their products pink; to the Committee on Agriculture and Forestry.

Resolutions of the Lake Carriers' Association, urging upon Congress the necessity of a liberal provision to enable the Secretary of War to furnish lake navigators with accurate and complete charts; to the Committee on Commerce.

By Mr. Gallinger: A memorial of citizens of Washington, D. C., remonstrating against permitting the Washington, Georgetown and Terminal Railroad Company from laying their tracks on K street SW.; to the Committee on the District of Columbia.

By Mr. Cullom: Two petitions of citizens of Illinois, praying for the appointment of a committee to investigate an alleged combine formed to depreciate the price of grain by the millers, elevators, and others at St. Louis and Minneapolis; to the Committee on Agriculture and Forestry.

By Mr. Hoar: A resolution of the New England Drug Exchange, remonstrating against any increase of the tax on alcohol; to the Committee on Finance.

By Mr. Voorhees: A petition of citizens of Indiana, praying that an appropriation be made for the jury of awards at the Columbian Exposition; to the Select Committee on the Quadro-Centennial.

By Mr. Sherman: A petition of citizens of Ohio praying for the establishment of a permanent census bureau, and for the collection and publication of statistics relating to farm mortgages; to the Committee on the Census.

By Mr. Vance: A memorial of the Eastern Band of Cherokee Indians of North Carolina for a final settlement of their claims against the United States; to the Committee on Indian Affairs, to accompany the bill S. 3831.

By Mr. Allison: Several petitions of citizens of Iowa, praying the repeal of the provision providing for the closing of the Columbian Exposition on the Sabbath day; to the Select Committee on the Quadro-Centennial.

Mr. Allison presented five petitions of citizens of Iowa, praying the passage of the antioption bill.

Ordered, That they lie on the table.

Mr. Wolcott presented a resolution of the legislature of Colorado, remonstrating against the repeal of the law providing for the purchase of silver bullion.

Ordered, That it lie on the table.

Petitions praying for the prohibition of the sale of intoxicating liquors on the grounds of the Columbian Exposition were presented as follows:

By Mr. Chandler: A petition of citizens of New Hampshire.

By Mr. Allison: A petition of citizens of Iowa.

Ordered, That they be referred to the Select Committee on the Quadro-Centennial.

Petitions praying the passage of a law for the restriction of immigration, and for the appointment of a commission to investigate the subject of immigration, were presented as follows:

By Mr. Faulkner: A petition of citizens of West Virginia.

By Mr. Vest: A petition of citizens of Missouri.

By Mr. Quay: Several petitions of citizens of Pennsylvania.

By Mr. Cockrell: A petition of citizens of Missouri.

By Mr. Sherman: A petition of citizens of Ohio.

By Mr. Chandler: A petition of citizens of New Hampshire.

By Mr. Voorhees: A petition of citizens of Indiana.

By Mr. Hiscock: A petition of citizens of New York.

Ordered, That they be referred to the Committee on Immigration.

Petitions praying the repeal of the law providing for the purchase of silver bullion were presented as follows:

By Mr. Hill: A petition of citizens of New York.

By Mr. Hiscock: A petition of citizens of New York.

By Mr. Hoar: A petition of the Arkwright Club of Boston, Mass., and a petition of the Commercial Club of Boston, Mass.

Ordered, That they lie on the table.

The Vice-President laid before the Senate a memorial of the Federation of Labor of the District of Columbia, remonstrating against any increase of the hours of labor in the Government Departments; which was referred to the Committee on Education and Labor.

Mr. Hiscock presented a resolution of the drug trade section of the New York Board of Trade, remonstrating against any increase of the tax on alcohol; which was referred to the Committee on Finance.

Mr. Pasco presented a resolution of the Tampa Board of Trade, praying for a continuance of the fast-mail service between New York, via Tampa, Fla., to Havana, Cuba; which was referred to the Committee on Appropriations.

REPORTS OF COMMITTEES.

Mr. Quay, from the Committee on the Library, to whom was referred the joint resolution (S. R. 145)authorizing the issue of duplicate medals where the originals have been lost or destroyed, reported it without amendment.

Mr. Vest, from the Committee on Commerce, to whom was referred the bill (S. 3826) authorizing the Velasco and Surfside Terminal Railway Company to construct a bridge across the Galveston and Brazos Canal, reported it without amendment.

The Senate proceeded, by unanimous consent, to consider the said bill as in Committee of the Whole; and no amendment being made, it was reported to the Senate.

Ordered, That it be engrossed and read a third time.

The said bill was read the third time.

Resolved, That it pass, and that the title thereof be as aforesaid.

Ordered, That the Secretary request the concurrence of the House of Representatives therein.

Mr. Dixon, from the Committee on Patents, to whom was referred the bill (S. 409) for the relief of John C. Howe, reported it without amendment and submitted a report (No. 1264) thereon.

Mr. Turpie, from the Committee on Pensions, to whom were referred the following bills, reported them severally without amendment and submitted written reports thereon as follows:

H. R. 3845. An act to increase the pension of Edward R. Chapman; Report No. 1265.

H. R. 2493. An act granting a pension to Jesse Cleaveland; Report No. 1266.

H. R. 8221. An act granting a pension to George W. Boyd; Report No. 1267.

H. R. 6914. An act granting a pension to Drake Nettie Barnett; Report No. 1268.

Mr. Vest, from the Committee on Commerce, to whom was referred the bill (S. 3800) to authorize the constructionof a bridge over the Tennessee River at or near Sheffield, Ala., reported it with amendments.

Mr. Vest, from the Committee on the Judiciary, to whom was referred the bill (S. 3768) relative to voluntary assignments by debtors for the benefit of creditors in the District of Columbia, and to amend section 782 of the Revised Statutes of the United States, relating to the District of Columbia, reported it without amendment.

On motion by Mr. Teller,

Ordered, That the Committee on the Judiciary be discharged from the further consideration of the following bills, and that they be referred to the Committee on Private Land Claims.

H. R. 7203. An act to amend an act entitled "An act to establish a court of private land claims and to provide for the settlement of private land claims in certain States and Territories," approved March 3, 1891; and

H. R. 8340. An act to amend an act establishing a court of private land claims and to provide for the settlement of private land claims in certain States and Territories, approved March 3, 1891.

MESSAGE FROM THE HOUSE.

A message from the Hous eof Representatives, by Mr. Towles, its chief clerk:

Mr. President: The House of Representatives has passed, without amendment, the joint resolution (S. R. 144) to provide for maintenance of order during the inaugural ceremonies, March, 1893.

The House of Representatives has passed the following resolutions, which I am directed to communicate to the Senate:

Resolved, That the business of the House be now suspended, that opportunity be given for tributes to the memory of Hon. Alexander K. Craig, late a Representative from the State of Pennsylvania.

Resolved, That as a further mark of respect to the memory of the deceased and in recognition of his eminent public and private virtues, the House, at the conclusion of these memorial proceedings, shall stand adjourned.

Resolved, That the Clerk communicate these resolutions to the Senate.

Resolved, That the Clerk be instructed to transmit a copy of these resolutions to the family of the deceased.

The Speaker of the House of Representatives having signed three enrolled bills, H. R. 6798, H. R. 9930, and H. R. 10010, I am directed to bring them to the Senate for the signature of its President.

ENROLLED BILLS SIGNED.

Mr. Dubois reported from the committee that they had examined and found duly enrolled the following bills:

H. R. 6798. An act to authorize the construction of a bridge across the Warrior River by the Montgomery, Tuscaloosa and Memphis Railway Company;

H. R. 9930. An act for the construction and maintenance of a bridge across the St. Lawrence River; and

H. R. 10010. An act to establish a court of appeals for the District of Columbia, and for other purposes;

Whereupon,

The Vice-President signed the same, and they were delivered to the committee to be presented to the President of the United States.

INTRODUCTION OF BILLS.

Bills were introduced, read the first and second times by unanimous consent, and referred as follows:

By Mr. Vance: A bill (S. 3831) for the relief of the Eastern Band of Cherokee Indians of the State of North Carolina; to the Committee on Indian Affairs.

By Mr. Allison: A bill (S. 3832) granting a pension to Orlando Van Ness; to the Committee on Pensions.

A bill (S. 3833) granting to William E. Biddison, Eighteenth Iowa Infantry, amount due as equalization of bounty; to the Committee on Military Affairs.

By Mr. Coke: A bill (S. 3834) authorizing Rockport and Harbor Island Suburban Railroad to construct a bridge across the Corpus Christi Channel, known as the Morris and Cummings Ship Channel, near its entrance into Aransas Bay, in Aransas County, Texas; to the Committee on Commerce.

By Mr. Hunton: A bill (S. 3835) to authorize the Washington, Alexandria and Mount Vernon Electric Railway Company to construct a bridge across the Potomac River opposite Observatory Hill, and to construct a railroad over the same and through certain streets and reservations; to the Committee on the District of Columbia.

By Mr. Quay: A bill (S. 3836) to authorize the Union Railroad Company to construct and maintain a bridge across the Monongahela River; to the Committee on Commerce.

SMITHSONIAN AND NATIONAL MUSEUM REPORTS.

Mr. Morrill submitted the following concurrent resolution; which was referred to the Committee on Printing:

Resolved by the Senate (the House of Representatives concurring), That there be printed of the reports of the Smithsonian Institution and of the National Museum for the year ending June 30, 1892, in two octavo volumes, 10,000 extra copies, of which 1,000 copies shall be for the use of the Senate, 2,000 copies for the use of the House of Representatives, 5,000 copies for the use of the Smithsonian Institution, and 2,000 copies for the use of the National Museum.

HEARINGS ON INDIAN DEPREDATION CLAIMS.

Mr. Shoup submitted the following resolution; which was referred to the Committee to Audit and Control the Contingent Expenses of the Senate:

Resolved, That the Select Committee on Indian Depredations be authorized to employ a stenographer to report hearings for it in relation to the number of Indian depredation claims filed in the Court of Claims, the number of cases entitled to priority of consideration, and the judgments rendered thereon; the expense thereof to be paid from the contingent fund of the Senate.

CREDENTIALS OF A SENATOR.

Mr. Jones, of Nevada, presented the credentials of William M. Stewart, elected a Senator by the legislature of Nevada for the term of six years commencing March 4, 1893; which were read and placed on file.

MESSAGE FROM THE PRESIDENT.

The following message was received from the President of the United States, by Mr. Pruden, his secretary:

To the Senate:

I transmit herewith, as desired by the resolution of the Senate of the 4th instant, a report from the Secretary of State on the 6th instant, with its accompanying correspondence, in relation to the draft of an uncompleted treaty with Hawaii made in 1854.

BENJ. HARRISON.

EXECUTIVE MANSION,
Washington, February 6, 1893.

The message was read.

Ordered, That it be referred to the Committee on Foreign Relations and printed.

RECOMMITAL OF BILL.

On motion by Mr. Sawyer,

The Senate proceeded to consider, as in Committee of the Whole, the bill (H. R. 7099) granting an increase of pension to Samuel S. Anderson, and

Ordered, That the bill be recommitted to the Committee on Pensions.

WITHDRAWAL OF MEMORIAL.

On motion by Mr. Cullom,
The Senate proceeded to consider the order submitted by him on the 3d instant to withdraw from the files of the Senate the memorial of Maria Helena America Vespucci; and having been amended, on the motion of Mr. Cockrell,
The order, as amended, was agreed to, as follows:
Ordered, That the rules be suspended and that the Secretary of the Senate be directed to withdraw from the files of the Senate, for exhibition at the World's Columbian Exposition, under the auspices of the Department of State, a memorial of Maria Helena America Vespucci, praying a donation of land and that she be admitted to the right of citizenship; and that the memorial be returned to the files of the Senate by the Secretary of State at the conclusion of the Exposition.

BRIDGE OVER THE MONONGAHELA RIVER.

On motion by Mr. Quay,
The Senate proceeded to consider, as in Committee of the Whole, the bill (S. 3825) to authorize the Homestead and Pittsburg Bridge Company to construct a bridge over the Monongahela River from Pittsburg to Homestead; and no amendment being made, it was reported to the Senate.
Ordered, That it be engrossed and read a third time.
The said bill was read the third time.
Resolved, That it pass, and that the title thereof be as aforesaid.
Ordered, That the Secretary request the concurrence of the House of Representatives therein.

RELIEF TO INDIAN CITIZENS.

The morning hour having expired,
The Vice-President laid before the Senate the unfinished business at its last adjournment, viz, the bill (S. 2068) extending relief to Indian citizens, and for other purposes;
When,
On motion by Mr. Hill, that the Senate proceed to the consideration of the bill (S. 3423) for the repeal of certain parts of the act directing the purchase of silver bullion and the issue of Treasury notes thereon, and for other purposes, approved July 14, 1890,
On motion by Mr. Voorhees, that the motion lie on the table,
Mr. Hoar raised a question of order, viz, that the motion to lay on the table was not one of the incidental motions in order pending a motion to proceed to the consideration of a bill under Rule 9; and
The Vice-President sustained the point of order.
On the question to proceed to the consideration of the bill S. 3423,

It was determined in the negative, { Yeas 23
{ Nays 42

On motion by Mr. Hoar,
The yeas and nays being desired by one-fifth of the Senators present,
Those who voted in the affirmative are,
Messrs. Brice, Caffery, Davis, Dawes, Dixon, Faulkner, Frye, Gallinger, Gibson, Gorman, Hale, Hawley, Hill, Hoar, McPherson, Mills, Morrill, Palmer, Proctor, Sherman, Vest, Vilas, White.
Those who voted in the negative are,
Messrs. Bate, Berry, Blackburn, Blodgett, Call, Carey, Cockrell, Coke, Cullom, Daniel, Dolph, Dubois, Felton, George, Gordon, Hansbrough, Harris, Hunton, Irby, Jones of Nevada, Kyle, McMillan, Manderson, Mitchell, Morgan, Pasco, Peffer, Perkins, Pettigrew, Platt, Power, Pugh, Ransom, Shoup, Squire, Stewart, Stockbridge, Teller, Turpie, Vance, Voorhees, Wolcott.
So the motion was not agreed to.
The Senate resumed, as in Committee of the Whole, the consideration of the bill (S. 2068) extending relief to Indian citizens, and for other purposes; and
The question being on the amendment proposed by Mr. Manderson to the reported amendment.
Mr. Manderson withdrew his amendment,
The reported amendment having been further amended on the motion of Mr. Cockrell, it was agreed to as amended; and the bill was reported to the Senate and the amendment as amended was concurred in.
Ordered, That it be engrossed and read a third time.
The said bill was read the third time.
Resolved, That it pass, and that the title thereof be as aforesaid.
Ordered, That the Secretary request the concurrence of the House of Representatives therein.

MESSAGE FROM THE HOUSE.

A message from the House of Representatives, by Mr. Towles, its chief clerk:
Mr. President: The House of Representatives has disagreed to the amendments of the Senate to the bill (H. R. 9923) making appropriations for fortifications and other works of defense, for the armament thereof, for the procurement of heavy ordnance for trial and service, and for other purposes. It asks a conference with the Senate on the disagreeing votes of the two Houses thereon, and has appointed

12 s

Mr. Breckinridge of Kentucky, Mr. Livingston, and Mr. Cogswell managers at the same on its part.
The House of Representatives has passed a bill (H. R. 10290) making appropriations for the support of the Military Academy for the fiscal year ending June 30, 1894, in which it requests the concurrence of the Senate.
The House of Representatives has passed the following resolutions, which I am directed to communicate to the Senate:
Resolved, That the business of the House of Representatives be now suspended that opportunity may be given for tribute to the memory of Hon. John W. Kendall, late a Representative from the State of Kentucky.
Resolved, That as a further mark of respect to the memory of the deceased and in recognition of his eminent ability as a distinguished public servant, the House of Representatives, at the conclusion of these memorial services, shall stand adjourned.
Resolved, That the Clerk communicate these resolutions to the Senate.
Resolved, That the Clerk send a copy of these resolutions to the family of the deceased.
The Speaker of the House of Representatives having signed twenty enrolled bills, H. R. 1318, H. R. 2400, H. R. 2407, H. R. 4047, H. R. 5705, H. R. 6272, H. R. 6345, H. R. 6507, H. R. 6508, H. R. 6649, H. R. 7036, H. R. 7226, H. R. 7238, H. R. 7257, H. R. 7682, H. R. 8106, H. R. 8275, H. R. 8925, H. R. 9220, and H. R, 9531, I am directed to bring them to the Senate for the signature of its President.

HOUSE BILL REFERRED.

The bill H. R. 10290, last received from the House of Representatives for concurrence, was read the first and second times by unanimous consent and referred to the Committee on Appropriations.

QUARANTINE SERVICE.

On motion by Mr. Harris,
The Senate proceeded to consider, as in Committee of the Whole, the bill (H. R. 9757) granting additional quarantine powers and imposing additional duties upon the Marine-Hospital Service; and the reported amendment having been agreed to, the bill was reported to the Senate and the amendment was concurred in.
Ordered, That the amendment be engrossed and the bill read a third time.
The said bill as amended was read the third time.
Resolved, That it pass, and that the Senate request a conference with the House of Representatives on the said bill and amendment.
Ordered, That the conferees on the part of the Senate be appointed by the Presiding Officer; and
The Presiding Officer (Mr. Turpie in the chair) appointed Mr. Harris, Mr. Berry, and Mr. Chandler.
Ordered, That the Secretary notify the House of Representatives thereof.

FORTIFICATIONS APPROPRIATION BILL.

The Presiding Officer laid before the Senate the message from the House of Representatives announcing its disagreement to the amendments of the Senate to the bill (H. R. 9923) making appropriations for fortifications and other works of defense, for the armament thereof, for the procurement of heavy ordnance for trial and service, and for other purposes, and asking a conference on the disagreeing votes of the two Houses thereon; and
On motion by Mr. Dawes,
Resolved, That the Senate insist upon its amendments to the said bill, and agree to the conference asked by the House on the disagreeing votes of the two Houses thereon.
Ordered, That the conferees on the part of the Senate be appointed by the Presiding Officer; and
The Presiding Officer appointed Mr. Dawes, Mr. Stewart, and Mr. Gorman.
Ordered, That the Secretary notify the House of Representatives thereof.

CAR-COUPLERS AND BRAKES.

The Senate proceeded to consider, as in Committee of the Whole, the bill (H. R. 9350) to promote the safety of employés and travelers upon railroads by compelling common carriers engaged in interstate commerce to equip their cars with automatic couplers and continuous brakes and their locomotives with driving-wheel brakes, and for other purposes; and
An amendment to the reported amendment having been proposed by Mr. George,
Pending debate,

EXECUTIVE SESSION.

On motion by Mr. Sherman,
The Senate proceeded to the consideration of executive business; and
After the consideration of executive business the doors were reopened, and
On motion by Mr. Hawley, at 5 o'clock and 16 minutes p. m.,
The Senate adjourned.

TUESDAY, FEBRUARY 7, 1893.

MESSAGE FROM THE PRESIDENT.

The following message was received from the President of the United States, by Mr. Pruden, his secretary:

To the Senate and House of Representatives:

I transmit herewith for the consideration of Congress a communication from the the Secretary of the Interior, dated 4th instant, accompanied by an agreement concluded by and between the Turtle Mountain Indians and the commission appointed under the provisions of the Indian appropriation act of July 13, 1892, to negotiate with the Turtle Mountain band of Chippewa Indians in North Dakota for the cession and relinquishment to the United States of whatever right or interest they have in and to any and all lands in said State to which they claim title, and for their removal to and settlement upon lands to be hereafter selected and determined upon by the Secretary of the Interior upon the recommendation of the proposed commissioners, subject to the approval of Congress.

BENJ. HARRISON.

EXECUTIVE MANSION, *February 6, 1893.*

The message was read.

Ordered, That it be referred to the Committee on Indian Affairs and printed.

EXECUTIVE COMMUNICATIONS.

The Vice-President laid before the Senate a letter of the Secretary of War, transmitting, in answer to a resolution of the Senate of the 4th instant, a copy of a report upon the routes for a ship canal between the Atlantic and Pacific oceans, known as the Nicaragua route and the Darien or Atrato route; which was referred to the Committee on Foreign Relations and ordered to be printed.

The Vice-President laid before the Senate a letter of the Secretary of War transmitting an abstract of the militia force of the United States for the year 1892; which was referred to the Committee on Military Affairs and ordered to be printed.

The Vice-President laid before the Senate a letter of the Chief of Engineers, United States Army, transmitting, in answer to a resolution of the Senate of January 30, 1893, a report relative to the character of the building material used in the construction of the building for the Library of Congress; which was referred to the Select Committee on Additional Accommodations for the Library of Congress and ordered to be printed.

The Vice-President laid before the Senate a letter of the Secretary of the Treasury, transmitting an estimate of appropriation submitted by the Secretary of War for hospital at Rock Island Arsenal; which was referred to the Committee on Appropriations and ordered to be printed.

The Vice-President laid before the Senate a letter of the Secretary of the Treasury, transmitting estimates of appropriation submitted by the Attorney-General for the support of prisoners, United States courts, 1890, and for defending suits in claims against the United States, 1892; which was referred to the Committee on Appropriations and ordered to be printed.

The Vice-President laid before the Senate a letter of the Secretary of the Treasury, transmitting an estimate of appropriation submitted by the Secretary of War for Index for Confederate Records, for service of the fiscal year 1894; which was referred to the Committee on Appropriations and ordered to be printed.

The Vice-President laid before the Senate a letter of the Secretary of the Treasury, transmitting additional estimates of appropriations for the District of Columbia, submitted by the Commissioners of the District; which was referred to the Committee on Appropriations and ordered to be printed.

PETITIONS AND MEMORIALS.

Petitions, memorials, etc., were presented and referred as follows:

By the Vice-President: A resolution of the legislature of the State of Nevada in favor of the passage of a law reimbursing said State the amount of money now due her on account of her rebellion war claims against the United States; to the Committee on Appropriations and ordered to be printed.

By Mr. Cockrell: Resolutions adopted at a meeting held at Guthrie, Okla., January 18, 1893, praying for the ratification of the treaty providing for the opening up to settlement of the Cherokee Outlet; to the Committee on Indian Affairs and ordered to be printed.

By Mr. Vest: A petition of the St. Louis Chapter of the American Institute of Architects, praying the passage of the bill relating to the appointment of architects for the erection of public buildings; to the Committee on Public Buildings and Grounds.

By Mr. Allison: A memorial of the Memorial Association of the District of Columbia, praying an appropriation for the purchase of the building in which Abraham Lincoln died, and to make repairs to the same; to the Committee on Appropriations.

By Mr. Daniel: A resolution of the Chamber of Commerce of Richmond, Va., praying an amendment to the present pilot laws as will place sailing vessels upon the same advantageous footing as steam vessels; to the Committee on Commerce.

By Mr. Cullom: A petition of citizens of Illinois, praying for the appointment of a committee to investigate an alleged combine formed to depreciate the price of grain by millers, elevators, and others at St. Louis and Minneapolis; to the Committee on Agriculture and Forestry.

By Mr. Turpie: A memorial of B. Steinhart in relation to the execution of the Secret-Service rules in the district of Cleveland, Ohio; to the Committee on Civil Service and Retrenchment.

By Mr. Voorhees: Papers relating to the application of the heirs of Bayless W. Hanna, deceased, late minister plenipotentiary to the Argentine Republic, for the difference between the pay as minister resident and consul-general to said Republic; to the Committee on Appropriations, to accompany an amendment intended to be proposed to the bill (H. R. 10267) making appropriations for the diplomatic and consular service, etc.

Mr. Teller presented a resolution of the legislature of Colorado, remonstrating against the repeal of the law providing for the purchase of silver bullion.

Ordered, That it lie on the table.

Mr. Daniel presented a resolution of the Chamber of Commerce of Richmond, Va., and a memorial of the Board of Trade of Roanoke, Va., praying the passage of a law for the extension of the Norfolk and Western Railroad into and within the District of Columbia, and for the erection of another bridge over the Potomac River.

Ordered, That they lie on the table.

Mr. Daniel presented a resolution of the Chamber of Commerce of Richmond, Va., and a resolution of the Board of Trade of Portsmouth, Va., praying the repeal of the law providing for the purchase of silver bullion.

Ordered, That they lie on the table.

Petitions, etc., praying the passage of a law for the suspension o immigration into the United States, and for the establishment of a national quarantine, were presented as follows:

By the Vice-President: A resolution of the College of Physicians, of Philadelphia, Pa.

By Mr. Teller: A petition of citizens of Colorado.

By Mr. Dawes: A petition of citizens of Massachusetts.

By Mr. Daniel: A petition of citizens of Virginia.

Ordered, That they be referred to the Committee on Immigration.

Mr. Chandler presented a petition of Charles T. Hurd, praying for the removal of the charge of desertion from his naval record; which was referred to the Committee on Naval Affairs, to accompany the bill S. 3838.

Mr. Chandler presented papers relating to the application of W. Marietta Chapman to be allowed a pension; which were referred to the Committee on Pensions, to accompany the bill S. 3839.

ENROLLED BILLS SIGNED.

Mr. Dubois reported from the committee that they had examined and found duly enrolled the following bills:

H. R. 2400. An act granting a pension to Willis Luttrell;

H. R. 5705. An act to increase the pension of Amelia Graham;

H. R. 6272. An act to pension Susan S. Murphy;

H. R. 6345. An act granting an honorable discharge to Frederick E. Colter;

H. R. 6507. An act granting a pension to Sarah A. Hagan;

H. R. 6508. An act granting a pension to Joseph Fortier;

H. R. 6649. An act to extend the provisions of an act to provide for the muster and pay of certain officers and enlisted men of the volunteer forces;

H. R. 2407. An act granting a pension to Samuel Luttrell;

H. R. 1318. An act granting a pension to Martha A. Harris;

H. R. 7257. An act granting a pension to Alonzo D. Barber;

H. R. 8106. An act for the correction of the army record of David R. Wallace, deceased;

H. R. 8275. An act granting a pension to Abraham B. Simmons, of Capt. Thomas Tripp's company, in Col. Brisbane's regiment, South Carolina Volunteers, in the Florida Indian war;

H. R. 7662. An act granting a pension to Marion Kern Sherman;

H. R. 8925. An act to increase the pension of Harvey Lyon;

H. R. 9220. An act granting a pension to Mrs. Carolina Hardee Dyall, widow of James R. Dyall, veteran of the Florida war, 1836;

H. R. 4047. An act granting a pension to Ellen Hewett;

H. R. 7238. An act granting a pension to Amanda Atherton;

H. R. 9631. An act to make Rockport, Tex., a subport of entry;

H. R. 7226. An act granting a pension to Julia P. Wright; and

H. R. 7036. An act granting a pension to Lillie Ries, late a nurse at Jefferson Barracks;

Whereupon,

The Vice-President signed the same, and they were delivered to the committee to be presented to the President of the United States.

REPORTS OF COMMITTEES.

On motion by Mr. Allison,

Ordered, That the Committee on Appropriations be discharged from the further consideration of the bill (S. 264) for the relief of William B. Morgan, and that it be referred to the Committee on Claims.

Mr. Teller, from the Committee on Private Land Claims, to whom was referred the bill (H. R. 8340) to amend an act establishing a court of private land claims and to provide for the settlement of private land claims in certain States and Territories, approved March 3, 1891, reported it without amendment.

Mr. Carey, from the Committee on Education and Labor, to whom was referred the joint resolution (H. Res. 71) to authorize the Secretary of the Interior to continue the report on wages by Joseph D. Weeks, reported it without amendment.

On motion by Mr. Hale,

Ordered, That the said resolution be referred to the Committee on the Census.

Mr. Jones, of Arkansas, from the Committee on Indian Affairs, to whom was referred the bill (S. 3702) granting to the Chicago, Rock Island and Pacific Railway Company the use of certain lands at the Chickasaw Station, and for a " Y " in the Chickasaw Nation, Indian Territory, reported it with an amendment.

Mr. Jones, of Arkansas, from the Committee on Indian Affairs, to whom were referred the following bills, reported them each with amendments:

H. R. 3697. An act to grant to the Gainesville, Oklahoma and Gulf Railway Company a right of way through the Indian Territory, and for other purposes; and

S. 3602. A bill to grant to the Chicago, Rock Island and Pacific Railway Company a right of way through the Indian Territory, and for other purposes.

Mr. Platt, from the Committee on Indian Affairs, to whom was referred the bill (H. R. 10206) to ratify and confirm an agreement made between the Seneca Nation of Indians and William B. Barker, reported it without amendment.

Mr. Mitchell, from the Committee on the Judiciary, to whom was referred the bill (S. 3409) to extend the jurisdiction of the justices of the peace in the District of Columbia, and to regulate the proceedings before them, reported it without amendment and submitted a report (No. 1269) thereon.

The Senate proceeded, by unanimous consent, to consider the said bill as in Committee of the Whole; and no amendment being made, it was reported to the Senate.

Ordered, That it be engrossed and read a third time.

The said bill was read the third time.

Resolved, That it pass, and that the title thereof be as aforesaid.

Ordered, That the Secretary request the concurrence of the House of Representatives therein.

PRESENTATION OF BILLS.

Mr. Dubois reported from the committee that on the 3d instant they presented to the President of the United States the following enrolled bills:

S. 509. An act granting an increase of pension to Thomas J. Matlock;

S. 3311. An act to refer the claim of Jessie Benton Fremont to certain lands and the improvements thereon, in San Francisco, Cal., to the Court of Claims; and

S. 3753. An act relating to the anchorage and movement of vessels in the port of Chicago.

MESSAGE FROM THE HOUSE.

A message from the House of Representatives, by Mr. Towles, its chief clerk:

Mr. President: The House of Representatives has agreed to the amendments of the Senate to the following bills of the House:

H. R. 9176. An act relating to contracts of common carriers and to certain obligations, duties, and rights in connection with the carriage of property;

H. R. 929. An act granting a pension to Mrs. Mary E. Donaldson;

H. R. 8268. An act to amend chapter 559, page 1095, volume 26, United Statutes at Large;

H. R. 2592. An act for the relief of Andrew B. Knapp;

H. R. 9592. An act authorizing the Secretary of the Treasury to obtain plans and specifications for public buildings to be erected under the supervision of the Treasury Department, and providing for local supervision of the construction of the same;

H. R. 5649. An act for the relief of Lieut. F. W. Davis, and granting him an honorable discharge;

H. R. 730. An act for the relief of James A. Finley; and

H. R. 4758. An act for the relief of Charles E. Heuston.

The House of Representatives has disagreed to the amendments of the Senate to the bill (H. R. 1036) for the benefit of Logan, Simpson, and Hart counties and of the city of Louisville, Ky., and of Sumner and Davidson counties, Tennessee. It agrees to the conference asked by the Senate on the disagreeing votes of the two Houses thereon, and has appointed Mr. Bunn, Mr. Cox, of Tennessee, and Mr. Wever managers at the same on its part.

The House of Representatives has disagreed to the amendments of the Senate to the bill (H. R. 7028) to protect settlement rights where two or more persons settle upon the same subdivision of agricultural public lands before survey thereof. It agrees to the conference asked by the Senate on the disagreeing votes of the two

Houses thereon, and has appointed Mr. McRae, Mr. Pendleton, and Mr. Pickler managers at the same on its part.

The House of Representatives has disagreed to the amendments of the Senate to the bill (H. R. 9286) to create the California Débris Commission and to regulate hydraulic mining in the State of California. It agrees to the conference asked by the Senate on the disagreeing votes of the two Houses thereon, and has appointed Mr. Cowles, Mr. Caminetti, and Mr. Townsend managers at the same on its part.

The Speaker of the House of Representatives having signed three enrolled bills, H. R. 730, H. R. 7234, and H. R. 9758, I am directed to bring the same to the Senate for the signature of its President.

ENROLLED BILLS SIGNED.

Mr. Dubois reported from the committee that they had examined and found duly enrolled the following bills:

H. R. 730. An act for the relief of James A. Finley;

H. R. 7234. An act granting a pension to Mary Millard; and

H. R. 9758. An act to amend the charter of the Eckington and Soldiers' Home Railway Company of the District of Columbia;

Whereupon,

The Vice-President signed the same, and they were delivered to the committee to be presented to the President of the United States.

INTRODUCTION OF BILLS AND JOINT RESOLUTION.

Bills and a joint resolution were introduced, read the first and second times by unanimous consent, and referred as follows:

By Mr. Gallinger: A bill (S. 3837) for the relief of Sarah J. Warren; to the Committee on Pensions..

By Mr. Chandler: A bill (S. 3838) to remove charge of desertion from the record of Charles T. Hurd, formerly a landsman in the United States Navy; to the Committee on Naval Affairs.

A bill (S. 3839) granting a pension to W. Marietta Chapman; and A bill (S. 3840) granting a pension to William H. Kimball; to the Committee on Pensions.

By Mr. Allison: A bill (S. 3841) to amend an act entitled "An act to provide for the establishment of a port of delivery at Council Bluffs, Iowa;" to the Committee on Commerce.

By Mr. Stewart: A bill (S. 3842) for the relief of Gustav Gade and Henry F. Meyer; to the Committee on Claims.

By Mr. Faulkner: A bill (S. 3843) to authorize the Chesapeake and Ohio Railway to renew its railroad bridge across the Big Sandy River, upon such plans and location as may be approved by the Secretary of War; to the Committee on Commerce.

By Mr. Daniel: A bill (S. 3844) to authorize the Washington, Alexandria and Mount Vernon Electric Railway Company to construct a bridge across the Potomac River, and to construct a railroad over the same and through certain streets and reservations of Washington; to the Committee on the District of Columbia.

By Mr. George: A joint resolution (S. R. 147) asking information as to the shoaling in Horn Island Channel, in the Mississippi Sound; to the Committee on Commerce.

IMMIGRATION FROM CUBA, ETC.

Mr. Chandler, from the Committee on Immigration, reported the following resolution; and it was considered by unanimous consent, and agreed to:

Resolved, That there shall be printed for the use of the Committee on Immigration 1,000 extra copies of the report, with the testimony, of the Cuba and Florida inquiry.

BANKING STATEMENTS.

Mr. Sherman submitted the following resolution; which was referred to the Committee on Printing:

Resolved, That there be printed for the use of the Senate 10,000 additional copies of Senate Executive Document 38, part 1, second session, Fifty-second Congress (report of the Secretary of the Treasury in reply to the Senate resolution of July 26 last, relating to bank statistics).

ASYLUM FOR POLITICAL OFFENSES.

Mr. Turpie submitted the following resolution for consideration; which was ordered to lie on the table and be printed:

Believing that the doctrine of asylum as practiced and approved by a very large majority of the members of the family of nations is highly expedient and that jurisdiction in what are known as political offenses ought not to be extraterritorial, it is concluded as the sense of the Senate that no treaty should be approved which proposes to oust the courts or magistrates of the United States of the right to deter mine in each case, under the allegations and proof therein, whether the offense charged be political or not political under the law of nations.

REPRINT OF REPORT.

Mr. Call submitted the following resolution; which was considered by unanimous consent and agreed to:

Resolved, That the report (No. 1263) made February 4, 1893, from the Committee on Immigration, be reprinted, with the testimony.

ADDITIONAL PAGES IN THE SENATE.

Mr. Sherman submitted the following resolution; which was referred to the Committee to Audit and Control the Contingent Expenses of the Senate:

Resolved, That the Sergeant-at-Arms be, and he is hereby, authorized to appoint two additional pages for the balance of the present session, to be paid at the rate of $2.50 per day each, to be paid from the miscellaneous items of the contingent fund of the Senate.

VISITORS TO THE MILITARY ACADEMY.

The Vice-President appointed Mr. Cullom and Mr. White members of the Board of Visitors on the part of the Senate to attend the next annual examination of cadets at the Military Academy at West Point, N. Y., under the requirement of section 1327 of the Revised Statutes.

CONSIDERATION OF BILLS ON CALENDAR.

The Senate proceeded to consider, as in Committee of the Whole, the following bills; and no amendment being made, they were severally reported to the Senate:

H. R. 8123. An act granting to the Santa Fe, Prescott and Phœnix Railway Company the right of way across the Whipple Barracks military reservation in Arizona;

H. R. 8780. An act to restore to the pension roll Mary Eleanor White as former widow of Capt. George W. Hazzard;

H. R. 8784. An act granting a pension to Edward Smitherman;

H. R. 8969. An act to grant a pension to Lydia Bollman, dependent sister;

H. R. 8924. An act granting a pension to the widow of James A. Kelly;

H. R. 8054. An act to increase the pension of Mary L. Bacon, widow of the late George B. Bacon, late lieutenant-commander of the United States Navy;

H. R. 4375. An act for the relief of Charles S. Blood;

H. R. 9437. An act for the removal of the charge of desertion against William H Holloway;

H. R. 4215. An act to correct the military record of Capt. William C. Knowlton;

H. R. 8727. An act for the relief of S. J. Brooks;

H. R. 9585. An act for the relief of Harriett E. Niles;

H. R. 3713. An act for increase of pension of Frances P. Gardener;

H. R. 2427. An act granting a pension to Margaret Byron;

H. R. 9011. An act to grant a pension to Ida A. Taylor;

H. R. 8298. An act to pension Emma Johnson, blind and dependent daughter of Daniel D. Johnson, Company B, One hundred and forty-second New York Volunteers;

H. R. 6194. An act to commission David P. Cordray as second lieutenant, to date from June 12, 1892;

H. R. 8550. An act to increase the pension of W. H. Philpot, a pensioner of the Mexican war;

H. R. 3845. An act to increase the pension of Edward R. Chapman;

H. R. 2493. An act granting a pension to Jesse Cleaveland;

H. R. 8221. An act granting a pension to George W. Boyd; and

H. R. 6914. An act granting a pension to Drake Nettie Barnett;

Ordered, That they pass to a third reading.

The said bills were severally read the third time.

Resolved, That they pass.

Ordered, That the Secretary notify the House of Representatives thereof.

The Senate proceeded to consider, as in Committee of the Whole, the following bills; and the reported amendments having been agreed to, the bills were severally reported to the Senate and the amendments were concurred in.

H. R. 1162. An act for the relief of Harlow L. Street;

H. R. 7762. An act to ratify and confirm agreement between the Puyallup Indians and the Northern Pacific Railroad Company for right of way through the Puyallup Indian Reservation; and

H. R. 9527. An act to restore to the public domain a portion of the White Mountain Apache Indian Reservation in the Territory of Arizona, and for other purposes.

Ordered, That the amendments be engrossed and the bills read a third time.

The said bills as amended were read the third time.

Resolved, That they pass.

Ordered, That the Secretary request the concurrence of the House of Representatives in the amendments.

On motion by Mr. Sawyer,

The vote on the passage of the bill (H. R. 8550) to increase the pension of W. H. Philpot, a pensioner of the Mexican war, was reconsidered and the bill recommitted to the Committee on Pensions.

The Senate resumed, as in Committee of the Whole, the consideration of the bill (S. 457) for the relief of the assignees or legal representatives of John Roach, deceased; to pay balance due on the United States steamship *Dolphin;* and no further amendment being proposed, the bill was reported to the Senate and the amendment made in Committee of the Whole was concurred in.

Ordered, That it be engrossed and read a third time.

The said bill was read the third time.

Resolved, That it pass, and that the title thereof be as aforesaid.

Ordered, That the Secretary request the concurrence of the House of Representatives therein.

The Senate proceeded to consider, as in Committee of the Whole, the bill (S. 443) granting to the Midland Pacific Railroad Company the right of way through the Crow Creek Indian Reservation, in the State of South Dakota; and the reported amendments having been agreed to, and the bill further amended on the motion of Mr. Cockrell, it was reported to the Senate and the amendments were concurred in.

Ordered, That it be engrossed and read a third time.

The said bill was read the third time.

Resolved, That it pass, and that the title be amended so as to read, "A bill granting to the Midland Pacific Railway Company the right of way through the Crow Creek Indian Reservation, in the State of South Dakota."

Ordered, That the Secretary request the concurrence of the House of Representatives therein.

On motion by Mr. Teller, and by unanimous consent,

The Senate proceeded to consider, as in Committee of the Whole, the bill (H. R. 8340) to amend an act establishing a court of private land claims and to provide for the settlement of private land claims in certain States and Territories, approved March 3, 1891; and no amendment being made, it was reported to the Senate.

Ordered, That it pass to a third reading.

The said bill was read the third time.

On the question, Shall the bill pass?

Ordered, That the further consideration thereof be postponed to to-morrow.

SAFETY OF LIFE ON RAILROADS.

The morning hour having expired,

The Vice-President laid before the Senate the unfinished business at its adjournment yesterday, viz, the bill (S. 9350) to promote the safety of employés and travelers upon railroads by compelling common carriers engaged in interstate commerce to equip their cars with automatic couplers and continuous brakes and their locomotives with driving-wheel brakes, and for other purposes.

When,

On motion by Mr. Blackburn, that the Senate proceed to the consideration of the bill (S. 2626), to authorize the New York and New Jersey Bridge Companies to construct and maintain a bridge across the Hudson River between New York City and the State of New Jersey,

It was determined in the negative, { Yeas 22
                                     { Nays 34

On motion by Mr. Blackburn,

The yeas and nays being desired by one-fifth of the Senators present,

Those who voted in the affirmative are,

Messrs. Blackburn, Blodgett, Brice, Caffery, Coke, Daniel, George, Gibson, Gorman, Harris, Hill, Hunton, Irby, Mills, Power, Ransom, Stewart, Turpie, Vance, Vest, Voorhees, Wolcott.

Those who voted in the negative are,

Messrs. Allison, Bate, Call, Carey, Chandler, Cockrell, Cullom, Davis, Dawes, Dolph, Dubois, Frye, Gallinger, Hale, Hansbrough, Hawley, Higgins, Hiscock, Hoar, McMillan, Mitchell, Morgan, Morrill, Palmer, Peffer, Platt, Proctor, Sawyer, Sherman, Shoup, Stockbridge, Teller, Vilas, Washburn.

So the motion was not agreed to.

The Senate thereupon resumed, as in Committee of the Whole, the consideration of the bill H. R. 9350; and,

The question being on the amendment proposed by Mr. George to the reported amendment,

After debate,

Mr. George withdrew his amendment.

After further debate,

On motion by Mr. Jones, of Arkansas, at 5 o'clock and 10 minutes p. m.,

The Senate adjourned.

WEDNESDAY, FEBRUARY 8, 1893.

VISITORS TO THE NAVAL ACADEMY.

The Vice-President appointed Mr. Dixon and Mr. Gray members of the Board of Visitors on the part of the Senate to attend the next annual examination of cadets at the Naval Academy at Annapolis, Md., under the requirement of the act of February 14, 1878.

EXECUTIVE COMMUNICATIONS.

The Vice-President laid before the Senate a letter of the Secretary of the Treasury, transmitting an estimate of appropriations submitted by the Secretary of the Interior for inspecting mines in the Territories for the fiscal year ending June 30, 1894; which was referred to the Committee on Appropriations and ordered to be printed.

The Vice-President laid before the Senate a letter of the Secretary of the Treasury, transmitting, in answer to a resolution of the

Senate of January 28, 1893, a copy of a communication from the Supervising Surgeon-General of the Marine-Hospital Service relative to the rules and regulations now in force at the port of New York for the prevention of the introduction of contagious or infectious diseases.

Ordered, That it lie on the table and be printed.

PETITIONS AND MEMORIALS.

The Vice-President laid before the Senate a resolution of the legislative assembly of the Territory of Oklahoma, praying for an extension of the term of this session of the second legislative assembly for thirty days, with power to employ and pay such employés as from time to time may be found necessary; which was referred to the Committee on Territories.

The Vice-President laid before the Senate a memorial of the legislature of Montana in favor of the passage of the bill (S. 2373) to establish the boundaries of the Yellowstone National Park, and for other purposes.

Ordered, That it lie on the table.

Petitions, memorials, etc., were presented and referred as follows:

By Mr. Dawes: A memorial of the Boston Congregational Ministers' meeting, praying such legislation as will prohibit the exportation of intoxicating liquors and firearms to the natives of the Pacific islands; to the Committee on Foreign Relations.

By Mr. White: A memorial of the Board of Trade of New Orleans, La., praying the passage of a law for the establishment of a uniform bill of lading; to the Committee on Commerce.

By Mr. Mitchell: A memorial of the legislature of Oregon, in favor of the passage of a law for the restriction of indiscriminate immigration into the United States; to the Committee on Immigration.

By Mr. Perkins: A resolution of the Post-Office Clerks Association of Wichita, Kans., praying the passage of the bill for the classification of post-office clerks in free-delivery offices; to the Committee on Post-Offices and Post-Roads.

By Mr. Brice: Three petitions of citizens of Ohio, praying the passage of a law for the restriction of immigration into the United States; to the Committee on Immigration.

Two petitions of citizens of Ohio, praying for the establishment of a permanent census bureau, and for the collection and publication of statistics relating to farm mortgages; to the Committee on the Census.

Resolutions of the Chamber of Commerce of Cincinnati, Ohio, praying the passage of a law conferring upon the Commissioners of Interstate Commerce the power to enforce the principles, etc., of the law upon common carriers; to the Committee on Interstate Commerce.

By Mr. Daniel: Memorials of the Board of Trade, of the board of public works, and of the common council of Roanoke, Va., praying the passage of a law for the establishment of a term of the United States court at that place; to the Committee on the Judiciary.

A resolution of the Board of Trade of Roanoke, Va., praying liberal appropriations for the expenses of the naval rendezvous in Hampton Roads; to the Select Committee on the Quadro-Centennial.

Mr. Perkins presented a petition of citizens of Kansas, praying the passage of a law for the opening up to settlement of the Cherokee Outlet.

Ordered, That it lie on the table.

Mr. Daniel presented a resolution of the Board of Trade of Roanoke, Va., praying the passage of a law for the early completion of the Nicaragua Canal under the direction and control of the United States Government.

Ordered, That it lie on the table.

Petition praying the repeal of the law providing for the purchase of silver bullion were presented as follows:

By Mr. Brice: A petition of the Commercial Club of Cincinnati, Ohio.

By Mr. McPherson: A petition of citizens of New Jersey.

Ordered, That they tie on the table.

Memorials remonstrating against the repeal of the law providing for the purchase of silver bullion were presented as follows:

By Mr. Perkins: A memorial of the legislature of Kansas.

By Mr. Teller: A memorial of citizens of Colorado.

Ordered, That they lie on the table.

Petitions praying the passage of a law for the restriction of immigration into the United States were presented as follows:

By Mr. Brice: A petition of citizens of Ohio.

By Mr. McPherson: Two petitions of citizens of New Jersey.

Ordered, That they be referred to the Committee on Immigration.

Mr. Brice presented a petition of citizens of Ohio, praying the passage of the anti-option bill.

Ordered, That it lie on the table.

Mr. Brice presented a petition of citizens of Ohio, praying the repeal of the provision providing for the closing of the Columbian Exposition on the Sabbath day; which was referred to the Select Committee on the Quadro-Centennial.

Mr. Brice presented a memorial of citizens of Ohio, remonstrating against the repeal of the provision providing for the closing of the Columbian Exposition; which was referred to the Select Committee on the Quadro-Centennial.

REPORTS OF COMMITTEES.

Mr. Manderson, from the Committee on Printing, to whom was referred the resolution submitted by Mr. Morrill on the 6th instant, to print 10,000 extra copies of the reports of the Smithsonian Institution and the National Museum for the year ending June 30, 1892, reported it without amendment and submitted a report (No. 1273) thereon.

The Senate proceeded, by unanimous consent, to consider the said resolution; and

Resolved, That the Senate agree thereto.

Ordered, That the Secretary request the concurrence of the House of Representatives therein.

Mr. Manderson, from the Committee on Printing, to whom was referred the resolution received from the House of Representatives for concurrence, on the 1st instant, to print 6,000 of House Report No. 2319, on the sweating system, reported it without amendment and submitted a report (No. 1274) thereon.

The Senate proceeded, by unanimous consent, to consider the said resolution; and

Resolved, That the Senate agree thereto.

Ordered, That the Secretary notify the House of Representatives thereof.

Mr. Harris, from the Committee on Finance, to whom was referred the bill (S. 3561) to encourage the construction of electric railroads, to facilitate the rapid transportation of the mails, to promote the interests of commerce and travel, and to aid in demonstrating the feasibility of the distribution of electrical power for agricultural and other purposes along the line of electric roads, and especially to aid in the construction of a pioneer electric railroad between the cities of Chicago and St. Louis by the Chicago and St. Louis Electric Railroad Company, and to secure to the Government the use of the same for postal, military, and other purposes at the existing rates, reported it with an amendment.

Mr. Blodgett, from the Committee on Pensions, to whom was referred the bill (S. 3819) granting a pension to Mary Doubleday, widow of Bvt. Maj. Gen. Abner Doubleday, reported it with an amendment and submitted a report (No. 1270) thereon.

Mr. Mitchell, from the Committee on Claims, to whom was referred the bill (H. R. 5504) to permit the withdrawal of certain papers and the signing of certain receipts by John Finn or his attorney, reported it with amendments and submitted a report (No. 1271) thereon.

Mr. McMillan, from the Committee on the District of Columbia, to whom was referred the bill (H. R. 8815) to extend North Capitol street to the Soldiers' Home, reported it with amendments and submitted a report (No. 1272) thereon.

Mr. Sherman, from the Committee on Foreign Relations, to whom was referred in executive session the message of the President of the United States, transmitting, in answer to a resolution of the Senate of January 23, 1890, the official correspondence of the Government of the United States and China relating to the acts of Congress forbidding immigration of Chinese, and the treaty stipulations between the two countries, reported the same with the recommendation that it be printed and recommitted to the Committee on Foreign Relations; which was agreed to.

Mr. Jones, of Nevada, from the Committee to Audit and Control the Contingent Expenses of the Senate, to whom was referred the resolution yesterday submitted by Mr. Sherman, to authorize the appointment of two additional pages for the balance of the present session, reported it without amendment.

The Senate proceeded by unanimous consent to consider the said resolution; and

Resolved, That the Senate agree thereto.

MESSAGE FROM THE HOUSE.

A message from the House of Representatives, by Mr. Towles, its chief clerk:

Mr. President: The Speaker of the House of Representatives having signed seven enrolled bills, S. 1933, S. 3798, H. R. 929, H. R. 2592, H. R. 5649, H. R. 6797, and H. R. 8268, and an enrolled joint resolution, S. R. 144, I am directed to bring them to the Senate for the signature of its President.

ENROLLED BILLS.

Mr. Dubois reported from the committee that they had examined and found duly enrolled the following bills and joint resolution:

H. R. 929. An act granting a pension to Mrs. Mary E. Donaldson;

H. R. 2592. An act for the relief of Andrew B. Knapp;

H. R. 5649. An act for the relief of Lieut. F. W. Davis and granting him an honorable discharge;

H. R. 6797. An act to authorize the construction of a bridge across the Cahaba River, in Bibb County, Alabama, by the Montgomery, Tuscaloosa and Memphis Railway;

H. R. 8268. An act to amend chapter 559, page 1095, volume 26, United States Statutes at Large;

S. 1933. An act in relation to testimony before the Interstate Commerce Commission and in cases of proceedings under or connected with an act entitled "An act to regulate commerce," approved February 4, 1887, and amendments thereto;

S. 3798. An act to authorize the building of a railroad bridge at Little Rock, Ark; and

S. R. 144. Joint resolution to provide for maintenance of order during inaugural ceremonies, March 4, 1893;

Whereupon,

The Vice-President signed the same, and they were delivered to the committee to be presented to the President of the United States.

PRESIDENTIAL APPROVALS.

A message from the President of the United States, by Mr. Pruden, his secretary:

Mr. President: The President of the United States approved and signed on the 6th instant the following acts:

S. 3753. An act relating to the anchorage and movement of vessels in the port of Chicago; and

S. 509. An act granting an increase of pension to Thomas J. Matlock.

Ordered, That the Secretary notify the House of Representatives thereof.

INTRODUCTION OF BILLS AND JOINT RESOLUTION.

Bills and a joint resolution were introduced, read the first and second times by unanimous consent, and referred as follows:

By Mr. Morgan: A bill (S. 3845) to provide for the provisional government of countries and places acquired by treaty or otherwise; to the Committee on Foreign Relations.

By Mr. Vance: A bill (S. 3846) for the relief of G. M. Woodruff; to the Committee on Claims.

By Mr. Davis: A bill (S. 3847) granting a pension to —— Sturgis, widow of Brig. Gen. Samuel Davis Sturgis; to the Committee on Pensions.

By Mr. Carey: A bill (S. 3848) to increase the pension of Juliet W. Hart; to the Committee on Pensions.

By Mr. Perkins: A bill (S. 3849) granting a pension to Henderson H. Boggs; to the Committee on Pensions.

By Mr. Pettigrew: A joint resolution (S. R. 148) authorizing the Secretary of the Smithsonian Institution to send articles illustrative of the life and development of the industries of women to the World's Columbian Exposition; to the Select Committee on the Quadro-Centennial.

THE ELECTORAL COUNT.

On motion by Mr. Hoar,

Ordered, That at 5 minutes before 1 o'clock to-day, the Senate, in pursuance of the concurrent resolution of the two Houses, proceed to the hall of the House of Representatives, to take part, under the Constitution and laws, in the count of the electoral votes for President and Vice-President of the United States.

SEAL ISLANDS FISHERIES.

Mr. Teller submitted the following resolution; which was considered by unanimous consent and agreed to:

Resolved, That the Secretary of the Treasury be directed to transmit to the Senate copies of all reports made by special agents to the Seal Islands during the years 1891 and 1892.

CONSIDERATION OF BILLS ON CALENDAR.

The Senate proceeded to consider, as in Committee of the Whole, the following bills; and no amendments being made, they were severally reported to the Senate:

S. 3811. A bill to amend an act entitled "An act to grant to the Mobile and Dauphin Island Railroad and Harbor Company the right to trestle across the shoal water between Cedar Point and Dauphin Island," approved September 26, 1890;

S. 3081. A bill to authorize the issue of a duplicate to Addison A. Hosmer of a certificate of location of certain land therein described, which has been lost or destroyed;

S. 203. A bill for the examination and allowance of certain awards made by a board of claims to certain citizens of Jefferson County, Kentucky;

S. 3248. A bill relating to acknowledgments of instruments affecting real estate within the District of Columbia;

S. 3050. A bill to amend an act entitled "An act to regulate the carriage of passengers by sea," approved August 2, 1882;

S. 3358. A bill providing for the collection of fees for furnishing certificates of title to vessels;

S. 2024. A bill to exempt veterans from competitive examinations in the classified service of the United States;

S. 3147. A bill to authorize the Gulf, Colorado and Santa Fe Railway Company to purchase certain lands for station purposes in the Chickasaw Nation, Indian Territory;

S. 2586. A bill to reimburse George C. Tanner, late consul, etc., the sum of $200, paid by him for rent of rooms;

S. 3309. A bill for the relief of Catherine E. Whitall; and

S. 3395. A bill to remit the penalties of gunboat No. 3, the *Concord,* and gunboat No. 4, the *Bennington.*

Ordered, That they be engrossed and read a third time.

The said bills were severally read the third time.

Resolved, That they pass, and that the respective titles thereof be as aforesaid.

Ordered, That the Secretary request the concurrence of the House of Representatives therein.

The Senate proceeded to consider, as in Committee of the Whole, the bill (H. R. 7625) for the relief of certain settlers on public lands in Tucson land district, in Arizona; and no amendment being made, it was reported to the Senate.

Ordered, That it pass to a third reading.

The said bill was read the third time.

Resolved, That it pass.

Ordered, That the Secretary notify the House of Representatives thereof.

The Senate proceeded to consider, as in Committee of the Whole, the following bills; and the reported amendments having been agreed to, the bills were severally reported to the Senate and the amendments were concurred in:

S. 3113. A bill to remove the charge of desertion standing against John W. Wacker;

S. 2422. A bill to amend the military record of John H. Skinner;

S. 2142. A bill for the relief of M. S. Hellman, of Canyon City, Oregon;

S. 3075. A bill for the relief of Maj. Gen. George S. Greene;

S. 3682. A bill to narrow California avenue, within Bel Air Heights, District of Columbia; and

S. 1808. A bill for the recognition of Henry C. Hill as captain and aid-de-camp on the staff of Maj. Gen. B. F. Butler, United States Volunteers.

Ordered, That they be engrossed and read a third time.

The said bills were severally read the third time.

Resolved, That they pass, and that the respective titles thereof be as aforesaid.

Ordered, That the Secretary request the concurrence of the House of Representatives therein.

The Senate proceeded to consider, as in Committee of the Whole, the bill (S. 1730) for the relief of A. P. H. Stewart and others; and the reported amendments having been agreed to, the bill was reported to the Senate and the amendments were concurred in.

Ordered, That the bill be engrossed and read a third time.

The said bill was read the third time.

Resolved, That it pass, and that the title thereof be amended so as to read, "A bill for the relief of A. P. H. Stewart."

Ordered, That the Secretary request the concurrence of the House of Representatives therein.

The Senate proceeded to consider, as in Committee of the Whole, the bill (S. 2783) authorizing the President to place upon the retired list of the Army Sergeant Long and others, late of the Signal Corps, United States, survivors of the Lady Franklin Bay expedition; and no amendment being made, it was reported to the Senate.

Ordered, That it be engrossed and read a third time.

The said bill was read the third time.

Resolved, That it pass, and that the title be amended as reported by the Committee on Military Affairs, so as to read, "A bill authorizing the President to place upon the retired list of the Army Sergeants Long and Connell, late of the Signal Corps, United States, survivors of the Lady Franklin Bay expedition."

Ordered, That the Secretary request the concurrence of the House of Representatives therein.

The Senate proceeded to consider, as in Committee of the Whole, the bill (S. 373) for the relief of Daniel Donovan; and the reported amendments having been agreed to, the bill was reported to the Senate and the amendments were concurred in.

Ordered, That the bill be engrossed and read a third time.

The said bill was read the third time.

Resolved, That it pass and that the title thereof be amended so as to read, "A bill for the relief of the heirs of Daniel Donovan."

Ordered, That the Secretary request the concurrence of the House of Representatives therein.

The Senate proceeded to consider, as in Committee of the Whole, the bill (S. 2966) to amend rule 7, section 4233, Revised Statutes; and having been amended on the motion of Mr. Frye, the bill was reported to the Senate and the amendments were concurred in.

Ordered, That the bill be engrossed and read a third time.

The said bill was read the third time.

Resolved, That it pass, and that the title thereof be amended so as to read, "A bill to amend rule 7, section 4233, Revised Statutes, relating to rules for preventing collisions on the water."

Ordered, That the Secretary request the concurrence of the House of Representatives therein.

MESSAGE FROM THE HOUSE.

A message from the House of Representatives, by Mr. Towles, its chief clerk:

Mr. President: The House of Representatives has passed, without amendment, the following bills and joint resolution of the Senate:

S. 3787. An act to authorize the construction of a bridge across the St. Marys River, between the States of Florida and Georgia;

S. 3825. An act to authorize the Homestead and Pittsburg Bridge Company to construct a bridge over the Monongahela River from Pittsburg to Homestead;

S. 3826. An act authorizing Velasco and Surfside Terminal Railway Company to construct a bridge across the Galveston and Brazos Canal; and

S. R. 134. A joint resolution authorizing the loan, for exhibition at the World's Columbian Exposition, of the picture entitled "The Recall of Columbus," by Angustus G. Heaton.

The House of Representatives has agreed to the amendments of the Senate to the following bills of the House:

H. R. 7762. An act to ratify and confirm agreement between the Puyallup Indians and the Northern Pacific Railroad Company for right of way through the Puyallup Indian Reservation; and

H. R. 9757. An act granting additional quarantine powers and imposing additional duties upon the Marine Hospital Service.

The House of Representatives has disagreed to the amendment of the Senate to the bill (H. R. 7633) to ratify and confirm an agreement with the Kickapoo Indians in Oklahoma Territory, and to make appropriations for carrying the same into effect. It agrees to the conference asked by the Senate on the disagreeing votes of the two Houses thereon, and has appointed Mr. Peel, Mr. Brawley, and Mr. Kem managers at the same on its part.

The House of Representatives has disagreed to the amendments of the Senate to the bill (H. R. 9527) to restore to the public domain a portion of the White Mountain Apache Indian Reservation, in the Territory of Arizona, and for other purposes. It asks a conference with the Senate on the disagreeing votes of the two Houses thereon, and has appointed Mr. Peel, Mr. English, and Mr. Wilson, of Washington, managers at the same on its part.

The Speaker of the House of Representatives having signed an enrolled bill, H. R. 9176, I am directed to bring the same to the Senate for the signature of its President.

CONSIDERATION OF BILLS ON CALENDAR.

The Senate proceeded to consider, as in Committee of the Whole, the bill (S. 3236) authorizing the Commissioners of the District of Columbia to refuse applications for water connections in certain cases; and, having been amended, on the motion of Mr. Sherman, the bill was reported to the Senate and the amendment was concurred in.

Ordered, That it be engrossed and read a third time.

The said bill was read the third time.

Resolved, That it pass, and that the title thereof be as aforesaid.

Ordered, That the Secretary request the concurrence of the House of Representatives therein.

The Senate resumed the consideration of the bill (H. R. 8340) to amend "An act establishing a court of private land claims and to provide for the settlement of private land claims in certain States and Territories," approved March 3, 1891; and

The question being, Shall the bill pass?

It was determined in the affirmative.

Ordered, That the Secretary notify the House of Representatives thereof.

The Senate proceeded to consider, as in Committee of the Whole, the bill (S. 1876) to incorporate the East Washington Crosstown Railway Company of the District of Columbia; and

On motion by Mr. McMillan,

Ordered, That it be recommitted to the Committee on the District of Columbia.

The Senate proceeded to consider, as in Committee of the Whole, the bill (S. 2637) to extend North Capitol street to Soldiers' Home; and,

On motion by Mr. McMillan,

Ordered, That it be postponed indefinitely.

The Senate proceeded to consider, as in Committee of the Whole, the bill (S. 1344) to make payment to Samuel J. Haynes of money erroneously and by mistake paid on his homestead entry; and no amendment being made, it was reported to the Senate.

Ordered, That it be engrossed and read a third time.

The said bill was read the third time.

Resolved, That it pass, that the preamble be stricken out, and that the title thereof be as aforesaid.

Ordered, That the Secretary request the concurrence of the House of Representatives therein.

The Senate proceeded to consider, as in Committee of the Whole, the bill (S. 3360) to amend section 6 of an act entitled "An act to prohibit the coming of Chinese persons into the United States," approved May 5, 1892; and

On motion by Mr. Hoar, to amend the bill by striking out all after the enacting clause, and in lien thereof inserting certain words,

Ordered, That the further consideration thereof be postponed to to-morrow.

COUNT OF THE ELECTORAL VOTE.

At 5 minutes before 1 o'clock p. m. the Senate, in pursuance of its order of this day, proceeded to the Hall of the House of Representatives; and

The two Houses being assembled,

The certificates of the electors of the several States for President and Vice-President of the United States were opened by the President of the Senate and handed to the tellers appointed for the purpose, who, having read the same in the presence and hearing of the two Houses, made a list thereof; and the votes having been ascertained and counted, the result was delivered to the President of the Senate, as follows:

List of votes for President and Vice-President of the United States for the term beginning March 4, 1893.

Number of electoral votes to which each State is entitled	States	For President			For Vice-President		
		Grover Cleveland, of New York	Benjamin Harrison, of Indiana	James B. Weaver, of Iowa	Adlai E. Stevenson, of Illinois	Whitelaw Reid, of New York	James G. Field, of Virginia
11	Alabama	11			11		
8	Arkansas	8			8		
9	California	8	1		8	1	
4	Colorado			4			4
6	Connecticut	6			6		
3	Delaware	3			3		
4	Florida	4			4		
13	Georgia	13			13		
3	Idaho			3			3
24	Illinois	24			24		
15	Indiana	15			15		
13	Iowa		13			13	
10	Kansas			10			10
13	Kentucky	13			13		
8	Louisiana	8			8		
6	Maine		6			6	
8	Maryland	8			8		
15	Massachusetts		15			15	
14	Michigan	5	9		5	9	
9	Minnesota		9			9	
9	Mississippi	9			9		
17	Missouri	17			17		
3	Montana	3			3		
8	Nebraska		8			8	
3	Nevada			3			3
4	New Hampshire		4			4	
10	New Jersey	10			10		
36	New York	36			36		
11	North Carolina	11			11		
3	North Dakota	1	1	1	1	1	1
23	Ohio	1	22		1	22	
23	Pennsylvania		23			23	
4	Rhode Island		4			4	
9	South Carolina	9			9		
	South Dakota						
12	Tennessee	12			12		
15	Texas	15			15		
4	Vermont		4			4	
12	Virginia	12			12		
4	Washington		4			4	
6	West Virginia	6			6		
12	Wisconsin	12			12		
3	Wyoming		3			3	
444	Total	277	145	22	277	145	22

EUGENE HALE,
JO. C. S. BLACKBURN,
Tellers on the part of the Senate.

J. LOGAN CHIPMAN,
HENRY CABOT LODGE,
Tellers on the part of the House of Representatives.

The President of the Senate thereupon announced the state of the vote, as follows:

The state of the vote for President of the United States, as delivered to the President of the Senate, is as follows:

The whole number of the electors appointed to vote for President of the United States is 444, of which a majority is 223.

Grover Cleveland, of the State of New York, has received for President of the United States 277 votes;

Benjamin Harrison, of the State of Indiana, has received 145 votes; and

James B. Weaver, of the State of Iowa, has received 22 votes.

The state of the vote for Vice-President of the United States, as delivered to the President of the Senate, is as follows:

The whole number of the electors appointed to vote for Vice-President of the United States is 444, of which a majority is 223.

Adlai E. Stevenson, of the State of Illinois, has received 277 votes;

Whitelaw Reid, of the State of New York, has received 145 votes; and

James G. Field, of the State of Virginia, has received 22 votes.

This announcement of the state of the vote by the President of the Senate is, by law, a sufficient declaration that Grover Cleveland, of the State of New York, is elected President of the United States, and that Adlai E. Stevenson, of the State of Illinois, is elected Vice-President of the United States, each for the term beginning March 4, 1893, and will be entered, together with a list of the votes, on the Journals of the Senate and House of Representatives.

The count of the electoral vote having been completed and the result announced, the joint meeting of the two Houses was dissolved; and

The Senate returned to its Chamber.

Mr. Hale, on the part of the tellers who were appointed on behalf of the Senate, in pursuance of the concurrent resolution of the two Houses, to ascertain the result of the election for President and Vice-President of the United States, reported that the two Houses met in joint convention, in pursuance of the resolution, and that thereupon the certificates of the electors of the various States of their votes for those officers were opened by the President of the Senate and delivered to the tellers; and on being examined it appeared that the votes of the several States had been cast in accordance with the list as hereinbefore stated.

That from those votes it appeared that the whole number of electors appointed to vote for President and Vice-President of the United States for the term of office beginning on the 4th day of March, 1893, was 444, of which a majority was 223.

The state of the vote for President of the United States appeared to be:

For Grover Cleveland, of the State of New York, 277.
For Benjamin Harrison, of the State of Indiana, 145.
For James B. Weaver, of the State of Iowa, 22.

The state of the vote for Vice-President of the United States appeared to be:

For Adlai E. Stevenson, of the State of Illinois, 277.
For Whitelaw Reid, of the State of New York, 145.
For James G. Field, of the State of Virginia, 22.

Which result having been ascertained and counted by the tellers, was delivered by them to the President of the Senate; whereupon, the President of the Senate announced the state of the vote to be that Grover Cleveland, of the State of New York, had received 277 electoral votes, and that Benjamin Harrison, of the State of Indiana, had received 145 electoral votes, and that James B. Weaver, of the State of Iowa, had received 22 electoral votes, for the office of President of the United States; and that Adlai E. Stevenson, of the State of Illinois, had received 277 electoral votes, that Whitelaw Reid, of the State of New York, had received 145 electoral votes, and that James G. Field, of the State of Virginia, had received 22 electoral votes for the office of Vice-President of the United States.

STATUE OF GEN. STARK.

The Senate proceeded to consider, as in Committee of the Whole, the bill (S. 2158) for the erection of equestrian statue of Maj. Gen. John Stark in the city of Manchester, N. H.; and no amendment being made, it was reported to the Senate.

Ordered, That it be engrossed and read a third time.
The said bill was read the third time.
On the question, Shall the bill pass?

It was determined in the affirmative, $\begin{cases} \text{Yeas.................... 39} \\ \text{Nays .... 7} \end{cases}$

On motion by Mr. Berry,
The yeas and nays being desired by one-fifth of the Senators present,
Those who voted in the affirmative are,
Messrs. Blodgett, Butler, Caffery, Call, Carey, Chandler, Cullom, Daniel, Dawes, Dolph, Dubois, Faulkner, Frye, Gallinger, George, Hawley, Hill, Hoar, Irby, Jones of Nevada, Manderson, Mills, Morgan, Morrill, Palmer, Perkins, Platt, Power, Proctor, Pugh, Sawyer, Shoup, Squire, Stewart, Stockbridge, Teller, Vest, White, Wolcott.

Those who voted in the negative are,
Messrs. Berry, Cockrell, Coke, Harris, Hunton, Kyle, Peffer.
So it was
Resolved, That the bill pass, and that the title thereof be as aforesaid.

Ordered, That the Secretary request the concurrence of the House of Representatives therein.

PRESENTATION OF BILLS.

Mr. Dubois reported from the committee that they this day presented to the President of the United States the following enrolled bills and joint resolution:

S. 1933. An act in relation to testimony before the Interstate Commerce Commission and in cases of proceedings under or connected with an act entitled "An act to regulate commerce," approved February 4, 1887, and amendments thereto;

S. R. 144. Joint resolution to provide for maintenance of order during inaugural ceremonies, March, 1893;

S. 3798. An act to authorize the building of a railroad bridge at Little Rock, Ark.

SAFETY OF LIFE ON RAILROADS.

The Senate resumed, as in Committee of the Whole, the consideration of the bill (H. R. 9350) to promote the safety of employés

and travelers upon railroads by compelling common carriers engaged in interstate commerce to equip their cars with automatic couplers and continuous brakes and their locomotives with driving-wheel brakes, and for other purposes; and

The question being on the amendment reported by the Committee on Interstate Commerce, viz: Strike out all after the enacting clause of the bill and in lieu thereof insert certain words; and

An amendment to the part proposed to be inserted having been submitted by Mr. Morgan,

On motion by Mr. Dolph to amend the amendment of Mr. Morgan,
Pending debate,
Ordered, That the bill be reprinted.
On motion of Mr. Sawyer,

The Senate proceeded to the consideration of executive business; and

After the consideration of executive business the doors were reopened, and

On motion by Mr. Stewart, at 3 o'clock and 30 minutes p. m.,
The Senate adjourned.

THURSDAY, FEBRUARY 9, 1893.

Mr. Teller raised the question as to the presence of a quorum;
Whereupon,
The Vice-President directed the roll to be called;
When,
Forty-six Senators answered to their names.
A quorum being present,

MESSAGE FROM THE PRESIDENT.

The following message was received from the President of the United States, by Mr. Pruden, his secretary:

To the Senate and House of Representatives:

I transmit herewith the Eighth Annual Report of the Commissioner of Labor. This report relates to industrial education in the United States and foreign countries.

BENJ. HARRISON.

EXECUTIVE MANSION,
Washington, D. C., February 8, 1893.

The message was read.
Ordered, That it be referred to the Committee on Education and Labor and printed.

WHITE MOUNTAIN APACHE INDIAN RESERVATION.

The Vice-President laid before the Senate the message of the House of Representatives announcing its disagreement to the amendments of the Senate to the bill (H. R. 9527) to restore to the public domain a portion of the White Mountain Apache Indian Reservation, in the Territory of Arizona.

On motion by Mr. Jones, of Arkansas,
Resolved, That the Senate insist upon its amendments to the said bill disagreed to by the House of Representatives, and agree to the conference asked by the House on the disagreeing votes of the two Houses thereon.

Ordered, That the conferees on the part of the Senate be appointed by the Vice-President; and

The Vice-President appointed Mr. Jones of Arkansas, Mr. Platt, and Mr. Manderson.

Ordered, That the Secretary notify the House of Representatives thereof.

EXECUTIVE COMMUNICATIONS.

The Vice-President laid before the Senate a letter of the Secretary of the Treasury, transmitting a communication from the Commissioner of Customs, submitting a draft of an amendment to the general deficiency appropriation bill for the allowance of certain amounts paid by officers of the Light-House Board; which was referred to the Committee on Appropriations and ordered to be printed.

The Vice-President laid before the Senate a letter of the Secretary of the Treasury, transmitting a communication from the Secretary of State, submitting an estimate of appropriation to defray the necessary expenses of the reception and entertainment of distinguished persons who have accepted invitations to attend the World's Columbian Exposition; which was referred to the Committee on Appropriations and ordered to be printed.

The Vice-President laid before the Senate the annual report of the Georgetown Barge, Dock, Elevator and Railroad Company of the District of Columbia; which was referred to the Committee on the District of Columbia and ordered to be printed.

PETITIONS AND MEMORIALS.

Petitions, memorials, etc., were presented and referred as follows:
By Mr. Washburn: A memorial of the legislature of Minnesota in favor of the passage of a law for the establishment of a national quarantine; to the Committee on Immigration.

Papers relating to the application of Christopher Schmidt, of St. Paul, Minn., for compensation for injuries received from accidental shot on the rifle range at Fort Snelling, July 14, 1882; to the Committee on Military Affairs and ordered to be printed.

By Mr. Vest: A memorial of S. D. Carpenter, praying an appropriation of £50,000 to enable him to complete and exhibit his new patent printing machine; to the Committee on Printing.

By Mr. Higgins: A memorial of citizens of Delaware, remonstrating against the repeal of the provision providing for the closing of the Columbian Exposition on the Sabbath day; to the Select Committee on the Quadro-Centennial.

By Mr. Hawley: Two petitions of citizens of Connecticut, praying the passage of a law for the restriction of immigration into the United States; to the Committee on Immigration.

By Mr. Power: A memorial of the legislature of Montana in favor of the passage of the bill (S. 2873) to establish the boundaries of the Yellowstone National Park, and for other purposes; to the Committee on Territories.

By Mr. McMillan: A paper relating to the proposed organization of a regular army and navy reserve; to the Committee on Military Affairs, to accompany the bill S. 3853.

By Mr. Dolph: A letter from J. H. Crane relative to ejectment suits brought against settlers by the Southern Pacific Railroad Company; to the Committee on Public Lands, to accompany the joint resolution S. R. 149.

By Mr. Hoar: A letter of the Attorney-General addressed to him as chairman of the Committee on the Judiciary, recommending an amendment to the statute relative to the jurisdiction of United States courts against corporations; to accompany the bill S. 3851.

By Mr. McMillan: A letter from the Secretary of the Lake Carriers' Association, urging an appropriation for the widening of the present channel at "the elbow" at the lower end of Lake George in St. Marys River, Michigan; to the Committee on Appropriations, to accompany an amendment intended to be proposed to the sundry civil appropriation bill, No. 10238.

By the Vice-President: A memorial of the legislature of the Territory of Oklahoma, praying the passage of a law reserving sections 13 and 19 of each township in said Territory for the benefit of certain schools thereof; to the Committee on Territories.

Mr. Washburn presented a petition of citizens of Minnesota, praying the passage of the antioption bill.

Ordered, That it lie on the table.

Mr. Washburn presented resolutions of the Board of Trade of Minneapolis, Minn., praying the early completion of the Nicaragua Canal under the direction of the Government.

Ordered, That they lie on the table.

Memorials praying the repeal of the law providing for the purchase of silver bullion were presented as follows:

By Mr. Dawes: A memorial of citizens of Massachusetts.

By Mr. Washburn: A memorial of the Clearing-House Association of Minneapolis, Minn.

Ordered, That they lie on the table.

Mr. Kyle presented a memorial of citizens of South Dakota, remonstrating against the repeal of the law providing for the purchase of silver bullion.

Ordered, That it lie on the table.

On motion by Mr. Carey,

Ordered, That the memorial of the legislature of Montana in relation to the boundaries of the Yellowstone National Park be taken from the table and referred to the Committee on Territories.

Mr. Hunton presented a memorial of the "Virginia Organization to Promote the Nicaragua Canal," praying for the early completion of the Nicaragua Canal under the direction of the Government.

Ordered, That it lie on the table and be printed.

CREDENTIALS OF A SENATOR.

Mr. Felton presented the credentials of Stephen M. White, elected a Senator by the legislature of California for the term of six years commencing March 4, 1893; which were read and placed on file.

RETURN OF BILL.

On motion by Mr. Dolph,

Ordered, That the Secretary request the House of Representatives to return to the Senate the bill (H. R. 9955) providing for sundry light-houses and other aids to navigation.

ENROLLED BILL SIGNED.

Mr. Dubois reported from the committee that they had examined and found duly enrolled the bill (H. R. 9176) relating to navigation of vessels, bills of lading, and to certain obligations, duties, and rights in connection with the carriage of property;

Whereupon,

The Vice-President signed the same, and it was delivered to the committee to be presented to the President of the United States.

REPORTS OF COMMITTEES.

Mr. Frye, from the Committee on Commerce, to whom was referred the bill (S. 3814) to establish a port of delivery at Bonners Ferry, Idaho, reported it without amendment.

Mr. Frye, from the Committee on Commerce, to whom was re-

13 s

ferred the bill (S. 3712) to grant the right of way for electric railroad purposes through certain lands of the United States in Richmond County, New York, reported it with amendments.

Mr. Frye, from the Committee on Commerce, to whom was referred the joint resolution (S. R. 147) asking information as to the shoaling in Horn Island Channel, in the Mississippi Sound, reported it without amendment.

The Senate proceeded, by unanimous consent, to consider the said resolution as in Committee of the Whole; and having been amended on the motion of Mr. Hoar, it was reported to the Senate and the amendment was concurred in.

Ordered, That the resolution be engrossed and read a third time.

The said resolution was read the third time.

Resolved, That it pass, and that the title thereof be as aforesaid.

Ordered, That the Secretary request the concurrence of the House of Representatives therein.

Mr. Frye, from the Committee on Commerce, to whom were referred the following bills, reported them without amendment:

S. 3836. A bill to authorize the Union Railroad Company to construct and maintain a bridge across the Monongahela River; and

S. 3843. A bill to authorize the Chesapeake and Ohio Railway Company to renew its railroad bridge across the Big Sandy River, upon such plans and location as may be approved by the Secretary of War.

The Senate proceeded, by unanimous consent, to consider the said bills as in Committee of the Whole; and no amendment being made, they were reported to the Senate.

Ordered, That they be engrossed and read a third time.

The said bills were read the third time.

Resolved, That they pass, and that the respective titles thereof be as aforesaid.

Ordered, That the Secretary request the concurrence of the House of Representatives therein.

Mr. Dawes, from the Committee on Indian Affairs, to whom was referred the bill (S. 3788) granting right of way to the Colorado River Irrigation Company through the Yuma Indian Reservation in California, reported it without amendment.

The Senate proceeded, by unanimous consent, to consider the said bill as in Committee of the Whole; and no amendment being made, it was reported to the Senate.

Ordered, That it be engrossed and read a third time.

The said bill was read the third time.

Resolved, That it pass, and that the title thereof be as aforesaid.

Ordered, That the Secretary request the concurrence of the House of Representatives therein.

Mr. Hoar, from the Committee on the Judiciary, reported a bill (S. 3851) to amend the act approved August 13, 1888, in relation to the jurisdiction of the circuit courts of the United States (Chap. 866, 25 Stats. at Large, page 433); which was read the first and second times by unanimous consent.

Mr. Jones, of Arkansas, from the Committee on Indian Affairs, to whom was referred the bill (H. R. 10146) to authorize the Oklahoma Midland Railway Company to construct and operate railway, telegraph, and telephone lines through the Indian and Oklahoma Territories, and for other purposes, reported it with amendments.

Mr. Coke, from the Committee on Commerce, to whom was referred the bill (H. R. 9502) to authorize the Trinity River Navigation Company to open to navigation the Trinity River in the State of Texas, reported it with amendments.

Mr. Pettigrew, from the Committee on Indian Affairs, to whom was referred the bill (S. 3392) to ratify and confirm an agreement entered into in March, 1892, between the Indians of the Rosebud Agency and certain Indians of the Lower Brulé Agency, both in South Dakota, and for other purposes, reported it with amendments and submitted a report (No. 1275) thereon.

MESSAGE FROM THE HOUSE.

A message from the House of Representatives, by Mr. Towles, its chief clerk:

Mr. President: The Speaker of the House of Representatives having signed twenty-three enrolled bills, H. R. 2427, H. R. 2493, H. R. 3713, H. R. 3845, H. R. 4215, H. R. 4375, H. R. 4758, H. R. 6194, H. R. 6311, H. R. 7625, H. R. 8054, R. R. 8221, H. R. 8298, H. R. 8727, H. R. 8780, H. R. 8784, H. R. 8924, H. R. 8969, H. R. 9011, H. R. 9437, H. R. 9585, H. R. 9592, and H. R. 9757, I am directed to bring the same to the Senate for the signature of its President.

I am directed to return to the Senate, in compliance with its request, the bill (H. R. 9955) providing for sundry light-houses and other aids to navigation.

ENROLLED BILLS SIGNED.

Mr. Dubois reported from the committee that they had examined and found duly enrolled the following bills:

H. R. 3713. An act for increase of pension of Frances P. Gardner;

H. R. 2493. An act granting a pension to Jesse Cleaveland;

H. R. 2427. An act granting a pension to Margaret Byron;

H. R. 8727. An act for the relief of S. J. Brooks;

H. R. 4758. An act for the relief of Charles E. Heuston;

H. R. 8221. An act granting a pension to George W. Boyd;

H. R. 9592. An act authorizing the Secretary of the Treasury to obtain plans and specifications for public buildings to be erected under the supervision of the Treasury Department, and providing for local supervision of the construction of the same;

H. R. 4375. An act for the relief of Charles S. Blood;

H. R. 4215. An act to correct the military record of Capt. William C. Knowlton;

H. R. 6194. An act to commission David P. Cordray as second lieutenant, to date from June 12, 1892;

H. R. 9437. An act for the removal of the charge of desertion against William H. Holloway;

H. R. 9585. An act for the relief of Harriett E. Niles;

H. R. 8969. An act to grant a pension to Lydia Ballman, a dependent sister;

H. R. 9011. An act to grant a pension to Ida A. Taylor;

H. R. 8924. An act granting a pension to the widow of James A. Kelly;

H. R. 8784. An act granting a pension to Edward Smitherman;

H. R. 8780. An act to restore to the pension roll Mary Eleanor White, as former widow of Capt. George W. Hazzard;

H. R. 8298. An act to pension Emma Johnson, blind and dependent daughter of Daniel D. Johnson, Company B, One hundred and forty-second New York Volunteers;

H. R. 8054. An act to increase the pension of Mary L. Bacon, widow of the late George B. Bacon, late lieutenant-commander of the United States Navy;

H. R. 6914. An act granting a pension to Druke Nettie Barnett;

H. R. 3845. An act to increase the pension of Edward R. Chapman;

H. R. 7625. An act for relief of certain settlers on public land in the Tucson land district of Arizona; and

H. R. 9757. An act granting additional quarantine powers and imposing additional duties upon the Marine-Hospital Service;

Whereupon,

The Vice-President signed the same, and they were delivered to the committee to be presented to the President of the United States.

INTRODUCTION OF BILLS AND JOINT RESOLUTION.

Bills and a joint resolution were introduced, read the first and second times by unanimous consent, and referred as follows:

By Mr. Washburn: A bill (S. 3850) for the relief of Christopher Schmidt; to the Committee on Military Affairs.

By Mr. Dawes: A bill (S. 3852) to pension Mrs. Eliza B. Peirce, widow of Charles Peirce, New Bedford, Mass.; to the Committee on Pensions.

By Mr. McMillan: A bill (S. 3853) to provide for the organization of a regular army and navy reserve; to the Committee on Military Affairs.

By Mr. Voorhees: A bill (S. 3854) providing for rebuilding lock No. 2, Green River, at Rumsey, Ky.; to the Committee on Commerce.

By Mr. Dolph: A joint resolution (S. R. 149) instructing the Attorney-General to defend settlers in California, who hold patents, against ejectment suits brought by the Southern Pacific Railroad Company to deprive them of their homes; to the Committee on Public Lands.

EXECUTIVE SESSION.

On motion by Mr. Morgan,

The Senate proceeded to the consideration of executive business; and

After the consideration of executive business the doors were reopened.

CORRESPONDENCE RELATIVE TO THE SANDWICH ISLANDS.

On motion by Mr. Morgan,

Ordered, That the message of the President of the United States, dated March 3, 1854, communicating, in answer to the resolution of the Senate of the 2d February, 1854, copies of correspondence with the British Government in regard to the Sandwich Islands, transmitted to the Senate in executive session, and the injunction of secrecy removed, be printed.

HOUR OF MEETING.

On motion by Mr. Wolcott, that when the Senate adjourn it be to to-morrow at 12 o'clock,

The yeas were 30 and the nays were 30.

On motion by Mr. Sherman,

The yeas and nays being desired by one-fifth of the Senators present, Those who voted in the affirmative are,

Messrs. Bate, Berry, Blackburn, Blodgett, Brice, Camden, Cockrell, Faulkner, Gallinger, Gordon, Harris, Hill, Jones of Arkansas, Jones of Nevada, Kyle, McMillan, McPherson, Palmer, Pasco, Peffer, Pugh, Quay, Ransom, Teller, Vance, Vest, Vilas, Voorhees, White, Wolcott.

Those who voted in the negative are,

Messrs. Call, Carey, Chandler, Coke, Cullom, Dawes, Dolph, Dubois, Felton, Frye, George, Hansbrough, Hawley, Higgins, Hoar, Hunton, Manderson, Mills, Morgan, Morrill, Perkins, Pettigrew, Platt, Power, Sawyer, Sherman, Shoup, Squire, Stockbridge, Washburn.

The Senate being equally divided,

The Vice-President voted in the affirmative and declared the motion agreed to.

WILLIAM SMITH AND OTHERS.

On motion by Mr. Davis, and by unanimous consent,

The vote on the passage of the bill (S. 1678) for the relief of William Smith and others was reconsidered; and

On motion by Mr. Davis,

Ordered, That it be postponed indefinitely.

SAFETY OF LIFE ON RAILROADS.

The Senate resumed, as in Committee of the Whole, the consideration of the bill (H. R. 9350) to promote the safety of employés and travelers upon railroads by compelling common carriers engaged in interstate commerce to equip their cars with automatic couplers and continuous brakes and their locomotives with driving-wheel brakes, and for other purposes; and

The question being on the amendment proposed by Mr. Dolph to the amendment of Mr. Morgan,

After debate,

On motion by Mr. Cullom to lay on the table the amendment of Mr. Morgan, as follows, viz: Insert as an additional section in the part proposed to be inserted by the committee the following:

That if the brake or coupling or device of any kind that shall be at any time adopted under the provisions of this act is under the protection of letters patent, it shall be the duty of the Attorney-General to institute judicial proceedings in the supreme court of the District of Columbia to condemn such device, brake, or coupling, and the letters patent protecting the same, to the public use, upon just compensation to be paid by the United States to the owners of such letters patent. Such proceeding shall be in the name and on behalf of the United States of America and against the owner of such letters patent. And full jurisdiction is hereby conferred upon said supreme court of the District of Columbia to hear and decide such proceedings of condemnation without reference to the residence of the defendant in such proceeding,

It was determined in the affirmative, { Yeas .... 36 / Nays .... 9 }

On motion by Mr. Wolcott,

The yeas and nays being desired by one-fifth of the Senators present, Those who voted in the affirmative are,

Messrs. Allison, Bate, Berry, Blackburn, Caffery, Call, Chandler, Cockrell, Cullom, Daniel, Dubois, Faulkner, Frye, Gallinger, George, Hansbrough, Harris, Higgins, Hoar, Hunton, Jones of Arkansas, Kyle, Manderson, Palmer, Peffer, Perkins, Platt, Quay, Sawyer, Sherman, Squire, Stockbridge, Vest, Vilas, Voorhees, White.

Those who voted in the negative are,

Messrs. Dolph, Felton, Gorman, Hill, McPherson, Mills, Morgan, Stewart, Wolcott.

So the motion to lay the amendment on the table was agreed to.

The reported amendment having been amended on the motion of Mr. Butler and the motion of Mr. Palmer,

On motion by Mr. George to amend section 5 of the part proposed to be inserted, as follows, viz: In lines 2 and 3 of the said section strike out the words "the American Railway Association is authorized hereby to designate to," and after the word "Commission" in line 3 insert the words *shall designate;* and in lines 8 and 9 in the same section strike out the words "upon their determination being certified to the Interstate Commerce Commission," and insert the word *and;* and after the word "standard" in line 14 strike out the following: "But should said association fail to determine a standard as above provided, it shall be the duty of the Interstate Commerce Commission to do so,"

After debate,

It was determined in the negative, { .... 17 / .... 27 }

On motion by Mr. Wolcott,

The yeas and nays being desired by one-fifth of the Senators present, Those who voted in the affirmative are,

Messrs. Bate, Berry, Brice, Caffery, Call, George, Gray, Hill, Jones of Arkansas, McPherson, Mills, Morgan, Pugh, Turpie, Vance, Vest, White.

Those who voted in the negative are,

Messrs. Carey, Chandler, Cockrell, Cullom, Dolph, Dubois, Felton, Gallinger, Hansbrough, Hawley, Higgins, Hoar, Hunton, Irby, Kyle, McMillan, Peffer, Perkins, Platt, Proctor, Sawyer, Sherman, Shoup, Squire, Stewart, Vilas, Washburn.

So the amendment to the amendment was not agreed to.

The reported amendment having been further amended on the motion of Mr. Butler and the motion of Mr. Gray,

On motion by Mr. Turpie, at 5 o'clock and 5 minutes p. m.,

The Senate adjourned.

FRIDAY, FEBRUARY 10, 1893.

Mr. Quay raised a question as to the presence of a quorum;

Whereupon,

The Vice-President directed the roll to be called;

When,

Forty-six Senators answered to their names.

A quorum being present,

PETITIONS AND MEMORIALS.

The Vice-President laid before the Senate resolutions of the Chamber of Commerce of Tacoma, Wash., praying for the annexation of the Hawaiian Islands to the United States; which were referred to the Committee on Foreign Relations.

Mr. Hansbrough presented a memorial of the legislature of North Dakota in favor of the passage of a law donating a portion of the abandoned Fort Abraham Lincoln military reservation to that State for the benefit and use of the State Reform School; which was referred to the Committee on Public Lands.

Mr. Cullom presented two petitions of citizens of Illinois, praying for the appointment of a committee to investigate an alleged combine formed to depreciate the price of grain by the millers, elevators, and others at St. Louis and Minneapolis; which were referred to the Committee on Agriculture and Forestry.

Mr. Sherman presented a petition of citizens of Ohio, praying for the establishment of a permanent census bureau, and for the collection and publication of statistics relating to farm mortgages; which was referred to the Committee on the Census.

Mr. Kyle presented a memorial of citizens of South Dakota, remonstrating against the repeal of the law providing for the purchase of silver bullion.

Ordered, That it lie on the table.

Petitions praying the passage of a law for the restriction of immigration were presented as follows:

By Mr. Chandler: A petition of citizens of New Hampshire.

By Mr. Quay: A petition of citizens of Pennsylvania.

Ordered, That they be referred to the Committee on Immigration.

Petitions praying the repeal of the provision providing for the closing of the Columbian Exposition on the Sabbath day were presented as follows:

By Mr. Power: Several petitions of citizens of Montana.

By Mr. Perkins: A petition of citizens of Kansas.

Ordered, That they be referred to the Select Committee on the Quadro-Centennial.

Memorials remonstrating against the repeal of the provision providing for the closing of the Columbian Exposition on the Sabbath day were presented as follows:

By Mr. Sherman: A memorial of citizens of Ohio.

By Mr. Carey: A memorial of citizens of Wyoming.

Ordered, That they be referred to the Select Committee on the Quadro-Centennial.

Mr. Hoar presented a memorial of citizens of Massachusetts, praying the passage of a law for the incorporation of the National Historical Society; which was referred to the Committee on the Library.

Mr. Quay presented a resolution of the legislature of Pennsylvania, remonstrating against any reduction of pensions; which was referred to the Committee on Pensions.

EXECUTIVE COMMUNICATIONS.

The Vice-President laid before the Senate a letter of the Secretary of the Treasury, recommending that authority be given him to use any unexpended balance of appropriations to pay for extra work performed in the Division of Warrants; which was referred to the Committee on Appropriations and ordered to be printed.

The Vice-President laid before the Senate a letter of the Secretary of the Treasury, transmitting a supplemental list of judgments rendered by the Court of Claims which have been presented to the Treasury Department for payment; which was referred to the Committee on Appropriations and ordered to be printed.

PAPERS REFERRED FROM FILES.

Papers in the cases hereinafter mentioned, to accompany bills introduced, were taken from the files and referred under the rule as follows:

William Dillon; to the Committee on Claims.

Enoch Davis; to the Committee on Military Affairs.

REPORTS OF COMMITTEES.

On motion by Mr. McMillan,

Ordered, That the Committee on the District of Columbia be discharged from the further consideration of the memorial of citizens of the District of Columbia, remonstrating against the proposition in the District of Columbia appropriation bill authorizing the Commissioners to reassess special assessments and taxes which have been, or shall hereafter be, declared void by the courts, and that it be referred to the Committee on Appropriations.

Mr. Bate, from the Committee on Military Affairs, to whom was referred the bill (H. R. 1422) for the relief of George M. Henry, reported it without amendment and submitted a report (No. 1277) thereon.

Mr. McMillan, from the Committee on the District of Columbia, to whom was referred the bill (S. 2177) to provide for the reassessment and relevying of taxes declared illegal and void, and for other purposes, reported adversely thereon.

Ordered, That it be postponed indefinitely.

Mr. McMillan, from the Committee on the District of Columbia, to whom was referred the bill (S. 3808) amending the charter of the

Maryland and Washington Railway Company, submitted an adverse report (No. 1278) thereon.

Ordered, That it be postponed indefinitely.

Mr. McMillan, from the Committee on the District of Columbia, to whom was referred the bill (H. R. 8125) to provide for the regulation of the equipment and operation of street-railroad lines within the District of Columbia by the Commissioners of said District, reported it with amendments and submitted a report (No. 1279) thereon.

Mr. Palmer, from the Committee on Military Affairs, to whom was referred the bill (H. R. 3184) correcting the muster of Lieut. Gilman L. Johnson, reported adversely thereon.

Ordered, That it be postponed indefinitely.

Mr. Palmer, from the Committee on Military Affairs, to whom were referred the following bills, reported them without amendment:

H. R. 5519. An act for the relief of Daniel Eldridge, Company D, Fifteenth Illinois Volunteers; and

H. R. 4071. An act for the relief of George W. Schachleiter.

Mr. Palmer, from the Committee on Military Affairs, to whom was referred the bill (S. 1968) for the relief of Dr. James Madison, reported it with an amendment.

Mr. Felton, from the Select Committee on Forest Reservations in California, reported a joint resolution (S. R. 150) to provide for the appointment of a commission by the Secretary of the Interior, to appraise the improvements made by actual settlers upon public lands, holding in good faith, under the United States, in the Sequoia and Yosemite reservations, in California, and for other purposes; which was read the first and second times by unanimous consent.

Mr. McMillan, from the Committee on the District of Columbia, to whom was referred the bill (S. 3792) to incorporate the American University, reported it with amendments.

On motion by Mr. Hunton,

Ordered, That the Committee on the District of Columbia be discharged from the further consideration of the bill (S. 3795) to authorize the Washington, Alexandria and Mount Vernon Electric Railway Company to construct a bridge across the Potomac River, and to construct a railroad over the same and through certain streets and reservations of Washington, and that it be referred to the Committee on Commerce.

EMPLOYMENT OF ARMED BODIES FOR PRIVATE PURPOSES.

Mr. Gallinger, from the Select Committee on the Employment of Armed Bodies of Men for Private Purposes, created by a resolution of the Senate of August 2, 1892, submitted a report (No. 1280).

Mr. Gallinger submitted the following concurrent resolution; which was referred to the Committee on Printing:

Resolved by the Senate (the House of Representatives concurring), That there be printed 6,000 copies of the report of the Senate select committee to investigate and report the facts in relation to the employment for private purposes of armed bodies of men or detectives in connection with differences between workmen and employers, 2,000 copies for the use of the Senate and 4,000 copies for the use of the House of Representatives.

CONFERENCE REPORT.

Mr. Jones, of Arkansas, from the committee of conference on the disagreeing votes of the two Houses on the amendments of the Senate to the bill H. R. 9527, submitted the following report:

The committee of conference on the disagreeing votes of the two Houses on the amendments of the Senate to the bill (H. R. 9527) to restore to the public domain a portion of the White Mountain Apache Indian Reservation in the Territory of Arizona, and for other purposes, having met, after full and free conference have agreed to recommend and do recommend to their respective Houses as follows:

That the House recede from its disagreement to the amendments of the Senate numbered 1, 2, and 3, and agree to the same.

That the House recede from its disagreement to the amendment of the Senate numbered 4 and agree to the same with an amendment as follows: In line 2 thereof strike out the word "Colville," and insert in lieu thereof the words White Mountain Apache Indian; and the Senate agree to the same.

JAMES K. JONES,
O. H. PLATT,
CHARLES F. MANDERSON,
Managers on the part of the Senate.

S. W. PEEL,
THOMAS DUNN ENGLISH,
JOHN W. WILSON,
Managers on the part of the House.

The Senate proceeded to consider the said report; and

On motion by Mr. Jones, of Arkansas,

Resolved, That the Senate agree thereto.

Ordered, That the Secretary notify the House of Representatives thereof.

MESSAGE FROM THE HOUSE.

A message from the House of Representatives, by Mr. Towles, its chief clerk:

Mr. President: The House of Representatives has passed, without amendment, the following bills of the Senate:

S. 3788. An act granting right of way to the Colorado River Irrigation Company through the Yuma Indian Reservation, in California; and

S. 3843. An act to authorize the Chesapeake and Ohio Railway Company to renew its railroad bridge across the Big Sandy River upon such plans and location as may be approved by the Secretary of War.

The House of Representatives has passed a joint resolution (H. R. 214) providing for additional telegraphic and electric-light facilities in the city of Washington during the inaugural ceremonies on the 4th day of March, 1893, in which it requests the concurrence of the Senate.

ELECTRIC-LIGHT FACILITIES DURING INAUGURAL CEREMONIES.

The joint resolution (H. R. 214) providing for additional telegraphic and electric-light facilities in the city of Washington during the inaugural ceremonies on the 4th day of March, 1893, this day received from the House of Representatives for concurrence, was read the first and second times by unanimous consent and considered as in Committee of the Whole; and no amendment being made, it was reported to the Senate.

Ordered, That it pass to a third reading.

The said resolution was read the third time by unanimous consent.

Resolved, That it pass.

Ordered, That the Secretary notify the House of Representatives thereof.

INTRODUCTION OF BILLS AND JOINT RESOLUTION.

Bills and a joint resolution were introduced, read the first and second times by unanimous consent, and referred as follows:

By Mr. Berry: A bill (S. 3855) granting the right of way for the construction of a railroad and other improvements through and on the Hot Springs Reservation, State of Arkansas; to the Committee on Public Lands.

By Mr. Chandler: A bill (S. 3856) to amend section 7 of the act approved February 15, 1892, relative to the construction of a bridge across the Mississippi River at South St. Paul, Minn.; to the Committee on Commerce.

By Mr. Quay: A bill (S. 3857) authorizing the construction of a bridge over the Monougahela River at the foot of Main street, in the borough of Belle Vernon, in the State of Pennsylvania; to the Committee on Commerce.

By Mr. Kyle: A bill (S. 3858) to incorporate the Washington Traction Company; to the Committee on the District of Columbia.

By Mr. Hill: A joint resolution (S. R. 151) extending the session of the thirteenth legislative assembly of the Territory of New Mexico from sixty to seventy days; to the Committee on Territories.

REPORT OF COMMISSIONER OF LABOR.

Mr. Manderson submitted the following resolution; which was referred to the Committee on Printing:

Resolved by the Senate (the House of Representatives concurring), That there be printed 35,000 additional copies, in cloth binding, of the Eighth Annual Report of the Commissioner of Labor, relating to industrial education in the United States and Europe, 16,000 copies for the use of the members of the House of Representatives, 8,000 copies for the use of the members of the Senate, and 11,000 copies for distribution by the Department of Labor.

WEATHER BUREAU REPORT.

Mr. Manderson submitted the following concurrent resolution; which was referred to the Committee on Printing:

Resolved by the Senate (the House of Representatives concurring), That there be printed, in quarto form, of the annual report of the Chief of the Weather Bureau, with appendices, 9,000 copies, of which 1,000 copies will be for the use of the Senate, 2,000 copies for the use of the House of Representatives, and 6,000 copies for the use of the Weather Bureau.

The report will cover the transactions of the Bureau from date of its transfer from the War to the Agricultural Department, July 1, 1891, to December 31, 1892.

LIGHT-HOUSES AND OTHER AIDS TO NAVIGATION.

On motion by Mr. Dolph, and by unanimous consent,

The vote on the passage of the bill (H. R. 9955) providing for sundry light-houses and other aids to navigation was reconsidered.

The vote ordering the amendments to be engrossed and the bill read a third time, and the vote concurring in the amendments made in Committee of the Whole having also been reconsidered, and

The question recurring on concurring in the amendments made in Committee of the Whole,

It was determined in the negative.

No further amendment being proposed,

Ordered, That the bill pass to a third reading.

The said bill was read the third time.

Resolved, That it pass.

Ordered, That the Secretary notify the House of Representatives thereof.

CONSIDERATION OF BILLS ON CALENDAR.

The Senate proceeded to consider, as in Committee of the Whole, the following bills; and no amendment being made, they were severally reported to the Senate:

S. 564. A bill for the relief of Israel Kimball;

S. 1018. A bill granting a pension to John Benn;

S. 1119. A bill for the relief of Hiram W. Love;

S. 1825. A bill granting a pension to David C. Canfield; and

S. 2126. A bill for the relief of Catherine E. Whitall.

Ordered, That they be postponed indefinitely.

The Senate proceeded to consider, as in Committee of the Whole, the following bills; and the reported amendments having been agreed to, the bills were severally reported to the Senate and the amendments were concurred in.

S. 707. A bill for the relief of George H. Plant, of the District of Columbia;

S. 1844. A bill to provide for the erection of a public building in the city of Laramie, Wyo.;

S. 3146. A bill to remove the charge of desertion from the military record of Peter Buckley;

S. 3711. A bill granting the right of way through the Arlington reservation for railroad purposes;

S. 1683. A bill for the relief of Mrs. Fanny N. Belger; and

S. 3294. A bill to authorize the construction of a dam across the Kansas River, near Kansas City, in the State of Kansas.

Ordered, That they be engrossed and read a third time.

The said bills were severally read the third time.

Resolved, That they pass, and that the respective titles thereof be as aforesaid.

Ordered, That the Secretary request the concurrence of the House of Representatives therein.

The Senate proceeded to consider, as in Committee of the Whole, the bill (S. 2993) authorizing the purchase of the Ourdan & Kolb letter-engraving machine for the use of the Navy Department; and having been amended on the motion of Mr. Cockrell,

Ordered, That the further consideration thereof be postponed to-morrow, and that the bill as amended be reprinted.

The Senate proceeded to consider, as in Committee of the Whole, the following bills and joint resolutions; and no amendment being made, they were severally reported to the Senate:

S. 3194. A bill for the relief of Jeronemus S. Underhill, of the city of New York;

S. 2598. A bill for the relief of George W. Quintard;

S. R. 102. Joint resolution to provide for the construction of a wharf as a means of approach to the monument to be erected at Wakefield, Va., to mark the birthplace of George Washington; and

S. R. 108. Joint resolution directing the appraisement of the library of Hubert Howe Bancroft.

Ordered, That they be engrossed and read a third time.

The said bills and resolutions were severally read the third time.

Resolved, That they pass, and that the respective titles thereof be as aforesaid.

Ordered, That the Secretary request the concurrence of the House of Representatives therein.

The Senate proceeded to consider, as in Committee of the Whole, the bill (S. 3510) to amend section 4347 of the Revised Statutes of the United States; and having been amended on the motion of Mr. Frye, the bill was reported to the Senate and the amendment was concurred in.

Ordered, That it be engrossed and read a third time.

The said bill was read the third time.

Resolved, That it pass, and that the title thereof be as aforesaid.

Ordered, That the Secretary request the concurrence of the House of Representatives therein.

The Senate proceeded to consider, as in Committee of the Whole, the bill (S. 3165) to incorporate the Holstein-Friesian Cattle Association of America; and having been amended on the motion of Mr. Manderson, the bill was reported to the Senate and the amendment was concurred in.

Ordered, That the bill be engrossed and read a third time.

The said bill was read the third time.

Resolved, That it pass, and that the title thereof be as aforesaid.

Ordered, That the Secretary request the concurrence of the House of Representatives therein.

The Senate proceeded to consider, as in Committee of the Whole, the bill (S. 2130) for the relief of Mrs. Mary P. C. Hooper; and having been amended on the motion of Mr. Cockrell, the bill was reported to the Senate and the amendment was concurred in.

Ordered, That the bill be engrossed and read a third time.

The said bill was read the third time.

Resolved, That it pass, and that the title thereof be as aforesaid.

Ordered, That the Secretary request the concurrence of the House of Representatives therein.

The Senate proceeded to consider, as in Committee of the Whole, the bill (S. 3297) granting to the Interstate Water and Electric Power Company of Kansas the right to erect and maintain a dam or dams across the Kansas River, within Wyandotte County, in the State of Kansas; and the reported amendments having been agreed to, the bill was reported to the Senate and the amendments were concurred in.

Ordered, That the bill be engrossed and read a third time.

The said bill was read the read third time.

Resolved, That it pass and that the title thereof be amended so as to read, "A bill granting to the Interstate Water and Electric Power Company, of Kansas, the right to erect and maintain a dam across the Kansas River, within Wyandotte County, in the State of Kansas."

Ordered, That the Secretary request the concurrence of the House of Representatives therein.

The Senate proceeded to consider, as in Committee of the Whole, the bill (H. R. 5504) to permit the withdrawal of certain papers and the signing of certain receipts by John Finn or his attorney; and the reported amendment having been agreed to, the bill was reported to the Senate and the amendment was concurred in.

Ordered, That the amendment be engrossed and the bill read a third time.

The said bill as amended was read the third time.

Resolved, That it pass and that the title thereof be amended so as to read, "An act to permit the withdrawal of certain papers and the signing of certain receipts by John Finn."

Ordered, That the Secretary request the concurrence of the House of Representatives in the amendments.

The Senate proceeded to consider, as in Committee of the Whole, the bill (S. 3702) granting to the Chicago, Rock Island and Pacific Railway Company the use of certain lands at Chickasaw Station, and for a "Y" in the Chickasaw Nation, Indian Territory; and the reported amendment having been agreed to, the bill was reported to the Senate and the amendment was concurred in.

Ordered, That the bill be engrossed and read a third time.

The said bill was read the third time.

Resolved, That it pass, and that the title thereof be amended so as to read, "A bill granting to the Chicago, Rock Island and Pacific Railway Company the use of certain lands at Chickasha Station, and for a "Y" in the Chickasaw Nation, Indian Territory."

Ordered, That the Secretary request the concurrence of the House of Representatives therein.

The Senate proceeded to consider, as in Committee of the Whole, the bill (H. R. 3627) to grant to the Gainesville, Oklahoma and Gulf Railway Company a right of way through the Indian Territory, and for other purposes; and the reported amendments having been agreed to, the bill was reported to the Senate and the amendments were concurred in.

Ordered, That the amendments be engrossed and the bill read a third time.

The said bill as amended was read the third time.

Resolved, That it pass, and that the Senate request a conference with the House of Representatives on the said bill and amendments.

Ordered, That the conferees on the part of the Senate be appointed by the Presiding Officer; and

The Presiding Officer (Mr. Hawley in the chair) appointed Mr. Jones of Arkansas, Mr. Platt, and Mr. Dawes.

Ordered, That the Secretary notify the House of Representatives thereof.

The Senate proceeded to consider, as in Committee of the Whole, the bill (S. 3831) to amend the act approved August 13, 1888, in relation to the jurisdiction of the circuit courts of the United States (chapter 866, 25 Statutes at Large, page 433); and having been amended on the motion of Mr. Hoar, the bill was reported to the Senate and the amendments were concurred in.

Ordered, That it be engrossed and read a third time.

The said bill was read the third time.

Resolved, That it pass, and that the title thereof be as aforesaid.

Ordered, That the Secretary request the concurrence of the House of Representatives therein.

MESSAGE FROM THE HOUSE.

A message from the House of Representatives, by Mr. Towles, its chief clerk:

Mr. President: The House of Representatives has passed the following bills, in which it requests the concurrence of the Senate:

H. R. 9786. An act authorizing the construction of a bridge over the Monongahela River at West Elizabeth, in the State of Pennsylvania, and

H. R. 10331. An act making appropriations for the legislative, executive and judicial expenses of the Government for the fiscal year ending June 30, 1894, and for other purposes.

The Speaker of the House of Representatives having signed two enrolled bills, H. R. 7762 and H. R. 8123, I am directed to bring them to the Senate for the signature of its President.

SAFETY OF LIFE ON RAILROADS.

The Senate resumed, as in Committee of the Whole, the consideration of the bill (H. R. 9350) to promote the safety of employés and travelers upon railroads by compelling common carriers engaged in interstate commerce to equip their cars with automatic couplers and continuous brakes and their locomotives with driving-wheel brakes, and for other purposes; and

The reported amendment having been further amended on the motion of Mr. Vilas,

On motion by Mr. George to further amend the amendment by striking out in line 2 section 5 of the part proposed to be inserted the words "American Railway Association," and in lieu thereof inserting the words *Brotherhood of American Trainmen,*

After debate,

It was determined in the negative { Yeas .... 10 } { Nays .... 37 }

On motion by Mr. George,

The yeas and nays being desired by one-fifth of the Senators present,

Those who voted in the affirmative are,

Messrs. Berry. Brice, Coke, Daniel, George, Harris, Mills, Pugh, Turpie, Voorhees.

Those who voted in the negative are,

Messrs. Bate, Blodgett, Caffery, Call, Carey, Chandler, Cockrell, Cullom, Davis, Dawes, Dolph, Dubois, Felton, Frye, Gallinger, Gray, Hansbrough, Hawley, Hiscock, Hoar, Irby, Jones of Nevada, Kyle, McPherson, Morrill, Palmer, Pasco, Peffer, Proctor, Sawyer, Sherman, Squire, Stewart, Stockbridge, Vilas, Washburn, White.

So the amendment to the amendment was not agreed to.

When, it was

Ordered, That the further consideration of the bill be postponed to to-morrow and that the bill as amended be reprinted.

HOUSE BILLS REFERRED.

The bills last received from the House of Representatives for concurrence were read the first and second times by unanimous consent.

Ordered, That the bill H. R. 9786 be referred to the Committee on Commerce, and that the bill H. R. 10331 be referred to the Committee on Appropriations.

HOUR OF MEETING.

On motion by Mr. Vilas,

Ordered, That when the Senate adjourn it be to 12 o'clock to-morrow.

EXECUTIVE SESSION.

On motion by Mr. Hoar,

The Senate proceeded to the consideration of executive business; and

After the consideration of executive business the doors were re-opened, and

On motion by Mr. Sawyer, at 5 o'clock and 15 minutes p. m.,

The Senate adjourned.

SATURDAY, FEBRUARY 11, 1893.

EXECUTIVE COMMUNICATIONS.

The Vice-President laid before the Senate a letter of the Attorney-General, transmitting a list of all final judgments for claims arising out of Indian depredations and not paid; which was referred to the Select Committee on Indian Depredation Claims and ordered to be printed.

The Vice-President laid before the Senate two communications from the Secretary of State, transmitting, in pursuance of the act of February 3, 1887, certified copies of the final ascertainment of the electors for President and Vice President appointed in the States of Montana and North Dakota.

Ordered, That they lie on the table.

Mr. Dolph presented a letter of the Secretary of the Interior addressed to him as chairman of the Committee on Public Lands, communicating all the information in the Interior Department relative to the claims of the Kaweah colony of Tulare county, California, in the Sequoia National Park; which was ordered to be printed.

Mr. Quay presented a letter of the Acting Supervising Architect of the Treasury Department relative to the purchase of a site for the Government Printing Office; which was referred to the Committee on Appropriations, to accompany an amendment intended to be proposed to the sundry civil appropriation bill, No. 10238, and ordered to be printed.

PETITIONS AND MEMORIALS.

Petitions, memorials, etc., were presented and referred as follows:

By the Vice-President; A resolution of the legislature of South Dakota in favor of the passage of a law for the establishment of a military post at or near the city of Pierre, in that State; to the Committee on Military Affairs.

By Mr. Quay: Resolutions of the College of Physicians of Philadelphia, Pa., praying the passage of a law for the establishment of a national quarantine and a national health commission; to the Committee on Epidemic Diseases.

By Mr. Hoar: A petition of citizens of Massachusetts, praying the passage of a law for the suppression of the traffic in intoxicating liquors and firearms with the natives of the islands of New Hebrides; to the Committee on Foreign Relations.

By Mr. Felton: A memorial of the Bar Association of San Francisco, Cal., praying for the establishment of a law library in San Francisco for the circuit court of appeals; to the Committee on the Judiciary.

By Mr. Carey: A petition of citizens of the District of Columbia, praying an amendment to the Constitution prohibiting the manufacture, importation, and sale of intoxicating liquors; to the Committee on the District of Columbia.

By Mr. Felton: A petition of citizens of Arizona, praying an appropriation for the construction of a deep-water harbor at San Pedro, Cal.; to the Committee on Commerce.

By Mr. Butler: A memorial of citizens of South Carolina, remonstrating against the repeal of the provision providing for the closing of the Columbian Exposition on the Sabbath day; to the Select Committee on the Quadro-Centennial.

By Mr. Kyle: A resolution of the legislature of South Dakota in favor of the passage of a law for the establishment of a military post at or near the city of Pierre, in that State; to the Committee on Military Affairs.

Mr. Butler presented a resolution of the New York Lumber Exchange, praying for the early completion of the Nicaragua Canal under the direction and control of the United States.

Ordered, That it lie on the table.

Petitions praying the passage of a law to restrict immigration into the United States were presented as follows:

By Mr. Gallinger: A petition of citizens of New Hampshire.

By Mr. Platt: A petition of citizens of Connecticut.

Ordered, That they be referred to the Committee on Immigration.

Mr. Frye presented several petitions of citizens of Maine, praying the appointment of a commission on the subject of the social vice; which were referred to the Committee on Education and Labor.

REPRINT OF DOCUMENT.

On motion by Mr. Stewart,

Ordered, That Mis. Doc. No. 203, first session, Fifty-second Congress, relating to an agreement with the Indians on the Pyramid and Walker River Reservations in Nevada, be reprinted and referred to the Committee on Appropriations, to accompany an amendment intended to be proposed to the Indian appropriation bill and ordered to be printed.

ENROLLED BILLS SIGNED.

Mr. Dubois reported from the committee that they had examined and found duly enrolled the following bills:

H. R. 7762. An act to ratify and confirm agreement between the Puyallup Indians and the Northern Pacific Railroad Company for right of way through the Puyallup Indian Reservation; and

H. R. 8123. An act granting to the Santa Fe, Prescott and Phœnix Railway Company the right of way across the Whipple Barracks military reservation in Arizona;

Whereupon,

The Vice President signed the same, and they were delivered to the committee to be presented to the President of the United States.

MESSAGE FROM THE HOUSE.

A message from the House of Representatives, by Mr. Towles, its chief clerk:

Mr. President: The House of Representatives has passed, without amendment, the following bill and joint resolution of the Senate:

S. 3510. An act to amend section 4347 of the Revised Statutes of the United States; and

S. R. 140. A joint resolution authorizing the Secretaries of War and of the Navy to loan to the committee on inaugural ceremonies flags, etc.

The House of Representatives has agreed to the amendments of the Senate to the following bills of the House:

H. R. 3627. An act to grant to the Gainesville, Oklahoma and Gulf Railway Company a right of way through the Indian Territory, and for other purposes; and

H. R. 5504. An act to permit the withdrawal of certain papers and the signing of certain receipts by John Finn or his attorney.

The House of Representatives has passed a bill (H. R. 10363) to remove the disabilities of William F. Robinson, a citizen of the State of Alabama, in which it requests the concurrence of the Senate.

The Speaker of the House of Representatives having signed four enrolled bills, S. 3787, S. 3825, S. 3826, and H. R. 8340, and an enrolled joint resolution S. R. 134, I am directed to bring the same to the Senate for the signature of its President.

ENROLLED BILLS SIGNED.

Mr. Dubois reported from the committee that they had examined and found duly enrolled the following bills and joint resolution;

S. 3787. An act to authorize the construction of a bridge across the St. Marys River, between the States of Florida and Georgia;

S. 3825. An act to authorize the Homestead and Pittsburg Bridge Company to construct a bridge over the Monongahela River from Pittsburg to Homestead;

S. 3826. An act authorizing Velasco and Surfside Terminal Railway Company to construct a bridge across the Galveston and Brazos Canal;

H. R. 8340. An act to amend an act establishing a court of private land claims and to provide for the settlement of private land claims in certain States and Territories, approved March 3, 1891; and

S. R. 134. A joint resolution authorizing the exhibition, at the World's Columbian Exposition, of the picture entitled "The Recall of Columbus," by Augustus G. Heaton;

Whereupon,

The Vice-President signed the same, and they were delivered to the committee to be presented to the President of the United States.

HOUSE BILLS REFERRED.

The bill H. R. 10363, last received from the House of Representatives for concurrence, was read the first and second times by unanimous consent and referred to the Committee on the Judiciary.

REPORTS OF COMMITTEES.

Mr. Frye, from the Committee on Commerce, reported a bill (S. 3859) to amend an act entitled "An act for the construction of a railroad and wagon bridge across the Mississippi River at South St. Paul, Minn.," approved April 26, 1890; which was read the first and second times by unanimous consent and considered as in Committee of the Whole; and no amendment being made, it was reported to the Senate.

Ordered, That it be engrossed and read a third time.

The said bill was read the third time by unanimous consent.

Resolved, That it pass, and that the title thereof be as aforesaid.

Ordered, That the Secretary request the concurrence of the House of Representatives therein.

Mr. Frye, from the Committee on Commerce, to whom was referred the bill (S. 3856) to amend section 7 of the act approved February 15, 1892, relative to the construction of a bridge across the Mississippi River at South St. Paul, Minn., reported adversely thereon.

Ordered, That it be postponed indefinitely.

Mr. Sawyer, from the Committee on Commerce, to whom was referred the bill (S. 3797) establishing a fog signal at Kewaunee, Wis., reported it without amendment.

The Senate proceeded, by unanimous consent, to consider the said bill as in Committee of the Whole; and no amendment being made, it was reported to the Senate.

Ordered, That it be engrossed and read a third time.

The said bill was read the third time.

Resolved, That it pass, and that the title thereof be as aforesaid.

Ordered, That the Secretary request the concurrence of the House of Representatives therein.

Mr. Frye, from the Committee on Commerce, to whom was referred the bill (H. R. 9786) authorizing the construction of a bridge over the Monongahela River at West Elizabeth, in the State of Pennsylvania, reported it without amendment.

The Senate proceeded, by unanimous consent, to consider the said bill as in Committee of the Whole; and no amendment being made, it was reported to the Senate.

Ordered, That it pass to a third reading.

The said bill was read the third time.

Resolved, That it pass.

Ordered, That the Secretary notify the House of Representatives thereof.

Mr. Manderson, from the Committee on the Census, to whom was referred the bill (H. R. 8582) to provide for the publication of the Eleventh Census, reported it without amendment and submitted a report (No. 1281) thereon.

Mr. Quay, from the Committee on Commerce, to whom was referred the bill (S. 3837) authorizing the construction of a bridge over the Monongahela River at the foot of Main street in the borough of Belle Vernon, in the State of Pennsylvania, reported it without amendment.

Mr. McMillan, from the Committee on the District of Columbia, to whom were referred the following bills, submitted written adverse reports thereon as follows:

S. 679. A bill to amend an act entitled "An act to provide for the settlement of all outstanding claims against the District of Columbia and conferring jurisdiction on the Court of Claims to hear the same, and for other purposes;" Report No. 1283.

S. 1102. A bill referring to the Court of Claims the claims of Elias E. Barnes and others; Report No. 1283.

S. 603. A bill referring to the Court of Claims the claims of James W. Walsh and others; Report No. 1284.

Ordered, That they be postponed indefinitely.

Mr. Shoup, from the Committee on Pensions, to whom was referred the bill (S. 3743) granting a pension to Julia E. Lock, formerly widow of the late Gen. Daniel McCook, reported it with amendments and submitted a report (No. 1285) thereon.

Mr. Chandler, from the Select Committee on Failed National Banks, to whom was referred the bill (S. 3730) in amendment of the provisions of the Revised Statutes relative to national banks, reported it without amendment and submitted a report (No. 1286) thereon.

INTRODUCTION OF BILLS.

Bills were introduced, read the first and second times by unanimous consent, and referred as follows:

By Mr. George: A bill (S. 3860) for the relief of J. R. Eggleston, of Hinds County, Mississippi; to the Committee on Claims.

By Mr. Hunton: A bill (S. 3861) to authorize the Washington, Alexandria and Mount Vernon Electric Railway Company to construct a bridge across the Potomac River opposite Observatory Hill, and to construct a railroad over the same and through certain streets and reservations; to the Committee on Commerce.

SEA PAY OF NAVAL OFFICERS.

Mr. Voorhees submitted the following resolution; which was considered by unanimous consent and agreed to:

Resolved, That the Secretary of the Treasury be, and he is hereby, directed to inform the Senate what amount, exclusive of payments from current appropriations, has been certified as due to naval officers for sea pay in accordance with the decision of the Supreme Court in the case of United States vs. Strong; how much of said amount has been paid; how much of the amount paid was paid without regard to the date when the services were rendered; and how much of the sums appropriated in payment of amounts so certified to be due remains unexpended because of proviso prohibiting payment for services rendered more than six years prior to the filing of the petition in said case. Also, whether officers on receiving ships are now, and have been since said decision was rendered, receiving sea pay, and from what date said decision has been construed by the Treasury Department to allow sea pay for such service.

CONFERENCE REPORT.

Mr. Dawes, from the committee of conference on the disagreeing votes of the two Houses on the amendments of the Senate to the bill H. R. 9923, submitted the following report:

The committee of conference on the disagreeing votes of the two Houses on the amendments of the Senate to the bill (H. R. 9923) "making appropriations for fortifications and other works of defense, for the armament thereof, for the procurement of heavy ordnance for trial and service, and for other purposes," having met, after full and free conference have agreed to recommend and do recommend to their respective Houses as follows:

That the Senate recede from its amendments numbered 3, 6, 7, 8, and 9.

That the House recede from its disagreement to the amendments of the Senate numbered 1 and 5, and agree to the same.

That the House recede from its disagreement to the amendment of the Senate numbered 2, and agree to the same with an amendment as follows: In lieu of the sum proposed in said amendment insert one hundred and seventy-five thousand dollars; and the Senate agree to the same.

That the House recede from its disagreement to the amendment of the Senate numbered 4, and agree to the same with amendments as follows: In lines 3 and 4, page 1, of said amendment, strike out the words "or so much thereof as may be necessary," and insert in lieu thereof the following: of the several sums available for allotment by the Board of Ordnance and Fortification for experimental and other purposes under the several "acts making appropriations for fortifications and other works of defense, for the armament thereof, for the procurement of heavy ordnance for trial and service, and for other purposes," which several acts were approved September twenty-second, eighteen hundred and eighty-eight, March second, eighteen hundred and eighty-nine, August eighteenth, eighteen hundred and ninety, February fourth, eighteen hundred and ninety-one, and July twenty-third, eighteen hundred and ninety-two, and this act, all of which sums are hereby set aside to the extent necessary, and made available and continued in force for this purpose; and strike out the words "eighty-five" where they occur in lines 16 and 20, page 2, of said amendment, and insert in lieu thereof the word sixty; and the Senate agree to the same.

That the House recede from its disagreement to the amendment of the Senate numbered 10, and agree to the same with amendments as follows: Strike out all of lines 17 to 24, inclusive, except the word "Provided," in line 24, on page 2, of said amendment, and at the end of said amendment add the following: or who is connected with or in the employ of any manufacturer who has, or shall have, contracts with the United States for any ordnance material; and the Senate agree to the same.

H. L. DAWES,
WILLIAM M. STEWART,
A. P. GORMAN,
Managers on the part of the Senate.
WILLIAM C. P. BRECKINRIDGE,
L. F. LIVINGSTON,
WILLIAM COGSWELL,
Managers on the part of the House.

The Senate proceeded to consider the said report; and
On motion by Mr. Dawes,
Resolved, That the Senate agree thereto.
Ordered, That the Secretary notify the House of Representatives thereof.

PRESIDENTIAL APPROVALS.

A message from the President of the United States, by Mr. Pruden, his secretary:

Mr. President: The President of the United States approved and signed on the 9th instant the joint resolution (S. R. 144) to provide for the maintenance of order during inaugural ceremonies, March, 1893.

He approved and signed on the 10th instant an act (S. 3311) to refer the claim of Jessie Benton Fremont to certain lands and the improvements thereon, in San Francisco, Cal., to the Court of Claims; and

He this day approved and signed an act (S. 3798) to amend an act entitled "An act to authorize the building of a railroad bridge at Little Rock, Ark."

Ordered, That the Secretary notify the House of Representatives thereof.

PRESENTATION OF BILLS.

Mr. Dubois reported from the committee that they this day presented to the President of the United States the following enrolled bills and joint resolution:

S. 3787. An act to authorize the construction of a bridge across St. Marys River, between the States of Florida and Georgia;

S. 3826. An act authorizing the Velasco and Surfside Terminal Railway Company to construct a bridge across the Galveston and Brazos Canal;

S. 3825. An act to authorize the Homestead and Pittsburg Bridge Company to construct a bridge over the Monongahela River from Pittsburg to Homestead; and

S. R. 134. A joint resolution authorizing the exhibition, at the World's Columbian Exposition, of the picture entitled "The Recall of Columbus," by Augustus G. Heaton.

SETTLERS ON RESERVATIONS IN CALIFORNIA.

On motion by Mr. Felton, that the Senate proceed to the consideration of the joint resolution (S. R. 150) to provide for the appointment of a commission by the Secretary of the Interior to appraise the improvements made by actual settlers upon public lands, holding in good faith under the United States, in the Sequoia and Yosemite reservations in California, and for other purposes,

It was determined in the affirmative, { Yeas 42
{ Nays 3

On motion by Mr. Dolph,

The yeas and nays being desired by one-fifth of the Senators present, Those who voted in the affirmative are,

Messrs. Berry, Blodgett, Brice, Butler, Caffery, Call, Carey, Chandler, Cockrell, Coke, Cullom, Dubois, Felton, Gallinger, George, Hansbrough, Harris, Hoar, Hunton, Jones of Arkansas, Kyle, McMillan, McPherson, Manderson, Mills, Morgan, Morrill, Palmer, Peffer, Perkins, Platt, Power, Pugh, Sawyer, Shoup, Stewart, Stockbridge, Teller, Turpie, Vance, Vilas, Voorhees.

Those who voted in the negative are,

Messrs. Dolph, Hawley, Sherman.

So the motion was agreed to; and

The Senate proceeded to consider the said resolution as in Committee of the Whole; and,

Pending debate,

SAFETY OF LIFE ON RAILROADS.

The Presiding Officer (Mr. Perkins in the chair) announced that the hour of 2 o'clock had arrived, and laid before the Senate the unfinished business of the Senate at its adjournment yesterday, viz, the bill (H. R. 9350) to promote the safety of employés and travelers upon railroads by compelling common carriers engaged in interstate commerce to equip their cars with automatic couplers and continuous brakes and their locomotives with driving-wheel brakes, and for other purposes; and

The Senate resumed, as in Committee of the Whole, the consideration of the bill; and the reported amendment having been further amended on the motion of Mr. Blodgett, the motion of Mr. Gorman, and the motion of Mr. Harris; and

A further amendment to the part proposed to be inserted by the committee having been proposed by Mr. George; and the same having been amended on the motion of Mr. Call,

On the question to agree to the amendment as amended, as follows, viz: Insert as an additional section in the part proposed to be inserted by the committee the following:

SEC. 8. That any employé of any such common carrier who may be injured by any locomotive, car, or train in use contrary to the provisions of this act, shall not be deemed thereby to have assumed the risk thereby occasioned, although continuing in the employment of such carrier after *the unlawful use of such locomotive, car, or train had been brought to his knowledge.*

It was determined in the affirmative, { Yeas 42
{ Nays 7

On motion by Mr. Gray,

The yeas and nays being desired by one-fifth of the Senators present,

Those who voted in the affirmative are,

Messrs. Bate, Berry, Blackburn, Call, Chandler, Coke, Cullom, Daniel, Davis, Dawes, Dolph, Dubois, Felton, Frye, Gallinger, George, Hansbrough, Harris, Hawley, Hoar, Jones of Arkansas, Jones of Nevada, Kyle, McMillan, McPherson, Mills, Morrill, Peffer, Perkins, Proctor, Pugh, Sherman, Squire, Stewart, Stockbridge, Teller, Turpie, Vance, Vilas, Voorhees, Washburn, White.

Those who voted in the negative are,

Messrs. Blodgett, Brice, Caffery, Camden, Gray, Morgan, Sawyer.

So the amendment to the amendment was agreed to.

No further amendment to the reported amendment having been made, it was agreed to as amended, and the bill was reported to the Senate and the amendment made in Committee of the Whole was concurred in.

Ordered, That the amendment be engrossed and the bill read the third time.

The said bill was read the third time,

When,

On motion by Mr. Hoar, that the Senate reconsider its vote ordering the amendment to be engrossed and the bill read a third time,

It was determined in the affirmative.

The vote concurring in the amendment made in Committee of the Whole having also been reconsidered; and

The question recurring on concurring in the amendment,

On motion by Mr. Hoar to amend the amendment by striking out, at the end of section 5 of the part proposed to be inserted, the following words: " And in order to enable said commission to perform the duties imposed upon them by this act, there is hereby appropriated, out of any money in the Treasury not otherwise appropriated, the sum of $3,000, or so much thereof as may be necessary,"

It was decided in the affirmative, { Yeas 39
{ Nays 11

On motion by Mr. Gorman,

The yeas and nays being desired by one-fifth of the Senators present,

Those who voted in the affirmative are,

Messrs. Allison, Bate, Berry, Caffery, Call, Carey, Chandler, Cockrell, Coke, Cullom, Davis, Dawes, Dolph, Dubois, Felton, Frye, Gallinger, Hansbrough, Hawley, Hoar, Jones of Nevada, Kyle, McPherson, Morrill, Palmer, Pasco, Peffer, Perkins, Proctor, Pugh, Sawyer, Sherman, Squire, Stockbridge, Turpie, Vilas, Voorhees, Washburn, White.

Those who voted in the negative are,

Messrs. Blodgett, Brice, Daniel, George, Gorman, Gray, Harris, McMillan, Morgan, Stewart, Vance.

So the amendment to the amendment was agreed to.

When,

The amendment made in Committee of the Whole as amended was concurred in.

Ordered, That the amendment be engrossed and the bill read a third time.

The said bill as amended was read the third time.

On the question, Shall the bill pass?

It was determined in the affirmative, { Yeas 39
{ Nays.................... 10

On motion by Mr. Blodgett,

The yeas and nays being desired by one-fifth of the Senators present,

Those who voted in the affirmative are,

Messrs. Allison, Berry, Caffery, Call, Carey, Chandler, Cockrell, Coke, Cullom, Davis, Dawes, Dolph, Dubois, Felton, Frye, Gallinger, Gray, Hansbrough, Hawley, Hoar, Jones of Nevada, Kyle, McMillan, McPherson, Morrill, Palmer, Pasco, Peffer, Perkins, Proctor, Pugh, Sherman, Squire, Teller, Turpie, Vilas, Voorhees, Washburn, White.

Those who voted in the negative are,

Messrs. Blodgett, Brice, Daniel, George, Gorman, Harris, Morgan, Sawyer, Stewart, Vance.

So it was

Resolved, That the bill pass; and

On motion by Mr. Cullom,

Resolved, That the Senate request a conference with the House of Representatives on the bill and amendment.

Ordered, That the conferees on the part of the Senate be appointed by the Vice-President; and

The Vice-President appointed Mr. Cullom, Mr. Wilson, and Mr. Harris.

Ordered, That the Secretary notify the House of Representatives thereof.

On motion by Mr. Sherman, that the Senate proceed to the consideration of the bill (S. 1218) to amend the act entitled "An act to incorporate the Maritime Canal Company of Nicaragua," approved February 20, 1889:

It was determined in the affirmative, { Yeas 33
{ Nays 19

On motion by Mr. Daniel,

The yeas and nays being desired by one-fifth of the Senators present,

Those who voted in the affirmative are,

Messrs. Allison, Brice, Carey, Chandler, Cullom, Dawes, Dolph, Dubois, Felton, Frye, Gallinger, Gorman, Hansbrough, Hawley, Hiscock, Hoar, Jones of Nevada, Kyle, McMillan, McPherson, Morgan, Morrill, Perkins, Proctor, Ransom, Sawyer, Sherman, Squire, Stockbridge, Teller, Vance, Washburn, White.

Those who voted in the negative are,

Messrs. Bate, Berry, Blodgett, Caffery, Call, Cockrell, Coke, Daniel, George, Harris, Jones of Arkansas, Mills, Palmer, Peffer, Power, Pugh, Turpie, Vilas, Voorhees.

So the motion was agreed to; and

The Senate proceeded to consider the said bill as in Committee of the Whole; and

Pending debate,

EXECUTIVE SESSION.

On motion by Mr. Hoar,

The Senate proceeded to the consideration of executive business; and

After the consideration of executive business the doors were reopened, and

On motion by Mr. Sherman, at 5 o'clock and 5 minutes p. m.,

The Senate adjourned.

MONDAY, FEBRUARY 13, 1893.

Mr. Faulkner raised a question as to the presence of a quorum;

Whereupon,

The Vice-President directed the roll to be called;

When,

Forty-six Senators answered to their names.

A quorum being present,

EXECUTIVE COMMUNICATIONS.

The Vice-President laid before the Senate a letter of the Secretary of the Treasury, transmitting a communication from the Secretary of the Interior submitting an additional estimate of appropriation for geological maps of the United States for the fiscal year ending June 30, 1894; which was referred to the Committee on Appropriations and ordered to be printed.

The Vice-President laid before the Senate a letter of the Secretary of the Treasury, recommending an appropriation to reimburse D. S. Alexander and Charles Deal for expenses incurred by them in defending a suit brought by Hugh O'Hara to recover the value of certain goods seized and sold by said Charles Deal, deputy collector of customs at Champlain, N. Y.; which was referred to the Committee on Appropriations and ordered to be printed.

The Vice-President laid before the Senate a letter of the Secretary of War submitting a communication from the Secretary of War submitting an estimate of appropriation for the support of the military prison at Fort Leavenworth, Kans., for the fiscal year ending June 30, 1893; which was referred to the Committee on Appropriations and ordered to be printed.

The Vice-President laid before the Senate a letter from the Attorney-General, recommending certain changes in the appropriations in the pending general deficiency appropriation bill, and recommending the insertion of certain other necessary items that have been omitted; which was referred to the Committee on Appropriations and ordered to be printed.

MOTION TO RECONSIDER.

Mr. Mitchell entered a motion to reconsider the vote of the Senate on the passage of the bill (S. 3851) to amend the act approved August 13, 1888, in relation to the jurisdiction of the circuit courts of the United States (chapter 866, 25 Statutes at Large, page 433); and

On motion by Mr. Mitchell,

Ordered, That the Secretary request the House of Representatives to return the said bill to the Senate.

CREDENTIALS OF SENATORS.

The Vice-President laid before the Senate the credentials of John L. Mitchell, elected a Senator by the legislature of the State of Wisconsin for the term of six years commencing March 4, 1893; which were read and placed on file.

Mr. Hill presented the credentials of Edward Murphy, jr., elected a Senator by the legislature of the State of New York for the term of six years commencing March 4, 1893; which were read and placed on file.

PETITIONS AND MEMORIALS.

Petitions, memorials, etc., were presented and referred as follows:

By Mr. Dolph: A resolution of the legislature of the State of Oregon in favor of an appropriation for the payment of the claim of that State for moneys expended to aid in the suppression of the rebellion; to the Committee on Appropriations and ordered to be printed.

By Mr. Turpie: A memorial of Eli Lilly & Co., remonstrating

against any increase of the tax on alcohol; to the Committee on Finance.

By Mr. Sherman: A petition of citizens of Ohio, praying the passage of a law to restrict immigration into the United States; to the Committee on Immigration.

A memorial of citizens of Ohio, remonstrating against the repeal of the provision providing for the closing of the Columbian Exposition on the Sabbath day; to the Select Committee on the Quadro-Centennial.

By Mr. Cullom: A petition of citizens of Illinois, praying for the appointment of a committee to investigate an alleged combine formed to depreciate the price of grain by the millers and others at St. Louis and Minneapolis; to the Committee on Agriculture and Forestry.

By Mr. Call: A petition of certain building contractors, praying for an extension of the time for receiving bids for the post-office building at Washington, D. C.; to the Committee on Public Buildings and Grounds, to accompany the joint resolution S. R. 153.

Petitions praying for the appointment of a commission on the subject of alcoholic liquor traffic were presented as follows:

By Mr. Hoar: Several petitions of citizens of Massachusetts.
By Mr. Dawes: A petition of citizens of Massachusetts.
By Mr. Peffer: Two petitions of citizens of Kansas.

Ordered, That they be referred to the Committee on Education and Labor.

MESSAGE FROM THE HOUSE.

A message from the House of Representatives, by Mr. Towles, its chief clerk:

Mr. President: The House of Representatives has passed, without amendment, the following bills of the Senate:

S. 741. An act to incorporate the Eclectic Medical Society of the District of Columbia;

S. 2852. An act to change the name of the Capitol, North O Street and South Washington Railway Company;

S. 3836. An act to authorize the Union Railroad Company to construct and maintain a bridge across the Monongahela River; and

S. 3859. An act to amend an act entitled "An act for the construction of a railroad and wagon bridge across the Mississippi River at South St. Paul, Minn.," approved April 26, 1890.

The House of Representatives has passed the following bills of the Senate, with amendments, in which it requests the concurrence of the Senate:

S. 1683. An act for the relief of Mrs. Fannie C. Belger; and
S. 2946. An act to amend an act entitled "An act to incorporate the Masonic Mutual Relief Association of the District of Columbia," approved March 3, 1869.

The House of Representatives has agreed to the resolution of the Senate to print 5,500 additional copies of the Reports of the Commissioners of the United States to the Paris Exposition of 1889.

The House of Representatives has passed the following bills, in which it requests the concurrence of the Senate:

H. R. 3253. An act to increase the pension of William G. Smith; and
H. R. 8450. An act to remove the charge of desertion from the record of Charles G. Pyer.

The House of Representatives has agreed to the reports of the committees of conference on the amendments of the Senate to the following bills of the House:

H. R. 2527. An act to restore to the public domain a portion of the White Mountain Apache Indian Reservation, in the Territory of Arizona, and for other purposes; and

H. R. 9923. An act making appropriations for fortifications and other works of defense, for the armament thereof, for the procurement of heavy ordnance for trial and service, and for other purposes.

I am directed by the House of Representatives to return to the Senate, in compliance with its request, the bill (S. 3851) to amend the act approved August 13, 1888, in relation to the jurisdiction of the circuit courts of the United States (chapter 866, 25 Statutes at Large, p. 433).

The Speaker of the House of Representatives having signed five enrolled bills, S. 3510, S. 3788, S. 3843, H. R. 5504, and H. R. 9955, and two enrolled joint resolutions S. R. 140 and H. R. 214, I am directed to bring the same to the Senate for the signature of its President.

ENROLLED BILLS SIGNED.

Mr. Dubois reported from the committee that they had examined and found duly enrolled the following bills and joint resolutions:

S. 3510. An act to amend section 4347 of the Revised Statutes of the United States;

S. 3788. An act granting right of way to the Colorado River Irrigation Company through the Yuma Indian Reservation in California;

S. 3843. An act to authorize the Chesapeake and Ohio Railway Company to renew its railroad bridge across the Big Sandy River, upon such plans and location as may be approved by the Secretary of War;

H. R. 5504. An act to permit the withdrawal of certain papers and the signing of certain receipts by John Finn;

14 s

H. R. 9955. An act providing for sundry light-houses and other aids to navigation;

S. R. 140. A joint resolution authorizing the Secretaries of War and of the Navy to loan to the committee on inaugural ceremonies flags, etc.; and

H. R. 214. A joint resolution providing for additional telegraphic and electric-light facilities in the city of Washington during the inaugural ceremonies on the 4th day of March, 1893;

Whereupon,

The Vice-President signed the same and they were delivered to the committee to be presented to the President of the United States.

HOUSE AMENDMENT TO SENATE BILL.

The Vice-President laid before the Senate the amendment of the House of Representatives to the bill (S. 2946) to amend an act entitled "An act to incorporate the Masonic Mutual Relief Association of the District of Columbia," approved March 3, 1869; and

On motion by Mr. Faulkner.

Resolved, That the Senate agree thereto.

Ordered, That the Secretary notify the House of Representatives thereof.

HOUSE BILLS REFERRED.

The bills last received from the House of Representatives for concurrence were read the first and second times by unanimous consent.

Ordered, That the bill H. R. 3253 be referred to the Committee on Pensions, and that the bill H. R. 8450 be referred to the Committee on Military Affairs.

REPORTS OF COMMITTEES.

Mr. Pugh, from the Committee on the Judiciary, to whom was referred the bill (H. R. 9612) to amend section 833 of the Revised Statutes of the United States relating to semiannual returns of fees by district attorneys, marshals, and clerks, reported it with an amendment.

The Senate proceeded, by unanimous consent, to consider the said bill as in Committee of the Whole; and the reported amendment having been agreed to, the bill was reported to the Senate and the amendment was concurred in.

Ordered, That the amendment be engrossed and the bill read a third time.

The said bill as amended was read the third time.

Resolved, That it pass, and that the title thereof be amended so as to read, "An act to prescribe the number of district attorneys and marshals in the judicial districts of the State of Alabama."

Resolved, That the Senate request a conference with the House of Representatives on the said bill and amendments.

Ordered, That the conferees on the part of the Senate be appointed by the Vice-President; and

The Vice-President appointed Mr. Pugh, Mr. Teller, and Mr. Platt.

Ordered, That the Secretary notify the House of Representatives thereof.

Mr. Allison, from the Committee on Appropriations, to whom was referred the bill (H. R. 10238) making appropriations for sundry civil expenses of the Government for the fiscal year ending June 30, 1894, and for other purposes, reported it with amendments, and submitted a report (No. 1287) thereon.

INTRODUCTION OF BILLS AND JOINT RESOLUTIONS.

Bills and joint resolutions were introduced, read the first and second times by unanimous consent, and referred as follows:

By Mr. Cockrell: A bill (S. 3862) to amend the act of Congress approved March 3, 1887, entitled "An act to authorize the construction of a bridge across the Missouri River at the most accessible point between the city of Kansas and the town of Sibley, in the county of Jackson and State of Missouri;" to the Committee on Commerce.

By Mr. Stewart: A bill (S. 3863) for the relief of George Q. Cannon, of Utah; to the Committee on Claims.

By Mr. Cullom: A joint resolution (S. R. 152) transferring the exhibit of the Naval Department known as the model battle ship Illinois, to the State of Illinois as a naval armory for the use of the naval militia of the State of Illinois, on the termination of the World's Columbian Exposition; to the Committee on Naval Affairs.

By Mr. Call: A joint resolution (S. R. 153) extending the time of receiving bids for the post-office building in Washington; to the Committee on Public Buildings and Grounds.

SAFETY OF BUSCH BUILDING.

Mr. Hunton submitted the following resolution; which was considered by unanimous consent and agreed to:

Resolved, That the Secretary of the Treasury and the Postmaster-General be requested to transmit to the Senate forthwith copies of any correspondence which may be on file in their respective Departments relating to the alleged unsafe condition of the Busch building, occupied by the money-order branch of the Sixth Auditor's office, caused by overloading the floors of said building, and what action has been taken to protect the persons employed therein from danger; also to report upon the advisability of transferring the Sixth Auditor's office to a safe fire-proof structure, and using the Busch building for such bureaus or divisions of the Post-Office Department as may be deemed desirable.

MESSAGE FROM THE HOUSE.

A message from the House of Representatives, by Mr. Towles, its chief clerk:

Mr. President: The House of Representatives has passed, without amendment, the joint resolution (S. R. 130) to amend an act entitled "An act making Saturday a half holiday for banking and trust companies in the District of Columbia," approved December 22, 1892.

The House of Representatives has passed the following bills, in which it requests the concurrence of the Senate:

H. R. 9730. An act to amend the charter of the Brightwood Railway Company of the District of Columbia;

H. R. 9873. An act to create a board of charities, and so forth, in the District of Columbia;

H. R. 10039. An act to narrow California avenue, within Bel Air Heights, District of Columbia; and

H. R. 10236. An act relative to voluntary assignments by debtors for the benefit of creditors, in the District of Columbia, and to amend section 782 of the Revised Statutes of the United States, relating to the District of Columbia.

The Speaker of the House of Representatives having signed three enrolled bills, H. R. 3627, H. R. 9527, and H. R. 9786, I am directed to bring the same to the Senate for the signature of its President.

ENROLLED BILLS EXAMINED.

Mr. Dubois reported from the committee that they had examined and found duly enrolled, the following bills:

H. R. 3627. An act to grant to the Gainesville, Oklahoma and Gulf Railway Company a right of way through the Indian Territory, and for other purposes;

H. R. 9527. An act to restore to the public domain a portion of the White Mountain Apache Indian Reservation, in the Territory of Arizona, and for other purposes; and

H. R. 9786. An act authorizing the construction of a bridge over the Monongahela River, at West Elizabeth, in the State of Pennsylvania.

HOUSE AMENDMENT TO SENATE BILL.

The Senate proceeded to consider the amendment of the House of Representatives to the bill (S. 1683) for the relief of Mrs. Fannie N. Belger; and

On motion by Mr. Bate,

Resolved, That the Senate agree thereto.

Ordered, That the Secretary notify the House of Representatives thereof.

COMMITTEE ON INDIAN DEPREDATIONS.

On motion by Mr. Chandler,

Ordered, That the Select Committee on Indian Depredations have leave to sit during the sessions of the Senate.

PRESENTATION OF BILLS.

Mr. Dubois reported from the committee that they this day presented to the President of the United States the following enrolled bills and joint resolution:

S. 3510. An act to amend section 4347 of the Revised Statutes of the United States;

S. 3788. An act granting right of way to the Colorado River Irrigation Company through the Yuma Indian Reservation in California;

S. 3843. An act to authorize the Chesapeake and Ohio Railway Company to renew its railroad bridge across the Big Sandy River upon such plans and location as may be approved by the Secretary of War; and

S. R. 140. Joint resolution authorizing the Secretaries of War and of the Navy to loan to the committee on inaugural ceremonies, flags, etc.

ADMISSION OF NEW MEXICO.

On motion by Mr. Carey, that the Senate proceed to the consideration of the bill (H. R. 7136) to enable the people of New Mexico to form a constitution and State government, and to be admitted into the Union on an equal footing with the original States,

It was determined in the negative, { Yeas .... 14 / Nays 30

On motion by Mr. Platt,

The yeas and nays being desired by one-fifth of the Senators present, Those who voted in the affirmative are,

Messrs. Blackburn, Butler, Carey, Felton, Gordon, Harris, McPherson, Mitchell, Palmer, Peffer, Pugh, Quay, Sawyer, Teller.

Those who voted in the negative are,

Messrs. Berry, Blodgett, Brice, Caffery, Call, Cockrell, Coke, Cullom, Dawes, Dolph, Faulkner, Frye, Gorman, Hawley, Hill, Hoar, Hunton, Jones of Arkansas, McMillan, Manderson, Mills, Morrill, Pasco, Platt, Sherman, Stockbridge, Voorhees, Washburn, White, Wolcott.

So the motion was not agreed to.

CONSIDERATION OF BUSINESS ON CALENDAR.

The Senate proceeded to consider, as in Committee of the Whole,

the following bills; and the reported amendments having been agreed to, the bills were severally reported to the Senate and the amendments were concurred in:

S. 706. A bill for the relief of the Potomac Steamboat Company;

S. 1565. A bill for the relief of the heirs of D. Fulford;

S. 2380. A bill for the relief of Joseph Redfern and Eliza J. Redfern, his wife;

S. 3792. A bill to incorporate The American University; and

S. 3819. A bill granting a pension to Mary Doubleday, widow of Bvt. Maj. Gen. Abner Doubleday.

Ordered, That they be engrossed and read a third time.

The said bills were severally read the third time.

Resolved, That they pass, and that the respective titles thereof be as aforesaid.

Ordered, That the Secretary request the concurrence of the House of Representatives therein.

The Senate proceeded to consider, as in Committee of the Whole, the bill (H. R. 3594) for the relief of the Stockbridge and Munsee tribe of Indians in the State of Wisconsin; and

On motion by Mr. Pettigrew, that the bill be recommitted to the Committee on Indian Affairs,

It was determined in the affirmative, { Yeas .... 24 / Nays 20

On motion by Mr. Jones of Arkansas,

The yeas and nays being desired by one-fifth of the Senators present, Those who voted in the affirmative are,

Messrs. Blackburn, Carey, Cullom, Davis, Dolph, Felton, Frye, Hale, Hansbrough, Hawley, Higgins, Manderson, Mitchell, Morrill, Peffer, Pettigrew, Platt, Proctor, Sawyer, Sherman, Stockbridge, Teller, Voorhees, Wolcott.

Those who voted in the negative are,

Messrs. Berry, Blodgett, Brice, Caffery, Call, Coke, Harris, Hunton, Jones of Arkansas, McPherson, Mills, Morgan, Palmer, Pasco, Pugh, Quay, Stewart, Turpie, Vilas, White.

So the motion to recommit was agreed to.

The Senate proceeded to consider, as in Committee of the Whole, the bill (S. 2977) for the relief of the Stockbridge and Munsee tribe of Indians in the State of Wisconsin; and

Ordered, That it be recommitted to the Committee on Indian Affairs.

The Senate proceeded to consider, as in Committee of the Whole, the bill (H. R. 3804) to confer jurisdiction upon the Court of Claims to hear and determine the claim of David Ryan against the United States; and

On motion by Mr. Palmer.

Ordered, That it be recommitted to the Committee on Claims.

The Senate proceeded to consider, as in Committee of the Whole, the following bills; and no amendment being made, they were severally reported to the Senate:

S. 2219. A bill for the relief of Eunice M. Brown;

S. 3278. A bill for the relief of R. Connable & Sons; and

S. 3280. A bill to provide for the enforcement of the provisions of the act of Congress for the protection of the salmon fisheries of Alaska, approved March 2, 1889.

Ordered, That they be engrossed and read a third time.

The said bills were severally read the third time.

Resolved, That they pass, and that the titles thereof be as aforesaid.

Ordered, That the Secretary request the concurrence of the House of Representatives therein.

The Senate proceeded to consider the resolution, submitted by Mr. Perkins July 5, 1892, to print 5,000 copies of Senate Mis. Doc. 48, first session, Fifty-second Congress, relating to legislation on the subject of bankruptcy; and

Ordered, That it be postponed indefinitely.

The Senate proceeded to consider, as in Committee of the Whole, the following bills; and no amendment being made, they were reported to the Senate.

S. 181. A bill for the relief of Eliza E. Phillips, Chesta M. Phillips, Charlean Phillips, and Nora Phillips, of the city of New Orleans, La., and Robert L. Phillips, of the town of Washington, Ark.; and

S. 2870. A bill to ratify and confirm an agreement with the Cherokee Nation of Indians, of the Indian Territory, to make appropriation for carrying out the same, and for other purposes.

Ordered, That they be postponed indefinitely.

The Senate proceeded to consider, as in Committee of the Whole, the bill (S. 3689) for the relief of the owners of the schooner *Henry R. Tilton,* and of personal effects thereon; and the reported amendment having been agreed to, the bill was reported to the Senate and the amendment was concurred in.

Ordered, That it be engrossed and read a third time.

The said bill was read the third time.

Resolved, That it pass, and that the title be amended to read, "A bill for the relief of the owners of the schooner *Henry R. Tilton* and the owners of the personal effects thereon."

Ordered, That the Secretary request the concurrence of the House of Representatives therein.

The Senate proceeded to consider, as in Committee of the Whole, the bill (H. R. 10266) to ratify and confirm an agreement made between the Seneca Nation of Indians and William B. Barker; and no amendment being made, it was reported to the Senate.

Ordered, That it pass to a third reading.

The said bill was read the third time.

Resolved, That it pass.

Ordered, That the Secretary notify the House of Representatives thereof.

NICARAGUA CANAL.

The Vice-President announced that the hour of 2 o'clock had arrived, and laid before the Senate the unfinished business at its adjournment on Saturday last, viz, the bill (S. 1218) to amend an act entitled "An act to incorporate the Maritime Canal Company of Nicaragua," approved February 20, 1889; and

The Senate resumed, as in Committee of the Whole, the consideration of the bill; and

Pending debate,

EXECUTIVE SESSION.

On motion by Mr. Sherman,

The Senate proceeded to the consideration of executive business; and

After the consideration of executive business the doors were reopened;

When,

On motion by Mr. Berry, at 5 o'clock and 40 minutes p. m.,

The Senate adjourned until 12 o'clock m. to-morrow.

TUESDAY, FEBRUARY 14, 1893.

ENROLLED BILLS SIGNED.

The Vice-President signed the three enrolled bills (H. R. 3627, H. R. 9527, and H. R. 9786) yesterday reported to have been examined, and they were delivered to the committee to be presented to the President of the United States.

MESSAGE FROM THE HOUSE.

A message from the House of Representatives, by Mr. Towles, its chief clerk:

Mr. President: The House of Representatives has passed, without amendment, the bill (S. 977) for the relief of B. F. Rockatellow.

The House of Representatives has agreed to the amendments of the Senate to the bill (H. R. 9612) to amend section 833 of the Revised Statutes of the United States relating to semiannual returns of fees by district attorneys, marshals, and clerks.

The House of Representatives has passed the following bills, in which it requests the concurrence of the Senate:

H. R. 9229. An act to incorporate the Washington and Georgetown Terminal Railway Company;

H. R. 10285. An act to amend the charter of the District of Columbia Suburban Railway Company;

H. R. 10304. An act to incorporate the American University; and

H. R. 10489. An act to amend the act of May 6, 1890, fixing the rate of interest to be charged on arrearages of general and special taxes now due the District of Columbia, and for other purposes.

The House of Representatives has passed the following resolutions, which I am directed to communicate to the Senate:

Resolved, That the business of the House be now suspended, that opportunity be given for tributes to the memory of Hon. Edward F. McDonald, late a Representative from the State of New Jersey.

Resolved, That as a further mark of respect to the memory of the deceased and in recognition of his eminent public and private virtues, the House at the conclusion of these memorial proceedings shall stand adjourned.

Resolved, That the Clerk communicate these resolutions to the Senate.

Resolved, That the Clerk be instructed to transmit a copy of these resolutions to the family of the deceased.

The Speaker of the House of Representatives having signed two enrolled bills, H. R. 9923 and H. R. 10206, I am directed to bring the same to the Senate for the signature of its President.

ENROLLED BILLS SIGNED.

Mr. Dubois reported from the committee that they had examined and found duly enrolled the following bills:

H. R. 9923. An act making appropriations for fortifications and other works of defense, for the armament thereof, for the procurement of heavy ordnance, for trial and service, and for other purposes; and

H. R. 10206. An act to ratify and confirm an agreement made between the Seneca Nation of Indians and William B. Barker;

Whereupon,

The Vice-President signed the same, and they were delivered to the committee to be presented to the President of the United States.

BRIGHTWOOD RAILWAY COMPANY.

The bill (H. R. 9730) to amend the charter of the Brightwood Railway Company of the District, yesterday received from the House of Representatives for concurrence, was read the first and second times by unanimous consent and considered as in Committee of the Whole;

and having been amended on the motion of Mr. Hoar, it was reported to the Senate and the amendment w. s concurred in.

Ordered, That the amendment be engrossed and the bill read a third time.

The said bill as amended was read the third time by unanimous consent.

Resolved, That it pass.

Ordered, That the Secretary request the concurrence of the House of Representatives in the amendment.

CALIFORNIA AVENUE.

The bill (H. R. 10039) to narrow California avenue, within Bel Air Heights, District of Columbia, yesterday received from the House of Representatives for concurrence, was read the first and second times by unanimous consent and considered as in Committee of the Whole; and no amendment being made, it was reported to the Senate.

Ordered, That it pass to a third reading.

The said bill was read the third time by unanimous consent.

Resolved, That it pass.

Ordered, That the Secretary notify the House of Representatives thereof.

AMERICAN UNIVERSITY.

The bill (H. R. 10304) to incorporate the American University, this day received from the House of Representatives for concurrence, was read the first and second times by unanimous consent and considered as in Committee of the Whole; and no amendment being made, it was reported to the Senate.

Ordered, That it pass to a third reading.

The said bill was read the third time by unanimous consent.

Resolved, That it pass.

Ordered, That the Secretary notify the House of Representatives thereof.

HOUSE BILLS REFERRED.

The bill H. R. 10873, yesterday received from the House of Representatives for concurrence, was read the first and second times by unanimous consent and referred to the Committee on the District of Columbia.

The bills H. R. 9229, H. R. 10 85, and H. R. 10489, this day received from the House of Representatives for concurrence, were severally read the first and second times by unanimous consent and referred to the Committee on the District of Columbia.

MESSAGES FROM THE PRESIDENT.

The following message was received from the President of the United States, by Mr. Pruden, his secretary:

To the Senate and House of Representatives:

I transmit herewith a special report of the Commissioner of Labor, relating to compulsory insurance of workingmen in Germany and other countries.

BENJ. HARRISON.

EXECUTIVE MANSION,
Washington, D. C., February 14, 1893.

The message was read.

Ordered, That it be referred to the Committee on Education and Labor and printed.

The following message was received from the President of the United States, by Mr. Pruden, his secretary:

To the Senate and House of Representatives:

I transmit herewith a communication of the 13th instant from the Secretary of the Interior, transmitting copy of reports of Lieuts. Brown, Gurovits, and Suplee, United States Army, who were charged with the duty of inspecting the Navajo country so that the Interior Department could be advised as to the practicability of restraining the Navajoes within their present reservations and of furnishing irrigation and water for their flocks, together with report of the Commissioner of Indian Affairs upon the matter, with draft of an item of appropriation to carry the same into effect.

BENJ. HARRISON.

EXECUTIVE MANSION, *February 14, 1893.*

The message was read.

Ordered, That it be referred to the Committee on Indian Affairs and printed.

PETITIONS AND MEMORIALS.

Petitions, memorials, etc., were presented and referred as follows:

By Mr. Teller: A memorial of the legislature of Colorado in favor of the annexation of the Hawaiian Islands to the United States; to the Committee on Foreign Relations.

By Mr. Daniel: A petition of Daniel Ruggles, late captain, Fifth Regiment of Infantry, United States Army, praying compensation for the commutation of an additional ration of subsistence alleged to be due him under the act of July 5, 1838; to the Committee on Military Affairs.

By Mr. Quay: Several petitions of citizens of Pennsylvania, praying the passage of a law for the restriction of immigration into the United States; to the Committee on Immigration.

By Mr. Blodgett: Papers relating to the application of Antoinette Acken to be allowed a pension; to the Committee on Pensions, to accompany the bill S. 3865.

By Mr. Caffery: Papers relating to the application of Peter Bro-mon to be allowed a pension; to the Committee on Pensions, to ac-company the bill S. 3867.

MESSAGE FROM THE HOUSE.

A message from the House of Representatives, by Mr. Towles, its chief clerk:

Mr. President: The House of Repre-entatives has agreed to the concurrent resolution of the Senate to print extra copies of the re-ports of the Smithsonian Institution and of the National Museum for the year ending June 30, 1892.

The House of Representatives has passed the following bills, in which it requests the concurrence of the Senate:

H. R. 9956. An act to incorporate the Washington, Burnt Mills, and Sandy Spring Railway Company;

H. R. 10053. An act for the relief of Robert C. Burton; and

H. R. 10266. An act regulating the sale of intoxicating liquors in the District of Columbia.

The House of Representatives has passed the following resolu-tions, in which it requests the concurrence of the Senate:

Resolved by the House of Representatives (the Senate concurring), That there be printed of the eulogies delivered in Congress upon the Hon. Melbourne H. Ford, late a Representative from the State of Michigan, 8,000 copies, of which 2,000 copies shall be delivered to the Representatives and Senators of that State, and of the remain-ing number 2,000 copies shall be for the use of the Senate and 4,000 copies for the use of the House; and of the quota of the House of Representatives the Public Printer shall set aside 50 copies, which he shall have bound in full morocco with gilt edges, the same to be delivered, when completed, to the family of the deceased. And the Secretary of the Treasury is hereby directed to have engraved and printed, at the earliest day possible, a portrait of the above to ac-company said eulogies.

Resolved by the House of Representatives (the Senate concurring), That there be printed of the eulogies delivered in Congress upon the Hon. John W. Kendall, late a Representative from the State of Kentucky, 8,000 copies. of which 2,000 copies shall be delivered to the Senators and Representatives of that State, and of the remain-ing number 2,000 copies shall be for the use of the Senate and 4,000 copies for the use of the House; and of the quota of the House the Public Printer shall set aside 50 copies, which he shall have bound in full morocco with gilt edges, the same to be delivered, when completed, to the family of the deceased. And the Secretary of the Treasury is hereby directed to have engraved and printed, at the earliest day practicable, a portrait of the deceased to accompany said eulogies.

The Speaker of the House Representatives having signed three enrolled bills, S. 741, S. 2852. and S. 3859; I am directed to bring them to the Senate for the signature of its President.

HOUSE BILLS REFERRED.

The bills last received from the House of Representatives for con-currence were severally read the first and second times by unani-mous consent.

Ordered, That the bills H. R. 9956 and H. R. 10266 be referred to the Committee on the District of Columbia, and that the bill H. R. 10053 be referred to the Committee on Patents.

ENROLLED BILLS SIGNED.

Mr. Dubois reported from the committee that they had examined and found duly enrolled the following bills:

S. 741. An act to incorporate the Eclectic Medical Society of the District of Columbia;

S. 2852. An act to change the name of the Capitol, North O Street and South Washington Railway Company; and

S. 3859. An act to amend the act entitled "An act for the con-struction of a railroad and wagon bridge across the Mississippi River at South St. Paul, Minnesota," approved April 26, 1890;

Whereupon,

The Vice-President signed the same, and they were delivered to the committee to be presented to the President of the United States.

HOUSE RESOLUTIONS REFERRED.

The resolutions to print the eulogies delivered in Congress upon the Hon. John W. Kendall and the Hon. Melbourne H. Ford were read and referred to the Committee on Printing.

REPORTS OF COMMITTEES.

Mr. Shoup, from the Committee on Indian Affairs, to whom were referred the following bills, reported adversely thereon:

S. 1634. A bill to provide for a final settlement with the Naalem band of the Tillamook tribe of Indians, of Oregon, in accordance with a certain agreement between the United States and the said Indians, dated the 6th day of August, 1851; and

S. 1635. A bill to provide for a final settlement with the Tillamook tribe of Indians, of Oregon, in accordance with a certain agreement between the United States and the said Indians, dated the 7th day of August, 1851.

Ordered, That they be postponed indefinitely.

Mr. Morrill, from the Committee on Finance, to whom was referred

the bill (S. 873) to establish an assay office at Baker City, in the State of Oregon, reported it without amendment.

Mr. Jones, of Arkansas, from the Committee on Indian Affairs, to whom was recommitted the bill (H. R. 3594) for the relief of the Stockbridge and Munsee tribe of Indians, in the State of Wiscon-sin, reported it without amendment.

Mr. Jones, of Arkansas, asked and obtained leave to submit the views of a minority of the Committee on Indian Affairs on the bill (S. 3392) to ratify and confirm an agreement entered into in March, 1892, between the Indians of the Rosebud Agency and certain In-dians of the Lower Brule Agency, both in South Dakota, and for other purposes; which were ordered to be printed, to accompany the re-port No. 1275.

Mr. Manderson, from the Committee on Printing, to whom was re-ferred the resolution submitted by him on the 10th instant, to print 35,000 extra copies of the Eighth Annual Report of the Commis-sioner of Labor, relating to industrial education in the United States and Europe, reported it without amendment and submitted a re-port (No. 1288) thereon.

The Senate proceeded, by unanimous consent, to consider the said resolution; and

Resolved, That the Senate agree thereto.

Ordered, That the Secretary request the concurrence of the House of Representatives therein.

Mr. Carey, from the Committee on Education and Labor, to whom was referred the resolution submitted by Mr. Dubois January 30, 1893, for the appointment of a committee to investigate and report the facts in relation to the recent difficulties between the silver-mine owners and miners in Idaho, reported it with an amendment, viz: Strike out the word "seven" before the word "Senators," and insert the word *five.*

Ordered, That the resolution be referred to the Committee to Audit and Control the Contingent Expenses of the Senate.

REPRINT OF BILL.

On motion by Mr. Platt,

Ordered, That the bill (H. R. 9190) to ratify and confirm an agree-ment with the Cherokee Nation of Indians of the Indian Territory, to make appropriation for carrying out the same, and for other pur-poses, be reprinted as passed by the Senate.

INTRODUCTION OF BILLS.

Bills were introduced, read the first and second times by unani-mous consent, and referred as follows:

By Mr. Manderson: A bill (S. 3864) for the relief of John M. Burke, James Manning, and C. S. Waite; to the Committee on Claims.

By Mr. Blodgett: A bill (S. 3865) for the relief of Antoinette Acken; to the Committee on Pensions.

By Mr. Quay: A bill (S. 3866) for the relief of William D. Har-tupee, administrator of Andrew Hartupee, surviving partner of the firm of Tomlinson & Hartupee & Co.; to the Committee on Claims.

By Mr. Caffery: A bill (S. 3867) granting a pension to Peter Bromon, of Patterson, State of Louisiana; to the Committee on Pensions.

By Mr. Mitchell: A bill (S. 3868) to provide for allotment of land in severalty to the Quapaws in Indian Territory, and for other pur-poses; to the Committee on Indian Affairs.

By Mr. Voorhees: A bill (S. 3869) for the relief of Lewis Pelham; to the Committee on Claims.

CLOSING OF WORLD'S FAIR ON SUNDAY.

Mr. Quay submitted the following resolution; which was consid-ered by unanimous consent and agreed to:

Resolved, That the Secretary of the Treasury shall be, and hereby is, directed forthwith to inform the Senate whether the appropria-tions, or any part thereof, made to the World's Columbian Exposi-tion by the act making appropriations for sundry civil expenses of the Government for the fiscal year ending June 30, 1893, and for other purposes, approved August 5, 1892, have been paid to the World's Columbian Commission; and if so, what rules, or modifica-tion of the rules of the said Commission have been made to effect the closing of the Exposition on the first day of the week, commonly called Sunday.

TESTIMONY BEFORE COMMITTEE ON APPROPRIATIONS.

Mr. Allison submitted the following resolution; which was re-ferred to the Committee to Audit and Control the Contingent Ex-penses of the Senate:

Resolved, That the Committee on Appropriations be, and is hereby, authorized to employ a stenographer from time to time, as may be necessary, to report such testimony as may be taken by said com-mittee and its subcommittees in connection with appropriation bills, and to have the same printed for its use; and that such stenog-rapher be paid out of the contingent fund of the Senate.

READING OF WASHINGTON'S FAREWELL ADDRESS.

Mr. Hoar submitted the following resolution for consideration:

Resolved, That on the 22d day of February, current, the anniver-sary of the birthday of George Washington, the Senate shall meet at 12 o'clock at noon, and after the reading of the Journal, shall listen to the reading of Washington's farewell address by the Senator from Nebraska, President *pro tempore* of the Senate.

SPOLIATION OF LANDS GRANTED THE STATE OF CALIFORNIA.

On motion by Mr. Dolph,

Ordered, That the letter of the Secretary of the Interior, laid before the Senate January 31, 1891, communicating, in answer to a resolution of the Senate of September 22, 1890, information relative to the spoliation of lands granted to the State of California on certain conditions by the act of June 30, 1864, be printed.

PRESIDENTIAL APPROVALS.

A message from the President of the United States, by Mr. Pruden, his secretary:

Mr. President: The President of the United States approved and signed on the 11th instant an act (S. 1933) concerning testimony in criminal cases or proceedings based upon or growing out of alleged violations of an act entitled "An act to regulate commerce," approved February 4, 1887, as amended March 2, 1889, and February 10, 1891.

He approved and signed on the 13th instant a joint resolution (S. R. 134) authorizing the loan, for exhibition at the World's Columbian Exposition, of the picture entitled "The Recall of Columbus," by Augustus Heaton: and

He this day approved and signed a joint resolution (S. R. 140) authorizing the Secretaries of War and the Navy to loan to the committee on inaugural ceremonies, flags, and so forth.

Ordered, That the Secretary notify the House of Representatives thereof.

SUNDRY CIVIL APPROPRIATION BILL.

On motion by Mr. Allison,

The Senate proceeded to consider, as in Committee of the Whole, the bill (H. R. 10238) making appropriations for sundry civil expenses of the Government for the fiscal year ending June 30, 1894, and for other purposes; and the reported amendments having been agreed to in part, and the bill further amended on the motion of Mr. Allison, from the Committee on Appropriations,

Pending debate,

NICARAGUA CANAL.

The Presiding Officer (Mr. Chandler in the chair) announced that the hour of 2 o'clock had arrived, and laid before the Senate the unfinished business at its adjournment yesterday, viz., the bill (S. 1218) to amend the act entitled "An act to incorporate the Maritime Canal Company of Nicaragua," approved February 20, 1889; and

The Senate resumed, as in Committee of the Whole, the consideration of the bill; and

Pending debate,

EXECUTIVE SESSION.

On motion by Mr. Quay,

The Senate proceeded to the consideration of executive business; and

After the consideration of executive business the doors were reopened;

When

SUNDRY CIVIL APPROPRIATION BILL.

On motion by Mr. Hale, and by unanimous consent,

The Senate resumed, as in Committee of the Whole, the consideration of the bill (H. R. 10238) making appropriations for sundry civil expenses of the Government for the fiscal year ending June 30, 1894, and for other purposes; and the reported amendments having been further agreed to in part,

On motion by Mr. Voorhees, at 5 o'clock and 40 minutes p. m.,

The Senate adjourned until 12 o'clock m. to-morrow.

WEDNESDAY, FEBRUARY 15, 1893.

EXECUTIVE COMMUNICATIONS.

The Vice-President laid before the Senate a letter of the Secretary of the Treasury, transmitting a communication from the Commissioner of Labor, submitting an estimate of appropriation for miscellaneous expenses, Department of Labor, for the fiscal year ending June 30, 1894; which was referred to the Committee on Appropriations and ordered to be printed.

The Vice-President laid before the Senate a letter of the Secretary of the Treasury, recommending an appropriation to pay C. S. Waite for services as engineer, and James Manning for services as fireman in the United States court-house and post-office building at Lincoln, Nebr.; which was referred to the Committee on Appropriations and ordered to be printed.

The Vice-President laid before the Senate a letter of the Secretary of the Treasury, transmitting a communication from the Secretary of State, submitting an estimate of appropriation to pay the expenses of the messenger sent to obtain the electoral vote of the State of Montana; which was referred to the Committee on Appropriations and ordered to be printed.

The Vice-President laid before the Senate a letter of the Secretary of the Treasury, transmitting, in answer to a resolution of the Senate of the 11th instant, a report of the Fourth Auditor relative to naval officers' claims for sea pay in accordance with the decision of the Supreme Court; which was referred to the Committee on Appropriations and ordered to be printed.

The Vice-President laid before the Senate a letter of the Secretary of the Treasury, transmitting a communication from the Secretary of the Interior, submitting an additional estimate of appropriation for salaries, office of surveyor-general of Montana; which was referred to the Committee on Appropriations and ordered to be printed.

PETITIONS AND MEMORIALS.

Petitions, memorials, etc., were presented and referred as follows:

By Mr. Hill: A memorial of the legislature of New York in favor of the passage of the bill (H. R. 3608) for classifying the salaries of clerks in the first and second class post-offices; to the Committee on Post-Offices and Post-Roads.

A memorial of the legislature of New York in favor of the passage of a law for the construction of a national harbor of refuge at the Bight of Canaveral, Florida; to the Committee on Commerce.

A memorial of the legislature of New York in favor of the annexation of the Hawaiian Islands to the United States; to the Committee on Foreign Relations.

A memorial of the Produce Exchange of New York, praying the passage of a law for the construction of a canal between the Great Lakes and the Hudson River; to the Committee on Commerce.

A resolution of the Merchant Tailors' Society of New York, praying the passage of the bill limiting the amount of clothing that may be admitted free of duty; to the Committee on Finance.

A petition of the Regular Army and Navy Union of the United States, praying an amendment to the law providing a retired list for enlisted men of the Army so as to include enlisted men of the Navy—to the Committee on Military Affairs.

By Mr. Voorhees: A memorial of certain physicians of the United States, remonstrating against the proposition to increase the hours of labor in the Departments from seven to eight hours—to the Committee on Appropriations.

By Mr. Stockbridge: Papers relating to the selection of lands by certain of the Stockbridge and Munsee tribe of Indians in Wisconsin—to the Committee on Indian Affairs and ordered to be printed.

By Mr. Cullom: Several petitions of citizens of Illinois, praying for the appointment of a committee to investigate an alleged combine formed to depreciate the price of grain by the millers and others at St. Louis and Minneapolis—to the Committee on Agriculture and Forestry.

By Mr. Hill: A petition of citizens of New York, praying the repeal of the provision providing for the closing of the Columbian Exposition on the Sabbath day—to the Select Committee on the Quadro-Centennial.

By Mr. Teller: A memorial of citizens of Colorado, remonstrating against the repeal of the provision providing for the closing of the Columbian Exposition on the Sabbath day—to the Select Committee on the Quadro-Centennial.

Mr. Hoar presented a petition of citizens of Massachusetts, praying for the repeal of the law providing for the purchase of silver bullion.

Ordered, That it lie on the table.

Petitions praying the passage of a law for the restriction of immigration into the United States were presented as follows:

By Mr. Cullom: A petition of citizens of Illinois.

By Mr. Hill: Two petitions of citizens of New York.

Ordered, That they be referred to the Committee on Immigration.

Mr. McPherson presented a tabular statement of revenue and expenditures of the United States for fourteen years since the resumption of specie payment; which was ordered to be printed.

CONFERENCE REPORT.

Mr. Turpie, from the committee of conference on the disagreeing votes of the two Houses on the amendment of the House of Representatives to the bill (S. 1303) granting an increase of pension to Mrs. S. A. Farquharson, submitted the following report:

The committee of conference on the disagreeing votes of the two Houses on the amendment of the House of Representatives to the bill (S. 1303) granting an increase of pension to Mrs. S. A. Farquharson, having met, after full and free conference have agreed to recommend and do recommend to their respective Houses as follows:

That the House recede from its amendment and agree to the same.

DAVID TURPIE,
JOHN M. PALMER,
Managers on the part of the Senate.
CHARLES BARWIG,
JOHN C. HOUK,
R. P. C. WILSON,
Managers on the part of the House.

The Senate proceeded to consider the said report; and

On motion by Mr. Turpie,

Resolved, That the Senate agree thereto.

Ordered, That the Secretary notify the House of Representatives thereof.

MESSAGE FROM THE HOUSE.

A message from the House of Representatives, by Mr. Towles, its chief clerk:

Mr. President: The House of Representatives has agreed to the report of the committee of conference on the disagreeing votes of the two Houses on the amendment of the House to the bill (S. 1303) to increase the pension of Mrs. S. A. Farquharson.

The House of Representatives has passed, without amendment, the following bills of the Senate:

S. 2826. An act for the relief of L. M. Garrett; and

S. 3819. An act granting a pension to Mary Doubleday, widow of Bvt. Maj. Gen. Abner Doubleday.

The House of Representatives has agreed to the resolution of the Senate providing for the printing of the Eighth Annual Report of the Commissioner of Labor.

The House of Representatives has agreed to the amendments of the Senate to the following bills of the House:

H. R. 9730. An act to amend the charter of the Brightwood Railway Company of the District of Columbia; and

H. R. 9826. An act granting certain rights and privileges to the commissioners of water works in the city of Erie, Pa.

The House of Representatives has passed the the following bills and joint resolution, in which it requests the concurrence of the Senate:.

H. R. 1479. An act to remove the charge of desertion from the record of James Morrison, alias James C. McIntosh;

H. R. 10241. An act to amend "An act making appropriations for the construction, repair, and preservation of certain public works on rivers and harbors, and for other purposes," approved July 13, 1892;

H. R. 10391. An act to amend an act entitled "An act to provide for the establishment of a port of delivery at Council Bluffs, Iowa;" and

H. R. 202. A joint resolution extending the session of the thirtieth legislative assembly of the Territory of New Mexico from sixty to seventy days.

The House of Representatives has passed the following resolutions, in which it requests the concurrence of the Senate:

Resolved by the House of Representatives (the Senate concurring), That there be printed in quarto form of the annual report of the Chief of the Weather Bureau, with appendices, 9,000 copies; of which 1,000 copies shall be for the use of the Senate, 2,000 copies for the use of the House of Representatives, and 6,000 copies for the use of the Weather Bureau. The report will cover the transactions of the Bureau from date of its transfer from the War to the Agricultural Department, July 1, 1891, to December 31, 1892.

Resolved by the House of Representatives (the Senate concurring), That the Secretary of War be requested to ascertain and report the present actual condition of the harbor improvement at Cumberland Sound and the entrance to the port of Fernandina, Fla., and whether any necessity exists for immediate legislation with regard thereto, with such recommendations as he may deem it proper to submit.

The Speaker of the House of Representatives having signed three enrolled bills, S. 1683, S. 2946, S. 3836, and an enrolled joint resolution, S. R. 130, I am directed to bring the same to the Senate for the signature of its President.

ENROLLED BILLS SIGNED.

Mr. Dubois reported from the committee that they had examined and found duly enrolled the following bills and joint resolution:

S. 1683. An act for the relief of Mrs. Fannie N. Belger;

S. 2946. An act to amend an act entitled "An act to incorporate the Masonic Mutual Relief Association of the District of Columbia," approved March 3, 1869;

S. 3836. An act to authorize the Union Railroad Company to construct and maintain a bridge across the Monongahela River; and

S. R. 130. A joint resolution to amend an act entitled "An act making Saturday a half holiday for banking and trust companies in the District of Columbia," approved December 22, 1892;

Whereupon,

The Vice President signed the same, and they were delivered to the committee to be presented to the President of the United States.

HOUSE BILLS AND RESOLUTIONS REFERRED.

The resolution to print 9,000 copies of the annual report of the Chief of the Weather Bureau, this day received from the House of Representatives for concurrence, was read and referred to the Committee on Printing.

The resolution calling for a report as to the condition of the harbor improvement at Cumberland Sound and the entrance to the port of Fernandina, Fla., this day received from the House of Representatives for concurrence, was read and referred to the Committee on Commerce.

The bills H. R. 1479, H. R. 10391 and the joint resolution H. R. 202, this day received from the House of Representatives, were severally read the first and second times by unanimous consent.

Ordered, That the bill H. R. 1479 be referred to the Committee on

Naval Affairs; that the bill H. R. 10391 be referred to the Committee on Commerce, and that the joint resolution H. R. 202 be referred to the Committee on Territories.

BILLS PRESENTED.

Mr. Dubois reported from the committee that they this day presented to the President of the United States the following enrolled bills:

S. 741. An act to incorporate the Eclectic Medical Society of the District of Columbia;

S. 2852. An act to change the name of the Capitol, North O street and South Washington Railroad Company; and

S. 3859. An act to amend the act entitled "An act for the construction of a railroad and wagon bridge across the Mississippi River at South St. Paul, Minn.," approved April 26, 1890.

REPORTS OF COMMITTEES.

Mr. Hale, from the Committee on Appropriations, to whom was referred the bill (H. R. 10267) making appropriations for the diplomatic and consular service of the United States for the fiscal year ending June 30, 1894, reported it with amendments and submitted a report (No. 1289) thereon.

Mr. Cullom, from the Committee on Appropriations, to whom was referred the bill (H. R. 10290) making appropriations for the support of the Military Academy for the fiscal year ending June 30, 1894, reported it with amendments, and submitted a report (No. 1290) thereon.

Mr. Peffer, from the Committee on Claims, to whom was referred the bill (S. 2793) for the relief of Crank & Hoffman, reported it with amendments and submitted a report (No. 1291) thereon.

Mr. Morrill, from the Committee on Finance, to whom was referred the bill (S. 3817) for the relief of W. W. Rollins, collector of internal revenue for the fifth collection district of North Carolina, reported it without amendment and submitted a report (No. 1292) thereon.

Mr. Stewart, from the Committee on Claims, to whom was referred the bill (H. R. 3508) for the relief of Nemiah Garrison, assignee of Moses Perkins, reported it without amendment and submitted a report (No. 1293) thereon.

Mr. Davis, from the Committee on Foreign Relations, to whom was referred the amendment intended to be proposed by Mr. Hunton to the diplomatic and consular appropriation bill, providing for the purchase of Haswell's "Chronological History of the Department of State and the Foreign Relations of the Government from September 5, 1774, to July 1, 1885," submitted a report (No. 1294); which, together with the proposed amendment, was referred to the Committee on Appropriations.

Mr. Mitchell, from the Committee on Claims, to whom was referred the bill (S. 3863) for the relief of George Q. Cannon, of Utah, reported it with an amendment and submitted a report (No. 1295) thereon.

INTRODUCTION OF BILLS.

Bills were introduced, read the first and second times by unanimous consent, and referred as follows:

By Mr. Hiscock: A bill (S. 3870) to incorporate mining companies in the Chickasaw Nation; to the Committee on Indian Affairs.

By Mr. Palmer: A bill (S. 3871) to authorize the construction of a bridge across the Calumet River; to the Committee on Commerce.

READING OF WASHINGTON'S FAREWELL ADDRESS.

The Vice-President laid before the Senate the following resolution yesterday submitted by Mr. Hoar:

Resolved, That on the 22d day of February, current, the anniversary of the birthday of Washington, the Senate shall meet at 12 o'clock at noon, and after the reading of the Journal, shall listen to the reading of Washington's farewell address by the Senator from Nebraska, President *pro tempore* of the Senate; and

Resolved, That the Senate agree to the resolution.

COMMITTEE ON THE DISTRICT OF COLUMBIA.

On motion by Mr. McMillan,

Ordered, That the Committee on the District of Columbia have leave to sit during the sessions of the Senate.

ARMY APPROPRIATION BILL.

Mr. Stewart, from the committee of conference on the disagreeing votes of the two Houses on the amendments of the Senate to the bill H. R. 9825, submitted the following report:

The committee of conference on the disagreeing votes of the two Houses on the amendments of the Senate to the bill (H. R. 9825) "making appropriations for the support of the Army for the fiscal year ending June 30, 1894, and for other purposes," having met, after full and free conference have agreed to recommend and do recommend to their respective Houses as follows:

That the Senate recede from its amendments numbered 5 and 13.

That the House recede from its disagreement to the amendments of the Senate numbered 2, 3, 4, 6, 7, 8, 9, 10, 11, 12, 14, 15, 16, 17, 18, and 22, and agree to the same.

That the House recede from its disagreement to the amendment of the Senate numbered 1, and agree to the same with an amendment as follows: Strike out in line 2 of said amendment the word "thirty," and insert in lieu thereof *twenty-five;* and the Senate agree to the same.

That the House recede from its disagreement to the amendment of the Senate numbered 19, and agree to the same with an amendment as follows: In lieu of the matter inserted by said amendment insert the following: *No part of this appropriation shall be expended for the manufacture of magazine rifles of foreign invention until such magazine rifles of American invention as may be presented for tests to the War Department within the next thirty days shall have been tested by a board of officers to be selected by the Secretary of War, which board shall report to the Board of Ordnance and Fortification on or before July first, eighteen hundred and ninety-three. If the decision of said board of officers shall be in favor of any American invention and shall also receive the approval of the Board of Ordnance and Fortification and the Secretary of War, then this appropriation, or such part thereof as the Secretary may direct, shall be expended in the manufacture of such American arms: Provided further, That if no such American invention shall be recommended by said board or receive the approval of the Secretary of War;* and the Senate agree to the same.

That the House recede from its disagreement to the amendment of the Senate numbered 20, and agree to the same with an amendment as follows: Insert after the word "appropriation," in line 19, page 22, of the bill, the following: *also, including the actual and necessary cost of transportation of accepted applicants from their homes to places of enlistment, when authorized by the Secretary of War;* and the Senate agree to the same.

That the House recede from its disagreement to the amendment of the Senate numbered 21, and agree to the same with an amendment as follows: Strike out in line 3 of the same amendment the word "person," and insert in lieu thereof the word *private;* and the Senate agree to the same.

WILLIAM STEWART,
W. B. ALLISON,
JO. C. S. BLACKBURN,
Managers on the part of the Senate.
JOS. H. OUTHWAITE,
W. C. NEWBERRY,
HENRY H. BINGHAM,
Managers on the part of the House.

Ordered, That the report and the bill as agreed upon be printed.

PRESIDENTIAL APPROVALS.

A message from the President of the United States, by Mr. Pruden, his secretary.

Mr. President: The President of the United States yesterday approved and signed the following acts:

S. 3787. An act to authorize the construction of a bridge across the St. Marys River between the States of Florida and Georgia;

S. 3825. An act to authorize the Homestead and Pittsburg Bridge Company to construct a bridge over the Monongahela River from Pittsburg to Homestead; and

S. 3826. An act authorizing Velasco and Surfside Railway Company to construct a bridge across the Galveston and Brazos Canal.

He this day approved and signed the following acts:

S. 3510. An act to amend section 4347 of the Revised Statutes of the United States; and

S. 3859. An act to amend an act entitled "An act for the construction of a railroad and wagon bridge across the Mississippi River at South St. Paul, Minn.," approved April 26, 1890.

Ordered, That the Secretary notify the House of Representatives thereof.

JOHN H. RUSSELL.

On motion by Mr. Peffer, and by unanimous consent,

The vote postponing indefinitely the bill (S. 376) for the relief of John H. Russell, was reconsidered and the bill recommitted to the Committee on Claims.

SUNDRY CIVIL APPROPRIATION BILL.

On motion by Mr. Allison,

The Senate resumed, as in Committee of the Whole, the consideration of the bill (H. R. 10238) making appropriations for sundry civil expenses of the Government for the fiscal year ending June 30, 1894, and for other purposes; and the reported amendments having been further agreed to in part, and in part amended, and as amended agreed to,

On the question to agree to the amendment reported in line 14, page 81,

Pending debate,

EXECUTIVE SESSION.

On motion by Mr. Sherman,

The Senate proceeded to the consideration of executive business; and

After the consideration of executive business the doors were opened;

When,

DEATH OF HON. EDWARD F. M'DONALD.

The Vice-President laid before the Senate the resolutions of the House of Representatives on the announcement of the death of the Hon. Edward F. McDonald.

The resolutions were read;

When,

Mr. McPherson submitted the following resolutions:

Resolved, That the Senate has heard with profound sorrow the announcement of the death of Hon. Edward F. McDonald, late a Representative from the State of New Jersey.

Resolved, That the business of the Senate be now suspended in order that fitting tributes may be paid to his memory.

Resolved, That a copy of these resolutions be transmitted by the Secretary of the Senate to the family of the deceased.

Resolved, That at the conclusion of these ceremonies the Senate stand adjourned.

The Senate proceeded, by unanimous consent, to consider the resolutions; and

After addresses by Mr. McPherson and Mr. Blodgett,

The resolutions were unanimously agreed to; and

The Senate adjourned.

THURSDAY, FEBRUARY 16, 1893.

CONNEAUT HARBOR, OHIO.

The bill (H. R. 10241) to amend "An act making appropriations for the construction, repair, and preservation of certain public works on rivers and harbors, and for other purposes," approved July 13, 1892, yesterday received from the House of Representatives for concurrence, was read the first and second times by unanimous consent, and considered as in Committee of the Whole; and no amendment being made, it was reported to the Senate.

Ordered, That it pass to a third reading.

The said bill was read the third time by unanimous consent.

Resolved, That it pass.

Ordered, That the Secretary notify the House of Representatives thereof.

EXECUTIVE COMMUNICATIONS.

The Vice-President laid before the Senate a letter of the Secretary of the Treasury, communicating, in answer to a resolution of the Senate of the 14th instant, information relative to the payments made to the World's Columbian Commission of the appropriation made in the sundry civil appropriation bill, approved August 5, 1892, upon the condition that the Fair be closed on the Sabbath day.

Ordered, That it lie on the table and be printed.

The Vice-President laid before the Senate a letter of the Postmaster-General, transmitting, in answer to a resolution of the Senate of the 13th instant, all correspondence relative to the alleged unsafe condition of the Busch Building occupied by the money-order branch of the Sixth Auditor's Office; which was referred to the Committee on Appropriations and ordered to be printed.

PETITIONS AND MEMORIALS.

Petitions, memorials, etc., were presented and referred as follows:

By Mr. Peffer: A petition of citizens of Kansas, praying the passage of a law for the restriction of immigration; to the Committee on Immigration.

By Mr. Hoar: A petition of citizens of Massachusetts, praying the establishment of a permanent census bureau, and for the collection and publication of statistics relating to farm mortgages; to the Committee on the Census.

By Mr. Frye: A petition of citizens of Maine, praying the passage of a law prohibiting the manufacture, importation, and sale of cigarettes; to the Committee on Finance.

By Mr. Hawley: A resolution of the Board of Trade of Hartford, Conn., praying the repeal of the so-called Chinese exclusion act; to the Committee on Foreign Relations.

By Mr. Squire: A memorial of the Chamber of Commerce of Seattle, Wash., praying an appropriation for coast defenses; to the Committee on Coast Defenses.

A petition of citizens of Washington, praying the passage of a law for the restriction of immigration into the United States; to the Committee on Immigration.

By Mr. Coke: A letter of the Commissioner of Fish and Fisheries, recommending an increase of the appropriation for the completion of the fish-cultural station in Texas; to the Committee on Appropriations, to accompany an amendment intended to be proposed to the general deficiency appropriation bill, No. 10258.

Mr. Voorhees presented a petition of citizens of the District of Columbia praying for the immediate repeal of the law prohibiting the sale of intoxicating liquors within one mile of the Soldiers' Home.

Ordered, That it lie on the table.

Mr. Call presented papers relating to the application of Mary A. McLeran to have issued her a land warrant for 500 acres of land; which were referred to the Committee on Public Lands, to accompany the bill S. 3874.

CONFERENCE REPORT.

Mr. Stewart, from the committee of conference on the disagreeing votes of the two Houses on the amendments of the Senate to the bill H. R. 9286, submitted the following report:

The committee of conference on the disagreeing votes of the two Houses on the amendments of the Senate to the bill of the House (H. R. 9286) to create the California Débris Commission and regulate hydraulic mining in the State of California, having met, after full and free conference have agreed to recommend and do recommend to their respective Houses as follows:

That the House recede from its disagreement to the amendments of the Senate numbered 3, 4, 5, 6, 7, 8, 9, 10, 11, 12, 13, 14, 15, 16, 17, 18, 19, 20, 21, 23, 25, 26, 28, and 29, and agree to the same.

That the House recede from its disagreement to the amendment of the Senate numbered 1, and agree to the same with an amendment as follows: Add, after the word "systems," in section 3, line 21, the words *in the State of California;* and the Senate agree to the same.

That the House recede from its disagreement to the amendment of the Senate numbered 2, and agree to the same with an amendment as follows: Add, after the word "carried," in section 4, line 16, the words *on, provided the same can be accomplished;* and the Senate agree to the same.

That the House recede from its disagreement to the amendment . or the Senate numbered 22, and agree to the same with amendments as follows: Add, after the word "process," in line 2 of the amendment to section 22, the words *directly or indirectly injuring the navigable waters of the United States;* and the Senate agree to the same.

Add at the end of section 22 the following:

Provided, That this section shall take effect on the first day of May, eighteen hundred and ninety-three.

And the Senate agree to the same.

That the House recede from its disagreement to the amendment of the Senate numbered 24, and agree to the same with an amendment as follows: Add, after the word "lands," in section 24, line 7, of the amendment, the words *or relating to the wording of hydraulic mines;* and the Senate agree to the same.

That the House recede from its disagreement to the amendment of the Senate numbered 27; and agree to the same with an amendment as follows: Strike out, after the word " in " in section 25, line 25, the word " which," and insert the word *which* before the word "in;" and the Senate agree to the same.

WM. M. STEWART, .
C. N. FELTON,
R. Q. MILLS,
Managers on the part of the Senate.
WM. H. H. COWLES,
A. CAMINETTI,
HOSEA TOWNSEND,
Managers on the part of the House.

The Senate proceeded to consider the said report; and

Resolved, That the Senate agree thereto.

Ordered, That the Secretary notify the House of Representatives thereof.

REPORTS OF COMMITTEES.

Mr. Davis, from the Committee on Military Affairs, to whom was referred the bill (S. 2905) for the relief of John M. Goodhue, reported it with an amendment and submitted a report (No. 1296) thereon.

The Senate proceeded, by unanimous consent, to consider the said bill as in Committee of the Whole; and the reported amendment having been agreed to, the bill was reported to the Senate and the amendment was concurred in.

Ordered, That the bill be engrossed and read a third time.

The said bill was read the third time.

Resolved, That it pass, and that the title thereof be as aforesaid.

Ordered, That the Secretary request the concurrence of the House of Representatives therein.

Mr. Davis, from the Committee on Pensions, to whom were referred the following bills, reported them without amendment and submitted written reports thereon as follows:

H. R. 6212. An act granting an increase of pension to Ellis P. Phipps, late lieutenant in Company A, Twelfth New Jersey Volunteer Infantry, invalid certificate No. 35619; Report No. 1297.

H. R. 7306. An act to pension Maud Case, of Dodge County, Minnesota; Report No. 1298.

Mr. Manderson, from the Committee on Military Affairs, to whom was referred the bill (H. R. 6554) to remove the charge of desertion against Charles H. Behle, reported it without amendment and submitted a report (No. 1299) thereon.

Mr. Perkins, from the Committee on the District of Columbia, to whom was referred the bill (H. R. 9873) to create a board of charities, and so forth, in the District of Columbia, reported it without amendment and submitted a report (No. 1300) thereon.

On motion by Mr. Perkins,

The Senate proceeded to consider, as in Committee of the Whole, the bill (S. 3330) to create a board of charities for the District of Columbia; and

Ordered, That it be postponed indefinitely.

Mr. Hausbrough, from the Committee on the District of Columbia, to whom was referred the bill (H. R. 10266) regulating the sale of intoxicating liquors in the District of Columbia, reported it without amendment and submitted a report (No. 1301) thereon.

On motion by Mr. Hausbrough,

The Senate proceeded to consider, as in Committee of the Whole, the bill (S. 2845) regulating the sale of distilled and fermented liquors in the District of Columbia; and

Ordered, That it be postponed indefinitely.

MESSAGE FROM THE HOUSE.

A message from the House of Representatives, by Mr. Towles, its chief clerk:

Mr. President: The House of Representatives has passed the bill of the Senate (S. 2931) to provide for the survey and transfer of that part of the Fort Randall military reservation in the State of Nebraska to said State for school and other purposes, with an amendment, in which it requests the concurrence of the Senate.

The House of Representatives has passed a bill (H. R. 10280) to authorize the construction of a bridge over the Tennessee River at or near Sheffield, Ala., in which it requests the concurrence of the Senate.

The Speaker of the House having signed six enrolled bills, S. 977, H. R. 9612, H. R. 9730, H. R. 9826, H. R. 10039, and H. R. 10304, I am directed to bring the same to the Senate for the signature of its President.

ENROLLED BILLS SIGNED.

Mr. Dubois reported from the committee that they had examined and found duly enrolled the following bills:

S. 977. An act for the relief of B. F. Rockafellow;

H. R. 9612. An act to prescribe the number of district attorneys and marshals in the judicial districts of the State of Alabama;

H. R. 9730. An act to amend the charter of the Brightwood Railway Company of the District of Columbia;

H. R. 9826. An act granting certain rights and privileges to the commissioners of water works in the city of Erie, Pa.;

H. R. 10039. An act to narrow California avenue, within Bel Air Heights, District of Columbia; and

H. R. 10304. An act to incorporate The American University;

Whereupon,

The Vice-President signed the same, and they were delivered to the committee to be presented to the President of the United States.

HOUSE BILL REFERRED.

The bill H. R. 10280, this day received from the House of Representatives for concurrence, was read the first and second times by unanimous consent and referred to the Committee on Commerce.

HOUSE AMENDMENT TO SENATE BILL.

The Vice-President laid before the Senate the amendment of the House of Representatives to the bill (S. 2931) to provide for the survey and transfer of that part of the Fort Randall military reservation in the State of Nebraska to said State for school and other purposes.

On motion by Mr. Paddock,

Resolved, That the Senate disagree to the amendment of the House of Representatives to the said bill and ask a conference with the House on the disagreeing votes of the two Houses thereon.

Ordered, That the conferees on the part of the Senate be appointed by the Vice-President; and

The Vice-President appointed Mr. Paddock, Mr. Pettigrew, and Mr. Pasco.

Ordered, That the Secretary notify the House of Representatives thereof.

INTRODUCTION OF BILLS AND JOINT RESOLUTIONS.

Bills and joint resolutions were introduced, read the first and second times by unanimous consent, and referred as follows:

By Mr. Peffer: A bill (S. 3872) to provide for the sale of the surplus lands belonging to certain tribes of Indians within limits of the Quapaw Agency, in the Indian Territory, and for other purposes; to the Committee on Indian Affairs.

By Mr. Cockrell: A bill (S. 3873) to authorize the Kansas City, Pittsburg and Gulf Railroad Company to construct and operate railroad, telegraph, and telephone lines through the Indian Territory, and for other purposes; to the Committee on Indian Affairs.

By Mr. Call: A bill (S. 3874) for the relief of Mary A. McLeron, and for the issue of a land warrant of 500 acres of land; to the Committee on Public Lands.

By Mr. Hunton: A joint resolution (S. R. 154) instructing the Commissioner of Internal Revenue to reopen and reexamine the claim of the Continental Fire Insurance Company and others, and certify the amount of taxes erroneously paid by said corporations, if any; to the Committee on Finance.

By Mr. Hill: A joint resolution (S. R. 155) authorizing and directing the Secretary of the Interior to purchase Report on Mineral Industry, etc., covering mineral statistics for 1892, etc.; to the Committee on Printing.

WITHDRAWAL OF PAPERS.

On motion by Mr. Pugh,

Ordered, That Patrick Doran have leave to withdraw his papers from the files of the Senate, there being no adverse report.

PERSONNEL OF THE NAVY.

Mr. Hale submitted the following resolution; which was referred to the Committee on Naval Affairs:

Whereas there are constantly before Congress numerous bills dealing with the question of rank and pay in the Navy, and other matters concerning the personnel of the same; and

Whereas the present laws relating to this subject are in many instances inconsistent, unjust, and the result of piecemeal legislation: Now, therefore,

Be it resolved by the Senate of the United States (the House of Representatives concurring), That a special joint committee, consisting of three members of the House who have been elected to the Fifty-third Congress and three members of the Senate who will continue Senators during such Congress, be appointed, respectively, by the Speaker of the House of Representatives and the President of the Senate, whose duty it shall be to fully investigate and consider the entire subject of the rank, pay, and all other matters relating to the personnel of the Navy; to have power to send for persons and papers, sit during the recess of both Houses, and to report to the next Congress, as soon after it convenes as may be convenient, what legislation, if any, is necessary in the premises; any bill so reported by them shall simplify, codify, and revise existing laws relating to the personnel of the Navy, so far as may be found possible. And said commission is hereby authorized to employ a clerk at $6 per day and a messenger at $3 per day while employed, and any expenses incurred by said commission in performing the duties herein required shall be defrayed equally from the contingent funds of the two Houses.

BRIDGE ACROSS THE MONONGAHELA RIVER.

On motion by Mr. Quay,

The Senate proceeded to consider, as in Committee of the Whole, the bill (S. 3857) authorizing the construction of a bridge over the Monongahela River, at the foot of Main street, in the borough of Belle Vernon, in the State of Pennsylvania; and no amendment being made, it was reported to the Senate.

Ordered, That it be engrossed and read a third time.

The said bill was read the third time.

Resolved, That it pass, and that the title thereof be as aforesaid.

Ordered, That the Secretary request the concurrence of the House of Representatives therein.

PRESIDENTIAL APPROVALS.

A message from the President of the United States, by Mr. Pruden, his secretary:

Mr. President: The President of the United States yesterday approved and signed the following acts:

S. 3788. An act granting right of way to the Colorado River Irrigation Company through the Yuma Indian Reservation in California; and

S. 3843. An act to authorize the Chesapeake and Ohio Railway Company to renew its railroad bridge across the Big Sandy River, upon such plans and location as may be approved by the Secretary of War.

Ordered, That the Secretary notify the House of Representatives thereof.

BILLS PRESENTED.

Mr. Dubois reported from the committee that they this day presented to the President of the United States the following enrolled bills and joint resolution:

S. 977. An act for the relief of B. F. Rockafellow;

S. 1693. An act for the relief of Mrs. Fannie N. Belger;

S. 2946. An act to amend an act entitled "An act to incorporate the Masonic Mutual Relief Association of the District of Columbia," approved March 3, 1869;

S. 3836. An act to authorize the Union Railroad Company to construct and maintain a bridge across the Monongahela River; and

S. R. 130. A joint resolution to amend an act entitled "An act making Saturday a half holiday for banking and trust companies in the District of Columbia," approved December 22, 1892.

SUNDRY CIVIL APPROPRIATION BILL.

On motion by Mr. Allison,

The Senate resumed, as in Committee of the Whole, the consideration of the bill (H. R. 10238) making appropriations for sundry civil expenses of the Government for the fiscal year ending June 30, 1894, and for other purposes; and

The question being on the following reported amendment, viz: In line 14, page 81, strike out the word "five," and in lieu thereof insert *three*,

It was determined in the negative $\left\{ \begin{array}{l} \text{Yeas} \dots\dots\dots\dots\dots 21 \\ \text{Nays} \dots\dots\dots\dots\dots 26 \end{array} \right.$

On motion by Mr. Quay,

The yeas and nays being desired by one-fifth of the Senators present,

15 s

Those who voted in the affirmative are,

Messrs. Allison, Berry, Blackburn, Call, Cockrell, Dawes, Frye, Gorman, Hale, Harris, Hawley, Jones of Arkansas, McMillan, Morrill, Proctor, Sawyer, Sherman, Stewart, Teller, Vilas, Voorhees.

Those who voted in the negative are,

Messrs. Blodgett, Brice, Butler, Caffery, Chandler, Coke, Davis, Dolph, Felton, Hansbrough, Hiscock, Hoar, Manderson, Mitchell, Morgan, Paddock, Palmer, Peffer, Pettigrew, Pugh, Quay, Shoup, Turpie, Vance, Vest, Washburn.

So the amendment was not agreed to.

On the question to agree to the following reported amendment, viz: In line 22, page 81, strike out the word "five," and in lieu thereof insert *three*,

It was determined in the negative $\left\{ \begin{array}{l} \text{Yeas} \dots\dots\dots\dots\dots 22 \\ \text{Nays} \dots\dots\dots\dots\dots 30 \end{array} \right.$

On motion by by Mr. Hiscock,

The yeas and nays being desired by one-fifth of the Senators present,

Those who voted in the affirmative are,

Messrs. Allison, Berry, Blackburn, Call, Cullom, Gibson, Gorman, Gray, Hale, Harris, Hawley, Hoar, Hunton, Morrill, Palmer, Proctor, Sawyer, Sherman, Shoup, Teller, Vilas, White.

Those who voted in the negative are,

Messrs. Butler, Caffery, Chandler, Coke, Daniel, Davis, Dolph, Felton, Frye, Hansbrough, Hill, Hiscock, Kyle, McMillan, Manderson, Mitchell, Morgan, Paddock, Peffer, Perkins, Pettigrew, Platt, Power, Pugh, Quay, Ransom, Squire, Stockbridge, Vest, Washburn.

So the amendment was not agreed to.

On the question to agree to the following reported amendment, viz: In line 10, page 82, strike out the word "eight," and in lieu thereof insert *seven*,

It was determined in the negative, $\left\{ \begin{array}{l} \text{Yeas} \dots\dots\dots\dots\dots 21 \\ \text{Nays} \dots\dots\dots\dots\dots 24 \end{array} \right.$

On motion by Mr. Allison,

The yeas and nays being desired by one-fifth of the Senators present,

Those who voted in the affirmative are,

Messrs. Allison, Blackburn, Call, Camden, Cullom, Daniel, Frye, Gibson, Hale, Harris, Hawley, Jones of Arkansas, Palmer, Perkins, Power, Proctor, Sherman, Shoup, Stewart, Vance, Voorhees.

Those who voted in the negative are,

Messrs. Blodgett, Brice, Butler, Caffery, Coke, Felton, George, Gray, Hansbrough, Hiscock, McMillan, Manderson, Mitchell, Morgan, Peffer, Pettigrew, Pugh, Quay, Ransom, Sawyer, Squire, Vest, Washburn, White.

So the amendment was not agreed to.

The reported amendments having been further agreed to in part, and the bill further amended on the motion of Mr. McMillan,

On the question to agree to the amendment reported in lines 21, 22, and 23, page 82, as follows: Strike out the words "one million four hundred and nineteen thousand two hundred and fifty" and in lieu thereof insert *eight hundred and sixty-nine thousand*,

On motion by Mr. Mitchell to amend the amendment by inserting in lieu of the part proposed to be inserted by the committee the words. *one million two hundred and thirty-nine thousand six hundred and fifty-three*.

It was determined in the affirmative, $\left\{ \begin{array}{l} \text{Yeas} \dots\dots\dots\dots\dots 24 \\ \text{Nays} \dots\dots\dots\dots\dots 20 \end{array} \right.$

On motion by Mr. Allison,

The yeas and nays being desired by one-fifth of the Senators present,

Those who voted in the affirmative are,

Messrs. Butler, Chandler, Coke, Davis, Dolph, Frye, Hansbrough, Hiscock, Hoar, Kyle, Manderson, Mitchell, Paddock, Peffer, Pettigrew, Platt, Pugh, Quay, Sawyer, Shoup, Squire, Stockbridge, Teller, Washburn.

Those who voted in the negative are,

Messrs. Allison, Berry, Blackburn, Caffery, Call, Cockrell, Dawes, Gorman, Hale, Harris, Hawley, Hunton, Morrill, Proctor, Sherman, Stewart, Turpie, Vest, Vilas, Voorhees.

So the amendment to the amendment was agreed to; and

The amendment as amended was agreed to.

On the question to agree to the amendment reported in line 9, page 83, as follows: Strike out the words "five hundred," and in lieu thereof insert *four hundred and fifty*,

It was determined in the negative, $\left\{ \begin{array}{l} \text{Yeas} \dots\dots\dots\dots\dots 18 \\ \text{Nays} \dots\dots\dots\dots\dots 26 \end{array} \right.$

On motion by Mr. Pugh,

The yeas and nays being desired by one-fifth of the Senators present,

Those who voted in the affirmative are,

Messrs. Allison, Berry, Blackburn, Chandler, Cockrell, Cullom, Dawes, Gorman, Gray, Harris, Hawley, Morrill, Paddock, Perkins, Sherman, Shoup, Stewart, Voorhees.

Those who voted in the negative are,

Messrs. Brice, Butler, Caffery, Coke, Daniel, Dolph, Frye, George, Hansbrough, Hiscock, Hunton, Manderson, Mitchell, Morgan, Peffer, Pettigrew, Platt, Pugh, Quay, Ransom, Sawyer, Vest, Washburn, White.

So the amendment was not agreed to.

The reported amendments having been further agreed to in part, and in part disagreed to, and the bill further amended on motion of Mr. Vest,

On the question to agree to the amendment reported in line 14, page 99,

Pending debate,

On motion by Mr. Harris, at 6 o'clock and 7 minutes p. m., The Senate adjourned until 12 o'clock m. to-morrow.

FRIDAY, FEBRUARY 17, 1893.

MESSAGE FROM THE PRESIDENT.

The following message was received from the President of the United States, by Mr. Pruden, his secretary:

To the Senate:

I transmit herewith a letter from the Secretary of State of the 15th instant, covering a report, with accompanying correspondence, respecting relations between the United States and the Hawaiian Islands, from September, 1820, to January, 1893.

BENJ. HARRISON.

EXECUTIVE MANSION,
Washington, February 16, 1893.

The message was read.

Ordered, That it be referred to the Committee on Foreign Relations and printed.

ASSIGNMENTS BY DEBTORS IN THE DISTRICT.

The bill (H. R. 10236) relative to voluntary assignments by debtors for the benefit of creditors in the District of Columbia, and to amend section 782 of the Revised Statues of the United States relating to the District of Columbia, received from the House of Representatives for concurrence on the 13th instant, was read the first and second times by unanimous consent and considered as in Committee of the Whole; and no amendment being made, it was reported to the Senate.

Ordered, That it pass to a third reading.

The said bill was read the third time by unanimous consent.

Resolved, That it pass.

Ordered, That the Secretary notify the House of Representatives thereof.

The Senate proceeded to consider, as in Committee of the Whole, the bill (S. 3768) relative to voluntary assignments by debtors for the benefit of creditors in the District of Columbia, and to amend section 782 of the Revised Statutes of the United States, relating to the District of Columbia; and

Ordered, That it be postponed indefinitely.

EXECUTIVE COMMUNICATION.

The Vice-President laid before the Senate a letter of the Secretary of the Treasury, communicating, in answer to a resolution of the Senate of the 13th instant, information relative to the alleged unsafe condition of the Busch Building, occupied by the Money-Order Division of the Sixth Auditor's Office; which was referred to the Committee on Appropriations and ordered to be printed.

PETITIONS AND MEMORIALS.

Petitions, memorials, etc., were presented and referred as follows:

By the Vice-President: Resolutions of the Pennsylvania Sabbath Convention, remonstrating against the opening of the Columbian Exposition on the Sabbath day; to the Select Committee on the Quadro-Centennial.

By Mr. Cullom: Six petitions of citizens of Illinois, praying for the appointment of a committee to investigate an alleged combine formed to depreciate the price of grain by the millers and others at St. Louis and Minneapolis; to the Committee on Agriculture and Forestry.

By Mr. Hoar: A petition of citizens of Massachusetts, praying the repeal of the so-called Chinese exclusion act; to the Committee on Foreign Relations.

By Mr. Teller: A petition of the Woman's Christian Temperance Union of the District of Columbia, praying that no exceptions in the liquor license bill be made in favor of incorporated clubs in the District of Columbia; to the Committee on the District of Columbia.

By Mr. Platt: A petition of citizens of Connecticut, praying the passage of a law to prohibit the importation, manufacture, and sale of cigarettes; to the Committee on Finance.

By Mr. Perkins: A resolution of the legislature of Kansas in favor of the passage of a law granting a service pension to the soldiers of the late war; to the Committee on Pensions.

By Mr. Vest: A petition of citizens of the Cherokee Nation, praying the passage of a law for the admission into the Union of the Territory of Oklahoma, and for a survey and allotment of lands in severalty in accordance with the treaty of 1866; to the Committee on Indian Affairs.

By Mr. McPherson: A petition of William Farr Goodwin, praying an extension of his patent for an improvement in railway tracks and trucks; to the Committee on Patents, to accompany the bill S. 3875.

By Mr. Paddock: Several petitions of citizens of the United

States, praying an appropriation for the continuance of the investigation for continuing tests of American timber and the speedy publication of the results; to the Committee on Appropriations, to accompany an amendment intended to be proposed to the agricultural appropriation bill, H. R. 10421.

By Mr. Quay: A resolution of the Pennsylvania Sabbath Convention, remonstrating against the opening of the Columbian Exposition on the Sabbath day; to the Select Committee on the Quadro-Centennial.

Petitions praying the repeal of the law providing for the purchase of silver bullion were presented as follows:

By Mr. Platt: A petition of citizens of Connecticut.

By Mr. Hiscock: A petition of merchants and manufacturers of New York.

Ordered, That they lie on the table.

Mr. Stewart presented a resolution of the legislature of Nevada in favor of the passage of the bill for the construction of the Nicaragua Canal.

Ordered, That it lie on the table.

REPORTS OF COMMITTEES.

Mr. Hunton, from the Committee on the District of Columbia, to whom was referred the bill (H. R. 10489) to amend the act of May 6, 1890, fixing the rate of interest to be charged on arrearages of general and special taxes now due the District of Columbia, and for other purposes, reported it without amendment.

The Senate proceeded, by unanimous consent, to consider the said bill as in Committee of the Whole; and no amendment being made, it was reported to the Senate.

Ordered, That it pass to a third reading.

The said bill was read the third time.

Resolved, That it pass.

Ordered, That the Secretary notify the House of Representatives thereof.

Mr. Frye, from the Committee on Commerce, to whom was referred the bill (H. R. 10391) to amend an act entitled "An act to provide for the establishment of a port of delivery at Council Bluffs, Iowa," reported it without amendment.

The Senate proceeded, by unanimous consent, to consider the said bill as in Committee of the Whole; and no amendment being made, it was reported to the Senate.

Ordered, That it pass to a third reading.

The said bill was read the third time.

Resolved, That it pass.

Ordered, That the Secretary notify the House of Representatives thereof.

Mr. Pettigrew, from the Select Committee on the Quadro-Centennial, to whom was referred the joint resolution (S. R. 148) authorizing the Secretary of the Smithsonian Institution to send articles illustrative of the life and development of the industries of women to the World's Columbian Exposition, reported it without amendment.

The Senate proceeded, by unanimous consent, to consider the said resolution as in Committee of the Whole; and no amendment being made, it was reported to the Senate.

Ordered, That it be engrossed and read a third time.

The said resolution was read the third time.

Resolved, That it pass, and that the title thereof be as aforesaid.

Ordered, That the Secretary request the concurrence of the House of Representatives therein.

Mr. Voorhees, from the Committee on the Library, to whom was referred the joint resolution (S. R. 146) for the restoration of the books of the Beaufort Library Society, of Beaufort, S. C., reported it without amendment, and submitted a report (No. 1302) thereon.

MESSAGE FROM THE HOUSE.

A message from the House of Representatives, by Mr. Towles, its chief clerk:

Mr. President: The House of Representatives insists upon its amendment to the bill (S. 2931) to provide for the survey and transfer of that part of the Fort Randall military reservation in the State of Nebraska to said State for school and other purposes. It agrees to the conference asked by the Senate on the disagreeing votes of the two Houses thereon, and has appointed Mr. McRae, Mr. Amerman, and Mr. Clark, of Wyoming, managers at the same on its part.

The House of Representatives has passed, without amendment, the following bills of the Senate:

S. 3629. An act to extend to the North Pacific Ocean the provisions of the statutes for the protection of fur seals and other fur-bearing animals; and

S. 3857. An act authorizing the construction of a bridge over the Monongahela River at the foot of Main street, in the borough of Belle Vernon, in the State of Pennsylvania.

The Speaker of the House of Representatives having signed four enrolled bills, S. 1303, S. 2828, S. 3819, and H. R. 10241, I am directed to bring the same to the Senate for the signature of its President.

ENROLLED BILLS SIGNED.

Mr. Dubois reported from the committee that they had examined and found duly enrolled the following bills:

S. 1303. An act to increase the pension of Mrs. S. A. Farquharson;

S. 2828. An act for the relief of L. M. Garrett;
S. 3819. An act granting a pension to Mary Doubleday, widow of Bvt. Maj. Gen. Abner Doubleday; and
H. R. 10241. An act to amend "An act making appropriations for the construction, repair, and preservation of certain public works on rivers and harbors, and for other purposes," approved July 13, 1892;
Whereupon,
The Vice-President signed the same, and they were delivered to the committee to be presented to the President of the United States.

VACANCY IN COMMITTEE FILLED.

On motion by Mr. Gorman,
Ordered, That the vacancy in the Select Committee on Indian Depredations, occasioned by the resignation of Mr. Carlisle, be filled by the Vice-President; and
The Vice-President appointed Mr. White.

INTRODUCTION OF BILLS AND JOINT RESOLUTIONS.

Bills and a joint resolution were introduced, read the first and second times by unanimous consent, and referred as follows:
By Mr. McPherson: A bill (S. 3875) to extend the patent granted to William Farr Goodwin, for an improvement in railway tracks and trucks; to the Committee on Patents.
By Mr. Vest: A bill (S, 3876) authorizing the St. Louis and Madison Transfer Company to construct a bridge over the Mississippi River; to the Committee on Commerce.
By Mr. Palmer: A bill (S. 3877) authorizing the construction of a bridge over the Mississippi River to the city of St. Louis, in the State of Missouri, from some suitable point between the north line of St. Clair County, State of Illinois, and the southwest line of said county; to the Committee on Commerce.
By Mr. Chandler. A joint resolution (S. R. 156) for the appointment of an immigration commission; to the Committee on Immigration.

WRECKING PRIVILEGES ON THE GREAT LAKES.

Mr. McMillan submitted the following resolution; which was referred to the Committee on Foreign Relations:
Resolved, That t e Secretary of State be requested, if not inconsistent with the public interests, to inform the Senate in regard to the present status of the arrangements to provide for reciprocal wrecking privileges to be enjoyed by the citizens of the United States and of the Dominion of Canada on the Great Lakes and their connecting waters, under the laws already enacted by the respective governments.

REPORT ON ROCK CREEK SEWER.

Mr. McMillan submitted the following resolution; which was referred to the Committee on Printing:
Resolved, That of the report of the Engineer Commissioner of the District of Columbia submitting estimates of the cost of converting Rock Creek into a closed sewer, being Senate Mis. Doc. No. 21, Fifty-second Congress, second session, 500 additional copies be printed, 250 of which shall be for the use of the Senate and 250 for the use of the Commissioners of the District of Columbia.

MESSAGE FROM THE HOUSE.

A message from the House of Representatives, by Mr. Towles, its chief clerk:
Mr. President: The House of Representatives has passed a bill (H. R. 10345) making appropriations for the payment of invalid and other pensions of the United States for the fiscal year ending June 30, 1894, and for other purposes, in which it requests the concurrence of the Senate.
The Speaker of the House of Representatives having signed three enrolled bills, H. R. 10236, H. R. 10391, and H. R. 10489, I am directed to bring them to the Senate for the signature of its President.

ENROLLED BILLS SIGNED.

Mr. Dubois reported from the committee that they had examined and found duly enrolled the following bills:
H. R. 10236. An act relative to voluntary assignments by debtors for the benefit of creditors in the District of Columbia, and to amend section 782 of the Revised Statutes of the United States relating to the District of Columbia;
H. R. 10489. An act to amend the act of May 6, 1890, fixing the rate of interest to be charged on arrearages of general and special taxes now due the District of Columbia, and for other purposes; and
H. R. 10391. An act to amend an act entitled "An act to provide for the establishment of a port of delivery at Council Bluffs, Iowa;"
Whereupon,
The Vice-President signed the same, and they were delivered to the committee to be presented to the President of the United States.

HOUSE BILL REFERRED.

The bill H. R. 10345, last received from the House of Representatives for concurrence, was read the first and second times by unanimous consent, and referred to the Committee on Appropriations.

SUNDRY CIVIL APPROPRIATION BILL.

On motion by Mr. Allison,
The Senate resumed, as in Committee of the Whole, the consideration of the bill (H. R. 10238) making appropriations for sundry civil expenses of the Government for the fiscal year ending June 30, 1894, and for other purposes; and

The question being on the amendment reported in line 14, page 15, viz: Strike out the words "or the laws relating to the election of members of Congress,"
It was determined in the affirmative, { Yeas .... 27 / Nays 24
On motion by Mr. Allison,
The yeas and nays being desired by one-fifth of the Senators present,
Those who voted in the affirmative are,
Messrs. Allison, Cullom, Davis, Dolph, Felton, Frye, Hale, Hansbrough, Hawley, Higgins, Hiscock, Hoar, McMillan, Manderson, Morrill, Paddock, Perkins, Pettigrew, Platt, Power, Quay, Sawyer, Sherman, Shoup, Stewart, Stockbridge, Washburn.
Those who voted in the negative are,
Messrs. Blackburn, Brice, Caffery, Call, Camden, Coke, George, Gibson, Gorman, Gray, Harris, Hunton, Jones of Arkansas, Kyle, McPherson, Palmer, Peffer, Pugh, Ransom, Turpie, Vance, Vest, Vilas, White.
So the amendment was agreed to.

EXECUTIVE SESSION.

On motion by Mr. Sherman,
The Senate proceeded to the consideration of executive business; and
After the consideration of executive business the doors were reopened;
When,

SUNDRY CIVIL APPROPRIATION BILL.

The Senate resumed, as in Committee of the Whole, the consideration of the bill H. R. 10238; and having been further amended on the motion of Mr. Allison, from the Committee on Appropriations, the motion of Mr. Hoar, and the motion of Mr. Quay,
On motion by Mr. Sherman, from the Committee on Finance, to further amend the bill by inserting after line 24, page 41, the following:
To enable the Secretary of the Treasury to provide for and to maintain the redemption of United States notes according to the provisions of the act approved January fourteenth, eighteen hundred and seventy-five, entitled "An act to provide for the resumption of specie payments," fifty thousand dollars; and, at the discretion of the Secretary, he is authorized to issue, sell, and dispose of, at not less than par in coin, either of the description of bonds authorized in said act, or bonds of the United States bearing not to exceed three per centum interest, payable semiannually and redeemable at the pleasure of the United States after five years from their date with like qualities, privileges, and exemptions provided in said act for the bonds therein authorized, to the extent necessary to carry said resumption act into full effect, and to use the proceeds thereof for the purposes provided in said act and none other,
Mr. Stewart raised the question of order, viz: that the amendment proposed general legislation to a general appropriation bill and was not in order under Rule XVI.
The Vice-President overruled the question of order and decided that the amendment made an appropriation to carry out existing law, limited the authority of the Secretary of the Treasury under existing law, and did not in the opinion of the Chair propose new legislation.
From the decision of the Chair Mr. Stewart appealed to the Senate; and
On the question, Shall the decision of the Chair stand as the judgment of the Senate?
On motion by Mr. Hoar, that the appeal lie on the table,
It was determined in the affirmative, { Yeas .... 28 / Nays 18
On motion by Mr. Hale,
The yeas and nays being desired by one-fifth of the Senators present,
Those who voted in the affirmative are,
Messrs. Allison, Brice, Butler, Caffery, Camden, Cullom, Felton, Frye, Gorman, Hale, Hawley, Higgins, Hiscock, Hoar, Jones of Arkansas, McMillan, McPherson, Morrill, Paddock, Palmer, Pasco, Ransom, Sawyer, Sherman, Stockbridge, Vilas, Voorhees, Washburn.
Those who voted in the negative are,
Messrs. Bate, Blackburn, Call, Cockrell, Coke, Dolph, George, Kyle, Mitchell, Peffer, Pettigrew, Power, Pugh, Shoup, Stewart, Teller, Vance, Wolcott.
So the appeal was laid on the table.
The question recurring on the amendment proposed by Mr. Sherman,
The Vice-President announced that the hour of 2 o'clock had arrived, and laid before the Senate the unfinished business, viz, the bill (S. 1218) to amend the act entitled "An act to incorporate the Maritime Canal Company of Nicaragua," approved February 20, 1889.
When,
On motion by Mr. Allison, that the Senate proceed with the consideration of the bill (H. R. 10238) making appropriations for sundry civil expenses of the Government for the fiscal year ending June 30, 1894, and for other purposes,
It was determined in the affirmative; and
The Senate resumed, as in Committee of the Whole, the consideration of the bill; and
The question being on the amendment proposed by Mr. Sherman, from the Committee on Finance,

On motion by Mr. Mills to amend the amendment,
Pending debate,
On motion by Mr. Allison, at 5 o'clock and 45 minutes p. m.,
The Senate adjourned.

SATURDAY, FEBRUARY 18, 1893.

MESSAGE FROM THE HOUSE.

A message from the House of Representatives, by Mr. Towles, its chief clerk:
Mr. President: The House of Representatives has passed, without amendment, the bill (S. 3811) to amend an act entitled "An act to grant to the Mobile and Dauphin Island Railroad and Harbor Company the right to trestle across the shoal water between Cedar Point and Dauphin Islands," approved September 26, 1890,
The House of Representatives has passed a bill (H. R. 8736) for the relief of the Shibley and Wood Grocer Company, of Van Buren, Crawford County, Arkansas, in which it requests the concurrence of the Senate.

HOUSE BILL REFERRED.

The bill H. R. 8736, last received from the House of Representatives for concurrence, was read the first and second times by unanimous consent and referred to the Committee on Finance.

EXECUTIVE COMMUNICATION.

The Vice-President laid before the Senate a letter of the Secretary of the Treasury, recommending an appropriation of $75,000 for furniture and repairs of furniture for public buildings; which was referred to the Committee on Appropriations and ordered to be printed.

PETITIONS AND MEMORIALS.

Petitions, memorials, etc., were presented and referred as follows:
By Mr. Paddock: A petition of Pierce & Bickford, architects, Elmira, N. Y., praying an appropriation of $40,000 for continuing the tests of American lumber; to the Committee on Appropriations.
A memorial of the city council of Oklahoma City, praying the passage of a law donating the Oklahoma military reservation to that city for school purposes; to the Committee on Military Affairs.
A resolution of the Trades League of Philadelphia, Pa., praying for more adequate postal facilities in the larger cities of the country; to the Committee on Post-Offices and Post-Roads.
A memorial of the Democratic and Republican Territorial Central Committees of Arizona, praying the passage of a law for the admission of that Territory into the Union as a State; to the Committee on Territories.
A petition of citizens of Nebraska, praying for the appointment of a committee to investigate an alleged combine formed to depreciate the price of grain by the millers and others at St. Louis and Minneapolis; to the Committee on Agriculture and Forestry.
By Mr. Quay: Two petitions of citizens of Pennsylvania, praying the passage of a law for the restriction of immigration into the United States; to the Committee on Immigration.
A petition of citizens of Pennsylvania, praying for the establishment of a permanent census bureau, and for the collection and publication of statistics relating to farm mortages; to the Committee on the Census.
By Mr. Stockbridge: A petition of citizens of Michigan, praying the passage of a law to prohibit the sale of intoxicating liquors on the grounds of the Columbian Exposition; to the Select Committee on the Quadro-Centennial.
Petitions praying the repeal of the provision providing for the closing of the Columbian Exposition on the Sabbath day were presented as follows:
By Mr. Paddock: A petition of citizens of Nebraska.
By Mr. Mills: A petition of citizens of Texas.
By Mr. Perkins: A petition of citizens of Kansas.
By Mr. Mitchell: A petition of citizens of Oregon.
By Mr. Stockbridge: A petition of citizens of Michigan.
By Mr. Sherman: A petition of citizens of Ohio.
Ordered, That they be referred to the Select Committee on the Quadro-Centennial.
Memorials remonstrating against the repeal of the provision providing for the closing of the Columbian Exposition on the Sabbath day were presented as follows:
By Mr. Quay: Several memorials of citizens of Pennsylvania.
By Mr. Paddock: Several memorials of citizens of Nebraska.
By Mr. Higgins: A memorial of citizens of Delaware.
Ordered, That they be referred to the Select Committee on the Quadro-Centennial.
Mr. Paddock presented a memorial of the New York Lumber Trade Association, praying the passage of the Nicaragua Canal bill.
Ordered, That it lie on the table.
Mr. Felton presented a resolution of the Chamber of Commerce of Salt Lake City, Utah, praying for the construction of a deep-water harbor at San Pedro, Cal.; which was referred to the Committee on Commerce.

Mr. Felton presented a resolution of the Chamber of Commerce of Salt Lake City, Utah, praying for the annexation of the Hawaiian Islands to the United States; which was referred to the Committee on Foreign Relations.
Mr. Hawley presented a petition of citizens of Connecticut, praying the repeal of the law providing for the purchase of silver bullion.
Ordered, That it lie on the table.

MESSAGE FROM THE HOUSE.

A message from the House of Representatives, by Mr. Towles, its chief clerk:
Mr. President: The House of Representatives has passed the bill (S. 1232) removing charge of desertion against Lucius W. Hayford, Worcester, Vt., with amendments, in which it requests the concurrence of the Senate.
The House of Representatives has passed the following bills, in which it requests the concurrence of the Senate:
H. R. 9564. An act to regulate the terms of the circuit and district courts of the United States in the district of Kentucky, and for other purposes; and
H. R. 10484. An act to amend an act approved July 27, 1892, entitled "An act to provide for the improvement of the outer bar of Brunswick, Ga."
The Speaker of the House of Representatives having signed three enrolled bills, S. 3629, S. 3811, and S. 3857, I am directed to bring them to the Senate for the signature of its President.

HOUSE BILLS REFERRED.

The bills last received from the House of Representatives for concurrence were read the first and second times by unanimous consent.
Ordered, That the bill H. R. 9564 be referred to the Committee on the Judiciary, and that the bill H. R. 10484 be referred to the Committee on Commerce.

REPORTS OF COMMITTEES.

Mr. Harris, from the Committee on the District of Columbia, to whom was referred the bill (H. R. 9956) to incorporate the Washington, Burnt Mills and Sandy Springs Railway Company, reported it with amendments and submitted a report (No. 1304) thereon.
Mr. Sawyer, from the Committee on Pensions, to whom was referred the bill (H. R. 7729) granting a pension to Mrs. Phebe Sigler, reported it without amendment and submitted a report (No. 1305) thereon.
Mr. Vest, from the Committee on Commerce, to whom were referred the following bills, reported them severally without amendment:
S. 3876. A bill authorizing the St. Louis and Madison Transfer Company to construct a bridge over the Mississippi River;
S. 3634. A bill authorizing Rockport and Harbor Island Suburban Railroad to construct a bridge across the Corpus Christi channel, known as the Morris and Cummings Ship Channel, near its entrance into Aransas Bay, in Aransas County, Texas; and
H. R. 10280. An act to authorize the construction of a bridge over the Tennessee River at or near Sheffield, Ala.
Mr. Manderson, from the Committee on Printing, to whom was referred the resolution submitted by him on the 10th instant, to print 9,000 copies of the annual report of the Chief of the Weather Bureau, reported it with amendments and submitted a report (No. 1303) thereon.
The Senate proceeded, by unanimous consent, to consider the said resolution; and the reported amendments having been agreed to, the resolution as amended was agreed to, as follows:
Resolved by the Senate (the House of Representatives concurring), That there be printed in quarto form of the annual report of the Chief of the Weather Bureau, with appendices, 5,500 copies, of which 1,000 copies shall be for the use of the Senate, and 2,000 copies for the use of the House of Representatives, and 2,500 copies for the use of the Weather Bureau.
Ordered, That the Secretary request the concurrence of the House of Representatives therein.
Mr. Harris, from the Committee on the District of Columbia, to whom were referred the following bills, reported adversely thereon:
S. 3343. A bill to amend the act to incorporate the Washington and Sandy Springs Narrow Gauge Railroad Company; and
S. 3655. A bill to incorporate the Washington, Burnt Mills and Sandy Springs Railway Company.
Ordered, That they be postponed indefinitely.
Mr. Sawyer, from the Committee on Pensions, to whom was referred the bill (H. R. 8498) to pension Sophia Kagwaich, reported it without amendment and submitted a report (No. 1306) thereon.
Mr. Mitchell, from the Committee on Claims, to whom was referred the bill (S. 728) for the relief of William A. Starkweather, of Oregon, reported it with amendments and submitted a report (No. 1307) thereon.
Mr. Jones, of Arkansas, from the Committee on Indian Affairs, to whom was referred the bill (S. 3873) to authorize the Kansas City, Pittsburg and Gulf Railroad Company to construct and operate a

railroad, telegraph, and telephone line through the Indian Territory, and for other purposes, reported it with amendments.

Mr. Dawes, from the Committee on Appropriations, to whom was referred the bill (H. R. 10831) making appropriations for the legislative, executive, and judicial expenses of the Government for the fiscal year ending June 30, 1894, and for other purposes, reported it with amendments and submitted a report (No. 1308) thereon.

Mr. Vest, from the Committee on Commerce, to whom was referred the bill (S. 3871) to authorize the construction of a bridge across the Calumet River, reported it with an amendment.

Mr. Proctor, from the Committee on Military Affairs, to whom was referred the bill (H. R. 8450) to remove the charge of desertion from the record of Charles G. Fyer, reported it without amendment and submitted a report (No. 1309) thereon.

Mr. Stewart, from the Committee on Mines and Mining, who were instructed by a resolution of the Senate of July 12, 1892, to investigate and report the average cost of the production of gold and silver bullion in the United States, submitted a report (No. 1310).

INTRODUCTION OF JOINT RESOLUTION.

Mr. Hawley introduced a joint resolution (S. R. 157) authorizing the Secretary of War to receive for instruction at the Military Academy at West Point, Albert Guirola, of Salvador; which was read the first and second times by unanimous consent and referred to the Committee on Military Affairs.

REPORT OF COMMISSIONER OF EDUCATION.

Mr. Manderson submitted the following concurrent resolution; which was referred to the Committee on Printing:

Be it resolved by the United States Senate (the House of Representatives concurring), That of the annual report of the Commissioner of Education for 1890-'91 there be printed 5,000 copies for the use of the Senate, 10,000 for the use of the House of Representatives, and 20,000 copies for distribution by the Commissioner.

REPORT ON LAW EDUCATION.

Mr. Higgins submitted the following resolution; which was referred to the Committee on Printing:

Resolved by the Senate, That there be printed for the use of the Senate 5,500 copies of the report of the Bureau of Education on law education.

BATH-HOUSE SITE AT HOT SPRINGS.

Mr. Jones, of Arkansas, submitted the following concurrent resolution; which was considered by unanimous consent and agreed to:

Resolved by the Senate (the House of Representatives concurring), That the Secretary of the Interior be, and he is hereby, directed to take no further steps looking to the lease of the Big Iron bath-house site at Hot Springs, Ark., until Congress shall have acted upon Senate bill 3822.

Ordered, That the Secretary request the concurrence of the House of Representatives therein.

CONFERENCE REPORT.

Mr. Mitchell, from the committee of conference on the disagreeing votes of the two Houses on the amendments of the Senate to the bill H. R. 1036, submitted the following report:

The committee of conference on the disagreeing votes of the two Houses on the amendments of the Senate to the bill (H. R. 1036) for the benefit of Logan, Simpson, Hardin, and Hart counties, and the city of Louisville, Ky., and Sumner and Davidson counties, Tennessee, having met, after full and free conference have agreed to recommend and do recommend to their respective Houses as follows:

That the House recede from its disagreement to the amendment of the Senate numbered 1, and agree to the same with amendments as follows:

First amendment: In line 10, page 1, strike out the word "State."

Second amendment: In line 12, page 1, after the word "Company," insert the following: and of said State for internal-revenue taxes collected and interest on railroad bonds of the railroad from Louisville to Lexington, and on dividends on stock of said railroads owned by said State.

Third amendment: In line 15, page 1, after the word "dividends," insert the words or interest.

And the Senate agree to the same.

That the House recede from its disagreement to the amendment of the Senate amending the title of the bill, and agree to the same.

JOHN H. MITCHELL,
W. A. PEFFER,
WILLIAM F. VILAS,
Managers on the part of the Senate.
B. H. BUNN,
N. N. COX,
J. M. WEVER,
Managers on the part of the House.

The Senate proceeded to consider the said report; and
On motion by Mr. Mitchell,
Resolved, That the Senate agree thereto.

Ordered, That the Secretary notify the House of Representatives thereof.

RIGHT OF WAY THROUGH INDIAN TERRITORY.

The Senate proceeded to consider, as in Committee of the Whole, the following bills; and the reported amendments having been agreed to, the bills were reported to the Senate and the amendments were concurred in:

S. 3602. A bill to grant to the Chicago, Rock Island and Pacific Railway Company a right of way through the Indian Territory, and for other purposes; and

S. 3873. A bill to authorize the Kansas City, Pittsburg and Gulf Railroad Company to construct and operate a railroad, telegraph, and telephone line through the Indian Territory, and for other purposes.

Ordered, That they be engrossed and read a third time.

The said bills were read the third time.

Resolved, That they pass, and that the respective titles thereof be as aforesaid.

Ordered, That the Secretary request the concurrence of the House of Representatives therein.

LUCIUS W. HAYFORD.

The Senate proceeded to consider the amendments of the House of Representatives to the bill (S. 1232) removing charge of desertion against Lucius W. Hayford, Worcester, Vt.; and

On motion by Mr. Proctor,

Resolved, That the Senate agree thereto.

Ordered, That the Secretary notify the House of Representatives thereof.

ENROLLED BILLS SIGNED.

Mr. Dubois reported from the committee that they had examined and found duly enrolled the following bills:

S. 3629. An act to extend to the North Pacific Ocean the provisions of the statutes for the protection of fur-seals and other fur-bearing animals;

S. 3811. An act to amend an act entitled "An act to grant to the Mobile and Dauphin Island Railroad and Harbor Company the right to trestle across the shoal water between Cedar Point and Dauphin Point," approved September 26, 1890; and

S. 3857. An act authorizing the construction of a bridge across the Monongahela River at the foot of Main street, in the borough of Belle Vernon, in the State of Pennsylvania;

Whereupon,

The Vice-President signed the same, and they were delivered to the committee to be presented to the President of the United States.

MESSAGE FROM THE HOUSE.

A message from the House of Representatives, by Mr. Towles, its chief clerk:

Mr. President: The House of Representatives has agreed to the report of the committee of conference on the disagreeing votes of the two Houses on the amendments of the Senate to the following bills of the House:

H. R. 1036. An act for the benefit of Logan, Simpson, Hardin, and Hart counties, and of the city of Louisville, Ky., and of Sumner and Davidson counties, Tennessee; and

H. R. 9286. An act to create the California Débris Commission and regulate hydraulic mining in the State of California.

The President of the United States has informed the House of Representatives that he has approved and signed acts and a joint resolution as follows:

On February 2, 1893:

H. R. 5597. An act for the relief of William Smith and others.

On February 3, 1893:

H. R. 5049. An act to amend the military record of Lucius L. Dyer;

H. R. 10062. An act to authorize the construction of a bridge across the Osage River, between the mouths of Pomme de Terre River and Buffalo Creek, in Benton County, Missouri;

H. R. 10189. An act relating to proof of citizenship of applicants for Indian war pensions under the act of Congress approved July 27, 1892; and

H. R. 10007. An act to provide for lowering the height of a bridge proposed to be constructed across the Ohio River between Cincinnati, Ohio, and Covington, Ky., by the Cincinnati and Covington Rapid Transit Bridge Company.

On February 6, 1893:

H. R. 8956. An act establishing a fog signal at Tibbets Point, Lake Ontario, New York.

On February 7, 1893:

H. R. 8602. An act to authorize the construction of a bridge across the Mobile River by the Chicago, Mobile and Gulf Ports Railroad Company;

H. R. 10063. An act to amend "an act authorizing the construction of a high wagon bridge across the Missouri River at or near Sioux City, Iowa," etc.; and

H. R. 5752. An act to amend an act approved August 6, 1888, entitled "An act to authorize the construction of a bridge across the Alabama River."

On February 8, 1893:

H. R. 1795. An act to increase the pension of A. J. Copenhaver, late a soldier in the Mexican war;

H. R. 5012. An act to increase the pension of Thomas Enloe; and

H. R. 9433. An act granting a pension to Mrs. Ann Mercer Slaughter.

On February 15, 1893:

H. R. 9757. An act granting additional quarantine powers and imposing additional duties upon the Marine-Hospital Service;

H. R. 9955. An act providing for sundry light-houses and other aids to navigation;

H. R. 7625. An act for the relief of certain settlers on public land in the Tucson land district in Arizona;

H. R. 9786. An act authorizing the construction of a bridge over the Monongahela River at West Elizabeth, in the State of Pennsylvania;

H. R. 2427. An act granting a pension to Margaret Byron;

H. R. 2493. An act granting a pension to Jesse Cleaveland;

H. R. 6914. An act granting a pension to Druke Nettie Barnett;

H. R. 8221. An act granting a pension to George W. Boyd;

H. R. 8784. An act granting a pension to Edward Smitherman;

H. R. 8924. An act granting a pension to the widow of James A. Kelly;

H. R. 9585. An act for the relief of Harriett E. Niles;

H. R. 8298. An act to pension Emma Johnson, blind and dependent daughter of Daniel D. Johnson, Company B, One hundred and forty-second New York Volunteers;

H. R. 8969. An act to grant a pension to Lydia Bollman, a dependent sister;

H. R. 9011. An act to grant a pension to Ida A. Taylor;

H. R. 8780. An act to restore to the pension roll Mary Eleanor White, a former widow of Capt. George W. Hazzard;

H. R. 8054. An act to increase the pension of Mary L. Bacon, widow of the late George D. Bacon, late lieutenant-commander of the United States Navy;

H. R. 3845. An act to increase the pension of Edward R. Chapman;

H. R. 3713. An act for increase of pension of Frances P. Gardener. ; and

H. R. 204. Joint resolution providing for additional telegraphic and electric-light facilities in the city of Washington during the inaugural ceremonies on the 4th day of March, 1893.

The bill (H. R. 8038) granting a pension to William M. Watson, of Georgia, having been presented to the President January 20, 1893, and not having been returned by him to the House of Congress in which it originated within the ten days prescribed by the Constitution, has become a law without his approval.

SUNDRY CIVIL APPROPRIATION BILL.

On motion by Mr. Allison,

The Senate resumed, as in Committee of the Whole, the consideration of the bill (H. R. 10238) making appropriations for sundry civil expenses of the Government for the fiscal year ending June 30, 1894, and for other purposes; and

The question being on the amendment submitted by Mr. Mills to the amendment proposed by Mr. Sherman, from the Committee on Finance,

After debate,

It was determined in the negative.

On motion by Mr. Stewart to amend the amendment of Mr. Sherman by adding thereto the following:

And the bonds issued under the provisions of this act shall not be used as security for the issuance of national-bank currency,

It was determined in the negative, { Yeas 21
                                      { Nays 32

On motion by Mr. George,

The yeas and nays being desired by one-fifth of the Senators present, Those who voted in the affirmative are,

Messrs. Bate, Blackburn, Call, Cockrell, Coke, Daniel, Hunton, Kyle, Mitchell, Morgan, Paddock, Peffer, Perkins, Power, Pugh, Ransom, Stewart, Teller, Vance, Vest, Wolcott.

Those who voted in the negative are,

Messrs. Allison, Brice, Carey, Chandler, Cullom, Davis, Dawes, Felton, Frye, Gibson, Gorman, Gray, Hale, Hansbrough, Hawley, Higgins, Hiscock, Hoar, McMillan, McPherson, Manderson, Morrill, Palmer, Platt, Proctor, Sawyer, Sherman, Squire, Stockbridge, Vilas, Voorhees, Washburn.

So the amendment to the amendment was not agreed to.

On motion by Mr. Pugh to amend the amendment of Mr. Sherman by adding thereto the following proviso:

Provided, That no bonds authorized to be issued and sold under this act shall be issued and sold by the Secretary of the Treasury until the amount of the coin redemption fund reserved in the Treasury under existing law shall be reduced to twenty-five million dollars by the actual redemption of the Treasury notes authorized to be redeemed under the act hereby amended; and in the event of such reduction to twenty-five million dollars in coin, no greater amount of said bonds shall be issued

and sold under this act than is necessary to keep said redemption fund equal to fifty million dollars in coin,

It was determined in the negative, { Yeas 21
                                    { Nays 31

On motion by Mr. Pugh,

The yeas and nays being desired by one-fifth of the Senators present, Those who voted in the affirmative are,

Messrs. Bate, Blackburn, Call, Cockrell, Coke, Daniel, Harris, Hunton, Kyle, Mitchell, Morgan, Peffer, Power, Pugh, Stewart, Teller, Turpie, Vance, Vest, Voorhees, Wolcott.

Those who voted in the negative are,

Messrs. Allison, Brice, Caffery, Chandler, Cullom, Dawes, Felton, Frye, Gorman, Gray, Hale, Hansbrough, Hawley, Hiscock, Hoar, McMillan, McPherson, Manderson, Morrill, Paddock, Palmer, Perkins, Platt, Proctor, Ransom, Sawyer, Sherman, Squire, Stockbridge, Vilas, Washburn.

So the amendment to the amendment was not agreed to.

On motion by Mr. Vance* to amend the amendment of Mr. Sherman by adding thereto the following proviso:

Provided, That all laws imposing any tax on the circulation of bank notes issued under the authority of any State be and the same are hereby repealed,

On motion by Mr. Gorman, that the amendment to the amendment lie on the table,

It was determined in the affirmative, { Yeas 40
                                       { Nays 16

On motion by Mr. Vance,

The yeas and nays being desired by one-fifth of the Senators present, Those who voted in the affirmative are,

Messrs. Aldrich, Allison, Brice, Chandler, Cullom, Davis, Dawes, Dixon, Felton, Frye, Gorman, Gray, Hale, Hansbrough, Hawley, Higgins, Hiscock, Hoar, Kyle, McMillan, McPherson, Mitchell, Morrill, Paddock, Palmer, Peffer, Perkins, Platt, Power, Proctor, Sawyer, Sherman, Squire, Stewart, Stockbridge, Teller, Vilas, Washburn, White, Wolcott.

Those who voted in the negative are,

Messrs. Bate, Caffery, Call, Coke, Daniel, Faulkner, George, Harris, Hunton, Morgan, Pugh, Ransom, Turpie, Vance, Vest, Voorhees.

So the motion to lay the amendment on the table was agreed to.

A further amendment to the amendment having been proposed by Mr. Brice,

Pending debate,

EXECUTIVE SESSION.

On motion by Mr. Hoar,

The Senate proceeded to the consideration of executive business; and

After the consideration of executive business the doors were reopened;

When,

SUNDRY CIVIL APPROPRIATION BILL.

The Senate resumed, as in Committee of the Whole, the consideration of the bill (H. R. 10238) making appropriations for sundry civil expenses of the Government for the fiscal year ending June 30, 1894, and for other purposes; and

The question being on the amendment proposed by Mr. Brice to the amendment of Mr. Sherman,

After debate,

Mr. Brice withdrew his amendment.

The question recurring on agreeing to the amendment reported by Mr. Sherman, from the Committee on Finance, viz: After line 24, page 41, insert the following:

To enable the Secretary of the Treasury to provide for and to maintain the redemption of United States notes according to the provisions of the act approved January fourteenth, eighteen hundred and seventy-five, entitled "An act to provide for the resumption of specie payments," fifty thousand dollars; and, at the discretion of the Secretary, he is authorized to issue, sell, and dispose of, at not less than par in coin, either of the description of bonds authorized in said act, or bonds of the United States bearing not to exceed three per centum interest, payable semi-annually and redeemable at the pleasure of the United States after five years from their date, with like qualities, privileges, and exemptions provided in said act for the bonds therein authorized, to the extent necessary to carry said resumption act into full effect, and to use the proceeds thereof for the purposes provided in said act and none other,

It was determined in the affirmative, { Yeas 30
                                       { Nays 16

On motion by Mr. Peffer,

The yeas and nays being desired by one-fifth of the Senators present, Those who voted in the affirmative are,

Messrs. Aldrich, Allison, Brice, Caffery, Chandler, Cullom, Davis, Dixon, Felton, Frye, Gorman, Gray, Hale, Hansbrough, Harris, Hawley, Higgins, Hiscock, Hoar, McMillan, McPherson, Morrill, Perkins, Sawyer, Sherman, Stockbridge, Vilas, Voorhees, Washburn, White.

Those who voted in the negative are,

Messrs. Bate, Call, Cockrell, Coke, George, Gordon, Jones of Nevada, Kyle, Mitchell, Peffer, Power, Pugh, Shoup, Stewart, Teller, Vest.

So the amendment was agreed to.

When,

On motion by Mr. Cockrell, at 5 o'clock and 40 minutes p. m., The Senate adjourned.

MONDAY, FEBRUARY 20, 1893.

Mr. Blackburn raised the question as to the presence of a quorum;

Whereupon,

The Vice-President directed the roll to be called;

When,

Forty-four Senators answered to their names.

A quorum being present,

PETITIONS AND MEMORIALS.

Petitions, memorials, etc., were presented and referred as follows:

By the Vice-President: A memorial of the legislature of Oregon in favor of the passage of a law for the payment of the claims of the States of California, Oregon, and Nevada for expenses incurred during the war of the rebellion; to the Committee on Appropriations.

A memorial of J. M. Dalzell, of Caldwell, Ohio, remonstrating against any change in the existing pension laws; to the Committee on Pensions.

A resolution of the National Live Stock Exchange, praying the passage of the bill for the opening of the Cherokee Outlet to settlement; to the Committee on Territories.

By Mr. Cockrell: A petition of citizens of Missouri, praying an appropriation to defray the expenses of the Pan-American Medical Congress, to be held in Washington in September, 1893; to the Committee on Appropriations.

By Mr. Wolcott: A memorial of the legislature of Colorado in favor of an amendment to the Constitution of the United States providing for the election of Senators by a direct vote of the people; to the Committee on Privileges and Elections.

By Mr. Vest: A petition of citizens of the Cherokee Nation, praying to be admitted into the Union separate from Oklahoma, and for the allotment of lands in severalty in accordance with the treaty of 1866; to the Committee on Indian Affairs.

Resolutions of the common council of Kansas City, Mo., remonstrating against any change in the franchise of the Winner bridge over the Missouri River between that city and Clay County; to the Committee on Commerce.

By Mr. Blackburn: A memorial of citizens of Kentucky, remonstrating against the passage of any law giving preference to the principle of any one religion over another; to the Committee on the Judiciary.

By Mr. Pettigrew: A resolution of the legislature of South Dakota in favor of the passage of a law to establish a military post at or near the city of Pierre, S. Dak.; to the Committee on Military Affairs.

By Mr. Sherman: A petition of citizens of Ohio, praying for the establishment of a permanent census bureau, and for the collection and publication of statistics relating to farm mortgages; to the Committee on the Census.

A petition of citizens of Ohio, praying the passage of a law for the restriction of immigration into the United States; to the Committee on Immigration.

By Mr. Peffer: A memorial of citizens of Kansas, remonstrating against the passage of any law respecting religion or the free exercise thereof; to the Committee on the Judiciary.

By Mr. Frye: Several petitions of citizens of the United States, praying the passage of a law to prevent the sale of intoxicating liquors on the grounds of the Columbian Exposition; to the Select Committee on the Quadro-Centennial.

Memorials remonstrating against the repeal of the provisions providing for the closing of the Columbian Exposition on the Sabbath day were presented as follows:

By Mr. Pasco: A memorial of citizens of Florida.

By Mr. Cullom: A memorial of citizens of Illinois.

Ordered, That they be referred to the Select Committee on the Quadro-Centennial.

Memorials praying for the repeal of the law providing for the purchase of silver bullion were presented as follows:

By Mr. Gallinger: A memorial of citizens of New Hampshire.

By Mr. Washburn: A memorial of the Board of Trade of Minneapolis, Minn.

Ordered, That they lie on the table.

Mr. Hansbrough presented a resolution of the legislature of North Dakota in favor of an amendment to the Constitution providing for the election of United States Senators by a direct vote of the people.

Ordered, That it lie on the table.

Mr. Manderson presented a letter of John G. Ames, superintendent of documents, Interior Department, recommending the preparation and publication of a comprehensive index of public documents; which was referred to the Committee on Printing, to accompany the resolution relating thereto.

The Vice-President laid before the Senate a memorial of the Scientific Publishing Company of New York, proposing to furnish the United States with its volume of mineral statistics, relating to mineral industries and mineral products for the year 1892; which was referred to the Committee on Printing.

Mr. Gordon presented a resolution of the Board of Trade of Brunswick, Ga., praying an appropriation for the deepening of the water in the harbor at that place; which was referred to the Committee on Commerce.

EXECUTIVE COMMUNICATIONS.

The Vice-President laid before the Senate a letter of the Secretary of the Treasury, transmitting a communication from the Secretary of State, submitting an estimate of appropriation for contingent expenses, Department of State; which was referred to the Committee on Appropriations and ordered to be printed.

The Vice-President laid before the Senate the annual report of the National Academy of Sciences for the year 1892; which was referred to the Committee on Printing.

MESSAGE FROM THE HOUSE.

A message from the House of Representatives, by Mr. Towles, its chief clerk:

Mr. President: The House of Representatives has passed the following resolutions, in which it requests the concurrence of the Senate:

Resolved by the House of Representatives (the Senate concurring), That there be printed the eulogies delivered in Congress upon Hon. Edward F. McDonald, late a Representative from the State of New Jersey, 8,000 copies, of which 2,000 copies shall be delivered to the Senators and Representatives of the State of New Jersey, and of those remaining 2,000 copies shall be for the use of the Senate and 4,000 copies for the use of the House; and the Secretary of the Treasury be, and he is hereby, directed to have printed a portrait of said Edward F. McDonald to accompany said eulogies. That of the quota of the House the Public Printer shall set apart 50 copies, which he shall have bound in full morocco with gilt edges, the same to be delivered, when completed, to the family of the deceased.

Resolved by the House of Representatives (the Senate concurring), That there be printed of the eulogies delivered in Congress upon Eli Thomas Stackhouse, late a Representative from the State of South Carolina, 8,000 copies, of which 2,000 copies shall be delivered to the Senators and Representatives of the State of South Carolina, and of those remaining 2,000 shall be for the use of the Senate and 4,000 for the use of the House of Representatives; and the Secretary of the Treasury be, and he is hereby, directed to have printed a portrait of the said Eli Thomas Stackhouse to accompany said eulogies. That of the quota of the House of Representatives the Public Printer shall set apart 50 copies, which he shall have bound in full morocco with gilt edges, the same to be delivered, when completed, to the family of the deceased.

Be it resolved by the House of Representatives of the United States (the Senate concurring), That of the annual report of the Commissioner of Education for 1890–'91 there be printed 5,000 copies for the use of the Senate, 10,000 for the use of the House of Representatives, and 20,000 copies for distribution by the Commissioner.

The House of Representatives has passed the following resolutions, which I am directed to communicate to the Senate:

Resolved, That the business of the House be now suspended that opportunity may be given for tributes to the memory of the Hon. John G. Warwick, lately a Representative from the State of Ohio.

Resolved, That as a particular mark of respect to the memory of the deceased, and in recognition of his eminent abilities as a distinguished public servant, the House, at the conclusion of these memorial proceedings, shall stand adjourned.

Resolved, That the Clerk communicate these resolutions to the Senate.

Resolved, That the Clerk be instructed to send a copy of these resolutions to the family of the deceased.

The House of Representatives has passed the bill (S. 43) for the relief of the personal representatives of Adelicia Cheatham, deceased, with an amendment, in which it requests the concurrence of the Senate.

The Speaker of the House of Representatives having signed an enrolled bill, H. R. 1036, I am directed to bring the same to the Senate for the signature of its President.

The President of the United States has informed the House of Representatives that he has approved and signed the following acts:

On February 8, 1893:

H. R. 730. An act for the relief of James Finley; and

H. R. 9531. An act to make Rockport, Tex., a subport of entry.

On February 9, 1893:

H. R. 6798. An act to authorize the construction of a bridge across the Warrior River by the Montgomery, Tuscaloosa and Memphis Railway Company;

H. R. 9930. An act for the construction and maintenance of a bridge across the St. Lawrence River;

H. R. 10010. An act to establish a court of appeals for the District of Columbia, and for other purposes;

H. R. 6649. An act to extend the provisions of an act to provide for the muster and pay of certain officers and enlisted men of the volunteer forces;

H. R. 6345. An act granting an honorable discharge to Frederick E. Kolter;

H. R. 8106. An act for the correction of the army record of David R. Wallace, deceased;

H. R. 7603. An act granting a pension to Marion Kerr Sharman;

H. R. 1318. An act granting a pension to Martha A. Harris;

H. R. 2400. An act granting a pension to Willis Luttrell;

H. R. . An act granting a pension to Samuel Luttrell;

H. R. . An act granting a pension to Sarah A. Hagan;

H. R. 3497. An act granting a pension to Ellen Hewett;

H. R. 7257. An act granting a pension to Alonzo D. Barber;

H. R. 7234. An act granting a pension to Mary Millard;

H. R. 6508. An act granting a pension to Joseph Fostier;

H. R. 7226. An act granting a pension to Julia P. Wright;

H. R. 8925. An act to increase the pension of Harvey Lyon;

H. R. 5705. An act to increase the pension of Amelia Graham;

H. R. 6272. An act to pension Susan S. Murphy;

H. R. 8275. An act granting a pension to Abraham B. Simmons, of Capt. Thomas Tripp's company in Col. Brisbane's regiment, South Carolina Volunteers, in the Florida Indian war;

H. R. 9290. An act granting a pension to Mrs. Caroline Hardee Dyall, widow of James R. Dyall, veteran of the Florida war, 1836;

H. R. 7096. An act granting a pension to Lillie Ries, late a nurse at Jefferson Barracks;

H. R. 7288. An act granting a pension to Amanda Atherton;

H. R. 5649. An act for the relief of Lieut. F. W. Davis, and granting him an honorable discharge;

H. R. 2592. An act for the relief of Andrew B. Knapp; and

H. R. 6797. An act to authorize the construction of a bridge across the Cahaba River, in Bibb County, Alabama, by the Montgomery, Tuscaloosa and Memphis Railway.

On February 13, 1893:

H. R. 8268. An act to extend the provisions of section 8 of the act entitled "An act to repeal timber-culture laws, and for other purposes," approved March 3, 1891, concerning prosecutions for cutting timber on public lands, to Wyoming, New Mexico, and Arizona;

H. R. 9758. An act to amend the charter of the Eckington and Soldiers' Home Railway of the District of Columbia; and

H. R. 9176. An act relating to navigation of vessels, bills of lading, and to certain obligations, duties, and rights in connection with the carriage of property.

On February 14, 1893:

H. R. 4758. An act for the relief of Charles E. Heuston;

H. R. 8727. An act for the relief of S. J. Brooks;

H. R. 4215. An act to correct the military record of Capt. William C. Knowlton;

H. R. 4375. An act for the relief of Charles S. Blood; and

H. R. 9437. An act for the removal of the charge of desertion against William H. Holloway.

ENROLLED BILL SIGNED.

Mr. Dubois reported from the committee that they had examined and found duly enrolled the bill (H. R. 1036) for the benefit of the State of Kentucky, Logan and Simpson counties, and of Louisville, Ky., and of Sumner and Davidson counties, Tennessee.

Whereupon,

The Vice-President signed the same, and it was delivered to the committee to be presented to the President of the United States.

HOUSE AMENDMENT TO SENATE BILL.

The Vice-President laid before the Senate the amendment of the House of Representatives to the bill (S. 43) for the relief of the personal representatives of Adelicia Cheatham, deceased; and,

On motion by Mr. Harris,

Resolved, That the Senate agree thereto.

Ordered, That the Secretary notify the House of Representatives thereof.

REPORTS OF COMMITTEES.

Mr. Manderson, from the Committee on Printing, to whom were referred the following resolutions received from the House of Representatives for concurrence on the 14th instant, reported them without amendment and submitted written reports thereon as follows:

A resolution to print the eulogies delivered in Congress upon the Hon. Melbourne H. Ford, late a Representative from the State of Michigan; Report No. 1312.

A resolution to print the eulogies delivered in Congress upon the Hon. John W. Kendall, late a Representative from the State of Kentucky; Report No. 1313.

The Senate proceeded, by unanimous consent, to consider the said resolutions and

Resolved, That the Senate agree thereto.

Ordered, That the Secretary notify the House of Representatives thereof.

Mr. Chandler, from the Committee on Naval Affairs, to whom was referred the bill (H. R. 1479) to remove the charge of desertion from

the record of James Morrison alias James C. McIntosh, reported it without amendment.

The Senate proceeded, by unanimous consent, to consider the said bill as in Committee of the Whole; and no amendment being made, it was reported to the Senate.

Ordered, That it pass to a third reading.

The said bill was read the third time.

Resolved, That it pass.

Ordered, That the Secretary notify the House of Representatives thereof.

Mr. Hoar from the Committee on the Judiciary, to whom was referred the bill (H. R. 456) to limit the jurisdiction of the district and and circuit courts of the United States, reported adversely thereon.

Ordered, That it be placed on the Calendar.

Mr. Sawyer, from the Committee on Post-Offices and Post-Roads, to whom was referred the bill (S. 2439) for the relief of J. M. Lyon, submitted an adverse report (No. 1341) thereon.

Ordered, That it be postponed indefinitely.

Mr. Voorhees, from the Select Committee on Additional Accommodations for the Library of Congress, to whom was referred the letter of the Chief of Engineers relative to the material used in the construction of the building for the Library of Congress, submitted a report (No. 1314).

INDEX OF GOVERNMENT PUBLICATIONS.

Mr. Manderson submitted the following concurrent resolution; which was referred to the Committee on Printing:

Resolved by the Senate (the House of Representatives concurring), That there be printed and bound, at the Government Printing Office, 3,000 copies of a comprehensive index of the publications of the Fifty-first and Fifty-second Congresses, prepared by John G. Ames, superintendent of documents—500 for the use of the Senate, 1,000 for the use of the House of Representatives, and 1,500 for distribution by the said superintendent of documents.

EULOGIES UPON THE LATE SENATOR BARBOUR.

Mr. Hunton submitted the following resolution; which was referred to the Committee on Printing:

Resolved by the Senate (the House of Representatives concurring), That there be printed of the eulogies delivered in Congress upon the Hon. John S. Barbour, late a Senator from the State of Virginia, 8,000 copies, of which 2,000 copies shall be delivered to the Senators and Representatives of that State, and of the remaining number 2,000 shall be for the use of the Senate and 4,000 copies for the use of the House; and of the quota of the Senate the Public Printer shall set aside 50 copies, which he shall have bound in full morocco with gilt edges, the same to be delivered, when completed, to the family of the deceased; and the Secretary of the Treasury is hereby directed to have engraved and printed at the earliest day practicable a portrait of the deceased to accompany said eulogies.

PRESIDENTIAL APPROVALS.

A message from the President of the United States, by Mr. Pruden, his secretary:

Mr. President: The President of the United States approved and signed on the 18th instant the following acts and joint resolution:

S. 741. An act to incorporate the Eclectic Medical Society of the District of Columbia;

S. 1683. An act for the relief of Mrs. Fannie N. Belger;

S. 2852. An act to change the name of the Capitol, North O Street and South Washington Railway Company;

S. 3836. An act to authorize the Union Railroad Company, to construct and maintain a bridge across the Monongahela River;

S. R. 130. Joint resolution to amend an act entitled "An act making Saturday a half holiday for banking and trust companies in the District of Columbia," approved December 22, 1892; and

He this day approved and signed an act (S. 2946) to amend "An act to incorporate the Masonic Mutual Relief Association of the District of Columbia," approved March 3, 1869.

Ordered, That the Secretary notify the House of Representatives thereof.

MESSAGE FROM THE PRESIDENT.

The following message was received from the President of the United States, by Mr. Pruden, his secretary:

To the Senate of the United States:

I transmit herewith a report submitted by the Acting Secretary of State in response to the resolution of the Senate of February 2, last, relating to the building of the Ozama River bridge at Santo Domingo City, by American citizens.

BENJ. HARRISON.

EXECUTIVE MANSION,
Washington, February 20, 1893.

The message was read.

Ordered, That it be printed and, with accompanying papers, referred to the Committee on Foreign Relations.

BILLS RECONSIDERED AND RECOMMITTED.

On motion by Mr. Dawes and by unanimous consent,

Ordered, That the votes of the Senate postponing indefinitely the following bills be reconsidered, and that they be recommitted to the Committee on Indian Affairs:

S. 1634. A bill to provide for a final settlement with the Naalem band of the Tillamook tribe of Indians, of Oregon, in accordance with a certain agreement between the United States and the said Indians, dated the 6th day of August, 1851; and

S. 1635. A bill to provide for a final settlement with the Tillamook tribe of Indians, of Oregon, in accordance with a certain agreement between the United States and the said Indians, dated the 7th day of August, 1851.

PUBLICATION OF THE CENSUS.

On motion by Mr. Manderson,

The Senate proceeded to consider, as in Committee of the Whole, the bill (H. R. 8582) to provide for the publication of the Eleventh Census; and no amendment being made, it was reported to the Senate.

Ordered, That it pass to a third reading.

The said bill was read the third time.

Resolved, That it pass,

Ordered, That the Secretary notify the House of Representatives thereof.

HOUSE RESOLUTIONS REFERRED.

The resolutions to print the eulogies delivered in Congress upon the late Edward F. McDonald and the late Eli Thomas Stackhouse, and the resolution to print additional copies of the report of the Commissioner of Education for 1890–'91, this day received from the House of Representatives for concurrence, were read and referred to the Committee on Printing.

MESSAGE FROM THE HOUSE.

A message from the House of Representatives, by Mr. Kerr, its Clerk:

Mr. President: The Speaker of the House of Representatives having signed two enrolled bills, S. 43 and S. 1232, I am directed to bring them to the Senate for the signature of its President.

ENROLLED BILLS SIGNED.

Mr. Dubois reported from the committee that they had examined and found duly enrolled the following bills:

S. 43. An act for the relief of the personal representatives of Adelicia Cheatham, deceased; and

S. 1232. An act removing the charge of desertion against Lucius W. Hayford, Worcester, Vt.;

Whereupon,

The Vice-President signed the same, and they were delivered to the committee to be presented to the President of the United States.

BILLS PRESENTED.

Mr. Dubois reported from the committee that they this day presented to the President of the United States the following enrolled bills:

S. 1303. An act to increase the pension of Mrs. S. A. Farquharson;

S. 2828. An act for the relief of L. M. Garrett;

S. 3419. An act granting a pension to Mary Doubleday, widow of Bvt. Maj. Gen. Abner Doubleday;

S. 3811. An act to amend an act entitled "An act to grant to the Mobile and Dauphin Island Railroad and Harbor Company the right to trestle across the shoal water between Cedar Point and Dauphin Island," approved September 26, 1890;

S. 3629. An act to extend to the North Pacific Ocean the provisions of the statutes for the protection of fur seals and other fur-bearing animals; and

S. 3857. An act authorizing the construction of a bridge over the Monongahela River at the foot of Main street, in the borough of Belle Vernon, in the State of Pennsylvania.

SUNDRY CIVIL APPROPRIATION BILL.

On motion by Mr. Allison,

The Senate resumed, as in Committee of the Whole, the consideration of the bill (H. R. 10238) making appropriations for sundry civil expenses of the Government for the fiscal year ending June 30, 1894, and for other purposes; and having been further amended on the motion of Mr. Platt and the motion of Mr. Morrill,

On motion by Mr. Morrill to further amend the bill by inserting after line 5, page 3, the following:

For completing the building at Saint Albans, Vermont, twenty-five thousand dollars,

It was determined in the affirmative, { Yeas .... 27 / Nays .... 20 }

On motion by Mr. Morrill,

The yeas and nays being desired by one-fifth of the Senators present, Those who voted in the affirmative are,

Messrs. Allison, Chandler, Davis, Felton, Frye, Gallinger, Hansbrough, Hawley, Hoar, McMillan, Manderson, Mitchell, Morrill,

16 s

Paddock, Peffer, Perkins, Platt, Power, Proctor, Quay, Sawyer, Stewart, Stockbridge, Teller, Vest, Washburn, Wolcott.

Those who voted in the negative are,

Messrs. Bate, Berry, Blackburn, Brice, Call, Cockrell, Coke, Gibson, Gorman, Harris, Hunton, Kyle, Morgan, Palmer, Pugh, Sherman, Turpie, Vance, Vilas, Voorhees.

So the amendment was agreed to.

On motion by Mr. Wolcott to amend the bill by striking out in line 9, page 60, the word "two" and inserting in lieu thereof the word one,

It was determined in the negative, { Yeas .... 18 / Nays .... 38 }

On motion by Mr. Wolcott,

The yeas and nays being desired by one-fifth of the Senators present, Those who voted in the affirmative are,

Messrs. Berry, Blodgett, Chandler, Coke, Felton, Hansbrough, Hiscock, Kyle, McMillan, Mitchell, Peffer, Power, Quay, Sawyer, Stewart, Teller, Vest, Wolcott.

Those who voted in the negative are,

Messrs. Allison, Bate, Blackburn, Brice, Caffery, Call, Cockrell, Cullom, Dawes, Dixon, Dubois, Faulkner, Frye, Gallinger, George, Gibson, Gorman, Hale, Harris, Hawley, Higgins, Hoar, Hunton, Jones of Arkansas, Manderson, Mills, Paddock, Palmer, Perkins, Platt, Proctor, Ransom, Shoup, Squire, Stockbridge, Vance, Voorhees, Washburn.

So the amendment was not agreed to.

The bill having been further amended on the motion of Mr. Hoar, the motion of Mr. Quay, from the Committee on Public Buildings and Grounds, and the motion of Mr. Allison, from the Committee on Appropriations,

On motion by Mr. Manderson, from the Committee on Printing, to further amend the bill by inserting at the end thereof the following:

That the sum of two hundred and fifty thousand dollars to provide accommodation for the Government Printing Office and the construction of the needed storage and distribution warehouses in connection therewith in the act making appropriations for sundry civil expenses of the Government, approved August thirtieth, eighteen hundred and ninety, and suspended by act making appropriations for sundry civil expenses of the Government for the fiscal year ending June thirtieth, eighteen hundred and ninety-two, approved March third, eighteen hundred and ninety-one, is hereby made available for the purposes provided for in the above act, approved August thirtieth, eighteen hundred and ninety; and the Secretary of the Treasury is hereby directed to pay out of this sum one hundred and six thousand dollars when a deed, duly approved by the Attorney-General of the United States, conveying to the United States the following-described block, or parcel of ground, situated in the city of Washington, District of Columbia, shall be delivered to him, namely: Block numbered seven hundred and thirteen, in the city of Washington, District of Columbia, which said block fronts four hundred and one and one-half feet on L street, three hundred and eleven feet on K street, three hundred and thirty-six feet on Delaware avenue, three hundred and twenty-three feet on First street east, in what is denominated "Northeast Washington,"

On motion by Mr. Vest, from the Committee on Public Buildings and Grounds, to amend the amendment by striking out all after the word "that" in the first line, and in lieu thereof inserting the following:

The Secretary of the Treasury be, and he hereby is, empowered and directed to employ the money appropriated in the "Act making appropriations for sundry civil expenses of the Government for the fiscal year ending June thirtieth, eighteen hundred and ninety-one, and for other purposes," and approved August thirtieth, eighteen hundred and ninety, as by section two of said act to provide accommodations for the Government Printing Office and the construction of the needed storage and distributing warehouse in connection therewith, for the purchase of the south half of square numbered six hundred and seventy-three, fronting on North Capitol street, containing about two hundred and thirteen thousand eight hundred and fifteen square feet and bounded as follows: Two hundred and seventy-three and one-fourth feet on North Capitol street, along the same from the intersection of L, thence therewith to what is called Pierce or Babcook street; thence along the same eastward for seven hundred and eighty-two and one-third feet to First street; thence along the same for two hundred and seventy-three and one-fourth feet to L street; thence west along the same to point of beginning; and that he pay over the said money, as appropriated, to the owners of the said south half of square numbered six hundred and seventy-three, on the presentation to him, the said Secretary, of a deed conveying the said parcel of ground to the United States, duly approved by the Attorney-General of the United States,

Pending debate,

EXECUTIVE SESSION.

On motion by Mr. Quay,

The Senate proceeded to the consideration of executive business; and

After the consideration of executive business the doors were reopened, and

On motion by Mr. Mills, at 6 o'clock p. m.,

The Senate adjourned.

TUESDAY, FEBRUARY 21, 1893.

CREDENTIALS OF SENATORS.

Mr. Blackburn presented the credentials of William Lindsay, elected a Senator by the legislature of the State of Kentucky to fill the vacancy occasioned by the resignation of John G. Carlisle in the term expiring March 3, 1895; which were read and placed on file.

Mr. Lindsay appeared, and the oath prescribed by law having been administered to him by the Vice-President, he took his seat in the Senate.

Mr. Paddock presented the credentials of William Vincent Allen, elected a Senator by the legislature of the State of Nebraska for the term of six years commencing March 4, 1893; which were read and placed on file.

MESSAGE FROM THE HOUSE.

A message from the House of Representatives, by Mr. Kerr, its Clerk:

Mr. President: The House of Representatives has agreed to the resolution of the Senate directing the Secretary of the Interior to take no further steps looking to the lease of the Big Iron bath-house site at Hot Springs, Ark.

The House of Representatives has passed, without amendment, the following bills of the Senate:

S. 3602. An act to grant to the Chicago, Rock Island and Pacific Railway Company a right of way through the Indian Territory, and for other purposes; and

S. 3873. An act to authorize the Kansas City, Pittsburg and Gulf Railroad Company to construct and operate a railroad, telegraph, and telephone line through the Indian Territory, and for other purposes.

The House of Representatives has passed the following bills, in which it requests the concurrence of the Senate:

H. R. 10488. An act making appropriations for the naval service for the fiscal year ending June 30, 1894, and for other purposes; and

H. R. 10589. An act to authorize the New York and New Jersey Bridge Companies to construct and maintain a bridge across the Hudson River between New York City and the State of New Jersey.

The Speaker of the House having signed three enrolled bills, H. R. 1479, H. R. 8582, and H. R. 9286, I am directed to bring the same to the Senate for the signature of its President.

ENROLLED BILLS SIGNED.

Mr. Dubois reported from the committee that they had examined and found duly enrolled the following bills:

H. R. 1479. An act to remove the charge of desertion from the record of James Morrison alias James C. McIntosh;

H. R. 8582. An act to provide for the publication of the Eleventh Census; and

H. R. 9286. An act to create the California Débris Commission and regulate hydraulic mining in the State of California;

Whereupon,

The Vice-President signed the same, and they were delivered to the committee to be presented to the President of the United States.

HOUSE BILLS REFERRED.

The bills H. R. 10488 and H. R. 10589, this day received from the House of Representatives for concurrence, were read the first and second times by unanimous consent.

Ordered, That the bill H. R. 10488 be referred to the Committee on Appropriations, and that the bill H. R. 10589 be referred to the Committee on Commerce.

MESSAGE FROM THE PRESIDENT.

The following message was received from the President of the United States, by Mr. Pruden, his secretary:

To the Senate and House of Representatives:

I transmit herewith a communication of the Secretary of State, transmitting the official report of the American delegates to the International Monetary Conference convened at Brussels on November 22, 1892, with its accompaniments.

BENJ. HARRISON.

EXECUTIVE MANSION,
Washington, February 21, 1893.

The message was read.

Ordered, That it be referred to the Committee on Foreign Relations and printed.

PETITIONS AND MEMORIAL.

Mr. Davis presented a memorial of the Board of Trade of Minneapolis, Minn., and a petition of citizens of Minnesota, praying the repeal of the law providing for the purchase of silver bullion.

Ordered, That they lie on the table.

Mr. Peffer presented a petition of citizens of Kansas, praying the passage of the antioption bill.

Ordered, That it lie on the table.

REPORTS OF COMMITTEES.

Mr. Turpie, from the Committee on Pensions, to whom was referred the bill (S. 2383) granting a pension to Rebecca H. Chambers, reported it with an amendment and submitted a report (No. 1315) thereon.

Mr. Turpie, from the Committee on Pensions, to whom were referred the following bills, reported them severally without amendment and submitted written reports thereon as follows:

H. R. 4320. An act granting a pension to Thomas S. Kennedy; Report No. 1316.

H. R. 8230. An act for the relief of Louis G. Sanderson, of Craighead County, Arkansas; Report No. 1317.

H. R. 3253. An act to increase the pension of William G. Smith; Report No. 1318.

H. R. 5958. An act for the relief of Elizabeth Carpenter; Report No. 1319.

H. R. 7100. An act to pension Jacob O'Neal; Report No. 1320.

H. R. 2901. An act to pension Ida Carroll; Report No. 1321.

Mr. Harris, from the Committee on Finance, to whom was referred the bill (H. R. 8736) for the relief of the Shibley & Wood Grocer Company, of Van Buren, Crawford County, Arkansas, reported it without amendment.

Mr. Frye, from the Committee on Commerce, to whom was referred the resolution received from the House of Representatives for concurrence on the 15th instant, calling for a report of the present actual condition of the harbor improvement at Cumberland Sound, and the entrance to the port of Fernandina, Fla., reported it without amendment.

The Senate proceeded, by unanimous consent, to consider the said resolution; and

Resolved, That the Senate agree thereto.

Ordered, That the Secretary notify the House of Representatives thereof.

Mr. Proctor, from the Committee on Military Affairs, to whom was referred the bill (H. R. 9925) to establish companies of the Hospital Corps, United States Army, and for other purposes, reported it with amendments and submitted a report (No 1322) thereon.

Mr. Davis, from the Committee on Pensions, to whom was referred the bill (S. 2706) for the relief of Mary M. Craddock, submitted an adverse report (No. 1323) thereon.

Ordered, That it be postponed indefinitely.

Mr. Sawyer, from the Committee on Pensions, to whom was referred the bill (H. R. 3118) to pension John S. Dunham, reported it without amendment and submitted a report (No. 1324) thereon.

Mr. Sawyer, from the Committee on Pensions, to whom was referred the bill (H. R. 7099) granting an increase of pension to Samuel S. Anderson, submitted an adverse report (No. 1325) thereon.

Ordered, That it be postponed indefinitely.

Mr. Gallinger, from the Committee on Pensions, to whom were referred the following bills, reported them without amendment and submitted written reports thereon as follows:

H. R. 9233. An act to grant a pension to Harriet Cota; Report No. 1326.

H. R. 8409. An act granting a pension to Mary Danahay, mother of Daniel Danahay, late a private Company H, Eighteenth New York Cavalry; Report No. 1327.

Mr. Manderson, from the Committee on Printing, to whom was referred the resolution submitted by Mr. Dawes January 26, 1893, providing for the printing of the contracts made with Indian tribes, or Indians respecting compensation to be paid attorneys, agents or other persons for services in preparing claims for settlement, reported it without amendment and submitted a report (No. 1328) thereon.

The Senate proceeded, by unanimous consent, to consider the said resolution; and

Resolved, That the Senate agree thereto.

Mr. Manderson, from the Committee on Printing, to whom was referred the resolution submitted by Mr. Gallinger on the 10th instant, to print 6,000 copies of Report No. 1280, of the select committee to investigate and report the facts in relation to the employment for private purposes of armed bodies of men, submitted an adverse report (No. 1329) thereon.

Ordered, That it be postponed indefinitely.

On motion by Mr. Manderson,

Ordered, That 2,000 copies of the foregoing report (No. 1280) be printed for the use of the Senate.

Mr. Paddock, from the Committee on Agriculture and Forestry, reported the following resolution; which was considered by unanimous consent and agreed to:

Resolved, That the powers conferred and duties imposed on the Committee on Agriculture and Forestry by, and all of the provisions of, the resolution of the Senate of April 19, 1892, be continued during the recess, after the expiration of this Congress.

Mr. Cockrell entered a motion to reconsider the vote of the Senate agreeing to the foregoing resolution.

On motion by Mr. Dawes,

Ordered, That the Committee on Indian Affairs be discharged from the further consideration of the joint resolution (S. R. 109) for the payment of an account to W. F. Niedringhaus, contractor for furnishing beef to the Indians, and that it be referred to the Committee on Claims.

INTRODUCTION OF BILL.

Mr. Quay introduced a bill (S. 3878) authorizing the construction of a bridge over the Monongahela River at Glenwood, Twenty-third ward, city of Pittsburg, in the State of Pennsylvania; which was read the first and second time by unanimous consent and referred to the Committee on Commerce.

PINE RIDGE INDIAN DEPREDATION CLAIMS.

Mr. Kyle submitted the following resolution; which was considered by unanimous consent and agreed to:

Resolved, That the Secretary of the Interior be directed to furnish to the Senate the following information:

(1) The number and value of claims presented by friendly Indians arising from depredations committed during the late Indian disturbance at Pine Ridge, S. Dak.

(2) A statement of the amount allowed on each claim and whether paid to claimant in person or to an agent or attorney; and if so, the name of such agent or attorney.

(3) A full statement as to the disbursement of the $100,000 appropriated by Congress for the settlement of such claims.

FOX AND WISCONSIN RIVERS IMPROVEMENT.

Mr. Sawyer submitted the following resolution; which was considered by unanimous consent and agreed to:

Resolved, That the Attorney-General be, and he is hereby, directed to furnish to the Senate a statement of the awards and judgments rendered by the commissioners or courts on file in his office against the United States arising under an act of Congress entitled "An act to aid in the improvement of the Fox and Wisconsin Rivers in the State of Wisconsin," approved March 3, 1875, from which awards and judgments no appeal has been taken and the time for such appeal has expired, which have not heretofore been reported to Congress, and if he knows any reason why the same should not be paid.

LIST OF CLAIMS ALLOWED.

Mr. Hale submitted the following resolution; which was considered by unanimous consent and agreed to:

Resolved, That the Secretary of the Treasury be directed to transmit to the Senate a list of all claims allowed by the several accounting officers of the Treasury Department under appropriations the balances of which have been exhausted or carried to the surplus fund under the provisions of section 5 of the act of June 20, 1874, since the allowance of those already transmitted to Congress during the present session; and also a list of judgments of the Court of Claims requiring an appropriation at the present session not already transmitted; said list to include all claims allowed up to and including the 25th instant.

BRIDGE AT LITTLE ROCK, ARK.

On motion by Mr. Jones, of Arkansas,

The Senate proceeded to consider, as in Committee of the Whole, the bill (S. 3725) authorizing the construction of a free bridge across the Arkansas River, connecting Little Rock and Argenta; and the reported amendments having been agreed to, and the bill further amended on the motion of Mr. Jones, of Arkansas, it was reported to the Senate and the amendments were concurred in.

Ordered, That the bill be engrossed and read a third time.

The said bill was read the third time.

Resolved, That it pass, and that the title thereof be as aforesaid.

Ordered, That the Secretary request the concurrence of the House of Representatives therein.

STREET RAILROADS IN THE DISTRICT.

Mr. Gorman submitted a motion to recommit to the Committee on the District of Columbia the bill (H. R. 8125) to provide for the regulation of the equipment and operation of street-railroad lines within the District of Columbia by the Commissioners of said District.

ALBERTO GUIROLA.

Mr. Hawley, from the Committee on Military Affairs, to whom was referred the joint resolution (S. R. 157) authorizing the Secretary of War to receive for instruction at the Military Academy at West Point Alberto Guirola, of Salvador, reported it without amendment.

The Senate proceeded, by unanimous consent, to consider the said resolution as in Committee of the Whole; and no amendment being made, it was reported to the Senate.

Ordered, That it be engrossed and read a third time.

The said resolution was read the third time.

Resolved, That it pass, and that the title thereof be as aforesaid.

Ordered, That the Secretary request the concurrence of the House of Representatives therein.

PRESIDENTIAL APPROVAL.

A message from the President of the United States, by Mr. Pruden, his secretary:

Mr. President: The President of the United States this day approved and signed an act (S. 977) for the relief of B. F. Rockafellow.

Ordered, That the Secretary notify the House of Representatives thereof.

BILLS PRESENTED.

Mr. Dubois reported from the committee that they yesterday presented to the President of the United States the following enrolled bills:

S. 43. An act for the relief of the personal representatives of Adelicia Cheatham, deceased; and

S. 1232. An act removing the charge of desertion against Lucius W. Hayford, Worcester, Vt.

MESSAGE FROM THE HOUSE.

A message from the House of Representatives, by Mr. Towles, its chief clerk:

Mr. President: The House of Representatives has passed a bill (H. R. 10421) making appropriations for the Department of Agriculture for the fiscal year ending June 30, 1894, in which it requests the concurrence of the Senate.

HOUSE BILL REFERRED.

The bill H. R. 10421, last received from the House of Representatives for concurrence, was read the first and second times by unanimous consent and referred to the Committee on Appropriations.

SUNDRY CIVIL APPROPRIATION BILL.

On motion by Mr. Allison,

The Senate resumed, as in Committee of the Whole, the consideration of the bill (H. R. 10238) making appropriations for sundry civil expenses of the Government for the fiscal year ending June 30, 1894, and for other purposes; and

The question being on the amendment proposed by Mr. Vest to the amendment of Mr. Manderson; and the same having been modified by Mr. Vest,

On the question to agree to the amendment as modified, viz: Strike out all after the word "That" in the first line of the amendment of Mr. Manderson, and in lieu thereof insert the following: *the Secretary of the Treasury be, and he hereby is, empowered and directed to employ the money appropriated in the "Act making appropriations for sundry civil expenses of the Government for the fiscal year ending June thirtieth, eighteen hundred and ninety-one, and for other purposes," and approved August thirtieth, eighteen hundred and ninety, as by section two of said act to provide accommodations for the Government Printing Office, and the construction of the needed storage and distributing warehouses in connection therewith, for the purchase of the south half of square numbered six hundred and seventy-three, fronting on North Capitol street, containing about two hundred and thirteen thousand eight hundred and fifteenth square feet, and bounded as follows: Two hundred and seventy-three and one-fourth feet on North Capitol street, along the same from the intersection of L; thence there-with to what is called Pierce or Babcock street; thence along the same eastward for seven hundred and eighty-two and one-third feet to First street; thence along the same for two hundred and seventy-three and one-fourth feet to L street; thence west along the same to point of beginning; and that he pay over the said money so appropriated to the owners of the said south half of square numbered six hundred and seventy-three on the presentation to him, the said Secretary, of a deed conveying the said parcel of ground to the United States, duly approved by the Attorney-General of the United States,*

It was determined in the negative, { Yeas 21   { Nays 24

On motion by Mr. Manderson,

The yeas and nays being desired by one-fifth of the Senators present,

Those who voted in the affirmative are,

Messrs. Allison, Brice, Butler, Carey, Cullom, Davis, Jones of Nevada, Lindsay, Mitchell, Perkins, Pettigrew, Power, Pugh, Quay, Sawyer, Sherman, Stewart, Teller, Vest, Washburn, Wolcott.

Those who voted in the negative are,

Messrs. Bate, Berry, Caffery, Chandler, Cockrell, Coke, Dubois, Faulkner, Gorman, Hansbrough, Harris, Hiscock, Hunton, Jones of Arkansas, McMillan, Manderson, Paddock, Palmer, Peffer, Shoup, Turpie, Vance, Vilas, Voorhees.

So the amendment to the amendment was not agreed to.

On motion by Mr. Gallinger to amend the amendment of Mr. Manderson by striking out after the word "ninety" in line 12 the following:

"And the Secretary of the Treasury is hereby directed to pay out of this sum one hundred and six thousand dollars when a deed, duly approved by the Attorney-General of the United States, conveying to the United States the following described block, or parcel of ground, situated in the city of Washington, D. C., shall be

delivered to him, namely: Block numbered seven hundred and thirteen, in the city of Washington, D. C., which said block fronts four hundred and one and one-half feet on L street, three hundred and eleven feet on K street, three hundred and thirty-six feet on Delaware avenue, three hundred and twenty-three feet on First street east, in what is denominated 'Northeast Washington.'"

And in lieu thereof inserting the following:

And that the Secretary of the Treasury, the Secretary of the Interior, and the Architect of the Capitol Extension, acting as a board, be, and they are hereby, empowered and instructed to acquire, as hereinafter provided, such additional part of square numbered six hundred and twenty-four, in the city of Washington, District of Columbia,, as may be deemed necessary for the needs of the Government Printing Office, which said square is bounded as follows: On the east by North Capitol street, on the north by H street north, on the west by First street west, and on the south by G street north; and the Secretary of the Treasury is hereby directed to pay out of the sum hereinbefore mentioned such amount as may be found necessary when deeds duly approved by the Attorney-General of the United States, conveying to the United States said property hereinbefore mentioned, shall be delivered to him: Provided, That such sum does not exceed the amount of said two hundred and fifty thousand dollars.

That for the purpose of acquiring said real estate the said board may purchase the same, or any part thereof, from the owner or owners; and if the said board shall be unable so to purchase the same, or any part or parts thereof, at a price that, in their opinion, is reasonable, they may institute legal proceedings for the condemnation thereof.

After debate,

It was determined in the negative, { Yeas .... 14 / Nays 34

On motion by Mr. Butler,

The yeas and nays being desired by one-fifth of the Senators present,

Those who voted in the affirmative are,

Messrs. Blodgett, Butler, Carey, Davis, Gallinger, Jones of Nevada, Perkins, Pettigrew, Power, Sawyer, Shoup, Stewart, Teller, Vest.

Those who voted in the negative are,

Messrs. Allison, Bate, Berry, Caffery, Chandler, Cockrell, Coke, Cullom, Dubois, Faulkner, Frye, Hansbrough, Harris, Hunton, Jones of Arkansas, Kyle, Lindsay, McMillan, Manderson, Mills, Mitchell, Morrill, Paddock, Palmer, Peffer, Platt, Pugh, Quay, Sherman, Turpie, Vance, Vilas, Voorhees, White.

So the amendment to the amendment was not agreed to.

The question recurring on agreeing to the amendment submitted by Mr. Manderson, from the Committee on Printing, viz: Insert at the end of the bill the following:

That the sum of two hundred and fifty thousand dollars, to provide accommodation for the Government Printing Office and the construction of the needed storage and distribution warehouses in connection therewith, in the act making appropriations for sundry civil expenses of the Government, approved August thirtieth, eighteen hundred and ninety, and suspended by act making appropriations for sundry civil expenses of the Government for the fiscal year ending June thirtieth, eighteen hundred and ninety-two, approved March third, eighteen hundred and ninety-one, is hereby made available for the purposes provided for in the above act, approved August thirtieth, eighteen hundred and ninety; and the Secretary of the Treasury is hereby directed to pay out of this sum one hundred and six thousand dollars when a deed duly approved by the Attorney-General of the United States, conveying to the United States the following described block, or parcel of ground, situated in the city of Washington, District of Columbia, shall be delivered to him, namely: Block numbered seven hundred and thirteen, in the city of Washington, District of Columbia, which said block fronts four hundred and one and one-half feet on L street, three hundred and eleven feet on K street, three hundred and thirty-six feet on Delaware avenue, three hundred and twenty-three feet on First street east, in what is denominated "Northeast Washington,"

It was determined in the negative, { Yeas .... 21 / Nays 28

On motion by Mr. Manderson,

The yeas and nays being desired by one-fifth of the Senators present,

Those who voted in the affirmative are,

Messrs. Bate, Caffery, Chandler, Cockrell, Coke, Dubois, Faulkner, Gorman, Hansbrough, Harris, Hiscock, Jones of Arkansas, Kyle, Lindsay, Manderson, Mills, Morrill, Paddock, Peffer, Turpie, Vilas.

Those who voted in the negative are,

Messrs. Allison, Berry, Blodgett, Brice, Butler, Carey, Cullom, Davis, Frye, Gallinger, Hunton, Jones of Nevada, Mitchell, Palmer, Pasco, Perkins, Pettigrew, Platt, Power, Pugh, Quay, Sawyer, Sherman, Stewart, Teller, Vest, Washburn, Wolcott.

So the amendment was not agreed to.

The bill having been further amended on the motion of Mr. Harris, the motion of Mr. Manderson, and the motion of Mr. Hiscock,

On motion by Mr. Hiscock to further amend the bill by inserting after line 16, page 2, the following:

That the sum of eight hundred thousand dollars, or so much thereof as may be necessary, is hereby appropriated, out of any moneys in the United States Treasury not otherwise appropriated, to enable the Secretary of

the Treasury to make payment of the damages awarded, and such costs as may have been or may hereafter necessarily be entailed upon the Government, in the proceedings in condemnation against the property selected for the site for the custom-house building in the city and State of New York,

On motion by Mr. Allison to amend the amendment by adding thereto the following proviso: *Provided, That section three of an act entitled "An act for the erection of a new custom-house in the city of New York, and for other purposes," approved March third, eighteen hundred and ninety-one, is hereby repealed,*

It was determined in the affirmative, { Yeas .... 41 / Nays 12

On motion by Mr. Hiscock,

The yeas and nays being desired by one-fifth of the Senators present,

Those who voted in the affirmative are,

Messrs. Allison, Bate, Berry, Blackburn, Brice, Butler, Caffery, Call, Cockrell, Coke, Cullom, Dawes, Faulkner, Frye, Gorman, Hale, Hansbrough, Hawley, Hoar, Hunton, Irby, Jones of Arkansas, Kyle, Lindsay, Morrill, Paddock, Palmer, Peffer, Power, Proctor, Quay, Ransom, Sherman, Stewart, Teller, Turpie, Vest, Vilas, Voorhees, White, Wolcott.

Those who voted in the negative are,

Messrs. Carey, Chandler, Davis, Dubois, Gallinger, Hiscock, Manderson, Mitchell, Perkins, Platt, Sawyer, Washburn.

So the amendment to the amendment was agreed to;

When,

The amendment as amended was agreed to.

The bill having been further amended on the motion of Mr. Hoar, the motion of Mr. Platt, the motion of McMillan, the motion of Mr. Hawley, the motion of Mr. Carey, the motion of Mr. Kyle, the motion of Mr. Voorhees, the motion of Mr. Coke, the motion of Mr. Frye, the motion of Mr. Vilas, the motion of Mr. White, the motion of Mr. Call, the motion of Mr. Hiscock, the motion of Mr. Allison, the motion of Mr. Quay, the motion of Mr Teller, the motion of Mr. Wolcott, the motion of Mr. Squire, the motion of Mr. Stewart, the motion of Pettigrew, and the motion of Mr. Gorman, it was reported to the Senate and the amendments were in part concurred in.

When,

On motion by Mr. Faulkner, at 10 o'clock and 25 minutes p. m.,

The Senate adjourned.

WEDNESDAY, FEBRUARY 22, 1893.

The Vice-President being absent, the President pro tempore assumed the chair.

WASHINGTON'S FAREWELL ADDRESS.

The President pro tempore laid before the Senate the resolution agreed to on the 15th, as follows:

Resolved, That on the 22d day of February, current, the anniversary of the birthday of George Washington, the Senate shall meet at 12 o'clock at noon, and after the reading of the Journal shall listen to the reading of Washington's farewell address by the Senator from Nebraska, President pro tempore of the Senate.

In pursuance of the order the farewell address was read by the President pro tempore;

When,

EXECUTIVE SESSION.

On motion by Mr. Sherman,

The Senate proceeded to the consideration of executive business; and

After the consideration of executive business the doors were reopened.

MESSAGE FROM THE HOUSE.

A message from the House of Representatives, by Mr. Towles, its chief clerk:

Mr. President: The House of Representatives has passed, without amendment, the following bill and joint resolutions of the Senate:

S. 3702. An act granting to the Chicago, Rock Island and Pacific Railway Company the use of certain lands at Chickasha Station, and for a "Y" in the Chickasaw Nation, Indian Territory;

S. R. 102. A joint resolution to provide for the construction of a wharf as a means of approach to the monument to be erected at Wakefield, Va., to mark the birthplace of George Washington; and

S. R. 121. A joint resolution authorizing payment, under act of August 30, 1890, to the State of Virginia, upon the assent of the governor, heretofore given, till adjournment of next session of the legislature thereof.

The House of Representatives has passed the following bills, in which it requests the concurrence of the Senate:

H. R. 3626. An act to grant to the Gainesville, McCallister and St. Louis Railway Company a right of way through the Indian Territory, and for other purposes;

H. R. 8518. An act to authorize the Commissioner of the General Land Office to issue a patent for Mace Clement's survey, No 386, in the Virginia military district of Ohio; and

H. R. 8677. An act to remove the cloud from the title to certain real estate in the city of Crawfordsville, Ind.

HOUSE BILLS REFERRED.

The bills last received from the House of Representatives for concurrence were severally read the first and second times by unanimous consent.

Ordered, That the bills H. R. 8518 and H. R. 8677 be referred to the Committee on Public Lands, and that the bill H. R. 3626 be referred to the Committee on Indian Affairs.

EXECUTIVE COMMUNICATIONS.

The President *pro tempore* laid before the Senate a letter of the Secretary of the Treasury, transmitting the claim of Charles Gallagher for fees alleged to have been unlawfully exacted from him under commercial intercourse regulations prescribed by the Secretary of the Treasury; which was referred to the Committee on Claims and ordered to be printed.

The President *pro tempore* laid before the Senate a letter of the Secretary of the Treasury, transmitting a communication from the Secretary of the Interior, submitting an estimate of deficiency of appropriation for salaries and expenses of pension agents for the fiscal year 1892; which was referred to the Committee on Appropriations and ordered to be printed.

The President *pro tempore* laid before the Senate a letter of the Secretary of the Treasury, transmitting a communication from the Secretary of War, submitting an estimate of deficiency in the appropriation for burial of indigent soldiers for fiscal year 1893; which was referred to the Committee on Appropriations and ordered to be printed.

PETITIONS AND MEMORIALS.

Petitions, memorials, etc., were presented and referred as follows:

By Mr. Paddock: Two petitions of citizens of Nebraska, praying an appropriation of $40,000 for continuing the tests of American timber; to the Committee on Appropriations.

A petition of citizens of Nebraska, praying for a reduction of the rate of letter postage to one cent per ounce; to the Committee on Post-Offices and Post-Roads.

By Mr. Cullom: Three petitions of citizens of Illinois, praying for the appointment of a committee to investigate an alleged combine formed for the depreciation of grain by the millers and others at St. Louis and Minneapolis; to the Committee on Agriculture and Forestry.

By Mr. Frye: A petition of citizens of Maine, praying the passage of a law for the establishment of a permanent census bureau, and for the collection and registration of statistics relating to farm mortgages; to the Committee on the Census.

By Mr. Pettigrew: A resolution of the legislature of South Dakota, remonstrating against the repeal of the dependent pension act; to the Committee on Pensions.

By Mr. McPherson: A memorial of manufacturers of tin in the United States, praying for the repeal of the duty on pig tin; to the Committee on Finance and ordered to be printed.

By Mr. Cockrell: A memorial of citizens of Clay County, Missouri, remonstrating against any change in the franchise of the Winner bridge so as to eliminate the clause providing for free transportation over the same between Kansas City and Clay County; to the Committee on Commerce.

REPORTS OF COMMITTEES

Mr. White, fr ... the Committee on Public Lands, to whom was referred the b''.) ('. 3302) reconveying to the original grantors the title to certain lands in the State of Louisiana conveyed by them to the United States, reported it without amendment.

The Senate proceeded, by unanimous consent, to consider the said bill as in Committee of the Whole; and no amendment being made, it was reported to the Senate.

Ordered, That it be engrossed and read a third time.

The said bill was read the third time.

Resolved, That it pass, and that the title thereof be as aforesaid.

Ordered, That the Secretary request the concurrence of the House of Representatives therein.

Mr. Morrill, from the Committee on Finance, to whom was referred the joint resolution (S. R. 154) instructing the Commissioner of Internal Revenue to reopen and reëxamine the claim of the Continental Fire Insurance Company and others, and certify the amount of taxes erroneously paid by said corporations, if any, reported it without amendment and without recommendation.

Mr. Sawyer, from the Committee on Pensions, to whom was referred the bill (H. R. 8017) granting a pension to Elizabeth Voss, reported it without amendment and submitted a report (No. 1330) thereon.

Mr. Mitchell, from the Committee on Claims, to whom was referred the bill (S. 264) for the relief of William B. Morgan, submitted an adverse report (? o. '531) thereon.

Ordered, That it be postponed indefinitely.

Mr. Mitchell, from the Committee on Claims, to whom was referred the bill (S. 3733) to empower Robert Adger and others to bring suit

in the Court of Claims for rent alleged to be due them, reported it without amendment and submitted a report (No. 1332) thereon.

Mr. Jones, of Arkansas, from the Committee on Indian Affairs, to whom was referred the bill (S. 3173) to authorize the Interoceanic Railway Company to construct and operate a railway, telegraph, and telephone line through the Indian Territory, reported it with an amendment.

Mr. Chandler, from the Committee on Immigration, submitted a report (No. 1333) to accompany the bill (S. 3786) establishing additional regulations concerning immigration to the United States, heretofore reported.

On motion by Mr. Chandler, and by unanimous consent,

Ordered, That 2,000 extra copies of the foregoing report (No. 1333) be printed for the use of Senate.

INTRODUCTION OF BILL.

Mr. Dubois introduced a bill (S. 3879) granting a pension to Charlotte M. Bryson, widow of Andrew Bryson, late rear-admiral, United States Navy; which was read the first and second times by unanimous consent and referred to the Committee on Pensions.

INAUGURATION ARRANGEMENTS.

Mr. Hale submitted the following resolution, for consideration:

Resolved, That the Secretary of War, the Commissioners of the District of Columbia, and the Engineer Officer in charge of public buildings and grounds in the District of Columbia, are directed to send forthwith to the Senate a statement of all places on the public grounds and streets where permits have been given to erect stands for seats to be used on inauguration day, and whether in any case such stands have been erected in front of any of the public buildings, and what, if any, conditions have been imposed as to the charges to be made to the public for the use of such stands, either public or private.

MESSAGE FROM THE HOUSE.

A message from the House of Representatives, by Mr. Towles, its chief clerk:

Mr. President: The House of Representatives has passed a bill (H. R. 10349) making appropriations for the service of the Post-Office Department for the fiscal year ending June 30, 1894 in which it requests the concurrence of the Senate.

CONFERENCE REPORT,

Mr. Proctor, from the committee of conference on the disagreeing votes of the two Houses on the amendments of the Senate to the bill (H. R. 4275) to grant to the Champlain and St. Lawrence Railroad Company the right of way across the Fort Mongomery military reservation, submitted the following report:

The committee of conference on the disagreeing votes of the two Houses on the amendment of the Senate to the bill (H. R. 4275) to grant to the Champlain and St. Lawrence Railroad Company a right of way across the Fort Montgomery military reservation, having met, after full and free conference have agreed to recommend and do recommend to their respective Houses as follows:

That the Senate recede from its amendment and the House agree to the same with an amendment as follows:

In line 4, strike out all after "New York," down to and including the word "consideration" in line 7, and insert in lieu thereof the following: *Subject, however, to the provisions of an act entitled "An act authorizing the Secretary of War to lease public property in certain cases," approved July twenty-eighth, eighteen hundred and ninety-two, and on condition;* and the Senate agree to the same.

REDFIELD PROCTOR,
C. K. DAVIS,
F. M. COCKRELL,
Managers on the part of the Senate.
JOHN L. MITCHELL,
D. H. PATTON,
C. E. BELKNAP,
Managers on the part of the House.

The Senate proceeded to consider the report; and

On motion by Mr. Proctor,

Resolved, That the Senate agree thereto.

Ordered, That the Secretary notify the House of Representatives thereof.

LEAVE TO WITHDRAW PAPERS.

On motion by Mr. Perkins,

Ordered, That Patrick Montgomery have leave to withdraw certain papers from the files of the Senate.

SUNDRY CIVIL APPROPRIATION BILL.

On motion by Mr. Allison,

The Senate resumed the consideration of the bill (H. R. 10238) making appropriations for sundry civil expenses of the Government for the fiscal year ending June 30, 1894 and for other purposes; and the residue of the amendments made in Committee of the Whole having been concurred in,

On motion by Mr. Davis to amend the bill by striking out on page 58 the following words:

"*Provided further,* That there be added to section 7 of "An act to repeal the timber-culture laws, and for other purposes," approved March 3, 1891, the following proviso: *Provided further* that nothing in this section shall be construed to apply in its provisions or to affect any case where a contest was pending in the Land Department prior to the date of the passage of said act, so as to in any manner impair rights which had been acquired under the preëmption, desert-land, or timber-culture laws prior to March 3, 1891,"

It was determined in the affirmative, { Yeas .... 28 Nays 18

On motion by Mr. Call,

The yeas and nays being desired by one-fifth of the Senators present, Those who voted in the affirmative are,

Messrs. Allison, Carey, Chandler, Dawes, Dixon, Dubois, Frye, Gallinger, Hale, Hansbrough, Hawley, Jones of Nevada, McMillan, Manderson, Morrill, Paddock, Peffer, Perkins, Pettigrew, Power, Quay, Sawyer, Sherman, Shoup, Squire, Stewart, Teller, Wolcott. Those who voted in the negative are,

Messrs. Berry, Blackburn, Blodgett, Coke, Faulkner, Gorman, Harris, Hill, Irby, Jones of Arkansas, McPherson, Mills, Morgan, Palmer, Pasco, Ransom, Vest, Vilas.

So the amendment was agreed to.

The bill having been further amended on the motion of Mr. Hawley, and no further amendment having been made,

Ordered, That the amendments be engrossed and the bill read a third time.

The said bill as amended was read the third time.

Resolved, That it pass.

Ordered, That the Secretary request the concurrence of the House of Representatives in the amendments.

ARMY APPROPRIATION BILL.

On motion by Mr. Stewart,

The Senate proceeded to consider the report of the committee of conference on the disagreeing votes of the two Houses on the amendments of the Senate to the bill (H. R. 9825) making appropriations for the support of the Army for the fiscal year ending June 30, 1894, and for other purposes; and

Resolved, That the Senate agree thereto.

Ordered, That the Secretary notify the House of Representatives thereof.

BRIDGE OVER THE MISSISSIPPI RIVER.

On motion by Mr. Vest,

The Senate proceeded to consider, as in Committee of the Whole, the bill (S. 3876) authorizing the St. Louis and Madison Transfer Company to construct a bridge over the Mississippi River; and no amendment being made, it was reported to the Senate.

Ordered, That it be engrossed and read a third time.

The said bill was read the third time.

Resolved, That it pass, and that the title thereof be as aforesaid.

Ordered, That the Secretary request the concurrence of the House of Representatives therein.

ALLOTMENT OF LANDS AT THE QUAPAW AGENCY.

The Presiding Officer (Mr. Berry in the chair) laid before the Senate the first bill on the calendar of special orders, viz, the bill (S. 3030) to provide for the allotment of lands among the several Indian tribes in the Quapaw Agency, in the Indian Territory, and for the sale of surplus lands of such tribes, and for the creation of the county of Cayuga, in the Territory of Oklahoma, and for other purposes;

When,

DIPLOMATIC AND CONSULAR APPROPRIATION BILL.

On motion by Mr. Hale,

The Senate proceeded to consider, as in Committee of the Whole, the bill (H. R. 10267) making appropriations for the diplomatic and consular service of the United States for the fiscal year ending June 30, 1894;

Pending which,

EXECUTIVE SESSION.

On motion by Mr. Hale,

The Senate proceeded to the consideration of executive business; and,

After the consideration of executive business the doors were reopened, and

On motion by Mr. Hale, at 5 o'clock and 40 minutes p. m.,

The Senate adjourned.

THURSDAY, FEBRUARY 23, 1893.

The Vice President resumed the chair.

MESSAGE FROM THE HOUSE.

A message from the House of Representatives, by Mr. Towles, its chief clerk:

Mr. President: The House of Representatives has passed, without amendment, the following bills and joint resolution of the Senate:

S. 1538. An act for the relief of the heir of James S. Ham;

S. 1539. An act for the relief of the heirs of John W. Vose;

S. 3725. An act authorizing the construction of a free bridge across the Arkansas River, connecting Little Rock and Argenta; and

S. R. 157. A joint resolution authorizing the Secretary of War to receive for instruction at the Military Academy at West Point, Alberto Guirola, of Salvador.

The Speaker of the House of Representatives having signed two enrolled bills, S. 3602 and S. 3873, I am directed to bring the same to the Senate for the signature of its President.

ENROLLED BILLS SIGNED.

Mr. Dubois reported from the committee that they had examined and found duly enrolled the following bills:

S. 3602. An act to grant to the Chicago, Rock Island and Pacific Railway Company a right of way through the Indian Territory, and for other purposes; and

S. 3873. An act to authorize the Kansas City, Pittsburg and Gulf Railroad Company to construct and operate a railroad, telegraph, and telephone line through the Indian Territory, and for other purposes;

Whereupon,

The Vice-President signed the same, and they were delivered to the committee to be presented to the President of the United States.

PETITIONS AND MEMORIALS.

Petitions, memorials, etc., were presented and referred as follows:

Mr. Hale presented a petition of citizens of Maine, praying the passage of a law for the establishment of a permanent census bureau, and for the collection and publication of statistics relating to farm mortgages; which was referred to the Committee on the Census.

Mr. Cullom presented several petitions of citizens of Illinois, praying for the appointment of a committee to investigate an alleged combine formed to depreciate the price of grain by the millers and others at St. Louis and Minneapolis; which were referred to the Committee on Agriculture and Forestry.

Mr. Sherman presented a memorial of citizens of Ohio, remonstrating against the repeal of the provision providing for the closing of the Columbian Exposition on the Sabbath day; which was referred to the Select Committee on the Quadro-Centennial.

HOUSE BILL REFERRED.

The bill H. R. 10349 yesterday received from the House of Representatives for concurrence, was read the first and second times by unanimous consent and referred to the Committee on Appropriations.

MESSAGE FROM THE HOUSE.

A message from the House of Representatives, by Mr. Towles, its chief clerk:

Mr. President: The House of Representatives has agreed to the report of the committee of conference on the disagreeing votes of the two Houses on the amendments of the Senate to the bill (H. R. 9825) making appropriations for the support of the Army for the fiscal year ending June 30, 1894, and for other purposes.

The House of Representatives has passed the bill of the Senate (S. 3317) extending the time for the construction of the Big Horn Southern Railroad through the Crow Indian Reservation, with an amendment in which it requests the concurrence of the Senate.

The House of Representatives has passed a bill (H. R. 9862) for the relief of George W. Jones, in which it requests the concurrence of the Senate.

BIG HORN SOUTHERN RAILROAD.

The Presiding Officer (Mr. Harris in the chair) laid before the Senate the amendment of the House of Representatives to the bill (S. 3317) extending the time for the construction of the Big Horn Southern Railroad through the Crow Indian Reservation; and

On motion by Mr. Jones, of Arkansas,

Resolved, That the Senate disagree to the amendment of the House of Representatives to the said bill and ask a conference with the House on the disagreeing votes of the two Houses thereon.

Ordered, That the conferees on the part of the Senate be appointed by the Presiding Officer; and

The Presiding Officer appointed Mr. Jones of Arkansas, Mr. Dawes, and Mr. Manderson.

Ordered, That the Secretary notify the House of Representatives thereof.

GEORGE W. JONES.

The bill (H. R. 9862) for the relief of George W. Jones, last received from the House of Representatives for concurrence, was read the first and second times by unanimous consent and considered as in Committee of the Whole; and no amendment being made, it was reported to the Senate.

Ordered, That it pass to a third reading.

The said bill was read the third time by unanimous consent.

Resolved, That it pass.

Ordered, That the Secretary notify the House of Representatives thereof.

The Senate proceeded to consider, as in Committee of the Whole, the bill (S. 3555) for the relief of George W. Jones; and

H. R. 8677. An act to remove the cloud from the title to certain real estate in the city of Crawfordsville, Ind.

HOUSE BILLS REFERRED.

The bills last received from the House of Representatives for concurrence were severally read the first and second times by unanimous consent.

Ordered, That the bills H. R. 8518 and H. R. 8677 be referred to the Committee on Public Lands, and that the bill H. R. 3626 be referred to the Committee on Indian Affairs.

EXECUTIVE COMMUNICATIONS.

The President *pro tempore* laid before the Senate a letter of the Secretary of the Treasury, transmitting the claim of Charles Gallagher for fees alleged to have been unlawfully exacted from him under commercial intercourse regulations prescribed by the Secretary of the Treasury; which was referred to the Committee on Claims and ordered to be printed.

The President *pro tempore* laid before the Senate a letter of the Secretary of the Treasury, transmitting a communication from the Secretary of the Interior, submitting an estimate of deficiency of appropriation for salaries and expenses of pension agents for the fiscal year 1892; which was referred to the Committee on Appropriations and ordered to be printed.

The President *pro tempore* laid before the Senate a letter of the Secretary of the Treasury, transmitting a communication from the Secretary of War, submitting an estimate of deficiency in the appropriation for burial of indigent soldiers for fiscal year 1893; which was referred to the Committee on Appropriations and ordered to be printed.

PETITIONS AND MEMORIALS.

Petitions, memorials, etc., were presented and referred as follows:

By Mr. Paddock: Two petitions of citizens of Nebraska, praying an appropriation of $40,000 for continuing the tests of American timber; to the Committee on Appropriations.

A petition of citizens of Nebraska, praying for a reduction of the rate of letter postage to one cent per ounce; to the Committee on Post-Offices and Post-Roads.

By Mr. Cullom: Three petitions of citizens of Illinois, praying for the appointment of a committee to investigate an alleged combine formed for the depreciation of grain by the millers and others at St. Louis and Minneapolis; to the Committee on Agriculture and Forestry.

By Mr. Frye: A petition of citizens of Maine, praying the passage of a law for the establishment of a permanent census bureau, and for the collection and publication of statistics relating to farm mortgages; to the Committee on the Census.

By Mr. Pettigrew: A resolution of the legislature of South Dakota, remonstrating against the repeal of the dependent pension act; to the Committee on Pensions.

By Mr. McPherson: A memorial of manufacturers of tin in the United States, praying for the repeal of the duty on pig tin; to the Committee on Finance and ordered to be printed.

By Mr. Cockrell: A memorial of citizens of Clay County, Missouri, remonstrating against any change in the franchise of the Winner bridge so as to eliminate the clause providing for free transportation over the same between Kansas City and Clay County; to the Committee on Commerce.

REPORTS OF COMMITTEES

Mr. White, from the Committee on Public Lands, to whom was referred the bill (. 3202) reconveying to the original grantors the title to certain lands in the State of Louisiana conveyed by them to the United States, reported it without amendment.

The Senate proceeded, by unanimous consent, to consider the said bill as in Committee of the Whole; and no amendment being made, it was reported to the Senate.

Ordered, That it be engrossed and read a third time.

The said bill was read the third time.

Resolved, That it pass, and that the title thereof be as aforesaid.

Ordered, That the Secretary request the concurrence of the House of Representatives therein.

Mr. Morrill, from the Committee on Finance, to whom was referred the joint resolution (S. R. 154) instructing the Commissioner of Internal Revenue to reopen and reexamine the claim of the Continental Fire Insurance Company and others, and certify the amount of taxes erroneously paid by said corporations, if any, reported it without amendment and without recommendation.

Mr. Sawyer, from the Committee on Pensions, to whom was referred the bill (H. R. 8017) granting a pension to Elizabeth Voss, reported it without amendment and submitted a report (No. 1330) thereon.

Mr. Mitchell, from the Committee on Claims, to whom was referred the bill (S. 264) for the relief of William B. Morgan, submitted an adverse report (No. 1331) thereon.

Ordered, That it be postponed indefinitely.

Mr. Mitchell, from the Committee on Claims, to whom was referred the bill (S. 3733) to empower Robert Adger and others to bring suit

in the Court of Claims for rent alleged to be due them, reported it without amendment and submitted a report (No. 1332) thereon.

Mr. Jones, of Arkansas, from the Committee on Indian Affairs, to whom was referred the bill (S. 3173) to authorize the Interoceanic Railway Company to construct and operate a railway, telegraph, and telephone line through the Indian Territory, reported it with an amendment.

Mr. Chandler, from the Committee on Immigration, submitted a report (No. 1333) to accompany the bill (S. 3786) establishing additional regulations concerning immigration to the United States, heretofore reported.

On motion by Mr. Chandler, and by unanimous consent, *Ordered,* That 2,000 extra copies of the foregoing report (No. 1333) be printed for the use of Senate.

INTRODUCTION OF BILL.

Mr. Dubois introduced a bill (S. 3879) granting a pension to Charlotte M. Bryson, widow of Andrew Bryson, late rear-admiral, United States Navy; which was read the first and second times by unanimous consent and referred to the Committee on Pensions.

INAUGURATION ARRANGEMENTS.

Mr. Hale submitted the following resolution, for consideration:

Resolved, That the Secretary of War, the Commissioners of the District of Columbia, and the Engineer Officer in charge of public buildings and grounds in the District of Columbia, are directed to send forthwith to the Senate a statement of all places on the public grounds and streets where permits have been given to erect stands for seats to be used on inauguration day, and whether in any case such stands have been erected in front of any of the public buildings, and what, if any, conditions have been imposed as to the charges to be made to the public for the use of such stands, either public or private.

MESSAGE FROM THE HOUSE.

A message from the House of Representatives, by Mr. Towles, its chief clerk:

Mr. President: The House of Representatives has passed a bill (H. R. 10349) making appropriations for the service of the Post-Office Department for the fiscal year ending June 30, 1894 in which it requests the concurrence of the Senate.

CONFERENCE REPORT.

Mr. Proctor, from the committee of conference on the disagreeing votes of the two Houses on the amendments of the Senate to the bill (H. R. 4275) to grant to the Champlain and St. Lawrence Railroad Company the right of way across the Fort Montgomery military reservation, submitted the following report:

The committee of conference on the disagreeing votes of the two Houses on the amendment of the Senate to the bill (H. R. 4275) to grant to the Champlain and St. Lawrence Railroad Company a right of way across the Fort Montgomery military reservation, having met, after full and free conference have agreed to recommend and do recommend to their respective Houses as follows:

That the Senate recede from its amendment and the House agree to the same with an amendment as follows:

In line 4, strike out all after "New York," down to and including the word "consideration" in line 7, and insert in lieu thereof the following: *Subject, however, to the provisions of an act entitled "An act authorizing the Secretary of War to lease public property in certain cases," approved July twenty-eighth, eighteen hundred and ninety-two, and on condition;* and the Senate agree to the same.

REDFIELD PROCTOR,
C. K. DAVIS,
F. M. COCKRELL,
Managers on the part of the Senate.

JOHN L. MITCHELL,
D. H. PATTON,
C. E. BELKNAP,
Managers on the part of the House.

The Senate proceeded to consider the report; and

On motion by Mr. Proctor,

Resolved, That the Senate agree thereto.

Ordered, That the Secretary notify the House of Representatives thereof.

LEAVE TO WITHDRAW PAPERS.

On motion by Mr. Perkins,

Ordered, That Patrick Montgomery have leave to withdraw certain papers from the files of the Senate.

SUNDRY CIVIL APPROPRIATION BILL.

On motion by Mr. Allison,

The Senate resumed the consideration of the bill (H. R. 10238) making appropriations for sundry civil expenses of the Government for the fiscal year ending June 30, 1894 and for other purposes; and the residue of the amendments made in Committee of the Whole having been concurred in,

On motion by Mr. Davis to amend the bill by striking out on page 58 the following words:

and telephone line through the Indian Territory, and for other purposes.

MILITARY ACADEMY APPROPRIATION BILL.

On motion by Mr. Cullom,
The Senate proceeded to consider, as in Committee of the Whole, the bill (H. R. 10290) making appropriations for the support of the Military Academy for the fiscal year ending June 30, 1894; and the reported amendments having been agreed to, the bill was reported to the Senate and the amendments were concurred in.

Ordered, That the amendments be engrossed and the bill read a third time.

The said bill as amended was read the third time.

Resolved, That it pass.

Ordered, That the Secretary request the concurrence of the House of Representatives in the amendments.

LEGISLATIVE APPROPRIATION BILL.

On motion by Mr. Dawes,
The Senate proceeded to consider, as in Committee of the Whole, the bill (H. R. 10331) making appropriations for the legislative, executive, and judicial expenses of the Government for the fiscal year ending June 30, 1894, and for other purposes; and the reported amendments having been agreed to in part and in part disagreed to, and in part amended and as amended agreed to, and the bill further amended on the motion of Mr. Dawes, from the Committee on Appropriations, and on motion of Mr. Hoar,
On motion by Mr. Harris, at 5 o'clock and 40 minutes p. m.,
The Senate adjourned.

FRIDAY, FEBRUARY 24, 1893.

The Vice-President being absent, the President *pro tempore* assumed the Chair.

MESSAGE FROM THE HOUSE.

A message from the House of Representatives, by Mr. Towles, its chief clerk:

Mr. President: The House of Representatives has disagreed to the amendments of the Senate to the bill (H. R. 10290) making appropriations for the support of the Military Academy for the fiscal year ending June 30, 1894. It asks a conference with the Senate on the disagreeing votes of the two Houses thereon, and has appointed Mr. Wheeler of Alabama, Mr. Newberry, and Mr. Bowers managers at the same on its part.

MILITARY ACADEMY APPROPRIATION BILL.

The President *pro tempore* laid before the Senate the message of the House of Representatives announcing its disagreement to the amendments of the Senate to the bill (H. R. 10290) making appropriations for the support of the Military Academy for the fiscal year ending June 30, 1894.

On motion by Mr. Cullom,
Resolved, That the Senate insist upon its amendments to the said bill disagreed to by the House of Representatives and agree to the conference asked by the House on the disagreeing votes of the two Houses thereon.

Ordered, That the conferees on the part of the Senate be appointed by the President *pro tempore*; and
The President *pro tempore* appointed Mr. Cullom, Mr. Stewart, and Mr. Call.

Ordered, That the Secretary notify the House of Representatives thereof.

EXECUTIVE COMMUNICATIONS.

The President *pro tempore* laid before the Senate a letter of the Secretary of the Treasury, transmitting, in obedience to law, a list of the names of the clerks and other persons employed in the several bureaus of the Treasury Department during the calendar year ended December 31, 1892; which was ordered to be printed and, with the accompanying documents, referred to the Committee on Printing.

The President *pro tempore* laid before the Senate a letter of the Secretary of the Treasury, transmitting an estimate of deficiency of appropriation for the postal service submitted by the Sixth Auditor; which was referred to the Committee on Appropriations and ordered to be printed.

PETITIONS AND MEMORIALS.

The President *pro tempore* laid before the Senate a petition of the Grand Army of the Republic of New York, praying the passage of the bill (S. 1598) to insure preference in appointment, employment, and retention therein in the public service of the United States to veterans of the late war.

Ordered, That it lie on the table.

Mr. Dubois presented a memorial of the legislature of Idaho in favor of the passage of the bill (H. R. 10412) to correct the northern boundary line of the Cœur d'Alene Indian Reservation; which was referred to the Committee on Indian Affairs.

Mr. Hiscock presented a resolution of the American Hebrew Association, remonstrating against the ratification of the treaty with Russia for the extradition of persons murdering or attempting to murder members of the royal family.

Ordered, That it lie on the table.

MOTION TO RECONSIDER WITHDRAWN.

Mr. Vest, with the consent of the Senate, withdrew the motion yesterday submitted by him that the Senate reconsider its vote on the passage of the bill (H. R. 10267) making appropriations for the diplomatic and consular service of the United States for the fiscal year ending June 30, 1894.

Ordered, That the Secretary request the concurrence of the House of Representatives in the amendments of the Senate to the bill.

PRESENTATION OF BILL AND JOINT RESOLUTION.

Mr. Dubois reported from the committee that they this day presented to the President of the United States the following enrolled bill and joint resolutions:

S. 3702. An act granting to the Chicago, Rock Island and Pacific Railway Company the use of certain lands at Chickasha Station, and for a "Y" In the Chickasaw Nation, Indian Territory;

S. R. 102. Joint resolution to provide for the construction of a wharf as a means of approach to the monument to be erected at Wakefield, Va., to mark the birthplace of George Washington; and

S. R. 121. Joint resolution authorizing payment, under act of August 30, 1890, to the State of Virginia, upon the assent of the governor, heretofore given, till adjournment of next session of the Legislature thereof.

REPORTS OF COMMITTEES.

Mr. Manderson, from the Committee on Military Affairs, to whom was referred the bill (H. R. 8004) donating the military reservation at Oklahoma City, in Oklahoma Territory, to said city for the use and benefit of the free public schools thereof, and for other purposes, reported it with amendments and submitted a report (No. 1338) thereon.

Mr. Quay, from the Committee on Commerce, to whom was referred the bill (S. 3878) authorizing the construction of a bridge over the Monongahela River at Glenwood, Twenty-third ward, city of Pittsburg, in the State of Pennsylvania, reported it with an amendment.

The Senate proceeded, by unanimous consent, to consider the said bill as in Committee of the Whole; and the reported amendment having been agreed to, the bill was reported to the Senate and the amendment was concurred in.

Ordered, That the bill be engrossed and read a third time.

The said bill was read the third time.

Resolved, That it pass, and that the title thereof be as aforesaid.

Ordered, That the Secretary request the concurrence of the House of Representatives therein.

Mr. Stewart, from the Committee on Claims, to whom was recommitted the bill (S. 1358) for the relief of Clara A. Graves, Lewis Smith Lee, Florence P. Lee, Mary S. Sheldon, and Elizabeth Smith, heirs of Lewis Smith, deceased, reported it with an amendment and submitted a report (No. 1336) thereon.

Mr. Jones, of Arkansas, from the Committee on Indian Affairs, to whom was referred the bill (H. R. 3626) to grant to the Gainesville, McCallister and St. Louis Railway Company a right of way through the Indian Territory, and for other purposes, reported it without amendment.

Mr. Wolcott, from the Committee on Post-Offices and Post-Roads, to whom was referred the amendment intended to be proposed by him to the general deficiency appropriation bill, No. 10258, providing for the payment of the claims of H. A. W Tabor, of William M. Keightley, and of Royal M. Hubbard, submitted a report (No. 1337) thereon; which, together with the proposed amendment, was referred to the Committee on Appropriations.

Mr. Manderson, from the Committee on Printing, to whom was referred the resolution submitted by Mr. Hunton on the 20th instant, to print the eulogies delivered in Congress on Hon. John S. Barbour, late a Senator from the State of Virginia, reported it without amendment and submitted a report (No. 1339) thereon.

The Senate proceeded, by unanimous consent, to consider the resolution; and

Resolved, That the Senate agree thereto.

Ordered, That the Secretary request the concurrence of the House of Representatives therein.

Mr. Manderson, from the Committee on Printing, to whom were referred the following resolutions received from the House of Representatives for concurrence on the 20th instant, reported them without amendment and submitted written reports thereon as follows:

Resolution to print the eulogies delivered in Congress on Hon. Eli Thomas Stackhouse, late a Representative from the State of South Carolina; Report No. 1340.

Resolution to print the eulogies delivered in Congress upon Hon. Edward F. McDonald, late a Representative from the State of New Jersey; Report No. 1341.

The Senate proceeded, by unanimous consent, to consider the resolutions; and

On motion by Mr. Sherman,
Ordered, That it be postponed indefinitely.

PRESIDENTIAL APPROVAL.

A message from the President of the United States, by Mr. Pruden, his secretary:

Mr. President: The President of the United States approved and signed, on the 21st instant, an act (S. 3629) to extend to the North Pacific Ocean the provisions of the statutes for the protection of fur seals and other fur-bearing animals.

Ordered, That the Secretary notify the House of Representatives thereof.

REPORTS OF COMMITTEES.

On motion by Mr. Vest,
Ordered, That the Committee on Commerce be discharged from the further consideration of the bill (S. 3681) to authorize the Washington, Alexandria and Mount Vernon Electric Railway Company to construct a bridge across the Potomac River, opposite Observatory Hill, and to construct a railroad over the same and through certain streets and reservations, and that it be referred to the Committee on the District of Columbia.

Mr. Vest, from the Committee on Commerce, reported a bill (S. 3880) to authorize the Washington, Alexandria and Mount Vernon Electric Railway Company to construct a bridge across the Potomac River opposite Observatory Hill; which was read the first and second times by unanimous consent.

Mr. Manderson, from the Committee on Printing, to whom was referred the resolution received from the House of Representatives for concurrence on the 20th instant, to print 35,000 copies of the Report of the Commissioner of Education for 1890–'91, reported it without amendment and submitted a report (No. 1334) thereon.

The Senate proceeded, by unanimous consent, to consider the said resolution; and

Resolved, That the Senate agree thereto.

Ordered, That the Secretary notify the House of Representatives thereof.

Mr. Manderson, from the Committee on Printing, to whom was referred the resolution submitted by him on the 18th instant to print 35,000 copies of the Report of the Commissioner of Education for 1890–'91, reported adversely thereon.

Ordered, That it be postponed indefinitely.

Mr. Mitchell, from the Committee on Claims, to whom was referred the amendment intended to be proposed by him to the general deficiency appropriation bill (H. R. 10258), to pay the claim of William Mulligan, administrator of George Wattles, submitted a report (No. 1335); which, together with the proposed amendment, was referred to the Committee on Appropriations.

Mr. Stewart, from the Committee on Appropriations, to whom was referred the bill (H. R. 10345) making appropriations for the payment of invalid and other pensions of the United States for the fiscal year ending June 30, 1894, and for other purposes, reported it without amendment.

INTRODUCTION OF BILLS.

Bills were introduced, read the first and second times by unanimous consent, and referred as follows:

By Mr. Gordon: A bill (S. 3881) relating to copyrights; to the Committee on Patents.

By Mr. Vest: A bill (S. 3882) granting a pension to Honora Shea; to the Committee on Pensions.

REPORT ON THE WOOLEN INDUSTRY.

Mr. Manderson submitted the following concurrent resolution; which was referred to the Committee on Printing:

Resolved by the Senate (the House of Representatives concurring therein), That there be printed a new edition of the special report of the Chief of the Bureau of Statistics of the Treasury Department relating to wool and the manufactures of wool, published by order of Congress in 1888, with the matter contained therein brought down to date—3,000 copies for the use of the Senate, 6,000 for the use of the House of Representatives, and 2,000 for distribution by the Bureau of Statistics of the Treasury Department.

INAUGURATION CEREMONIES.

The Vice-President laid before the Senate the resolution yesterday submitted by Mr. Hale, calling for information relative to the permits granted for the erection of stands in the public grounds and streets to be used on inauguration day; and having been amended on the motion of Mr. Faulkner,

The resolution as amended was agreed to, as follows:

Resolved, That the Secretary of War, the Commissioners of the District of Columbia, and the Engineer Officer in charge of public buildings and grounds in the District of Columbia are directed to send forthwith to the Senate a statement of all places on the public grounds and streets where permits have been given to erect stands for seats to be used on inauguration day, and whether in any case such stands have been erected in front of any of the public buildings; informing the Senate of any difference in location of said

stands under the resolution approved the 26th of January, 1893, from the places designated under former resolutions authorizing the erection of stands at former inaugurations; and what, if any, conditions have been imposed as to the charges to be made to the public for the use of such stands.

MESSAGE FROM THE HOUSE.

A message from the House of Representatives, by Mr. Towles, its chief clerk:

Mr. President: The Speaker of the House of Representatives having signed two enrolled bills, S. 3702, H. R. 9825, and two enrolled joint resolutions, S. R. 102 and S. R. 121, and I am directed to bring them to the Senate for the signature of its President.

ENROLLED BILLS AND RESOLUTIONS SIGNED.

Mr. Dubois reported from the committee that they had examined and found duly enrolled the following bills and joint resolutions:

S. 3702. An act granting to the Chicago, Rock Island and Pacific Railway Company the use of certain lands at Chickasha Station, and for a "Y" in the Chickasaw Nation, Indian Territory;

H. R. 9825. An act making appropriations for the support of the Army for the fiscal year ending June 30, 1894, and for other purposes;

S. R. 102. Joint resolution to provide for the construction of a wharf as a means of approach to the monument to be erected at Wakefield, Va., to mark the birthplace of George Washington; and

S. R. 121. Joint resolution authorizing payment, under act of August 30, 1890, to the State of Virginia, upon the assent of the governor, heretofore given, till adjournment of next session of the legislature thereof;

Whereupon,

The Vice-President signed the same, and they were delivered to the committee to be presented to the President of the United States.

CONSIDERATION OF BILLS ON THE CALENDAR.

The Senate proceeded to consider, as in Committee of the Whole, the following bills; and no amendment being made, they were reported to the Senate:

H. R. 8450. A bill to remove the charge of desertion from the record of Charles G. Pyer; and

H. R. 9069. A bill for the further continuance of the publication of the supplement of the Revised Statutes of the United States.

Ordered, That they pass to a third reading.

The said bills were read the third time.

Resolved, That they pass.

Ordered, That the Secretary notify the House of Representatives thereof.

The Senate proceeded to consider, as in Committee of the Whole, the following bills; and the reported amendments having been agreed to, and the bills were reported to the Senate and the amendments were concurred in:

S. 3696. A bill for the relief of Brig. Gen. John R. Brooke, United States Army; and

S. 3712. A bill to grant the right of way for electric-railroad purposes through certain lands of the United States in Richmond County, New York.

Ordered, That they be engrossed and read a third time.

The said bills were read the third time.

Resolved, That they pass and that the respective titles thereof be as aforesaid.

Ordered, That the Secretary request the concurrence of the House of Representatives therein.

DIPLOMATIC AND CONSULAR APPROPRIATION BILL.

On motion by Mr. Hale,

The Senate resumed, as in Committee of the Whole, the consideration of the bill (H. R. 10267) making appropriations for the diplomatic and consular service of the United States, for the fiscal year ending June 30, 1894; and the reported amendments having been agreed to, and the bill further amended on the motion of Mr. Hunton, it was reported to the Senate and the amendments were concurred in.

Ordered, That the amendments be engrossed and the bill read a third time.

The said bill as amended was read the third time.

Resolved, That it pass.

Mr. Vest entered a motion that the Senate reconsider its vote on the passage of the foregoing bill.

PRESENTATION OF BILLS.

Mr. Dubois reported from the committee that they this day presented to the President of the United States the following enrolled bills:

S. 3602. An act to grant to the Chicago, Rock Island and Pacific Railway Company a right of way through the Indian Territory, and for other purposes; and

S. 3873. An act to authorize the Kansas City, Pittsburg and Gulf Railroad Company to construct and operate a railroad, telegraph,

Hiscock, Hunton, Jones of Arkansas, Kyle, McMillan, McPherson, Manderson, Morrill, Paddock, Palmer, Pasco, Perkins, Platt, Power, Proctor, Pugh, Ransom, Sawyer, Sherman, Shoup, Stockbridge, Teller, Vance, Vest, Vilas, Washburn, Wolcott.

Those who voted in the negative are,

Messrs. Berry, Blackburn, Call, Dubois, Gallinger, Lindsay, Peffer, Turpie, Voorhees.

So the motion was agreed to; and

The Senate proceeded to consider the said bill as in Committee of the Whole; and

On motion by Mr. Hansbrough to amend the bill by striking out after the word "further" in line 15, page 6, the following words: "That any duly incorporated club having a license under this act may sell intoxicating liquor to its members at any time till the hour of 1 o'clock antemeridian;" and in lieu thereof inserting the following:

That the said excise board may, in its discretion, issue a license to any duly incorporated club on the petition of the officers of the club, and that the said excise board may, in its discretion, grant a permit to such club to sell intoxicating liquors to members and guests between such hours as the board aforesaid may designate in such permit,

It was determined in the affirmative, } Yeas .... 47 Nays 9

On motion by Mr. Peffer,

The ayes and nays being desired by one-fifth of the Senators present, Those who voted in the affirmative are,

Messrs. Bate, Berry, Blackburn, Brice, Butler, Call, Carey, Cockrell, Coke, Daniel, Davis, Dubois, Faulkner, Felton, Gorman, Hansbrough, Harris, Hawley, Higgins, Hill, Hiscock, Hunton, Irby, Jones of Arkansas, Kyle, McMillan, McPherson, Manderson, Mitchell, Paddock, Palmer, Pasco, Power, Pugh, Ransom, Sawyer, Shoup, Squire, Turpie, Vance, Vest, Vilas, Voorhees, Warren, Washburn, White, Wolcott.

Those who voted in the negative are,

Messrs. Chandler, Frye, Gallinger, Morrill, Peffer, Platt, Sherman, Teller, Wilson.

So the amendment was agreed to.

On motion by Mr. Hunton to amend the bill by striking out in section 21 the following words: "Except such laws as are applicable to the sale of liquor within one mile of the Soldiers' Home,"

On motion by Mr. Faulkner to amend the part proposed to be stricken out,

Pending debate,

LEGISLATIVE APPROPRIATION BILL.

The President pro tempore announced that the hour of 1 o'clock had arrived, and laid before the Senate the unfinished business at its adjournment yesterday, viz, the bill (H. R. 10331) making appropriations for the legislative, executive, and judicial expenses of the Government for the fiscal year ending June 30, 1894, and for other purposes; and

The Senate resumed, as in Committee of the Whole, the consideration of the bill; and the residue of the reported amendments having been agreed to in part, and the bill further amended on the motion of Mr. Sherman, and the motion of Mr. Dawes, from the Committee on Appropriations,

On the question to agree to the amendment reported after line 19, page 7,

On motion by Mr. Hawley to amend the amendment,

It was determined in the affirmative;

When,

The amendment as amended was agreed to.

On the question to agree to the following reported amendment, viz: On page 62 strike out the following words:

"That so much of section 9 of the act entitled 'An act to amend section 5352 of the Revised Statutes of the United States, in reference to bigamy, and for other purposes,' approved March 22, 1882, as authorizes the President to appoint a board of five persons to exercise certain powers and duties prescribed in said section, be, and the same is hereby, repealed; and the said board is hereby abolished, and all powers and duties conferred upon said board are hereby imposed upon and shall be discharged, without additional compensation, by a board hereby created, to be constituted of the governor, chief justice, and secretary of the Territory of Utah,"

After debate,

It was determined in the affirmative, } Yeas .... 36 Nays 20

On motion by Mr. Gorman,

The yeas and nays being desired by one-fifth of the Senators present, Those who voted in the affirmative are,

Messrs. Allison, Carey, Chandler, Cullom, Davis, Dawes, Dubois, Felton, Frye, Gallinger, Hale, Hansbrough, Hawley, Higgins, Hiscock, Jones of Arkansas, Jones of Nevada, Kyle, Manderson, Mitchell, Morrill, Paddock, Palmer, Peffer, Perkins, Platt, Power, Sawyer, Sherman, Shoup, Stewart, Stockbridge, Teller, Voorhees, Washburn, Wolcott.

Those who voted in the negative are,

Messrs Bate, Brice, Butler, Caffery, Coke, Faulkner, Gibson, Gorman, Gray, Harris, Hill, Hunton, Irby, Lindsay, McPherson, Mills, Pugh, Ransom, Turpie, Vest.

So the amendment was agreed to.

The residue of the reported amendments having been agreed to in part,

On the question to agree to the following reported amendment viz: After line 5, page 63, insert the following:

For the following expenses of the Commission, namely: For traveling expenses, printing, stationery, clerk hire, and office rent, seven thousand dollars: Provided, That out of this sum the Commission is hereby authorized to pay the secretary of the Territory, who is its secretary and disbursing agent, a reasonable sum for such service, not exceeding three hundred dollars, for the fiscal year eighteen hundred and ninety-four: Provided further, That it shall be the duty of the Commission to direct and require the registration officers of each precinct of said Territory, at the time of making the annual revision of the registration list as now required by law, to erase from the preceding registration list the names of all persons who have died or removed from such precinct or who can not be found as permanent residents therein, and to otherwise revise said list as now required by the laws of said Territory of Utah: And provided further, That said Commission, as soon as practicable after the completion of said revision of the registration lists, and upon the basis of the census of said Territory taken in the year eighteen hundred and ninety, shall redistrict said Territory, and apportion representatives in the same in such manner as to provide, as nearly as the same may be, for an equal representation of the people, excepting Indians not taxed, according to numbers, and by single districts as nearly compact as possible, in the legislative assembly, and to the number of members of the council and house of representatives thereof, respectively, as now established by law, and cause a record of the establishment of such new districts, and the apportionment of representatives thereto, to be made in the office of the secretary of said Territory, and such establishment and representation shall continue until Congress shall otherwise provide,

On motion by Mr. Stewart to amend the amendment by adding thereto the following:

Provided further, That whenever the legislature of Utah shall have provided by law for officers to execute the laws of Congress relating to registration of voters and elections in said Territory, said Commission shall cease to exist, and thereafter said legislature shall have jurisdiction in matters of registration and election; and the legislature shall have power by a vote of two-thirds of each branch thereof to pass any laws relating to said matters of election and registration over the veto of the governor,

Mr. Dawes raised a question of order, viz, that the amendment of Mr. Stewart proposed general legislation to a general appropriation bill, and was not in order under Rule 16.

The President pro tempore submitted the question to the Senate: Is the amendment in order under Rule 16? and

It was determined in the negative, } Yeas .... 26 Nays 26

On motion by Mr. Stewart,

The yeas and nays being desired by one-fifth of the Senators present, Those who voted in the affirmative are,

Messrs. Bate, Blackburn, Butler, Carey, Cockrell, Coke, Faulkner, Gibson, Gorman, Gray, Hale, Hansbrough, Higgins, Hill, Jones of Nevada, Lindsay, McPherson, Mills, Mitchell, Peffer, Perkins, Pugh, Stewart, Teller, Vest, Wolcott.

Those who voted in the negative are,

Messrs. Allison, Berry, Chandler, Cullom, Davis, Dawes, Dubois, Frye, Gallinger, Harris, Hawley, Hiscock, Irby, Jones of Arkansas, Kyle, Manderson, Morrill, Paddock, Palmer, Power, Sawyer, Sherman, Shoup, Stockbridge, Voorhees, Washburn.

So it was determined that the amendment was not in order.

The question recurring on agreeing to the reported amendment, Mr. Platt demanded a division of the question; and

On the question to agree to the first branch, vis: After line 5, page 63, insert the following:

For the following expenses of the Commission, namely: For traveling expenses, printing, stationery, clerk hire, and office rent, seven thousand dollars: Provided, That out of this sum the Commission is hereby authorized to pay the secretary of the Territory, who is its secretary and disbursing agent, a reasonable sum for such service, not exceeding three hundred dollars, for the fiscal year eighteen hundred and ninety-four,

It was determined in the affirmative.

The question recurring on the remaining portion of the amendment,

Mr. Gorman demanded a division of the question; and

On the question to agree to the first branch thereof, as follows: After line 12, page 63, insert the following:

Provided further, That it shall be the duty of the Commission to direct and require the registration officers of each precinct of said Territory, at the time of making the annual revision of the registration list as now required by law, to erase from the preceding registration list the names of all persons who have died or removed from such precinct or who can not be found as permanent residents therein, and to otherwise revise said list as now required by the laws of said Territory of Utah,

On motion by Mr. Paddock to amend the amendment by inserting

before the words "said Territory" where they last occur the words *Congress and,*
It was determined in the affirmative;
When,
The amendment as amended was agreed to.
On the question to agree to the remaining portion of the amendment as follows: After the word "Utah" in line 21, page 63, insert the following:

And provided further, That said Commission, as soon as practicable after the completion of said revision of the registration lists, and upon the basis of the census of said Territory taken in the year eighteen hundred and ninety, shall redistrict said Territory, and apportion representatives in the same in such manner as to provide, as nearly as the same may be, for an equal representation of the people, excepting Indians not citizens, according to numbers, and by single districts as nearly compact as possible, in the legislative assembly, and to the number of members of the council and house of representatives thereof, respectively, as now established by law, and to cause a record of the establishment of such new districts, and the apportionment of representatives thereto, to be made in the office of the secretary of said Territory, and such establishment and representation shall continue until Congress shall otherwise provide,

Mr. Platt raised a question of order, viz, that the amendment proposed general legislation to a general appropriation bill and was not in order under Rule 16, clause 3.
The President *pro tempore* submitted the question to the Senate: Is the amendment in order under clause 3, Rule 16? and

It was determined in the negative, { Yeas 18
                                    { Nays 27

On motion by Mr. Gorman,
The yeas and nays being desired by one-fifth of the Senators present,
Those who voted in the affirmative are,
Messrs. Butler, Cockrell, Coke, Daniel, Faulkner, Gorman, Gray, Hill, Jones of Arkansas, Lindsay, McPherson, Mills, Pasco, Peffer, Pugh, Stewart, Vest, Voorhees.
Those who voted in the negative are,
Messrs. Allison, Carey, Chandler, Cullom, Davis, Dixon, Dubois, Felton, Frye, Gallinger, Hale, Hansbrough, Hawley, Higgins, Hiscock, Irby, Kyle, Manderson, Mitchell, Paddock, Perkins, Sawyer, Sherp, Teller, Turpie, Washburn, Wolcott.
So it was determined that the amendment was not in order.
The residue of the reported amendments having been agreed to, and the bill further amended on the motion of Mr. Dawes, from the Committee on Appropriations, the motion of Mr. Wolcott, from the Committee on Civil Service and Retrenchment, and
A further amendment having been proposed by Mr. Allison,
Pending debate,
On motion by Mr. Manderson, at 6 o'clock and 15 minutes p. m., The Senate adjourned.

SATURDAY, FEBRUARY 25, 1893.

The Vice-President resumed the chair.

ENROLLED BILLS SIGNED.

The Vice-President signed the enrolled bills S. 1538, S. 1539, S. 3725, H. R. 8450, H. R. 9069, H. R. 9862, and the enrolled joint resolution S. R. 157, yesterday reported to have been examined, and they were delivered to the committee to be presented to the President of the United States.

MESSAGE FROM THE HOUSE.

A message from the House of Representatives, by Mr. Towles, its chief clerk:
Mr. President: The House of Representatives has disagreed to the amendments of the Senate to the bill (H. R. 10267) making appropriations for the diplomatic and consular service of the United States for the fiscal year ending June 30, 1894. It asks a conference with the Senate on the disagreeing votes of the two Houses thereon, and has appointed Mr. Blount, Mr. McCreery, and Mr. Hitt managers at the same on its part.
The House of Representatives has passed the following resolutions, in which it requests the concurrence of the Senate:
Resolved by the House of Representatives (the Senate concurring), That the report of the Director of the Mint on the production of the precious metals in the United States for the year 1892 be printed, and that 9,000 extra copies be printed, 4,000 copies for the use of the House of Representatives, 2,000 copies for the use of the Senate, and 3,000 copies for the use of the Director of the Mint.
Resolved by the House of Representatives (the Senate concurring), That there be printed of the eulogies delivered in Congress upon John G. Warwick, late a Representative from the State of Ohio, 8,000 copies, of which 2,000 copies shall be delivered to the Senators and Representatives of the State of Ohio, and of those remaining 2,000 copies shall be for the use of the Senate and 4,000 for the House of Representatives; and the Secretary of the Treasury be, and he is hereby, directed to have printed a portrait of the said John G. Warwick to accompany said eulogies. That of the quota of the House of Representatives the Public Printer shall set apart 50 copies, which he shall have bound in full morocco with gilt

edges, the same to be delivered, when completed, to the family of the deceased.
The House of Representatives has passed, without amendment, the following bills of the Senate:
S. 2772. An act for the relief of Seaton Norman; and
S. 3871. An act to authorize the construction of a bridge across the Calumet River.
The House of Representatives has agreed to the resolution of the Senate requesting the President of the United States to return to the Senate the bill (S. 3811) to amend an act giving the Mobile and Dauphin Island Railroad and Harbor Company the right to trestle across the shoal water between Cedar Point and Dauphin Island.
The Speaker of the House of Representatives having signed an enrolled bill, H. R. 3594, I am directed to bring the same to the Senate for the signature of its President.

ENROLLED BILL SIGNED.

Mr. Dubois reported from the committee that they had examined and found duly enrolled a bill (H. R. 3594) for the relief of the Stockbridge and Munsee tribe of Indians in the State of Wisconsin;
Whereupon,
The Vice-President signed the same, and it was delivered to the committee to be presented to the President of the United States.

DIPLOMATIC AND CONSULAR APPROPRIATION BILL.

The Vice-President laid before the Senate the message of the House of Representatives announcing its disagreement to the amendments of the Senate to the bill (H. R. 10267) making appropriations for the diplomatic and consular service of the United States for the fiscal year ending June 30, 1894; and
On motion by Mr. Hale,
Resolved, That the Senate insist upon its amendments to the said bill disagreed to by the House of Representatives and agree to the conference asked by the House on the disagreeing votes of the two Houses thereon.
Ordered, That the conferees on the part of the Senate be appointed by the Vice-President; and
The Vice-President appointed Mr. Hale, Mr. Allison, and Mr. Blackburn.
Ordered, That the Secretary notify the House of Representatives thereof.

HOUSE RESOLUTIONS REFERRED.

The resolution to print 9,000 extra copies of the report of the Director of the Mint on the precious metals of the United States for the year 1892, and the resolution to print 8,000 copies of the eulogies delivered in Congress upon the late Hon. John G. Warwick, this day received from the House of Representatives for concurrence, were read and referred to the Committee on Printing.

EXECUTIVE COMMUNICATION.

The Vice-President laid before the Senate a letter of the Attorney-General, transmitting, in answer to a resolution of the Senate of the 21st instant, a list of unappealed awards and judgments for flowage damages caused by the improvement of the Fox and Wisconsin rivers; which was referred to the Committee on Appropriations and ordered to be printed.

PETITIONS AND MEMORIALS.

The Vice-President laid before the Senate a communication from the committee appointed by the Chamber of Commerce of New York, urging an appropriation by Congress sufficient to defray the expenses for the entertainment of distinguished foreigners who may pass through New York on their way to the Columbian Exposition; which was referred to the Committee on Appropriations and ordered to be printed.
Mr. Gordon presented a petition of citizens of Georgia, praying the passage of a law to prohibit the sale of intoxicating liquors on the grounds of the Columbian Exposition; which was referred to the Select Committee on the Quadro-Centennial.
Mr. Mitchell presented a memorial of the legislature of the State of Oregon in favor of the construction of a breakwater and harbor of refuge at Port Orford, in said State; which was referred to the Committee on Commerce.
Mr. Caffery presented papers relating to the application of the heirs of Hilary B. Cenas to be relieved from responsibility as surety on the bond of Joseph M. Kennedy; which were referred to the Committee on Claims, to accompany the bill S. 3889.
Mr. Call presented two memorials of citizens of Florida, remonstrating against the repeal of the provision providing for the closing of the Columbian Exposition; which were referred to the Select Committee on the Quadro-Centennial.
Mr. Call presented several petitions of citizens of Florida, praying the passage of a law for the restriction of immigration into the United States; which were referred to the Committee on Immigration.

EXECUTIVE COMMUNICATION.

The Vice-President laid before the Senate a letter of the Secretary of War, transmitting, in answer to a concurrent resolution of the

Senate and the House of Representatives, a copy of a report of the Chief of Engineers upon the present condition of the harbor improvement at Cumberland Sound and the entrance to the port of Fernandina, Fla.; which was referred to the Committee on Commerce and ordered to be printed.

REPORTS OF COMMITTEES.

Mr. Washburn, from the Committee on Commerce, to whom was referred the bill (S. 3793) to authorize the construction of a bridge over the St. Louis River, between the States of Wisconsin and Minnesota, reported it with an amendment.

The Senate proceeded, by unanimous consent, to consider the said bill as in Committee of the Whole; and the reported amendment having been agreed to, the bill was reported to the Senate and the amendment was concurred in.

Ordered, That the bill be engrossed and read a third time.

The said bill was read the third time.

Resolved, That it pass, and that the title thereof be as aforesaid.

Ordered, That the Secretary request the concurrence of the House of Representatives therein.

Mr. Daniel, from the Committee on Claims, to whom was referred the bill (H. R. 5948) for the relief of Louisa Q. Lovell, submitted a report (No. 1342), and stated that under the provisions of the act of March 3, 1885, they had referred the same to the Court of Claims.

Mr. Peffer, from the Committee on Claims, to whom was referred the bill (H. R. 1484) for the relief of Mary A. Lewis, reported it without amendment and submitted a report (No. 1343) thereon.

Mr. Peffer, from the Committee on Claims, to whom was referred the bill (S. 97) for the relief of Mary A. Lewis, widow of Joseph N. Lewis, reported adversely thereon.

Ordered, That it be postponed indefinitely.

Mr. Vest, from the Committee on Commerce, to whom was referred the bill (S. 3886) to authorize the Montgomery Bridge Company to construct and maintain a bridge across the Alabama River near the city of Montgomery, Ala., reported it without amendment.

The Senate proceeded, by unanimous consent, to consider the said bill as in Committee of the Whole; and no amendment being made, it was reported to the Senate.

Ordered, That it be engrossed and read a third time.

The said bill was read the third time.

Resolved, That it pass, and that the title thereof be as aforesaid.

Ordered, That the Secretary request the concurrence of the House of Representatives therein.

Mr. Hale, from the Committee on Appropriations, to whom was referred the bill (H. R. 10488) making appropriations for the naval service for the fiscal year ending June 30, 1894, and for other purposes, reported it with amendments and submitted a report (No. 1344) thereon.

MESSAGE FROM THE HOUSE.

A message from the House of Representatives, by Mr. Towles, its chief clerk:

Mr. President: The House of Representatives has agreed to the report of the committee of conference on the disagreeing votes of the two Houses on the amendment of the House to the bill (S. 3317) extending the time for the construction of the Big Horn Southern Railroad through the Crow Indian Reservation.

The House of Representatives has passed a bill (H. R. 9741) to increase the pension of Capt. E. R. Chase from $20 to $72 a month, in which it requests the concurrence of the Senate.

The Speaker of the House of Representatives having signed an enrolled bill, S. 3876, I am directed to bring the same to the Senate for the signature of its President.

ENROLLED BILL SIGNED.

Mr. Dubois reported from the committee that they had examined and found duly enrolled the bill (S. 3876) authorizing the St. Louis and Madison Transfer Company to construct a bridge over the Mississippi River;

Whereupon,

The Vice-President signed the same, and it was delivered to the committee to be presented to the President of the United States.

HOUSE BILL REFERRED.

The bill H. R. 9741, this day received from the House of Representatives for concurrence, was read the first and second times by unanimous consent and referred to the Committee on Pensions.

PRESIDENTIAL APPROVALS.

A message from the President of the United States, by Mr. Pruden, his secretary:

Mr. President: The President of the United States approved and signed on the 24th instant, the following acts:

S. 1232. An act removing charge of desertion against Lucius W. Hayford, Worcester, Vt.;

S. 3857. An act authorizing the construction of a bridge over the Monongahela River at the foot of Main street, in the borough of Belle Vernon, in the State of Pennsylvania;

S. 3819. An act granting a pension to Mary Doubleday, widow of Bvt. Maj Gen. Abner Doubleday;

S. 1303. An act to increase the pension of Mrs. S. A. Farquharson; and

He this day approved and signed a joint resolution (S. R. 102) to provide for the construction of a wharf as a means of approach to the monument to be erected at Wakefield, Va., to mark the birthplace of George Washington.

Ordered, That the Secretary notify the House of Representatives thereof.

CONFERENCE REPORT.

Mr. Jones, of Arkansas, from the committee of conference on the disagreeing votes of the two Houses on the amendment of the House of Representatives to the bill S. 3317, submitted the following report:

The committee of conference on the disagreeing votes of the two Houses on the amendment of the House to the bill (S. 3317) extending the time for the construction of the Big Horn Southern Railroad through the Crow Indian Reservation, having met, after full and free conference have agreed to recommend and do recommend to their respective Houses as follows:

That the Senate recede from its disagreement to the amendment of the House of Representatives, and agree to the same with an amendment, as follows: On page 2, line 10, after "reservation," insert *said grant of a right of way through the military reservation to be subject to the consent and approval of the Secretary of War;* and the House agree to the same.

> JAMES K. JONES,
> H. L. DAWES,
> CHARLES F. MANDERSON,
> *Managers on the part of the Senate.*
> S. W. PEEL,
> L. M. TURPIN,
> JOHN L. WILSON,
> *Managers on the part of the House.*

The Senate proceeded to consider the said report; and

Resolved, That the Senate agree thereto.

Ordered, That the Secretary notify the House of Representatives thereof.

INTRODUCTION OF BILLS.

Bills were introduced, read the first and second times by unanimous consent, and referred as follows:

By Mr. Proctor: A bill (S. 3887) for the relief of L. A. Noyes; to the Committee on Claims.

By Mr. George: A bill (S. 3888) for the relief of Julia A. Nutt, widow and executrix of Haller Nutt, deceased, late of Natchez, State of Mississippi; to the Committee on Claims.

By Mr. Caffery: A bill (S. 3889) for the relief of the heirs of Hilary B. Cenas; to the Committee on Claims.

By Mr. Cullom: A bill (S. 3890) to authorize the Lake Shore and Michigan Southern Railroad Company to renew its railroad bridge across the Calumet River; to the Committee on Commerce.

LIST OF CLAIMS ALLOWED.

Mr. Hale submitted the following resolution; which was considered by unanimous consent and agreed to:

Resolved, That the Secretary of the Treasury be directed to transmit to the Senate a list of all claims allowed by the several accounting officers of the Treasury Department under appropriations the balances of which have been exhausted or carried to the surplus fund under the provisions of section 5 of the act of June 20, 1874, since the allowance of those already transmitted to Congress during the present session; and also a list of judgments of the Court of Claims requiring an appropriation at the present session not already transmitted; said list to include all claims allowed up to and including the 1st day of March next.

JUDGMENTS AGAINST THE UNITED STATES.

Mr. Gorman submitted the following resolution; which was considered by unanimous consent and agreed to:

Resolved, That the Attorney-General be directed to report to the Senate under section 11 of the act of March 3, 1887, entitled "An act to provide for the bringing of suits against the United States," all judgments rendered in the circuit and district courts of the United States against the United States, not heretofore reported, which require an appropriation for their payment.

REPORT ON COST ON PRODUCTION OF PRECIOUS METALS.

Mr. Hawley submitted the following concurrent resolution; which was referred to the Committee on Printing.

Resolved by the Senate (the House of Representatives concurring), That there be printed 6,000 copies of the report of the Committee on Mines and Mining on the cost of the production of gold and silver, 2,000 copies of it to be for the use of the Senate and 4,000 for the use of the House.

REPORTS ON LABOR IN EUROPE.

Mr. Chandler, from the Committee on Immigration, reported the following concurrent resolution; which was referred to the Committee on Printing:

Resolved by the Senate (the House of Representatives concurring),

That there shall be printed and bound 5,000 copies of the report on the condition of labor in Europe by Mr. Walter T. Griffin, commercial agent at Limoges, France, and 5,000 copies of the report of Mr. W. H. Edwards, consul-general at Berlin, on the "Labor statistics of the German trades unions for the year 1891," 1,000 copies of each report to be for the use of the Senate, 2,000 copies for the use of the House, and 2,000 copies to be distributed by the Secretary of State; that said report shall be edited and prepared for publication by the Commissioner of Labor, who shall also insert in said reports the equivalents in American money of all statements of prices or other sums now given in foreign money; and that only such photographs, maps, and other plates shall be reproduced as the Commissioner of Labor may deem essential to a fair illustration of the text of the reports.

EULOGIES ON FRANCIS B. SPINOLA.

Mr. Hill submitted the following resolution; which was considered by unanimous consent and agreed to.

Resolved, That this day, at 5 o'clock p. m., be set apart for paying tribute to the memory of Hon. Francis B. Spinola, late a member of the House of Representatives for the Tenth district of New York.

REPORT ON LABOR IN EUROPE.

Mr. Chandler, from the Committee on Immigration, reported the following resolution; which was considered by unanimous consent and agreed to:

Resolved, That the report on the condition of labor on the continent of Europe made to the Secretary of State by Mr. Walter T. Griffin, commercial agent at Limoges, France, dated April 25, 1892, and the report of Mr. W. H. Edwards, consul-general at Berlin, dated November 29, 1892, being a translation of the work entitled "Labor statistics of the German trades unions for the year 1891," transmitted to the Senate by the President in response to the resolutions of December 20, 1892, and January 5, 1893, be returned to the Secretary of State.

WITHDRAWAL OF PAPERS.

On motion by Mr. Perkins,
Ordered, That the papers in the case of Richard J. Hukle be withdrawn from the files of the Senate, subject to the rules.

REBECCA H. CHAMBERS.

On motion by Mr. Turpie,
The Senate proceeded to consider, as in Committee of the Whole, the bill (S. 2383) granting a pension to Rebecca H. Chambers; and the reported amendment having been agreed to, the bill was reported to the Senate, and the amendment was concurred in.
Ordered, That it be engrossed and read a third time.
The said bill was read the third time.
Resolved, That it pass, and that the title thereof be as aforesaid.
Ordered, That the Secretary request the concurrence of the House of Representatives therein.

ORSEMUS B. BOYD.

The Senate proceeded to consider, as in Committee of the Whole, the bill (S. 1920) for the relief of the legal representatives of Orsemus B. Boyd; and no amendment being made, it was reported to the Senate.
Ordered, That it be engrossed and read a third time.
The said bill was read the third time.
Resolved, That it pass, and that the title thereof be as aforesaid.
Ordered, That the Secretary request the concurrence of the House of Representatives therein.

MOTION TO RECONSIDER.

Mr. Washburn entered a motion to reconsider the vote of the Senate on the passage of the bill (S. 3703) to authorize the construction of a bridge over the St. Louis River between the States of Wisconsin and Minnesota; and
On motion by Mr. Washburn,
Ordered, That the Secretary request the House of Representatives to return the said bill to the Senate.

MESSAGE FROM THE PRESIDENT.

The following message was received from the President of the United States, by Mr. Pruden, his secretary:

To the Senate of the United States:

In compliance with a resolution of the Senate (the House of Representatives concurring) I return herewith the bill (S. 3811) entitled "An act to amend an act entitled 'An act to grant to the Mobile and Dauphin Island Railroad and Harbor Company the right to trestle across the shoal water between Cedar Point and Dauphin Island,' approved September 26, 1890."

BENJ. HARRISON.

EXECUTIVE MANSION, *February 25, 1893.*

The message was read.
Whereupon,

CORRECTION OF ENROLLED BILL.

Mr. Vest submitted the following resolution; which was considered by unanimous consent and agreed to:

Resolved by the Senate (the House of Representatives concurring), That the Committee on Enrolled Bills be, and they are hereby, authorized to correct the enrolled bill (S. 3811) to amend an act entitled "An act to grant to the Mobile and Dauphin Island Railroad and Harbor Company the right to trestle across the shoal water between Cedar Point and Dauphin Island," approved September 26, 1890, by striking out the word "six" in the second line, and inserting the word *four,* and the figure "6" in the sixth line, and inserting the figure *4.*
Ordered, That the Secretary request the concurrence of the House of Representatives therein.

PRESENTATION OF BILLS.

Mr. Dubois reported from the committee that they this day presented to the President of the United States the following enrolled bills and joint resolution:

S. 1538. An act for the relief of the heirs of James S. Ham;
S. 1539. An act for the relief of the heirs of John W. Vose;
S. 3725. An act for the construction of a free bridge across the Arkansas River, connecting Little Rock and Argenta; and
S. R. 157. A joint resolution authorizing the Secretary of War to receive for instruction at the Military Academy at West Point, Alberto Guirola, of Salvador.

EXECUTIVE COMMUNICATION.

The Vice-President laid before the Senate a letter of the Secretary of the Treasury, transmitting estimates of amounts found due by the First Comptroller on account of appropriations for expenses of the diplomatic and consular service; which was referred to the Committee on Appropriations and ordered to be printed.

CALENDAR BILLS CONSIDERED.

The Senate proceeded to consider, as in Committee of the Whole, the following bills; and no amendment being made, they were reported to the Senate:

H. R. 3508. An act for the relief of Nemiah Garrison, assignee of Moses Perkins; and
H. R. 8736. An act for the relief of the Shibley and Wood Grocer Company, of Van Buren, Crawford County, Arkansas.
Ordered, That they pass to a third reading.
The said bills were read the third time.
Resolved, That they pass.
Ordered, That the Secretary notify the House of Representatives thereof.

LEGISLATIVE APPROPRIATION BILL.

On motion by Mr. Dawes,
The Senate resumed, as in Committee of the Whole, the consideration of the bill (H. R. 10331) making appropriations for the legislative, executive, and judicial expenses of the Government for the fiscal year ending June 30, 1894, and for other purposes; and
The question being on the amendment proposed by Mr. Allison, and the same having been modified by Mr. Allison,
The amendment, as modified, was agreed to.
The bill having been further amended on the motion of Mr. Voorhees, the motion of Mr. Perkins, the motion of Mr. Dubois, the motion of Mr. Power, the motion of Mr. Carey, the motion of Mr. Hansbrough, the motion of Mr. Mitchell, the motion of Mr. Stewart, the motion of Mr. Gorman, and the motion of Mr. Turpie, it was reported to the Senate and the amendments were concurred in.
Ordered, That the amendments be engrossed and the bill read a third time.
The said bill as amended was read the third time.
Resolved, That it pass, and that the Senate request a conference with the House of Representatives on the said bill and amendment.
Ordered, That the conferees on the part of the Senate be appointed by the Presiding Officer; and
The Presiding Officer (Mr. Platt in the chair) appointed Mr. Dawes, Mr. Allison, and Mr. Cockrell.
Ordered, That the Secretary notify the House of Representatives thereof.

EXECUTIVE BUSINESS.

On motion by Mr. Sherman, that the Senate proceed to the consideration of executive business,

It was determined in the negative, { Yeas .... 21 { Nays 26

On motion by Mr. Gorman,
The yeas and nays being desired by one-fifth of the Senators present,
Those who voted in the affirmative are,
Messrs. Chandler, Cullom, Davis, Dawes, Felton, Gallinger, Hawley, Higgins, Hoar, Jones of Nevada, McMillan, Manderson, Mitchell, Morrill, Paddock, Platt, Sherman, Shoup, Squire, Stockbridge, Washburn.
Those who voted in the negative are,
Messrs. Berry, Blackburn, Butler, Call, Cockrell, Coke, Daniel, Gibson, Gorman, Hale, Harris, Hill, Hunton, Kyle, McPherson, Mills, Pasco, Peffer, Power, Pugh, Ransom, Teller, Turpie, Vance, Vest, Voorhees.
So the motion was not agreed to.

SALE OF LIQUOR IN THE DISTRICT.

On motion by Mr. Hansbrough,

The Senate resumed, as in Committee of the Whole, the consideration of the bill (H. R. 10266) regulating the sale of intoxicating liquors in the District of Columbia; and

The question being on the amendment proposed by Mr. Faulkner to the text of the bill proposed to be stricken out by the amendment of Mr. Hunton, viz: After the word "Home," in line 6, page 13, insert the following: *which law is hereby declared to be amended by reducing the limit prescribed in said act to one-half of a mile from the Soldiers' Home property,*

After debate,

It was determined in the affirmative, { Yeas 28
{ Nays 23

On motion by Mr. Gallinger,

The yeas and nays being desired by one-fifth of the Senators present,

Those who voted in the affirmative are,

Messrs. Berry, Blackburn, Call, Cockrell, Coke, Daniel, Davis, Gibson, Gorman, Hansbrough, Harris, Higgins, Hill, Hunton, McMillan, Manderson, Mills, Paddock, Pugh, Ransom, Sherman, Shoup, Stewart, Turpie, Vance, Vest, Voorhees, Washburn.

Those who voted in the negative are,

Messrs. Allison, Carey, Chandler, Cullom, Dubois, Felton, Gallinger, Gordon, Hawley, Hoar, Irby, Kyle, McPherson, Mitchell, Pasco, Peffer, Perkins, Platt, Power, Proctor, Teller, Warren, Wilson.

So the amendment was agreed to.

The question recurring on the amendment proposed by Mr. Hunton to strike out a part of the text of the bill as amended as follows: On page 13, line 5, after the word "act," strike out the following words: "Except such laws as are applicable to the sale of liquor within 1 mile of the Soldiers' Home, which law is hereby declared to be amended by reducing the limit prescribed in said act to one-half of a mile from the Soldiers' Home property,"

After debate,

It was determined in the negative, { Yeas 7
{ Nays 44

On motion by Mr. Gallinger,

The yeas and nays being desired by one-fifth of the Senators present.

Those who voted in the affirmative are,

Messrs. Butler, Carey, Harris, Mills, Power, Turpie, Voorhees.

Those who voted in the negative are,

Messrs. Allison, Bate, Berry, Blackburn, Call, Casey, Chandler, Cockrell, Coke, Daniel, Davis, Dubois, Felton, Gallinger, Gibson, Gorman, Hansbrough, Hawley, Higgins, Hill, Hoar, Irby, Kyle, McMillan, McPherson, Manderson, Mitchell, Paddock, Pasco, Peffer, Perkins, Proctor, Pugh, Ransom, Sherman, Shoup, Squire, Stewart, Stockbridge, Teller, Vance, Vest, Washburn, Wilson.

So the amendment was not agreed to.

A further amendment having been proposed by Mr. Peffer,

Pending debate,

EULOGIES ON HON. FRANCIS B. SPINOLA.

The Vice-President laid before the Senate the resolutions of the House of Representatives on the announcement of the death of Hon. Francis B. Spinola, as follows:

IN THE HOUSE OF REPRESENTATIVES,
March 26, 1893.

Resolved, That the business of the House be now suspended that opportunity may be given for tributes to the memory of the Hon. Francis B. Spinola, late a Representative from the State of New York.

Resolved, That as a particular mark of respect to the memory of the deceased, and in recognition of his eminent abilities as a distinguished public servant, the House, at the conclusion of these memorial proceedings, shall stand adjourned.

Resolved, That the Clerk communicate these resolutions to the Senate

Resolved, That the Clerk be instructed to send a copy of these resolutions to the family of the deceased.

The resolutions were read.

When,

Mr. Hill submitted the following resolutions; which were considered by unanimous consent and unanimously agreed to:

Resolved, That the Senate has heard with profound sorrow the announcement of the death of Hon. Francis B. Spinola, late a Representative from the State of New York.

Resolved, That in the death of Gen. Spinola the country has lost a gallant soldier, an able and faithful Representative in Congress, and an esteemed and patriotic citizen.

Resolved, That the business of the Senate be now suspended in order that fitting tribute be paid to his memory.

After addresses by Mr. Hill and Mr. Hiscock,

On motion by Mr. Hiscock, as an additional mark of respect to the memory of the deceased,

The Senate adjourned.

MONDAY, FEBRUARY 27, 1893.

Mr. Alfred H. Colquitt, from the State of Georgia, attended.

MESSAGE FROM THE HOUSE.

A message from the House of Representatives, by Mr. Towles, its chief clerk:

Mr. President: The House of Representatives has passed, without amendment, the bill (S. 3886) to authorize the Montgomery Bridge Company to construct and maintain a bridge across the Alabama River near the city of Montgomery, Ala.

The House of Representatives has passed the following resolutions, which I am directed to communicate to the Senate:

Resolved, That the business of the House be now suspended, that opportunity may be given for tribute to the memory of Hon. John S. Barbour, lately a United States Senator from the State of Virginia.

Resolved, That, as a particular mark of respect to the memory of the deceased and in recognition of his eminent abilities as a distinguished public servant, the House of Representatives, at the conclusion of these memorial services, adjourn.

Resolved, That the Clerk communicate these resolutions to the Senate.

Resolved, That the Clerk be instructed to send a copy of these resolutions to the family of the deceased.

The Speaker of the House of Representatives having signed two enrolled bills, H. R. 3508 and H. R. 8736, I am directed to bring the same to the Senate for the signature of its President.

ENROLLED BILLS SIGNED.

Mr. Dubois reported from the committee that they had examined and found duly enrolled the following bills:

H. R. 3508. An act for the relief of Nemiah Garrison, assignee of Moses Perkins; and

H. R. 8736. An act for the relief of the Shibley and Wood Grocer Company, of Van Buren, Crawford County, Arkansas;

Whereupon,

The Vice-President signed the same, and they were delivered to the committee to be presented to the President of the United States.

EXECUTIVE COMMUNICATIONS.

The Vice-President laid before the Senate a letter of the Attorney-General, transmitting, in answer to a resolution of the Senate of the 24th instant, a list of all judgments rendered by the Court of Claims in Indian depredation cases since February 6, 1893, and copies of all recent correspondence with the Secretary of the Interior relative to the payment of such claims; which was referred to the Select Committee on Indian Depredations and ordered to be printed.

The Vice-President laid before the Senate a letter of the Secretary of the Treasury, submitting an estimate of amounts found due naval officers for moneys expended by them under orders; which was referred to the Committee on Appropriations and ordered to be printed.

The Vice-President laid before the Senate a letter of the Secretary of the Interior, transmitting, in answer to a resolution of the Senate of the 21st instant, a communication from the Commissioner of Indian Affairs, relative to the number and value of claims presented by friendly Indians arising from depredations committed during the late disturbance at Pine Ridge, S. Dak.; which was referred to the Committee on Indian Affairs and ordered to be printed.

The Vice-President laid before the Senate a letter of the Secretary of War, transmitting, in answer to a resolution of the Senate of the 23d instant, a report of the engineer officer in charge of public buildings and grounds in the District of Columbia, relative to the erection of stands for seats to be used on inauguration day.

Ordered, That it lie on the table and be printed.

The Vice-President laid before the Senate a letter of the Secretary of the Smithsonian Institution, transmitting the annual report of the American Historical Association for the year 1892; which was referred to the Committee on Printing.

CREDENTIALS OF A SENATOR.

Mr. Blodgett presented the credentials of James Smith, jr., elected a Senator by the legislature of the State of New Jersey for the term of six years commencing March 4, 1893; which were read and placed on file.

PETITIONS AND MEMORIALS.

Petitions, memorials, etc., were presented and referred as follows:

Mr. Squire presented a memorial of the Chamber of Commerce of Port Townsend, Wash., praying liberal appropriations for the erection of coast defenses on Puget Sound; which was referred to the Committee on Appropriations.

Mr. Squire presented a memorial of the Chamber of Commerce of Seattle, Wash., praying such legislation as will guard against foreign interference in the affairs of the Hawaiian Islands; which was referred to the Committee on Foreign Relations.

Mr. Squire presented a memorial of the legislature of Washington in favor of the passage of a law for the establishment of an additional light-house district in that State; to the Committee on Commerce.

Mr. Sherman presented a memorial of citizens of Ohio, remonstrating against the repeal of the interstate-commerce law; which was referred to the Committee on Interstate Commerce.

Mr. Sherman presented a petition of citizens of Ohio, praying for the repeal of the law providing for the purchase of silver bullion.

Ordered, That it lie on the table.

Petitions praying the passage of the bill for the suspension of immigration into the United States were presented as follows:

By Mr. Quay: Five petitions of citizens of Pennsylvania.

By Mr. Manderson: A petition of citizens of Nebraska.

Ordered, That they be referred to the Committee on Immigration.

Memorials remonstrating against the repeal of the provision providing for the closing of the Columbian Exposition on the Sabbath day were presented as follows:

By Mr. Sherman: A memorial of citizens of Ohio.

By Mr. Quay: Two memorials of citizens of Pennsylvania.

Ordered, That they be referred to the Select Committee on the Quadro-Centennial.

Mr. Jones, of Arkansas, presented papers relating to the application of the Choctaw Nation to be reimbursed certain moneys with interest advanced by order of the Commissioner of Indian Affairs for the relief of the loyal Cherokee Indians; which were referred to the Committee on Indian Affairs, to accompany an amendment intended to be proposed to the Indian appropriation bill, H. R. 10415.

The Vice-President laid before the Senate a memorial of citizens of Washington, D. C., remonstrating against the adoption of the provision in section 5 of the license bill granting licenses to hotels or taverns having twenty-five chambers for lodging, without the consent of the real-estate owners and housekeepers in the locality.

Ordered, That it lie on the table.

REPORTS OF COMMITTEES.

Mr. Allison, from the Committee on Appropriations, to whom was referred the bill (H. R. 10421) making appropriations for the Department of Agriculture for the fiscal year ending June 30, 1894, reported it with amendments and submitted a report (No. 1345) thereon.

Mr. Pasco, from the Committee on Claims, to whom was referred the bill (H. R. 1231) for the relief of J. P. Randolph, administrator of J. G. Randolph, deceased, reported it with amendments and submitted a report (No. 1346) thereon.

Mr. Pasco, from the Committee on Claims, to whom was referred the bill (H. R. 5818) for the relief of William B. Morrow, reported it with an amendment and submitted a report (No. 1347) thereon.

Mr. Pugh, from the Committee on the Judiciary, to whom was referred the bill (H. R. 10363) to remove the disabilities of William F. Robinson, a citizen of the State of Alabama, reported it without amendment.

The Senate proceeded, by unanimous consent, to consider the said bill as in Committee of the Whole; and no amendment being made, it was reported to the Senate.

Ordered, That it pass to a third reading.

The said bill was read the third time.

Resolved, That it pass.

Ordered, That the Secretary notify the House of Representatives thereof.

Mr. Manderson, from the Committee on Printing, to whom was referred the resolution received from the House of Representatives for concurrence on the 15th instant, to print 9,000 copies of the annual report of the Chief of the Weather Bureau, reported it without amendment and submitted a report (No. 1348) thereon.

The Senate proceeded, by unanimous consent, to consider the said resolution; and

Resolved, That the Senate agree thereto.

Ordered, That the Secretary notify the House of Representatives thereof.

Mr. Daniel, from the Committee on Claims, to whom was referred the bill (H. R. 2122) for the relief of Cumberland Female College, of McMinnville, Tenn., reported it with an amendment and submitted a report (No. 1349) thereon.

Mr. Berry, from the Committee on Public Lands, to whom was referred the bill (H. R. 8677) to remove a cloud from the title to certain real estate in the city of Crawfordsville, Ind., reported it without amendment.

The Senate proceeded, by unanimous consent, to consider the said bill as in Committee of the Whole, and no amendment being made, it was reported to the Senate.

Ordered, That it pass to a third reading.

The said bill was read the third time.

Resolved, That it pass.

Ordered, That the Secretary notify the House of Representatives thereof.

Mr. Frye, from the Committee on Commerce, to whom was referred the bill (H. R. 10484) to amend an act approved July 27, 1892, entitled "An act to provide for the improvement of the outer bar of Brunswick, Ga," reported it without amendment.

The Senate proceeded, by unanimous consent, to consider the said bill as in Committee of the Whole, and no amendment being made, it was reported to the Senate.

Ordered, That it pass to a third reading.

The said bill was read the third time.

Resolved, That it pass.

Ordered, That the Secretary notify the House of Representatives thereof.

Mr. Manderson, from the Committee on Printing, to whom was referred the question of printing the list of persons employed in the Treasury Department during the year 1892, reported adversely thereon; and

The report was agreed to.

Mr. Vest, from the Committee on Commerce, to whom was referred the bill (S. 3890), to authorize the Lake Shore and Michigan Southern Railroad Company to renew its railroad bridge across the Calumet River upon or near the site of its present bridge, and upon a location and plans to be approved by the Secretary of War, and to operate the same, reported it without amendment.

MESSAGE FROM THE PRESIDENT.

The following message was received from the President of the United States, by Mr. Pruden, his secretary:

To the Senate and House of Representatives:

I herewith transmit for the information of Congress a communication from the Acting Secretary of State, forwarding certain bulletins of the Bureau of the American Republics.

BENJ. HARRISON.

EXECUTIVE MANSION,
Washington, February 27, 1893.

The message was read.

Ordered, That it be referred to the Committee on Foreign Relations and printed.

INTRODUCTION OF BILLS.

Bills were introduced, read the first and second times by unanimous consent, and referred as follows:

By Mr. Quay: A bill (S. 3891) extending the time for the completion of its railroad by the Choctaw Coal and Railway Company, and for other purposes; to the Committee on Indian Affairs.

By Mr. Stockbridge: A bill (S. 3892) for the removal of the charge of desertion from the record of John Cassidy; to the Committee on Naval Affairs.

By Mr. Squire: A bill (S. 3893) to increase the number of lighthouse districts, and for other purposes; to the Committee on Commerce.

By Mr. Perkins: A bill (S. 3894) granting to the Purcell Bridge and Transfer Company the consent of the United States to construct and maintain a bridge over the South Canadian River at or within one mile of the town of Lexington, county of Cleveland, Territory of Oklahoma; to the Committee on Commerce.

WOOL SAMPLES.

Mr. Sherman submitted the following resolution; which was considered by unanimous consent and agreed to:

Resolved, That the Secretary of the Treasury be directed to communicate to the Senate the reports made by the commission to select wool samples for use in the custom-houses of the United States, and all information in the Department in respect to such samples.

PHILADELPHIA HARBOR IMPROVEMENT.

Mr. Quay submitted the following resolution; which was considered by unanimous consent and agreed to:

Resolved, That the Secretary of War be required to furnish, for the information of the Senate, copies of all papers and documents relating to the proposals for the improvement of the harbor of Philadelphia under date of January 31, A. D. 1893, and that he be requested to suspend action upon said proposals until the information has been received and considered by the Senate.

MESSAGE FROM THE HOUSE.

A message from the House of Representatives, by Mr. Kerr, its Clerk:

Mr. President: The House of Representatives has disagreed to the amendments of the Senate to the bill (H. R. 10331) making appropriations for the legislative, executive, and judicial expenses of the Government for the fiscal year ending June 30, 1894, and for other purposes. It agrees to the conference asked by the Senate on the disagreeing votes of the two Houses thereon, and has appointed Mr. Dockery, Mr. Holman, and Mr. Henderson, of Iowa, managers at the same on its part.

The House of Representatives has disagreed to the report of the committee of conference on the disagreeing votes of the two Houses on the amendment of the House to the bill (S. 2931) to provide for the survey and transfer of that part of the Fort Randall military reservation in the State of Nebraska to said State for school purposes. It asks a further conference with the Senate on the disagreeing votes of the two Houses thereon, and has appointed Mr. McRae, Mr. Amerman, and Mr. Clark, of Wyoming, managers at the same on its part.

The House of Representatives has disagreed to the amendments of the Senate to the bill (H. R. 10238) making appropriations for sundry civil expenses of the Government for the fiscal year ending

June 30, 1894, and for other purposes. It asks a conference with the Senate on the disagreeing votes of the two Houses thereon, and has appointed Mr. Holman, Mr. Sayers, and Mr. Cogswell managers at the same on its part.

The House of Representatives has passed, without amendment, the following resolutions of the Senate:

Resolution authorizing the Committee on Enrolled Bills to correct an error in the bill (S. 3811) to amend an act entitled "An act to grant to the Mobile and Dauphin Island Railroad and Harbor Company the right to trestle across the shoal water between Cedar Point and Dauphin Island," approved September 26, 1890; and

Resolution to print the eulogies delivered in Congress upon Hon. John S. Barbour, late a Senator f om the State of Virginia.

I am directed by the House of Representatives to return to the Senate in compliance with its request the bill (S. 3793) to authorize the construction of a bridge over the St. Louis River, between the States of Wisconsin and Minnesota.

The Speaker of the House of Representatives having signed three enrolled bills, S. 2772, S. 3317, and S. 3871, I am directed to bring the same to the Senate for the signature of its President.

ENROLLED BILLS SIGNED.

Mr. Dubois reported from the committee that they had examined and found duly enrolled the following bills:

S. 2772. An act for the relief of Seaton Norman;

S. 3317. An act extending the time for the construction of the Big Horn Southern Railroad through the Crow Indian Reservation, and

S. 3871. An act to authorize the construction of a bridge across the Calumet River;

Whereupon,

The Vice-President signed the same, and they were delivered to the committee to be presented to the President of the United States.

SUNDRY CIVIL APPROPRIATION BILL.

The Presiding Officer (Mr. Faulkner in the chair) laid before the Senate the message of the House of Representatives announcing its disagreement to the amendments of the Senate to the bill (H. R. 10238) making appropriations for sundry civil expenses of the Government for the fiscal year ending June 30, 1894, and for other purposes.

On motion by Mr. Allison,

Resolved, That the Senate insist upon its amendments to the said bill disagreed to by the House of Representatives and agree to the conference asked by the House on the disagreeing votes of the two Houses thereon.

Ordered, That the conferees on the part of the Senate be appointed by the Presiding Officer; and

The Presiding Officer appointed Mr. Allison, Mr. Hale, and Mr. Gorman.

Ordered, That the Secretary notify the House of Representatives thereof.

PRESIDENTIAL APPROVAL.

A message from the President of the United States, by Mr. Pruden, his secretary:

Mr. President: The President of the United States approved and signed, on the 25th instant, a joint resolution (S. R. 121) authorizing payment, under act of August 30, 1890, to the State of Virginia, upon the assent of the governor, heretofore given, till adjournment of the next session of the legislature

Ordered, That the Secretary notify the House of Representatives thereof.

CONFERENCE REPORTS.

Mr. Cullom, from the committee of conference on the disagreeing votes of the two Houses on the amendments of the Senate to the bill H. R. 10290, submitted the following report:

The committee of conference on the disagreeing votes of the two Houses on the amendments of the Senate to the bill (H. R. 10290) making appropriations for the support of the Military Academy for the fiscal year ending June 30, 1894, having met, after full and free conference have agreed to recommend and do recommend to their respective Houses as follows:

That the House recede from its disagreement to the amendments of the Senate numbered 2, 3, 4, 5, 6, 7, and 8, and agree to the same.

That the House recede from its disagreement to the amendment of the Senate numbered 1, and agree to the same with an amendment as follows: Insert after the word "Academy," in line 2 of said amendment, the following: from the Army; and the Senate agree to the same.

S. M. CULLOM,
WILLIAM M. STEWART,
WILKINSON CALL,
Managers on the part of the Senate.

JOS. WHEELER,
W. C. NEWBERRY,
W. W. BOWERS,
Managers on the part of the House.

The Senate proceeded to consider the said report; and

On motion by Mr. Cullom,

Resolved, That the Senate agree thereto.

Ordered, That the Secretary notify the House of Representatives thereof.

Mr. Hale, from the committee of conference on the disagreeing votes of the two Houses on the amendments of the Senate to the bill H. R. 10267, submitted the following report:

The c mmittee of conference on the disagreeing votes of the two Houses on the amendments of the Senate to the bill (H. R. 10267) making appropriations for the diplomatic and consular service of the United States for the fiscal year ending June 30, 1894, having met, after full and free conference have agreed to recommend and do recommend to their respective Houses as follows:

That the Senate recede from its amendments numbered 3, 4, 9, 13, and 15.

That the House recede from its disagreement to the amendments of the Senate numbered 1, 2, 5, 6, 7, 8, 10, 11, 12, 14, 16, and 17, and agree to the same.

EUGENE HALE,
W. B. ALLISON,
JO. C. S. BLACKBURN,
Managers on the part of the Senate.

JAMES H. BLOUNT,
JAMES B. McCREARY,
ROBERT R. HITT,
Managers on the part of the House.

The Senate proceeded to consider the said report.

On motion by Mr. Hale,

Resolved, That the Senate agree thereto.

Ordered, That the Secretary notify the House of Representatives thereof.

PRIVILEGES OF THE FLOOR.

On motion by Mr. Manderson, and by unanimous consent,

Ordered, That the privileges of the floor be granted to members-elect of the House of Representatives for the present week.

PUBLIC LANDS TO CORPORATIONS.

On motion by Mr. Call,

The Senate proceeded to consider, as in Committee of the Whole, the joint resolution (S. R. 125) to suspend approval of list of public lands to States or corporations until the further action of the Congress of the United States of America; and having been amended on the motion of Mr. Wolcott, that the bill be referred to the Committee on Public Lands,

It was determined in the negative, { Yeas 25
{ Nays 31

On motion by Mr. Call,

The yeas and nays being desired by one-fifth of the Senators present,

Those who voted in the affirmative are,

Messrs. Brice, Carey, Dawes, Felton, Frye, Hale, Hansbrough, Harris, Hawley, Hiscock, Hoar, McMillan, Manderson, Mills, Morrill, Platt, Power, Sawyer, Shoup, Stewart, Teller, Vilas, Washburn, White, Wolcott.

Those who voted in the negative are,

Messrs. Bate, Berry, Blodgett, Butler, Call, Chandler, Coke, Daniel, Davis, Dubois, Gallinger, Gibson, Higgins, Hill, Hunton, Irby, Jones of Arkansas, Kyle, Lindsay, McPherson, Mitchell, Pad.dock, Palmer, Peffer, Perkins, Pugh, Squire, Turpie, Vance, Vest, Voorhees.

So the motion was not agreed to.

On motion by Mr. Call,

Ordered, That the bill as amended be reprinted.

PENSION APPROPRIATION BILL.

On motion by Mr. Stewart,

The Senate proceeded to consider, as in Committee of the Whole, the bill (H. R. 10345), making appropriations for the payment of invalid and other pensions of the United States for the fiscal year ending June 30, 1894, and for other purposes; and no amendment being made, it was reported to the Senate.

Ordered, That it pass to a third reading.

The said bill was read the third time.

Resolved, That it pass.

Ordered, That the Secretary notify the House of Representatives thereof.

CONSIDERATION OF BILLS ON CALENDAR.

On motion by Mr. Coke,

The Senate proceeded to consider, as in Committee of the Whole, the bill (H. R. 3626) to grant to the Gainesville, McCallister and St. Louis Railway Company a right of way through the Indian Territory, and for other purposes; and no amendment being made, it was reported to the Senate.

Ordered, That it pass to a third reading.

The said bill was read the third time.

Resolved, That it pass.

Ordered, That the Secretary notify the House of Representatives thereof.

On motion by Mr. Vest,

The Senate proceeded to consider, as in Committee of the Whole, the bill (S. 2782) to restore Eugene Wells to the Army; and no amendment being made, it was reported to the Senate.

Ordered, That it be engrossed and read a third time.

The said bill was read the third time.

Resolved, That it pass, and that the title thereof be as aforesaid.

Ordered, That the Secretary request the concurrence of the House of Representatives therein.

MESSAGE FROM THE HOUSE.

A message from the House of Representatives, by Mr. Towles, its chief clerk:

Mr. President: The House of Representatives has passed a bill (H. R. 10415) making appropriations for current and contingent expenses and fulfilling treaty stipulations with Indian tribes for fiscal year ending June 30, 1894, and for other purposes, in which it requests the concurrence of the Senate.

The House of Representatives has agreed to the amendment of the Senate to the bill (H. R. 9350) to promote the safety of employés and travelers upon railroads by compelling common carriers engaged in interstate commerce to equip their cars with automatic couplers and continuous brakes and their locomotives with driving-wheel brakes, and for other purposes.

The Speaker of the House of Representatives having signed four enrolled bills, S. 3886, H. R. 8677, H. R. 10345, and H. R. 10363, I am directed to bring the same to the Senate for the signature of its President.

ENROLLED BILLS EXAMINED.

Mr. Dubois reported from the committee that they had examined and found duly enrolled the following bills:

S. 3886. An act to authorize the Montgomery Bridge Company to construct and maintain a bridge across the Alabama River near the city of Montgomery, Ala.;

H. R. 8677. An act to remove a cloud from the title to certain real estate in the city of Crawfordsville, Ind.;

H. R. 10345. An act making appropriations for the payment of invalid and other pensions of the United States for the fiscal year ending June 30, 1894, and for other purposes; and

H. R. 10363. An act to remove the disabilities of William F. Robinson, a citizen of the State of Alabama.

HOUSE BILLS REFERRED.

The bill H. R. 10415, last received from the House of Representatives for concurrence, was read the first and second times by unanimous consent and referred to the Committee on Appropriations.

SALE OF INTOXICATING LIQUORS IN THE DISTRICT.

The Senate resumed, as in Committee of the Whole, the consideration of the bill (H. R. 10266) regulating the sale of intoxicating liquors in the District of Columbia; and

The question being on the amendment proposed by Mr. Peffer, viz: After the word "license," in line 32, page 8, insert:

Provided, That no screens, tables, chairs, stands, or other furniture of any description, except the bar fixtures, shall be kept or used in any barroom, saloon, or other place where intoxicating liquors are permitted to be sold under the provisions of this act; and there shall be no painting, staining, curtaining, or other means used in said places for the purpose of obstructing the view from the outside thereof. And no place where liquors are authorized to be sold by the provisions of this act shall be opened, kept, or maintained within one-fourth of a mile from any schoolhouse, place of religious worship, or building occupied by any department or bureau of the public service: Provided further, That it shall be unlawful for any person to sell any of such liquors to any inmate of the Soldiers' Home under penalty of forfeiture of his or her license, if any exist. Any person offending against the foregoing provisions shall be liable to a further penalty of one hundred dollars for each offense,

On motion by Mr. Harris that the amendment lie on the table,

It was determined in the affirmative, { Yeas .... 39 / Nays 15

On motion by Mr. Gallinger,

The yeas and nays being desired by one-fifth of the Senators present,

Those who voted in the affirmative are,

Messrs. Bate, Berry, Blackburn, Brice, Butler, Caffery, Call, Cockrell, Daniel, Dubois, Faulkner, Felton, Hansbrough, Harris, Hawley, Higgins, Hiscock, Hunton, Irby, Jones of Arkansas, Kyle, Lindsay, McMillan, McPherson, Mills, Mitchell, Morrill, Palmer, Pasco, Power, Proctor, Ransom, Sawyer, Turpie, Vance, Vest, Voorhees, White, Wolcott.

Those who voted in the negative are,

Messrs. Carey, Casey, Chandler, Dawes, Frye, Gallinger, Hoar, Peffer, Perkins, Platt, Shoup, Squire, Stockbridge, Teller, Wilson.

So the motion was agreed to.

The bill having been further amended on the motion of Mr. Hansbrough, from the Committee on the District of Columbia,

On motion by Mr. Hoar to amend the bill by adding thereto the following proviso:

Provided, That it shall be unlawful for any person to sell intoxicating liquors knowingly to any inmate of the Soldiers' Home, under penalty of forfeiture of his or her license, if any exists. Any person offending against the foregoing provisions shall be liable to a further penalty of one hundred dollars for each offense,

It was determined in the negative, { Yeas .... 20 / Nays 42

On motion by Mr. Gorman,

The yeas and nays being desired by one-fifth of the Senators present,

Those who voted in the affirmative are,

Messrs. Allison, Chandler, Dawes, Frye, Gallinger, Hansbrough, Higgins, Hiscock, Hoar, Kyle, McPherson, Morrill, Peffer, Perkins, Platt, Proctor, Sherman, Stockbridge, Washburn, Wilson.

Those who voted in the negative are,

Messrs. Bate, Berry, Blackburn, Brice, Butler, Carey, Casey, Cockrell, Daniel, Dubois, Faulkner, Felton, Gibson, Gordon, Gorman, Harris, Hawley, Hill, Hunton, Irby, Jones of Nevada, Lindsay, McMillan, Manderson, Mills, Mitchell, Pasco, Power, Pugh, Ransom, Sawyer, Shoup, Squire, Stewart, Teller, Turpie, Vance, Vest, Voorhees, Warren, White, Wolcott.

So the amendment was not agreed to.

On motion by Mr. Gallinger to amend the bill by striking out the proviso after the word "tavern" in line 33, page 5, down to and including the word "consent" in line 46, and in lieu thereof inserting:

Provided, That nothing herein contained shall be construed to repeal sections one thousand one hundred and eighty-one, one thousand one hundred and eighty-two, and one thousand one hundred and eighty-three of the Revised Statutes relating to the District of Columbia, or any part thereof.

On motion by Mr. Faulkner, that the amendment lie on the table,

It was determined in the affirmative, { Yeas .... 29 / Nays 22

On motion by Mr. Gallinger,

The yeas and nays being desired by one-fifth of the Senators present,

Those who voted in the affirmative are,

Messrs. Bate, Berry, Blackburn, Butler, Call, Daniel, Faulkner, Gibson, Gordon, Gorman, Hansbrough, Harris, Irby, Jones of Arkansas, Lindsay, McMillan, Mills, Pasco, Pugh, Ransom, Sawyer, Sherman, Stewart, Turpie, Vest, Voorhees, Washburn, White, Wolcott.

Those who voted in the negative are,

Messrs. Carey, Casey, Chandler, Dawes, Dubois, Frye, Gallinger, Hawley, Higgins, Hiscock, Mitchell, Morrill, Peffer, Perkins, Platt, Power, Proctor, Shoup, Squire, Stockbridge, Teller, Wilson.

So the motion was agreed to.

On motion by Mr. Gallinger to amend the bill by striking out after the word "license" in line 11, page 7, the following words: "The fee for a wholesale license shall be two hundred and fifty dollars per annum, and for a barroom license four hundred dollars per annum;" and in lieu thereof inserting: *The fee for a wholesale license shall be five hundred dollars per annum, and for a barroom license one thousand dollars per annum.*

It was determined in the negative, { Yeas .... 21 / Nays 31

On motion by Mr. Gallinger,

The yeas and nays being desired by one-fifth of the Senators present,

Those who voted in the affirmative are,

Messrs. Carey, Casey, Chandler, Cullom, Dubois, Frye, Gallinger, Higgins, Hoar, Irby, Peffer, Platt, Power, Proctor, Sherman, Squire, Stockbridge, Teller, Warren, Washburn, Wilson.

Those who voted in the negative are,

Messrs. Bate, Berry, Blackburn, Butler, Call, Coke, Daniel, Faulkner, Gibson, Gorman, Gray, Hansbrough, Harris, Hawley, Hill, McMillan, McPherson, Mills, Mitchell, Morrill, Pasco, Pugh, Ransom, Sawyer, Shoup, Stewart, Turpie, Vest, Voorhees, White, Wolcott.

So the amendment was not agreed to.

The bill having been further amended on the motion of Mr. Gallinger,

Pending debate,

EULOGIES ON THE LATE SENATOR KENNA.

Mr. Faulkner, pursuant to notice, submitted the following resolutions:

Resolved, That the Senate has heard with profound sorrow of the death of Hon. John E. Kenna, late a Senator from the State of West Virginia, and extends to his afflicted family sincere sympathy and condolence in their bereavement.

Resolved, That as an additional mark of respect to the memory of Mr. Kenna the legislative business of the Senate be now suspended in order that his former associates in this body may pay fitting tribute to his memory.

Resolved, That the Secretary of the Senate be directed to transmit to the family of the deceased, and also to the governor of West Virginia, a certified copy of these resolutions, with a statement of the action of the Senate thereon.

Resolved, That the Secretary of the Senate communicate these resolutions to the House of Representatives.

Resolved, That as a further testimonial of respect to the memory of the deceased Senator that the Senate do now adjourn.

18 s

The Senate proceeded, by unanimous consent, to consider the resolutions, and

After addresses by Mr. Faulkner, Mr. Frye, Mr. Gorman, Mr. Blackburn, Mr. Cullom, Mr. Gray, Mr. Vest, Mr. Stewart, Mr. Daniel, Mr. Hawley, and Mr. Camden,

The resolutions were unanimously agreed to, and

The Senate adjourned.

TUESDAY, FEBRUARY 28, 1893.

ENROLLED BILLS SIGNED.

The Vice-President signed the four enrolled bills, S. 3886, H. R. 8677, H. R. 10345, and H. R. 10363, yesterday reported to have been examined, and they were delivered to the committee to be presented to the President of the United States.

MESSAGE FROM THE HOUSE.

A message from the House of Representatives, by Mr. Kerr, its Clerk:

Mr. President: The House of Reprentatives has agreed to the reports of the committees of conference on the disagreeing votes of the two Houses on the amendments of the Senate to the following bills of the House:

H. E. 4275. An act to grant to the Champlain and St. Lawrence Railroad Company a right of way across the Fort Montgomery military reservation;

H. R. 10290. An act making appropriations for the support of the Military Academy for the fiscal year ending June 30, 1894; and

H. R. 10267. An act making appropriations for the diplomatic and consular service of the United States for the fiscal year ending June 30, 1894.

The House of Representatives has agreed to the report of the committee of conference on the disagreeing votes of the two Houses on the amendments of the House to the bill (S. 1307) to provide a permanent system of highways in that part of the District of Columbia lying outside of cities.

The House of Representatives has passed a bill (H. R. 10351) to continue the duties on certain manufactures of flax at the rate now provided by law, in which it requests the concurrence of the Senate.

The House of Representatives has passed the following resolutions, in which it requests the concurrence of the Senate:

Resolved by the House of Representatives (the Senate concurring), That there be printed and bound at the Government Printing Office, 4,000 copies of the official report of the American delegates to the International Monetary Conference, convened at Brussels, November 22, 1892, and the accompaniments—1,000 copies for the use of the Senate, 2,000 copies for the use of the House of Representatives, and 1,000 copies for the use of the State Department.

Resolved by the House of Representatives (the Senate concurring), That there be printed of the eulogies delivered in Congress upon the Hon. Alexander K. Craig, late a Representative from the State of Pennsylvania, 8,000 copies, of which 2,000 copies shall be delivered to the Senators and Representatives of that State; and of the remaining number 2,000 shall be for the use of the Senate and 4,000 copies shall be for the use of the House; and of the quota of the House the Public Printer shall set aside 50 copies, which he shall have bound in full morocco with gilt edges, the same to be delivered, when completed, to the family of the deceased; and the Secretary of the Treasury is hereby directed to have engraved and printed at the earliest day practicable a portrait of the deceased to accompany said eulogies.

The Speaker of the House of Representatives having signed four enrolled bills, H. R. 4275, H. R. 9350, H. R. 10290, and H. R. 10484, I am directed to bring the same to the Senate for the signature of its President.

The President of the United States has informed the House of Representatives that he approved and signed on the 18th instant the following acts:

H. R. 9923. An act making appropriations for fortifications and other works of defense, for the armament thereof, for the procurement of heavy ordnance for trial and service, and for other purposes;

H. R. 8123. An act granting to the Santa Fe, Prescott and Phœnix Railway Company the right of way across the Whipple Barracks military reservation in Arizona;

H. R. 5504. An act to permit the withdrawal of certain papers and the signing of certain receipts by John Finn;

H. R. 9592. An act authorizing the Secretary of the Treasury to obtain plans and specifications for public buildings to be erected under the supervision of the Treasury Department, and providing for local supervision of the construction of the same;

H. R. 3627. An act to grant to the Gainesville, Oklahoma and Gulf Railroad Company a right of way through the Indian Territory, and for other purposes;

H. R. 7762. An act to ratify and confirm agreement between the Puyallup Indians and the Northern Pacific Railroad Company for right of way through the Puyallup Indian Reservation;

H. R. 10206. An act to ratify and confirm an agreement made between the Seneca Nation of Indians and William B. Barker;

H. R. 9527. An act to restore to the public domain a portion of the White Mountain Apache Indian Reservation, in the Territory of Arizona, and for other purposes; and

H. R. 8340. An act to amend an act establishing a court of private land claims and to provide for the settlement of private land claims in certain States and Territories, approved March 3, 1891.

ENROLLED BILLS SIGNED.

Mr. Dubois reported from the committee that they had examined and found duly enrolled the following bills:

H. R. 4275. An act to grant to the Champlain and St. Lawrence Railroad Company a right of way across the Fort Montgomery military reservation;

H. R. 9350. An act to promote the safety of employés and travelers upon railroads by compelling common carriers to equip their cars with automatic couplers and continuous brakes and their locomotives with driving-wheel brakes, and for other purposes;

H. R. 10290. An act making appropriations for the support of the Military Academy for the fiscal year ending June 30, 1894; and

H. R. 10484. An act to amend an act approved July 27, 1892, entitled "An act to provide for the improvement of the outer harbor of Brunswick, Ga;"

Whereupon,

The Vice President signed the same, and they were delivered to the committee to be presented to the President of the United States.

HOUSE BILL AND RESOLUTIONS REFERRED.

The bill H. R. 10351, last received from the House of Representatives for concurrence, was read the first and second times by unanimous consent and referred to the Committee on Finance.

The resolution to print 4,000 copies of the report of the American delegates to the International Monetary Conference, and the resolution to print 8,000 copies of the eulogies delivered in Congress upon the Hon. Alexander K. Craig, late a Representative from the State of Pennsylvania, this day received from the House of Representatives for concurrence, were read and referred to the Committee on Printing.

EXECUTIVE COMMUNICATIONS.

The Vice-President laid before the Senate a letter of the Attorney-General, transmitting, in answer to a resolution of the Senate of the 25th instant, a list of all judgments rendered by the circuit and district courts of the United States as provided for in the act of March 3, 1887, and which have not heretofore been reported to Congress; which was referred to the Committee on Appropriations and ordered to be printed.

The Vice-President laid before the Senate a letter of the Secretary of the Treasury, transmitting, in answer to a resolution of the Senate of the 8th instant, copies of reports made by special agents to the Seal Islands of Alaska during the years 1891 and 1892.

Ordered, That it lie on the table and be printed.

PETITIONS AND MEMORIALS.

Petitions, memorials, etc., were presented and referred as follows:

By the Vice-President: A resolution of the legislative assembly of Oklahoma Territory in favor of the passage of a law granting a charter to the Lexington and Purcell Railway Company; to the Committee on Indian Affairs.

A resolution of the legislative assembly of the Territory of Oklahoma in favor of the passage of a law approving the act of said legislative assembly providing for the employment of additional employés other than provided for by the organic act; to the Committee on Territories.

A resolution of the legislative assembly of the Territory of Oklahoma in favor of the passage of a law creating a new department to be known as the Department of Labor; to the Committee on Education and Labor.

By Mr. Cullom: Three petitions of citizens of Illinois, praying for the appointment of a committee to investigate an alleged combine formed to depreciate the price of grain by millers and others at St. Louis and Minneapolis; to the Committee on Agriculture and Forestry.

By Mr. Squire: A memorial of the chamber of commerce of Port Townsend, Wash., praying the establishment of a fog-signalvessel off Umatilla Reef, Flattery Rocks, in aid of the navigation of the coast and strait of Fuca; to the Committee on Commerce.

By Mr. Sherman: A memorial of citizens of Ohio, remonstrating against the issuance by the Post-Office Department of stamped envelopes to purchasers at the face value of the stamps printed thereon; to the Committee on Post-Offices and Post-Roads.

By Mr. Hawley: A petition of citizens of Philadelphia, Pa., praying the repeal of the so-called Chinese exclusion act; to the Committee on Foreign Relations.

By Mr. Cockrell: A petition of citizens of Missouri, praying the repeal of the so-called Chinese exclusion act; to the Committee on Foreign Relations.

By Mr. Faulkner: Papers relating to the application of J. H. Van Buren, assistant index clerk of the House of Representatives, to be

Ordered, That the Secretary notify the House of Representatives thereof.

On motion by Mr. Vest,

The Senate proceeded to consider, as in Committee of the Whole, the bill (S. 2782) to restore Eugene Wells to the Army; and no amendment being made, it was reported to the Senate.

Ordered, That it be engrossed and read a third time.

The said bill was read the third time.

Resolved, That it pass, and that the title thereof be as aforesaid.

Ordered, That the Secretary request the concurrence of the House of Representatives therein.

MESSAGE FROM THE HOUSE.

A message from the House of Representatives, by Mr. Towles, its chief clerk:

Mr. President: The House of Representatives has passed a bill (H. R. 10415) making appropriations for current and contingent expenses and fulfilling treaty stipulations with Indian tribes for fiscal year ending June 30, 1894, and for other purposes, in which it requests the concurrence of the Senate.

The House of Representatives has agreed to the amendment of the Senate to the bill (H. R. 9350) to promote the safety of employés and travelers upon railroads by compelling common carriers engaged in interstate commerce to equip their cars with automatic couplers and continuous brakes and their locomotives with driving-wheel brakes, and for other purposes.

The Speaker of the House of Representatives having signed four enrolled bills, S. 3886, H. R. 8677, H. R. 10345, and H. R. 10363, I am directed to bring the same to the Senate for the signature of its President.

ENROLLED BILLS EXAMINED.

Mr. Dubois reported from the committee that they had examined and found duly enrolled the following bills:

S. 3886. An act to authorize the Montgomery Bridge Company to construct and maintain a bridge across the Alabama River near the city of Montgomery, Ala.;

H. R. 8677. An act to remove a cloud from the title to certain real estate in the city of Crawfordsville, Ind.;

H. R. 10345. An act making appropriations for the payment of invalid and other pensions of the United States for the fiscal year ending June 30, 1894, and for other purposes; and

H. R. 10363. An act to remove the disabilities of William F. Robinson, a citizen of the State of Alabama.

HOUSE BILLS REFERRED.

The bill H. R. 10415, last received from the House of Representatives for concurrence, was read the first and second times by unanimous consent and referred to the Committee on Appropriations.

SALE OF INTOXICATING LIQUORS IN THE DISTRICT.

The Senate resumed, as in Committee of the Whole, the consideration of the bill (H. R. 10266) regulating the sale of intoxicating liquors in the District of Columbia; and

The question being on the amendment proposed by Mr. Peffer, viz: After the word "license," in line 32, page 8, insert:

Provided, That no screens, tables, chairs, stands, or other furniture of any description, except the bar fixtures, shall be kept or used in any barroom, saloon, or other place where intoxicating liquors are permitted to be sold under the provisions of this act; and there shall be no painting, staining, curtaining, or other means used in said places for the purpose of obstructing the view from the outside thereof. And no place where liquors are authorized to be sold by the provisions of this act shall be opened, kept, or maintained within one-fourth of a mile from any schoolhouse, place of religious worship, or building occupied by any department or bureau of the public service: Provided further, That it shall be unlawful for any person to sell any of such liquors to any inmate of the Soldiers' Home under penalty of forfeiture of his or her license, if any exist. Any person offending against the foregoing provisions shall be liable to a further penalty of one hundred dollars for each offense,

On motion by Mr. Harris that the amendment lie on the table,

It was determined in the affirmative, { Yeas .... 39 / Nays 15

On motion by Mr. Gallinger,

The yeas and nays being desired by one-fifth of the Senators present,

Those who voted in the affirmative are,

Messrs. Bate, Berry, Blackburn, Brice, Butler, Caffery, Call, Cockrell, Daniel, Dubois, Faulkner, Felton, Hansbrough, Harris, Hawley, Higgins, Hiscock, Hunton, Irby, Jones of Arkansas, Kyle, Lindsay, McMillan, McPherson, Mills, Mitchell, Morrill, Palmer, Pasco, Power, Proctor, Ransom, Sawyer, Turpie, Vance, Vest, Voorhees, White, Wolcott.

Those who voted in the negative are,

Messrs. Carey, Casey, Chandler, Dawes, Frye, Gallinger, Hoar, Peffer, Perkins, Platt, Shoup, Squire, Stockbridge, Teller, Wilson.

So the motion was agreed to.

The bill having been further amended on the motion of Mr. Hansbrough, from the Committee on the District of Columbia,

On motion by Mr. Hoar to amend the bill by adding thereto the following proviso:

18 s

Provided, That it shall be unlawful for any person to sell intoxicating liquors knowingly to any inmate of the Soldiers' Home, under penalty of forfeiture of his or her license, if any exists. Any person offending against the foregoing provisions shall be liable to a further penalty of one hundred dollars for each offense,

It was determined in the negative, { Yeas .... 20 / Nays 42

On motion by Mr. Gorman,

The yeas and nays being desired by one-fifth of the Senators present,

Those who voted in the affirmative are,

Messrs. Allison, Chandler, Dawes, Frye, Gallinger, Hansbrough, Higgins, Hiscock, Hoar, Kyle, McPherson, Morrill, Peffer, Perkins, Platt, Proctor, Sherman, Stockbridge, Washburn, Wilson.

Those who voted in the negative are,

Messrs. Bate, Berry, Blackburn, Brice, Butler, Carey, Casey, Cockrell. Daniel, Dubois, Faulkner, Felton, Gibson, Gordon, Gorman, Harris, Hawley, Hill, Hunton, Irby, Jones of Nevada, Lindsay, McMillan, Manderson, Mills, Mitchell, Pasco, Power, Pugh, Ransom, Sawyer, Stewart, Teller, Turpie, Vance, Vest, Voorhees, Warren, White, Wolcott.

So the amendment was not agreed to.

On motion by Mr. Gallinger to amend the bill by striking out the proviso after the word "tavern" in line 33, page 5, down to and including the word "consent" in line 46, and in lieu thereof inserting:

Provided, That nothing herein contained shall be construed to repeal sections one thousand one hundred and eighty-one, one thousand one hundred and eighty-two, and one thousand one hundred and eighty-three of the Revised Statutes relating to the District of Columbia, or any part thereof.

On motion by Mr. Faulkner, that the amendment lie on the table,

It was determined in the affirmative, { Yeas .... 29 / Nays 22

On motion by Mr. Gallinger,

The yeas and nays being desired by one-fifth of the Senators present,

Those who voted in the affirmative are,

Messrs. Bate, Berry, Blackburn, Butler, Call, Daniel, Faulkner, Gibson, Gordon, Gorman, Hansbrough, Harris, Irby, Jones of Arkansas, Lindsay, McMillan, Mills, Pasco, Pugh, Ransom, Sawyer, Sherman, Stewart, Turpie, Vest, Voorhees, Washburn, White, Wolcott.

Those who voted in the negative are,

Messrs. Carey, Casey, Chandler, Dawes, Dubois, Frye, Gallinger, Hawley, Higgins, Hiscock, Mitchell, Morrill, Peffer, Perkins, Platt, Power, Proctor, Shoup, Squire, Stockbridge, Teller, Wilson.

So the motion was agreed to.

On motion by Mr. Gallinger to amend the bill by striking out after the word "license" in line 11, page 7, the following words: "The fee for a wholesale license shall be two hundred and fifty dollars per annum, and for a barroom license four hundred dollars per annum;" and in lieu thereof inserting: *The fee for a wholesale license shall be five hundred dollars per annum, and for a barroom license one thousand dollars per annum.*

It was determined in the negative, { Yeas .... 21 / Nays 31

On motion by Mr. Gallinger,

The yeas and nays being desired by one-fifth of the Senators present,

Those who voted in the affirmative are,

Messrs. Carey, Casey, Chandler, Cullom, Dubois, Frye, Gallinger, Higgins, Hoar, Irby, Peffer, Platt, Power, Proctor, Sherman, Squire, Stockbridge, Teller, Warren, Washburn, Wilson.

Those who voted in the negative are,

Messrs. Bate, Berry, Blackburn, Butler, Call, Coke, Daniel, Faulkner, Gibson, Gorman, Gray, Hansbrough, Harris, Hawley, Hill, McMillan, McPherson, Mills, Mitchell, Morrill, Pasco, Pugh, Ransom, Sawyer, Shoup, Stewart, Turpie, Vest, Voorhees, White, Wolcott.

So the amendment was not agreed to.

The bill having been further amended on the motion of Mr. Gallinger,

Pending debate,

EULOGIES ON THE LATE SENATOR KENNA.

Mr. Faulkner, pursuant to notice, submitted the following resolutions:

Resolved, That the Senate has heard with profound sorrow of the death of Hon. John E. Kenna, late a Senator from the State of West Virginia, and extends to his afflicted family sincere sympathy and condolence in their bereavement.

Resolved, That as an additional mark of respect to the memory of Mr. Kenna the legislative business of the Senate be now suspended in order that his former associates in this body may pay fitting tribute to his memory.

Resolved, That the Secretary of the Senate be directed to transmit to the family of the deceased, and also to the governor of West Virginia, a certified copy of these resolutions, with a statement of the action of the Senate thereon.

Resolved, That the Secretary of the Senate communicate these resolutions to the House of Representatives.

Resolved, That as a further testimonial of respect to the memory of the deceased Senator that the Senate do now adjourn.

enrolled bills, H. R. 3626 and H. R. 10267, I am directed to bring the same to the Senate for the signature of its President.

ENROLLED BILLS SIGNED.

Mr. Dubois reported from the committee that they had examined and found duly enrolled the following bills:

H. R. 3626. An act to grant to the Gainesville, McCallister and St. Louis Railway Company a right of way through the Indian Territory, and for other purposes; and

H. R. 10267. An act making appropriations for the diplomatic and consular service of the United States for the fiscal year ending June 30, 1894;

Whereupon,

The Vice-President signed the same, and they were delivered to the committee to be presented to the President of the United States.

NAVAL APPROPRIATION BILL.

On motion by Mr. Hale,

The Senate proceeded to consider, as in Committee of the Whole, the bill (H. R. 10488) making appropriations for the naval service for the fiscal year ending June 30, 1894, and for other purposes; and the reported amendments having been agreed to in part,

On the question to agree to the amendment reported from line 13, page 42, to line 14, page 43,

On motion by Mr. Gorman to amend the amendment by striking out of the part proposed to be inserted the following words: "and the number of persons who may at one time be enlisted into the Navy of the United States, including seamen, ordinary seamen, landsmen, mechanics, firemen, and coal heavers, and including 1,500 apprentices and boys, hereby authorized to be enlisted annually, shall not exceed 9,000."

After debate,

It was determined in the negative, { Yeas...................... 23
                                    { Nays...................... 26

On motion by Mr. Gorman,

The yeas and nays being desired by one-fifth of the Senators present,

Those who voted in the affirmative are,

Messrs. Bate, Blackburn, Caffery, Call, Camden, Cockrell, Gibson, Gorman, Hill, Jones of Arkansas, Kyle, Lindsay, Mills, Palmer, Pasco, Peffer, Ransom, Sherman, Turpie, Vance, Vest, Vilas, Voorhees.

Those who voted in the negative are,

Messrs. Casey, Chandler, Davis, Dubois, Felton, Frye, Gallinger, Hale, Hansbrough, Hawley, Higgins, Hiscock, Hoar, Hunton, Jones of Nevada, McMillan, McPherson, Manderson, Platt, Power, Proctor, Sawyer, Squire, Stewart, Stockbridge, Teller.

So the amendment to the amendment was not agreed to.

The amendment having been amended on the motion of Mr. Vest, was agreed to as amended.

The residue of the reported amendments having been agreed to, and the bill further amended on the motion of Mr. Hale, from the Committee on Appropriations, and the motion of Mr. Squire, the bill was reported to the Senate and the amendments were concurred in.

Ordered, That the amendments be engrossed and the bill read a third time.

The said bill as amended was read the third time.

Resolved, That it pass.

Ordered, That the Secretary request the concurrence of the House of Representatives in the amendments.

EXECUTIVE BUSINESS.

On motion by Mr. Sherman, that the Senate proceed to the consideration of executive business,

It was determined in the negative, { Yeas...................... 27
                                    { Nays...................... 29

On motion by Mr. Sherman,

The yeas and nays being desired by one-fifth of the Senators present,

Those who voted in the affirmative are,

Messrs. Carey, Casey, Chandler, Davis, Dawes, Dubois, Felton, Frye, Gallinger, Hale, Hansbrough, Hawley, Hiscock, Hoar, McMillan, Manderson, Morrill, Peffer, Pettigrew, Platt, Proctor, Sawyer, Sherman, Squire, Stewart, Stockbridge, Warren.

Those who voted in the negative are,

Messrs. Bate, Berry, Blackburn, Blodgett, Brice, Call, Camden, Cockrell, Coke, Daniel, Faulkner, Gibson, Gordon, Gorman, Harris, Hill, Hunton, Irby, Jones of Arkansas, Kyle, Lindsay, Palmer, Pasco, Pugh, Turpie, Vance, Vest, Vilas, Voorhees.

So the motion was not agreed to.

SALE OF INTOXICATING LIQUORS IN THE DISTRICT.

The Senate resumed, as in Committee of the Whole, the consideration of the bill (H. R. 10266) regulating the sale of intoxicating liquors in the District of Columbia; and having been further amended on the motion of Mr. Hansbrough, the bill was reported to the Senate and the amendments were in part concurred in.

On the question to concur, in the following amendment made in Committee of the Whole, viz:

On page 6, line 15, after the word "further," strike out the words "That any duly incorporated club having a license under this act may sell intoxicating liquors to its members at any time till the hour of 1 o'clock a. m," and in lieu thereof insert the following:

That the said excise board, may, in its discretion, issue a license to any duly incorporated club on the petition of the officers of the club, and that the said excise board may, in its discretion, grant a permit to such club to sell intoxicating liquors to members and guests between such hours as the board aforesaid may designate in said permit,

On motion by Mr. Gallinger to amend the amendment by inserting at the end of the part proposed to be inserted the words except on Sunday,

It was determined in the negative, { Yeas...................... 20
                                    { Nays...................... 36

On motion by Mr. Gallinger,

The yeas and nays being desired by one-fifth of the Senators present,

Those who voted in the affirmative are,

Messrs. Bate, Berry, Carey, Chandler, Dawes, Frye, Gallinger, Hawley, Irby, Kyle, Lindsay, Mills, Mitchell, Morrill, Peffer, Perkins, Platt, Pugh, Teller, Wilson.

Those who voted in the negative are,

Messrs. Blackburn, Blodgett, Caffery, Call, Coke, Daniel, Dubois, Faulkner, Felton, Gibson, Gordon, Gorman, Hansbrough, Harris, Higgins, Hill, Hiscock, Jones of Arkansas, McMillan, McPherson, Manderson, Power, Ransom, Sawyer, Sherman, Shoup, Squire, Stewart, Stockbridge, Vance, Vest, Vilas, Voorhees, Warren, White, Wolcott.

So the amendment to the amendment was not agreed to.

The question recurring on concurring in the amendment,

It was determined in the affirmative.

On the question to concur in the following amendment, made in Committee of the Whole, viz: After the word "Home," in line 6, page 13, insert the following words: Which law is hereby declared to be amended by reducing the limit prescribed in said act to one-half of a mile from the Soldiers' Home property.

It was determined in the negative, { Yeas...................... 24
                                    { Nays...................... 32

On motion by Mr. Faulkner,

The yeas and nays being desired by one-fifth of the Senators present,

Those who voted in the affirmative are,

Messrs. Bate, Blackburn, Cockrell, Coke, Daniel, Faulkner, Gibson, Gorman, Hansbrough, Harris, Hill, Lindsay, McMillan, Manderson, Mills, Morrill, Pugh, Sawyer, Stewart, Vance, Vest, Vilas, Voorhees, White.

Those who voted in the negative are,

Messrs. Allison, Berry, Blodgett, Caffery, Carey, Casey, Chandler, Dawes, Dubois, Felton, Frye, Gallinger, Hawley, Higgins, Hiscock, Hoar, Irby, Jones of Arkansas, Kyle, McPherson, Mitchell, Palmer, Pasco, Peffer, Perkins, Platt, Power, Sherman, Squire, Stockbridge, Teller, Wilson.

So the amendment was not concurred in.

No further amendment being proposed,

Ordered, That the amendments be engrossed and the bill read a third time.

The said bill as amended was read the third time.

On the question, Shall the bill pass?

It was determined in the affirmative, { Yeas...................... 41
                                       { Nays...................... 15

On motion by Mr. Mills,

The yeas and nays being desired by one-fifth of the Senators present,

Those who voted in the affirmative are,

Messrs. Berry, Blackburn, Caffery, Carey, Casey, Coke, Dawes, Dubois, Faulkner, Felton, Gibson, Gorman, Hansbrough, Harris, Hawley, Higgins, Hill, Hiscock, Irby, Jones of Arkansas, Kyle, Lindsay, McMillan, McPherson, Manderson, Mitchell, Morrill, Palmer, Pasco, Perkins, Power, Sawyer, Sherman, Shoup, Stewart, Stockbridge, Teller, Vance, Vilas, Warren, White.

Those who voted in the negative are,

Messrs. Bate, Blodgett, Chandler, Frye, Gallinger, Gordon, Hoar, Mills, Peffer, Platt, Pugh, Turpie, Vest, Voorhees, Wilson.

So it was

Resolved, That the bill pass; and

On motion by Mr. Hansbrough,

Resolved, That the Senate request a conference with the House of Representatives in the bill and amendments.

Ordered, That the conferees on the part of the Senate be appointed by the Presiding Officer; and

The Presiding Officer (Mr. Chandler in the chair) appointed Mr. Faulkner, Mr. McMillan, and Mr. Hansbrough.

Ordered, That the Secretary notify the House of Representatives thereof.

EXECUTIVE BUSINESS.

On motion by Mr. Frye, that the Senate proceed to the consideration of executive business,

It was determined in the negative, { Yeas...................... 30
                                    { Nays...................... 32

On motion by Mr. Hill,

The yeas and nays being desired by one-fifth of the Senators present,

Those who voted in the affirmative are,

Messrs. Allison, Carey, Casey, Chandler, Cullom, Davis, Dawes, Dubois, Frye, Gallinger, Hale, Hawley, Higgins, Hiscock, Hoar, Mc-

Millan, Manderson, Mitchell, Morrill, Paddock, Platt, Power, Sawyer, Sherman, Shoup, Squire, Stockbridge, Teller, Warren, Wolcott.

Those who voted in the negative are,

Messrs. Berry, Blackburn, Blodgett, Caffery, Cockrell, Coke, Daniel, Gibson, Gordon, Gorman, Gray, Harris, Hill, Hunton, Irby, Jones of Arkansas, Kyle, Lindsay, McPherson, Mills, Palmer, Pasco, Peffer, Pugh, Ransom, Stewart, Turpie, Vance, Vest, Vilas, Voorhees, White.

So the motion was not agreed to.

NEW YORK AND NEW JERSEY BRIDGE.

On motion by Mr. Hill, that the Senate proceed to the consideration of the bill (S. 2626) to authorize the New York and New Jersey Bridge Companies to construct and maintain a bridge across the Hudson River between New York City and the State of New Jersey,

It was determined in the affirmative, { Yeas 33
{ Nays 29

On motion by Mr. Hill,

The yeas and nays being desired by one-fifth of the Senators present, Those who voted in the affirmative are,

Messrs. Bate, Berry, Blackburn, Blodgett, Caffery, Call, Coke, Daniel, Faulkner, Gibson, Gray, Hansbrough, Harris, Hill, Hunton, Irby, Jones of Arkansas, Kyle, Lindsay, Mills, Palmer, Pasco, Pettigrew, Power, Pugh, Ransom, Squire, Stewart, Turpie, Vance, Vilas, Voorhees, White.

Those who voted in the negative are,

Messrs. Allison, Carey, Casey, Chandler, Cullom, Davis, Dubois, Frye, Gallinger, Gordon, Hawley, Higgins, Hiscock, Hoar, McMillan, McPherson, Manderson, Mitchell, Morrill, Paddock, Peffer, Platt, Proctor, Sawyer, Sherman, Shoup, Stockbridge, Teller, Wolcott.

So the motion was agreed to; and

Pending the consideration of the bill,

AGRICULTURAL APPROPRIATION BILL.

On motion by Mr. Allison,

The Senate proceeded to consider, as in Committee of the Whole, the bill (H. R. 10421) making appropriations for the Department of Agriculture for the fiscal year ending June 30, 1894; and the reported amendments having been agreed to, and the bill further amended on the motion of Mr. Allison, from the Committee on Appropriations, and the motion of Mr. Paddock, from the Committee on Agriculture and Forestry, it was reported to the Senate and the amendments were concurred in.

Ordered, That the amendments be engrossed and the bill read a third time.

The said bill as amended was read the third time.

Resolved, That it pass.

Ordered, That the Secretary request the concurrence of the House of Representatives in the amendments.

CONFERENCE REPORTS.

Mr. Harris, from the committee of conference on the disagreeing votes of the two Houses on the amendments of the House to the bill (S. 1307) to provide a permanent system of highways in that part of the District of Columbia lying outside of cities, submitted the following report:

The committee of conference on the disagreeing votes of the two Houses on the amendments of the House to the bill S. 1307, "A bill to provide a permanent system of highways in that part of the District of Columbia lying outside of cities," having met, after full and free conference have agreed to recommend and do recommend to their respective Houses as follows:

That the Senate recede from its disagreement to the first amendment of the House, and agree to the same amended to read as follows: "That the amount awarded by said court as damages for each highway or reservation or part thereof, condemned and established under this act, shall be one-half assessed against the land benefited thereby, and the other half shall be charged up to the revenues of the District of Columbia;" and that the House agree to the same.

That the Senate recede from its disagreement to the second amendment, and agree to the same amended to read as follows: "That one-half of the amount awarded by said court as damages for each highway or reservation or part thereof, condemned and established under this act, shall be charged upon the lands benefited by the laying out and opening of such highway or reservation or part thereof, and the remainder of said amount shall be charged to the revenues of the District of Columbia;" and that the House agree to the same.

That the Senate recede from its disagreement to the third amendment, and agree to the same with an amendment which inserts one-half instead of "one-third;" and that the House agree to the same.

That the Senate recede from its disagreement to the fourth amendment of the House, and agree to the same amended to read as follows:

That no expense for the improvement of any street, circle, reservation, or avenue laid out under the provisions of this act, outside the cities of Washington and Georgetown, shall be chargeable to the Treasury of the United States, but such expense shall be paid solely out of the revenues of the District of Columbia; and that the House agree to the same.

That the House recede from its fifth amendment.

That the Senate recede from its disagreement to the sixth amendment of the House, and agree to the same with an amendment to read as follows: In case the court shall enter judgment of condemnation in any case, and appropriation is not made by Congress for the payment of such award within the period of six months, Congress being in session for that time after such awards, or for the period of six months after the meeting of the next session of Congress, the proceedings shall be void, and the land shall revert to the owners; and that the House agree to the same.

That the House recede from its seventh amendment.

That the House recede from its eighth amendment.

That the House recede from its ninth amendment.

ISHAM G. HARRIS,
JAMES McMILLAN,
B. W. PERKINS,
Managers on the part of the Senate.

JNO. J. HEMPHILL,
JNO. F. HEARD,
P. S. POST,
Managers on the part of the House.

The Senate proceeded to consider the said report; and

On motion by Mr. Harris,

Resolved, That the Senate agree thereto.

Ordered, That the Secretary notify the House of Representatives thereof.

DISTRICT APPROPRIATION BILL.

Mr. Allison, from the committee of conference on the disagreeing votes of the two Houses on the amendments of the Senate to the bill H. R. 10038, submitted the following report:

The committee of conference on the disagreeing votes of the two Houses on the amendments of the Senate to the bill (H. R. 10038) making appropriations for the expenses of the government of the District of Columbia for the fiscal year ending June 30, 1894, and for other purposes, having met, after full and free conference have agreed to recommend and do recommend to their respective Houses as follows:

That the Senate recede from its amendments numbered 1, 4, 5, 11, 22, 26, 27, 28, 29, 33, 47, 48, 55, 65, 70, 71, 73, 74, 78, 85, 89, 109, 112, 114, and 116.

That the House recede from its disagreements to the amendments of the Senate numbered 2, 6, 7, 8, 9, 10, 13, 20, 21, 24, 30, 31, 32, 35, 39, 40, 41, 42, 43, 44, 45, 46, 49, 50, 51, 53, 54, 56, 57, 58, 59, 60, 61, 62, 64, 68, 72, 75, 76, 77, 79, 80, 82, 83, 84, 86, 87, 88, 90, 101, 102, 105, 106, 110, 111, and 115, and agree to the same.

Amendment numbered 3: That the House recede from its disagreement to the amendment of the Senate numbered 3, and agree to the same with an amendment as follows: In lieu of the sum proposed insert: forty-six thousand one hundred and forty-one dollars; and the Senate agree to the same.

Amendment numbered 12: That the House recede from its disagreement to the amendment of the Senate numbered 12, and agree to the same with an amendment as follows: Strike out the matter inserted by said amendment and insert after the word "dollars," in line 27, page 10, of the bill, the following: And this appropriation shall be available for removing and repairing parking on New York avenue between Ninth and Tenth streets, under the provisions of the compulsory permit system; and the Senate agree to the same.

Amendment numbered 14: That the House recede from its disagreement to the amendment of the Senate numbered 14, and agree to the same with an amendment as follows: In lieu of the sum proposed insert: two hundred thousand dollars; and the Senate agree to the same.

Amendment numbered 15: That the House recede from its disagreement to the amendment of the Senate numbered 15, and agree to the same with an amendment as follows: In lieu of the sum proposed insert: seventeen thousand dollars; and the Senate agree to the same.

Amendment numbered 16: That the House recede from its disagreement to the amendment of the Senate numbered 16, and agree to the same with an amendment as follows: In lieu of the sum proposed insert: seventy-six thousand dollars; and the Senate agree to the same.

Amendment numbered 17: That the House recede from its disagreement to the amendment of the Senate numbered 17, and agree to the same with an amendment as follows: In lieu of the sum proposed insert: twenty-six thousand dollars; and the Senate agree to the same.

Amendment numbered 18: That the House recede from its disagreement to the amendment of the Senate numbered 18, and agree to the same with an amendment as follows: In lieu of the sum proposed insert: thirty-eight thousand dollars; and the Senate agree to the same.

Amendment numbered 19: That the House recede from its disagreement to the amendment of the Senate numbered 19, and agree to the same with an amendment as follows: In lieu of the sum proposed insert: *forty-three thousand dollars*; and the Senate agree to the same.

Amendment numbered 23: That the House recede from its disagreement to the amendment of the Senate numbered 23, and agree to the same with an amendment as follows: In lieu of the sum proposed insert: *one hundred and twenty-three thousand nine hundred and fifty dollars*; and the Senate agree to the same.

Amendment numbered 25: That the House recede from its disagreement to the amendment of the Senate numbered 25, and agree to the same with an amendment as follows: In lieu of the sum proposed insert: *eighty-two thousand two hundred and fifty-five dollars*; and the Senate agree to the same.

Amendment numbered 34: That the House recede from its disagreement to the amendment of the Senate numbered 34, and agree to the same with an amendment as follows: Insert after said amendment as a new paragraph the following:

For grading Massachusetts avenue extended, ten thousand dollars.

And the Senate agree to the same.

Amendment numbered 36: That the House recede from its disagreement to the amendment of the Senate numbered 36, and agree to same with an amendment as follows: In lieu of the sum proposed insert: *thirty-nine thousand dollars*; and the Senate agree to the same.

Amendment numbered 37: That the House recede from its disagreement to the amendment of the Senate numbered 37, and agree to the same with an amendment as follows: In lieu of the sum proposed insert: *one hundred and twenty-five thousand dollars*; and the Senate agree to the same.

Amendment numbered 38; That the House recede from its disagreement to the amendment of the Senate numbered 38, and agree to the same with an amendment as follows: In lieu of the sum proposed insert: *one hundred and forty-six thousand dollars*; and the Senate agree to the same.

Amendment numbered 52: That the House recede from its disagreement to the amendment of the Senate numbered 52, and agree to the same with an amendment as follows: Strike out, in line 5 of said amendment the word "seventy-five," and insert in lieu thereof the word *sixty*; and the Senate agree to the same.

Amendment numbered 63: That the House recede from its disagreement to the amendment of the Senate numbered 63, and agree to the same with an amendment as follows: In lieu of the number proposed insert *fourteen*; and the Senate agree to the same.

Amendment numbered 66: That the House recede from its disagreement to the amendment of the Senate numbered 66, and agree to the same with an amendment as follows: In lieu of the sum proposed insert: *seven thousand seven hundred and fifty dollars*; and the Senate agree to the same.

Amendment numbered 67: That the House recede from its disagreement to the amendment of the Senate numbered 67, and agree to the same with an amendment as follows: In lieu of the sum proposed insert: *twenty-three thousand one hundred and fifty dollars*; and the Senate agree to the same.

Amendment numbered 69: That the House recede from its disagreement to the amendment of the Senate numbered 69, and agree to the same with an amendment as follows: In lieu of the matter proposed to be inserted by said amendment insert the following:

For one light wagon, harness and horse, three hundred and sixty-five dollars.

And the Senate agree to the same.

Amendment numbered 81: That the House recede from its disagreement to the amendment of the Senate numbered 81, and agree to the same with an amendment as follows: Strike out, in line 5 of said amendment, the word "ten," and insert in lieu thereof the word *five*; and the Senate agree to the same.

Amendment numbered 91: That the House recede from its disagreement to the amendment of the Senate numbered 91, and agree to the same with an amendment as follows: In lieu of the sum named in said amendment insert: *one thousand one hundred and eighty-one dollars*; and the Senate agree to the same.

Amendment numbered 92: That the House recede from its disagreement to the amendment of the Senate numbered 92, and agree to the same with an amendment as follows: In lieu of the sum named in said amendment insert: *one thousand one hundred and eighty-one dollars*; and the Senate agree to the same.

Amendment numbered 93; That the House recede from its disagreement to the amendment of the Senate numbered 93, and agree to the same with an amendment as follows: In lieu of the sum named in said amendment insert: *seven thousand six hundred and eighty dollars*; and the Senate agree to the same.

Amendment numbered 94: That the House recede from its disagreement to the amendment of the Senate numbered 94, and agree to the same with an amendment as follows: In lieu of the sum named in said amendment insert: *three thousand eight hundred and forty dollars*; and the Senate agree to the same.

Amendment numbered 95: That the House recede from its disagreement to the amendment of the Senate numbered 95, and agree to the same with an amendment as follows: In lieu of the sum named

in said amendment insert: *one thousand one hundred and eighty-one dollars*; and the Senate agree to the same.

Amendment numbered 96: That the House recede from its disagreement to the amendment of the Senate numbered 96, and agree to the same with an amendment as follows: In lieu of the sum named in said amendment insert: *one hundred and fifty dollars*; and the Senate agree to the same.

Amendment numbered 97: That the House recede from its disagreement to the amendment of the Senate numbered 97, and agree to the same with an amendment as follows: In lieu of the sum named in said amendment insert *one thousand one hundred and eighty-one dollars*; and the Senate agree to the same.

Amendment numbered 98: That the House recede from its disagreement to the amendment of the Senate numbered 98, and agree to the same with an amendment as follows: In lieu of the sum named in said amendment insert *one thousand seven hundred and seventy-three dollars*; and the Senate agree to the same.

Amendment numbered 99: That the House recede from its disagreement to the amendment of the Senate numbered 99, and agree to the same with an amendment as follows: In lieu of the sum named in said amendment insert *seven thousand six hundred and eighty dollars*; and the Senate agree to the same.

Amendment numbered 100: That the House recede from its disagreement to the amendment of the Senate numbered 100, and agree to the same with an amendment as follows: In lieu of the sum named in said amendment insert *two thousand nine hundred and fifty-three dollars*; and the Senate agree to the same.

Amendment numbered 103: That the House recede from its disagreement to the amendment of the Senate numbered 103, and agree to the same with an amendment as follows: In lieu of the sum proposed insert *nineteen thousand two hundred dollars*; and the Senate agree to the same.

Amendment numbered 104: That the House recede from its disagreement to the amendment of the Senate numbered 104, and agree to the same with an amendment as follows: In lieu of the sum proposed insert *twenty-four thousand two hundred dollars*; and the Senate agree to the same.

Amendment numbered 107: That the House recede from its disagreement to the amendment of the Senate numbered 107, and agree to the same with an amendment as follows: Strike out all of said amendment down to and including the word "dollars," in line 4 of said amendment; and the Senate agree to the same.

Amendment numbered 108. That the House recede from its disagreement to the amendment of the Senate numbered 108, and agree to the same with an amendment as follows: Strike out of said amendment the words "twelve thousand dollars" and insert in lieu thereof the following: *ten thousand dollars; in all, fifteen thousand dollars*; and the Senate agree to the same.

Amendment numbered 113. That the House recede from its disagreement to the amendment of the Senate numbered 113, and agree to the same with an amendment as follows: In lieu of the sum proposed insert *forty-five thousand eight hundred and sixty-four dollars*; and the Senate agree to the same.

W. B. ALLISON,
H. L. DAWES,
F. M. COCKRELL,
Managers on the part of the Senate.

ALEX. M. DOCKERY,
BARNES COMPTON,
D. B. HENDERSON,
Managers on the part of the House.

On motion by Mr. Allison, at 5 o'clock and 55 minutes p. m.,
The Senate adjourned.

WEDNESDAY, MARCH 1, 1893.

The Vice-President being absent, the President *pro tempore* assumed the chair.

HOUSE BILL REFERRED.

The bill H. R. 10567, yesterday received from the House of Representatives for concurrence, was read the first and second times by unanimous consent and referred to the Committee on Finance.

HOUSE AMENDMENTS TO SENATE BILLS.

The President *pro tempore* laid before the Senate the message of the House of Representatives announcing its disagreement to the report of the committee of conference on the disagreeing votes of the two Houses on the amendment of the House to the bill (S. 2931) to provide for the survey and transfer of that part of the Fort Randall military reservation in the State of Nebraska to said State for school and other purposes, and asking a further conference with the Senate thereon.

On motion by Mr. Paddock,

Resolved, That the Senate recede from its disagreement to the amendment of the House of Representatives to the said bill, and agree to the same.

Ordered, That the Secretary notify the House of Representatives thereof.

The President *pro tempore* laid before the Senate the amendment of the House of Representatives to the bill (S. 782) to provide for the adjustment of the sales of lands in the late reservation of the Confederated Otoe and Missouria tribes of Indians in the States of Nebraska and Kansas; and
On motion by Mr. Paddock,
Resolved, That the Senate agree thereto.
Ordered, That the Secretary notify the House of Representatives thereof.

EXECUTIVE SESSION.

On motion by Mr. Sherman,
The Senate proceeded to the consideration of executive business; and
After the consideration of executive business, the doors were reopened.

MESSAGE FROM THE HOUSE.

A message from the House of Representatives, by Mr. Towles, its chief clerk:
Mr. President: The House of Representatives has disagreed to the amendments of the Senate to the bill (H. R. 10488) making appropriations for the naval service for the fiscal year ending June 30, 1894, and for other purposes. It asks a conference with the Senate on the disagreeing votes of the two Houses thereon, and has appointed Mr. Herbert, Mr. Elliott, and Mr. Boutelle managers at the same on its part.
The House of Representatives has passed a bill (H. R. 10375) establishing a standard gauge for sheet and plate iron and steel, in which it requests the concurrence of the Senate.
The House of Representatives has passed the following resolution, in which it requests the concurrence of the Senate:
Resolved by the House of Representatives (the Senate concurring), That there be printed a new edition of the special report of the Chief of the Bureau of Statistics of the Treasury Department relating to wool and the manufactures of wool, published by order of Congress in 1888, with the matter contained therein brought down to date—3,000 copies for the use of the Senate, 6,000 for the use of the House of Representatives, and 2,000 for distribution by the Bureau of Statistics of the Treasury Department.

HOUSE BILL AND RESOLUTION REFERRED.

The bill H. R. 10375, last received from the House of Representatives for concurrence, was read the first and second times by unanimous consent and referred to the Committee on Finance.
The resolution to print 11,000 copies of the report of the Bureau of Statistics relating to wool and the manufactures of wool, this day received from the House of Representatives for concurrence, was read and referred to the Committee on Printing.

NAVAL APPROPRIATION BILL.

The President *pro tempore* laid before the Senate the message of the House of Representatives announcing its disagreement to the amendments of the Senate to the bill (H. R. 10488) making appropriations for the naval service for the fiscal year ending June 30, 1894, and for other purposes.
On motion by Mr. Hale,
Resolved, That the Senate insist upon its amendments to the said bill disagreed to by the House of Representatives and agree to the conference asked by the House on the disagreeing votes of the two Houses thereon.
Ordered, That the conferees on the part of the Senate be appointed by the President *pro tempore;* and
The President *pro tempore* appointed Mr. Hale, Mr. Allison, and Mr. Gorman.
Ordered, That the Secretary notify the House of Representatives thereof.

PETITIONS AND MEMORIALS.

Mr. Dawes presented a memorial of the Presbyterian Ministerial Association of Pittsburg, Pa., praying the repeal of the so-called Chinese exclusion act; which was referred to the Committee on Foreign Relations.
Petitions praying the passage of a law restricting immigration into the United States were presented as follows:
By Mr. Sherman: Several petitions of citizens of Ohio.
By Mr. Stockbridge: Three petitions of citizens of Michigan.
By Mr. Hoar: A petition of citizens of Massachusetts.
By Mr. McPherson: Several petitions of citizens of New Jersey.
By Mr. Voorhees: A petition of citizens of Indiana.
By Mr. Hiscock: Three petitions of citizens of New York.
By Mr. Cockrell: Four petitions of citizens of Missouri.
By Mr. Faulkner: Several petitions of citizens of West Virginia.
Ordered, That they be referred to the Committee on Immigration.
Mr. Teller presented a memorial of the Colorado Marble and Mining Company, remonstrating against the letting of contracts for marble to be used in the construction of the building for the Library of Congress; which was referred to the Select Committee on Additional Accommodations for the Library of Congress.
Mr. Wolcott presented a similar memorial for a like purpose; which was similarly referred.

EXECUTIVE COMMUNICATIONS.

The President *pro tempore* laid before the Senate a letter of the Secretary of the Treasury, recommending an appropriation for the payment of the publication of the Supplement to the Revised Statutes, compiled under the act of February 27, 1893; which was referred to the Committee on Appropriations and ordered to be printed.
The President *pro tempore* laid before the Senate a letter of the Secretary of the Treasury, submitting an estimate of appropriation by the Fourth Auditor for the payment of amounts found due certain naval officers for moneys expended by them when traveling under orders; which was referred to the Committee on Appropriations and ordered to be printed.
The President *pro tempore* laid before the Senate a letter of the Secretary of the Treasury transmitting a list of claims allowed by the accounting officers of the Treasury Department under appropriations the balances of which have been exhausted or carried to the surplus fund under the provisions of section 5 of the act of June 20, 1874; which was referred to the Committee on Appropriations and ordered to be printed.
The President *pro tempore* laid before the Senate a letter of the Secretary of the Treasury, transmitting a supplemental list of claims allowed by the accounting officers of the Treasury Department under appropriations the balances of which have been exhausted or carried to the surplus fund, since those transmitted February 28, 1893; which was referred to the Committee on Appropriations and ordered to be printed.
The President *pro tempore* laid before the Senate a letter of the Commissioners of the District of Columbia, communicating, in answer to a resolution of the Senate of February 23, 1893, information in relation to reviewing stands erected on certain reservations in the city of Washington, to be used on inauguration day; which was referred to the Select Committee on Inaugural Ceremonies.
The President *pro tempore* laid before the Senate a letter of the Secretary of War, transmitting, in answer to a resolution of the Senate of February 27, 1893, copies of all papers and documents relating to the proposals for the improvement of the harbor at Philadelphia, etc.; which was referred to the Committee on Commerce and ordered to be printed.

PETITIONS AND MEMORIALS.

Petitions, memorials, etc., were presented and referred as follows:
The president *pro tempore* laid before the Senate a memorial of the League of American Wheelmen, praying for increased appropriations for the topographical and geological surveys of the United States; which was referred to the Committee on Appropriations.
Mr. Felton presented a memorial of citizens of California, remonstrating against the passage of any law in regard to the observance of the Sabbath day; which was referred to the Committee on the Judiciary.
Mr. Felton presented a petition of owners, agents, and masters, praying the passage of the bill (S. 1224) legalizing the payment of advanced wages to seamen; which was referred to the Committee on Commerce.
Mr. Vest presented a petition of citizens of Missouri, praying the repeal of the so-called Chinese exclusion act.
Ordered, That it lie on the table.

SENATOR FROM IDAHO.

On motion by Mr. Teller,
The Senate proceeded to consider the motion submitted by Mr. Morgan, March 7, 1892, that the Senate reconsider its vote agreeing to the resolution declaring Fred. T. Dubois entitled to a seat in the Senate from the State of Idaho; and
On the question to agree thereto,
It was determined in the negative.
On motion by Mr. Teller,
The Senate proceeded to consider the motion submitted by Mr. Morgan, March 7, 1892, that the Senate reconsider its vote declaring William H. Clagett not entitled to a seat in the Senate; and
On the question to agree thereto,
It was determined in the negative.

PRESENTATION OF BILL.

Mr. Dubois reported from the committee that they yesterday presented to the President of the United States an enrolled bill (S. 3886) to authorize the Montgomery Bridge Company to construct and maintain a bridge across the Alabama River near the city of Montgomery, Ala.

REPORTS OF COMMITTEES.

Mr. Sherman, from the Committee on Foreign Relations, reported a joint resolution (S. R. 160) to authorize Thomas Adamson to accept a medal from the Government of China; which was read the first and second times by unanimous consent and considered as in Committee of the Whole; and no amendment being made, it was reported to the Senate.
Ordered, That it be engrossed and read a third time.
The said resolution was read the third time, by unanimous consent.

Resolved, That it pass, and that the title thereof be as aforesaid.

Ordered, That the Secretary request the concurrence of the House of Representatives therein.

Mr. Davis, from the Committee on Pensions, to whom were referred the following bills, reported them severally without amendment and submitted written reports thereon as follows:

H. R. 2123. An act granting a pension to John Fields; Report No. 1354.

H. R. 7305. An act to pension Martin McDermott; Report No. 1355.

H. R. 4955. An act granting a pension to Susannah Chadwick; Report No. 1356.

Mr. Frye, from the Committee on Commerce, to whom was referred the resolution submitted by Mr. Higgins February 24, 1893, calling for an estimate of the survey of the Back Creek route, reported in lien thereof a joint resolution (S. R. 161), requesting the Secretary of War to furnish revised estimate of survey of the Back Creek route, etc.; which was read the first and second times by unanimous consent and considered as in Committee of the Whole; and no amendment being made, it was reported to the Senate.

Ordered, That it be engrossed and read a third time.

The said resolution was read the third time by unanimous consent.

Resolved, That it pass, and that the title thereof be as aforesaid.

Ordered, That the Secretary request the concurrence of the House of Representatives therein.

Mr. Mitchell, from the Committee on Claims, to whom was referred the bill (H. R. 4464) for the benefit of J. C. Rudd, submitted an adverse report (No. 1358) thereon.

Ordered, That it be postponed indefinitely.

Mr. Cullom, from the Committee on Appropriations, to whom was referred the bill (H. R. 10349) making appropriations for the service of the Post-Office Department for the fiscal year ending June 30, 1894, reported it with amendments and submitted a report (No. 1353) thereon.

Mr. Dawes, from the Committee on Appropriations, to whom was rererred the bill (H. R. 10415) making appropriations for current and contingent expenses and fulfilling treaty stipulations with Indian tribes for the fiscal year ending June 30, 1894, reported it with amendments and submitted a report (No. 1357) thereon.

Mr. Mitchell, from the Committee on Claims, to whom was referred the bill (S. 721) for the relief of Peter Grant Stewart, of Oregon, reported it with amendments and submitted a report (No. 1359) thereon.

INTRODUCTION OF BILL.

Mr. Higgins introduced a bill (S. 3895) to protect the revenues of the United States; which was read the first and second times by unanimous consent and referred to the Committee on Finance.

PRESIDENTIAL APPROVALS.

A message from the President of the United States, by Mr. Pruden, his secretary:

Mr. President: The President of the United States approved and signed, February 27, 1893, the following acts:

S. 3602. An act to grant the Chicago, Rock Island and Pacific Railway Company a right of way through the Indian Territory, and for other purposes; and

S. 3873. An act to authorize the Kansas City, Pittsburg and Gulf Railway Company to construct and operate a railroad, telegraph, and telephone line through the Indian Territory, and for other purposes.

He approved and signed, February 28, 1893, the following acts and joint resolutions:

S. 3811. An act to amend an act entitled " An act to grant to the Mobile and Dauphin Island Railroad and Harbor Company the right to trestle across the shoal water between Cedar Point and Dauphin Island," approved September 26, 1890;

S. 3702. An act granting to the Chicago, Rock Island and Pacific Railway Company the use of certain lands at Chickasha Stafton, and for a " Y" in the Chickasaw Nation, Indian Territory;

S. 1538. An act for the relief of the heirs of James S. Ham;

S. 1539. An act for the relief of the heirs of John W. Vose;

S. 3725. An act authorizing the construction of a free bridge across the Arkansas River, connecting Little Rock and Argenta;

S. 3876. An act authorizing the St. Louis and Madison Tranfer Company to construct a bridge over the Mississippi River;

S. 3871. An act to authorize the construction of a bridge across the Calumet River;

S. 3828. An act for the relief of L. M. Garret; and

S. R. 157. A joint resolution authorizing the Secretary of War to receive for instruction at the Military Academy at West Point, Alberto Gnirola, of Salvador.

Ordered, That the Secretary notify the House of Representatives thereof.

WITHDRAWAL OF PAPERS.

On motion by Mr. Felton,

Ordered, That the papers in the case of Morgan Everts be withdrawn from the files of the Senate, subject to the rules.

DISTRICT APPROPRIATION BILL.

On motion by Mr. Allison,

The Senate proceeded to consider the report of the committee of conference on the disagreeing votes of the two Houses on the amendments of the Senate to the bill (H. R. 10038) making appropriations for the expenses of the government of the District of Columbia for the fiscal year ending June 30, 1894, and for other purposes; and

After debate,

Resolved, That the Senate agree thereto.

Ordered, That the Secretary notify the House of Representatives thereof.

CLAIM OF WILLIAM M'GARRAHAN.

On motion by Mr. Teller, that the Senate proceed to the consideration of the bill (S. 3741) to submit to the court of private land claims, established by an act of Congress approved March 3, 1891, the title of William McGarrahan to the Rancho Panoche Grande, in the State of California, and for other purposes,

It was determined in the affirmative, { Yeas 54
                                      { Nays 5

On motion by Mr. Morrill,

The yeas and nays being desired by one-fifth of the Senators present, Those who voted in the affirmative are,

Messrs. Bate, Berry, Brice, Butler, Caffery, Call, Cameron, Carey, Chandler, Cockrell, Coke, Colquitt, Daniel, Davis, Dawes, Dubois, Frye, Gordon, Gorman, Hansbrough, Harris, Hawley, Higgins, Hill, Hiscock, Hoar, Hunton, Irby, Jones of Arkansas, Jones of Nevada, Kyle, McMillan, McPherson, Manderson, Mitchell, Paddock, Peffer, Pettigrew, Platt, Pugh, Ransom, Sawyer, Shoup, Squire, Stockbridge, Teller, Turpie, Vance, Vest, Vilas, Voorhees, Warren, Washburn, Wolcott.

Those who voted in the negative are,

Messrs. Morrill, Palmer, Proctor, Sherman, Stewart.

So the motion was agreed to; and

The Senate proceeded to consider the said bill as in Committee of the Whole; and

Pending debate,

The President pro tempore announced that the hour of 1 o'clock had arrived, and laid before the Senate the first bill on the calendar of special orders, viz., the bill (S. 825) relating to the pay and retirement of the mates in the Navy;

When,

NEW YORK AND NEW JERSEY BRIDGE.

On motion by Mr. Hill, that the Senate proceed to the consideration of the bill (S. 2636) to authorize the New York and New Jersey Bridge Companies to construct and maintain a bridge across the Hudson River between New York City and the State of New Jersey,

It was determined in the affirmative, { Yeas 26
                                      { Nays 24

On motion by Mr. Wolcott,

The yeas and nays being desired by one-fifth of the Senators present, Those who voted in the affirmative are,

Messrs. Berry, Blackburn, Blodgett, Butler, Caffery, Call, Cockrell, Daniel, Faulkner. Gibson, Hansbrough, Hill, Hunton, Jones of Arkansas, Lindsay, Palmer, Pettigrew, Power, Pugh, Squire, Stewart, Turpie, Vance, Vest, Vilas, Voorhees.

Those who voted in the negative are,

Messrs. Allison, Cameron, Davis, Dawes, Frye, Hawley, Hiscock, Hoar, Jones of Nevada, McMillan, McPherson, Manderson, Mitchell, Morrill, Paddock, Peffer, Platt, Proctor, Sawyer, Shoup, Stockbridge, Teller, Washburn, Wolcott.

So the motion was agreed to.

When,

POST-OFFICE APPROPRIATION BILL.

On motion by Mr. Cullom, and by unanimous consent,

The Senate proceeded to consider, as in Committee of the Whole, the bill (H. R. 10349) making appropriations for the service of the Post-Office Department for the fiscal year ending June 30, 1894; and the reported amendments having been agreed to in part,

On the question to agree to the following reported amendment, viz:

On page 4, after line 23, strike out the following words:

"For necessary and special facilities on trunk lines from Springfield, Mass., via New York and Washington, to Atlanta and New Orleans, one hundred and ninety-six thousand six hundred and fourteen dollars and twenty-two cents: *Provided,* That no part of the appropriation made by this paragraph shall be expended unless the Postmaster-General shall deem such expenditure necessary in order to promote the interest of the postal service,"

On motion by Mr. Call to amend the part proposed to be stricken out by striking out the words "from Springfield, Mass., via New York and Washington, to Atlanta and New Orleans,"

Pending debate,

MESSAGE FROM THE HOUSE.

A message from the House of Representatives, by Mr. Towles, its chief clerk:

Mr. President: The House of Representatives has disagreed to the amendments of the Senate to the bill (H. R. 10421) making appropriations for the Department of Agriculture for the fiscal year ending June 30, 1894. It asks a conference with the Senate on the disagreeing votes of the two Houses thereon, and has appointed Mr. Hatch, Mr. Forman, and Mr. Funston managers at the same on its part.

The House of Representatives has agreed to the report of the committee of conference on the disagreeing votes of the two Houses on the amendments of the Senate to the bill (H. R. 10038) making appropriations for the expenses of the District of Columbia for the fiscal year ending June 30, 1894.

The House of Representatives has disagreed to the amendments of the Senate to the bill (H. R. 7203) to amend an act entitled "An act to establish a court of private land claims and to provide for the settlement of private land claims in certain States and Territories," approved March 3, 1891. It agrees to the conference asked by the Senate on the bill and amendments, and has appointed Mr. Buchanan, of Virginia, Mr. Layton, and Mr. Ray managers at the same on its part.

The House of Representatives has passed, without amendment, the following bills of the Senate:

S. 2596. An act for the relief of William and Mary College, of Virginia;

S. 2966. An act to amend rule 7, section 4233, Revised Statutes, relating to rules for preventing collisions on the water; and

S. 3892. An act for the removal of the charge of desertion from the record of John Cassidy.

The Speaker of the House of Representatives having signed an enrolled bill, S. 1307, I am directed to bring the same to the Senate for the signature of its President.

AGRICULTURAL APPROPRIATION BILL.

The President pro tempore laid before the Senate the message of the House of Representatives announcing its disagreement to the amendments of the Senate to the bill (H. R. 10421) making appropriations for the Department of Agriculture for the fiscal year ending June 30, 1894.

On motion by Mr. Cullom,

Resolved, That the Senate insist upon its amendments to the said bill disagreed to by the House of Representatives, and agree to the conference asked by the House on the disagreeing votes of the two Houses thereon.

Ordered, That the conferees on the part of the Senate be appointed by the President pro tempore; and

The President pro tempore appointed Mr. Allison, Mr. Cullom, and Mr. Call.

Ordered, That the Secretary notify the House of Representatives thereof.

ENROLLED BILL SIGNED.

Mr. Dubois reported from the committee that they had examined and found duly enrolled a bill (S. 1307) to provide for a permanent system of highways in that part of the District of Columbia lying outside of cities;

Whereupon,

The President pro tempore signed the same, and it was delivered to the committee to be presented to the President of the United States.

SUNDRY CIVIL APPROPRIATION BILL.

Mr. Allison, from the committee of conference on the disagreeing votes of the two Houses on the amendments of the Senate to the bill (H. R. 10238) making appropriations for sundry civil expenses of the Government for the fiscal year ending June 30, 1894, and for other purposes, submitted the following report:

The committee of conference on the disagreeing votes of the two Houses on the amendments of the Senate to the bill (H. R. 10238) "making appropriations for sundry civil expenses of the Government for the fiscal year ending June 30, 1894, and for other purposes," having met, after full and free conference have agreed to recommend and do recommend to their respective Houses as follows:

That the Senate recede from its amendments numbered 13, 32, 35, 38, 44, 45, 48, 49, 57, 58, 74, 76, 82, 89, 90, 91, 92, 95, 96, 106, 111, 112, 113, 114, 115, 116, 121, 125, 130, 131, 122, 133, 142, 144, 146, 185, 201, and 202.

That the House recede from its disagreement to the amendments of the Senate numbered 1, 2, 5, 7, 9, 10, 14, 16, 18, 20, 21, 22, 24, 25, 26, 28, 29, 30, 31, 34, 36, 39, 40, 46, 47, 50, 52, 53, 54, 55, 61, 62, 64, 66, 72, 73, 77, 78, 80, 84, 85, 88, 96, 97, 100, 101, 102, 105, 108, 117, 119, 126, 134, 138, 141, 143, 144, 147, 148, 149, 150, 151, 152, 153, 154, 155, 157, 158, 159, 160, 161, 162, 163, 164, 165, 166, 167, 168, 169, 170, 171, 172, 173, 174, 177, 181, 184, 186, 187, 188, 190, 192, 195, 196, 197, 198, 199, 200, 203, 204, 205, 206, and 207.

That the House recede from its disagreement to the amendment of the Senate numbered 3, and agree to the same with an amendment as follows: In lieu of the matter proposed to be inserted by said amendment insert the following: and the limit of cost of said building and site therefor is hereby fixed at four hundred and twenty-five thousand dollars; and the Senate agree to the same.

That the House recede from its disagreement to the amendment of the Senate numbered 4, and agree to the same with an amendment as follows: In lieu of the sum proposed in said amendment

insert seventy-five thousand dollars; and the Senate agree to the same.

That the House recede from its disagreement to the amendment of the Senate numbered 6, and agree to the same with an amendment as follows: In lieu of the matter proposed to be inserted by said amendment insert the following:

For post-office and court-house at San Francisco, California: That the limit of cost of the public building at San Francisco, California, for post-office, court-house, and other offices, exclusive of site, is hereby fixed at two million five hundred thousand dollars.

And the Senate agree to the same.

That the House recede from its disagreement to the amendment of the Senate numbered 8, and agree to the same with an amendment as follows: In line 2 of said amendment, after the word "construct," insert the words and complete; and the Senate agree to the same.

That the House recede from its disagreement to the amendment of the Senate numbered 11, and agree to the same with an amendment as follows: In lines 11 and 12 of said amendment strike out the words "five hundred thousand;" and the Senate agree to the same.

That the House recede from its disagreement to the amendment of the Senate numbered 12, and agree to the same with an amendment as follows: In lieu of the matter proposed to be inserted by said amendment insert the following:

For custom-house at New York, New York: That section three of an act entitled "An act for the erection of a new custom-house in the city of New York, and for other purposes," approved March third, eighteen hundred and ninety-one, is hereby repealed.

And the Senate agree to the same.

That the House recede from its disagreement to the amendment of the Senate numbered 15, and agree to the same with an amendment as follows: In lieu of the sum proposed insert two hundred thousand dollars; and the Senate agree to the same.

That the House recede from its disagreement to the amendment of the Senate numbered 17, and agree to the same with an amendment as follows: In lieu of the sum proposed in said amendment insert one hundred thousand dollars; and the Senate agree to the same.

That the House recede from its disagreement to the amendment of the Senate numbered 19, and agree to the same with an amendment as follows: In lieu of the matter proposed to be inserted by said amendment insert the following:

For public building at Portland, Oregon: That the limit of cost of the public building at Portland, Oregon, for custom-house and other Government offices and site therefor, is hereby fixed at seven hundred and fifty thousand dollars.

And the Senate agree to the same.

That the House recede from its disagreement to the amendment of the Senate numbered 23, and agree to the same with an amendment, as follows: In lieu of the sum proposed in said amendment insert twenty thousand dollars; and the Senate agree to the same.

That the House recede from its disagreement to the amendment of the Senate numbered 27, and agree to the same with an amendment as follows: In lieu of the matter proposed to be stricken out by said amendment insert the following:

Rockland Lake light station, New York: For establishment of a light-house and fog signal at or near Oyster Bed Shoal, Hudson River, opposite Rockland Lake dock, thirty-five thousand dollars.

And the Senate agree to the same.

That the House recede from its disagreement to the amendment of the Senate numbered 33, and agree to the same with an amendment as follows: In lieu of the matter proposed to be inserted by said amendment insert the following:

For Brazos River light-station, Texas: For a light-house, fog signal, and range lights at such points as the Light-House Board may determine, fifty thousand dollars.

And the Senate agree to the same.

That the House recede from its disagreement to the amendment of the Senate numbered 37, and agree to the same with an amendment as follows: In lieu of the sum proposed in said amendment insert three thousand three hundred dollars; and the Senate agree to the same.

That the House recede from its disagreement to the amendment of the Senate numbered 41, and agree to the same with an amendment as follows: In lieu of the sum proposed in said amendment insert one hundred thousand dollars; and the Senate agree to the same.

That the House recede from its disagreement to the amendment of the Senate numbered 42, and agree to the same with an amendment as follows: In lieu of the sum proposed insert: six hundred and seventy thousand dollars; and the Senate agree to the same.

That the House recede from its disagreement to the amendment of the Senate numbered 43, and agree to the same with an amendment as follows: In lieu of the sum proposed insert: three hundred and seventy thousand dollars; and at the end of the amended paragraph insert the words to be immediately available; and the Senate agree to the same.

That the House recede from its disagreement to the amendment of the Senate numbered 51, and agree to the same with an amendment as follows: In lieu of the sum named in said amendment insert: twenty-five thousand dollars; and the Senate agree to the same.

That the House recede from its disagreement to the amendment of the Senate numbered 56, and agree to the same with an amendment as follows: In lieu of the matter stricken out by said amendment insert the following:

That the Secretary of the Treasury shall examine and report to the next Congress at its first session what reduction can be made in the number and salaries of the employés of the Coast and Geodetic Survey.

And the Senate agree to the same.

That the House recede from its disagreement to the amendment of the Senate numbered 59, and agree to the same with the amendments as follows: In lieu of the sum proposed insert *nine thousand dollars;* and the Senate agree to the same.

That the House recede from its disagreement to the amendment of the Senate numbered 60, and agree to the same with an amendment as follows: In lieu of the sum proposed insert *fourteen thousand five hundred dollars;* and the Senate agree to the same.

That the House recede from its disagreement to the amendment of the Senate numbered 63, and agree to the same with an amendment as follows: In line 4 of said amendment, strike out the words "*Provided, That,*" and in the last line of said amendment, strike out the words "*one thousand dollars;*" and the Senate agree to the same.

That the House recede from its disagreement to the amendment of the Senate numbered 65, and agree to the same with an amendment as follows: In lieu of the sum proposed insert *thirty-five thousand dollars;* and the Senate agree to the same.

That the House recede from its disagreement to the amendment of the Senate numbered 79, and agree to the same with an amendment as follows: In lieu of the sum proposed in said amendment insert *four thousand dollars;* and the Senate agree to the same.

That the House recede from its disagreement to the amendment of the Senate numbered 81, and agree to the same with an amendment as follows: In lieu of the sum proposed in said amendment insert *six thousand dollars;* and the Senate agree to the same.

That the House recede from its disagreement to the amendment of the Senate numbered 83, and agree to the same with an amendment as follows: After the word "*and*" in said amendment insert the words *in such emergency;* and the Senate agree to the same.

That the House recede from its disagreement to the amendment of the Senate numbered 93, and agree to the same with an amendment as follows: In lieu of the sum proposed insert *five hundred and twenty thousand dollars;* and the Senate agree to the same.

That the House recede from its disagreement to the amendment of the Senate numbered 98, and agree to the same with an amendment as follows: In lieu of the sum proposed insert *ten thousand dollars;* and the Senate agree to the same.

That the House recede from its disagreement to the amendment of the Senate numbered 99, and agree to the same with an amendment as follows: In lieu of the sum proposed insert *two hundred thousand dollars;* and the Senate agree to the same.

That the House recede from its disagreement to the amendment of the Senate numbered 103, and agree to the same with an amendment as follows: Add at the end of said amendment the following: *But no person shall be permitted to acquire more than one hundred and sixty acres of public land through the location of any such certificates;* and the Senate agree to the same.

That the House recede from its disagreement to the amendment of the Senate numbered 107, and agree to the same with an amendment as follows: In line 5 of said amendment strike out the word "*forty,*" and insert in lieu thereof the word *twenty;* and the Senate agree to the same.

That the House recede from its disagreement to the amendment of the Senate numbered 109, and agree to the same with an amendment as follows: In lieu of the sum named in said amendment insert *twenty thousand dollars;* and the Senate agree to the same.

That the House recede from its disagreement to the amendment of the Senate numbered 110, and agree to the same with amendments as follows: In line 9 of said amendment, after the word "*patents,*" insert the words *their heirs or assigns;* and in line 17 of said amendment strike out the word "*ten,*" and insert in lieu thereof the word *eight,* and add at the end of said amendment the following: *to be immediately available, and the said secretary shall make report thereon at the first session of the Fifty-third Congress;* and the Senate agree to the same.

That the House recede from its disagreement to the amendment of the Senate numbered 118, and agree to the same with an amendment as follows: In lieu of the sum proposed insert *fifty-five thousand dollars;* and the Senate agree to the same.

That the House recede from its disagreement to the amendment of the Senate numbered 120, and agree to the same with an amendment as follows: In lieu of the sum proposed insert *four hundred and fourteen thousand dollars;* and the Senate agree to the same.

That the House recede from its disagreement to the amendment of the Senate numbered 122, and agree to the same with an amendment as follows: In lieu of the sum proposed insert *thirteen thousand dollars;* and the Senate agree to the same.

That the House recede from its disagreement to the amendment of the Senate numbered 123, and agree to the same with an amendment as follows: In lieu of the sum proposed insert *sixty-two thousand five hundred dollars;* and the Senate agree to the same.

That the House recede from its disagreement to the amendment of the Senate numbered 124, and agree to the same with an amendment as follows: In lieu of the sum proposed insert *twenty-three thousand five hundred dollars;* and the Senate agree to the same.

That the House recede from its disagreement to the amendment of the Senate numbered 127, and agree to the same with an amendment as follows: In lieu of the sum proposed insert *twenty-eight thousand eight hundred dollars;* and the Senate agree to the same.

That the House recede from its disagreement to the amendment of the Senate numbered 128, and agree to the same with an amendment as follows: In lieu of the sum proposed insert *eight thousand five hundred dollars;* and the Senate agree to the same.

That the House recede from its disagreement to the amendment of the Senate numbered 129, and agree to the same with an amendment as follows: In lieu of the sum proposed insert *forty-five thousand dollars;* and the Senate agree to the same.

That the House recede from its disagreement to the amendment of the Senate numbered 135, and agree to the same with an amendment as follows: In lieu of the sum proposed insert *three hundred and fifty thousand dollars;* and the Senate agree to the same.

That the House recede from its disagreement to the amendment of the Senate numbered 136, and agree to the same with an amendment as follows: In the last line of said amendment strike out the words "*and fifty;*" and the Senate agree to the same.

That the House recede from its disagreement to the amendment of the Senate numbered 137, and agree to the same with an amendment as follows: In lieu of the sum proposed insert *thirty thousand dollars;* and the Senate agree to the same.

That the House recede from its disagreement to the amendment of the Senate numbered 139, and agree to the same with an amendment as follows: After the word "*field,*" in line 5 of said amendment, strike out the following: "*and for the purchase and condemnation of land of historical importance;*" and the Senate agree to the same.

That the House recede from its disagreement to the amendment of the Senate numbered 140, and agree to the same with an amendment as follows: In lieu of the sum proposed insert *six hundred and forty-five thousand dollars;* and the Senate agree to the same.

That the House recede from its disagreement to the amendment of the Senate numbered 156, and agree to the same with an amendment as follows: In line 3 of said amendment, after the word "Iowa," insert the following: *to be expended under the direction of the Secretary of War;* and the Senate agree to the same.

That the House recede from its disagreement to the amendment of the Senate numbered 175, and agree to the same with an amendment as follows: In lieu of the sum proposed insert *seventy-six thousand dollars;* and the Senate agree to the same.

That the House recede from its disagreement to the amendment of the Senate numbered 176, and agree to the same with an amendment as follows: In lieu of the sum proposed insert *four thousand dollars;* and the Senate agree to the same.

That the House recede from its disagreement to the amendment of the Senate numbered 178, and agree to the same with an amendment as follows: In lieu of the sum proposed insert *eighty-six thousand six hundred and three dollars and forty-seven cents;* and the Senate agree to the same.

That the House recede from its disagreement to the amendment of the Senate numbered 179, and agree to the same with an amendment as follows: In lieu of the sum proposed insert *seventy-one thousand two hundred and forty dollars;* and the Senate agree to the same.

That the House recede from its disagreement to the amendment of the Senate numbered 180, and agree to the same with an amendment as follows: In lieu of the sum proposed insert *one thousand four hundred dollars;* and the Senate agree to the same.

That the House recede from its disagreement to the amendment of the Senate numbered 182, and agree to the same with an amendment as follows: In lieu of the sum proposed insert *one hundred and sixty-four thousand one hundred and seventy-five dollars and thirty-eight cents;* and the Senate agree to the same.

That the House recede from its disagreement to the amendment of the Senate numbered 183 and agree to the same, with an amendment as follows: In lieu of the sum proposed insert *two million three hundred and seventy-eight thousand five hundred and sixty-three dollars and eighty-nine cents;* and the Senate agree to the same.

That the House recede from its disagreement to the amendment of the Senate numbered 191, and agree to the same with amendments as follows: Before the words inserted by said amendment insert the words *the nearest;* and on page 86, lines 7 and 8, of the bill, strike out the words "before said court;" and the Senate agree to the same.

On amendments numbered 67, 68, 69, 70, 71, 75, 86, 87, 104, 189, 193, and 194 the committee of conference have been unable to agree.

W. B. ALLISON,
EUGENE HALE,
A. P. GORMAN,
Managers on the part of the Senate.

W. S. HOLMAN,
JOSEPH D. SAYERS,
WILLIAM COGSWELL,
Managers on the part of the House.

On motion by Mr. Allison,
The Senate proceeded to consider the report; and
After debate,
Resolved, That the Senate agree thereto and
On motion by Mr. Allison, that the Senate recede from its amendment numbered 75,
After debate,
It was determined in the affirmative.
On motion by Mr. Allison,
Resolved, That the Senate further insist upon its amendments numbered 67, 68, 69, 70, 71, 86, 87, 104, 189, 193, and 194, and ask a further conference with the House of Representatives on the disagreeing votes of the two Houses thereon.
Ordered, That the conferees on the part of the Senate be appointed by the President *pro tempore;* and
The President *pro tempore* appointed Mr. Allison, Mr. Hale, and Mr. Gorman.
Ordered, That the Secretary notify the House of Representatives thereof.

MESSAGE FROM THE HOUSE.

A message from the House of Representatives by Mr. Towles, its chief clerk:
Mr. President: The Speaker of the House of Representatives having signed two enrolled bills, S. 782 and S. 2931, I am directed to bring the same to the Senate for the signature of its President.

ENROLLED BILLS EXAMINED.

Mr. Dubois reported from the committee that they had examined and found duly enrolled the following bills:
S. 782. An act to provide for the adjustment of certain sales of lands in the late reservation of the Confederated Otoe and Missouri a tribes of Indians in the States of Nebraska and Kansas; and
S. 2931. An act to provide for the survey and transfer of that part of the Fort Randall military reservation in the State of Nebraska to said State for school and other purposes.

EULOGIES ON THE LATE SENATOR GIBSON.

Pursuant to notice Mr. White submitted the following resolutions:
Resolved, That the Senate has heard with profound sorrow of the death of the honorable Randall Lee Gibson, late a Senator from the State of Louisiana, and it extends to his afflicted family its sincere sympathy in their bereavement.
Resolved further, That as an additional mark of respect to the memory of Senator Gibson the legislative business of the Senate be now suspended, in order that his associates in this body may pay tribute to his memory.
Resolved, That the Secretary of the Senate be directed to transmit to the family of the deceased certified copies of these resolutions, with statement of the action of the Senate thereon.
Resolved, That the Secretary of the Senate be directed to communicate these resolutions to the House of Representatives.
Resolved, That as a mark of testimonial to the memory of the deceased the Senate do now adjourn.
The Senate proceeded to consider the said resolutions; and
After addresses by Mr. White, Mr. Wolcott, Mr. Gordon, Mr. Voorhees, Mr. Mills, Mr. McPherson, Mr. Manderson, and Mr. Caffery.
The resolutions were unanimously agreed to, and
The Senate adjourned.

THURSDAY, MARCH 2, 1893.

The Vice-President resumed the chair.

ENROLLED BILL SIGNED.

The Vice-President signed the two enrolled bills (S. 782 and S. 2931) yesterday reported to have been examined, and they were delivered to the committee to be presented to the President of the United States.

EXECUTIVE COMMUNICATIONS.

The Vice-President laid before the Senate a letter of the Secretary of the Treasury, transmitting, in answer to a resolution of the Senate of February 21, 1893, a supplemental list of judgments rendered by the Court of Claims requiring an appropriation for their payment; which was referred to the Committee on Appropriations and ordered to be printed.
The Vice-President laid before the Senate a letter of the Secretary of the Interior, transmitting a report of disbursements made in all States and Territories under the provisions of the act approved August 30, 1890, to apply a portion of the proceeds of the sales of public lands to the more complete endowment and support of colleges for the benefit of agriculture and the mechanic arts; which was referred to the Committee on Public Lands and ordered to be printed.
The Vice-President laid before the Senate a letter of the Secretary of the Treasury, transmitting an estimate of appropriation submitted by the Commissioner of Fish and Fisheries for the completion of the fish hatchery in Texas; which was referred to the Committee on Appropriations and ordered to be printed.

PETITIONS AND MEMORIALS.

Petitions, memorials, etc., were presented and referred as follows:
Mr. Power presented a memorial of the legislature of the State of Montana in favor of the passage of an amendment to the Constitution of the United States providing for the election of United States Senators by a direct vote of the people; which was referred to the Committee on Privileges and Elections.
Mr. Cameron presented a petition of citizens of Pennsylvania, praying the passage of a law to prevent the sale of intoxicating liquors on the grounds of the Columbian Exposition; which was referred to the Select Committee on the Quadro-Centennial.
Petitions praying the passage of a law to restrict immigration into the United States were presented as follows:
By Mr. Cameron: Several petitions of citizens of Pennsylvania.
By Mr. McPherson: A petition of citizens of New Jersey.
By Mr. Blodgett: Several petitions of citizens of New Jersey.
By Mr. Manderson: A petition of citizens of Nebraska.
By Mr. Cullom: A petition of citizens of Illinois.
By Mr. Chandler: A petition of citizens of New Hampshire.
Ordered, That they be referred to the Committee on Immigration.
Mr. Felton, from the Select Committee on Forest Reservations in California, presented certain documents relating to the titles of settlers on lands within the limits of the Yosemite National Park and Sequoia Park, California; which were ordered to be printed.

REPORTS OF COMMITTEES.

Mr. Manderson, from the Committee on Printing, to whom were referred the following concurrent resolutions, reported them severally without amendment and submitted written reports thereon as follows:
Resolution received from the House of Representatives for concurrence February 25, 1893, to print 9,000 copies of the report of the Director of the Mint on the production of precious metals in the United States for the year 1892; Report No. 1364.
Resolution received from the House of Representatives for concurrence February 25, 1893, to print and bind 4,000 copies of the official report of the American delegates to the International Monetary Conference; Report No. 1365.
Resolution received from the House of Representatives for concurrence February 25, 1893, to print 8,000 copies of the eulogies delivered in Congress upon Hon. John G. Warwick, late a Representative from the State of Ohio; Report No. 1366.
Resolution received from the House of Representatives for concurrence February 28, 1893, to print 8,000 copies of the eulogies delivered in Congress upon Hon. Alexander K. Craig, late a Representative from the State of Pennsylvania; Report No. 1367.
The Senate proceeded, by unanimous consent, to consider the said resolutions; and
Resolved, That the Senate agree thereto.
Ordered, That the Secretary notify the House of Representatives thereof.
Mr. Manderson, from the Committee on Printing, to whom was referred the resolution submitted by Mr. Hawley February 25, 1893, to print 6,000 copies of the report of the Committee on Mines and Mining on the cost of production of gold and silver, reported it without amendment and submitted a report (No. 1368) thereon.
The Senate proceeded by unanimous consent to consider the said resolution; and
Resolved, That the Senate agree thereto.
Ordered, That the Secretary request the concurrence of the House of Representatives therein.
Mr. Manderson, from the Committee on Printing, to whom was referred the resolution submitted by Mr. Higgins, February 18, 1893, to print 5,000 additional copies of the report of the Bureau of Education on law education, reported it without amendment and submitted a report (No. 1369) thereon.
The Senate proceeded, by unanimous consent, to consider the said resolution; and
Resolved, That the Senate agree thereto.
Mr. Manderson, from the Committee on Printing, to whom was referred the annual report of the National Academy of Sciences, submitted a report (No. 1370), accompanied by the following resolution; which was considered by unanimous consent and agreed to:
Resolved, That the usual number of the report of the operations of the National Academy of Sciences for the year 1892, transmitted under the requirements of the act of March 3, 1863, be printed.
Mr. Manderson, from the Committee on Printing, to whom was referred the letter of the Secretary of the Smithsonian Institution transmitting the annual report of the American Historical Association, submitted a report (No. 1371), accompanied by the following resolution; which was considered by unanimous consent and agreed to:
Resolved, That there be printed of the annual report of the American Historical Association for the year 1892 the usual number.
Mr. Cameron, from the Committee on Military Affairs, to whom was referred the bill (S. 3177) for the relief of J. E. Gillingwaters, reported it without amendment and submitted a report (No. 1360) thereon.
Mr. Turpie, from the Committee on Pensions, to whom was referred the bill (H. R. 8550) to increase the pension of W. H. Philpot, a pen-

sioner of the Mexican war, reported it without amendment and submitted a report (No. 1361) thereon.

Mr. Cockrell, from the Committee on Military Affairs, to whom was referred the bill (H. R. 2432) for the relief of Lansing Shear, reported it without amendment and submitted a report (No. 1363) thereon.

The Senate proceeded, by unanimous consent, to consider the said bill as in Committee of the Whole; and no amendment being made, it was reported to the Senate.

Ordered, That it pass to a third reading.

The said bill was read the third time.

Resolved, That it pass.

Ordered, That the Secretary notify the House of Representatives thereof.

Mr. Gallinger, from the Committee on Pensions, to whom was referred the bill (S. 3557) granting a pension to William O. Lyman, reported it with amendments and submitted a report (No. 1362) thereon.

Mr. Palmer, from the Committee on Pensions, to whom was referred the bill (H. R. 4496) to place upon the pension rolls of the United States the name of Thomas F. Sheldon, late captain Company A, One hundred and twenty-fifth New York Infantry, reported it without amendment.

Mr. Hale, from the Committee on Appropriations, to whom was referred the bill (H. R. 10258) making appropriations to supply deficiencies in the appropriations for the fiscal year ending June 30, 1893, and for prior years, and for other purposes, reported it with amendments.

Mr. Sawyer, from the Committee on Pensions, to whom were referred the following bills, reported them severally without amendment and submitted written reports thereon as follows:

S. 3882. A bill granting a pension to Honora Shea; Report No. 1372.

H. R. 1100. An act granting a pension to Mary Catherine Reardon; Report No. 1373.

H. R. 8246. An act granting a pension to Bridget Brennan, widow of Thomas Brennan, late of Companies C, and G, Second Regiment Rhode Island Volunteers; Report No. 1374.

Mr. Gallinger, from the Committee on Pensions, to whom were referred the following bills, reported them severally without amendment and submitted written reports thereon as follows:

H. R. 5508. An act to place the name of Sabra Wolcott upon the pension rolls; Report No. 1375.

H. R. 4804. An act to place the name of Sarah L. Van Nest on the pension list; Report No. 1376.

H. R. 5022. An act for the relief of Lucy Spotberry; Report No. 1377.

Mr. Gallinger, from the Committee on Pensions, to whom was referred the bill (H. R. 4916) granting a pension to Thomas Tucker, of Battery A, Fourth United States Artillery, reported it with an amendment and submitted a report (No. 1378) thereon.

MESSAGE FROM THE HOUSE.

A message from the House of Representatives, by Mr. Towles, its chief clerk:

Mr. President: The House of Representatives has agreed to the report of the committee of conference on the disagreeing votes of the two Houses on the amendments of the Senate to the bill (H. R. 7633) to ratify and confirm an agreement with the Kickapoo Indians in Oklahoma Territory, and to make appropriations for carrying the same into effect.

The House of Representatives has passed, without amendment, the bill (S. 203) for the examination and allowance of certain awards made by a board of claims to certain citizens of Jefferson County, Kentucky.

The House of Representatives has agreed to the amendments of the Senate to the bill (H. R. 10266) regulating the sale of intoxicating liquors in the District of Columbia.

The House of Representatives has passed the following resolutions, in which it requests the concurrence of the Senate:

Resolved by the House of Representatives (the Senate concurring), That there be printed and bound at the Government Printing Office 3,000 copies of the comprehensive index of the publications of the Fifty-first and Fifty-second Congresses, prepared by John G. Ames, superintendent of documents—500 for the use of the Senate, 1,000 for the use of the House of Representatives, and 1,500 for distribution by said superintendent of documents.

Resolved by the House of Representatives (the Senate concurring), That there be printed of the eulogies delivered in Congress upon the Hon. John E. Kenna, late a Senator from the State of West Virginia, 8,000 copies, of which 2,000 copies shall be delivered to the Senators and Representatives of that State; and of the remaining number 2,000 shall be for the use of the Senate, and 4,000 copies for the use of the House; and of the quota of the Senate the Public Printer shall set aside 50 copies, which he shall have bound in full morocco with gilt edges, the same to be delivered, when completed, to the family of the deceased; and the Secretary of the Treasury is hereby directed to have engraved and printed, at as early a date as practicable, the portrait of the deceased to accompany said eulogies.

The Speaker of the House of Representatives having signed four enrolled bills, S. 2566, S. 2966, S. 3892, and H. R. 10038, I am directed to bring the same to the Senate for the signature of its President.

ENROLLED BILLS SIGNED.

Mr. Dubois reported from the committee that they had examined and found duly enrolled the following bills:

S. 2566. An act for the relief of William and Mary College, of Virginia;

S. 2966. An act to amend rule 7, section 4283, Revised Statutes, relating to rules for preventing collisions on the water;

S. 3892. An act for the removal of the charge of desertion from the record of John Cassidy; and

H. R. 10038. An act making appropriations for the expenses of the government of the District of Columbia for the fiscal year ending June 30, 1894, and for other purposes;

Whereupon,

The Vice-President signed the same, and they were delivered to the committee to be presented to the President of the United States.

HOUSE RESOLUTION REFERRED.

The resolution to print 3,000 copies of the comprehensive index of publications of the Fifty-first and Fifty-second Congresses, prepared by John G. Ames; and the resolution to print 8,000 copies of the eulogies delivered in Congress upon Hon. John E. Kenna, late a Senator from the State of West Virginia, this day received from the House of representatives for concurrence, were read and referred to the Committee on Printing.

CONFERENCE REPORT.

Mr. Platt, from the committee of conference on the disagreeing votes of the two Houses on the amendments of the Senate to the bill H. R. 7633, submitted the following report:

The committee of conference on the disagreeing votes of the two Houses on the amendment of the Senate to the bill (H. R. 7633) "to ratify and confirm an agreement with the Kickapoo Indians in Oklahoma Territory, and make appropriations for carrying the same into effect," having met, after full and free conference have agreed to recommend and do recommend to their respective Houses as follows:

The House recedes from its disagreement to the amendment of the Senate, and agrees to the same with an amendment to read as follows: Strike out in said amendment all after "confirmed," line 2, page 1, down to and including "*Provided,*" line 26, page 2, and in lieu thereof insert:

That for the purpose of carrying into effect the provisions of the foregoing agreement there is hereby appropriated, out of any moneys in the Treasury of the United States not otherwise appropriated, the sum of sixty-four thousand six hundred and fifty dollars. And after first paying to John T. Hill the sum of five thousand one hundred and seventy-two dollars for services rendered said Kickapoo Indians and in discharge of a written contract made with said Indians and recommended by the Secretary of the Interior, the remainder to be expended for the use of said Indians as stipulated in said contract: Provided, That should said Indians elect to leave any portion of said remaining balance in the Treasury, the amount so left shall bear interest at the rate of five per centum per annum.

And the Senate agreed to the same.

Change section 3 of said amendment of the Senate to section 3.

Change section 4 of said amendment of the Senate to section 3.

O. H. PLATT,
JAMES K. JONES,
Managers on the part of the Senate.

S. W. PEEL,
O. M. KEM,
WILLIAM H. BRAWLEY,
Managers on the part of the House.

The Senate proceeded to consider the said report; and

On motion, by Mr. Platt,

Resolved, That the Senate agree thereto.

Ordered, That the Secretary notify the House of Representatives thereof.

INTRODUCTION OF BILL.

Mr. Kyle, from the Committee on Patents, to whom was referred the bill (S. 3881) relating to copyrights, reported it with an amendment.

POST-OFFICE APPROPRIATION BILL.

On motion by Mr. Cullom,

The Senate resumed, as in Committee of the Whole, the consideration of the bill (H. R. 10349) making appropriations for the service of the Post-Office Department for the fiscal year ending June 30, 1894; and

The question being on the amendment proposed by Mr. Call to the part proposed to be stricken out by the amendment of the committee, after line 22, page 4,

Mr. Call withdrew his amendment;

When,

The reported amendment having been modified by Mr. Cullom, from the Committee on Appropriations, was agreed to as modified.

The residue of the reported amendments having been agreed to, the bill was reported to the Senate and the amendments were concurred in.

Ordered, That the amendments be engrossed and the bill read a third time.

The said bill was read the third time.

Resolved, That it pass.

Ordered, That the Secretary request the concurrence of the House of Representatives in the amendments.

CONSIDERATION OF BILLS ON CALENDAR.

On motion by Mr. Harris,

The Senate proceeded to consider, as in Committee of the Whole, the bill (H. R. 2122) for the relief of Cumberland Female College, of McMinnville, Tenn.; and the reported amendment having been agreed to, the bill was reported to the Senate and the amendment was concurred in.

Ordered, That the amendment be engrossed and the bill read a third time.

The said bill as amended was read the third time.

Resolved, That it pass, and that the Senate request a conference with the House of Representatives on the said bill and amendment.

Ordered, That the conferees on the part of the Senate be appointed by the Vice-President; and

The Vice-President appointed Mr. Daniel, Mr. Peffer, and Mr. Pasco.

Ordered, That the Secretary notify the House of Representatives thereof.

The Senate proceeded to consider, as in Committee of the Whole, the following bills; and no amendment being made, they were reported to the Senate:

S. 3880. A bill to authorize the Washington, Alexandria and Mount Vernon Electric Railway Company to construct a bridge across the Potomac River, opposite Observatory Hill; and

S. 3890. A bill to authorize the Lake Shore and Michigan Southern Railroad Company to renew its railroad bridge across the Calumet River upon or near the site of its present bridge, and upon a location and plans to be approved by the Secretary of War, and to operate the same.

Ordered, That they be engrossed and read a third time.

The said bills were read the third time.

Resolved, That they pass, and that the respective titles thereof be as aforesaid.

Ordered, That the Secretary request the concurrence of the House of Representatives therein.

CONFERENCE REPORT.

Mr. Pettigrew, from the committee of conference on the disagreeing votes of the two Houses on the amendments of the Senate to the bill H. R. 7028, submitted the following report:

The committee of conference on the disagreeing votes of the two Houses on the amendments of the Senate to the bill H. R. 7028, entitled "An act to protect settlement rights where two or more persons settle upon the same subdivision of agricultural public lands before survey thereof," having met, after full and free conference have agreed to recommend and do recommend to their respective Houses as follows:

That the House recede from its disagreement to the amendments of the Senate and agree to the same amended as follows:

In line 4 of said Senate amendments, after the word "provision," strike out the words "*And provided further,* That any person who has made entry of any public lands of the United States under the timber-culture laws, and who has heretofore for a period of eight years in good faith attempted to comply with the provisions of said laws, and who at the time of making the entry was a bona fide resident of the State or Territory in which said land is located or residing within 5 miles of the boundary line of such State or Territory, and where there was no pending contest on March 3, 1891, shall be entitled to make final proof thereto and acquire title to the same by payment of the customary fee for final proofs in homestead entries," and insert—

SEC. —. *That section one shall not be construed so as to interfere with any valid right of contest initiated prior to the passage of this act: And provided further, That any person qualified to make entry, and who has a subsisting entry under the timber-culture laws, and who has for at least eight years in good faith attempted to comply with the provisions of said laws, shall be entitled to make final proof, upon the payment of the fees required in homestead entry, and such attempts in good faith to comply with said laws shall be construed to entitle the entryman to all the benefits of said timber-culture laws and amendments thereto; and in computing the time before final proof under said timber-culture laws and acts amendatory thereof the same shall commence at date of entry.*

Strike out lines 27 to 33, inclusive, and insert—

SEC. —. *That any public lands embraced within the limits of any forest reservation made under section twenty-four of the act approved March third, eighteen hundred and ninety-one, which after the examination shall be found better adapted to agricultural than forest uses, may be restored to the public domain upon the recommendation of the Secretary of the Interior, with the approval of the President, after sixty days' public notice in two newspapers of general circulation in the State where the reservation is situated.*

SEC. —. *That the Secretary of the Interior, with the assistance and co-operation of the Secretary of War, shall make provision for the protection against fire and depredations of the forest reservations, and the Secretary of the Interior shall make such proper rules and regulations for the occupancy and utilization of said reservations as will preserve the forest cover from destruction and insure the objects of the reservations.*

Strike out lines 63 to 69, inclusive, of the second amendment of the Senate, and all of the third amendment of the Senate, and insert in lieu thereof the following:

SEC. —. *That the proper officers of the Department of the Interior and of the Treasury shall finally adjust and settle the claims of any State against the United States for all lands which have been sold or located by warrant or scrip that were included in any grant of swamp and overflowed lands, and in such settlement and adjustment such State shall, upon filing proper relinquishment and waiver to the land in place, in the manner to be prescribed by the Secretary of the Interior, be allowed, credited, and paid the purchase money to the amount of one dollar and twenty-five cents per acre for all such lands situated therein as have been erroneously located by warrant or scrip therein, the amount of indemnity to be limited to the price at which the lands were held at the date of location, but not to exceed one dollar and twenty-five cents per acre: Provided, That all claims for land or indemnity under any of the swamp-land laws or under this act shall be forever barred for lands now surveyed, unless presented to the Secretary of the Interior within one year from the passage of this act, and for lands unsurveyed, unless presented within one year after the filing in the proper local land office of a copy of the officially approved township plat of the survey of the township in which said lands may be situated: Provided further, That under no circumstances shall more than two million dollars be paid under the provisions of this act for lands sold or located by warrant or scrip since March third, eighteen hundred and fifty-seven, and no money shall be paid to any State until the claim of each State, under the swamp-land grant, and under this act, has been adjusted, so far as the surveyed land in each State will permit of such adjustment; and should the claims of the various States amount to more than the said two million dollars, the claims shall be settled by the payment of said sum pro rata among the States according to the number of acres each State is found to be entitled to under said adjustment.*

SEC. —. *That in those States which elected to make the field notes of the United States Government survey the basis for determining what lands passed to them under the swamp grant, together with the State of California, the State will not be permitted to offer any other evidence in support of any claim to any tract of land as swamp, but said field notes shall be final in determining the character of the land; and in those States where evidence is to be taken as to the character of the land, the Commissioner of the General Land Office shall notify the governor of the State of the amount of estimated cost of the investigation into the character of any tract or tracts of land claimed by the State as swamp, and request that said amount be deposited in the Treasury of the United States, and after said investigation is concluded, if the claim of the State is allowed, said sum shall be returned to the State; but if the claim of the State is rejected, the balance only, if any, above the cost of the investigation, shall be returned, and it shall be the duty of the Secretary of the Treasury to return said money upon an account rendered by the Commissioner of the General Land Office, approved by the Secretary of the Interior; and if any State shall neglect or refuse, for a period of ninety days after notice, to deposit said sum, the claim of the State to the tract or tracts of land in question shall be considered as abandoned and forever barred without further investigation: Provided, That the Secretary of the Interior shall have the power to determine what shall be satisfactory and sufficient evidence as to the character of the land at the date of the swamp grant: Provided further, That any agent or inspector appointed by the Department of the Interior to investigate the claims under this or prior acts shall have the power to administer oaths and take affidavits of witnesses, both on behalf of the State and the United States, and any witness swearing falsely before such agent or inspector shall be deemed guilty of perjury, and shall, on conviction, be punished as now prescribed by law: Provided further, That nothing in this act shall deprive the Government of the right to investigate the matter, in any alleged fraudulent returns of Government surveys, and if land is falsely returned as swamp the claim to the same shall be rejected.*

SEC. —. *That upon the relinquishment, release, and quitclaim, in such form as may be approved by the Secretary of the Interior, to the United States by the State of Arkansas of all her claims and demands against the United States for the five per centum fund allowances under the act approved June twenty-third, eighteen hundred and thirty-six, for keeping prisoners under the executive order of February fifth, eighteen hundred and sixty-seven, for a portion of the distribution fund under the act approved September fourth, eighteen hundred and forty-one, for indemnity under the acts approved March second, eighteen hundred and fifty-five, March third, eighteen hundred and fifty-seven, and under this act, and for all swamp and overflowed lands under the act approved September twenty-eighth, eighteen hundred and fifty, not heretofore approved to the State, and all other claims of whatever kind or nature, the Secretary of the Treasury may, in his discretion, cancel or deliver to the proper officer of the said State of Arkansas all the bonds and coupons issued by the said State now in the possession of the Treasurer of the United States and owned or held in trust by the United States as a full and final compromise and settlement of accounts between the said State and United States.*

SEC. —. *That where soldiers' additional homestead entries have been*

mittee of conference on the disagreeing votes of the two Houses on the amendments of the Senate to the bill (H. R. 10238) making appropriations for the sundry civil expenses of the Government for the fiscal year ending June 30, 1894, and for other purposes. It further insists upon its disagreement to the amendments numbered 67, 68, 69, 70, 71, 86, 87, 104, 189, 193, 194, agrees to the further conference asked by the Senate on the disagreeing votes of the two Houses thereon, and has appointed Mr. Holman, Mr. Sayers, and Mr. Cogswell managers at the same on its part.

The House of Representatives has disagreed to the amendments of the Senate to the bill (H. R. 10415) making appropriation for current and contingent expenses and fulfilling treaty stipulations with Indian tribes for fiscal year ending June 30, 1894. It asks a conference with the Senate on the disagreeing votes of the two Houses thereon, and has appointed Mr. Peel, Mr. Allen, and Mr. Wilson, of Washington, managers at the same on its part.

The Speaker of the House of Representatives having signed an enrolled bill, H. R. 7633, I am directed to bring the same to the Senate for the signature of its President.

ENROLLED BILL SIGNED.

Mr. Dubois reported from the committee that they had examined and found duly enrolled a bill (H. R.7633) to ratify and confirm an agreement with the Kickapoo Indians in Oklahoma Territory and to make appropriations for carrying the same into effect;

Whereupon,

The President *pro tempore* signed the same, and it was delivered to the committee to be presented to the President of the United States.

INDIAN APPROPRIATION BILL.

The President *pro tempore* laid before the Senate the message of the House of Representatives announcing its disagreement to the amendments of the Senate to the bill (H. R. 10415) making appropriations for current and contingent expenses and fulfilling treaty stipulations with Indian tribes for fiscal year ending June 30, 1894.

On motion by Mr. Cullom,

Resolved, That the Senate insist upon its amendments to the said bill disagreed to by the House of Representatives, and agree to the conference asked by the House on the disagreeing votes of the two Houses thereon.

Ordered, That the conferees on the part of the Senate be appointed by the President *pro tempore;* and

The President *pro tempore* appointed Mr. Dawes, Mr. Cullom, and Mr. Call.

Ordered, That the Secretary notify the House of Representatives thereof.

EULOGIES ON DECEASED REPRESENTATIVES.

ALEXANDER K. CRAIG.

The President *pro tempore* laid before the Senate the resolutions of the House of Representatives on the announcement of the death of the Hon. Alexander K. Craig, late a Representative from the State of Pennsylvania; which were read.

Whereupon,

Mr. Cameron submitted the following resolutions:

Resolved, That the Senate has heard with profound sorrow the announcement of the death of Hon. Alexander K. Craig, late a Representative from the State of Pennsylvania.

Resolved, That the business of the Senate be now suspended in order that fitting tribute may be paid to his memory.

Resolved, That a copy of these resolutions be transmitted by the Secretary of the Senate to the family of the deceased.

The Senate proceeded, by unanimous consent, to consider the said resolutions; and

After addresses by Mr. Cameron, Mr. Peffer, Mr. Call, and Mr. Vilas, the resolutions were unanimously agreed to.

JOHN G. WARWICK.

The President *pro tempore* laid before the Senate the resolutions of the House of Representatives on the announcement of the death of Hon. John G. Warwick, late a Representative from the State of Ohio; which were read.

Whereupon,

Mr. Brice submitted the following resolutions:

Resolved, That the Senate has heard with profound sorrow the announcement of the death of Hon. John G. Warwick, late a Representative from the State of Ohio, and tenders to the relatives of the deceased the assurance of their sympathy with them under the bereavement they have been called to sustain.

Resolved, That the Secretary of the Senate be directed to transmit to the family of Mr. Warwick a certified copy of the foregoing resolution.

The Senate proceeded, by unanimous consent, to consider the said resolutions; and

After addresses by Mr. Brice and Mr. Daniel, the resolutions were unanimously agreed to.

JOHN W. KENDALL.

The President *pro tempore* laid before the Senate the resolutions of the House of Representatives on the announcement of the death of Hon. John W. Kendall, late a Representative from the State of Kentucky; which were read.

Whereupon,

Mr. Lindsay submitted the following resolutions; which were considered by unanimous consent, and unanimously agreed to:

Resolved, That the Senate has heard with profound sorrow of the announcement of the death of Hon. John W. Kendall, late a Representative from the State of Kentucky.

Resolved, That the business of the Senate be now suspended, in order that fitting tribute be paid to his memory.

After addresses by Mr. Lindsay, Mr. Cullom, Mr. Pasco, and Mr. Blackburn,

On motion by Mr. Blackburn, as a further mark of respect to the memory of the deceased representatives.

The Senate adjourned.

FRIDAY, MARCH 3, 1893.

The Vice-President laid before the Senate the credentials of Samuel Pasco, appointed a Senator by the governor of the State of Florida to fill the vacancy happening in the Senate of the United States by the expiration of the term of Samuel Pasco on March 3, 1893, during the recess of the legislature of said State; which were read and placed on file.

Mr. Hansbrough presented the credentials of William N. Roach, elected a Senator by the legislature of the State of North Dakota for the term of six years commencing March 4, 1893; which were read and placed on file.

HARBOR AT SAN PEDRO, CAL.

Mr. Felton presented a resolution of the common council of Salt Lake City, Utah, praying an appropriation for the construction of a deep-water harbor at San Pedro, Cal.; which was referred to the Committee on Commerce.

EXECUTIVE COMMUNICATIONS.

The Vice-President laid before the Senate a letter of the Secretary of the Interior, transmitting, in answer to a resolution of the Senate of January 25, 1893, a report of the Commissioner of the General Land Office, relative to the grant made to the Northern Pacific Railroad Company; which was referred to the Committee on Public Lands and ordered to be printed.

The Vice-President laid before the Senate a letter of the Civil Service Commissioners, transmitting, in answer to a resolution of the Senate of December 14, 1892, a statement of the positions of the Government service now embraced under civil-service regulations, etc.; which was referred to the Committee on Civil Service and Retrenchment and ordered to be printed.

PETITIONS AND MEMORIALS.

Petitions, memorials, etc., were presented and referred as follows:

Mr. Carey presented a memorial of the legislature of Wyoming in favor of an amendment to the Constitution of the United States providing for the election of United States Senators by a direct vote of the people.

Ordered, That it lie on the table.

Mr. Carey presented a memorial of the legislature of Wyoming in favor of the passage of a law to restore silver to the position occupied in the currency prior to the demonetization act of 1873; which was referred to the Committee on Finance.

Mr. Carey presented a memorial of the legislature of Wyoming in favor of the admission of the Territories of Utah, New Mexico, and Arizona into the Union as States; which was referred to the Committee on Territories.

Mr. Carey presented resolutions of the Fremont County Business Men's Club, of Lander, Wyo., praying the passage of the Torrey bankruptcy bill; which was referred to the Committee on the Judiciary and ordered to be printed.

Mr. Gibson presented several petitions of citizens of Maryland, praying for the closing of the World's Columbian Exposition on the Sabbath day; which were referred to the Select Committee on the Quadro-Centennial.

Mr. Vilas presented a resolution of the legislature of Wisconsin in favor of the passage of a joint resolution permitting that State to place a statue of Pere Marquette in the old Hall of the House of Representatives at Washington.

Ordered, That it lie on the table.

Mr. Hawley presented a memorial of the legislature of Connecticut in favor of the passage of the bill providing for an increase of the pay of letter-carriers after four years of service; which was referred to the Committee on Post-Offices and Post-Roads.

Mr. Stewart presented extracts from the annual report of the Commissioner of Railroads relative to the proposed settlement of Pacific Railroad debts; which were ordered to be printed.

MESSAGE FROM THE HOUSE.

A message from the House of Representatives, by Mr. Kerr, its Clerk:

Mr. President: The House of Representatives has passed, without amendment, the following bills of the Senate:

S. 3240. An act to facilitate the enforcement of the immigration and contract-labor laws of the United States, and

S. 3890. An act authorizing the Lake Shore and Michigan Southern Railroad Company to renew its railroad bridge across the Calumet River, upon or near the site of its present bridge and upon a location and plans to be approved by the Secretary of War, and to operate the same.

The House of Representatives has disagreed to the amendments of the Senate to the bill (H. R. 10258) making appropriations to supply deficiencies in the appropriations for the fiscal year ending June 30, 1893, and for prior years, and for other purposes. It asks a conference with the Senate on the disagreeing votes of the two Houses thereon, and has appointed Mr. Sayers, Mr. Holman, and Mr. Dingley managers at the same on its part.

The House of Representatives has disagreed to the amendments of the Senate to the bill (H. R. 2122) for the relief of Cumberland Female Collage, of McMinnville, Tenn. It agrees to the conference asked by the Senate on the disagreeing votes of the two Houses thereon, and has appointed Mr. Enloe, Mr. Stone, of Kentucky, and Mr. Houk, of Tennessee, managers at the same on its part.

The House of Representatives has agreed to the concurrent resolution of the Senate providing for the printing of 6,000 copies of the report of the Committee on Mines and Mining on the cost of the production of gold and silver.

The House of Representatives has passed a joint resolution (H. R. 196) authorizing members to certify monthly the amount paid by them for clerk hire, and directing the same to be paid out of the contingent fund of the House, in which it requests the concurrence of the Senate.

DEFICIENCY APPROPRIATION BILL.

The Vice-President laid before the Senate the message of the House of Representatives announcing its disagreement to the amendments of the Senate to the bill (H. R. 10258) making appropriations to supply deficiencies in the appropriations for the fiscal year ending June 30, 1893, and for prior years, and for other purposes.

On motion by Mr. Hale,

Resolved, That the Senate insist upon its amendments to the said bill disagreed to by the House of Representatives, and agree to the conference asked by the House on the disagreeing votes of the two Houses thereon.

Ordered, That the conferees on the part of the Senate be appointed by the Vice-President; and,

The Vice-President appointed Mr. Hale, Mr. Allison,. and Mr. Cockrell.

Ordered, That the Secretary notify the House of Representatives thereof.

CLERKS FOR MEMBERS.

The joint resolution (H. R. 196) authorizing members to certify monthly the amount paid by them for clerk hire, and directing the same to be paid out of the contingent fund of the House, this day received from the House of Representatives for concurrence, was read the first and second times by unanimous consent and considered as in Committee of the Whole; and no amendment being made, it was reported to the Senate.

Ordered, That it pass to a third reading.

The said resolution was read the third time by unanimous consent.

Resolved, That it pass.

Ordered, That the Secretary notify the House of Representatives thereof.

CONFERENCE REPORTS.

LEGISLATIVE APPROPRIATION BILL.

Mr. Dawes, from the committee of conference on the disagreeing votes of the two Houses on the amendments of the Senate to the bill H. R. 10331, submitted the following report:

The committee of conference on the disagreeing votes of the two Houses on the amendments of the Senate to the bill (H. R. 10331) making appropriations for the legislative, executive, and judicial expenses of the Government for the fiscal year ending June 30, 1894, and for other purposes, having met, after full and free conference have agreed to recommend and do recommend to their respective Houses as follows:

That the Senate recede from its disagreement to the amendments numbered 13, 14, 15, 19, 20, 21, 24, 25, 26, 27, 33, 34, 37, 38, 40, 42, 43, 44, 45, 52, 58, 59, 70, 71, 72, 73, 74, 75, 78, 79, 81, 105, 106, 107, and 109.

That the House recede from its disagreement to the amendments of the Senate numbered 2, 3, 4, 5, 6, 7, 10, 11, 12, 18, 29, 30, 31, 35, 39, 41, 46, 47, 48, 53, 54, 55, 56, 57, 60, 61, 62, 63, 64, 65, 67, 68, 69, 76, 82, 82, 101, 102, 103, 104, 110, 113, 114, 116, and 117, and agree to the same.

That the House recede from its disagreement to the amendment of the Senate numbered 1, and agree to the same with an amendment as follows: In lieu of the sum proposed insert: *four hundred and eighteen thousand five hundred and fifty-eight dollars and ninety cents;* and the Senate agree to the same.

That the House recede from its disagreement to the amendment of the Senate numbered 8, and agree to the same with an amendment as follows: In lieu of the matter stricken out by said amendment insert the following:

For twenty-three clerks to committees, at one thousand four hundred and forty dollars each, thirty-three thousand one hundred and twenty dollars, to be immediately available.

And the Senate agree to the same.

That the House recede from its disagreement to the amendment

20 s

---

of the Senate numbered 9, and agree to the same with an amendment as follows: In lieu of the matter inserted by said amendment insert the following:

For thirty-five annual clerks to Senators who are not chairman of committees, at one thousand two hundred dollars each, forty-two thousand dollars to be immediately available.

And the Senate agree to the same.

That the House recede from its disagreement to the amendment of the Senate numbered 16, and agree to the same with an amendment as follows: In lieu of the number proposed insert *ten;* and the Senate agree to the same.

That the House recede from its disagreement to the amendment of the Senate numbered 17, and agree to the same with an amendment as follows: In lieu of the sum proposed insert: *forty-three thousand eight hundred dollars;* and the Senate agree to the same.

That the House recede from its disagreement to the amendment of the Senate numbered 22, and agree to the same with an amendment as follows: In lieu of the sum proposed insert: *six thousand dollars;* and the Senate agree to the same.

That the House recede from its disagreement to the amendment of the Senate numbered 23, and agree to the same with an amendment as follows: In lieu of the matter stricken out by said amendment insert the following:

That a joint commission, consisting of three Senators, members of the Fifty-third Congress, to be appointed by the present President of the Senate, and three members-elect of the House of Representatives of the Fifty-third Congress, to be appointed by the Speaker of the House of Representatives of the Fifty-second Congress, shall, during the Fifty-third Congress, inquire into and examine the status of the laws organizing the Executive Departments, bureaus, divisions, and other Government establishments at the national capital; the rules, regulations, and methods for the conduct of the same; the time and attention devoted to the operations thereof by the persons employed therein, and the degree cf efficiency of all such employés; whether any modification of these laws can be made to secure greater efficiency and economy; and whether a reduction in the number or compensation of the persons authorized to be employed in said Executive Department or bureaus can be made without injury to the public service: Provided, That the commission herein authorized shall have no jurisdiction to inquire into and report on pension legislation. Said commission is authorized to employ not exceeding three experts, who shall render such assistance as the commission may require in the prosecution of the investigation herein required, and shall receive such compensation as the commission shall determine to be just and reasonable. The heads of the respective Executive Departments shall detail from to time to time such officers and employés as may be requested by said commission in their investigations. Said commission or any subcommittee thereof shall have power to send for persons and papers, and to administer oaths, and such process shall be issued and such oaths administered by the chairman of the commission or subcommittee, and the commission may report, by bill or otherwise, to their respective Houses of the Fifty-third Congress. All necessary expenses of said commission shall be paid out of any money in the Treasury not otherwise appropriated, upon vouchers approved jointly by the chairmen of said commission.

And the Senate agree to the same.

That the House recede from its disagreement to the amendment of the Senate numbered 28, and agree to the same with an amendment as follows: In line 1 of said amendment, before the word "act" where it first occurs, insert the words approved *May twenty-four, eighteen hundred and ninety, entitled "An act;"* and the Senate agree to the same.

That the House recede from its disagreement to the amendment of the Senate numbered 32, and agree to the same with amendments as follows: On page 41, in line 25, of the bill, strike out the words 'by striking out the," and insert in lieu thereof the words *so as to read as follows;* and in line 27 of said amendment, strike out all after the word "commodities," and insert in lieu thereof the following: *shall have been delivered to the collector of customs, as above required, by the person exporting such commodities, or by his agent, on information satisfactory to such customs officer as to the kind, quantities, and values of the domestic and foreign free or duty-paid commodities laden on such car. The agent or employé of any railway or transportation company who shall transport such commodities into a foreign country before the delivery to the collector of customs of the manifests, as above required, shall be liable to a penalty of fifty dollars for each offense: Provided, that the provisions of this law shall apply to commodities transported to the frontier in railway cars for exportation and transshipment across the frontier into the adjacent foreign territory in ferryboats or vehicles, so far as to require the person in charge thereof to furnish to the collector of customs information of the kinds, qualities, and values of such commodities: And provided further, That nothing contained in the foregoing shall be held as applicable to goods in transit between American ports by routes passing through foreign territory, or to merchandise in transit between places in the Dominion of Canada by routes passing through the United States, or to merchandise arriving at the ports designated under the authority of section three thousand and five of the Revised Statutes, and which may be destined for places in the Republic of Mexico;* and the Senate agree to the same.

That the House recede from its disagreement to the amendment of the Senate numbered 36, and agree to the same with an amendment as follows: In lieu of the sum proposed insert *four hundred dollars;* and the Senate agree to the same.

That the House recede from its disagreement to the amendment of the Senate numbered 49, and agree to the same with an amendment as follows: In lieu of the number proposed insert *five;* and the Senate agree to the same.

That the House recede from its disagreement to the amendment of the Senate numbered 50, and agree to the same with an amendment as follows: Strike out of said amendment the words "and one at Sand Point;" and the Senate agree to the same.

That the House recede from its disagreement to the amendment of the Senate numbered 51, and agree to the same with an amendment as follows: In lieu of the sum proposed insert: *twenty-three thousand dollars;* and the Senate agree to the same.

That the House recede from its disagreement to the amendment of the Senate numbered 66, and agree to the same with an amendment as follows: In lieu of the sum proposed insert: *fifteen thousand five hundred dollars;* and the Senate agree to the same.

That the House recede from its disagreement to the amendment of the Senate numbered 77, and agree to the same with an amendment as follows: In lieu of the sum proposed insert: *one thousand five hundred dollars;* and the Senate agree to the same.

That the House recede from its disagreement to the amendment of the Senate numbered 80, and agree to the same with an amendment as follows: In lieu of the matter inserted by said amendment insert the following:

Bureau of Education, four thousand dollars.

Indian Office, six thousand dollars; General Land Office, four thousand eight hundred dollars; storage of documents, two thousand dollars, and Civil Service Commission, four thousand dollars; in all, thirty thousand eight hundred dollars.

And the Senate agree to the same.

That the House recede from its disagreement to the amendment of the Senate numbered 83, and agree to the same with an amendment as follows: In lieu of the sum proposed insert: *six thousand dollars;* and the Senate agree to the same.

That the House recede from its disagreement to the amendment of the Senate numbered 84, and agree to the same with an amendment as follows: In lieu of the sum proposed insert: *eight thousand dollars;* and the Senate agree to the same.

That the House recede from its disagreement to the amendment of the Senate numbered 85, and agree to the same with an amendment as follows: In lieu of the sum proposed insert: *five thousand dollars;* and the Senate agree to the same.

That the House recede from its disagreement to the amendment of the Senate numbered 86, and agree to the same with an amendment as follows: In lieu of the sum proposed insert: *six thousand eight hundred dollars;* and the Senate agree to the same.

That the House recede from its disagreement to the amendment of the Senate numbered 87, and agree to the same with an amendment as follows: In lieu of the sum proposed insert: *ten thousand dollars;* and the Senate agree to the same.

That the House recede from its disagreement to the amendment of the Senate numbered 88, and agree to the same with an amendment as follows: In lieu of the sum proposed insert: *twelve thousand dollars;* and the Senate agree to the same.

That the House recede from its disagreement to the amendment of the Senate numbered 89, and agree to the same with an amendment as follows: In lieu of the sum proposed insert: *one thousand five hundred dollars;* and the Senate agree to the same.

That the House recede from its disagreement to the amendment of the Senate numbered 90, and agree to the same with an amendment as follows: In lieu of the sum proposed insert: *three thousand three hundred dollars;* and the Senate agree to the same.

That the House recede from its disagreement to the amendment of the Senate numbered 91, and agree to the same with an amendment as follows: In lieu of the sum proposed insert: *five thousand five hundred dollars;* and the Senate agree to the same.

That the House recede from its disagreement to the amendment of the Senate numbered 92, and agree to the same with an amendment as follows: In lieu of the sum proposed insert: *seven thousand five hundred dollars;* and the Senate agree to the same.

That the House recede from its disagreement to the amendment of the Senate numbered 93, and agree to the same with an amendment as follows: In lieu of the sum proposed insert: *three thousand dollars;* and the Senate agree to the same."

That the House recede from its disagreement to the amendment of the Senate numbered 94, and agree to the same with an amendment as follows: In lieu of the sum proposed insert: *five thousand dollars;* and the Senate agree to the same.

That the House recede from its disagreement to the amendment of the Senate numbered 95, and agree to the same with an amendment as follows: In lieu of the sum proposed insert: *eight thousand dollars;* and the Senate agree to the same.

That the House recede from its disagreement to the amendment of the Senate numbered 96, and agree to the same with an amendment as follows: In lieu of the sum proposed insert: *ten thousand dollars;* and the Senate agree to the same.

That the House recede from its disagreement to the amendment of the Senate numbered 97, and agree to the same with an amendment as follows: In lieu of the sum proposed insert *eight thousand five hundred dollars;* and the Senate agree to the same.

That the House recede from its disagreement to the amendment of the Senate numbered 98, and agree to the same with an amendment as follows: In lieu of the sum proposed insert *ten thousand five hundred dollars;* and the Senate agree to the same.

That the House recede from its disagreement to the amendment of the Senate numbered 99, and agree to the same with an amendment as follows: In lieu of the sum proposed insert *five thousand five hundred dollars;* and the Senate agree to the same.

That the House recede from its disagreement to the amendment of the Senate numbered 100, and agree to the same with an amendment as follows: In lieu of the sum proposed insert *seven thousand five hundred dollars;* and the Senate agree to the same.

That the House recede from its disagreement to the amendment of the Senate numbered 108, and agree to the same with an amendment as follows: In lieu of the sum proposed by said amendment insert *forty-seven thousand five hundred dollars;* and the Senate agree to the same.

That the House recede from its disagreement to the amendment of the Senate numbered 111, and agree to the same with amendments as follows: In line 2 of said amendment strike out the word "two" and insert the word *one,* and in line 3 strike out the word "five" and insert the word *four;* and the Senate agree to the same.

That the House recede from its disagreement to the amendment of the Senate numbered 112, and agree to the same with an amendment as follows: In lieu of the amended paragraph insert the following:

Supreme court of the District of Columbia: For salaries of the chief justice of the supreme court of the District of Columbia and the five associate judges, thirty thousand dollars. One-half of the foregoing amounts for the court of appeals and the supreme court of the District of Columbia shall be paid from the revenues of the District of Columbia.

And the Senate agree to the same.

That the House recede from its disagreement to the amendment of the Senate numbered 115, and agree to the same with an amendment as follows: In lieu of the sum proposed in said amendment insert *two hundred and fifty dollars;* and the Senate agree to the same.

That the House recede from its disagreement to the amendment of the Senate numbered 118, and agree to the same with an amendment as follows: In lieu of the matter stricken out by said amendment insert the following:

SEC. 5. That on and after July first, eighteen hundred and ninety-three, it shall be the duty of the heads of the several Executive Departments, in the interest of the public service, to require of all clerks and other employés of whatever grades or class in their respective Departments, not less than seven hours of labor each day, except Sundays and days declared to be public holidays by law or executive order : Provided, That the heads of the Departments may by special order, stating the reason, further extend or limit the hours of service of any clerk or employé in their Departments, respectively; but in case of an extension it shall be without additional compensation : And provided further, That the head of any Department may grant thirty days' annual and thirty days' sick leave with pay in any one year to each clerk or employé, the sick leave to be allowed in cases of personal illness only, or where some member of the immediate family is afflicted with a contagious disease and requires the care and attendance of such employé, or where his or her presence in the Department would jeopardize the health of fellow clerks : And be it provided further, That in exceptional and meritorious cases where to limit such sick leave would work peculiar hardship, it may be extended, in the discretion of the head of the Department, with pay not exceeding sixty days in any one case or in any one calendar year.

This section shall not be construed to mean that so long as the clerk or employé is borne upon the rolls of the Department in excess of the time herein provided for or granted that he or she shall be entitled to pay during the period of such excessive absence, but that the pay shall stop upon the expiration of the granted leave.

And the Senate agree to the same.

That the House recede from its disagreement to the amendment of the Senate numbered 119, and agree to the same with an amendment as follows: In lieu of the number proposed insert *six;* and the Senate agree to the same.

H. L. DAWES,
W. B. ALLISON,
F. M. COCKRELL,
Managers on the part of the Senate.

ALEX. M. DOCKERY,
W. S. HOLMAN,
D. B. HENDERSON,
Managers on the part of the House.

The Senate proceeded to consider the report; and
On the question to agree thereto,

It was determined in the affirmative, { Yeas 41
                                       { Nays 21

On motion by Mr. Wolcott,
The yeas and nays being desired by one-fifth of the Senators present,

Those who voted in the affirmative are,

Messrs. Allison, Bate, Berry, Blackburn, Brice, Butler, Call, Cockrell, Coke, Cullom, Davis, Dawes, Dixon, Faulkner, Felton, Frye, Gibson, Gorman, Harris, Hawley, Hunton, Irby, Jones of Arkansas, Lindsay, McMillan, McPherson, Mills, Morrill, Palmer, Pasco, Platt, Sawyer, Sherman, Stewart, Stockbridge, Turpie, Vance, Vest, Vilas, Voorhees, White.

Those who voted in the negative are,

Messrs. Blodgett, Cameron, Carey, Casey, Chandler, Dubois, Gallinger, Hansbrough, Higgins, Hiscock, Kyle, Manderson, Mitchell, Peffer, Perkins, Power, Proctor, Pugh, Shoup, Teller, Wolcott.

So the report was agreed to.

Ordered, That the Secretary notify the House of Representatives, thereof.

POST-OFFICE APPROPRIATION BILL.

Mr. Cullom, from the committee of conference on the disagreeing votes of the two Houses on the amendments of the Senate to the bill H. R. 10349, submitted the following report:

The committee of conference on the disagreeing votes of the two Houses on the amendments of the Senate to the bill (H. R. 10349) "making appropriations for the service of the Post-Office Department for the fiscal year ending June 30, 1894," having met, after full and free conference have agreed to recommend and do recommend to their respective Houses as follows:

That the Senate recede from its amendments numbered 2 and 4.

That the House recede from its disagreement to the amendments of the Senate numbered 3 and 6, and agree to the same.

That the House recede from its disagreement to the amendment of the Senate numbered 1, and agree to the same with an amendment as follows: In lieu of the matter inserted by said amendment insert the following: *And of this sum not exceeding fifty thousand dollars may, in the discretion of the Postmaster-General, be expended for the rental of canceling machines;* and the Senate agree to the same.

That the House recede from its disagreement to the amendment of the Senate numbered 5, and agree to the same with an amendment as follows: In lieu of the sum proposed, insert *one million six hundred thousand dollars;* and the Senate agree to the same.

S. M. CULLOM,
WM. M. STEWART,
JO. C. S. BLACKBURN,
Managers on the part of the Senate.
JOHN S. HENDERSON,
JAMES H. BLOUNT,
JNO. A. CALDWELL,
Managers on the part of the House.

The Senate proceeded to consider the report; and
On the question to agree thereto,

It was determined in the affirmative, { Yeas .... 35 Nays 25

On motion by Mr. Pasco,

The yeas and nays being desired by one-fifth of the Senators present,

Those who voted in the affirmative are,

Messrs. Allison, Berry, Blackburn, Brice, Butler, Cockrell, Coke, Cullom, Daniel, Dawes, Felton, Frye, Gallinger, Gordon, Hale, Hawley, Hiscock, Hunton, Jones of Arkansas, Jones of Nevada, Lindsay, McPherson, Mills, Mitchell, Morrill, Palmer, Platt, Pugh, Ransom, Sawyer, Sherman, Vest, Voorhees, Warren, White.

Those who voted in the negative are,

Messrs. Bate, Call, Cameron, Casey, Chandler, Dubois, Faulkner, Gorman, Hansbrough, Harris, Higgins, Hoar, Kyle, McMillan, Manderson, Paddock, Pasco, Peffer, Perkins, Pettigrew, Proctor, Shoup, Stockbridge, Teller, Washburn.

So the report was agreed to.

Ordered, That the Secretary notify the House of Representatives thereof.

AGRICULTURAL APPROPRIATION BILL.

Mr. Allison, from the committee of conference on the disagreeing votes of the two Houses on the amendments of the Senate to the bill H. R. 10421, submitted the following report:

The committee of conference on the disagreeing votes of the two Houses on the amendments of the Senate to the bill (H. R. 10421) making appropriations for the Department of Agriculture for the fiscal year ending June 30, 1894, having met, after full and free conference have agreed to recommend and do recommend to their respective Houses as follows:

That the Senate recede from its amendment numbered 7.

That the House recede from its disagreement to the amendments of the Senate numbered 1, 2, 3, 4, 5, 6, 8, 9, and 10, and agree to the same.

That the House recede from its disagreement to the amendment of the Senate numbered 11, and agree to the same with an amendment as follows: In lieu of the number proposed insert *eleven;* and the Senate agree to the Same.

That the House recede from its disagreement to the amendment of the Senate numbered 12, and agree to the same with an amendment as follows: In lieu of the sum proposed insert *fifteen thousand 'our hundred dollars;* and the Senate agree to the same.

That the House recede from its disagreement to the amendment of the Senate numbered 13, and agree to the same with an amendment as follows: In lieu of the sum proposed insert *thirty-one;* and the Senate agree to the same.

That the House recede from its disagreement to the amendment of the Senate numbered 14, and agree to the same with an amendment as follows: In lieu of the sum proposed insert *thirty-seven thousand two hundred dollars;* and the Senate agree to the same.

That the House recede from its disagreement to the amendment of the Senate numbered 15, and agree to the same with an amendment as follows: Strike out "one" and insert in lieu therof *five;* and the Senate agree to the same.

W. B. ALLISON,
S. M. CULLOM,
WILKINSON CALL,
Managers on the part of the Senate.
W. H. HATCH,
W. S. FORMAN,
E. H. FUNSTON,
Managers on the part of the House.

The Senate proceeded to consider the report; and
On motion by Mr. Allison,

Resolved, That the Senate agree thereto.

Ordered, That the Secretary notify the House of Representatives thereof.

NAVAL APPROPRIATION BILL.

Mr. Hale, from the committee of conference on the disagreeing votes of the two Houses on the amendments of the Senate to the bill H. R. 10488, submitted the following report:

The committee of conference on the disagreeing votes of the two Houses on the amendments of the Senate to the bill (H. R. 10488) "making appropriations for the naval service for the fiscal year ending June 30, 1894, and for other purposes," having met, after full and free conference have agreed to recommend and do recommend to their respective Houses as follows:

That the Senate recede from its amendments numbered 2, 3, 7, 11, 14, 15, and 18.

That the House recede from its disagreement to the amendment of the Senate numbered 1, 4, 8, 9, 10, 12, 13, 17, 20, 21, 23, 24, 25, 26, 27, 28, 29, 30, and 31, and agree to the same.

That the House recede from its disagreement to the amendment of the Senate numbered 5, and agree to the same with an amendment insert the following:

And in time of peace the President may, in his discretion, under such rules and upon such conditions as he may prescribe, permit any enlisted man to purchase his discharge from the Navy or the Marine Corps, the amounts received therefrom to be covered into the Treasury; and the Senate agree to the same.

That the House recede from its disagreement to the amendment of the Senate numbered 6, and agree to the same with an amendment as follows: Add at the end of said amendment the following: *to be taken from the balances of appropriations on hand July first, eighteen hundred and ninety-three, to the credit of armor and armament of vessels heretofore authorized;* and the Senate agree to the same.

That the House recede from its disagreement to the amendment of the Senate numbered 16, and agree to the same with an amendment as follows: In line 17, page 35 of the bill, strike out "fifteen," and insert in lieu thereof *nineteen;* and the Senate agree to the same.

That the House recede from its disagreement to the amendment of the Senate numbered 19, and agree to the same with an amendment as follows: In lieu of the matter inserted by said amendment insert the following: *three light-draft protected gunboats;* and the Senate agree to the same.

That the House recede from its disagreement to the amendment of the Senate numbered 22, and agree to the same with an amendment insert the following: *Either of said gunboats,* and strike out after the word "contain," in lines 23 and 24, page 38 of the bill, all down to and including the word "dollars," in line 6, page 38 of the bill, and insert in lieu thereof the following: *Such provisions as to speed and premiums and penalties affected by speed as may, in the judgment of the Secretary of the Navy, be deemed proper and fitting;* and the Senate agree to the same.

That the House recede from its disagreement to the amendments of the Senate numbered 32, and agree to the same with an amendment as follows: Strike out, in lines 8 and 9, page 40 of the bill, the words "six hundred and fifty," and insert in lieu thereof *eight hundred and seventy-five;* and the Senate agree to the same.

EUGENE HALE,
W. B. ALLISON,
A. P. GORMAN,
Managers on the part of the Senate.
H. A. HERBERT,
WILLIAM ELLIOTT,
C. A. BOUTELLE,
Managers on the part of the House.

The Senate proceeded to consider the report; and
On motion by Mr. Hale,
Resolved, That the Senate agree thereto.
Ordered, That the Secretary notify the House of Representatives thereof.

PRESENTATION OF BILL.

Mr. Dubois reported from the committee that they yesterday presented to the President of the United States an enrolled bill (S. 203) for the examination and allowance of certain awards made by a board of claims to certain citizens of Jefferson County, Kentucky.

REPORTS OF COMMITTEES.

Mr. Gorman, from the Select Committee on Corporations in the District of Columbia, who were authorized by a resolution of the Senate of July 27, 1892, to ascertain and report upon the amount of capital stock, bonds, etc., issued by incorporated institutions of the District of Columbia, submitted a report (No. 1379).

Mr. Morrill, from the Committee on Finance, to whom was referred the bill (H. R. 10375) establishing a standard gauge for sheet and plate iron and steel, reported it without amendment.

Mr. Manderson, from the Committee on Printing, to whom was referred the resolution submitted by him February 20, 1893, to print 3,000 copies of a comprehensive index of public documents prepared by John G. Ames, submitted an adverse report (No. 1381) thereon.

Ordered, That it be postponed indefinitely.

Mr. Bate, from the Committee on Military Affairs, to whom was referred the bill (H. R. 6965) to perfect the military record of Warren Alonzo Alden, reported it without amendment and submitted a report (No. 1382) thereon.

Mr. Faulkner, from the Committee on the District of Columbia, to whom was referred the bill (S. 3799) to amend "An act to incorporate the Georgetown and Tennallytown Railway Company of the District of Columbia," which became a law August 10, A. D. 1888, reported it with an amendment.

Mr. McPherson, from the Committee on Finance, to whom was referred the bill (H. R. 10597) to repeal paragraph No. 209 of the "act to reduce the revenue and equalize duties on imports, and for other purposes," reported it with amendments.

Mr. Proctor, from the Committee on Military Affairs, to whom was referred the bill (H. R. 2077) for the relief of William B. Price, reported it without amendment and submitted a report (No. 1383) thereon.

The Senate proceeded, by unanimous consent, to consider the said bill as in Committee of the Whole; and no amendment being made it was reported to the Senate.

Ordered, That it pass to a third reading.
The said bill was read the third time.
Resolved, That it pass.
Ordered, That the Secretary notify the House of Representatives thereof.

Mr. Proctor, from the Select Committee to Establish the University of the United States, to whom was referred the bill (S. 3824) to establish a national university, reported it without amendment and submitted a report (No. 1384) thereon.

Mr. Sawyer, from the Committee on Pensions, to whom was referred the bill (H. R. 6233) granting a pension to Thomas T. Prather, reported it without amendment and submitted a report (No. 1385) thereon.

The Senate proceeded, by unanimous consent, to consider the said bill as in the Committee of the Whole; and no amendment being made, it was reported to the Senate.

Ordered, That it pass to a third reading.
The said bill was read the third time.
Resolved, That it pass.
Ordered, That the Secretary notify the House of Representatives thereof.

Mr. Hiscock, from the Committee on Finance, to whom was referred the bill (H. R. 10351) to continue the duties on certain manufactures of flax at the rate now provided by law, reported it without amendment.

The Senate proceeded, by unanimous consent, to consider the said bill as in Committee of the Whole; and no amendment being made, it was reported to the Senate.

Ordered, That it pass to a third reading.
The said bill was read the third time.
Resolved, That it pass.
Ordered, That the Secretary notify the House of Representatives thereof.

Mr. Voorhees, from the Committee on the Library, to whom was referred the joint resolution (H. Res. 107) authorizing the State of Wisconsin to place in Statuary Hall at the Capitol the statue of Pere Marquette, reported it without amendment.

The Senate proceeded, by unanimous consent, to consider the said resolution as in Committee of Whole; and no amendment being made, it was reported to the Senate.

Ordered, That it pass to a third reading.
The said resolution was read the third time.
Resolved, That it pass.

Ordered, That the Secretary notify the House of Representatives thereof.

Mr. Manderson, from the Committee on Printing, to whom were referred the following concurrent resolutions, reported them severally without amendment and submitted written reports thereon as follows:

Resolution received from the House of Representatives for concurrence, March 2, 1893, to print 2,400 copies of the annual report of the health officer of the District of Columbia for the years 1891 and 1892; Report No. 1386.

Resolution received from the House of Representatives for concurrence, March 2, 1893, to print 8,000 copies of the eulogies delivered in Congress upon Hon. John E. Kenna, late a Senator from the State of West Virginia; Report No. 1387.

Resolution received from the House of Representatives for concurrence, March 1, 1893, to print 11,000 copies of the report of the Chief of the Bureau of Statistics of the Treasury Department relating to wool and the manufactures of wool; Report No. 1388.

Resolution received from the House of Representatives for concurrence, March 2, 1893, to print and bind 3,000 copies of the comprehensive index of public documents of the Fifty-first and Fifty-second Congresses, prepared by John G. Ames; Report No. 1389.

The Senate proceeded, by unanimous consent, to consider the said resolutions; and

Resolved, That the Senate agree thereto.
Ordered, That the Secretary notify the House of Representatives thereof.

Mr. Manderson, from the Committee on Printing, to whom referred the resolution submitted by Mr. Sherman, February 7, 1893, to print 10,000 additional copies of Senate Ex. Doc. 38, Part 1, second session, Fifty-second Congress, being a report of the Secretary of the Treasury relative to bank statistics, reported it without amendment and submitted a report (No. 1391) thereon.

The Senate proceeded, by unanimous consent, to consider the said resolution; and

Resolved, That the Senate agree thereto.

Mr. Manderson, from the Committee on Printing, to whom was referred the joint resolution (S. R. 155) authorizing and directing the Secretary of the Interior to purchase report on mineral industry, etc., covering mineral statistics for 1892, etc., submitted an adverse report (No. 1380) thereon.

Ordered, That it be postponed indefinitely.

Mr. Manderson, from the Committee on Printing, to whom was referred the resolution submitted by Mr. Chandler, February 3, 1893, to print 7,000 copies of the testimony taken by the Select Committee on Failed National Banks, together with the report of the committee thereon, reported it with amendments and submitted a report (No. 1390) thereon.

The Senate proceeded, by unanimous consent, to consider the said resolution, and the reported amendments having been agreed to, the resolution as amended was agreed to, as follows:

Resolved by the Senate (the House of Representatives concurring), That the Public Printer be, and he is hereby, directed to print and bind in muslin 5,200 copies of the testimony taken by the Senate Select Committee on Failed National Banks, together with the report of the committee, of which 800 copies shall be for the use of the House, 400 copies for the use of the Senate, and 4,000 copies to be distributed by the Comptroller of the Currency.

Ordered, That the Secretary request the concurrence of the House of Representatives therein.

Mr. Manderson, from the Committee on Printing, reported the following resolution; which was considered by unanimous consent and agreed to:

Resolved, That an extra edition of the Congressional Directory be compiled under the direction of the Joint Committee on Printing, corrected and revised to cover the principal and meet changes incident to the change of administration, the expense of which shall be paid out of the contingent fund of the Senate.

Mr. Aldrich, from the Committee on Finance, who were instructed, by a resolution of the Senate of March 3, 1891, to ascertain and report from time to time the effect of the tariff laws upon imports and exports, the growth, development, production, and prices of agricultural and manufactured articles at home and abroad, submitted a report (No. 1394) on wholesale prices and wages.

Mr. Harris asked and obtained leave to submit, should he so desire, the views of a minority of the Committee on Finance on the subject-matter of the foregoing report, and to be printed, to accompany the said report No. 1394.

PATENTS AND TRADE-MARKS.

Mr. Platt submitted the following resolution; which was considered by unanimous consent and agreed to:

Resolved, That the Secretary of the Interior be requested to ascertain what legislation, if any, is necessary to enforce the provisions of existing treaties or conventions with foreign countries with respect to patents and trade-marks, or to secure to citizens of the United States the enjoyment of privileges in foreign countries corresponding to those enjoyed by the citizens or subjects of such countries in the United States, and to report his conclusions to the Senate at the next session of Congress.

PHAROS B. BRUBAKER.

Mr. Hansbrough submitted the following resolution; which was considered by unanimous consent and agreed to:

Resolved, That the Secretary of State be, and he hereby is, directed to forward to the Senate, at the earliest date possible, all information in his possession with respect to the alleged capture and imprisonment by Honduras officials of Capt. Pharos B. Brubaker, a citizen of the United States, and a resident of the city of Fargo, State of North Dakota.

WRITING SET FOR THE VICE-PRESIDENT.

Mr. McPherson submitted the following resolution; which was considered by unanimous consent and agreed to:

Resolved, That the Vice-President is hereby authorized to retain for his personal use the writing set and appendages used by him during his term of office.

HISTORY OF THE RED CROSS.

Mr. Manderson submitted the following concurrent resolution; which was referred to the Committee on Printing:

Resolved by the Senate (the House of Representatives concurring), That there be printed of the History of the Red Cross, the Treaty of Geneva, and its adoption by the United States, 2,000 additional copies, 700 for use of the Senate and 1,300 for use of the House.

REPORT OF NATIONAL ACADEMY OF SCIENCES.

Mr. Manderson submitted the following concurrent resolution; which was referred to the Committee on Printing:

Resolved by the Senate (the House of Representatives concurring), That there be printed 3,500 additional copies of the report of the National Academy of Sciences for the year 1892, 500 copies for the use of the Senate, 1,000 copies for the use of the House, and 2,000 copies for use of the National Academy of Sciences.

CONSIDERATION OF BILLS ON CALENDAR.

The Senate proceeded to consider as in Committee of the Whole the following bills; and no amendment being made, they were severally reported to the Senate:

H. R. 6212. An act granting an increase of pension to Ellis P. Phipps, late lieutenant in Company A, Twelfth New Jersey Volunteer Infantry, invalid certificate No. 35719;

H. R. 7306. An act to pension Maud Case, of Dodge County, Minnesota;

H. R. 7729. An act granting a pension to Miss Phebe Sigler;

H. R. 8498. An act to pension Sophia Kagwaich;

H. R. 3118. An act to pension John S. Dunham;

H. R. 9233. An act to grant a pension to Harriet Cota;

H. R. 8409. An act granting a pension to Mary Danahay, mother of Daniel Danahay, late a private, Company H, Eighteenth New York Cavalry;

H. R. 4320. An act granting a pension to Thomas S. Kennedy;

H. R. 3230. An act for the relief of Louis G. Sanderson, of Craighead County, Arkansas.

H. R. 3253. An act to increase the pension of William G. Smith;

H. R. 7100. An act to pension Jacob O'Neal;

H. R. 2901. An act to pension Ida Cassell;

H. R. 8017. An act granting a pension to Elizabeth Voss;

H. R. 9741. An act to increase the pension of Capt. E. R. Chase from $20 to $72;

H. R. 2128. An act granting a pension to John Fields;

H. R. 7306. An act to pension Martin McDermott;

H. R. 4955. An act granting a pension to Susannah Chadwick;

H. R. 1422. An act for the relief of George M. Henry;

H. R. 6554. An act to remove the charge of desertion against Charles H. Behle;

H. R. 5519. An act for the relief of Daniel Eldridge, Company D, Fifteenth Illinois Volunteers;

H. R. 4071. An act for the relief of George W. Schachleiter;

H. R. 8550. An act to increase the pension of W. H. Philpot, a pensioner of the Mexican war;

H. R. 4496. An act to place upon the pension rolls of the United States the name of Thomas F. Sheldon, late captain, Company A, One hundred and twenty-fifth New York Infantry;

H. R. 1100. An act granting a pension to Mary Catherine Reardon;

H. R. 8246. An act granting a pension to Bridget Brennan, widow of Thomas Brennan, late of Companies C and G, Second Regiment of Rhode Island Volunteers;

H. R. 5508. An act to place the name of Sabra Wolcott upon the pension rolls;

H. R. 4804. An act to place the name of Sarah L. Van Nest on the pension list;

H. R. 5022. An act for the relief of Lucy Spotberry; and

H. R. 1484. An act for the relief of Mary A. Lewis.

Ordered, That they pass to a third reading.

The said bills were read the third time.

Resolved, That they pass.

Ordered, That the Secretary notify the House of Representatives thereof.

CONFERENCE REPORT.

Mr. Platt, from the committee of conference on the disagreeing votes of the two Houses, on the amendment of the House of Repre-

sentatives to the bill (S. 2171) to amend section 766 of the Revised Statutes of the United States, submitted the following report:

The committee of conference on the disagreeing votes of the two Houses on the amendments of the House to the bill (S. 2171) to amend section 766 of the Revised Statutes of the United States, having met, after full and free conference have agreed to recommend and do recommend to their respective Houses as follows: That the Senate recede from its disagreement to the amendment of the House and agree to the same.

O. H. PLATT,
J. L. PUGH,
Managers on the part of the Senate.
JAMES BUCHANAN,
JOHN A. BUCHANAN,
Managers on the part of the House.

The Senate proceeded to consider the report; and

On motion by Mr. Platt,

Resolved, That the Senate agree thereto.

Ordered, That the Secretary notify the House of Representatives thereof.

J. P. RANDOLPH.

On motion by Mr. Harris,

The Senate proceeded to consider, as in Committee of the Whole, the bill (H. R. 1231) for the relief of J. P. Randolph, administrator of J. F. Randolph, deceased; and the reported amendments having been agreed to, the bill was reported to the Senate and the amendments were concurred in.

Ordered, That the amendments be engrossed and the bill read a third time.

The said bill as amended was read the third time.

Resolved, That it pass, and that the Senate request a conference with the House of Representatives on the said bill and amendments.

Ordered, That the conferees on the part of the Senate be appointed by the Vice-President; and

The Vice-President appointed Mr. Pasco, Mr. Mitchell, and Mr. Daniel.

Ordered, That the Secretary notify the House of Representatives thereof.

WASHINGTON, BURNT MILLS AND SANDY SPRINGS RAILROAD.

The Senate proceeded to consider, as in Committee of the Whole, the bill (H. R. 9956) to incorporate the Washington, Burnt Mills and Sandy Springs Railroad Company; and the reported amendments having been disagreed to, and no amendments being proposed, the bill was reported to the Senate.

Ordered, That it pass to a third reading.

The said bill was read the third time.

Resolved, That it pass.

Ordered, That the Secretary notify the House of Representatives thereof.

MESSAGE FROM THE HOUSE.

A message from the House of Representatives, by Mr. Towles, its chief clerk:

Mr. President: The House of Representatives has agreed to the reports of the committees of conference on the disagreeing votes of the two Houses on the amendments of the Senate to the following bills:

H. R. 10421. An act making appropriations for the Department of Agriculture for the fiscal year ending June 30, 1894;

H. R. 10488. An act making appropriations for the naval service for the fiscal year ending June 30, 1894, and for other purposes; and

H. R. 10349. An act making appropriations for the service of the Post-Office Department for the fiscal year ending June 30, 1894.

The House of Representatives has agreed to the report of the second committee of conference on the disagreeing votes of the two Houses on certain amendments of the Senate to the bill (H. R. 10238) making appropriations for sundry civil expenses of the Government for the fiscal year ending June 30, 1894, and for other purposes. It further insists upon the disagreement to the amendments of the Senate numbered 67, 68, 69, 70, 71, and 104, and asks a further conference with the Senate on the disagreeing votes of the two Houses thereon, and has appointed Mr. Holman, Mr. Sayers, and Mr. Cogswell managers at the same on its part.

The Speaker of the House of Representatives having signed three enrolled bills, S. 3240, S. 3890, and H. R. 4071, and an enrolled joint resolution, H. R. 196, I am directed to bring the same to the Senate for the signature of its President.

ENROLLED BILLS SIGNED.

Mr. Dubois reported from the committee that they had examined and found duly enrolled the following bills and joint resolution:

S. 3240. An act to facilitate the enforcement of the immigration and contract-labor laws of the United States;

S. 3890. An act to authorize the Lake Shore and Michigan Southern Railroad Company to renew its railroad bridge across the Calumet River upon or near the site of its present bridge, and upon a location and plans to be approved by the Secretary of War, and to operate the same;

H. R. 4071. An act for the relief of George W. Schachleiter; and

H. Res. 196. A joint resolution authorizing members to certify monthly the amount paid by them for clerk hire, and directing the same to be paid out of the contingent fund of the House;

Whereupon,

The Vice-President signed the same, and they were delivered to the committee to be presented to the President of the United States.

CONSIDERATION OF BILLS ON CALENDAR.

On motion by Mr. Cameron, and by unanimous consent,

The Senate proceeded to consider, as in Committee of the Whole, the bill (H. R. 10375) establishing a standard gauge for sheet and plate iron and steel; and no amendment being made, it was reported to the Senate.

Ordered, That it pass to a third reading.

The said bill was read the third time.

Resolved, That it pass.

Ordered, That the Secretary notify the House of Representatives thereof.

The Senate proceeded to consider, as in Committee of the Whole, the bill (H. R. 5818) for the relief of William B. Morrow; and the reported amendment having been agreed to, the bill was reported to the Senate and the amendment was concurred in.

Ordered, That the amendment be engrossed and the bill read a third time.

The said bill as amended was read the third time.

Resolved, That it pass, and that the Senate request a conference with the House of Representatives on the said bill and amendment.

Ordered, That the conferees on the part of the Senate be appointed by the Vice-President; and

The Vice-President appointed Mr. Pasco, Mr. Mitchell, and Mr. Peffer.

Ordered, That the Secretary notify the House of Representatives thereof.

The Senate proceeded to consider, as in Committee of the Whole, the bill (S. 3881) relating to copyrights; and the reported amendment having been agreed to, the bill was reported to the Senate and the amendment was concurred in.

Ordered, That it be engrossed and read a third time.

The said bill was read the third time.

Resolved, That it pass, and that the title thereof be as aforesaid.

Ordered, That the Secretary request the concurrence of the House of Representatives therein.

The Senate proceeded to consider, as in Committee of the Whole, the following bills; and the reported amendments having been agreed to, the bills were severally reported to the Senate and the amendments were concurred in:

H. R. 4916. An act granting a pension to Thomas Tucker, of Battery A, Fourth United States Artillery;

H. R. 9004. An act donating the military reservation at Oklahoma City, in Oklahoma Territory, to said city, for the use and benefit of the free public schools thereof, and for other purposes; and

H. R. 9925. An act to establish companies of the Hospital Corps, United S. ates Army, and for other purposes.

Ordered, That the amendments be engrossed and the bills read a third time.

The said bills as amended were read the third time.

Resolved, That they pass.

Ordered, That the Secretary request the concurrence of the House of Representatives in the amendment.

RECESS.

On motion by Mr. Allison,

Ordered, That at 5 o'clock and 30 minutes the Senate take a recess until 8 o'clock p. m.

EXECUTIVE SESSION.

On motion by Stewart,

The Senate proceeded to the consideration of executive business; and

After the consideration of executive business the doors were reopened;

When,

The hour of 5 o'clock and 30 minutes having arrived, the Senate, in pursuance of its order, took a recess until 8 o'clock p. m.

AT 8 O'CLOCK P. M.

On motion by Mr. Cockrell,

The Senate took a further recess until 8 o'clock and 15 minutes p. m.

AT 8 O'CLOCK AND 15 MINUTES P. M.

DEFICIENCY APPROPRIATION BILL.

Mr. Hale, from the committee of conference on the disagreeing votes of the two Houses on the amendments of the Senate to the bill H. R. 10258, submitted the following report:

The committee of conference on the disagreeing votes of the two Houses on the amendments of the Senate to the bill (H. R. 10258) making appropriations to supply deficiencies in the appropriations for the fiscal year ending June 30, 1893, and for other purposes, having met, after full and free conference have agreed to recommend and do recommend to their respective Houses as follows:

That the Senate recede from its amendments numbered 4, 13, 15, 16, 19, 24, 25, 26, 27, 28, 32, 35, 37, 51, 52, 59, 61, 62, 84, 85, 86, 87, 88, 89, 90, 91, 92, 93, 103, 104, 106, 113, 136, 149, 153, 162, 172, and 178.

That the House recede from its disagreement to the amendments of the Senate numbered 1, 2, 3, 5, 6, 7, 8, 9, 10, 11, 17, 18, 20, 21, 22, 23, 29, 31, 33, 34, 36, 38, 39, 40, 41, 42, 43, 44, 45, 46, 47, 48, 49, 53, 54, 55, 56, 57, 65, 80, 81, 83, 100, 101, 102, 106, 107, 109, 110, 112, 114, 115, 116, 117, 118, 119, 120, 121, 122, 123, 124, 125, 126, 127, 128, 129, 130, 131, 132, 133, 134, 135, 137, 138, 139, 140, 141, 142, 143, 144, 145, 146, 147, 148, 151, 154, 155, 156, 157, 158, 163, and 164, and agree to the same.

That the House recede from its disagreement to the amendment of the Senate numbered 12, and agree to the same with an amendment as follows: In lieu of the sum proposed in said amendment insert *five thousand dollars;* and the Senate agree to the same.

That the House recede from its disagreement to the amendment of the Senate numbered 14, and agree to the same with an amendment as follows: In lieu of the sum proposed in said amendment insert *two thousand dollars;* and the Senate agree to the same.

That the House recede from its disagreement to the amendment of the Senate numbered 50, and agree to the same with an amendment as follows: At the end of the amended paragraph insert the following: *Provided, That on and after March fifteenth, eighteen hundred and ninety-three, the existing clerical force of the Record and Pension Office be, and the same is hereby, reduced as follows: One clerk of class I and four clerks at one thousand dollars each;* and the Senate agree to the same.

That the House recede from its disagreement to the amendment of the Senate numbered 58, and agree to the same with an amendment as follows: In lieu of the amended paragraph insert the following: *For care and preservation of the bridge and viaduct and expenses of maintaining and operating the draw of the Rock Island bridge, two thousand five hundred dollars;* and the Senate agree to the same.

That the House recede from its disagreement to the amendment of the Senate numbered 60, and agree to the same with an amendment as follows: In lieu of the matter inserted by said amendment insert the following: *To pay the owners of the Bellevue Rifle Range, Omaha, Nebraska, for use and occupation thereof, five hundred dollars; the said sum to be in full for such use and occupation for the years eighteen hundred and ninety-two and eighteen hundred and ninety-three;* and the Senate agree to the same.

That the House recede from its disagreement to the amendment of the Senate numbered 82, and agree to the same with an amendment as follows: In line 2 of the matter inserted by said amendment strike out the words "*on duty,*" and insert in lieu thereof the words *and traveling on duty outside of the District of Columbia;* and on page 20 of the bill, strike out lines 21 to 27, inclusive, and line 1 on page 21 of the bill; and the Senate agree to the same.

That the House recede from its disagreement to the amendment of the Senate numbered 111, and agree to the same with an amendment as follows: In lieu of the sum proposed insert *one thousand one hundred and thirty-two dollars and eighty cents;* and insert as a new paragraph the following:

For expenses of defending suits in claims against the United States, being for the service of the fiscal year eighteen hundred and ninety-three, five thousand dollars.

And the Senate agree to the same.

That the House recede from its disagreement to the amendment of the Senate numbered 152, and agree to the same with an amendment as follows: In lieu of the matter inserted by said amendment insert as follows:

To pay for a clerk for the Senator in charge of the conference room of the minority of the Senate, which shall be in lieu of any Senator's or committee clerk for such Senator, and shall commence on March fourth, eighteen hundred and ninety-three, two thousand two hundred and twenty dollars.

And the Senate agree to the same.

That the House recede from its disagreement to the amendment of the Senate numbered 159, and agree to the same with an amendment as follows: In lieu of the sum named in said amendment insert *six thousand three hundred and sixty-seven dollars and eighty-four cents;* and the Senate agree to the same.

That the House recede from its disagreement to the amendment of the Senate numbered 175, and agree to the same with an amendment as follows: On page 6 of said amendment strike out lines 24, 25, and 26, and on page 8 of said amendment strike out all after the word "cents" in line 24, down to and including line 28; and on page 9 strike out all of lines 1 to 12, inclusive; and the Senate agree to the same.

On amendments numbered 30, 63, 64, 66, 67, 68, 69, 70, 71, 72, 73, 74, 75, 76, 77, 78, 79, 94, 95, 96, 97, 98, 99, 108, 150, 160, 161, 165, 166, 167, 168, 169, 170, 171, 173, 174, 176, and 177, the committee of conference have been unable to agree.

EUGENE HALE,
W. B. ALLISON,
F. M. COCKRELL,
Managers on the part of the Senate.
JOSEPH D. SAYERS,
W. S. HOLMAN,
NELSON DINGLEY, JR.,
Managers on the part of the House.

The Senate proceeded to consider the report; and
On motion by Mr. Hale,
Resolved, That the Senate agree thereto.
Ordered, That the Secretary notify the House of Representatives thereof.
On motion by Mr. Hale,
Resolved, That the Senate further insist upon its amendments numbered 30, 63, 64, 66, 67, 68, 69, 70, 71, 72, 73, 74, 75, 76, 77, 78, 79, 94, 95, 96, 97, 98, 99, 108, 150, 160, 161, 165, 166, 167, 168, 169, 170, 171, 173, 174, 176, and 177, disagreed to by the House of Representatives, and ask a further conference with the House on the disagreeing votes of the two Houses thereon.
Ordered, That the conferees on the part of the Senate be appointed by the Vice-President; and
The Vice-President appointed Mr. Hale, Mr. Allison, and Mr. Cockrell.
Ordered, That the Secretary notify the House of Representatives thereof.

COMPILATION OF LABOR LAWS.

Mr. Manderson, from the Committee on Printing, to whom was referred the resolution received from the House of Representatives for concurrence on the 2d instant, to print 5,500 copies of House Report No. 1960, being a compilation of the labor laws of the various States and Territories, reported it without amendment and submitted a report (No. 1392) thereon.
The Senate proceeded, by unanimous consent, to consider the said resolution; and
Resolved, That the Senate agree thereto.
Ordered, That the Secretary notify the House of Representatives thereof.

REPORT OF NATIONAL ACADEMY OF SCIENCES.

Mr. Hawley, from the Committee on Printing, to whom was referred the resolution this day submitted by him to print 3,500 copies of the annual report of the National Academy of Sciences, reported it without amendment and submitted a report (No. 1393) thereon.
The Senate proceeded, by unanimous consent, to consider the said resolution; and
Resolved, That the Senate agree thereto.
Ordered, That the Secretary request the concurrence of the House of Representatives therein.

MESSAGE FROM THE HOUSE.

A message from the House of Representatives, by Mr. Kerr, its Clerk:
Mr. President: The House of Representatives has agreed to the report of the committee of conference on the disagreeing votes of the two Houses on the amendment of the Senate to the bill (H. R. 2122) for the relief of Cumberland Female College, of McMinnville, Tenn.
The Speaker of the House of Representatives having signed sixteen enrolled bills, S. 2171, H. R. 1422, H. R. 3253, H. R. 3118, H. R. 5519, H. R. 6554, H. R. 7100, H. R. 7306, H. R. 7729, H. R. 8017, H. R. 8230, H. R. 8409, H. R. 8498, H. R. 9233, H. R. 10331, and H. R. 10421, I am directed to bring the same to the Senate for the signature of its President.

ENROLLED BILLS SIGNED.

Mr. Dubois reported from the committee that they had examined and found duly enrolled the following bills:
H. R. 1422. An act for the relief of George M. Henry;
H. R. 3253. An act to increase the pension of William G. Smith;
H. R. 3118. An act to pension John O. Dunham;
H. R. 5519. An act for the relief of Daniel Eldredge, Company D, Fifteenth Illinois Volunteers;
H. R. 6554. An act to remove the charge of desertion against Charles R. Behle;
H. R. 7100. An act to pension Jacob O'Neal;
H. R. 7306. An act to pension Maud Case, of Dodge County, Minnesota;
H. R. 7729. An act granting a pension to Mrs. Phœbe Sigler;
H. R. 8017. An act granting a pension to Elizabeth Voss;
H. R. 8230. An act for the relief of Louis G. Sanderson, of Craighead County, Arkansas;
H. R. 8409. An act granting a pension to Mary Danahay, mother of Daniel Danahay, late a private Company H, Eighteenth New York Cavalry;
H. R. 8498. An act to pension Sophia Kagwaich;
H. R. 9233. An act to grant a pension to Harriet Cota;
H. R. 10331. An act making appropriations for the legislative, executive, and judicial expenses of the Government for the fiscal year ending June 30, 1894, and for other purposes;
H. R. 10421. An act making appropriations for the Department of Agriculture for the fiscal year ending June 30, 1894; and
S. 2171. An act to amend section 766 of the Revised Statutes of the United States;
Whereupon,
The Vice-President signed the same, and they were delivered to the committee to be presented to the President of the United States.

CONFERENCE REPORTS.

Mr. Pasco, from committee of conference on the disagreeing votes of the two Houses on the amendment of the Senate to the bill H. R. 2122, submitted the following report:
The committee of conference on the disagreeing votes of the two Houses on the amendment of the Senate to the bill (H. R. 2122) for the relief of Cumberland Female College, of McMinnville, Tenn., having met, after full and free conference have agreed to recommend and do recommend to their respective Houses as follows:
That the Senate recede from its amendment, and agree to an amendment as follows: Strike out all after the word "appropriated," in line 6, and insert in lieu thereof the following: *the sum of five thousand dollars for use and occupation of the college buildings and premises as a hospital during the years eighteen hundred and sixty-two, eighteen hundred and sixty three, eighteen hundred and sixty-four, and eighteen hundred and sixty-five, by the military authorities of the United States, the same to be accepted and receipted for in full of all claims of the said Cumberland Female College against the United States;* and the House agree to the same.

JOHN W. DANIEL,
S. PASCO,
W. A. PEFFER.
Managers on the part of the Senate.

B. A. ENLOE,
W. J. STONE,
JOHN C. HOUK,
Managers on the part of the House.

The Senate proceeded to consider the said report; and
On motion by Mr. Pasco,
Resolved, That the Senate agree thereto.
Ordered, That the Secretary notify the House of Representatives thereof.

SUNDRY CIVIL APPROPRIATION BILL.

Mr. Allison, from the second committee of conference on the disagreeing votes of the two Houses on certain amendments of the Senate to the bill H. R. 10238, submitted the following report:
The committee of conference on the disagreeing votes of the two Houses on certain amendments of the Senate to the bill (H. R. 10238) "making appropriations for sundry civil expenses of the Government for the fiscal year ending June 30, 1894, and for other purposes," having met, after full and free conference have agreed to recommend and do recommend to their respective Houses as follows:
That the Senate recede from its amendments numbered 86, 87, 193, and 194.
That the House recede from its disagreement to the amendment of the Senate numbered 189, and agree to the same.
On amendments numbered 67, 68, 69, 70, 71, and 104, the committee of conference have been unable to agree.

W. B. ALLISON,
EUGENE HALE,
A. P. GORMAN,
Managers on the part of the Senate.

W. S. HOLMAN,
JOSEPH D. SAYERS,
WILLIAM COGSWELL,
Managers on the part of the House.

The Senate proceeded to consider the report; and
On motion by Mr. Allison,
Resolved, That the Senate agree thereto.
On motion by Mr. Allison, that the Senate further insist upon its amendments to the said bill numbered 67, 68, 69, 70, and 71,
After debate,
It was determined in the affirmative, { Yeas.................... 54 / Nays.................... 11
On motion by Mr. Allison,
The yeas and nays being desired by one-fifth of the Senators present,
Those who voted in the affirmative are,
Messrs. Aldrich, Allison, Blackburn, Blodgett, Brice, Butler, Camden, Cameron, Carey, Casey, Chandler, Cullom, Davis, Dawes. Dubois, Faulkner, Felton, Frye, Gallinger, Gibson, Gorman, Gray, Hale, Hansbrough, Hawley. Hill, Hiscock, Hoar, Jones of Nevada, Kyle, Lindsay, McMillan, Manderson, Mitchell, Morrill, Paddock, Palmer, Peffer, Perkins, Pettigrew, Platt, Power, Proctor, Sawyer, Sherman, Shoup, Stewart, Stockbridge, Teller, Voorhees, Warren, Washburn, White, Wolcott.
Those who voted in the negative are,
Messrs. Bate, Berry, Cockrell, Coke, Harris, Hunton, Jones of Arkansas, Mills, Pugh, Turpie, Vest
So it was,
Resolved, That the Senate further insist upon the said amendments; and
On motion by Mr. Allison,
Resolved, That the Senate also further insist upon its amendment to the said bill numbered 104, and agree to the further conference asked by the House of Representatives on the disagreeing votes of the two Houses on the several amendments.

Ordered, That the conferees on the part of the Senate be appointed by the Vice President; and

The Vice President appointed Mr. Allison, Mr. Hale, and Mr. Gorman,

Ordered, That the Secretary notify the House of Representatives thereof.

MESSAGE FROM THE HOUSE.

A message from the House of Representatives, by Mr. Towles, its chief clerk:

Mr. President: The House of Representatives has passed, without amendment, the bill of the Senate (S. 3881) relating to copyrights.

The Speaker of the House of Representatives having signed four enrolled bills, H. R. 4496, H. R. 8550, H. R. 9741, and H. R. 10351, I am directed to bring the same to the Senate for the signature of its President.

ENROLLED BILLS SIGNED.

Mr. Dubois reported from the committee that they had examined and found duly enrolled the following bills:

H. R. 4496. An act to place upon the pension rolls of the United States the name of Thomas F. Sheldon, late captain Company A, One hundred and twenty-fifth New York Infantry;

H. R. 8550. An act to increase the pension of W. H. Philpot, a pensioner of the Mexican war;

H. R. 9741. An act to increase the pension of Capt. E. R. Chase from $20 to $72 a month; and

H. R. 10351. An act to continue the duties on certain manufactures of flax at the rate now provided by law;

Whereupon,

The Vice-President signed the same, and they were delivered to the committee to be presented to the President of the United States.

INDIAN APPROPRIATION BILL.

Mr. Dawes, from the committee of conference on the disagreeing votes of the two Houses on the amendments of the Senate to the bill H. R. 10415, submitted the following report:

The committee of conference on the disagreeing votes of the two Houses on the amendments of the Senate to the bill (H. R. 10415) making appropriation for the current and contingent expenses and fulfilling treaty stipulations with Indian tribes for the fiscal year ending June 30, 1894, and for other purposes, having met, after full and free conference have agreed to recommend and do recommend to their respective Houses as follows:

That the Senate recede from its amendments numbered 5, 12, 15, 25, 37, 38, 45, 47, 52, 58, 67, and 69.

That the House recede from its disagreement to the amendments of the Senate numbered 2, 3, 4, 6, 7, 8, 9, 10, 11, 13, 14, 16, 17, 18, 19, 20, 21, 22, 23, 24, 26, 27, 28, 29, 31, 32, 33, 35, 36, 39, 40, 41, 42, 43, 46, 48, 50, 51, 53, 54, 55, 56, 57, 59, 60, 61, 62, 64, 70, 71, 72, 73, 76, 77, 78, 79, 80, 81, 82, 85, 87, 88, 89, 90, 91, and 93, and agree to the same.

That the House recede from its disagreement to the amendment of the Senate numbered 1, and agree to the same with an amendment as follows: After the word "agents," in line 7, page 1 of the bill, insert the following: *where civilians are employed;* and the Senate agree to the same.

That the House recede from its disagreement to the amendment of the Senate numbered 30, and agree to the same with an amendment as follows: In line 3 of said amendment strike out "sixty-four," and insert in lieu thereof *forty,* and in line 5 of said amendment strike out "seventy-one," and insert in lieu thereof *forty-seven;* and the Senate agree to the same.

That the House recede from its disagreement to the amendment of the Senate numbered 34, and agree to the same with an amendment as follows: After the word "purchase," in line 1 of said amendment, insert the words *land and;* and the Senate agree to the same.

That the House recede from its disagreement to the amendment of the Senate numbered 44, and agree to the same with an amendment as follows: In lieu of the matter inserted by said amendment insert the following: *Provided, That of this sum a sufficient amount may be used to sink one artesian well at each of the three following places, namely: Rosebud Reservation, Standing Rock Reservation, and Pine Ridge Reservation, in South Dakota, neither of said wells to cost more than five thousand dollars;* and the Senate agree to the same.

That the House recede from its disagreement to the amendment of the Senate numbered 49, and agree to the same with an amendment as follows: In lieu of the sum named in said amendment insert *one thousand dollars;* and the Senate agree to the same.

That the House recede from its disagreement to the amendment of the Senate numbered 63, and agree to the same with an amendment as follows: In lieu of the sum proposed insert *twenty thousand dollars;* and the Senate agree to the same.

That the House recede from its disagreement to the amendment of the Senate numbered 65, and agree to the same with an amendment as follows: In lieu of the sum proposed insert *twenty thousand dollars;* and the Senate agree to the same.

That the House recede from its disagreement to the amendment of the Senate numbered 66, and agree to the same with an amendment as follows: Strike out, in lines 18 and 19, page 50 of the bill, the following "for the establishment of an industrial boarding school on the Navajo Reservation;" and the Senate agree to the same.

That the House recede from its disagreement to the amendment of the Senate numbered 68, and agree to the same with an amendment as follows: Strike out after the word "used," in line 20, page 50 of the bill, all down to and including the word "service" in line 27, same page of the bill; and the Senate agree to the same.

That the House recede from its disagreement to the amendment of the Senate numbered 74, and agree to the same with an amendment as follows: In lieu of the sum proposed insert *twenty-five thousand dollars;* and the Senate agree to the same.

That the House recede from its disagreement to the amendment of the Senate numbered 75, and agree to the same with an amendment as follows: In lieu of the sum named in said amendment insert the following: *one million one hundred and eighty-one thousand dollars;* and the Senate agree to the same.

That the House recede from its disagreement to the amendment of the Senate numbered 83, and agree to the same with an amendment as follows: In lieu of the matter inserted by said amendment insert the following: *For improvement of buildings, two thousand dollars; for purchase, in the discretion of the Secretary of the Interior, of one hundred and twenty acres of land adjoining said Indian farm school, ten thousand dollars;* and the Senate agree to the same.

That the House recede from its disagreement to the amendment of the Senate numbered 84, and agree to the same with an amendment as follows: In lieu of the sum proposed insert *thirty-seven thousand three hundred and seventy-five dollars;* and the Senate agree to the same.

That the House recede from its disagreement to the amendment of the Senate numbered 86, and agree to the same with an amendment as follows: Add at the end of said amendment the following: *Provided, That any amount that may be found due by the Secretary shall be credited to the Choctaw fund and charged to the Cherokee fund;* and the Senate agree to the same.

That the House recede from its disagreement to the amendment of the Senate numbered 92, and agree to the same with an amendment as follows: Insert after the word "lands," in line 13 of page 4 of said amendment, the following: *Provided, Said railroad shall be relieved from any further payments of compensation to said Cherokee Nation as required by law for running said railroad across the Cherokee Outlet;* and strike out, after the word "paid," in line 16, down to and including the word "same" in line 18, same page of said amendment; at the end of line 25, same page, insert the following: *Provided, That if the legislative council of the Cherokee Nation shall deem it more advantageous to their people they may issue a loan for the principal and interest of the deferred payment, pledging said amounts of interest and principal to secure payment of such debt;* strike out, in line 17, page 5 of said amendment, the words "one year after the approval of this act," and insert in lieu thereof the following: *six months after the approval of this act, and the acceptance of the same by the Cherokee Nation as herein provided;* and after the word "delay," in line 22, page 7 of said amendment, strike out the word "to" and insert in lieu thereof the word *by;* and the Senate agree to the same.

That the House recede from its disagreement to the amendment of the Senate numbered 94, and agree to the same with an amendment as follows: Strike out, in lines 19, 20, and 21, on page 4 of said amendment, the words "and all other Indian tribes and bands now owning lands or residing upon lands within the Indian Territory;" strike out, in the last line of page 5 of said amendment, the words "tribes and bands," and insert after the word "Indians," in line 1, page 6, of said amendment, the words *as aforesaid;* and the Senate agree to the same.

H. L. DAWES,
S. M. CULLOM,
WILKINSON CALL,
Managers on the part of the Senate.
S. W. PEEL,
JOHN L. WILSON,
Managers on the part of the House.

The Senate proceeded to consider the report; and

On motion by Mr. Dawes,

Resolved, That the Senate agree thereto.

Ordered, That the Secretary notify the House of Representatives thereof.

RECONSIDERATION OF BILL VETOED.

The Senate proceeded to reconsider the bill (H. R. 9612) entitled "An act to prescribe the number of district attorneys and marshals in the judicial districts of the State of Alabama," returned by the President of the United States to the House of Representatives in which it originated with his objections thereto, and passed by the House of Representatives on a reconsideration of the same.

The message of the President of the United States returning the bill to the House of Representatives having been read, as follows:

To the House of Representatives:

I return herewith, without my approval, an act (H. R. 9612) entitled "An act to prescribe the number of district attorneys and marshals in the judicial districts of the State of Alabama."

Under the present law there is a district attorney for the southern district of Alabama, a district attorney for the northern and middle districts, a marshal for the northern district, and a marshal for the southern and middle districts.

An examination of the records of the Attorney-General's office as to the amount of business in these courts in these districts leads me to believe that two districts would provide amply for the disposition of all public and private cases. The law creates two new officers whose aggregate compensation may be $12,000 per annum, without, it seems to me, a justifying necessity. But the most serious objection to the legislation is that it creates at once, upon the taking effect of the law, the offices of district attorney and marshal for each of the three districts; and the effect, it seems to me, must be to abolish the offices as they now exist.

No provision is made for a continued discharge of the duties of marshal and district attorney by the present incumbents. A serious question would be raised as to whether these officers were not at once legislated out of office and vacancies created. As these vacancies could not be filled immediately, the business of the courts would seriously suffer. The law should at least have contained a provision for the continued discharge of their duties by the incumbents until the new officers were appointed and qualified.

BENJ. HARRISON.

EXECUTIVE MANSION, *February 27, 1893.*

The Vice President stated the question to be, Shall the bill pass, the objections of the President of the United States notwithstanding? and

It was determined in the affirmative, $\begin{cases} \text{Yeas} \dots\dots\dots\dots\dots 58 \\ \text{Nays} \dots\dots\dots\dots\dots 1 \end{cases}$

Those who voted in the affirmative are,

Messrs. Aldrich, Bate, Berry, Blackburn, Blodgett, Brice, Butler, Call, Cameron, Carey, Chandler, Cockrell, Coke, Cullom, Daniel, Davis, Dawes, Dubois, Faulkner, Felton, Gallinger, Gray, Hansbrough, Harris, Hawley, Hill, Hiscock, Hoar, Hunton, Jones of Arkansas, Jones of Nevada, Lindsay, McMillan, McPherson, Manderson, Mills, Mitchell, Morrill, Paddock, Palmer, Peffer, Perkins, Pettigrew, Platt, Power, Pugh, Sherman, Shoup, Squire, Stewart, Stockbridge, Teller, Turpie, Vest, Voorhees, Washburn, White, Wolcott.

Mr. Frye voted in the negative.

So it was

Resolved, That the bill do pass, two-thirds of the Senators present voting in the affirmative.

Ordered, That the Secretary notify the House of Representatives thereof.

MESSAGE FROM THE HOUSE.

A message from the House of Representatives, by Mr. Towles, its chief clerk :

Mr. President, The House of Representatives has agreed to the report of the committee of conference on the disagreeing votes of the two Houses on the amendments of the Senate to the bill (H. R. 10258) making appropriations to supply deficiencies in the appropriations for the fiscal year ending June 30, 1893, and for prior years, and for other purposes. It further insists on its disagreement to the amendments numbered 30, 63, 64, 66, 67, 68, 69, 70, 71, 72, 73, 74, 75, 76, 77, 78, 79, 94, 95, 96, 97, 98, 99, 108, 150, 160, 161, 165, 166, 167, 168, 169, 170, 171, 173, 174, 176, and 177, agrees to the further conference asked by the Senate on the disagreeing votes of the two Houses thereon, and has appointed Mr. Sayers, Mr. Holman, and Mr. Dingley managers at the same on its part.

The Speaker of the House of Representatives having signed an enrolled bill, S. 3881, I am directed to bring the same to the Senate for the signature of its President.

ENROLLED BILL SIGNED.

Mr. Dubois reported from the committee that they had examined and found duly enrolled a bill (S. 3881) relating to copyrights;

Whereupon,

The Vice-President signed the same, and it was delivered to the committee to be presented to the President of the United States.

PRESENTATION OF BILLS.

Mr. Dubois reported from the committee that they this day presented to the President of the United States the following enrolled bills:

S. 3240. An act to facilitate the enforcement of the immigration and contract-labor laws of the United States; and

S. 3890. An act authorizing the Lake Shore and Michigan Southern Railroad Company to renew its railroad bridge across the Calumet River upon or near the site of its present bridge and upon a location and plans to be approved by the Secretary of War, and to operate the same.

CLAIM OF WILLIAM M'GARRAHAN.

On motion by Mr. Teller, that the Senate proceed to the consideration of the bill (S. 3741) to submit to the Court of Private Land Claims, established by an act of Congress approved March 3, 1891, the title of William McGarrahan to the Rancho Panoche Grande, in the State of California, and for other purposes,

It was determined in the affirmative, $\begin{cases} \text{Yeas} \dots\dots\dots\dots\dots 46 \\ \text{Nays} \dots\dots\dots\dots\dots 8 \end{cases}$

On motion by Mr. Morrill,

21 s

The yeas and nays being desired by one-fifth of the Senators present, Those who voted in the affirmative are,

Messrs. Bate, Berry, Blackburn, Blodgett, Brice, Butler, Call, Cameron, Casey, Chandler, Coke, Cullom, Dubois, Felton, Frye, Gallinger, Gorman, Gray, Hansbrough, Harris, Hawley, Higgins, Hiscock, Hoar, Jones of Nevada, Kyle, Lindsay, McMillan, McPherson, Manderson, Mitchell, Peffer, Pettigrew, Platt, Power, Pugh, Shoup, Squire, Stockbridge, Teller, Turpie, Vance, Voorhees, Warren, Washburn, Wolcott.

Those who voted in the negative are,

Messrs. Mills, Morrill, Palmer, Pasco, Perkins, Proctor, Sherman, Vest.

So the motion was agreed to; and

The Senate proceeded to consider the said bill as in Committee of the Whole; and the reported amendments having been agreed to in part, and in part amended, and as amended agreed to,

On motion by Mr. Morrill to amend the bill by striking out after the words "to the" in line 8, page 1, the words "Court of Private Land Claims, established by an act of Congress approved March 3, 1891," and in lieu thereof inserting *United States district court for the southern district of California,*

After debate,

It was determined in the negative, $\begin{cases} \text{Yeas} \dots\dots\dots\dots\dots 10 \\ \text{Nays} \dots\dots\dots\dots\dots 39 \end{cases}$

On motion by Mr. Morrill,

The yeas and nays being desired by one-fifth of the Senators present, Those who voted in the affirmative are,

Messrs. Aldrich, Frye, Hiscock, McPherson, Mills, Morrill, Proctor, Sherman, Stewart, White.

Those who voted in the negative are,

Messrs. Allison, Bate, Brice, Call, Camden, Cameron, Chandler, Coke, Daniel, Davis, Dubois, Felton, Gallinger, Gorman, Gray, Hansbrough, Hawley, Hill, Hoar, Hunton, Jones of Arkansas, Jones of Nevada, Lindsay, McMillan, Manderson, Mitchell, Paddock, Peffer, Pettigrew, Platt, Power, Pugh, Shoup, Squire, Stockbridge, Teller, Warren, Washburn, Wolcott.

So the amendment was not agreed to.

The bill having been further amended on the motion of Mr. Morrill, On motion by Mr. Morrill to further amend the bill by inserting after line 47, page 3, the following:

SEC. —. *That to enable the United States to be represented by competent legal counsel, and to procure the attendance of necessary witnesses, the sum of twenty thousand dollars, or so much thereof as may be necessary, is hereby appropriated out of any money in the Treasury not otherwise appropriated,*

It was determined in the negative, $\begin{cases} \text{Yeas} \dots\dots\dots\dots\dots 10 \\ \text{Nays} \dots\dots\dots\dots\dots 39 \end{cases}$

On motion by Mr. Mills,

The yeas and nays being desired by one-fifth of the Senators present, Those who voted in the affirmative are,

Messrs. Chandler, Cockrell, Faulkner, Hiscock, McPherson, Mills, Morrill, Palmer, Proctor, Stewart.

Those who voted in the negative are,

Messrs. Allison, Berry, Blodgett, Brice, Camden, Cameron, Carey, Coke, Daniel, Davis, Dawes, Dubois, Felton, Frye, Gallinger, Gorman, Hansbrough, Harris, Hawley, Hill, Hoar, Hunton, Jones of Nevada, McMillan, Manderson, Mitchell, Paddock, Peffer, Perkins, Pettigrew, Platt, Power, Shoup, Squire, Stockbridge, Teller, Warren, Washburn, Wolcott.

So the amendment was not agreed to.

On motion by Mr. Palmor to amend the bill by inserting after the word "evidence," in line 3, section 2, the words *so far as the same are competent legal evidence.*

The yeas were 10 and the nays were 31.

On motion by Mr. Mills,

The yeas and nays being desired by one-fifth of the Senators present, Those who voted in the affirmative are,

Messrs. Bate, Berry, Cockrell, Hiscock, McPherson, Mills, Morrill, Palmer, Perkins, Stewart.

Those who voted in the negative are,

Messrs. Blodgett, Butler, Cameron, Carey, Chandler, Daniel, Davis, Dubois, Felton, Frye, Gallinger, Hansbrough, Harris, Hawley, Hill, Hunton, Kyle, Manderson, Mitchell, Paddock, Peffer, Pettigrew, Platt, Pugh, Shoup, Stockbridge, Teller, Voorhees, Warren, Washburn, Wolcott.

The number of Senators voting not constituting a quorum, The Vice-President directed the roll to be called;

When,

Forty-eight Senators answered to their names.

A quorum being present, and

The question being again taken on the amendment,

It was determined in the negative, $\begin{cases} \text{Yeas} \dots\dots\dots\dots\dots 14 \\ \text{Nays} \dots\dots\dots\dots\dots 38 \end{cases}$

Those who voted in the affirmative are,

Messrs. Aldrich, Bate, Berry, Blackburn, Cockrell, Cullom, Faulkner, Hiscock, Lindsay, McPherson, Mills, Palmer, Proctor, Sawyer.

Those who voted in the negative are,

Messrs. Allison, Blodgett, Butler, Call, Cameron, Carey, Chandler, Coke, Daniel, Davis, Dawes, Dubois, Felton, Frye, Gallinger, Gor-

tered, That the conferees on the part of the Senate be appointed he Vice President; and

e Vice President appointed Mr. Allison, Mr. Hale, and Mr. Gor-

rdered, That the Secretary notify the House of Representatives reof.

MESSAGE FROM THE HOUSE.

A message from the House of Representatives, by Mr. Towles, its tief clerk:

Mr. President: The House of Representatives has passed, without amendment, the bill of the Senate (S. 3881) relating to copyrights.

The Speaker of the House of Representatives having signed four anrolled bills, H. R. 4496, H. R. 8550, H. R. 9741, and H. R. 10351, I am directed to bring the same to the Senate for the signature of its President.

ENROLLED BILLS SIGNED.

Mr. Dubois reported from the committee that they had examined and found duly enrolled the following bills:

H. R. 4496. An act to place upon the pension rolls of the United States the name of Thomas F. Sheldon, late captain Company A, One hundred and twenty-fifth New York Infantry;

H. R. 8550. An act to increase the pension of W. H. Philpot, a pensioner of the Mexican war;

H. R. 9741. An act to increase the pension of Capt. E. R. Chase from $20 to $72 a month; and

H. R. 10351. An act to continue the duties on certain manufactures of flax at the rate now provided by law;

Whereupon,

The Vice-President signed the same, and they were delivered to the committee to be presented to the President of the United States.

INDIAN APPROPRIATION BILL.

Mr. Dawes, from the committee of conference on the disagreeing votes of the two Houses on the amendments of the Senate to the bill H. R. 10415, submitted the following report:

The committee of conference on the disagreeing votes of the two Houses on the amendments of the Senate to the bill (H. R. 10415) making appropriation for the current and contingent expenses and fulfilling treaty stipulations with Indian tribes for the fiscal year ending June 30, 1894, and for other purposes, having met, after full and free conference have agreed to recommend and do recommend to their respective Houses as follows:

That the Senate recede from its amendments numbered 5, 12, 15, 25, 37, 38, 45, 47, 52, 58, 67, and 69.

That the House recede from its disagreement to the amendments of the Senate numbered 2, 3, 4, 6, 7, 8, 9, 10, 11, 13, 14, 16, 17, 18, 19, 20, 21, 22, 23, 24, 26, 27, 28, 29, 31, 32, 33, 35, 36, 39, 40, 41, 42, 43, 46, 48, 50, 51, 53, 54, 55, 56, 57, 59, 60, 61, 62, 64, 70, 71, 72, 73, 76, 77, 78, 79, 80, 81, 82, 85, 87, 88, 89, 90, 91, and 93, and agree to the same.

That the House recede from its disagreement to the amendment of the Senate numbered 1, and agree to the same with an amendment as follows: After the word "agents," in line 7, page 1 of the bill, insert the following: *where civilians are employed;* and the Senate agree to the same.

That the House recede from its disagreement to the amendment of the Senate numbered 30, and agree to the same with an amendment as follows: In line 3 of said amendment strike out "sixty-four," and insert in lieu thereof *forty,* and in line 5 of said amendment strike out "seventy-one," and insert in lieu thereof *forty-seven;* and the Senate agree to the same.

That the House recede from its disagreement to the amendment of the Senate numbered 34, and agree to the same with an amendment as follows: After the word "purchase," in line 1 of said amendment, insert the words *land and;* and the Senate agree to the same.

That the House recede from its disagreement to the amendment of the Senate numbered 44, and agree to the same with an amendment as follows: In lieu of the matter inserted by said amendment insert the following: *Provided, That of this sum a sufficient amount may be used to sink one artesian well at each of the three following places, namely: Rosebud Reservation, Standing Rock Reservation, and Pine Ridge Reservation, in South Dakota, neither of said wells to cost more than five thousand dollars;* and the Senate agree to the same.

That the House recede from its disagreement to the amendment of the Senate numbered 49, and agree to the same with an amendment as follows: In lieu of the sum named in said amendment insert *one thousand dollars;* and the Senate agree to the same.

That the House recede from its disagreement to the amendment of the Senate numbered 63, and agree to the same with an amendment as follows: In lieu of the sum proposed insert *twenty thousand dollars;* and the Senate agree to the same.

That the House recede from its disagreement to the amendment of the Senate numbered 65, and agree to the same with an amendment as follows: In lieu of the sum proposed insert *twenty thousand dollars;* and the Senate agree to the same.

That the House recede from its disagreement to the amendment of the Senate numbered 66, and agree to the same with an amendment as follows: Strike out, in lines 18 and 19, page 50 of the bill, the following "for the establishment of an industrial boarding school ... Reservation;" and the Senate agree to the same.

That the House recede from its disagreement to the amendment of the Senate numbered 68, and agree to the same with an amendment as follows: Strike out after the word "used," in line 20, page 50 of the bill, all down to and including the word "service" in line 27, same page of the bill; and the Senate agree to the same.

That the House recede from its disagreement to the amendment of the Senate numbered 74, and agree to the same with an amendment as follows: In lieu of the sum proposed insert *twenty-five thousand dollars;* and the Senate agree to the same.

That the House recede from its disagreement to the amendment of the Senate numbered 75, and agree to the same with an amendment as follows: In lieu of the sum named in said amendment insert the following: *one million one hundred and eighty-one thousand dollars;* and the Senate agree to the same.

That the House recede from its disagreement to the amendment of the Senate numbered 83, and agree to the same with an amendment as follows: In lieu of the matter inserted by said amendment insert the following: *For improvement of buildings, two thousand dollars; for purchase, in the discretion of the Secretary of the Interior, of one hundred and twenty acres of land adjoining said Indian farm school, ten thousand dollars;* and the Senate agree to the same.

That the House recede from its disagreement to the amendment of the Senate numbered 84, and agree to the same with an amendment as follows: In lieu of the sum proposed insert *thirty-seven thousand three hundred and seventy-five dollars;* and the Senate agree to the same.

That the House recede from its disagreement to the amendment of the Senate numbered 86, and agree to the same with an amendment as follows: Add at the end of said amendment the following: *Provided, That any amount that may be found due by the Secretary shall be credited to the Choctaw fund and charged to the Cherokee fund;* and the Senate agree to the same.

That the House recede from its disagreement to the amendment of the Senate numbered 92, and agree to the same with an amendment as follows: Insert after the word "lands," in line 13 of page 4 of said amendment, the following: *Said railroad shall be relieved from any further payments of compensation to said Cherokee Nation as required by law for running said railroad across the Cherokee Outlet;* and strike out, after the word "paid," in line 16, down to and including the word "same" in line 18, same page of said amendment; as the end of line 25, same page, insert the following: *Provided, That if the legislative council of the Cherokee Nation shall deem it more advantageous to their people they may issue a loan for the principal and interest of the deferred payment, pledging said amounts of interest and principal to secure payment of such debt;* strike out, in line 17, page 5 of said amendment, the words "one year after the approval of this act," and insert in lieu thereof the following: *six months after the approval of this act, and the acceptance of the same by the Cherokee Nation as herein provided;* and after the word "delay," in line 22, page 7 of said amendment, strike out the word "to" and insert in lieu thereof the word *by;* and the Senate agree to the same.

That the House recede from its disagreement to the amendment of the Senate numbered 94, and agree to the same with an amendment as follows: Strike out, in lines 19, 20, and 21, on page 4 of said amendment, the words "and all other Indian tribes and bands now owning lands or residing upon lands within the Indian Territory;" strike out, in the last line of page 5 of said amendment, the words "tribes and bands," and insert after the word "Indians," in line 1, page 6, of said amendment, the words *as aforesaid;* and the Senate agree to the same.

H. L. DAWES,
S. M. CULLOM,
WILKINSON CALL,
Managers on the part of the Senate.

S. W. PEEL,
JOHN L. WILSON,
Managers on the part of the House.

The Senate proceeded to consider the report; and

On motion by Mr. Dawes,

Resolved, That the Senate agree thereto.

Ordered, That the Secretary notify the House of Representative thereof.

RECONSIDERATION OF BILL VETOED.

The Senate proceeded to reconsider the bill (H. R. 9612) entit "An act to prescribe the number of district attorneys and mars in the judicial districts of the State of Alabama," returned by President of the United States to the House of Representative which it originated with his objections thereto, and passed by House of Representatives on a reconsideration of the same.

The message of the President of the United States returning bill to the House of Representatives having been read, as follow

To the House of Representatives:

I return herewith, without my approval, an act (H. R. 961 titled "An act to prescribe the number of district attorney marshals in the judicial districts of the State of Alabama."

Under the present law there is a district attorney for the so district of Alabama, a district attorney for the northern and districts, a marshal for the northern district, and a marshal for the southern and middle districts.

An examination of the records of the Attorney-General's office as to the amount of business in these courts in these districts leads me to believe that two districts would provide amply for the disposition of all public and private cases. The law creates two new officers whose aggregate compensation may be $12,000 per annum, without, it seems to me, a justifying necessity. But the most serious objection to the legislation is that it creates at once, upon the taking effect of the law, the offices of district attorney and marshal for each of the three districts; and the effect, it seems to me, must be to abolish the offices as they now exist.

No provision is made for a continued discharge of the duties of marshal and district attorney by the present incumbents. A serious question would be raised as to whether these officers were not at once legislated out of office and vacancies created. As these vacancies could not be filled immediately, the business of the courts would seriously suffer. The law should at least have contained a provision for the continued discharge of their duties by the incumbents until the new officers were appointed and qualified.

BENJ. HARRISON.

EXECUTIVE MANSION, *February 27, 1893.*

The Vice President stated the question to be, Shall the bill pass, the objections of the President of the United States notwithstanding? and

It was determined in the affirmative, { Yeas .... 58 { Nays 1

Those who voted in the affirmative are,

Messrs. Aldrich, Bate, Berry, Blackburn, Blodgett, Brice, Butler, Call, Cameron, Carey, Chandler, Cockrell, Coke, Cullom, Daniel, Davis, Dawes, Dubois, Faulkner, Felton, Gallinger, Gray, Hansbrough, Harris, Hawley, Hill, Hiscock, Hoar, Hunton, Jones of Arkansas, Jones of Nevada, Lindsay, McMillan, McPherson, Manderson, Mills, Mitchell, Morrill, Paddock, Palmer, Peffer, Perkins, Pettigrew, Platt, Power, Pugh, Sherman, Shoup, Squire, Stewart, Stockbridge, Teller, Turpie, Vest, Voorhees, Washburn, White, Wolcott.

Mr. Frye voted in the negative.

So it was

Resolved, That the bill do pass, two-thirds of the Senators present voting in the affirmative.

Ordered, That the Secretary notify the House of Representatives thereof.

MESSAGE FROM THE HOUSE.

A message from the House of Representatives, by Mr. Towles, its chief clerk:

Mr. President, The House of Representatives has agreed to the report of the committee of conference on the disagreeing votes of the two Houses on the amendments of the Senate to the bill (H. R. 10258) making appropriations to supply deficiencies in the appropriations for the fiscal year ending June 30, 1893, and for prior years, and for other purposes. It further insists on its disagreement to the amendments numbered 30, 63, 64, 66, 67, 68, 69, 70, 71, 72, 73, 74, 75, 76, 77, 78, 79, 94, 95, 96, 97, 98, 99, 108, 150, 160, 161, 165, 166, 167, 168, 169, 170, 171, 173, 174, 176, and 177, agrees to the further conference asked by the Senate on the disagreeing votes of the two Houses thereon, and has appointed Mr. Sayers, Mr. Holman, and Mr. Dingley managers on its part.

The Speaker of the House of Representatives having signed an enrolled bill, S. 3881, I am directed to bring the same to the Senate for the signature of its President.

ENROLLED BILL SIGNED.

Mr. Dubois reported from the committee that they had examined and found duly enrolled a bill (S. 3881) relating to copyrights;

Whereupon,

The Vice-President signed the same, and it was delivered to the committee to be presented to the President of the United States.

PRESENTATION OF BILLS.

Mr. Dubois reported from the committee that they this day presented to the President of the United States the following enrolled bills:

S. 3240. An act to facilitate the enforcement of the immigration and contract-labor laws of the United States; and

S. 3890. An act authorizing the Lake Shore and Michigan Southern Railroad Company to renew its railroad bridge across the Calumet River upon or near the site of its present bridge and upon a location and plans to be approved by the Secretary of War, and to operate the same.

CLAIM OF WILLIAM M'GARRAHAN.

On motion by Mr. Teller, that the Senate proceed to the consideration of the bill (S. 3741) to submit to the Court of Private Land Claims, established by an act of Congress approved March 3, 1891, the title of William McGarrahan to the Rancho Panoche Grande, in the State of California, and for other purposes,

It was determined in the affirmative, { Yeas .... 46 { Nays 8

On motion by Mr. Morrill,

21 s

The yeas and nays being desired by one-fifth of the Senators present, Those who voted in the affirmative are,

Messrs. Bate, Berry, Blackburn, Blodgett, Brice, Butler, Call, Cameron, Casey, Chandler, Coke, Cullom, Dubois, Felton, Frye, Gallinger, Gorman, Gray, Hansbrough, Harris, Hawley, Higgins, Hiscock, Hoar, Jones of Nevada, Kyle, Lindsay, McMillan, McPherson, Manderson, Mitchell, Peffer, Pettigrew, Platt, Power, Pugh, Shoup, Squire, Stockbridge, Teller, Turpie, Vance, Voorhees, Warren, Washburn, Wolcott.

Those who voted in the negative are,

Messrs. Mills, Morrill, Palmer, Pasco, Perkins, Proctor, Sherman, Vest.

So the motion was agreed to; and

The Senate proceeded to consider the said bill as in Committee of the Whole; and the reported amendments having been agreed to in part, and in part amended, and as amended agreed to,

On motion by Mr. Morrill to amend the bill by striking out after the words "to the" in line 8, page 1, the words "Court of Private Land Claims, established by an act of Congress approved March 3, 1891," and in lieu thereof inserting *United States district court for the southern district of California,*

After debate,

It was determined in the negative, { Yeas .... 10 { Nays 39

On motion by Mr. Morrill,

The yeas and nays being desired by one-fifth of the Senators present, Those who voted in the affirmative are,

Messrs. Aldrich, Frye, Hiscock, McPherson, Mills, Morrill, Proctor, Sherman, Stewart, White.

Those who voted in the negative are,

Messrs. Allison, Bate, Brice, Call, Camden, Cameron, Chandler, Coke, Daniel, Davis, Dubois, Felton, Gallinger, Gorman, Gray, Hansbrough, Hawley, Hill, Hoar, Hunton, Jones of Arkansas, Jones of Nevada, Lindsay, McMillan, Manderson, Mitchell, Paddock, Peffer, Pettigrew, Platt, Power, Pugh, Shoup, Squire, Stockbridge, Teller, Warren, Washburn, Wolcott.

So the amendment was not agreed to.

The bill having been further amended on the motion of Mr. Morrill,

On motion by Mr. Morrill to further amend the bill by inserting after line 47, page 3, the following:

SEC. —. *That to enable the United States to be represented by competent legal counsel, and to procure the attendance of necessary witnesses, the sum of twenty thousand dollars, or so much thereof as may be necessary, is hereby appropriated out of any money in the Treasury not otherwise appropriated,*

It was determined in the negative, { Yeas .... 10 { Nays 39

On motion by Mr. Mills,

The yeas and nays being desired by one-fifth of the Senators present, Those who voted in the affirmative are,

Messrs. Chandler, Cockrell, Faulkner, Hiscock, McPherson, Mills, Morrill, Palmer, Proctor, Stewart.

Those who voted in the negative are,

Messrs. Allison, Berry, Blodgett, Brice, Camden, Cameron, Carey, Coke, Daniel, Davis, Dawes, Dubois, Felton, Frye, Gallinger, Gorman, Hansbrough, Harris, Hawley, Hill, Hoar, Hunton, Jones of Nevada, McMillan, Manderson, Mitchell, Paddock, Peffer, Perkins, Pettigrew, Platt, Power, Shoup, Squire, Stockbridge, Teller, Warren, Washburn, Wolcott.

So the amendment was not agreed to.

On motion by Mr. Palmer to amend the bill by inserting after the word "evidence," in line 3, section 2, the words *so far as the same are competent legal evidence.*

The yeas were 10 and the nays were 31.

On motion by Mr. Mills,

The yeas and nays being desired by one-fifth of the Senators present, Those who voted in the affirmative are,

Messrs. Bate, Berry, Cockrell, Hiscock, McPherson, Mills, Morrill, Palmer, Perkins, Stewart.

Those who voted in the negative are,

Messrs. Blodgett, Butler, Cameron, Carey, Chandler, Daniel, Davis, Dubois, Felton, Frye, Gallinger, Hansbrough, Harris, Hawley, Hill, Hunton, Kyle, Manderson, Mitchell, Paddock, Peffer, Pettigrew, Platt, Pugh, Shoup, Stockbridge, Teller, Voorhees, Warren, Washburn, Wolcott.

The number of Senators voting not constituting a quorum,

The Vice-President directed the roll to be called;

When,

Forty-eight Senators answered to their names.

A quorum being present, and

The question being again taken on the amendment,

It was determined in the negative, { Yeas .... 14 { Nays 38

Those who voted in the affirmative are,

Messrs. Aldrich, Bate, Berry, Blackburn, Cockrell, Cullom, Faulkner, Hiscock, Lindsay, McPherson, Mills, Palmer, Proctor, Sawyer.

Those who voted in the negative are,

Messrs. Allison, Blodgett, Butler, Call, Cameron, Carey, Chandler, Coke, Daniel, Davis, Dawes, Dubois, Felton, Frye, Gallinger, Gorman, Hansbrough, Hawley, Higgins, Hunton, Kyle, McMillan, Manderson, Mitchell, Paddock, Peffer, Pettigrew, Platt, Power, Pugh, Shoup, Squire, Stockbridge, Teller, Voorhees, Warren, Washburn, Wolcott.

So the amendment was not agreed to.

The bill having been further amended on the motion of Mr. Palmer,

On motion by Mr. Faulkner to amend the bill by inserting after the word "case," in line 29, page 4, the following:

Provided, however, That the weight, value, legal effect, and relevancy of all such evidence shall be determined by the said court,

It was determined in the negative, { Yeas .... 11 / Nays .... 35 }

On motion by Mr. Faulkner,

The yeas and nays being desired by one-fifth of the Senators present,

Those who voted in the affirmative are,

Messrs. Bate, Cockrell, Faulkner, Gray, Hiscock, Lindsay, McPherson, Palmer, Perkins, Proctor, Stewart.

Those who voted in the negative are,

Messrs. Allison, Berry, Blodgett, Call, Cameron, Coke, Cullom, Daniel, Davis, Dawes, Felton, Frye, Gallinger, Gibson, Gorman, Hawley, Higgins, Hill, Hunton, Jones of Nevada, Kyle, McMillan, Manderson, Mitchell, Paddock, Peffer, Platt, Power, Pugh, Shoup, Squire, Stockbridge, Teller, Voorhees, Wolcott.

So the amendment was not agreed to.

The bill having been further amended on the motion of Mr. Teller, it was reported to the Senate, and the amendments made in Committee of the Whole were concurred in.

The bill having been further amended on the motion of Mr. Cockrell,

Ordered, That it be engrossed and read a third time.

The said bill was read the third time.

On the question, Shall the bill pass?

It was determined in the affirmative, { Yeas .... 37 / Nays .... 12 }

On motion by Mr. Palmer,

The yeas and nays being desired by one-fifth of the Senators present,

Those who voted in the affirmative are,

Messrs. Brice, Butler, Call, Cameron, Carey, Chandler, Coke, Daniel, Davis, Dubois, Felton, Frye, Gibson, Gorman, Hale, Hansbrough, Hawley, Higgins, Hill, Hunton, Jones of Nevada, Kyle, McMillan, Mitchell, Paddock, Peffer, Pettigrew, Power, Pugh, Shoup, Squire, Stockbridge, Teller, Voorhees, Warren, Washburn, Wolcott.

Those who voted in the negative are,

Messrs. Blackburn, Cockrell, Faulkner, Hiscock, Lindsay, McPherson, Palmer, Pasco, Proctor, Sawyer, Stewart, White.

So it was

Resolved, That the bill pass, and that the title thereof be as aforesaid,

Ordered, That the Secretary request the concurrence of the House of Representatives therein.

MESSAGE FROM THE HOUSE.

A message from the House of Representatives, by Mr. Towles, chief clerk:

Mr. President: The House of Representatives has agreed to the report of the second committee of conference on the disagreeing votes of the two Houses on the amendments of the Senate to the bill (H. R. 10258) making appropriations to supply deficiencies in the appropriations for the fiscal year ending June 30, 1893, and for prior years, and for other purposes, numbered 30, 63, 64, 66, 67, 68, 69, 70, 71, 72, 73, 74, 75, 76, 77, 78, 79, 94, 95, 96, 97, 98, 99, 108, 150, 160, 161, 165, 166, 167, 168, 169, 170, 171, 173, 174, and 176.

The Speaker of the House of Representatives having signed ten enrolled bills, H. R. 5022, H. R. 2077, H. R. 1100, H. R. 6212, H. R. 6233, H. R. 4955, H. R. 4804, H. R. 5508, H. R. 10349, and H. R. 10488, I am directed to bring them to the Senate for the signature of its President.

ENROLLED BILLS SIGNED.

Mr. Dubois reported from the committee that they had examined and found duly enrolled the following bills:

H. R. 5022. An act for the relief of Lucy Sprotberry;

H. R. 2077. An act for the relief of William B. Price;

H. R. 1100. An act granting a pension to Mary Catherine Reardon;

H. R. 6212. An act granting an increase of pension to Ellis P. Phipps, late lieutenant in Company A, Twelfth New Jersey Volunteer Infantry, invalid certificate No. 35619;

H. R. 6233. An act granting a pension to Thomas T. Prather;

H. R. 4955. An act granting a pension to Susannah Chadwick;

H. R. 4804. An act to place the name of Sarah L. Van Nest on the pension list;

H. R. 5508. An act to place the name of Sabra A. Wolcott upon the pension rolls;

H. R. 10349. An act making appropriations for the service of the Post-Office Department for the fiscal year ending June 30, 1894; and

H. R. 10488. An act making appropriations for the naval service for the fiscal year ending June 30, 1894, and for other purposes;

Whereupon,

The President *pro tempore* signed the same, and they were delivered to the committee to be presented to the President of the United States.

DEFICIENCY APPROPRIATION BILL.

Mr. Hale, from the second committee of conference on the disagreeing votes of the two Houses on certain amendments of the Senate to the bill H. R. 10258, submitted the following report:

The committee of conference on the disagreeing votes of the two Houses on certain amendments of the Senate to the bill (H. R. 10258) "making appropriations to supply deficiencies in the appropriations for the fiscal year ending June 30, 1893, and for prior years, and for other purposes," having met, after full and due conference have agreed to recommend and do recommend to their respective Houses as follows:

That the Senate recede from its amendments numbered 30, 63, 64, 66, 67, 68, 69, 70, 71, 72, 73, 74, 75, 76, 77, 78, 79, 94, 95, 96, 97, 98, 99, 108, 150, 165, 166, 167, 168, 169, 170, 171, 173, 174, and 176.

That the House recede from its disagreement to the amendment of the Senate numbered 177, and agree to the same.

That the House recede from its disagreement to the amendment of the Senate numbered 160, and agree to the same with an amendment as follows: Strike out all after the word "dollars" in line 24, page 1, of said amendment, down to and including line 30, and lines 1, 2, and 3, and the words "and thirty-two cents" in line 4, page 2, of said amendment; and the Senate agree to the same.

That the House recede from its disagreement to the amendment of the Senate numbered 161, and agree to the same with an amendment as follows: In lieu of the sum proposed insert *three hundred and thirty-four thousand one hundred and sixty-five dollars and ninety-six cents;* and the Senate agree to the same.

    EUGENE HALE,
    W. B. ALLISON,
    F. M. COCKRELL,
    Managers on the part of the Senate.
    JOSEPH D. SAYERS,
    W. S. HOLMAN,
    NELSON DINGLEY, JR.,
    Managers on the part of the House.

The Senate proceeded to consider the report; and

On motion by Mr. Hale

Resolved, That the Senate agree thereto.

Ordered, That the Secretary notify the House of Representatives thereof.

MESSAGE FROM THE HOUSE.

A message from the House of Representatives, by Mr. Towles, its chief clerk:

Mr. President: The House of Representatives has disagreed to the report of the committee of conference on the disagreeing votes of the two Houses on the amendments of the Senate to the bill (H. R. 10415) making appropriation for current and contingent expenses and fulfilling treaty stipulations with Indian tribes for the fiscal year ending June 30, 1894, and for other purposes. It asks a further conference with the Senate on the disagreeing votes of the two Houses thereon, and has appointed Mr. Peel, Mr. Allen, and Mr. Wilson, of Washington, managers at the same on its part.

INDIAN APPROPRIATION BILL.

The President *pro tempore* laid before the Senate the message of the House of Representatives announcing its disagreement to the report of the committee of conference on the disagreeing votes of the two Houses on the amendments of the Senate to the foregoing bill H. R. 10415, and asking a further conference thereon.

On motion by Mr. Cullom,

Resolved, That the Senate further insist upon its amendments to the said bill further disagreed to by the House of Representatives, and agree to the further conference asked by the House on the disagreeing votes of the two Houses thereon.

Ordered, That the conferees on the part of the Senate be appointed by the President *pro tempore;* and

The President *pro tempore* appointed Mr. Dawes, Mr. Cullom, and Mr. Call.

Ordered, That the Secretary notify the House of Representatives thereof.

CONSIDERATION OF BILLS ON CALENDAR.

On motion by Mr. Vest,

The Senate proceeded to consider, as in Committee of the Whole, the bill (S. 3882) granting a pension to Honora Shea; and no amendment being made, it was reported to the Senate.

Ordered, That it be engrossed and read a third time.

The said bill was read the third time.

Resolved, That it pass, and that the title thereof be as aforesaid.

Ordered, That the Secretary request the concurrence of the House of Representatives therein.

On motion by Mr. Teller,

The Senate resumed, as in the Committee of the Whole, the consideration of the bill (H. R. 5816) to regulate the manner in which property shall be sold under orders and decrees of any United States court; and

On motion by Mr. Teller,
The votes agreeing to the several amendments heretofore made in Committee of the Whole were reconsidered;
When,
The reported amendments having been agreed to in part, and in part amended, and as amended agreed to, the bill was reported to the Senate and the amendments were concurred in.

Ordered, That the amendments be engrossed and the bill read a third time.

The said bill as amended was read the third time.

Resolved, That it pass.

Ordered, That the Secretary request the concurrence of the House of Representatives in the amendments.

On motion by Mr. Perkins,
The Senate proceeded to consider, as in Committee of the Whole, the bill (H. R. 10146) to authorize the Oklahoma Midland Railway Company to construct and operate a railway, telegraph, and telephone line through the Indian and Oklahoma Territories, and for other purposes; and the reported amendments having been agreed to, the bill was reported to the Senate and the amendments were concurred in.

Ordered, That the amendments be engrossed and the bill read a third time.

The said bill as amended was read the third time.

Resolved, That it pass.

Ordered, That the Secretary request the concurrence of the House of Representatives in the amendments.

CONFERENCE REPORTS.

Mr. Allison, from the third committee of conference on the disagreeing votes of the two Houses on certain amendments of the Senate to the bill H. R. 10238, submitted the following report:

The committee of conference on the disagreeing votes of the two Houses on certain amendments of the Senate to the bill (H. R. 10238) "making appropriations for sundry civil expenses of the Government for the fiscal year ending June 30, 1894, and for other purposes," having met, after full and free conference have agreed to recommend and do recommend to their respective Houses as follows:

That the Senate recede from its amendments numbered 86, 87, 193, and 194.

That the House recede from its disagreement to the amendments of the Senate numbered 71 and 104, and agree to the same.

That the House recede from its disagreement to the amendment of the Senate numbered 67, and agree to the same with an amendment as follows: In lines 13 and 14, page 1, of said amendment, strike out *two hundred and one thousand seven hundred and fifty dollars,* and insert in lieu thereof *one hundred and fifty thousand seven hundred and fifty dollars;* and the Senate agree to the same.

That the House recede from its disagreement to the amendment of the Senate numbered 69, and agree to the same with an amendment as follows: Strike out, in line 2 of said amendment, the word "thirty-six," and insert in lieu thereof the word *eleven;* and in line 3 of said amendment strike out the word "ninety-eight," and insert in lieu thereof the word *ninety-three;* and the Senate agree to the same.

That the House recede from its disagreement to the amendment of the Senate numbered 70, and agree to the same with an amendment as follows: On page 2, in line 7 of said amendment, after the word "dollars," insert the following: *or so much thereof as, in the judgment of the Lady Managers, may be necessary.* And add at the end of said amendment the following:

And provided further, That said sum of five hundred and seventy thousand eight hundred and eighty dollars shall be a charge against the World's Columbian Exposition, and that of the moneys appropriated for the benefit of the World's Columbian Exposition, amounting to two million five hundred thousand dollars under the act of August five, eighteen hundred and ninety-two, five hundred and seventy thousand eight hundred and eighty dollars shall be retained by the Secretary of the Treasury until said World's Columbian Exposition shall have furnished, to the satisfaction of the Secretary of the Treasury, full and adequate security for the return and repayment by said World's Columbian Exposition to the Treasury of the sum of five hundred and seventy thousand eight hundred and eighty dollars on or before October one, eighteen hundred and ninety-three; and until such security shall have been furnished by said World's Columbian Exposition this appropriation, or any portion thereof, shall not be available.

And the Senate agree to the same.

W. B. ALLISON,
EUGENE HALE,
A. P. GORMAN,
Managers on the part of the Senate.

W. S. HOLMAN,
JOSEPH D. SAYERS,
WILLIAM COGSWELL,
Managers on the part of the House.

The Senate proceeded to consider the report; and
On motion by Mr. Allison,
Resolved, That the Senate agree thereto.

Ordered, That the Secretary notify the House of Representatives thereof.

INDIAN APPROPRIATION BILL.

Mr. Cullom, from the second committee of conference on the disagreeing votes of the two Houses on the amendments of the Senate to the bill H. R. 10415, submitted the following report:

The committee of conference on the disagreeing votes of the two Houses on the amendments of the Senate to the bill (H. R. 10415) making appropriations for the current and contingent expenses and fulfilling treaty stipulations with Indian tribes for the fiscal year ending June 30, 1894, and for other purposes, having met, after full and free conference have agreed to recommend and do recommend to their respective Houses as follows:

That the Senate recede from its amendments numbered 5, 12, 15, 25, 37, 38, 45, 47, 50, 52, 58, 67, and 69.

That the House recede from its disagreement to the amendments of the Senate numbered 2, 3, 4, 6, 7, 8, 9, 10, 11, 13, 14, 16, 17, 18, 19, 20, 21, 22, 23, 24, 26, 27, 28, 29, 31, 32, 33, 35, 36, 39, 40, 41, 42, 43, 46, 48, 51, 53, 54, 55, 56, 57, 59, 60, 61, 62, 64, 70, 71, 72, 73, 76, 77, 78, 79, 80, 81, 82, 85, 87, 88, 89, 90, 91, and 93, and agree to the same.

That the House recede from its disagreement to the amendment of the Senate numbered 1, and agree to the same with an amendment as follows: After the word "agents," in line 7, page 1 of the bill, insert the following: *where civilians are employed;* and the Senate agree to the same.

That the House recede from its disagreement to the amendment of the Senate numbered 30, and agree to the same with an amendment as follows: In line 3 of said amendment strike out "sixty-four," and insert in lieu thereof *forty;* and in line 5 of said amendment strike out "seventy-one," and insert in lieu thereof *forty-seven;* and the Senate agree to the same.

That the House recede from its disagreement to the amendment of the Senate numbered 30, and agree to the same with an amendment as follows: In line 3 of said amendment strike out after the word "purchase," and in line 1 of said amendment insert the words *land and;* and the Senate agree to the same.

That the House recede from its disagreement to the amendment of the Senate numbered 44, and agree to the same with amendment as follows: In lieu of the matter inserted by said amendment insert the following: *Provided, That of this sum a sufficient amount may be used to sink one artesian well at each of the three following places, namely: Rosebud Reservation, Standing Rock Reservation, and Pine Ridge Reservation, in South Dakota, neither of said wells to cost more than five thousand dollars;* and the Senate agree to the same.

That the House recede from its disagreement to the amendment of the Senate numbered 49, and agree to the same with an amendment as follows: In lieu of the sum named in said amendment insert *one thousand dollars;* and the Senate agree to the same.

That the House recede from its disagreement to the amendment of the Senate numbered 63, and agree to the same with an amendment as follows: In lieu of the sum proposed insert *twenty thousand dollars;* and the Senate agree to the same.

That the House recede from its disagreement to the amendment of the Senate numbered 65, and agree to the same with an amendment as follows: In lieu of the sum proposed insert *twenty thousand dollars;* and the Senate agree to the same.

That the House recede from its disagreement to the amendment of the Senate numbered 66, and agree to the same with an amendment as follows: Strike out, in lines 18 and 19, page 50 of the bill, the following: "for the establishment of an industrial boarding school on the Navajo Reservation;" and the Senate agree to the same.

That the House recede from its disagreement to the amendment of the Senate numbered 68, and agree to the same with an amendment as follows: Strike out, after the word "used," in line 20, page 50 of the bill, all down to and including the word "service," in line 27, same page of the bill; and the Senate agree to the same.

That the House recede from its disagreement to the amendment of the Senate numbered 74, and agree to the same with an amendment as follows: In lieu of the sum proposed insert *twenty-five thousand dollars;* and the Senate agree to the same.

That the House recede from its disagreement to the amendment of the Senate numbered 75, and agree to the same with an amendment as follows: In lieu of the sum named in said amendment insert the following: *one million one hundred and eighty-one thousand dollars;* and the Senate agree to the same.

That the House recede from its disagreement to the amendment of the Senate numbered 83, and agree to the same with an amendment as follows: In lieu of the matter inserted by said amendment insert the following: *For improvement of buildings, two thousand dollars; for purchase, in the discretion of the Secretary of the Interior, of one hundred and twenty acres of land adjoining said Indian farm school, ten thousand dollars;* and the Senate agree to the same.

That the House recede from its disagreement to the amendment of the Senate numbered 84, and agree to the same with an amendment as follows: In lieu of the sum proposed insert *thirty-seven thousand three hundred and seventy-five dollars;* and the Senate agree to the same.

That the House recede from its disagreement to the amendment of the Senate numbered 86, and agree to the same with an amendment as follows: Add at the end of said amendment the following: *Provided, That any amount that may be found due by the Secretary shall be credited to the Choctaw fund and charged to the Cherokee fund;* and the Senate agree to the same.

That the House recede from its disagreement to the amendment of the Senate numbered 92, and agree to the same with amendments as follows: Strike out the first six lines of said amendment, and insert in lieu thereof the following:

CHEROKEE OUTLET.

SEC. 10. *That the sum of two hundred and ninety-five thousand seven hundred and thirty-six dollars, payable as hereinafter provided, is hereby appropriated out of any money in the Treasury not otherwise appropriated, and the Secretary of the Interior is hereby authorized and directed to contract to pay eight million three hundred thousand dollars, or so much thereof as may be necessary in addition, to pay the Cherokee Nation of Indians.*

Strike out after the word "be," in line 22, down to and including the word "ninety-eight" in line 30, page 2 of said amendment, and insert in lieu thereof the following: *immediately available, and the remaining sum of eight million three hundred and sixty thousand dollars or so much thereof as is required to carry out the provisions of said agreement as amended and according to this act, to be payable in five equal annual installments, commencing on the fourth day of March, 1896, and ending on the fourth day of March, 1890.*

Insert after the word "lands," in line 13 of page 4 of said amendment, the following: *Provided said railroad shall be relieved from any further payments of compensation to said Cherokee Nation as required by law for running said railroad across the Cherokee Outlet;* and strike out in line 15, page 4 of said amendment, the word "five," and insert in lieu thereof the word *two,* and strike out after the word "paid," in line 16, down to and including the word "same," in line 18, same page of said amendment.

At the end of line 25, same page, insert the following: *Provided, That if the legislative council of the Cherokee Nation shall deem it more advantageous to their people they may issue a loan for the principal and interest of the deferred payment, pledging said amounts of interest and principal to secure payment of such debt.*

Strike out, in line 17, page 5, of said amendment, the words "one year after the approval of this act," and insert in lieu thereof the following: *six months after the approval of this act and the acceptance of the same by the Cherokee Nation as herein provided.*

And after the word "delay," in line 22, page 7, of said amendment, strike out the word "to," and insert in lieu thereof the word *by;* and the Senate agree to the same.

That the House recede from its disagreement to the amendment of the Senate numbered 94, and agree to the same with an amendment as follows: Strike out, in lines 19, 20, and 21, on page 4 of said amendment, the words "and all other Indian tribes and bands now owning lands or residing upon lands within the Indian Territory;" strike out in the last line on page 5 of said amendment the words "tribes and bands," and insert after the word "Indians," in line 1, page 6, of said amendment, the words *as aforesaid;* and the Senate agree to the same.

H. L. DAWES,
S. M. CULLOM,
WILKINSON CALL,
Managers on the part of the Senate.

S. M. PEEL,
JOHN M. ALLEN,
JOHN L. WILSON,
Managers on the part of the House.

The Senate proceeded to consider the report; and
On motion by Mr. Cullom,
Resolved, That the Senate agree thereto.
Ordered, That the Secretary notify the House of Representatives thereof.

NEW YORK AND NEW JERSEY BRIDGE BILL.

On motion by Mr. Hill that the Senate proceed to the consideration of the bill (S. 2626) to authorize the New York and New Jersey Bridge Companies to construct and maintain a bridge across the Hudson River between New York City and the State of New Jersey, The yeas were 25 and the nays were 16.

On motion by Mr. Hiscock,
The yeas and nays being desired by one-fifth of the Senators present, Those who voted in the affirmative are,
Messrs. Bate, Berry, Blackburn, Brice, Butler, Call, Coke, Daniel, Faulkner, Felton, Gibson, Hansbrough, Harris, Hill, Hunton. Kyle, Lindsay, Palmer, Pasco, Pettigrew, Pugh, Squire, Stewart, Vest, Voorhees.

Those who voted in the negative are,
Messrs. Cameron, Dubois, Frye, Gallinger, Higgins, McMillan, McPherson, Manderson, Paddock, Peffer, Proctor, Shoup, Stockbridge, Teller, Washburn, Wolcott.
The number of Senators voting not constituting a quorum,
The President *pro tempore* directed the roll to be called;

When,
Forty-nine Senators answered to their names.
A quorum being present, and
The question being again taken on the motion of Mr. Hill,
The yeas were 26, and the nays were 16.
Those who voted in the affirmative are,
Messrs. Bate, Berry, Blackburn, Brice, Butler, Call, Coke, Daniel, Faulkner, Felton, Gibson, Hansbrough, Harris, Hill, Hunton, Kyle, Lindsay, Palmer, Pasco, Pettigrew, Pugh, Squire, Stewart, Vest, Voorhees, White.
Those who voted in the negative are,
Messrs. Cameron, Cullom, Dubois, Frye, Gallinger, Higgins, McPherson, Manderson, Paddock, Peffer, Shoup, Stockbridge, Teller, Warren, Washburn, Wolcott.
The number of Senators voting not constituting a quorum,
The President *pro tempore* directed the roll to be called;
When,
Fifty Senators answered to their names.
A quorum being present,
On motion by Mr. Harris, that the Sergeant-at-Arms be directed to request the attendance of absent Senators,
Mr. Cockrell raised a question of order, viz, that it was not competent for the Senate under its rules to order the attendance of absent Senators when a quorum is present.
The President *pro tempore* overruled the point of order, and held that it was a right inherent in every legislative body to compel the attendance of absent members who are not present for duty and who have not been excused; and
On the question to agree to the motion of Mr. Harris,
It was determined in the affirmative.
The question recurring on the motion of Mr. Hill that the Senate proceed to the consideration of the bill S. 2626,
The yeas were 21 and the nays were 16.
Those who voted in the affirmative are,
Messrs. Bate, Berry, Blackburn, Brice, Butler, Call, Coke, Faulkner, Hansbrough, Harris, Hill, Hunton, Kyle, Lindsay, Palmer, Pasco, Pettigrew, Pugh, Stewart, Vest, Voorhees.
Those who voted in the negative are,
Messrs. Carey, Dubois, Frye, Gallinger, Higgins, McPherson, Manderson, Paddock, Peffer, Proctor, Sawyer, Stockbridge, Teller, Warren, Washburn, Wolcott.
The number of Senators voting not constituting a quorum,
The President *pro tempore* directed the roll to be called;
When,
Fifty-one Senators answered to their names.
A quorum being present, and
The question being again taken on the motion of Mr. Hill,
The yeas were 24 and the nays were 18.
Those who voted in the affirmative are,
Messrs. Bate, Berry, Blackburn, Brice, Butler, Call, Coke, Faulkner, Felton, Gibson, Hansbrough, Harris, Hill, Hunton, Kyle, Palmer, Pasco, Pettigrew, Pugh, Squire, Stewart, Vest, Voorhees, White.
Those who voted in the negative are,
Messrs. Cameron, Carey, Cullom, Dubois, Frye, Gallinger, Higgins, McPherson, Manderson, Peffer, Proctor, Sawyer, Shoup, Stockbridge, Teller, Warren, Washburn, Wolcott.
The number of Senators voting not constituting a quorum,
On motion by Mr. Butler, that the Sergeant-at-Arms be directed to compel the attendance of absent Senators,
It was determined in the affirmative, { Yeas .... 24 }
{ Nays .... 13 }
On motion by Mr. Frye,
The yeas and nays being desired by one-fifth of the Senators present, Those who voted in the affirmative are,
Messrs. Bate, Blackburn, Butler, Call, Carey, Coke, Daniel, Dubois, Faulkner, Gallinger, Gibson, Hansbrough, Harris, Hill, Hunton, Kyle, Manderson, Mitchell, Peffer, Squire, Stewart, Teller, Vest, Wolcott.
Those who voted in the negative are,
Messrs. Berry, Frye, Hawley, Higgins, Lindsay, Palmer, Pasco, Pettigrew, Proctor, Pugh, Sawyer, Shoup, Stockbridge.
So the motion was agreed to.
The number of Senators voting not constituting a quorum,
The President *pro tempore* directed the roll to be called;
When,
Forty-five Senators answered to their names.
A quorum being present, and
The question being again taken on the motion of Mr. Hill,
The yeas were 21 and the nays were 18.
Those who voted in the affirmative are,
Messrs. Bate, Berry, Blackburn, Brice, Butler, Caffery, Coke, Faulkner, Harris, Hill, Hunton, Irby, Jones of Arkansas, Kyle, Lindsay, Mills, Pasco, Pettigrew, Squire, Stewart, White.
Those who voted in the negative are,
Messrs. Allison, Cameron, Carey, Dubois, Frye, Gallinger, Higgins, Hiscock, Manderson, Paddock, Peffer, Proctor, Sawyer, Shoup, Teller, Warren, Washburn, Wolcott.
The number of Senators voting not constituting a quorum,

The President *pro tempore* directed the roll to be called;
When,
Fifty Senators answered to their names.
The Sergeant-at-Arms submitted the following report:

> SERGEANT-AT-ARMS, UNITED STATES SENATE,
> *Washington, March 4, 1893—2:25 a. m.*

SIR: I have the honor to report that, in obedience to the order of the Senate received by me at 2:08 this a. m., directing the Sergeant-at-Arms to request the attendance of absent Senators, I found Senators Allison, Gorman, and Mitchell in the committee rooms of the Senate, and that I requested their attendance in obedience to the order of the Senate, and that they replied that they would appear in the Senate Chamber at once. Deputies have been sent after other absentees.

Very respectfully,
E. K. VALENTINE,
Sergeant-at-Arms, United States Senate.
Hon. CHARLES F. MANDERSON,
President pro tempore, United States Senate.

A quorum being present on the last roll call, and
The question being again taken on the motion of Mr. Hill,
The yeas were 27 and the nays were 16.
Those who voted in the affirmative are,

Messrs. Bate, Berry, Blackburn, Brice, Butler, Caffery, Call, Cockrell, Coke, Daniel, Faulkner, Gibson, Harris, Hill, Hunton, Irby, Jones of Arkansas, Kyle, Lindsay, Mills, Palmer, Pasco, Pettigrew, Squire, Stewart, Vest, White.

Those who voted in the negative are,
Messrs. Allison, Cameron, Carey, Dubois, Frye, Gallinger, Higgins, Hiscock, Manderson, Paddock, Peffer, Proctor, Shoup, Stockbridge, Teller, Warren.

The number of Senators voting not constituting a quorum,
The President *pro tempore* directed the roll to be called;
When,
Forty-seven Senators answered to their names.
The Sergeant-at-Arms submitted the following report:

> SERGEANT-AT-ARMS, UNITED STATES SENATE,
> *Washington, March 4, 1893—3:27 a. m.*

SIR: I have the honor to report that in obedience to the order of the Senate, received at 2:35 this a. m., directing me to compel the attendance of all absent Senators, I sent deputies to their various residences and have up to this time received the following replies: Senator Caffery reported at once. Senators Dixon and Vilas said they would report immediately. Senators George and Ransom report themselves sick. Senators Morgan, Quay, Gordon, Allen, and Sanders are absent from the city. Senator Blodgett declined to come. My deputies are still visiting residences of absent Senators.

Very respectfully,
E. K. VALENTINE,
Sergeant-at-Arms, United States Senate.
Hon. CHARLES F. MANDERSON,
President pro tempore, United States Senate.

A quorum being present on the last roll call, and
The question being again taken on the motion of Mr. Hill, to proceed to the consideration of the bill S. 2626,
The yeas were 23 and the nays were 9.
Those who voted in the affirmative are,

Messrs. Bate, Berry, Blackburn, Butler, Caffery, Call, Cockrell, Coke, Faulkner, Gibson, Harris, Hill, Irby, Jones of Arkansas, Kyle, Lindsay, Mills, Palmer, Squire, Stewart, Vest, Vilas, White.

Those who voted in the negative are,
Messrs. Allison, Cameron, Carey, Hiscock, Manderson, Peffer, Proctor, Sawyer, Teller.

The number of Senators voting not constituting a quorum,
The Presiding Officer (Mr. Faulkner in the chair) directed the roll to be called;
When,
Forty-five Senators answered to their names.
A quorum being present, and
The question being again taken on the motion of Mr. Hill,
The yeas were 21 and the nays were 14.
Those who voted in the affirmative are,

Messrs. Bate, Berry, Blackburn, Brice, Butler, Caffery, Call, Cockrell, Coke, Faulkner, Gibson, Harris, Hill, Jones of Arkansas, Lindsay, Mills, Palmer, Pasco, Stewart, Vest, Vilas, White.

Those who voted in the negative are,
Messrs. Allison, Cameron, Carey, Dubois, Gallinger, Hiscock, Manderson, Paddock, Peffer, Proctor, Sawyer, Stockbridge, Teller, Warren.

The number of Senators voting not constituting a quorum,
The Presiding Officer directed the roll to be called;
When,
Forty-five Senators answered to their names.
A quorum being present,
On motion by Mr. Manderson, that the Senate proceed to the consideration of executive business,

---

The yeas were 15 and the nays were 13.
On motion by Mr. Hill,
The yeas and nays being desired by one-fifth of the Senators present,
Those who voted in the affirmative are,

Messrs. Bate, Carey, Dubois, Frye, Gallinger, Higgins, Hiscock, Manderson, Paddock, Pettigrew, Sawyer, Shoup, Squire, Teller, Warren.

Those who voted in the negative are,
Messrs. Blackburn, Call, Cameron, Faulkner, Harris, Hawley, Lindsay, Palmer, Pasco, Peffer, Perkins, Proctor, Stewart.

The number of Senators voting not constituting a quorum,
The Presiding Officer directed the roll to be called;
When,
Fifty Senators answered to their names.
A quorum being present,
Mr. Manderson, by unanimous consent, withdrew his motion.
The question recurring on the motion of Mr. Hill, that the Senate proceed to the consideration of the bill S. 2626,
The yeas were 22 and the nays were 18.
Those who voted in the affirmative are,

Messrs. Bate, Blackburn, Brice, Call, Cockrell, Coke, Faulkner, Gibson, Gorman, Harris, Hill, Irby, Jones of Arkansas, Kyle, Lindsay, Palmer, Pasco, Pettigrew, Squire, Vest, Vilas, White.

Those who voted in the negative are,
Messrs. Allison, Carey, Cullom, Dubois, Frye, Gallinger, Hawley, Higgins, Hiscock, Manderson, Paddock, Peffer, Proctor, Sawyer, Shoup, Stockbridge, Teller, Warren.

The number of Senators voting not constituting a quorum,
The President *pro tempore* directed the roll to be called;
When,
Forty-five Senators answered to their names.
A quorum being present,
On motion by Mr. Harris,
Ordered, That further proceedings under the call of the Senate be dispensed with.

RECESS.

On motion by Mr. Hill, at 6 o'clock and 27 minutes a. m. (Saturday),
The Senate took a recess until 9 o'clock and 30 minutes a. m.

AT 9 O'CLOCK AND 30 MINUTES A. M. (SATURDAY).

On motion by Mr. Berry,
The Senate took a further recess until 9 o'clock and 45 minutes a. m.

AT 9 O'CLOCK AND 45 MINUTES A. M.

MESSAGE FROM THE HOUSE.

A message from the House of Representatives, by Mr. Towles, its chief clerk:

Mr. President: The House of Representatives has agreed to the reports of the committees of conference on the disagreeing votes of the two Houses on the amendments of the Senate to the following bills of the House:

H. R. 10238. An act making appropriations for sundry civil expenses of the Government for the fiscal year ending June 30, 1894, and for other purposes; and

H. R. 10415. An act making appropriations for the current and contingent expenses, and fulfilling treaty stipulations with Indian tribes for the fiscal year ending June 30, 1894.

The House of Representatives has passed the following resolution, in which it requests the concurrence of the Senate:

Resolved by the House of Representatives (the Senate concurring), That there be printed of the eulogies delivered in Congress upon the Hon. George Hearst, late a Senator from the State of California, 8,000 copies, of which 2,000 copies shall be delivered to the Senators and Representatives of that State; and of the remaining number 2,000 shall be for the use of the Senate and 4,000 copies for the use of the House; and of the quota of the Senate the Public Printer shall set aside 50 copies, which he shall have bound in full morocco with gilt edges, the same to be delivered, when completed, to the family of the deceased; and the Secretary of the Treasury is hereby directed to have engraved and printed, at as early a date as practicable, the portrait of the deceased, to accompany said eulogies.

The Speaker of the House of Representatives having signed four enrolled bills, H. R. 4320, H. R. 7305, H. R. 8246, and H. R. 10258, I am directed to bring the same to the Senate for the signature of its President.

The President of the United States has informed the House of Representatives that he this day approved and signed an enrolled bill (H. R. 10331) making appropriations for the legislative, executive, and judicial expenses of the Government for the fiscal year ending June 30, 1894, and for other purposes.

ENROLLED BILLS SIGNED.

Mr. Dubois reported from the committee that they had examined and found duly enrolled the following bills:

H. R. 4320. An act granting a pension to Thomas C. Kennedy;
H. R. 7305. An act to pension Martha McDermott;
H. R. 8246. An act granting a pension to Bridget Brennan, widow

of Thomas Brennan, late of Companies C and G, Second Regiment Rhode Island Volunteers; and

H. R. 10258. An act making appropriations to supply deficiencies in the appropriations for the fiscal year ending June 30, 1893, and for prior years, and for other purposes;

Whereupon,

The President *pro tempore* signed the same, and they were delivered to the committee to be presented to the President of the United States.

EULOGIES ON THE LATE SENATOR HEARST.

The resolution first received from the House of Representatives for concurrence providing for the printing of the eulogies delivered in Congress upon Hon. George Hearst, late a Senator from the State of California, was read and referred to the Committee on Printing.

THANKS TO THE VICE-PRESIDENT.

Mr. Harris submitted the following resolution; which was considered by unanimous consent and unanimously agreed to:

Resolved, That the thanks of the Senate are hereby tendered to Hon. Levi P. Morton, Vice-President, for the dignified, impartial, and courteous manner with which he has presided over its deliberations during the present session.

COMMISSION TO EXAMINE THE STATUS OF THE LAWS RELATING TO THE EXECUTIVE DEPARTMENTS.

The President *pro tempore* appointed Mr. Cockrell, Mr. Jones of Arkansas, and Mr. Cullom members of the joint commission on the part of the Senate to inquire into and examine the status of the laws organizing the Executive Departments, bureaus, divisions, and other Government establishments at the national capital, authorized by the act approved this day, making appropriations for the legislative, executive, and judicial expenses of the Government for the fiscal year ending June 30, 1894.

Ordered, That the Secretary notify the House of Representatives thereof.

MOTION TO RECONSIDER WITHDRAWN.

Mr. Cockrell, with the consent of the Senate, withdrew the motion entered by him February 21, 1893, to reconsider the vote of the Senate on the passage of the resolution reported from the Committee on Agriculture and Forestry, conferring the powers and duties imposed upon said committee by the resolution of the Senate of April 19, 1892.

MESSAGE FROM THE HOUSE.

A message from the House of Representatives, by Mr. Kerr, its Clerk:

Mr. President: The House of Representatives has passed, without amendment, the following bill and joint resolution of the Senate:

S. 3473. An act to authorize the Interoceanic Railway Company to construct and operate railway, telegraph, and telephone lines through the Indian Territory; and

S. R. 148. A joint resolution authorizing the Secretary of the Smithsonian Institution to send articles illustrative of the life and development of the industries of women to the World's Columbian Exposition.

The House of Representatives has appointed a committee, consisting of Mr. Springer, Mr. Holman, and Mr. Reed, to join such committee as may be appointed on the part of the Senate to wait upon the President and inform him that unless he may have some further communication to make, the two Houses, having completed the business before them, are ready to adjourn.

The Speaker of the House of Representatives having signed eight enrolled bills, H. R. 1484, H. R. 9956, H. R. 2122, H. R. 5816, H. R. 4955, H. R. 10238, and H. R. 10375, and H. R. 10415, I am directed to bring the same to the Senate for the signature of its President.

ENROLLED BILLS SIGNED.

Mr. Dubois reported from the committee that they had examined and found duly enrolled the following bills:

H. R. 1484. An act for the relief of Mary A. Lewis;

H. R. 9956. An act to incorporate the Washington, Burnt Mills and Sandy Spring Railway Company;

H. R. 2122. An act for the relief of Cumberland Female College, of McMinnville, Tenn.;

H. R. 5816. An act to regulate the manner in which property shall be sold by decree of any United States court;

H. R. 4955. An act granting a pension to Susannah Chadwick;

H. R. 10238. An act making appropriations for sundry civil expenses of the Government for the fiscal year ending June 30, 1894, and for other purposes;

H. R. 10375. An act establishing a standard gauge for sheet and plate iron and steel; and

H. R. 10415. An act making appropriations for current and contingent expenses and fulfilling treaty stipulations with Indian tribes for fiscal year ending June 30, 1894;

Whereupon,

The Vice-President signed the same, and they were delivered to the committee to be presented to the President of the United States.

THANKS TO THE PRESIDENT PRO TEMPORE.

Mr. Gorman submitted the following resolution; which was considered by unanimous consent and unanimously agreed to:

Resolved, That the thanks of the Senate are due and are hereby tendered to Hon. Charles F. Manderson, President *pro tempore* of the Senate, for the uniformly able, courteous, and impartial manner in which he has presided over its deliberations.

COMMITTEE TO WAIT ON THE PRESIDENT.

Mr. Sherman submitted the following resolution; which was considered by unanimous consent and agreed to:

Resolved, That a committee of two Senators be appointed by the Chair, to join a similar committee appointed by the House of Representatives, to wait upon the President of the United States and inform him that the two Houses, having completed the business of the present session, are ready to adjourn unless the President has some further communication to make to them.

Whereupon,

The Vice-President appointed Mr. Sherman and Mr. Gorman members of the said committee on the part of the Senate.

Ordered, That the Secretary notify the House of Representatives thereof.

EULOGIES ON THE LATE SENATOR HEARST.

Mr. Hawley, from the Committee on Printing, to whom was referred the resolution this day received from the House of Representatives for concurrence, to print the eulogies delivered in Congress upon Hon. George Hearst, late a Senator from the State of California, reported it without amendment.

The Senate proceeded, by unanimous consent, to consider the said resolution; and

Resolved, That the Senate agree thereto.

Ordered, That the Secretary notify the House of Representatives thereof.

MESSAGE FROM THE HOUSE.

A message from the House of Representatives, by Mr. Towles, its chief clerk:

Mr. President: The House of Representatives has passed, without amendment, the following bills and joint resolutions of the Senate:

S. 3711. An act granting the right of way through the Arlington reservation for railroad purposes;

S. 762. An act granting a pension to Mrs. Elise Alden McCawley;

S. 204. An act to authorize the pay of Rear-Admiral James E. Jouett, retired;

S. 3075. An act for the relief of Maj. Gen. George S. Greene;

S. R. 57. A joint resolution authorizing Commander Dennis W. Mullan, United States Navy, to accept a medal presented to him by the Chilean Government; and

S. R. 159. A joint resolution authorizing the loan, for exhibition at the World's Columbian Exposition, of certain paintings therein stated.

By virtue of the authority conferred on the Speaker of the House by the legislative, executive, and judicial appropriation bill, he has appointed Mr. Dockery, of Missouri; Mr. Richardson, of Tennessee, and Mr. Dingley, of Maine, as the members on the part of the House of the joint commission of the two Houses to investigate the Executive Departments of the Government.

The House of Representatives has agreed to the amendments of the Senate to the bill (H. R. 1231) for the relief of J. P. Randolph, administrator of J. B. Randolph, deceased.

The Speaker of the House of Representatives having signed four enrolled bills, S. 3473, H. R. 1231, H. R. 2128, and H. R. 2901, and an enrolled joint resolution, S. R. 148, I am directed to bring the same to the Senate for the signature of its President.

ENROLLED BILLS SIGNED.

Mr. Dubois reported from the committee that they had examined and found duly enrolled the following bills and joint resolution:

S. 3473. An act granting the Interoceanic Railway Company the right to construct and operate railway, telegraph, and telephone lines through the Indian Territory;

H. R. 1231. An act for the relief of J. P. Randolph, administrator of J. B. Randolph, deceased;

H. R. 2128. An act granting a pension to John Fields;

H. R. 2901. An act to pension Ida Cassell; and

S. R. 148. A joint resolution authorizing the Secretary of the Smithsonian Institution to send articles illustrative of the life and development of the industries of women to the World's Columbian Exposition;

Whereupon,

The Vice-President signed the same, and they were delivered to the committee to be presented to the President of the United States.

MESSAGE FROM THE HOUSE.

A message from the House of Representatives, by Mr. Kerr, its Clerk:

Mr. President: The House of Representatives has passed, without amendment the bill (S. 3882) granting a pension to Honora Shea.

The Speaker of the House of Representatives having signed three enrolled bills, S. 204, S. 762, and S. 3711, and an enrolled joint resolution, S. R. 159, I am directed to bring the same to the Senate for th signature of its President.

ENROLLED BILLS SIGNED.

Mr. Dubois reported from the committee that they had examined and found duly enrolled the following bills and joint resolution:

S. 204. An act in relation to the pay of Rear-Admiral James E. Jouett, retired;

S. 762. An act granting a pension to Elise Alden McCawley;

S. 3711. An act granting the right of way through the Arlington reservation for railroad purposes; and

S. R. 159. A joint resolution authorizing the loan, for exhibition at the World's Columbian Exposition, of certain paintings therein stated.

Whereupon,

The Vice-President signed the same, and they were delivered to the Committee to be presented to the President of the United States.

MESSAGE FROM THE HOUSE.

A message from the House of Representatives, by Mr. Kerr, its Clerk:

Mr. President: The Speaker of the House of Representatives having signed an enrolled bill, S. 3882, I am directed to bring the same to the Senate for the signature of its President.

ENROLLED BILL SIGNED.

Mr. Dubois reported from the committee that they had examined and found duly enrolled a bill (S. 3882) granting a pension to Honora Shea;

Whereupon,

The Vice-President signed the same, and it was delivered to the committee to be presented to the President of the United States.

PRESIDENTIAL APPROVALS.

A message from the President of the United States, by Mr. Pruden, his secretary:

Mr. President: The President of the United States has this day approved and signed the following acts and joint resolutions:

S. 2931. An act to provide for the survey and transfer of that part of the Fort Randall military reservation in the State of Nebraska to said State for school and other purposes;

S. 3892. An act for the removal of the charge of desertion from the record of John Cassidy;

S. 2966. An act to amend rule 7, section 4233, Revised Statutes, relating to rules for preventing collisions on the water;

S. 203. An act for the examination and allowance of certain awards made by a board of claims to certain citizens of Jefferson County, Kentucky;

S. 782. An act to provide for the adjustment of certain sales of lands in the late reservation of the Confederated Otoe and Missouria tribes of Indians in the States of Nebraska and Kansas;

S. 3240. An act to facilitate the enforcement of the immigration and contract-labor laws of the United States;

S. 3890. An act to authorize the Lake Shore and Michigan Southern Railroad Company to renew its railroad bridge across the Calumet River upon or near the site of its present bridge, and upon a location and plans to be approved by the Secretary of War, and to operate the same;

S. 3566. An act for the relief of William and Mary College, of Virginia;

S. 2171. An act to amend section 766 of the Revised Statutes of the United States;

S. 3478. An act to authorize the Interoceanic Railway Company to construct and operate railway, telegraph, and telephone lines through the Indian Territory;

S. 3882. An act granting a pension to Honora Shea;

S. 3711. An act granting the right of way through the Arlington reservation for railroad purposes;

S. 762. An act granting a pension to Elise Alden McCawley;

S. 204. An act in relation to the pay of Rear-Admiral James E. Jouett, retired;

S. 3881. An act relating to copyrights;

S. 148. A joint resolution authorizing the Secretary of the Smithsonian Institution to send articles illustrative of the life and development of the industries of women to the World's Columbian Exposition; and

S. R. 159. A joint resolution authorizing the loan, for exhibition at the World's Columbian Exposition, of certain paintings therein stated.

The bill (S. 43) for the relief of the personal representatives of Adelicia Cheatham, deceased, having been presented to the President of the United States on the 20th of February for his approval, and not having been returned by him to the House of Congress in which it originated within the time prescribed by the Constitution, has become a law without his approval.

Ordered, That the Secretary notify the House of Representatives thereof.

REPORT OF COMMITTEE TO WAIT ON THE PRESIDENT.

Mr. Sherman, from the joint committee appointed by the two Houses to wait upon the President of the United States and inform

him that the two Houses, having completed the business of the present session, are ready to adjourn unless he have some further communication to make, reported that they had performed the duty assigned them, and that the President replied that he had no further communication to make.

PRESIDENTIAL APPROVALS.

A message from the House of Representatives, by Mr. Kerr, its Clerk:

Mr. President: The President of the United States has informed the House of Representatives that he has approved and signed acts and a joint resolution as follows:

On February 21, 1893:

H. R. 10391. An act to amend an act entitled "An act to provide for the establishment of a port of delivery at Council Bluffs, Iowa."

On February 23, 1893:

H. R. 9826. An act granting certain rights and privileges to the commissioners of waterworks in the city of Erie, Pa.; and

H. R. 8582. An act to provide for the publication of the Eleventh Census.

On February 24, 1893:

H. R. 10236. An act relative to voluntary assignments by debtors for the benefit of creditors in the District of Columbia, and to amend section 782 of the Revised Statutes of the United States relating to the District of Columbia;

H. R. 10304. An act to incorporate the American University;

H. R. 10241. An act to amend an act making appropriations for the construction, repair, and preservation of certain public works on rivers and harbors, and for other purposes, approved July 13, 1892; and

H. R. 10099. An act to narrow California avenue within Bel Air, Heights, D. C.

On February 25, 1893:

H. R. 10489. An act to amend the act of May 6, 1890, fixing the rate of interest to be charged on arrearages of general and special taxes now due the District of Columbia, and for other purposes;

H. R. 1036. An act for the benefit of the State of Kentucky, Logan and Simpson counties, and of Louisville, Ky., and of Sumner and Davidson counties, Tennessee; and

H. R. 1479. An act to remove the charge of desertion from the record of James Morrison alias James C. McIntosh.

On February 27, 1893:

H. R. 9069. An act for the further continuance of the publication of the Supplement to the Revised Statutes of the United States;

H. R. 9862. An act for the relief of George W. Jones;

H. R. 9730. An act to amend the charter of the Brightwood Railway Company of the District of Columbia;

H. R. 929. An act granting a pension to Mrs. Mary E. Donaldson; and

H. R. 9825. An act making appropriations for the support of the Army for the fiscal year ending June 30, 1894, and for other purposes.

On February 28, 1893:

H. R. 8450. An act to remove the charge of desertion from the record of Charles E. Pyer;

H. R. 3508. An act for the relief of Nemiah Garrison, assignee of Moses Perkins; and

H. R. 10363. An act to remove the disabilities of William F. Robinson, a citizen of the State of Alabama.

On March 1, 1893:

H. R. 10267. An act making appropriations for the diplomatic and consular service of the United States for the fiscal year ending June 20, 1894;

H. R. 9286. An act to create the California Débris Commission and regulate hydraulic mining in the State of California;

H. R. 10290. An act making appropriations for the support of the Military Academy for the fiscal year ending June 30, 1894;

H. R. 10345. An act making appropriations for the payment of invalid and other pensions of the United States for the fiscal year ending June 30, 1894, and for other purposes;

H. R. 4275. An act to grant to the Champlain and St. Lawrence Railroad Company a right of way across the Fort Montgomery military reservation;

H. R. 10484. An act to amend an act approved July 27, 1892, entitled "An act to provide for the improvement of the outer bar of Brunswick, Ga.;"

H. R. 3626. An act to grant to the Gainesville, McAllister and St. Louis Railway Company a right of way through the Indian Territory, and for other purposes.

On March 2, 1893:

H. R. 8736. An act for the relief of the Shibley and Wood Grocer Company, of Van Buren, Crawford County, Arkansas; and

H. R. 9350. An act to promote the safety of employés and travelers upon railroads by compelling common carriers engaged in interstate commerce to equip their cars with automatic couplers and continuous brakes and their locomotives with driving-wheel brakes, and for other purposes; and

H. R. 8677. An act to remove a cloud from the title to certain real estate in the city of Crawfordsville, Ind.

On March 3, 1893:

H. R. 10038. An act making appropriations for the expenses of the Government of the District of Columbia for the fiscal year ending June 30, 1894, and for other purposes;

H. R. 2432. An act for the relief of Lansing Shear;

H. R. 5958. An act for the relief of Elizabeth Carpenter;

H. R. 10280. An act to authorize the construction of a bridge over the Tennessee River at or near Sheffield, Ala.;

H. R. 7633. An act to ratify and confirm an agreement with the Kickapoo Indians in Oklahoma Territory, and to make appropriations for carrying the same into effect;

H. R. 10266. An act regulating the sale of intoxicating liquors in the District of Columbia;

H. R. 3504. An act for the relief of the Stockbridge and Munsee tribe of Indians in the State of Wisconsin;

H. R. 10331. An act making appropriations for the legislative, executive, and judicial expenses of the Government for the fiscal year ending June 30, 1894, and for other purposes;

H. R. 10421. An act making appropriations for the Department of Agriculture for the fiscal year ending June 30, 1894;

H. R. 9233. An act to grant a pension to Harriet Cota;

H. R. 3253. An act to increase the pension of William G. Smith;

H. R. 3118. An act to pension John S. Dunham;

H. R. 8498. An act to pension Sophia Kagwaich;

H. R. 7100. An act to pension Jacob O'Neal;

H. R. 7306. An act to pension Maud Case, of Dodge County, Minnesota.

H. R. 8409. An act granting a pension to Mary Danahay, mother of Daniel Danahay, late a private, Company H, Eighteenth New York Cavalry;

H. R. 7729. An act granting a pension to Mrs. Phœbe Sigler;

H. R. 8017. An act granting a pension to Elizabeth Voss;

H. R. 6654. An act to remove the charge of desertion against Charles H. Behle;

H. R. 5519. An act for the relief of Daniel Eldridge, Company D, Fifteenth Illinois Volunteers;

H. R. 1422. An act for the relief of George M. Henry;

H. R. 4071. An act for the relief of George W. Schachleiter;

H. R. 8230. An act for the relief of Louis G. Sanderson, of Craighead County, Arkansas;

H. R. 10349. An act making appropriations for the service of the Post-Office Department for the fiscal year ending June 30, 1894;

H. R. 10488. An act making appropriations for the naval service for fiscal year ending June 30, 1894, and for other purposes;

H. R. 10351. An act to continue the duties on certain manufactures of flax at the rate now provided by law;

H. R. 1100. An act granting a pension to Mary Catherine Reardon;

H. R. 4955. An act granting a pension to Susannah Chadwick;

H. R. 6233. An act granting a pension to Thomas T. Prather;

H. R. 5022. An act for the relief of Lucy Sprotberry;

H. R. 4496. An act to place upon the pension rolls of the United States the name of Thomas F. Sheldon, late captain Company A, One hundred and twenty-fifth New York Infantry;

H. R. 5508. An act to place the name of Sabra A. Wolcott upon the pension roll;

H. R. 4804. An act to place the name of Sarah L. Van Nest on the pension list;

H. R. 6212. An act granting an increase of pension to Ellis P. Phipps, late lieutenant in Company A, Twelfth New Jersey Volunteer Infantry, invalid certificate No. 35619;

H. R. 9741. An act to increase the pension of Capt. E. R. Chase from $20 to $72 per month;

H. R. 2077. An act for the relief of William B. Price;

H. R. 10258. An act making appropriations to supply deficiencies in the appropriations for the fiscal year ending June 30, 1893, and for prior years, and for other purposes;

H. R. 10415. An act making appropriations for current and contingent expenses and fulfilling treaty stipulations with Indian tribes for fiscal year ending June 30, 1894;

H. R. 10238. An act making appropriations for sundry civil expenses of the Government for the fiscal year ending June 30, 1894, and for other purposes;

H. R. 8550. An act to increase the pension of W. H. Philpot, a pensioner of the Mexican war;

H. R. 8246. An act granting a pension to Bridget Brennan, widow of Thomas Brennan, late of Companies C and G, Second Regiment Rhode Island Volunteers;

H. R. 4320. An act granting a pension to Thomas S. Kennedy;

H. R. 2128. An act granting a pension to John Fields;

H. R. 7305. An act to pension Martin McDermott;

H. R. 2901. An act to pension Ida Cassell;

H. R. 10375. An act establishing a standard gauge for sheet and plate iron and steel;

H. R. 1231. An act for the relief of J. P. Randolph, administrator of J. G. Randolph, deceased;

H. R. 5816. An act to regulate the manner in which property shall be sold under orders and decrees of any United States court;

H. R. 1484. An act for the relief of Mary A. Lewis;

H. Res. 196. A joint resolution authorizing members to certify monthly the amount paid by them for clerk hire, and directing the same to be paid out of the contingent fund of the House.

The bill (H. R. 6194) to commission David P. Cordway as second lieutenant to date from June 12, 1892, having been presented to the President of the United States February 12, 1893, and not having been returned by him to the House of Congress in which it originated within the ten days prescribed by the Constitution, has become a law without his approval.

OATH OF OFFICE ADMINISTERED TO THE VICE-PRESIDENT.

The Hon. Adlai E. Stevenson, Vice-President elect having entered the Senate Chamber accompanied by the committee of arrangements, was conducted to a seat on the right of the Chair;

The Vice-President then addressed the Senate as follows:

Senators, the time fixed by the Constitution for the termination of the Fifty-second Congress has arrived, and I shall soon resign the gavel of the President of the Senate to the honored son of Illinois who has been chosen as my successor.

I can not, however, take my leave of this distinguished body without offering my most grateful acknowledgments for the honor conferred by the resolution just adopted, declaring your approval of the manner in which I have discharged the duties of the Chair, and expressing my deep sense of the uniform courtesy and kindness, even in critical and complicated situations, extended to me as the Presiding Officer by every member of this body.

If I have committed errors, you have refrained from rebuking them, and I have never appealed in vain to your sense of justice, and have ever received your support.

My association with the representatives of the forty-four States of this great nation in this Chamber will be among the most cherished memories of my life, and I can express no better wish for my successor than that he may enjoy the same relations of mutual regard, and that the same courtesy and kindness that have never been limited by party lines or controlled by political affiliations, and which have so happily marked my intercourse with Senators, may be extended to him.

And now, Senators and officers of the Senate, from whom I have received so many good offices in the discharge of my duties, accept a feeble expression of my grateful appreciation of your kindness, with my heartfelt wishes for your future welfare and happiness in life.

Thereupon,

The Vice-President administered to Mr. Stevenson the oath of office prescribed by law, and declared the Senate adjourned without day.

PROCEEDINGS OF A SESSION SPECIALLY CALLED.

BY THE PRESIDENT OF THE UNITED STATES OF AMERICA.

A PROCLAMATION.

Whereas public interests require that the Senate should be convened at 12 o'clock on the 4th day of March next, to receive such communications as may be made by the Executive:

Now, therefore, I, Benjamin Harrison, President of the United States, do hereby proclaim and declare that an extraordinary occasion requires the Senate of the United States to convene at the Capitol in the city of Washington, on the 4th day of March next, at 12 o'clock noon, of which all persons who shall at that time be entitled to act as members of that body are hereby required to take notice.

Given under my hand and the seal of the United States at Washington, this twenty-fifth day of February, in the year of our Lord one thousand eight hundred and ninety-three, and of the Independence of the United States of America the one hundred and seventeenth.

[SEAL.]   BENJ. HARRISON.

By the President:
WILLIAM F. WHARTON,
   Acting Secretary of State.

In conformity with the foregoing proclamation of the President of the United States, the Senate assembled in its Chamber in the city of Washington.

SATURDAY, MARCH 4, 1893.

PRESENT.

From the State of Alabama:
  Mr. James L. Pugh.

From the State of Arkansas:
  Messrs. James H. Berry and James K. Jones.

From the State of Colorado:
  Messrs. Henry M. Teller and Edward O. Wolcott.

From the State of Connecticut:
  Mr. Orville H. Platt.

From the State of Delaware:
  Mr. Anthony Higgins.

From the State of Florida:
  Mr. Wilkinson Call.

From the State of Georgia:
  Mr. John B. Gordon.

From the State of Idaho:
  Messrs. Fred. T. Dubois and George L. Shoup.

From the State of Illinois:
  Messrs. Shelby M. Cullom and John M. Palmer.

From the State of Indiana:
  Mr. Daniel W. Voorhees.

From the State of Iowa:
  Messrs. William B. Allison and James F. Wilson.

From the State of Kansas:
  Mr. William A. Peffer.

From the State of Kentucky:
  Messrs. Joseph C. S. Blackburn and William Lindsay.

From the State of Louisiana:
  Messrs. Donelson Caffery and Edward D. White.

From the State of Maine:
  Mr. William P. Frye.

From the State of Maryland:
  Mr. Charles H. Gibson.

From the State of Massachusetts:
  Mr. George F. Hoar.

From the State of Michigan:
  Mr. James McMillan.

From the State of Minnesota:
  Mr. William D. Washburn.

From the State of Missouri:
  Mr. George G. Vest.

From the State of Montana:
  Mr. Thomas C. Power.

From the State of Nebraska:
  Mr. Charles F. Manderson.

From the State of Nevada:
  Mr. John P. Jones.

From the State of New Hampshire:
  Messrs. William E. Chandler and Jacob H. Gallinger.

From the State of New Jersey:
  Mr. John R. McPherson.

From the State of New York:
  Mr. David B. Hill.

From the State of North Carolina:
  Messrs. Matt. W Ransom and Zebulon B. Vance.

From the State of North Dakota:
  Mr. Henry C. Hansbrough.

From the State of Ohio:
  Mr. John H. Mitchell.

From the State of Oregon:
  Mr. James Donald Cameron.

From the State of Pennsylvania:
  Mr. James Donald Cameron.

From the State of Rhode Island and Providence Plantations:
  Mr. Nathan F. Dixon.

From the State of South Carolina:
  Messrs. Matthew C. Butler and John L. M. Irby.

From the State of South Dakota:
  Messrs. James H. Kyle and Richard F. Pettigrew.

From the State of Tennessee:
  Mr. Isham G. Harris.

From the State of Texas:
  Mr. Richard Coke.

From the State of Vermont:
  Mr. Justin S. Morrill.

From the State of Virginia:
  Mr. Eppa Hunton.

From the State of Washington:
        Mr. Watson C. Squire.
From the State of West Virginia:
        Mr. Johnson N. Camden.
From the State of Wisconsin:
        Mr. William F. Vilas.
From the State of Wyoming:
        .Mr. Joseph M. Carey.

The honorable Adlai E. Stevenson, Vice-President of the United States and President of the Senate, took the chair and addressed the Senate as follows:

I am not unmindful of the fact that among the occupants of this chair during the one hundred and four years of our constitutional history have been statesmen eminent alike for their talents and for their tireless devotion to public duty. Adams, Jefferson, and Calhoun honored its incumbency during the early days of the Republic, while Arthur, Hendricks, and Morton have at a later period of our history shed luster upon the office of President of the most august deliberative assembly known to men.

I assume the duties of the great trust confided to me with no feeling of self-confidence, but rather with that of grave distrust of my ability satisfactorily to meet its requirements. I may be pardoned for saying that it shall be my earnest endeavor to discharge the important duties which lie before me with no less of impartiality and courtesy than of firmness and fidelity. Earnestly invoking the coöperation, the forbearance, the charity of each of its members, I now enter upon my duties as Presiding Officer of the Senate.

The Secretary of the Senate will read the proclamation of the President of the United States convening the Senate in extraordinary session.

The proclamation of the President convening the Senate was read by the Secretary.

SENATORS SWORN.

The credentials of the following-named Senators having been heretofore presented to the Senate, the oath prescribed by law was administered to them by the Vice-President, and they took their seats in the Senate.

Mr. Nelson W. Aldrich, from the State of Rhode Island and Providence Plantations.
Mr. William V. Allen, from the State of Nebraska.
Mr. William B. Bate, from the State of Tennessee.
Mr. Francis M. Cockrell, from the State of Missouri.
Mr. John W. Daniel, from the State of Virginia.
Mr. Cushman K. Davis, from the State of Minnesota.
Mr. Charles J. Faulkner, from the State of West Virginia.
Mr. James Z. George, from the State of Mississippi.
Mr. Arthur P. Gorman, from the State of Maryland.
Mr. George Gray, from the State of Delaware.
Mr. Eugene Hale, from the State of Maine.
Mr. Joseph R. Hawley, from the State of Connecticut.
Mr. Henry Cabot Lodge, from the State of Massachusetts.
Mr. Roger Q. Mills, from the State of Texas.
Mr. John L. Mitchell, from the State of Wisconsin.
Mr. Edward Murphy, jr., from the State of New York.
Mr. Samuel Pasco, from the State of Florida.
Mr. Redfield Proctor, from the State of Vermont.
Mr. William N. Roach, from the State of North Dakota.
Mr. John Sherman, from the State of Ohio.
Mr. James Smith, jr., from the State of New Jersey.
Mr. William M. Stewart, from the State of Nevada.
Mr. Francis B. Stockbridge, from the State of Michigan.
Mr. David Turpie, from the State of Indiana.
Mr. Stephen M. White, from the State of California.

CREDENTIALS OF A SENATOR.

Mr. Peffer presented the credentials of John Martin, elected a Senator by the legislature of the State of Kansas to fill the vacancy occasioned by the death of Preston B. Plumb, in the term expiring March 3, 1895; which were read and placed on file.

Mr. Martin appeared, and the oath prescribed by law having been administered to him by the Vice-President, he took his seat in the Senate.

INAUGURAL ADDRESS.

The President of the United States, the ex-President, the ex-Vice-President, the Chief Justice and the associate justices of the Supreme Court of the United States, foreign ministers, and other persons entitled to admission by order of the committee of arrangements, having entered the Senate Chamber, the Senate proceeded, accompanied by them, to the eastern center portico of the Capitol, where the President of the United States delivered the following address:

My Fellow-Citizens: In obedience to the mandate of my countrymen, I am about to dedicate myself to their service under the sanction of a solemn oath. Deeply moved by the expression of confidence and personal attachment which has called me to this service, I am sure my gratitude can make no better return than the pledge I now give before God and these witnesses of unreserved and

complete devotion to the interests and welfare of those who have honored me.

I deem it fitting on this occasion, while indicating the opinions I hold concerning public questions of present importance, to also briefly refer to the existence of certain conditions and tendencies among our people which seem to menace the integrity and usefulness of their Government.

While every American citizen must contemplate with the utmost pride and enthusiasm the growth and expansion of our country, the sufficiency of our institutions to stand against the rudest shocks of violence, the wonderful thrift and enterprise of our people, and the demonstrated superiority of our free government, it behooves us to constantly watch for every symptom of insidious infirmity that threatens our national vigor.

The strong man who, in the confidence of sturdy health, courts the sternest activities of life and rejoices in the hardihood of constant labor may still have lurking near his vitals the unheeded disease that dooms him to sudden collapse.

It can not be doubted that our stupendous achievements as a people and our country's robust strength have given rise to heedlessness of those laws governing our national health which we can no more evade than human life can escape the laws of God and nature.

Manifestly, nothing is more vital to our supremacy as a nation and to the beneficent purposes of our Government than a sound and stable currency. Its exposure to degradation should at once arouse to activity the most enlightened statesmanship; and the danger of depreciation in the purchasing power of the wages paid to toil should furnish the strongest incentive to prompt and conservative precaution.

In dealing with our present embarrassing situation as related to this subject, we will be wise if we temper our confidence and faith in our national strength and resources with the frank concession that even those will not permit us to defy with impunity the inexorable laws of finance and trade. At the same time, in our efforts to adjust differences of opinion we should be free from intolerance or passion, and our judgments should be unmoved by alluring phrases and unvexed by selfish interests.

I am confident that such an approach to the subject will result in prudent and effective remedial legislation. In the meantime, so far as the Executive branch of the Government can intervene, none of the powers with which it is invested will be withheld when their exercise is deemed necessary to maintain our national credit or avert financial disaster.

Closely related to the exaggerated confidence in our country's greatness which tends to a disregard of the rules of national safety, another danger confronts us not less serious. I refer to the prevalence of a popular disposition to expect from the operation of the Government especial and direct individual advantages.

The verdict of our voters, which condemns the injustice of maintaining protection for protection's sake, enjoins upon the people's servants the duty of exposing and destroying the brood of kindred evils which are the unwholesome progeny of paternalism. This is the bane of republican institutions and the constant peril of our Government by the people. It degrades to the purposes of wily craft the plan of rule our fathers established and bequeathed to us as an object of our love and veneration. It perverts the patriotic sentiments of our countrymen, and tempts them to pitiful calculation of the sordid gain to be derived from their Government's maintenance. It undermines the self-reliance of our people, and substitutes in its place dependence upon governmental favoritism. It stifles the spirit of true Americanism and stupefies every ennobling trait of American citizenship.

The lessons of paternalism ought to be unlearned and the better lesson taught, that while the people should patriotically and cheerfully support their Government its functions do not include the support of the people.

The acceptance of this principle leads to a refusal of bounties and subsidies, which burden the labor and thrift of a portion of our citizens, to aid ill-advised or languishing enterprises in which they have no concern. It leads also to a challenge of wild and reckless pension expenditure, which overleaps the bounds of grateful recognition of patriotic service and degenerates to vicious uses the people's prompt and generous impulse to aid those disabled in their country's defense.

Every thoughtful American must realize the importance of checking at its beginning any tendency in public or private station to regard frugality and economy as virtues which we may safely outgrow. The toleration of this idea results in the waste of the people's money by their chosen servants, and encourages prodigality and extravagance in the home life of our countrymen.

Under our scheme of government the waste of public money is a crime against the citizen; and the contempt of our people for economy and frugality in their personal affairs deplorably saps the strength and sturdiness of our national character.

It is a plain dictate of honesty and good government that public expenditures should be limited by public necessity, and that this should be measured by the rules of strict economy; and it is equally clear that frugality among the people is the best guaranty of a contented and strong support of free institutions.

One mode of the misappropriation of public funds is avoided when appointments to office, instead of being the rewards of partisan activity, are awarded to those whose efficiency promises a fair return of work for the compensation paid to them. To secure the fitness and competency of appointees to office, and remove from political action the demoralizing madness for spoils, civil-service reform has found a place in our public policy and laws. The benefits already gained through this instrumentality and the further usefulness it promises entitle it to the hearty support and encouragement of all who desire to see our public service well performed or who hope for the elevation of political sentiment and the purification of political methods.

The existence of immense aggregations of kindred enterprises and combinations of business interests, formed for the purpose of limiting production and fixing prices, is inconsistent with the fair field which ought to be open to every independent activity. Legitimate strife in business should not be superseded by an enforced concession to the demands of combinations that have the power to destroy; nor should the people to be served lose the benefit of cheapness which usually results from wholesome competition. These aggregations and combinations frequently constitute conspiracies against the interests of the people, and in all their phases they are unnatural and opposed to our American sense of fairness. To the extent that they can be reached and restrained by Federal power, the General Government should relieve our citizens from their interference and exactions.

Loyalty to the principles upon which our Government rests positively demands the equality before the law which it guarantees to every citizen should be justly and in good faith conceded in all parts of the land. The enjoyment of this right follows the badge of citizenship wherever found, and, unimpaired by race or color, it appeals for recognition to American manliness and fairness.

Our relations with the Indians located within our border impose upon us responsibilities we can not escape. Humanity and consistency require us to treat them with forbearance, and in our dealings with them to honestly and considerately regard their rights and interests. Every effort should be made to lead them, through the paths of civilization and education, to self-supporting and independent citizenship. In the meantime, as the nation's wards they should be promptly defended against the cupidity of designing men and shielded from every influence or temptation that retards their advancement.

The people of the United States have decreed that on this day the control of their Government in its legislative and executive branches shall be given to a political party pledged in the most positive terms to the accomplishment of tariff reform. They have thus determined in favor of a more just and equitable system of Federal taxation. The agents they have chosen to carry out their purposes are bound by their promises not less than by the command of their masters, to devote themselves unremittingly to this service.

While there should be no surrender of principle, our task must be undertaken wisely and without heedless vindictiveness. Our mission is not punishment, but the rectification of wrongs. If, in lifting burdens from the daily life of our people, we reduce inordinate and unequal advantages too long enjoyed, this is but a necessary incident of our return to right and justice. If we exact from unwilling minds acquiescence in the theory of an honest distribution of the fund of the governmental beneficence treasured up for all, we but insist upon a principle which underlies our free institutions. When we tear aside the delusions and misconceptions which have blinded our countrymen to their condition under vicious tariff laws, we but show them how far they have been led away from the paths of contentment and prosperity. When we proclaim that the necessity for revenue to support the Government furnishes the only justification for taxing the people, we announce a truth so plain that its denial would seem to indicate the extent to which judgment may be influenced by familiarity with perversions of the taxing power; and when we seek to reinstate the self-confidence and business enterprise of our citizens, by discrediting an abject dependence upon governmental favor, we strive to stimulate those elements of American character which support the hope of American achievement.

Anxiety for the redemption of the pledges which my party has made, and solicitude for the complete justification of the trust the people have reposed in us, constrain me to remind those with whom I am to coöperate that we can succeed in doing the work which has been especially set before us only by the most sincere, harmonious, and disinterested effort. Even if insuperable obstacles and opposition prevent the consummation of our task, we shall hardly be excused; and if failure can be traced to our fault or neglect, we may be sure the people will hold us to a swift and exacting accountability.

The oath I now take to preserve, protect, and defend the Constitution of the United States, not only impressively defines the great responsibility I assume, but suggests obedience to constitutional commands as the rule by which my official conduct must be guided. I shall, to the best of my ability, and within my sphere of duty, preserve the Constitution by loyally protecting every grant of Federal power it contains, by defending all its restraints when attacked by impatience and restlessness, and by enforcing its limitations and reservations in favor of the States and the people.

Fully impressed with the gravity of the duties that confront me, and mindful of my weakness, I should be appalled if it were my lot to bear unaided the responsibilities which await me. I am, however, saved from discouragement when I remember that I shall have the support and the counsel and coöperation of wise and patriotic men who will stand at my side in Cabinet places or will represent the people in their legislative halls.

I find also much comfort in remembering that my countrymen are just and generous and in the assurance that they will not condemn those who by sincere devotion to their service deserve their forbearance and approval.

Above all, I know there is a Supreme Being who rules the affairs of men and whose goodness and mercy have always followed the American people; and I know He will not turn from us now if we humbly and reverently seek His powerful aid.

The President having concluded his address, the oath prescribed by the Constitution was administered to him by the Chief Justice of the United States;

When,

The Senate returned to its Chamber, and the Vice-President resumed the chair.

NOTIFICATION TO THE PRESIDENT.

Mr. Blackburn submitted the following resolution; which was considered by unanimous consent and agreed to:

Resolved, That a committee, to consist of two Senators, be appointed to wait on the President of the United States and inform him that the Senate is assembled and is ready to receive any communication he may be pleased to make.

The Vice-President appointed Mr. Blackburn and Mr. Allison as the committee.

HOUR OF MEETING.

On motion by Mr. Harris,

Ordered, That the daily hour of meeting of the Senate be 12 o'clock m. until otherwise ordered.

On motion by Mr. Gorman, at 2 o'clock and 5 minutes p. m.,

The Senate adjourned.

MONDAY, MARCH 6, 1893.

Mr. Alfred H. Colquitt, from the State of Georgia; Mr. Joseph N. Dolph, from the State of Oregon; Mr. Leland Stanford, from the State of California; and Mr. Edward C. Walthall, from the State of Mississippi, attended.

MESSAGE FROM THE PRESIDENT.

Mr. Blackburn, from the committee appointed to wait upon the President of the United States and inform him that a quorum of the Senate is assembled, and that the Senate is ready to receive any communication he may be pleased to make, reported that they had discharged the duties assigned them, and that they were requested by the President to state that he would very soon to-day communicate to the Senate in writing.

Whereupon,

A message in writing was received from the President of the United States, by Mr. Pruden, his secretary.

EXECUTIVE SESSION.

On motion by Mr. Harris,

The Senate proceeded to the consideration of executive business; and

After the consideration of executive business the doors were reopened.

ADJOURNMENT TO THURSDAY.

On motion by Mr. Gorman,

Ordered, That when the Senate adjourn it be to Thursday next.

SWAMP LAND PATENTS.

Mr. Call submitted the following resolution; which was ordered to lie on the table and be printed:

Resolved by the Senate, That the Secretary of the Interior be, and he is hereby, requested to suspend the approval or the issuing of patents to land under acts of Congress granting swamp and overflowed land until under the act of May 17, 1856, granting land to the States of Alabama and Florida in aid of the construction of certain lines of railway, until Congress shall hereafter authorize the approval of lists of such lands.

INTRODUCTION OF JOINT RESOLUTION.

Mr. Sherman introduced a joint resolution (S. R. 1) proposing an amendment to the Constitution of the United States; which was read the first and second times by unanimous consent and ordered to lie on the table.

On motion by Mr. Harris, at 12 o'clock and 32 minutes p. m.,

The Senate adjourned.

THURSDAY, MARCH 9, 1893.

CREDENTIALS OF A SENATOR.

Mr. Teller presented credentials of Lee Mantle, appointed a Senator by the governor of the State of Montana, to fill a vacancy existing from that State in the term commencing March 4, 1893; which were read.

Ordered, That they lie on the table and be referred to the Committee on Privileges and Elections, when appointed.

ADJOURNMENT TO MONDAY.

On motion by Mr. Gray,
Ordered, That when the Senate adjourn it be to Monday next.

LEAVE TO WITHDRAW PAPERS.

On motion by Mr. Proctor,
Ordered, That N. J. Coffin have leave to withdraw his papers from the files of the Senate, subject to the rule.

JOINT RESOLUTIONS.

Mr. Mitchell, of Oregon, introduced a joint resolution (S. R. 2) proposing an amendment to the Constitution of the United States, providing for the election of Senators by the votes of the qualified electors of the States; which was read the first and second times by unanimous consent.

Ordered, That it lie on the table.

Mr. Dolph offered a joint resolution calling on the President to take such measures as he may deem necessary to consummate the agreement between the Governments of Spain and the United States for the release of Antonio Maximo Mora, a naturalized citizen of the United States.

When,
Mr. Harris interposed an objection to its introduction.

BUSINESS OF THE SESSION.

Mr. Manderson submitted the following resolution for consideration; which was ordered to be printed:

Resolved, That it is the sense of the Senate that at this extraordinary session of the Senate the business transacted shall be confined to executive matters and those requiring the action of the Senate only.

Mr. Hale submitted the following resolution for consideration; which was ordered to be printed:

Resolved, That no legislative business, excepting treaties, shall be received or entertained at the present session of the Senate.

IMMIGRATION AND CONTRACT LABOR LAWS.

Mr. Chandler submitted the following resolution; which was ordered to lie on the table and be referred to the Committee on Printing, when appointed:

Resolved, That there be printed for the use of the Senate 2,000 copies of the act of March 3, 1893, "to facilitate the enforcement of the immigration and contract-labor laws of the United States," supplemented by Senate report No. 787, of the first session of the present Congress, which accompanied the bill when reported to the Senate.

NATIONAL UNIVERSITY.

Mr. Proctor submitted the following resolution; which was ordered to lie on the table and be referred to the Committee on Printing, when appointed:

Resolved, That 5,000 copies of Senate bill No. 3824, "to establish a national university," and of the Senate report thereon, be printed in document form for the use of the Senate.

MESSAGE FROM THE PRESIDENT.

The following message was received from the President of the United States, by Mr. Pruden, his secretary:

To the Senate of the United States:

I transmit herewith a report submitted by the Secretary of State, in compliance with the resolution of the Senate of the 3d instant, calling for information relating to the capture and imprisonment of Capt. Pharos B. Brubaker by Honduras officials.

GROVER CLEVELAND.

EXECUTIVE MANSION,
Washington, March 9, 1893.

The message was read.

Ordered, That it lie on the table and be printed, and be referred to the Committee on Foreign Relations, when appointed.

EXECUTIVE SESSION.

On motion by Mr. Gorman,
The Senate proceeded to the consideration of executive business; and

After the consideration of executive business the doors were reopened, and

On motion by Mr. Turpie, at 12 o'clock and 50 minutes p. m.,
The Senate adjourned.

MONDAY, MARCH 13, 1893.

ADJOURNMENT TO WEDNESDAY.

On motion by Mr. Gorman,
Ordered, That when the Senate adjourn it be to Wednesday next.

SWAMP LAND PATENTS.

The Vice-President laid before the Senate the resolution submitted by Mr. Call, on the 6th instant, requesting the Secretary of the Interior to suspend the approval or the issuing of patents to lands in certain cases in Alabama and Florida; and

On motion by Mr. Gorman,
Ordered, That the resolution lie on the table.

BUSINESS OF THE SESSION.

The Vice-President laid before the Senate the resolution submitted by Mr. Manderson on the 9th instant, confining the business of the present session to executive matters, and those requiring the action of the Senate only; and

The resolution having been modified by Mr. Manderson to read as follows:

Resolved, That it is the sense of the Senate that at this extraordinary session of the Senate the business transacted shall be confined to the consideration of treaties and other executive matters, and those requiring the action of the Senate only,

An amendment to the resolution having been proposed by Mr. Hale, viz: Strike out all after the word "*Resolved*," and in lieu thereof insert the following: *That no legislative business, excepting treaties, shall be received or entertained at the present session of the Senate.*

On motion by Mr. Hoar to amend the amendment by adding to the part proposed to be inserted the following proviso:

Provided, That petitions and resolutions of State legislatures may be received, to be referred to the appropriate committees at the next session,

Pending debate,

HARBOR AT PHILADELPHIA.

Mr. Frye, by unanimous consent, submitted the following resolution; which was considered by unanimous consent and agreed to;

Resolved, That so much of Senate resolution of February 27 last as requested the Secretary of War to suspend action in relation to the improvement of the harbor of Philadelphia, is hereby rescinded.

On motion by Mr. Vest, at 12 o'clock and 45 minutes p. m.,
The Senate adjourned.

WEDNESDAY, MARCH 15, 1893.

CREDENTIALS OF A SENATOR.

Mr. Vance presented the credentials of Asahel C. Beckwith, appointed a Senator by the governor of the State of Wyoming to fill the vacancy from said State in the Senate of the United States in the term commencing March 4, 1893; which were read.

Ordered, That they lie on the table and be referred to the Committee on Privileges and Elections, when appointed.

EXECUTIVE COMMUNICATION.

The Vice-President laid before the Senate a letter of the Secretary of the Interior, communicating, in answer to a resolution of the Senate of February 28, 1893, information relative to the use of the building of the Pension Office on the first day of the week, commonly called Sunday, for musical concerts, etc.

Ordered, That it lie on the table and be printed.

RESOLUTION OF A LEGISLATURE.

The Vice-President laid before the Senate a resolution of the legislature of Massachusetts in favor of the annexation of the Hawaiian Islands to the United States.

Ordered, That it lie on the table.

EXECUTIVE SESSION.

On motion by Mr. Gorman,
The Senate proceeded to the consideration of executive business; and

After the consideration of executive business the doors were reopened.

On motion by Mr. Gorman,
The Senate took a recess until 3 o'clock and 30 minutes p. m.

AT 3 O'CLOCK AND 30 MINUTES P. M.

NOTICE OF AMENDMENT TO THE RULES.

Mr. Sherman submitted the following notice:

Notice is hereby given of a motion to amend Rule XVI by adding after the words "Committee on Commerce," in clause 1, the words *and bills making appropriations for the District of Columbia, which shall be referred to the Committee on the District of Columbia,* so as to read: "All general appropriation bills shall be referred to the Committee on Appropriations, except bills making appropriations for rivers and harbors, which shall be referred to the Committee on Commerce, and bills making appropriations for the District of Columbia, which shall be referred to the Committee on the District of Columbia," etc.

Ordered, That the notice lie on the table and be printed.

APPOINTMENT OF COMMITTEES.

On motion by Mr. Gorman, and by unanimous consent, *Ordered,* That so much of Rule XXIV of the Senate as provides for the appointment of the standing and other committees of the Senate by ballot be suspended.

Mr. Gorman submitted the following resolution, which was considered by unanimous consent and agreed to:

Resolved, That the following constitute the standing and select committees of the Senate of the United States for the Fifty-third Congress:

STANDING COMMITTEES.

On Agriculture and Forestry: Messrs. George (chairman), Bate, Ransom, Peffer, Roach, McMillan, Washburn, Proctor, Hansbrough.

On Appropriations: Messrs. Cockrell (chairman), Call, Gorman, Blackburn, Brice, Allison, Hale, Teller.

To Audit and Control the Contingent Expenses of the Senate: Messrs. White of Louisiana (chairman), Camden, Jones of Nevada.

On the Census: Messrs. Turpie (chairman), Berry, White, of California, Murphy, Peffer, Hale, Stockbridge, Dixon, Hansbrough.

On Civil Service and Retrenchment: Messrs. Call (chairman), Walthall, Gordon, Irby, Cockrell, Stanford, Washburn, Morrill, Lodge.

On Claims: Messrs. Pasco (chairman), Daniel, Berry, Caffery, Allen of Nebraska, Mitchell, of Oregon, Davis, Stewart, Peffer.

On Coast Defenses: Messrs. Gordon (chairman), Irby, Mills, White of California, Smith, Squire, Dolph, Hawley, Higgins.

On Commerce: Messrs. Ransom (chairman), Coke, Vest, Gorman, White of Louisiana, White of California, Murphy, Frye, Jones of Nevada, Dolph, Cullom, Washburn, Quay.

On the District of Columbia: Messrs. Harris (chairman), Faulkner, Gibson, Hubton, Smith, Martin, McMillan, Wolcott, Gallinger, Hansbrough, Proctor.

On Education and Labor: Messrs. Kyle (chairman), George, Hunton, Caffery, Murphy, Carey, Stanford, Washburn, Lodge.

On Engrossed Bills: Messrs. Allison (chairman), Cockrell, Martin.

On Enrolled Bills: Messrs. Caffery (chairman), Mitchell of Wisconsin, Dubois.

On Epidemic Diseases: Messrs. Jones of Nevada (chairman), Stockbridge, Gallinger, Quay, Harris, Irby, White of Louisiana.

To Examine the Several Branches of the Civil Service: Messrs. Peffer (chairman), Gray, Vilas, Power, Gallinger.

On Finance: Messrs. Voorhees (chairman), McPherson, Harris, Vance, Vest, Jones of Arkansas, Morrill, Sherman, Jones of Nevada, Allison, Aldrich.

On Fisheries: Messrs. Coke (chairman), Call, Gibson, Hill, Mitchell of Wisconsin, Stockbridge, Stanford, Squire, Power.

On Foreign Relations: Messrs. Morgan (chairman), Butler, Gray, Turpie, Daniel, Sherman, Frye, Dolph, Davis.

On Immigration: Messrs. Hill (chairman), Voorhees, McPherson, Faulkner, Harris, Stewart, Chandler, Squire, Proctor, Dubois, Lodge.

On Improvement of the Mississippi River and its Tributaries: Messrs. Bate (chairman), Walthall, Palmer, Peffer, Washburn, Pettigrew, Power.

On Indian Affairs: Messrs. Jones of Arkansas (chairman), Morgan, Smith, Roach, Allen of Nebraska, Stewart, Platt, Stockbridge, Manderson, Pettigrew, Shoup.

On Indian Depredations: Messrs. Lindsay (chairman), Faulkner, Kyle, White of Louisiana, Cockrell, Shoup, Chandler, Pettigrew, Carey.

On Interstate Commerce: Messrs. Butler (chairman), Gorman, Brice, White of Louisiana, Camden, Lindsay, Cullom, Wilson, Chandler, Wolcott, Higgins.

On Irrigation and Reclamation of Arid Lands: Messrs. White of California (chairman), Jones of Arkansas, Kyle, Roach, Brice, Stewart, Dubois, Carey, Hansbrough.

On the Judiciary: Messrs. Pugh (chairman), Coke, George, Vilas, Hill, Lindsay, Hoar, Wilson, Teller, Platt, Mitchell of Oregon.

On the Library: Messrs. Mills (chairman), Voorhees, Wolcott.

On Manufactures: Messrs. Gibson (chairman), Smith, Caffery, Higgins, Gallinger.

On Military Affairs: Messrs. Walthall (chairman), Cockrell, Bate, Palmer, Mitchell of Wisconsin, Hawley, Cameron, Manderson, Davis.

On Mines and Mining: Messrs. Stewart (chairman), Bate, Call, Irby, Mills, Jones of Nevada, Power, Shoup, Allison.

On Naval Affairs: Messrs. McPherson (chairman), Butler, Blackburn, Gibson, Camden, Cameron, Hale, Stanford, Stockbridge.

On Organization, Conduct, and Expenditures of the Executive Departments: Messrs. Smith (chairman), Cockrell, Hill, Walthall, Caffery, Wilson, Proctor, Dubois, Lodge.

On Pacific Railroads: Messrs. Brice (chairman), Morgan, Faulkner, White of Louisiana, Murphy, Davis, Carey, Wolcott, McMillan.

On Patents: Messrs. Gray (chairman), Kyle, Mills, Berry, Dixon, Platt, Wilson.

On Pensions: Messrs. Palmer (chairman), Brice, Vilas, Camden, Caffery, Gorman, Shoup, Hansbrough, Gallinger, Hawley.

On Post-Offices and Post-Roads: Messrs. Colquitt (chairman), Vilas, Irby, Mills, Hunton, Hill, Mitchell of Oregon, McMillan, Wolcott, Dixon, Washburn.

On Printing: Messrs. Gorman (chairman), Ransom, Manderson.

On Private Land Claims: Messrs. Hale (chairman), Teller, Dixon, Ransom, Colquitt, Pasco, Berry.

On Privileges and Elections: Messrs. Vance (chairman), Gray, Pugh, Turpie, Palmer, Hoar, Mitchell of Oregon, Chandler, Higgins.

On Public Buildings and Grounds: Messrs. Vest (chairman), Daniel, Pasco, Brice, Gordon, Stanford. Morrill, Quay, Squire.

On Public Lands: Messrs. Berry (chairman), Walthall, Pasco, Vilas, Martin, Allen of Nebraska, Dolph, Pettigrew, Carey, Power, Dubois.

On Railroads: Messrs. Camden (chairman), Berry, Gordon, Palmer, Martin, Blackburn, Hawley, Stockbridge, Pettigrew, Power, Peffer.

On Relations with Canada: Messrs. Murphy (chairman), Pugh, Quitt, Hunton, Mitchell of Wisconsin, Hoar, Hale, Dolph, Higgins.

On the Revision of the Laws of the United States: Messrs. Daniel (chairman), Call, Lindsay, Wilson, Platt.

On Revolutionary Claims: Messrs. Cameron (chairman), Frye, Aldrich, Coke, Pugh.

On Rules: Messrs. Blackburn (chairman), Harris, Gorman, Aldrich, Manderson.

On Territories: Messrs. Faulkner (chairman), Hill, Blackburn, Bate, Call, White of California, Platt, Davis, Carey, Shoup, Hansbrough.

On Transportation Routes to the Seaboard: Messrs. Irby (chairman), George, Turpie, Gordon, Ransom, Gallinger, Squire, Mitchell of Oregon, Aldrich.

SELECT COMMITTEES.

To Investigate the Condition of the Potomac River Front of Washington: Messrs. Frye (chairman), Sherman, Proctor, McPherson, Ransom, Hunton.

To Inquire into all Claims of Citizens of the United States against the Government of Nicaragua: Messrs. Hawley (chairman), Stewart, Mitchell of Oregon, Morgan, Palmer.

On Woman Suffrage: Messrs. Hoar (chairman), Quay, Vance, George, Blackburn, McPherson.

On Additional Accommodations for the Library of Congress: Messrs. Morrill (chairman), Dixon, Voorhees, Butler, Pugh.

On the Five Civilized Tribes of Indians: Messrs. Teller (chairman), Platt, Butler, Pasco, Roach.

On Transportation and Sale of Meat Products: Messrs. Platt (chairman), Power, Vest, Coke, Allen of Nebraska.

To Establish the University of the United States: Messrs. Hunton (chairman), Kyle, Vance, Jones of Arkansas, Turpie, Proctor, Sherman, Dolph, Washburn.

On the Quadro-Centennial: Messrs. Vilas (chairman), Colquitt, Vest, Gray, Daniel, Gibson, Voorhees, Lindsay, Pettigew, Sherman, Cameron, Hawley, Wilson, Cullom.

To Investigate the Geological Survey: Messrs. Martin (chairman), Jones of Arkansas, Ransom, Wolcott, Carey.

On National Banks: Messrs. Mitchell of Wisconsin (chairman). Vance, Colquitt, Chandler, Manderson.

On Forest Reservations: Messrs. Allen of Nebraska (chairman), Kyle, Morgan, Teller, Davis.

On Corporations in the District of Columbia: Messrs. Aldrich (chairman), McMillan, Gorman, Brice, Harris.

To Investigate Trespassers upon Indian Lands: Messrs. Roach (chairman), Butler, Higgins.

On motion by Mr. Manderson, *Ordered,* That the list of committees be printed.

CLERK TO COMMITTEE.

Mr. Brice submitted the following resolution; which was referred to the Committee to Audit and Control the Contingent Expenses of the Senate:

Resolved, That the Committee on Pacific Railroads be, and is hereby, authorized to employ a clerk at an annual salary of $2,220 per annum, to be paid out of the contingent fund of the Senate until otherwise provided for.

On motion by Mr. Mills, at 3 o'clock and 45 minutes p. m., The Senate adjourned.

THURSDAY, MARCH 16, 1893.

RESOLUTIONS OF LEGISLATURES.

The Vice-President laid before the Senate resolutions of the legislature of the State of Washington; which were referred as follows:

A resolution in favor of the creation of a new light-house district on the Pacific coast; and

A resolution in favor of an appropriation for the improvement of the Ozette River; and the harbor at the mouth of the Quillayute River; to the Committee on Commerce.

A resolution in favor of the annexation of the Hawaiian Islands to the United States; and

A resolution in favor of the early completion of the Nicaragua Canal by the United States Government; to the Committee on Foreign Relations.

A resolution in favor of the establishment of a system of coast defenses on the coast of that State; to the Committee on Coast Defenses.

A resolution in favor of the passage of a national quarantine law; to the Committee on Epidemic Diseases.

A resolution in favor of an amendment to the Constitution providing for the election of United States Senators by a direct vote of the people; to the Committee on Privileges and Elections.

The Vice-President laid before the Senate a resolution of the legislative assembly of the Territory of Oklahoma, praying that the provisions of section 2301 of the Revised Statutes be made applicable to that portion of the Territory formerly known as the Public Land Strip, now known as Beaver County, and that part of said Territory known as the Cheyenne and Arapaho Reservation; which was referred to the Committee on Public Lands.

Mr. Hansbrough presented resolutions of the legislature of the State of North Dakota; which were referred as follows:

A resolution in favor of a change in the plans of the penitentiary building to be erected at Grafton, N. Dak., so that the building may be used as an institute for the feeble-minded; to the Committee on Public Buildings and Grounds.

A resolution in favor of the passage of a law creating a new department to be known as the Road Department; to the Committee on Agriculture and Forestry.

A resolution in favor of the passage of a law to secure governmental control of all telegraph lines; to the Committee on the Judiciary.

A resolution in favor of the removal of the duty on binding twine; to the Committee on Finance.

A resolution in favor of an amendment to the law regulating the allotment of the national militia fund between the States so that the same shall be based upon the effective militia force organized and maintained by the several States, instead of upon Congressional representation; to the Committee on Military Affairs.

A resolution in favor of the passage of a graduated income tax law; to the Committee on Finance.

GEOLOGICAL SURVEY.

The Vice-President laid before the Senate a resolution of the National Assembly, League of American Wheelmen, urging increased appropriations for completing the work of the United States Geological Survey; which was referred to the Committee on Appropriations.

ADJOURNMENT TO MONDAY.

On motion by Mr. Bate,
Ordered, That when the Senate adjourn it be to Monday next.

CLERK TO COMMITTEE.

Mr. Mitchell, of Wisconsin, submitted the following resolution; which was referred to the Committee to Audit and Control the Contingent Expenses of the Senate:

Resolved, That the Select Committee on National Banks be, and is hereby, authorized to employ a clerk at an annual salary of $1,440, to be paid out of the contingent fund of the Senate until otherwise provided for.

On motion by Mr. Gorman, at 12 o'clock and 10 minutes p. m., The Senate adjourned.

MONDAY, MARCH 20, 1893.

ADJOURNMENT TO WEDNESDAY.

On motion by Mr. Faulkner,
Ordered, That when the Senate adjourn it be to Wednesday next.

REGENT OF SMITHSONIAN INSTITUTION.

The Vice-President appointed Mr. Gray a member of the Board of Regents of the Smithsonian Institution in obedience to the provisions of section 5580 of the Revised Statutes, to fill the vacancy occasioned by the expiration of his term.

REPORT ON PHOSPHATE INDUSTRY.

The Vice-President laid before the Senate a letter of the Commissioner of Labor, transmitting, in answer to a resolution of the Senate of December 4, 1890, a special report relating to the phosphate industry of the United States; which was referred to the Committee on Printing.

CREDENTIALS OF JOHN B. ALLEN.

Mr. Squire presented the credentials of John B. Allen, appointed a Senator by the governor of the State of Washington to fill a vacancy existing from that State in the Senate of the United States, in the term commencing March 4, 1893; which were read and referred to the Committee on Privileges and Elections.

Mr. Hawley presented a resolution of the legislature of the State of Connecticut in favor of the erection of suitable coast defenses at the eastern entrance of Long Island Sound; which was referred to the Committee on Coast Defenses.

REPORTS OF COMMITTEES.

Mr. White of Louisiana, from the Committee to Audit and Control the Contingent Expenses of the Senate, to whom was referred the resolution submitted by Mr. Mitchell, of Wisconsin, on the 15th instant, authorizing the Select Committee on National Banks to employ a clerk, reported it with an amendment, as follows: Strike out all after the word "*Resolved*," and insert the following:

That the Secretary of the Senate be, and he is hereby, authorized and directed to pay the clerks to the following committees their salaries at the rate of one thousand four hundred and forty dollars per annum, from the sixteenth day of March, instant, or so soon thereafter as they shall qualify:

To Investigate the Geological Survey; On National Banks; On Forest Reservations in California; On Corporations in the District of Columbia; and To Investigate Trespassers upon Cherokee Lands; the said salaries to be paid from the contingent fund of the Senate.

Mr. White of Louisiana, from the Committee to Audit and Control the Contingent Expenses of the Senate, to whom was referred the resolution submitted by Mr. Brice on the 15th instant, authorizing the Committtee on Pacific Railroads to employ a clerk, reported it with an amendment.

The Senate proceeded, by unanimous consent, to consider the said resolution; and the reported amendment having been agreed to, the resolution as amended was agreed to, as follows:

Resolved, That the Committee on Pacific Railroads be, and it is hereby, authorized to employ a clerk at an annual salary of one thousand four hundred and forty dollars, from the sixteenth day of March, instant, or so soon thereafter as the said clerk shall qualify, and that the Secretary of the Senate be, and he is hereby, authorized and directed to pay the salary of the said clerk out of the contingent fund of the Senate.

AMENDMENT OF THE RULES—DISTRICT APPROPRIATION BILLS.

Mr. Sherman, in pursuance of notice given on the 15th instant, submitted the following resolution; which was referred to the Committee on Rules and ordered to be printed:

Resolved, That Rule XVI be amended by adding after the words "Committee on Commerce," in clause 1, the words, *and bills making appropriations for the District of Columbia; which shall be referred to the Committee on the District of Columbia,* so as to read:

"All general appropriation bills shall be referred to the Committee on Appropriations, except bills making appropriations for rivers and harbors, which shall be referred to the Committee on Commerce, and bills making appropriations for the District of Columbia, which shall be referred to the Committee on the District of Columbia," etc.

REFERENCE OF APPROPRIATION BILLS.

Mr. Butler submitted the following resolution; which was referred to the Committee on Rules and ordered to be printed:

Resolved, That paragraph 1 of Rule XVI of the standing rules of the Senate be amended by striking out the words "All general appropriation bills shall be referred to the Committee on Appropriations, except bills making appropriations for rivers and harbors, which shall be referred to the Committee on Commerce," and inserting the following:

The general appropriation bills shall be referred to committees as follows:

To the Committee on Appropriations: The bills for legislative, executive, and judicial expenses, for sundry civil expenses, for pensions, and for all deficiencies.

To the Committee on Agriculture: The bill for the Agricultural Department.

To the Committee on Foreign Relations: The consular and diplomatic bill.

To the Committee on Military Affairs: The bill for the military establishment, including the Military Academy.

To the Committee on Naval Affairs: The bill for the naval establishment.

To the Committee on Post-Offices and Post-Roads: The Post-Office appropriation bill.

To the Committee on Indian Affairs: The bill for Indians and Indian tribes.

To the Committee on Commerce: The bill for rivers and harbors.

To the Committee on Coast Defenses: The fortifications bill; and

To the Committee on the District of Columbia: The bill making appropriations for the District.

REPORT ON COST OF MANUFACTURED PRODUCTS.

Mr. McPherson submitted the following resolution; which was referred to the Committee on Finance.

Resolved, That the Commissioner of Labor is hereby directed to make a report to the Senate at the opening of the Fifty-third Congress, comprehending the facts already collected by him, or to be obtained from other sources, of the total cost and also actual labor cost of producing various iron and steel products, such as bar iron, steel rails, etc., and leading articles in the textile industry, and of such other articles for which the cost of production has been or may be approximately obtained, and in his report to state the facts in parallel columns for this and other countries for which they have been or may be obtained.

INDIAN DEPREDATION CLAIMS.

Mr. Kyle submitted the following resolution; which was referred to the Committee on Indian Depredations:

Resolved, That the Committee on Indian Depredations be, and hereby is, directed to make inquiry concerning all Indian depredation claims which at any time have been or may be presented in the Court of Claims under the act of March 3, 1891, especially those in which unpaid judgments have been hitherto rendered, or may be rendered prior to the conclusion of the inquiry; and also into the manner in which such claims have been defended in behalf of the Indians and the United States; and generally into the workings of said act of March 3, 1891; and concerning all other Indian depredation claims not covered by said act, and to make such recommendations relative to any or all of said claims and for additional legislation as said committee may deem expedient; said committee, either as a full committee or through subcommittees, being hereby empowered to sit during the recess of the Senate, to send for persons and papers, and to employ a stenographer and expert, the expenses of the inquiry to be paid from the contingent fund of the Senate.

PHOTOGRAPHS OF ANCIENT EXECUTIVE DOCUMENTS.

Mr. Allison submitted the following resolution; which was referred to the Committee on Rules:

Resolved, That the Secretary of the Senate be, and he is hereby, directed to allow, under his supervision, the representative of the Department of Justice on the board of management of the World's Columbian Exposition to have photographic copies made of certain ancient executive communications on file in the archives of the United States Senate, for exhibition at the World's Columbian Exposition as follows: The nominations by the President of the Chief Justices and the Associate Justices of the Supreme Court of the United States, embraced in Nos. 1, 2, 6, 7, 14, 16, 27, 28, 31, 35, 37, 40; also nominations of Ellsworth and Fuller, and Jefferson's address to the Senate on taking the oath of office.

REPORT ON IMMIGRATION.

Mr. Chandler submitted the following resolution; which was referred to the Committee on Printing:

Resolved, That there be printed and bound, in paper covers, for the use of the Senate, 1,000 copies of the report No. 1333 of the Committee on Immigration, made at the second session of the Fifty-second Congress, with the testimony accompanying said report.

REPORT ON FAILED NATIONAL BANKS.

Mr. Chandler submitted the following resolution; which was referred to the Committee on Printing:

Resolved, That there be printed and bound, in paper covers, for the use of the Senate, 2,250 copies of the Report No. 1286, of the Committee on Failed National Banks, made at the second session of the Fifty-second Congress, with the testimony accompanying said report.

STATE QUARANTINE PROPERTY.

Mr. Chandler submitted the following resolution; which was referred to the Committee on Epidemic Diseases:

Resolved, That the Secretary of the Treasury is hereby directed to ascertain, by means of a suitable board of officers appointed for that purpose, or otherwise, the value of the real or personal property belonging to any State or municipal government designed or used for quarantine purposes; also to ascertain at what price such property may be purchased by the United States, and to report the result of these inquiries at the first session of the next Congress.

COMMITTEE MEMBERSHIP.

Mr. Call submitted the following resolution; which was ordered to lie on the table and be printed:

Resolved, That the Committees on Naval Affairs, Military Affairs, Judiciary, Foreign Relations, Appropriations, Commerce, Interstate Commerce, shall each consist of fifteen members.

CLERK TO SELECT COMMITTEE ON GEOLOGICAL SURVEY.

Mr. Martin submitted the following resolution; which was referred to the Committee to Audit and Control the Contingent Expenses of the Senate:

Resolved, That the Select Committee to Investigate the Geological Survey be, and it hereby is, authorized to employ a clerk at an annual salary of $1,440, to be paid out of the contingent fund of the Senate, until otherwise provided for.

REPRINT OF INDIAN APPROPRIATION ACT.

Mr. Cockrell submitted the following resolution; which was considered by unanimous consent and agreed to:

Resolved, That there be printed for the use of the Senate 500 additional copies of public act No. 125, being "An act making appro-

priations for current and contingent expenses, and fulfilling treaty stipulations with Indian tribes, for fiscal year ending June 30, 1894."

EXECUTIVE SESSION.

On motion by Mr. Vest,
The Senate proceeded to the consideration of executive business; and
After the consideration of executive business the doors were reopened,
On motion by Mr. Berry, at 1 o'clock and 42 minutes p. m.,
The Senate adjourned.

WEDNESDAY, MARCH 22, 1893.

MEMORIALS.

The Vice-President laid before the Senate a resolution of the National Citizens' Industrial Alliance, praying relief from the unjust and extortionate rates and charges of the Bell telephone monopoly; which was referred to the Committee on Patents.

The Vice-President laid before the Senate a resolution of the senate of the legislature of the State of Kansas in favor of the passage of the bill for the raising of additional revenue by the levying and collection of a graduated tax; which was referred to the Committee on Finance.

REPORT ON COST OF MANUFACTURED PRODUCTS.

Mr. McPherson, from the Committee on Finance, to whom was referred the resolution submitted by him on the 20th instant, calling for a report of the total cost and also actual labor cost of producing various iron and steel products, such as bar iron, steel rails, etc., reported in lieu thereof the following resolution; which was referred to the Committee to Audit and Control the Contingent Expenses of the Senate:

Resolved, That the Commissioner of Labor is hereby directed to make a report to the Senate at the opening of the Fifty-third Congress comprehending the facts already collected by him, or to be obtained from other sources, of the total cost, including all the elements thereof, and also actual labor cost of producing various iron and steel products, such as bar iron, steel rails, and other articles of iron and steel, and also the leading articles of textile industry, and of such other articles for which the cost of production has been or may be approximately obtained, and in his report to state the facts in parallel columns for this and other countries from which they have been or may be obtained; and that the Committee on Finance, or any subcommittee thereof, is hereby authorized to make such further investigations in respect to the same matters as it shall deem important, and with power to summon and examine witnesses, to send for persons and papers, and to administer oaths; and the expenses of such investigations, when made by said Finance Committee, shall be paid out of the contingent fund of the Senate.

CLERKS TO SELECT COMMITTEES.

The Vice-President laid before the Senate the resolution submitted by Mr. Mitchell, of Wisconsin, on the 15th instant, authorizing the Select Committee on National Banks to employ a clerk; and the amendment reported by the Committee to Audit and Control the Contingent Expenses of the Senate having been amended on the motion of Mr. Cockrell, was agreed to as amended, and the resolution as amended was agreed to, as follows:

Resolved, That the Secretary of the Senate be, and he is hereby, authorized and directed to pay the clerks of the following committees their salaries at the rate of $1,440 per annum, from the 16th day of March, instant, or so soon thereafter as they shall qualify:
To investigate the Geological Survey; On National Banks; On Forest Reservations; On Corporations in the District of Columbia; and To Investigate Trespassers upon Indian Lands; the said salaries to be paid from the contingent fund of the Senate.

RESIGNATION AND ELECTION OF PRESIDENT PRO TEMPORE.

Mr. Manderson tendered his resignation as President *pro tempore* of the Senate and addressed the Senate as follows:

Mr. PRESIDENT: Two years ago there came to me the distinguished honor of election as the President *pro tempore* of the Senate. No suitable time has seemed to come when I could make that recognition of this distinction which I should like to do, and I desire now to express my deep sense of obligation and my very hearty thanks to my political associates on this side of the Chamber, by whom the distinction was proposed, and at the same time to thank very heartily those of opposing politics, who made no nomination against the selection of the Republican caucus. There came, therefore, to me this place by the unanimous vote of the Senate of the United States. I thank all from the depths of my heart for this distinction, and I further want to express my obligation for that forbearance on the part of all which has enabled me when I have been the occupant of the chair to administer, I hope with some satisfaction to the Senate, the duties that devolved upon me.

Recognizing a change of condition and perhaps, also a change of theory, I now tender my resignation of the position to the Senate and ask to be excused from further duty in that regard.

The resignation was then accepted;

Whereupon,

Mr. Gorman submitted the following resolution; which was considered by unanimous consent and agreed to;

Resolved, That the Senate now proceed to elect a President *pro tempore* of the Senate.

In pursuance of the foregoing resolution,

Mr. Cockrell submitted the following resolution; which was considered by unanimous consent and agreed to:

Resolved, That Isham G. Harris, a Senator from the State of Tennessee, be, and he hereby is, elected President *pro tempore* of the Senate, to hold office during the pleasure of the Senate and in accordance with the resolution of the Senate adopted on the 12th day of March, 1890, on the subject.

Mr. Harris appeared at the desk, and the oath of office was administered to him by the Vice-President.

Mr. McPherson submitted the following resolution; which was considered by unanimous consent and agreed to:

Resolved, That the Secretary wait upon the President of the United States and inform him that the Senate has elected Hon. Isham G. Harris, a Senator from the State of Tennessee, President of the Senate pro tempore, in place of Charles F. Manderson, resigned, to hold and exercise the office in the absence of the Vice-President from time to time, during the pleasure of the Senate, in accordance with its resolution passed March 12, 1890.

LABOR TROUBLES IN IDAHO.

Mr. Dubois submitted the following resolution; which was referred to the Committee to Audit and Control the Contingent Expenses of the Senate:

Resolved, That a select committee of seven Senators be appointed by the President of the Senate, whose duty it shall be to investigate and report to the Senate the facts in relation to the recent serious difficulties existing between the employing silver-mine owners and the working miners of Idaho, as to the employment for private purposes of armed bodies of men, or detectives, in connection with said difficulties. The investigation shall extend to and embrace, in addition, an inquiry into the causes and necessity for the employment of United States soldiers, and the conduct of such soldiers. The committee shall ascertain if present serious difficulties exist between employers and employés, or if justice has been or is being denied anyone through a suspension of the writ of habeas corpus, or through any dereliction of duty on the part of United States courts.

The committee shall also inquire into the character, objects, and purposes of the miners' union; and whether the obligations required of its members conflicts or conflicted with the obligations and duties these members owe to the State and Governments as law-abiding citizens. In addition to the testimony and conclusions of fact the committee will consider and report, by bill or otherwise, what legislation, if any, will tend to prevent a recurrence of similar troubles. Said committee, either as a full committee or through subcommittees thereof, shall have authority to send for persons and papers, administer oaths to witnesses, and take testimony in Washington or elsewhere, according to its discretion, during the present session or approaching recess of Congress, and to employ a clerk, messenger, and stenographer; the expenses of the investigation to be paid from the contingent fund of the Senate.

EXECUTIVE SESSION.

On motion by Mr. McPherson,

The Senate proceeded to the consideration of executive business; and

After the consideration of executive business the doors were reopened, and

On motion by Mr. Gorman, at 2 o'clock p. m.,

The Senate adjourned.

THURSDAY, MARCH 23, 1893.

The Vice-President appointed Mr. Walthall a member of the board of directors of the Columbia Institute for the Deaf and Dumb for the Fifty-third Congress, in pursuance of the provisions of section 4863 of the Revised Statutes of the United States.

JOINT COMMISSION ON EXECUTIVE DEPARTMENTS.

Mr. Call submitted the following resolution; which was ordered to lie on the table and be printed:

Resolved, That the enactment in the act making appropriations for legislative, executive, and judicial expenses of the Government for the fiscal year ending June 30, 1894, and for other purposes, approved March 3, 1893, creating a commission to be composed of members of the Senate and the House, appointed by a President of the Senate and a Speaker of the House whose terms of office expired on the 4th day of March current, to examine into the civil service in the executive branches of the United States and to report

and recommend to the present and future Congresses their opinion in relation to the exercise of the legislative powers of each and both Houses of the Congress which shall convene in December, 1893, in respect to the civil service of the United States, is in derogation of the constitutional right, power, and prerogative of each House and otherwise violative of the Constitution, and is absolutely null and void.

Resolved, second, That the Constitution confers on "each House" the sovereign and exclusive power to prescribe its rules of proceeding, and therein of the creation of its committees and the duties and powers which shall be imposed and conferred upon them, both to recommend changes in existing law and to enact new laws, and to obtain the information necessary for the exercise of their legislative power, and the members of each House can derive no power or authority or right in respect to any exercise of legislative functions from any other source than the separate and exclusive power of "each House" as they shall be organized, and during their constitutional term of official life to prescribe, regulate, and direct all their rules of procedure and the exercise of their legislative function.

AMENDMENT OF RULES—PENSION APPROPRIATION BILLS.

Mr. Palmer submitted the following resolution; which was referred to the Committee on Rules:

Resolved, That Rule XVI be amended by adding, after the words "Committee on Commerce," in clause I, the words, *and pension appropriation bills, which shall be referred to the Committee on Pensions,* so as to read:

"All general appropriation bills shall be referred to the Committee on Appropriations, except for rivers and harbors, which shall be referred to the Committee on Commerce, and pension appropriation bills, which shall be referred to the Committee on Pensions."

CLERK TO SELECT COMMITTEE ON LIBRARY OF CONGRESS.

Mr. Voorhees submitted the following resolution; which was referred to the Committee to Audit and Control the Contingent expenses of the Senate:

Resolved, That the Committee on Additional Accommodations for the Library of Congress be, and hereby is, authorized to employ a clerk from March 16 to June 30, 1893, inclusive, at the rate of $1,440 per annum, to be paid out of the contingent fund of the Senate.

ADJOURNMENT TO MONDAY.

On motion by Mr. Gorman,

Ordered, That when the Senate adjourn it be to meet Monday next.

EXECUTIVE SESSION.

On motion by Mr. Daniel,

The Senate proceeded to the consideration of executive business; and

After the consideration of executive business the doors were reopened, and

On motion by Mr. Butler, at 12 o'clock and 51 minutes p. m.,

The Senate adjourned.

MONDAY, MARCH 27, 1893.

EXECUTIVE COMMUNICATION.

The Vice-President laid before the Senate a letter of the Secretary of the Treasury, transmitting, in answer to a resolution of the Senate of February 27, 1893, a copy of the report made by the commission to select wool samples for the use of the custom-houses of the United States.

Ordered, That it lie on the table and be printed.

SENATOR FROM MONTANA.

Mr. Hoar, from the Committee on Privileges and Elections, to whom were referred the credentials of Lee Mantle, appointed a Senator by the governor of the State of Montana, submitted a report (No. 1) thereon, accompanied by the following resolution, for consideration:

Resolved, That Lee Mantle is entitled to be admitted to a seat as a Senator from the State of Montana.

Mr. Vance asked and obtained leave to submit at some future time the views of a minority of the Committee on Privileges and Elections to accompany the foregoing report, and to be printed in connection therewith.

SENATOR FROM WYOMING.

Mr. Hoar, from the Committee on Privileges and Elections, to whom were referred the credentials of Asahel C. Beckwith, appointed a Senator by the governor of the State of Wyoming, submitted a report (No. 2) thereon, accompanied by the following resolution, for consideration:

Resolved, That Asahel C. Beckwith is entitled to be admitted to a seat as a Senator from the State of Wyoming.

Mr. Vance asked and obtained leave to submit at some future time the views of a minority of the Committee on Privileges and Elections to accompany the foregoing report, and to be printed in connection therewith.

SENATOR FROM WASHINGTON.

Mr. Hoar, from the Committee on Privileges and Elections, to whom were referred the credentials of John B. Allen, appointed a Senator by the governor of the State of Washington, submitted a report (No. 3) thereon, accompanied by the following resolution for consideration:

Resolved, That John B. Allen is entitled to be admitted to a seat as a Senator from the State of Washington.

Mr. Vance asked and obtained leave to submit at some future time the views of a minority of the Committee on Privileges and Elections to accompany the foregoing report, and to be printed in connection therewith.

EXECUTION OF IMMIGRATION ACT.

Mr. Chandler submitted the following resolution for consideration; which was ordered to be printed:

Resolved, That the Secretary of the Treasury be directed to transmit to the Senate copies of any orders, regulations, and forms of lists, manifests, and certificates, prepared and issued by the Treasury Department in execution of the immigration act of March 3, 1893, together with copies of all correspondence concerning such orders, regulations, and forms between said Department and Government officials, steamship agents, and other persons.

INQUIRY BY COMMITTEE ON IMMIGRATION.

Mr. Chandler submitted the following resolution; which was referred to the Committee to Audit and Control the Contingent Expenses of the Senate, and ordered to be printed:

Resolved, That the Committee on Immigration be authorized and directed to make inquiry into the condition and character of the alien immigrants coming to the United States for the purpose of supplying labor for the coal, iron, and other mines of the country, and further to inquire whether the laws against the admission of laborers under contract are effectually enforced, and whether the immigration laws are economically administered, without an excessive force of officers, clerks, inspectors, special agents, and other employés, and also generally to inquire into the workings of the new immigration law of March 3, 1893, and prior immigration laws, and concerning any suspected evasion and violations thereof, for the purpose of which inquiry the committee may act as a full committee, or through subcommittees duly appointed by its chairman, and may take testimony during the recess of the Senate at such places as may be most convenient, and send for persons and papers and employ a stenographer, the expenses of the inquiry to be paid from the contingent fund of the Senate.

JOINT COMMISSION ON EXECUTIVE DEPARTMENTS.

On motion by Mr. Call,

The Senate proceeded to consider the resolution submitted by him on the 23d instant, declaring null and void the commission authorized by the act approved March 3, 1893, making appropriations for the legislative, executive, and judicial expenses of the Government for the fiscal year ending June 30, 1894, to inquire into and examine the status of the laws organizing the Executive Departments, bureaus, divisions, and other Government establishments at the national capital; and

After debate,

Ordered, That the further consideration thereof be postponed to to-morrow.

EXECUTIVE SESSION.

On motion by Mr. Coke,

The Senate proceeded to the consideration of executive business; and

After the consideration of executive business the doors were reopened, and

On motion by Mr. Gorman, at 2 o'clock and 20 minutes p. m., The Senate adjourned.

TUESDAY, MARCH 28, 1893.

EMPLOYMENT OF COMMITTEE CLERKS.

Mr. White, of Louisiana, from the Committee to Audit and Control the Contingent Expenses of the Senate, to whom was referred the resolution submitted by Mr. Voorhees on the 23d instant, to authorize the Select Committee on Additional Accommodations for the Library of Congress to employ a clerk, reported it with an amendment.

The Senate proceeded, by unanimous consent, to consider the said resolution; and the reported amendment having been agreed to, the resolution as amended was agreed to, as follows:

Resolved, That the Select Committee on Additional Accommodations for the Library of Congress be, and hereby is, authorized to sit during the recess of the Senate, and to employ a clerk.

Mr. White, of Louisiana, from the Committee to Audit and Control the Contingent Expenses of the Senate, to whom was referred the resolution submitted by Mr. Martin on the 20th instant, authorizing the Select Committee to Investigate the Geological Survey to employ a clerk, reported adversely thereon.

Ordered, That it be postponed indefinitely.

23 s

OFFICERS OF THE SENATE.

Mr. Gorman submitted the following resolutions; which were ordered to lie on the table and be printed:

Resolved, That the Senate do now proceed to the election of its Secretary, Sergeant-at-Arms and Doorkeeper, and Chaplain.

Resolved, That the officers to be elected, as aforesaid, shall, unless said offices become vacant in the meanwhile by death, resignation, or otherwise, only enter upon the discharge of their duties on the 30th day of June next, being the end of the present fiscal year, and the present incumbents of said offices as aforesaid shall continue to be the incumbents thereof, and exercise the duties of their respective offices until the end of the present fiscal year, as aforesaid, when the officers to be elected as hereinbefore provided shall, as hereinbefore stated, enter upon the discharge of their duties.

Mr. Gorman submitted the following resolution; which was ordered to lie on the table and be printed:

Resolved, That William R. Cox, of North Carolina, be, and he is hereby, elected Secretary of the Senate, his term of office to begin on the 30th day of June next, being the end of the present fiscal year, until which time the present incumbent shall continue to be Secretary of the Senate unless the office of Secretary becomes vacant by death, resignation, or otherwise, before the end of the present fiscal year, in which event the said William R. Cox shall be at once Secretary of the Senate, and enter upon the discharge of his duties as Secretary.

Mr. Gorman submitted the following resolution; which was ordered to lie on the table and be printed:

Resolved, That Richard J. Bright, of Indiana, be, and is hereby, elected Sergeant-at-Arms and Doorkeeper of the Senate, his term of office to begin on the 30th day of June next, being the end of the present fiscal year, until which time the present incumbent shall continue to be Sergeant-at-Arms and Doorkeeper, unless the office of Sergeant-at-Arms and Doorkeeper becomes vacant by death, resignation, or otherwise before the end of the present fiscal year, in which event the said Richard J. Bright shall be at once Sergeant-at-Arms and Doorkeeper of the Senate, and enter upon the discharge of his duties in said office.

Mr. Gorman submitted the following resolution; which was ordered to lie on the table and be printed:

Resolved, That William H. Milburn, D. D., of Illinois, be, and he is hereby, elected Chaplain of the Senate, his term of office to begin on the 30th day of June next, being the end of the present fiscal year, until which time the present incumbent shall continue to be Chaplain of the Senate, unless the office of Chaplain becomes vacant by death, resignation, or otherwise, before the end of the present fiscal year, in which event the said William H. Milburn, D. D., shall be at once Chaplain of the Senate, and enter upon the discharge of his duties as Chaplain.

SENATOR FROM NORTH DAKOTA.

Mr. Hoar submitted the following resolution for consideration; which was ordered to be printed:

Resolved, That the Committee on Privileges and Elections be directed to investigate the allegations recently extensively made in the public press, charging William N. Roach, a Senator from the State of North Dakota, with the offense of criminal embezzlement, to report the facts of the transactions referred to, and further, to report what is the duty of the Senate in regard thereto. For that purpose the committee shall have authority to send for persons and papers, to administer oaths, to employ a stenographer, and to act through a subcommittee.

REPORT OF THE CIVIL SERVICE COMMISSION.

Mr. Cockrell submitted the following resolution; which was considered by unanimous consent and agreed to:

Resolved, That the Public Printer be directed to inform the Senate as to the causes of delay in the printing of the last report of the Civil Service Commission.

EXECUTION OF THE IMMIGRATION ACT.

The Vice-President laid before the Senate the resolution yesterday submitted by Mr. Chandler, calling for copies of any orders, regulations, etc., prepared and issued by the Treasury Department in execution of the immigration act of March 3, 1893, together with copies of correspondence concerning the same and between said Department and Government officials, steamship agents, and other persons; and

Resolved, That the Senate agree thereto.

EXECUTIVE SESSION.

On motion by Mr. Harris,

The Senate proceeded to the consideration of executive business; and

After the consideration of executive business the doors were reopened, and

On motion by Mr. Butler, at 12 o'clock and 32 minutes p. m., The Senate adjourned.

WEDNESDAY, MARCH 29, 1893.

LETTER OF THE PUBLIC PRINTER.

The Vice-President laid before the Senate a letter of the Public Printer, communicating, in answer to a resolution of the Senate of the 28th instant, the causes for the delay in the printing of the last report of the Civil Service Commission.

Ordered, That it lie on the table and be printed.

MEMORIAL.

Mr. Teller presented a memorial of B. F. Rice, praying the appointment of a committee [to investigate the cause of the continuous financial depression throughout the country, and to ascertain how far the present mode of Federal taxation is responsible for such depression, and for appropriate legislation to correct any evils found to exist; which was referred to the Committee on Finance and ordered to be printed.

REPORTS OF COMMITTEE.

Mr. Gorman, from the Committee on Printing, to whom were referred the following resolutions, reported them severally without amendment and submitted written reports thereon as follows:

Resolution submitted by Mr. Proctor on the 9th instant, to print 5,000 copies of Senate bill No. 3824, to establish a national university; Report No. 4.

Resolution submitted by Mr. Chandler on the 9th instant, to print 2,000 copies of the act of March 3, 1893, to facilitate the enforcement of the immigration and contract-labor laws of the United States, and the report of the Senate thereon; Report No. 5.

Resolution submitted by Mr. Chandler on the 20th instant, to print 1,000 copies of Report No. 1333, of the Committee on Immigration, made at the second session of the Fifty-second Congress; Report No. 6.

Resolution submitted by Mr. Chandler on the 20th instant, to print 2,250 copies of Report No. 1286, of the Select Committee on Failed National Banks, made at the second session of the Fifty-second Congress; Report No. 7.

The Senate proceeded, by unanimous consent, to consider the said resolutions; and

Resolved, That the Senate agree thereto.

INTERSTATE COMMERCE INVESTIGATION.

Mr. Higgins submitted the following resolution; which was referred to the Committee on Interstate Commerce:

Resolved, That the Committee on Interstate Commerce be, and is hereby, authorized to inquire whether or not the methods prevailing in the transportation of freight and passengers over the great railroad lines of the country, and the conditions and the necessities of travelers and shippers and of the transportation companies justify or require a repeal or modification of section 5 of the interstate commerce act of February 4, 1887, which prohibits pooling under any circumstances; and that said committee be further authorized to inquire whether the system of closing and sealing cars engaged in transporting merchandise from one of the States of the Union into another State through foreign territory, or from such territory into any State, or from such territory through the United States into foreign territory, or any system of bonding merchandise so transported, needs to be abolished, modified, or further regulated by law, and whether all railroads engaged in such traffic should either be required to conform to all the provisions of the said interstate commerce act, or be prohibited from continuing such transportation business; the said committee being hereby empowered to sit during the recess of the Senate, to act by subcommittees if deemed necessary, to take testimony at convenient points, to send for witnesses, books, and papers, and employ a stenographer, and to have its expenses paid from the contingent fund of the Senate.

REPORT ON PHOSPHATES.

Mr. Call submitted the following resolution; which was referred to the Committee on Printing:

Resolved, That the number of copies authorized by law of the report of the Commissioner of Labor on phosphates, made by direction of the Senate, shall be printed.

SENATOR FROM MONTANA.

On motion by Mr. Hoar,

The Senate proceeded to consider the resolution reported from the Committee on Privileges and Elections on the 27th instant, declaring Lee Mantle entitled to be admitted to a seat in the Senate from the State of Montana; and

Pending debate,

CHARGES AGAINST SENATOR POWER.

Mr. Power, by unanimous consent, rose to a question of privilege and referred to certain aspersions cast upon him by the public press, and also to certain remarks made upon the floor of the Senate, and asked for an investigation by a special committee;

Whereupon,

Mr. Chandler, by unanimous consent, submitted the following resolution for consideration; which was ordered to be printed:

Resolved, That the request of the Senator from Montana, that an investigation be made into the facts alleged against him in the public press, be referred to the Committee on Privileges and Elections.

EXECUTIVE SESSION.

On motion by Mr. Gorman, that the Senate proceed to the consideration of executive business,

Mr. Manderson raised a question of order, viz: That, pending the consideration of a resolution for the admission of a Senator, which, being privileged, and under Rule VI must be proceeded with until disposed of, no other business, either legislative or executive, could intervene, except by unanimous consent, and the motion was not in order.

The Vice-President overruled the point of order; and

On the question to agree to the motion of Mr. Gorman,

It was determined in the affirmative.

Whereupon,

The Senate proceeded to the consideration of executive business; and,

After the consideration of executive business the doors were reopened, and

On motion by Mr. Harris, at 3 o'clock and 26 minutes p. m.,

The Senate adjourned.

THURSDAY, MARCH 30, 1893.

Mr. Manderson raised a question as to the presence of a quorum;

Whereupon,

The Vice-President directed the roll to be called;

When,

Forty-seven Senators answered to their names.

A quorum being present,

SENATORS FROM MONTANA.

The Vice-President laid before the Senate the resolution reported from the Committee on Privileges and Elections on the 27th instant declaring Lee Mantle entitled to a seat in the Senate from the State of Montana; and

The Senate resumed the consideration of the resolution;

Pending which,

Mr. Chandler, by unanimous consent, withdrew the resolution yesterday submitted by him to refer the request of the Senator from Montana for an investigation into certain allegations against him made in the public press to the Committee on Privileges and Elections; and

He submitted, in lieu thereof, the following resolution for consideration; which was ordered to be printed:

Resolved, That the Committee on Privileges and Elections be, and hereby is, directed to investigate the statements derogatory to the Senator from Montana (Mr. Power) contained in the Washington Post of Wednesday, March 29, 1893, and to report whether any, and if so, what action should be taken thereon by the Senate; and said committee is hereby empowered to send for and examine persons and papers, to employ a stenographer, and to have its expenses paid from the contingent fund of the Senate.

LEAVE OF ABSENCE.

Mr. Teller, at his own request, was granted leave of absence for the remainder of the present session.

WITHDRAWAL OF PAPERS.

On motion by Mr. Cullom, and by unanimous consent,

Ordered, That Maria N. Flint have leave to withdraw her papers from the files of the Senate.

On motion by Mr. Dolph, and by unanimous consent,

Ordered, That Arthur M. Thorp have leave to withdraw his papers from the files of the Senate.

INDIAN DEPREDATION CLAIMS.

Mr. Kyle, from the Committee on Indian Depredations, to whom was referred the resolution submitted by him on the 20th instant, directing said committee to make inquiry concerning all Indian depredation claims which at any time have been or may be presented in the Court of Claims under the act of March 3, 1891, reported it without amendment; and

On motion by Mr. Kyle,

Ordered, That the resolution be referred to the Committee to Audit and Control the Contingent Expenses of the Senate.

ADJOURNMENT TO MONDAY.

On motion by Mr. Harris,

Ordered, That when the Senate adjourn it be to Monday next.

EXECUTIVE SESSION.

On motion by Mr. Gorman,

The Senate proceeded to the consideration of executive business; and

After the consideration of executive business the doors were reopened, and

On motion by Mr. Gorman, at 4 o'clock and 7 minutes p. m.,

The Senate adjourned.

MONDAY, APRIL 3, 1893.

SENATOR FROM MONTANA.

The Vice-President laid before the Senate the resolution reported from the Committee on Privileges and Elections, March 27, 1893, declaring Lee Mantle entitled to a seat in the Senate from the State of Montana; and

The Senate resumed the consideration of the resolution;

Pending which,

PETITIONS AND MEMORIALS.

Mr. Hoar presented a petition of Joseph W. Ady, claiming a seat in the Senate as Senator from the State of Kansas for the term ending March 3, 1895; which was referred to the Committee on Privileges and Elections.

Mr. Hoar, by unanimous consent, presented a petition of Albert A. Pope, of Boston, Mass., praying that a subcommittee of the Committee on Agriculture and Forestry be instructed to make an extended tour throughout the country for the purpose of investigating the subject of wagon roads in relation to the agricultural interests of the country; which was referred to the Committee on Agriculture and Forestry and ordered to be printed.

Mr. Stewart, by unanimous consent, presented a resolution of the legislature of the State of Nevada in favor of legislation providing for the adjustment or refunding of the indebtedness of the Central Pacific Railroad Company; which was referred to the Committee on Pacific Railroads and ordered to be printed.

SPEECHES IN CONGRESS.

Mr. Hoar, by unanimous consent, submitted the following resolution; which was referred to the Committee on Printing:

Resolved, That the Public Printer be directed to deposit in the Senate Library ten copies each of all speeches made in either House of Congress, which shall hereafter be by him printed in pamphlet form; the same to be bound, under the direction of the Senate Committee on Printing, and preserved in said library for the use of the Senate.

AMENDMENT OF THE CONSTITUTION—ELECTION OF SENATORS.

Mr. Hoar, by unanimous consent, submitted the following resolution; which was ordered to lie on the table and be printed:

Resolved, That it is inexpedient that the resolution sent to the Senate by the House of Representatives during the last Congress, providing for an amendment of the Constitution securing the election of Senators by the people of the several States be adopted.

Such a method of election would essentially change the character of the Senate as conceived by the convention that framed the Constitution and the people who adopted it.

It would transfer, practically, the selection of the members of this body from the legislatures who are intrusted with all legislative powers of the States to bodies having no other responsibilities, whose election can not be regulated by law, whose members act by proxy, whose tenure of office is for a single day, whose votes and proceedings are not recorded, who act under no personal responsibility, whose mistakes, ordinarily, can only be corrected by the choice of Senators who do not represent the opinions concerning public measures and policies of the people who choose them.

It requires the substitution of pluralities for majorities in the election.

It will transfer the seat of political power in great States, now distributed evenly over their territory, to the great cities and masses of population.

It will create new temptations to fraud, corruption, and other illegal practices, and in close cases will give rise to numerous election contests which must tend seriously to weaken the confidence of the people in the Senate.

It will absolve the larger States from the constitutional obligation which secures the equal representation of all the States in the Senate by providing that no State shall be deprived of that equality without its consent.

It implies what the whole current of our history shows to be untrue, that the Senate has during the past century failed to meet the just expectations of the people, and that the State legislatures have proved themselves unfit to be the depositaries of the power of electing Senators.

The reasons which require this change, if acted upon and carried to their logical result, will lead to the election by the direct popular vote, and by popular majorities, of the President and of the judiciary, and will compel the placing of these elections under complete national control.

It will result in the overthrow of the whole scheme of the Senate and, in the end, of the whole scheme of the national Constitution as designed and established by the framers of the Constitution and the people who adopted it.

DEEP-WATER HARBOR ON PACIFIC COAST.

Mr. Ransom, by unanimous consent, submitted the following resolution; which was referred to the Committee to Audit and Control the Contingent Expenses of the Senate:

Resolved, That the Committee on Commerce be, and they are here-by, authorized and directed to sit, by subcommittee not exceeding five in number, to be appointed by the chairman of said committee, during the recess of Congress, and to visit and examine the Pacific coast between Points Duma and Capistrano, with a view to determining the best location for the construction of a deep-water harbor. Said subcommittee is hereby also authorized to visit and examine such other works of river and harbor improvement on the Pacific coast, existing or proposed, as in their judgment the interests of commerce shall demand, and shall have power to subpoena witnesses, to administer oaths and take testimony, to employ a stenographer, and to appoint a sergeant-at-arms from the messengers of the Senate; and that the actual necessary expenses of the said subcommittee, properly incurred, shall be paid out of the contingent fund of the Senate in the usual manner.

EXECUTIVE SESSION.

On motion by Mr. Vest,

The Senate proceeded to the consideration of executive business; and

After the consideration of executive business the doors were reopened, and

On motion by Mr. Sherman, at 3 o'clock and 7 minutes p. m.,

The Senate adjourned.

TUESDAY, APRIL 4, 1893.

SENATOR FROM MONTANA.

The Vice-President laid before the Senate the resolution reported from the Committee on Privileges and Elections, March 27, 1893, declaring that Lee Mantle is entitled to a seat in the Senate from the State of Montana;

When,

Mr. Hoar raised a question as to the presence of a quorum;

Whereupon,

The Vice-President directed the roll to be called;

When,

Forty-five Senators answered to their names.

A quorum being present,

The Senate resumed the consideration of the resolution declaring Lee Mantle entitled to a seat in the Senate.

Pending debate,

On motion by Mr. Vance,

The Senate proceeded to the consideration of executive business; and

After the consideration of executive business the doors were reopened, and

On motion by Mr. Gorman, at 1 o'clock and 42 minutes p. m.,

The Senate adjourned.

WEDNESDAY, APRIL 5, 1893.

SENATOR FROM MONTANA.

The Vice-President laid before the Senate the resolution reported from the Committee on Privileges and Elections, March 27, 1893, declaring that Lee Mantle is entitled to a seat in the Senate from the State of Montana;

When,

Mr. Hoar raised a question as to the presence of a quorum;

Whereupon,

The Vice-President directed the roll to be called;

When,

Forty-four Senators answered to their names.

A quorum being present,

The Senate resumed the consideration of the resolution declaring Lee Mantle entitled to a seat in the Senate; and

Pending debate, by unanimous consent,

COST OF IRON AND STEEL PRODUCTS.

Mr. White, of Louisiana, from the Committee to Audit and Control the Contingent Expenses of the Senate, to whom was referred the resolution reported by Mr. McPherson, from the Committee on Finance, March 22, 1893, calling for information concerning the cost of producing certain iron and steel products, etc., and to make investigations respecting the same, reported it without amendment.

DEEP-WATER HARBOR ON THE PACIFIC COAST.

Mr. White, of Louisiana, from the Committee to Audit and Control the Contingent Expenses of the Senate, to whom was referred the resolution submitted by Mr. Ransom on the 3d instant, directing the Committee on Commerce to make certain investigations with a view to determining the best location of a deep-water harbor on the Pacific coast, reported it with an amendment, viz: Strike out all after the word *Resolved,* and in lieu thereof insert the following:

That the Committee on Commerce be, and they are hereby, authorized and directed to sit, by subcommittee not exceeding five in number, to be appointed by the chairman of said committee, during the recess of Congress, and to visit and examine the Pacific coast between Points Duma and Capistrano, with a view to determining the best location for the construction of a deep-water harbor. Said subcommittee is hereby also authorized to visit and examine such other works of river and harbor improvement on the Pacific coast, existing or proposed, as in their judgment the interests of commerce shall demand, and shall have power to subpœna witnesses, to administer oaths and take testimony, to employ a stenographer, and to appoint a sergeant-at-arms from the messengers of the Senate; and that the actual necessary expenses of the said subcommittee, properly incurred, shall be paid out of the contingent fund of the Senate in the usual manner: Provided, That no compensation be paid for a clerk to said subcommittee, the chairman being authorized, if necessary, to detail the regular clerk of said committee to attend the said subcommittee, the clerk so assigned to receive no extra allowance or compensation.

INDIAN DEPREDATION CLAIMS.

Mr. White, of Louisiana, from the Committee to Audit and Control the Contingent Expenses of the Senate, to whom was referred the resolution submitted by Mr. Kyle, March 20, 1893, directing the Committee on Indian Depredations to make certain inquiries concerning Indian depredation claims, reported it with an amendment.

The Senate proceeded, by unanimous consent, to consider the said resolution; and the reported amendment having been agreed to, the resolution as amended was agreed to, as follows:

Resolved, That the Committee on Indian Depredations be, and hereby is, directed to make inquiry concerning all Indian depredation claims which at any time have been or may be presented in the Court of Claims under the act of March 3, 1891, especially those in which unpaid judgments have been hitherto rendered, or may be rendered prior to the conclusion of the inquiry; and also into the manner in which such claims have been defended in behalf of the Indians and the United States; and generally into the workings of said act of March 3, 1891; and concerning all other Indian depredation claims not covered by said act, and to make such recommendatious relative to any or all of said claims and for additional legislation as said committee may deem expedient; said committee, either as a full committee or through subcommittees, being hereby empowered to sit during the recess of the Senate, to send for persons and papers, and to employ a stenographer and expert, the expenses of the inquiry to be paid from the contingent fund of the Senate: *Provided,* That no extra expense be incurred for a clerk to said committee, any clerical work required by the committee or subcommittee to be performed by the regular clerk of the committee without extra allowance or compensation.

INQUIRY BY COMMITTEE ON IMMIGRATION.

Mr. White, of Louisiana, from the Committee to Audit and Control the Contingent Expenses of the Senate, to whom was referred the resolution submitted by Mr. Chandler, March 27, 1893, directing the Committee on Immigration to make inquiry into the condition and character of the alien immigrants coming to the United States for the purpose of supplying labor for the coal, iron, and other mines of the country, reported it with an amendment.

The Senate proceeded, by unanimous consent, to consider the said resolution; and the reported amendment having been agreed to, the resolution as amended was agreed to, as follows:

Resolved, That the Committee on Immigration be authorized and directed to make inquiry into the condition and character of the alien immigrants coming to the United States for the purpose of supplying labor for the coal, iron, and other mines of the country; and further to inquire whether the laws against the admission of laborers under contract are effectually enforced, and whether the immigration laws are economically administered, without an excessive force of officers, clerks, inspectors, special agents, and other employés; and also generally to inquire into the workings of the new immigration law of March 3, 1893, and prior immigration laws, and concerning any suspected evasions and violations thereof; for the purpose of which inquiry the committee may act as a full committee or through subcommittees duly appointed by its chairman, and may take testimony during the recess of the Senate at such places as may be most convenient, and send for persons and papers, and employ a stenographer, the expenses of the inquiry to be paid from the contingent fund of the Senate: *Provided,* That no extra expense be incurred for a clerk to said committee, any clerical work required by the committee or subcommittee to be performed by the regular clerk of the committee without extra allowance or compensation.

COMMITTEE ON PRINTING.

Mr. Gorman submitted the following resolution; which was considered by unanimous consent and agreed to:

Resolved, That the Committee on Printing be, and is hereby, authorized to sit during the coming recess for the performance of any and all duties devolving upon it.

CUTTING OF TIMBER IN THE BLACK HILLS DISTRICT.

Mr. Kyle submitted the following resolution; which was considered by unanimous consent and agreed to:

Resolved, That the Secretary of the Interior be directed to furnish for the Senate copies of all reports and correspondence relating to the unlawful cutting of timber on public mineral lands in the district known as the Black Hills, South Dakota.

INVESTIGATION OF THE CIVIL SERVICE.

Mr. Call submitted the following resolution; which was referred to the Committee to Audit and Control the Contingent Expenses of the Senate:

Resolved, That the Committee on Civil Service and Retrenchment be, and is hereby, directed to sit during the recess of Congress, either as an entire committee or as a subcommittee, to examine and investigate the civil service of the United States, and report by bill or otherwise the legislation proper for its reformation or change, and shall have power to send for and examine persons and papers, to employ a stenographer, and to have its expenses paid from the contingent fund of the Senate.

REPORTS OF THE CITIZENS' NATIONAL BANK.

Mr. Chandler submitted the following resolution for consideration:

Resolved, That the Secretary of the Treasury be, and he is hereby, directed to transmit to the Senate copies of all reports of the Citizens' National Bank of Washington, D. C., from 1875 to 1882, inclusive, and of any reports that may have been made by the bank examiners as to the condition of the said bank during that period.

EXECUTIVE SESSION.

On motion by Mr. Vance,
The Senate proceeded to the consideration of executive business; and

After the consideration of executive business the doors were reopened, and

On motion by Mr. Faulkner, at 3 o'clock and 18 minutes p. m.,
The Senate adjourned.

THURSDAY, APRIL 6, 1893.

ELECTION OF OFFICERS OF THE SENATE.

On motion by Mr. Gorman, and by unanimous consent,
The Senate proceeded to consider the resolutions submitted by him, March 28, 1893, providing for the election of officers of the Senate, and fixing the time at which their terms of office shall commence; and

The resolution having been modified by Mr. Gorman,
Mr. Hoar raised a question as to the presence of a quorum;
Whereupon,
The Vice-President directed the roll to be called;
When,
Forty-seven Senators answered to their names.
A quorum being present,
By unanimous consent the further consideration of the resolutions was postponed until 2 o'clock p. m.

INQUIRY BY COMMITTEE ON TERRITORIES.

Mr. Carey, from the Committee on Territories, by unanimous consent, reported the following resolution; which was referred to the Committee to Audit and Control the Contingent Expenses of the Senate:

Resolved, That the Committee on Territories, or any subcommittee thereof appointed for the purpose, are hereby authorized during the recess of Congress to visit the Territories of New Mexico, Arizona, Utah, and Oklahoma for the purpose of obtaining information with regard to the resources, population, and condition of said Territories, and as to the propriety of the admission of the same as States, and that the expenses of said committee be paid out of the contingent fund of the Senate.

COST OF IRON AND STEEL PRODUCTS.

On motion by Mr. McPherson, and by unanimous consent,
The Senate proceeded to consider the resolution reported by him from the Committee on Finance, March 22, 1893, calling for information relative to the cost of production of various iron and steel products; and

The resolution was agreed to, as follows:

Resolved, That the Commissioner of Labor is hereby directed to make a report to the Senate at the opening of the Fifty-third Congress comprehending the facts already collected by him, or to be obtained from other sources, of the total cost, including all the elements thereof, and also actual labor cost, of producing various iron and steel products, such as bar iron, steel rails, and other articles of iron and steel; and also the leading articles of textile industry, and of such other articles for which the cost of production has been or may be approximately obtained, and in his report to state the facts in parallel columns for this and other countries from which they have been or may be obtained; and that the Committee on Finance, or any subcommittee thereof, is hereby authorized to make such further investigation in respect to the same matters as it shall deem important, and with power to summon and examine witnesses, to send for persons and papers, and to administer oaths; and the expenses of such investigations, when made by said Finance Committee, shall be paid out of the contingent fund of the Senate.

SENATOR FROM MONTANA.

The Senate resumed the consideration of the resolution reported from the Committee on Privileges and Elections, March 27, 1893, declaring Lee Mantle entitled to a seat in the Senate from the State of Montana; and

Pending debate,

ELECTION OF OFFICERS OF THE SENATE.

The hour of 2 o'clock having arrived,

The Senate, by unanimous consent, resumed the consideration of the resolutions providing for the election of officers of the Senate; and

After debate,

The resolutions, as modified, were agreed to, as follows:

Resolved, That the Senate do now proceed to the election of its Secretary, Sergeant-at-Arms and Doorkeeper, and Chaplain.

Resolved, That the officers to be elected as aforesaid shall, unless said offices become vacant in the meanwhile, only enter upon the discharge of their duties on the first day of the meeting of the Fifty-third Congress, whether in extraordinary or regular session, and the present incumbents of said offices as aforesaid shall continue to be the incumbents thereof and exercise the duties of their respective offices until the said first day of the meeting of the Fifty-third Congress as aforesaid, when the officers to be elected as hereinabove provided shall, as hereinabove stated, enter upon the discharge of their duties.

ELECTION OF SECRETARY.

On motion by Mr. Gorman, and by unanimous consent,

The Senate proceeded to consider the resolution submitted by him, March 28, 1893, for the election of William R. Cox, of North Carolina, as Secretary of the Senate; and having been modified by Mr. Gorman.

The resolution, as modified, was agreed to, as follows:

Resolved, That William R. Cox, of North Carolina, be, and he is hereby, elected Secretary of the Senate, his term of office to begin on the first day of the meeting of the Fifty-third Congress, whether in extraordinary or regular session, until which time the present incumbent shall continue to be Secretary of the Senate, unless the office of Secretary becomes vacant before the said first day of the meeting of the Fifty-third Congress, in which event the said William R. Cox shall be at once Secretary of the Senate and enter upon the discharge of his duties as Secretary.

ELECTION OF SERGEANT-AT-ARMS AND DOORKEEPER.

On motion by Mr. Gorman, and by unanimous consent,

The Senate proceeded to consider the resolution submitted by him, March 28, 1893, for the election of Richard J. Bright, of Indiana, as Sergeant-at-Arms and Doorkeeper of the Senate; and having been modified by Mr. Gorman.

The resolution, as modified, was agreed to, as follows:

Resolved, That Richard J. Bright, of Indiana, be, and is hereby, elected Sergeant-at-Arms and Doorkeeper of the Senate, his term of office to begin on the first day of the meeting of the Fifty-third Congress, whether in extraordinary or regular session, until which time the present incumbent shall continue to be Sergeant-at-Arms and Doorkeeper, unless the office of Sergeant-at-Arms and Doorkeeper becomes vacant before the said first day of the meeting of the Fifty-third Congress, in which event the said Richard J. Bright shall be at once Sergeant-at-Arms and Doorkeeper of the Senate and enter upon the discharge of his duties in said office.

ELECTION OF CHAPLAIN.

On motion by Mr. Gorman, and by unanimous consent,

The Senate proceeded to consider the resolution submitted by him, March 28, 1893, for the election of William H. Milburn, D. D., of Illinois, as Chaplain of the Senate; and having been modified by Mr. Gorman.

The resolution, as modified, was agreed to, as follows:

Resolved, That William H. Milburn, doctor of divinity, of Illinois, be, and he is hereby, elected Chaplain of the Senate, his term of office to begin on the first day of the meeting of the Fifty-third Congress, whether in extraordinary or regular session, until which time the present incumbent shall continue to be Chaplain of the Senate, unless the office of Chaplain becomes vacant before the said first day of the meeting of the Fifty-third Congress, in which event the said William H. Milburn, doctor of divinity, shall be at once Chaplain of the Senate, and enter upon the discharge of his duties as Chaplain.

MODE OF ELECTION OF SENATORS.

On motion by Mr. Hoar, and by unanimous consent,

The Senate proceeded to consider the resolution submitted by him on the 3d instant, declaring that it is inexpedient that the resolution sent to the Senate by the House of Representatives during the last Congress, providing for an amendment to the Constitution, securing the election of Senators by the people of the several States, be adopted; and

Pending debate,

On motion by Mr. Gorman,

The Senate proceeded to the consideration of executive business; and

After the consideration of executive business the doors were reopened, and

On motion by Mr. Gray, at 2 o'clock and 50 minutes p. m.,

The Senate adjourned.

FRIDAY, APRIL 7, 1893.

EXECUTIVE COMMUNICATION.

The Vice-President laid before the Senate a letter of the Secretary of the Treasury, transmitting, in answer to a resolution of the Senate of March 28, 1893, copies of all orders, regulations, etc., prepared and issued by the Treasury Department in execution of the immigration act of March 3, 1893, together with copies of all correspondence covering the same and between said Department and Government officials, steamboat agents, and other persons; which was referred to the Committee on Immigration and ordered to be printed.

Mr. Chandler presented correspondence with the Secretary of the Treasury in relation to the regulation of immigration; which was ordered to be printed as an appendix to the foregoing letter and referred to the same committee.

QUESTION OF QUORUM.

Mr. Chandler raised a question as to the presence of a quorum;

Whereupon,

The Vice-President directed the roll to be called;

When,

Forty-seven Senators answered to their names.

A quorum being present,

REPORT OF CIVIL SERVICE COMMISSION.

Mr. Cockrell, by unanimous consent, submitted the following resolution; which was considered by unanimous consent and agreed to.

Resolved, That the United States Civil Service Commission is hereby directed to report to the Senate the cause of delay in furnishing the Public Printer with the copy for the completion of the publication of their last annual report.

INQUIRY BY COMMITTEE ON INTERSTATE COMMERCE.

Mr. Voorhees, by unanimous consent, submitted the following resolution; which was referred to the Committee on Interstate Commerce and ordered to be printed:

Whereas the tenth section of the act of Congress approved February 4, 1887, known as the interstate-commerce act, contains the following enactment:

"That any common carrier subject to the provisions of this act, or, whenever such common carrier is a corporation, any director or officer thereof, or any receiver, trustee, lessee, agent, or person acting for or employed by such corporation, who, alone or with any other corporation, company, person, or party, shall willfully do or cause to be done, or shall willingly suffer or permit to be done, any act, matter, or thing in this act prohibited or declared to be unlawful, or who shall aid or abet therein, or shall willfully omit or fail to do any act, matter, or thing in this act required to be done, or shall cause or willingly suffer or permit any act, matter, or thing so directed or required by this act to be done not to be so done, or shall aid or abet any such omission or failure, or shall be guilty of any infraction of this act, or shall aid or abet therein, shall be deemed guilty of a misdemeanor, and shall, upon conviction thereof in any district court of the United States within the jurisdiction of which such offense was committed, be subject to a fine of not to exceed $5,000 for each offense;"

And whereas it is alleged that said section of the law as it now stands has been construed by the judges of the circuit and district courts of the United States in recent decisions at Toledo, Ohio, to mean that "the duties of an employé of a public corporation are such that he can not always choose his own time for quitting that service," but that in attempting to leave the employment of such corporation of his own free will and to escape from its control and consequent servitude, such employé is guilty of a misdemeanor and liable to severe penalties: Therefore,

Resolved, That the Interstate Commerce Committee of the Senate be, and is hereby, instructed to inquire into the question here presented and to report to this body what action may be necessary, either by the repeal of said tenth section of the existing law, or by the enactment of additional legislation for the better protection of the laboring people of the United States in their natural and inalienable rights, and for their greater security from the encroachments of corporation power.

DEEP-WATER HARBOR ON PACIFIC COAST.

On motion by Mr. Ransom, and by unanimous consent,

The Senate proceeded to consider the resolution submitted by him on the 3d instant, directing the Committee on Commerce to make certain investigations with a view to determining the best location for the construction of a deep-water harbor on the Pacific coast: and the amendment reported by the Committee to Audit and Control the Contingent Expenses of the Senate having been agreed to, the resolution as amended was agreed to, as follows:

Resolved, That the Committee on Commerce be, and they are hereby, authorized and directed to sit, by subcommittee not exceeding five in number, to be appointed by the chairman of said committee, during the recess of Congress, and to visit and examine the Pacific coasts between Points Duma and Capistrano, with a view to determining the best location for the construction of a deep-water harbor. Said subcommittee is hereby also authorized to visit and examine such other works of river and harbor improvement on the Pacific coast, existing or proposed, as in their judgment the interests of commerce shall demand, and shall have power to subpœna witnesses, to administer oaths and take testimony, to employ a stenographer, and to appoint a sergeant-at-arms from the messengers of the Senate; and that the actual necessary expenses of the said subcommittee, properly incurred, shall be paid out of the contingent fund of the Senate in the usual manner: *Provided,* That no compensation be paid for a clerk to said subcommittee, the chairman being authorized, if necessary, to detail the regular clerk of said committee to said subcommittee, the clerk so assigned to receive no extra allowance or compensation.

ELECTION OF SENATORS.

The Senate resumed, by unanimous consent, the consideration of the resolution submitted by Mr. Hoar on the 3d instant, declaring that it is inexpedient that the resolution sent to the Senate by the House of Representatives during the last Congress, providing for an amendment to the Constitution, securing the election of Senators by the people of the several States, be adopted; and

After debate,

SENATOR FROM MONTANA.

The Senate resumed the consideration of the resolution reported from the Committee on Privileges and Elections, March 27, 1893, declaring Lee Mantle entitled to a seat in the Senate from the State of Montana;

Pending which,

EXECUTIVE SESSION.

On motion by Mr. Sherman,
The Senate proceeded to the consideration of executive business; and

After the consideration of executive business the doors were reopened, and

On motion by Mr. Butler, at 2 o'clock and 15 minutes p. m.,
The Senate adjourned.

SATURDAY, APRIL 8, 1893.

SENATOR FROM MONTANA.

The Vice-President laid before the Senate the resolution reported from the Committee on Privileges and Elections, March 27, 1893, declaring Lee Mantle entitled to a seat in the Senate from the State of Montana;

Pending which,
On motion by Mr. Martin, and by unanimous consent,

WITHDRAWAL OF PAPERS.

Ordered, That Lucy A. Dewey have leave to withdraw her petition and papers from the files of the Senate.

MEMBERSHIP OF CERTAIN COMMITTEES.

On motion by Mr. Call, and by unanimous consent,
The Senate proceeded to consider the resolution submitted by him, March 20, 1893, to increase the membership of certain committees of the Senate; and

The resolution having been modified by Mr. Call to read as follows: *Resolved,* That the Committees on Finance, Naval Affairs, Military Affairs, Judiciary, Foreign Relations, Appropriations, Commerce, and Interstate Commerce shall each consist of fifteen members,

On motion by Mr. Faulkner,
The Senate proceeded to the consideration of executive business; and

After the consideration of executive business the doors were reopened, and

On motion by Mr. Gorman, at 12 o'clock and 40 minutes p. m.,
The Senate adjourned.

MONDAY, APRIL 10, 1893.

SENATOR FROM MONTANA.

The Vice-President laid before the Senate the resolution reported by Mr. Hoar from the Committee on Privileges and Elections, March 27, 1893, declaring Lee Mantle entitled to a seat in the Senate from the State of Montana;

Pending which, and by unanimous consent,

PETITION AND MEMORIAL.

Mr. Peffer presented a petition of the National Citizens' Industrial Alliance, praying legislation to relieve the people from the un-

just and extortionate rates and charges of the Bell Telephone Company monopoly; which was referred to the Committee on Interstate Commerce.

Mr. Hoar presented a memorial of Joseph W. Ady, praying an investigation of the election of United States Senator from the State of Kansas, to fill the vacancy caused by the death of the late Preston B. Plumb; which was referred to the Committee on Privileges and Elections and ordered to be printed.

INQUIRY BY THE COMMITTEE ON INTERSTATE COMMERCE.

Mr. Butler, from the Committee on Interstate Commerce, to whom were referred the resolution submitted by Mr. Higgins, March 29, 1893, and the resolution submitted by Mr. Voorhees on the 7th instant, directing the said committee to inquire into certain questions relative to the operation of the interstate commerce act, reported in lieu thereof the following resolution; which was referred to the Committee to Audit and Control the Contingent Expenses of the Senate and ordered to be printed:

Resolved, That the Committee on Interstate Commerce be, and is hereby, authorized to inquire whether or not the methods prevailing in the transportation of freight and passengers over the great railroad lines of the country and the conditions and necessities of travelers and shippers and of the transportation companies justify or require a repeal or modification of section 5 of the interstate-commerce act of February 4, 1887, which prohibits pooling under any circumstances; and that said committee be further authorized to inquire whether the system of closing and sealing cars engaged in transporting merchandise from one of the States of the Union into another State through foreign territory, or from such territory into any State, or from such territory through the United States into foreign territory, or any system of bonding merchandise so transported, needs to be modified, or further regulated by law, and whether all railroads engaged in such traffic should either be required to conform to all the provisions of the said interstate-commerce act or be prohibited from continuing such transportation business; and whether any modifications should be made of the existing provisions of law concerning the relations between common carriers and their employés; the said committee being hereby empowered to sit during the recess of the Senate, to act by subcommittees, if deemed necessary, to take testimony at convenient points, to send for witnesses, books, and papers, and employ a stenographer, and to have its expenses paid from the contingent fund of the Senate; and it is expressly provided that no additional expense whatever shall be allowed for clerical hire under the terms of this resolution.

SENATOR FROM NORTH DAKOTA.

Mr. Hoar submitted the following resolution for consideration; which was ordered to be printed:

Resolved, That the Committee on Privileges and Elections be directed to examine the allegations recently made in the public press charging William N. Roach, a Senator from the State of North Dakota, with certain criminal offenses committed while cashier or officer of a bank in the city of Washington, and to ascertain the facts and circumstances so far as to enable the committee to determine and report what are the duty and power of the Senate in regard thereto; and for that purpose the committee shall have authority to send for persons and papers, to employ a stenographer, to sit during the recess of the Senate, and to act through a subcommittee; and its expenses shall be paid from the contingent fund of the Senate.

INVESTIGATION BY COMMITTEE ON INDIAN AFFAIRS.

Mr. Jones, of Arkansas, submitted the following resolution for consideration; which was ordered to be printed:

Resolved, That the Committee on Indian Affairs be instructed, either by full committee or such subcommittee or committees as may be appointed by the chairman thereof, with the full power of such committee to continue, during the recess of Congress, the investigations authorized by the resolutions of May 13, 1890, and February 27, 1891, with the authority and in the manner and to the extent provided in said resolutions, and in the pursuance of such investigations to visit the several Indian reservations, Indian schools supported in whole or in part by the Government, and the five nations in the Indian Territory, or any reservation where, in the opinion of said committee, it may be necessary to extend their investigations.

2. That said committee or subcommittee shall have power to send for persons and papers, to administer oaths, and to examine witnesses under oath touching the matters which they are hereby empowered to investigate, and may hold their sessions during the recess of the Senate at such place or places as they may determine; and the necessary and proper expense incurred in the execution of this order shall be paid out of the contingent fund of the Senate upon vouchers approved by the chairman of said committee.

ADJOURNMENT WITHOUT DAY.

Mr. Harris submitted the following resolution; which was considered by unanimous consent and agreed to:

Resolved, That a committee consisting of two Senators be appointed by the Chair to wait upon the President of the United States and inform him that, unless he may have some further communication to make, the Senate is ready to adjourn without day.

Mr. Hoar entered a motion that the Senate reconsider its vote agreeing to the foregoing resolution.

SENATOR FROM MONTANA.

Mr. Chandler submitted the following resolution for consideration; which was ordered to be printed:

Resolved, That the Committee on Privileges and Elections be, and hereby is, directed to examine the statements derogatory to the Senator from Montana, Mr. Power, contained in the Washington Post of Wednesday, March 29, 1893, and to ascertain the facts and circumstances so far as to enable the committee to determine and report what are the duty and power of the Senate in regard thereto; and said committee is hereby empowered to sit during the recess of the Senate, to send for persons and papers, to employ a stenographer, to act through a subcommittee, and to have its expenses paid from the contingent fund of the Senate.

INVESTIGATION BY THE COMMITTEE ON AGRICULTURE AND FORESTRY.

Mr. George submitted the following resolution for consideration; which was ordered to be printed:

Resolved, That the Secretary of the Senate be, and he is hereby, instructed to set apart for the investigation of the condition of agriculture in the United States, etc., as directed by the resolution of the Senate to be made by the Committee on Agriculture and Forestry, the sum of $5,000, $1,000 of which to be paid out of the contingent fund available for the present fiscal year and the remainder out of the contingent fund for the next fiscal year.

PHOTOGRAPHIC COPIES OF CERTAIN EXECUTIVE COMMUNICATIONS.

Mr. Blackburn, from the Committee on Rules, to whom was referred the resolution submitted by Mr. Allison, March 20, 1893, authorizing the Secretary of the Senate to allow photographic copies to be made of certain ancient executive communications, reported it with an amendment.

The Senate proceeded, by unanimous consent, to consider the said resolution; and the reported amendment having been agreed to, the resolution as amended was agreed to, as follows:

Resolved, That the Secretary of the Senate be, and he is hereby, directed to allow, under his supervision and subject to his directions, the representative of the Department of Justice on the board of management of the World's Columbian Exposition to have photographic copies made of certain ancient executive communications on file in the archives of the United States Senate, for exhibition at the World's Columbian Exposition, as follows: The nominations by the President of the Chief Justice and the associate justices of the Supreme Court of the United States, embraced in Nos. 1, 2, 3, 6, 7, 14, 16, 27, 28, 31, 35, 37, 40; also nominations of Ellsworth and Fuller, and Jefferson's address to the Senate on taking the oath of office: *Provided,* That the copies above referred to are to be used solely for the purposes of exhibition at the Columbian Exposition, and upon its conclusion are to be delivered to the Secretary of the Senate: *And provided further,* That the negatives from which the copies are printed shall also be delivered to the Secretary of the Senate.

LEAVE TO WITHDRAW PAPERS.

On motion by Mr. Faulkner,

Ordered, That John J. Farnsworth have leave to withdraw his papers from the files of the Senate, subject to the rule.

EXECUTIVE BUSINESS.

On motion by Mr. Gorman, that the Senate proceed to the consideration of executive business,

The yeas were 24 and the nays were 10.

On motion by Mr. Gorman,

The yeas and nays being desired by one-fifth of the Senators present,

Those who voted in the affirmative are,

Messrs. Bate, Blackburn, Brice, Caffery, Call, Coke, Faulkner, George, Gibson, Gorman, Gray, Harris, Hill, Hunton, Kyle, McPherson, Martin, Murphy, Palmer, Pasco, Peffer, Pugh, Vance, Vest.

Those who voted in the negative are,

Messrs. Cullom, Hansbrough, Hawley, Higgins, Hoar, Mitchell of Oregon, Morrill, Platt, Sherman, Stockbridge.

The number of Senators voting not constituting a quorum,

The Vice-President directed the roll to be called,

When,

Forty-one Senators answered to their names.

No quorum being present,

On motion by Mr. Gorman, at 3 o'clock and 35 minutes p. m., The Senate adjourned.

TUESDAY, APRIL 11, 1893.

SENATOR FROM MONTANA.

The Vice-President laid before the Senate the resolution reported from the Committee on Privileges and Elections, March 27, 1893, declaring Lee Mantle entitled to a seat in the Senate from the State of Montana;

When,

EXECUTIVE SESSION.

On motion by Mr. Gorman, that the Senate proceed to the consideration of executive business,

It was determined in the affirmative, { Yeas .... 39 { Nays 16

On motion by Mr. Chandler,

The yeas and nays being desired by one-fifth of the Senators present,

Those who voted in the affirmative are,

Messrs. Bate, Berry, Blackburn, Brice, Butler, Caffery, Call, Camden, Cockrell, Coke, Colquitt, Faulkner, George, Gibson, Gordon, Gorman, Gray, Harris, Hill, Hunton, Irby, Jones of Arkansas, Kyle, Lindsay, McPherson, Martin, Mitchell of Wisconsin, Murphy, Palmer, Pasco, Peffer, Pugh, Roach, Stewart, Turpie, Vance, Vest, Voorhees, White of Louisiana.

Those who voted in the negative are,

Messrs. Cameron, Carey, Chandler, Cullom, Dolph, Dubois, Hansbrough, Hawley, Hoar, Manderson, Morrill, Power, Proctor, Sherman, Stockbridge, Washburn.

So the motion was agreed to; and

The Senate proceeded to the consideration of executive business; and

After the consideration of executive business the doors were reopened, and

On motion by Mr. Faulkner, at 3 o'clock and 15 minutes p. m., The Senate adjourned.

WEDNESDAY, APRIL 12, 1893.

SENATOR FROM MONTANA.

The Vice-President laid before the Senate the resolution reported by Mr. Hoar, from the Committee on Privileges and Elections, March 27, 1893, declaring Lee Mantle entitled to a seat in the Senate from the State of Montana;

Pending which, and by unanimous consent,

MEMBERSHIP OF CERTAIN COMMITTEES.

On motion by Mr. Call,

The Senate proceeded to consider the resolution submitted by him, March 20, 1893, and modified by him on the 8th instant, to increase the membership of certain standing committees of the Senate, and

After debate,

INVESTIGATION BY THE COMMITTEE ON INDIAN AFFAIRS.

On motion by Mr. Jones, of Arkansas, and by unanimous consent,

The Senate proceeded to consider the resolution submitted by him on the 10th instant, instructing the Committee on Indian Affairs to make certain investigations during the recess of Congress; and

Ordered, That it be referred to the Committee to Audit and Control the Contingent Expenses of the Senate.

SENATOR FROM KANSAS.

Mr. Vance, from the Committee on Privileges and Elections, reported the following resolution; which was referred to the Committee to Audit and Control the Contingent Expenses of the Senate;

Resolved, That the Committee on Privileges and Elections, or any subcommittee thereof, be authorized to investigate the right of Mr. Joseph W. Ady, who claims a seat in this body as Senator from Kansas; and, if in their judgment it be necessary, to employ a stenographer, send for persons and papers, to administer oaths, and to sit during the recess of the Senate.

EXECUTIVE SESSION.

On motion by Mr. Faulkner,

The Senate proceeded to the consideration of executive business; and

After the consideration of executive business the doors were reopened, and

On motion by Mr. Faulkner, at 3 o'clock p. m., The Senate adjourned.

THURSDAY, APRIL 13, 1893.

Mr. Platt raised a question as to the presence of a quorum;

Whereupon,

The Vice-President directed the roll to be called;

When,

Forty-eight Senators answered to their names.

A quorum being present,

SENATOR FROM MONTANA.

The Vice-President laid before the Senate the resolution reported by Mr. Hoar, from the Committee on Privileges and Elections, March 27, 1893, declaring Lee Mantle entitled to a seat in the Senate from the State of Montana;

Pending which,

MEMORIAL OF THE LEGISLATURE OF MAINE.

The Vice-President laid before the Senate a memorial of the legislature of Maine in favor of an appropriation for the construction of a bridge over the St. Johns River at Fort Kent; which was referred to the Committee on Commerce.

SENATOR FROM KANSAS.

Mr. Sherman presented a memorial of 77 members of the legislature of the State of Kansas relating to the election of United States Senator from that State to fill the vacancy caused by the death of Preston B. Plumb, and protesting against the admission of John Martin; which was referred to the Committee on Privileges and Elections and ordered to be printed.

INVESTIGATION BY THE COMMITTEE ON TERRITORIES.

Mr. White, from the Committee to Audit and Control the Contingent Expenses of the Senate, to whom was referred the resolution submitted by Mr. Carey on the 6th instant, authorizing the Committee on Territories to visit the Territories of New Mexico, Arizona, Utah, and Oklahoma for the purpose of obtaining information with regard to the resources, population, etc., of said Territories, reported it with an amendment, viz: Add at the end of the resolution the following proviso:

Provided, That no expense be incurred for clerical service, any clerical service required by the said committee, or any subcommittee thereof, to be performed by the regular clerical force of the committee without extra compensation.

SENATOR FROM KANSAS.

Mr. White, of Louisiana, from the Committee to Audit and Control the Contingent Expenses of the Senate, to whom was referred the resolution submitted by Mr. Vance on the 12th instant, authorizing the Committee on Privileges and Elections to investigate the right of Mr. Joseph W. Ady to a seat in the Senate, reported it with an amendment, viz: Add to the resolution the following words: *the expense thereof to be paid from the contingent fund of the Senate.*

EXECUTIVE SESSION.

On motion by Mr. Vest, that the Senate proceed to the consideration of executive business,

It was determined in the affirmative, { Yeas 33
{ Nays 19

On motion by Mr. Hawley,

The yeas and nays being desired by one-fifth of the Senators present,

Those who voted in the affirmative are,

Messrs. Bate, Butler, Caffery, Call, Cockrell, Coke, Daniel, Faulkner, George, Gibson, Gordon, Gorman, Gray, Harris, Hill, Hunton, Irby, Jones of Arkansas, Kyle, McPherson, Martin, Mitchell of Wisconsin, Murphy, Palmer, Pasco, Peffer, Pugh, Roach, Smith, Turpie, Vest, Voorhees, White of Louisiana.

Those who voted in the negative are,

Messrs. Cameron, Carey, Chandler, Cullom, Davis, Dolph, Dubois, Hansbrough, Hawley, Higgins, Hoar, Jones of Nevada, Lodge, Morrill, Platt, Proctor, Sherman, Squire, Stockbridge.

So the motion was agreed to; and

The Senate proceeded to the consideration of executive business; and

After the consideration of executive business the doors were reopened, and

On motion by Mr. Gorman, at 12 o'clock and 55 minutes, p. m., The Senate adjourned.

FRIDAY, APRIL 14, 1893.

CHARGES AGAINST SENATOR ROACH.

On motion by Mr. Chandler, and by unanimous consent,

The Senate proceeded to consider the resolution submitted by Mr. Hoar on the 10th instant, directing the Committee on Privileges and Elections to examine certain allegations recently made against William N. Roach, a Senator from the State of North Dakota.

Pending which, by unanimous consent,

DISBURSEMENTS BY COMMITTEES DURING RECESS.

Mr. Cockrell submitted the following resolution; which was referred to the Committee to Audit and Control the Contingent Expenses of the Senate:

Resolved, That the Committee to Audit and Control the Contingent Expenses of the Senate be instructed to ascertain and fix the sums necessary to be disbursed by the various standing or special committees authorized to sit during the recess; that when the said sum or sums be so ascertained and fixed by the said committee, the expenses of the various committees, standing or select, authorized to sit during the recess, be absolutely limited to the amount so fixed by the said committee.

Resolved further, That the said Committee to Audit and Control the Contingent Expenses of the Senate, in ascertaining and fixing

---

the said sums, be, and hereby is, directed to so fix the amounts as to keep the aggregate sum within the appropriation.

REPORT OF IMMIGRANT COMMISSIONER SCHULTEIS.

Mr. Chandler submitted the following resolution; which was referred to the Committee on Printing:

Resolved, That the Public Printer be, and is hereby, directed to print for the use of the Senate, with a title page, 12,000 additional copies of the report of Immigration Commissioner H. J. Schulteis, contained in Part I, House Executive Document No. 235, first session Fifty-first Congress, pages 263 to 323, inclusive.

SENATOR FROM KANSAS.

On motion by Mr. Hoar,

The Senate proceeded to consider the resolution reported by Mr. Vance, from the Committee on Privileges and Elections, on the 12th instant, authorizing said committee to investigate the right of Mr. Joseph W. Ady to a seat in the Senate from the State of Kansas; and the amendment reported from the Committee to Audit and Control the Contingent Expenses of the Senate having been agreed to, the resolution as amended was agreed to, as follows:

Resolved, That the Committee on Privileges and Elections, or any subcommittee thereof, be authorized to investigate the right of Mr. Joseph W. Ady, who claims a seat in this body as Senator from Kansas; and, if in their judgment it be necessary, to employ a stenographer, send for persons and papers, to administer oaths, and to sit during the recess of the Senate, the expense thereof to be paid from the contingent fund of the Senate.

INVESTIGATION BY THE COMMITTEE ON TERRITORIES.

On motion by Mr. Harris,

The Senate proceeded to consider the resolution submitted by Mr. Carey on the 6th instant, authorizing the Committee on Territories to visit certain Territories for the purpose of obtaining information with regard to the resources, population, etc., of said Territories; and the amendment reported by the Committee to Audit and Control the Contingent Expenses of the Senate having been agreed to, the resolution as amended was agreed to, as follows:

Resolved, That the Committee on Territories, or any subcommittee thereof appointed for the purpose, are hereby authorized during the recess of Congress to visit the Territories of New Mexico, Arizona, Utah, and Oklahoma, for the purpose of obtaining information with regard to the resources, population, and condition of said Territories, and as to the propriety of the admission of the same as States, and that the expenses of said committee be paid out of the contingent fund of the Senate: *Provided,* That no expense be incurred for clerical service, any clerical service required by the said committee or any subcommittee thereof to be performed by the regular clerical force of the committee without extra compensation.

WITHDRAWAL OF PAPERS.

On motion by Mr. Cullom,

Ordered, That Goff A. Hall have leave to withdraw his papers from the files of the Senate.

On motion by Mr. Higgins,

Ordered, That William W. S. Davis have leave to withdraw his papers from the files of the Senate.

On motion by Mr. Cockrell,

Ordered, That G. W. Harbaugh have leave to withdraw his papers from the files of the Senate.

DISBURSEMENTS BY COMMITTEES DURING RECESS.

Mr. White, of Louisiana, from the Committee to Audit and Control the Contingent Expenses of the Senate, to whom was referred the resolution this day submitted by Mr. Cockrell, instructing that committee to ascertain and fix the sums necessary to be disbursed by the various standing or special committees authorized to sit during the recess, reported it without amendment.

CHARGES AGAINST SENATOR ROACH.

The Senate resumed the consideration of the resolution to examine the allegation against William N. Roach; and

An amendment having been proposed by Mr. Gorman,

After debate,

SENATOR FROM MONTANA.

The Senate resumed the consideration of the resolution reported by Mr. Hoar, from the Committee on Privileges and Elections, March 27, 1893, declaring that Lee Mantle is entitled to a seat in the Senate from the State of Montana;

When,

EXECUTIVE SESSION.

On motion by Mr. Gorman,

The Senate proceeded to the consideration of executive business; and

After the consideration of executive business the doors were reopened, and

On motion by Mr. Gorman, at 4 o'clock and 40 minutes p. m., The Senate adjourned.

SATURDAY, APRIL 15, 1893.

SENATOR FROM MONTANA.

The Vice-President laid before the Senate the resolution reported by Mr. Hoar from the Committee on Privileges and Elections, March 27, 1893, declaring Lee Mantle entitled to a seat in the Senate from the State of Montana;

Pending which, by unanimous consent,

WITHDRAWAL OF PAPERS.

On motion by Mr. Mitchell, of Oregon,

Ordered, That Austin Herr have leave to withdraw his papers from the files of the Senate.

On motion by Mr. Coke,

Ordered, That leave be granted to withdraw from the files of the Senate the papers in the case of Daniel Woodson and Ely Moore, and also in the case of John A. Whitfield.

HAWAIIAN AFFAIRS.

Mr. Lodge submitted the following resolution for consideration:

Resolved, That the Secretary of State be, and he is hereby, directed to inform the Senate by whose authority the American flag was hauled down from the Government building at Honolulu on April 1.

INTERNATIONAL MONETARY CONFERENCE.

Mr. Davis submitted the following resolution; which was referred to the Committee on Printing:

Resolved, That there be printed and bound for the use of the Senate 1,500 additional copies of Executive Document No. 82, Fifty-second Congress, second session, being the proceedings of the International Monetary Conference.

NOTIFICATION TO THE PRESIDENT.

Mr. Hoar, with the consent of the Senate, withdrew the motion entered by him on the 10th instant, that the Senate reconsider its vote agreeing to the resolution for the appointment of a committee to wait upon the President of the United States and inform him that, unless he may have some further communication to make, the Senate was ready to adjourn without day;

When,

The Presiding Officer (Mr. Manderson in the chair), appointed as the committee Mr. Harris and Mr. Sherman.

DISBURSEMENTS BY RECESS COMMITTEES.

On motion by Mr. White, of Louisiana, the Senate proceed to the consideration of the resolution yesterday submitted by Mr. Cockrell relative to the disbursements by the committees authorized to sit during the coming recess,

It was determined in the affirmative, { Yeas 33
{ Nays 16

On motion by Mr. Hoar,

The yeas and nays being desired by one-fifth of the Senators present, Those who voted in the affirmative are,

Messrs. Bate, Berry, Blackburn, Brice, Caffery, Call, Camden, Cockrell, Coke, Faulkner, George, Gibson, Gordon, Gorman, Gray, Harris, Hill, Hunton, Jones of Arkansas, Kyle, Martin, Mills, Mitchell of Wisconsin, Murphy, Palmer, Pasco, Peffer, Pugh, Roach, Turpie, Vance, White of Louisiana.

Those who voted in the negative are,

Messrs. Chandler, Cullom, Davis, Dolph, Dubois, Hansbrough, Hawley, Hoar, Jones of Nevada, Lodge, McMillan, Manderson, Morrill, Platt, Proctor, Sherman.

So the motion was agreed to; and

The Senate proceeded to the consideration of the said resolution, and

Pending debate,

REPORT OF COMMITTEE TO WAIT ON THE PRESIDENT.

Mr. Harris, from the committee appointed to wait upon the President of the United States and inform him that unless he may have some further communication to make the Senate is ready to adjourn without day, reported that they had performed the duty assigned to them, and that the President had replied that he had no further communication to make.

ANTITRUST AND INTERSTATE-COMMERCE DECISIONS.

Mr. Manderson submitted the following resolution; which was considered by unanimous consent and agreed to:

Resolved, That the late decisions of Judge Speer, of Georgia; Judge Ricks, of Ohio, and Judge Taft, of Ohio, made in certain cases involving the rights and duties of railroad employés and construction of the antitrust and interstate-commerce laws, be printed in document form for the use of the Senate.

EXECUTIVE SESSION.

On motion by Mr. Gorman,

The Senate proceeded to the consideration of executive business; and

After the consideration of executive business the doors were reopened.

THANKS TO THE VICE-PRESIDENT.

Mr. Manderson submitted the following resolution; which was

24 s

considered by unanimous consent and unanimously agreed to:

Resolved, That the thanks of the Senate are due, and are hereby tendered, to the Vice-President for the impartiality and courtesy with which he has presided over the Senate during its present extraordinary session.

REPORTS OF COMMITTEES.

Mr. Gorman, from the Committee on Printing, to whom were referred the following resolutions, reported them without amendment and submitted written reports thereon as follows:

Resolution this day submitted by Mr. Davis, to print 1,400 additional copies of the proceedings of the International Monetary Conference; Report No. 9.

Resolution yesterday submitted by Mr. Chandler to print 12,000 additional copies of the report of the immigrant commissioner, H. J. Schulteis; Report No. 10.

The Senate proceeded by unanimous consent to consider the said resolutions; and

Resolved, That the Senate agree thereto.

Mr. White, of Louisiana, from the Committee to Audit and Control the Contingent Expenses of the Senate, to whom was referred the following resolution, reported it without amendment:

Resolved, That the Committee on Indian Affairs be instructed, either by full committee or such subcommittee or committees as may be appointed by the chairman thereof, with the full power of such committee to continue, during the recess of Congress, the investigations authorized by the resolution of May 13, 1890, and February 27, 1891, with the authority and in the manner and to the extent provided in said resolutions, and in the pursuance of such investigations to visit the several Indian reservations, Indian schools supported in whole or in part by the Government, and the five nations in the Indian Territory, or any reservation where, in the opinion of said committee, it may be necessary to extend their investigations.

2. That said committee or subcommittee shall have power to send for persons and papers, to administer oaths, and to examine witnesses under oath touching the matters which they are hereby empowered to investigate, and may hold their sessions during the recess of the Senate at such place or places as they may determine; and the necessary and proper expense incurred in the execution of this order shall be paid out of the contingent fund of the Senate upon vouchers approved by the chairman of said committee.

The Senate proceeded, by unanimous consent, to consider the said resolution; and

Resolved, That the Senate agree thereto.

Mr. White of Louisiana, from the Committee to Audit and Control the Contingent Expenses of the Senate, to whom was referred the resolution reported by Mr. Butler on the 10th instant, authorizing certain inquiries by the Committee on Interstate Commerce, reported it without amendment.

The Senate proceeded, by unanimous consent, to consider the said resolution; and having been amended, on the motion of Mr. Hoar, by inserting after the word "circumstances," in line 9, the following words: *and also the provisions of the statute relating to long and short hauls,*

The resolution as amended was agreed to, as follows:

Resolved, That the Committee on Interstate Commerce be, and is hereby, authorized to inquire whether or not the methods prevailing in the transportation of freight and passengers over the great railroad lines of the country and the conditions and necessities of travelers and shippers and of the transportation companies justify or require a repeal or modification of section 5 of the interstate-commerce act of February 4, 1887, which prohibits pooling under any circumstances, and also the provisions of the statute relating to long and short hauls; and that said committee be further authorized to inquire whether the system of closing and sealing cars engaged in transporting merchandise from one of the States of the Union into another State through foreign territory, or from such territory into any State, or from such territory through the United States into foreign territory, or any system of bonding merchandise so transported, needs to be modified, or further regulated by law, and whether all railroads engaged in such traffic should either be required to conform to all the provisions of the interstate-commerce act or be prohibited from continuing such transportation business; and whether any modifications should be made of the existing provisions of law concerning the relations between common carriers and their employés; the said committee being hereby empowered to sit during the recess of the Senate, to act by subcommittees, if deemed necessary, to take testimony at convenient points, to send for witnesses, books, and papers, and employ a stenographer, and to have its expenses paid from the contingent fund of the Senate; and it is expressly provided that no additional expense whatever shall be allowed for clerical hire under the terms of this resolution.

INVESTIGATION BY THE COMMITTEE ON AGRICULTURE.

On motion by Mr. George, that the Senate proceed to the consideration of the resolution submitted by him on the 10th instant, instructing the Secretary of the Senate to set apart the sum of $5,000 for the investigation directed to be made by the Committee on Agriculture and Forestry,

On motion by Mr. Cockrell, that the Senate adjourn *sine die*,

It was determined in the negative, { Yeas 23
                                     { Nays 23

On motion by Mr. George,

The yeas and nays being desired by one-fifth of the Senators present,

Those who voted in the affirmative are,

Messrs. Berry, Blackburn, Brice, Butler, Carey, Cockrell, Dolph, Faulkner, Gibson, Gorman, Harris, Hawley, Hill, Jones of Arkansas, Lodge, McMillan, Morrill, Palmer, Pasco, Platt, Pugh, Turpie, Vest.

Those who voted in the negative are,

Messrs. Bate, Call, Chandler, Coke, Cullom, Davis, Dubois, George, Gordon, Hansbrough, Higgins, Hoar, Hunton, Jones of Nevada, Kyle, Manderson, Martin, Murphy, Peffer, Roach, Stockbridge, Voorhees, White of Louisiana.

So the motion was not agreed to.

The question recurring upon the motion of Mr. George to proceed to the consideration of the resolution submitted by him on the 10th instant,

It was determined in the negative, { Yeas 21
                                    { Nays 26

On motion by Mr. George,

The yeas and nays being desired by one-fifth of the Senators present,

Those who voted in the affirmative are,

Messrs. Bate, Butler, Caffery, Call, Coke, Davis, George, Gordon, Hunton, Kyle, McMillan, Manderson, Martin, Morrill, Murphy, Peffer, Proctor, Roach, Stockbridge, Turpie, Voorhees.

Those who voted in the negative are,

Messrs. Berry, Blackburn, Brice, Chandler, Cockrell, Cullom, Dolph, Dubois, Faulkner, Gibson, Gorman, Hansbrough, Harris, Hawley, Higgins, Hill, Hoar, Jones of Arkansas, Jones of Nevada, Lodge, Palmer, Pasco, Platt, Pugh, Vest, White of Louisiana.

So the motion was not agreed to.

DISBURSEMENTS BY RECESS COMMITTEES.

The Senate resumed the consideration of the resolution yesterday submitted by Mr. Cockrell relative to the disbursements by the committee authorized to sit during the recess; and

After debate,

The resolution was agreed to, as follows:

Resolved, That the Committee to Audit and Control the Contingent Expenses of the Senate be instructed to ascertain and fix the sums necessary to be disbursed by the various standing or special committees authorized to sit during the recess; that when the said sum or sums be so ascertained and fixed by the said committee, the expenses of the various committees, standing or select, authorized to sit during the recess be absolutely limited to the amount so fixed by the said committee.

Resolved further, That the said Committee to Audit and Control the Contingent Expenses of the Senate, in ascertaining and fixing the said sums, be, and hereby is, directed to so fix the amounts as to keep the aggregate sum within the appropriation.

EMPLOYÉS AT THE MALTBY BUILDING.

Mr. White, of Louisiana, from the Committee to Audit and Control the Contingent Expenses of the Senate, reported the following resolution; which was considered by unanimous consent and agreed to:

Resolved, That the Sergeant-at-Arms be, and he is hereby, authorized to continue the present session employés at the Maltby Building, authorized under the resolution of July 26, 1892, until June 30, 1893.

ADJOURNMENT SINE DIE.

On motion by Mr. Hill, at 6 o'clock and 15 minutes p. m., that the Senate adjourn without day,

It was determined in the affirmative;

When,

The Vice-President addressed the Senate as follows:

Senators, before announcing the result of the vote just taken, I beg to express my earnest appreciation of the uniform courtesy shown me by the members and officers of this body during the session now closing.

For the resolution personal to myself, so kindly adopted by the Senate, I am profoundly grateful.

In accordance with the vote just taken, I now declare this extraordinary session of the Senate adjourned without day.

APPENDIX.

SENATORS OF THE UNITED STATES WHOSE SEATS WILL BECOME VACANT IN—

1895. Class 2.	1897. Class 3.	1899. Class 1.
Mr. Berry, of Arkansas.	Mr. Allison, of Iowa.	Mr. Aldrich, of Rhode Island.
Butler, of South Carolina.	Blackburn, of Kentucky.	Allen, of Nebraska.
Caffery, of Louisiana.*	Brice, of Ohio.	Bate, of Tennessee.
Camden, of West Virginia.	Call, of Florida.	Cockrell, of Missouri.
Carey, of Wyoming.	Cameron, of Pennsylvania.	Daniel, of Virginia.
Chandler, of New Hampshire.	Dubois, of Idaho.	Davis, of Minnesota.
Coke, of Texas.	Gallinger, of New Hampshire.	Faulkner, of West Virginia.
Colquitt, of Georgia.	Gibson, of Maryland.	George, of Mississippi.
Cullom, of Illinois.	Gordon, of Georgia.	Gorman, of Maryland.
Dixon, of Rhode Island.	Hansbrough, of North Dakota.	Gray, of Delaware.
Dolph, of Oregon.	Hill, of New York.	Hale, of Maine.
Frye, of Maine.	Irby, of South Carolina.	Hawley, of Connecticut.
Harris, of Tennessee.	Jones, of Arkansas.	Lodge, of Massachusetts.
Higgins, of Delaware.	Jones, of Nevada.	Mitchell, of Wisconsin.
Hoar, of Massachusetts.	Kyle, of South Dakota.	Mills, of Texas.
Hunton, of Virginia.*	Mitchell, of Oregon.	Murphy, of New York.
Lindsay, of Kentucky.	Morrill, of Vermont.	Pasco, of Florida.*
McMillan, of Michigan.	Palmer, of Illinois.	Proctor, of Vermont.
McPherson, of New Jersey.	Peffer, of Kansas.	Quay, of Pennsylvania.†
Manderson, of Nebraska.	Platt, of Connecticut.	Roach, of North Dakota.
Martin, of Kansas.	Pugh, of Alabama.	Sherman, of Ohio.
Morgan, of Alabama.	Squire, of Washington.	Smith, of New Jersey.
Pettigrew, of South Dakota.	Stanford, of California.	Stewart, of Nevada.
Power, of Montana.	Teller, of Colorado.	Stockbridge, of Michigan.
Ransom, of North Carolina.	Vance, of North Carolina.	Turpie, of Indiana.
Shoup, of Idaho.	Vest, of Missouri.	White, of California.
Walthall, of Mississippi.	Vilas, of Wisconsin.	Vacant:
Washburn, of Minnesota.	Voorhees, of Indiana.	Montana, 1.
Wilson, of Iowa.	White, of Louisiana.	Washington, 1.
Wolcott, of Colorado.		Wyoming, 1.

*Appointed by the governor.   †Elected, but not sworn.

EXECUTIVE PROCEEDINGS OF THE SENATE OF THE UNITED STATES FROM WHICH THE INJUNCTION OF SECRECY HAS BEEN REMOVED, DURING THE SECOND SESSION OF THE FIFTY-SECOND CONGRESS, ENDING MARCH 3, 1893.

MONDAY, FEBRUARY 6, 1893.

Resolved, That the injunction of secrecy be removed from the draft of an uncompleted treaty between the United States and His Majesty the King of the Hawaiian Islands, made in 1854.

[PRINTED AS EX. DOC. NO. 45, FIFTY-SECOND CONGRESS, SECOND SESSION.]

THURSDAY, FEBRUARY 9, 1893.

Resolved, That the injunction of secrecy be removed from the message of the President of the United States, transmitting copies of correspondence between the Governments of the United States and Great Britain relative to the Sandwich Islands, in 1843 and 1844; and the said correspondence transmitted therewith.

[PRINTED AS EX. DOC. NO. 57, FIFTY-SECOND CONGRESS, SECOND SESSION.]

FRIDAY, FEBRUARY 17, 1893.

Resolved, That the injunction of secrecy be removed from the message of the President of the United States, transmitting the treaty of annexation concluded on the 14th day of February, 1893, between the United States and the Provisional Government of the Hawaiian Islands; together with the said treaty, and the correspondence accompanying the same.

[PRINTED AS EX. DOC. NO. 76, FIFTY-SECOND CONGRESS, SECOND SESSION.]

BILLS OF THE SENATE.

189

25

26

SENATE JOINT RESOLUTIONS.

HOUSE BILLS.

27

HOUSE JOINT RESOLUTIONS.

. INDEX.

29

31

32

○

Lightning Source UK Ltd.
Milton Keynes UK
UKHW010000160219
337399UK00011B/1033/P